BEYOND

CALVINISM AND ARMINIANISM

AN INDUCTIVE, MEDIATE THEOLOGY OF SALVATION

C. Gordon Olson

Global Gospel Publishers

BEYOND CALVINISM AND ARMINIANISM
AN INDUCTIVE, MEDIATE THEOLOGY OF SALVATION

GLOBAL GOSPEL MINISTRIES, INC
adba GLOBAL GOSPEL PUBLISHERS
74 Mountain Avenue
Cedar Knolls, New Jersey 07927
Telephone: 973-267-2511

ISBN 0-9624850-4-7

Cover layout is by the courtesy of Gerry Pruden of Bible Basics, International, Odessa, FL.

First edition: November, 2002

TABLE OF CONTENTS

APPENDICES

DEDICATED TO:

Brother Hidayat Masih, Elder and Evangelist of Bethany Assembly in Lahore, Pakistan for half a century, a faithful servant of Yisu Masih (Jesus the Messiah), a man of one book, the Bible. He is representative of myriads of indigenous pastors, elders, evangelists, and missionaries in the two-thirds world, who because of limited education probably have never heard of Calvinism and Arminianism, but whose effective ministries have suffered not the least thereby. I suspect that I, as a seminary graduate and missionary, learned far more of eternal significance from him than he did from me.

PREFACE

As the gospel of the Lord Jesus Christ penetrates into thousands of people groups around the world and Christ's church is planted among them, the global church is increasingly becoming non-western. One of the most astounding phenomena of the last quarter century has been the explosion of tens of thousands of non-western missionaries of the cross, who have joined their western colleagues in fulfilling the Greatest Decree of the Sovereign of the universe. The decline of the churches in Europe, the battleground of the Reformation, raises real questions about the soundness of the form of Christianity which developed from the Reformation. It was the radical Reformation which sought to break free from the overhanging legacy of medieval scholasticism and thus took the lead in world evangelization.

The greatest theologian of the apostolic church, the apostle Paul, was also its greatest missionary. Western churches desperately need an inductive biblical theology, which will break free from the deadening influence of deductive scholasticism and our polarized traditions. They are a crippling legacy of western church history. We must move on to a missions-centered theology, which will be conducive to world evangelization before the return of our Lord Jesus the Messiah, who was given for the whole world of lost sinners.

It is my earnest prayer and hope that this present work will somehow advance this goal. I have tried to set out positively what the Bible actually teaches about God's wonderful plan of salvation. Unfortunately, that legacy of the past has required me to first deal with the serious misconceptions and distortions of God's truth found among us. There is such a strong tradition of misinterpretation and even of mistranslation of the Scriptures that we desperately need a paradigm shift in our whole approach to God's truth.

Jody Dillow cites an experience Stephen Covey had on a New York subway train on a peaceful Sunday morning, when the passengers were sitting quietly enjoying a tranquil ride. That is, until a man and his children entered the car. The children were so loud and rambunctious that people obviously became distracted and upset. The man sat down next to Covey and closed his eyes, apparently oblivious to the situation. The children were yelling, throwing things, and even grabbing people's newspapers. Covey tried to restrain himself, but finally he could stand it no longer and remonstrated with the man. He seemed to come back to consciousness and said softly, "Oh, you're right. I guess I should do something about it. We just came from the hospital where their mother died about an hour ago. I don't know what to think, and I guess they don't know how to handle it either." Covey continued: "Can you imagine what I felt at that moment? My paradigm shifted. Suddenly I **saw** things differently, and because I **saw** differently, I **thought** differently. My irritation vanished. . . . Feelings of sympathy and compassion flowed freely. . . . Everything changed in an instant."[1]

Many of my readers may need to undergo a radical paradigm shift. I have been on a more gradual theological pilgrimage for the last quarter century. I am finding many others who are thoroughly dissatisfied with the polarized traditions of our western theology. Many in those traditions will be upset with this book. I get encouragement from the fact that the Lord Jesus spent His whole ministry countering the religious traditions of a nation which desperately need a paradigm shift. He spared no words in rebuffing adherence to the human traditions of His day.

Although I have had no significant organization or support staff to help me get this book to press, I am grateful for four ladies from Bethlehem Church who have helped in proof-reading the manuscript: Vicki Burnor, Susie Rickershauser, Beverly Funk, and Holly DiGiosaffatte. Christian friends at Bethlehem have been waiting encouragingly and patiently, year after year, for this book to see the light of day. Pastor Ken Spence graciously allowed me to preach popularized versions of many of these chapters. I also appreciate encouragement from Dr. James Bjornstad, my former colleague, and from Dr. Thomas Edgar. Pastor Gary Becker, one of my early students, has made some of my chapters available on the website of his ministry. Bibliophile Pat Minichello has provided invaluable help in alerting me to relevant books. Dr. Glen Carnagey, whom I have never met, has not only distributed chapters of my material to theologically alert pastors and colleagues, but has also stimulated them to pray for my health to finish this work. One of those encouraging colleagues is Dr. Stephen Lewis, whom I met at ETS 2001 in Colorado. Most providential has been God's putting a CD of the manuscript into the hands of Dr. Harold Holmyard, whom I have never met, but who has expertly proof-read the whole and made many suggestions. He has been like an angel from heaven to help me in this last stage. My wife, Miriam, has continued to be a spiritual encouragement over the years, my son Doug has kept my computer functioning for its task, and my daughter Joyce has been encouraging and praying for me from a distance.

C. Gordon Olson
Cedar Knolls, New Jersey
October 7, 2002

---

1. Stephen R. Covey, *The Seven Habits of Highly Effective People,* (NY: Simon and Schuster, 1989), pp. 30-31.

Introduction

Biblical Doctrine Is Foundational

In his first letter to Timothy, the apostle Paul emphasized again and again the importance of sound doctrine and teaching. He showed a great concern for the truth of the message which Timothy was to preach and teach and spoke frequently of the importance of holding to "the faith" as an objective body of essential truth. He encouraged Timothy to stay on in Ephesus to deal with false teachings and teachers in the churches there (1:3-11). In emphasizing God's desire that all men might be saved, he makes their coming **"to the knowledge of the truth"** synonymous with this (2:3-4). Therefore it is essential that local church leaders be"**able to teach**" (2:2) and must hold "**to the mystery of the faith with a clear conscience**" (2:9) since the church of the living God is "**the pillar and support of the truth**" (2:15).

Paul warns that "**in the latter times some will fall away from the faith, paying attention to deceitful spirits and doctrines of demons**" (4:1) and that to "**be a good servant of Christ Jesus**" Timothy will not only have to be "**nourished on the words of the faith and of the sound doctrine**" but also point out this apostasy to the brethren (4:6). Paul exhorts him to "**prescribe and teach**" that "**the living God . . . is the Savior of all men, especially of believers**" (4:10-11), and twice reminds him that by giving attention to his teaching he will insure salvation for his hearers (4:13, 16). In the concluding section, Paul shows a great concern that he teach "**doctrine conforming to godliness**" and warn those whose lifestyle is moving them away from "**the faith**" (5:8, 17; 6:2-3, 10, 17). Paul's letter to Titus emphasizes most of these same concerns (1:1, 9-14; 2:1, 7, 10).

Based on the preceding, it is no overstatement to say that biblical doctrine is foundational to the life, witness, and ministry of individual Christians, and to the life of the church. Yet today, we see little concern for doctrine in most evangelical churches, so serious that it could be called a crisis.

A Crisis in Theology

Theology used to be called the queen of the sciences, but today evangelical theology is in a sorry state. We hear very little doctrinal preaching in most evangelical pulpits, and works of evangelical theology are not best sellers. Music in the average evangelical church is fast becoming doctrinally vapid. Much of this can be attributed to the relativistic culture in which we live. There are no absolutes either of truth or morality. Certainly, Christians are greatly influenced by this kind of thinking.

Although membership in the Evangelical Theological Society has mushroomed to 2800 members, many of the members are more interested in one of the related disciplines, such as, historical theology, philosophy, apologetics, archaeology, Old or New Testament literature, etc. Only a small percentage of the papers given at the meetings of the society focus upon theology itself.

The polarization of theology. We who call ourselves theologians are mainly to blame. Evangelical theologians of great scholarly credentials have come to radically differing conclusions in important areas of theology and have developed radically contradicting systems of theology. As a result, the whole theological process is discredited. This would be a matter of concern in less significant areas of theology, but one would think that in the area of the theology of salvation things would be different. After all, salvation truth is what unites us as Evangelicals. However, it seems that the opposite is true.

There is today, unfortunately, a radical polarization in evangelical theology, as has been the case for over four centuries. Calvinists and Arminians are at antipodes as to just how God applies the merits of Christ's saving death to sinners. There has been very little dialogue, right up to the present, between the two polarized camps.[1] Furthermore, there is very little recognition by those at the antipodes that there is a whole spectrum of distinct positions between extreme, scholastic Calvinism and extreme forms of Arminianism. To make matters worse, now we must deal with a more radical kind of Arminianism, known as Open Theism. However, there is a vast mainstream of Evangelicals in the middle who are not committed fully to either system. Unfortunately, there are few voices which have articulated a clear middle position. Then there are the Lutherans, who hold aspects of both and feel that these truths are in paradox and need not be resolved.

Causes and solutions. I believe that we can come to a resolution of the conflicts in the theology of salvation, if we will work on our distorted perspectives, our defective attitudes, and our faulty methodologies. I will discuss these in the Prolegomena, since these are the roots of the tension. Far too much of our theology has been developed deductively, rather than inductively. Both are valid, but we must always start with an inductive process, as in all sciences. Failure to do so has been the major cause of the tension and conflict. In this present work I give priority to an inductive methodology in developing a fresh theology of salvation.

The neglect of salvation theology. Today we have a plethora of books about end-time prophecy (eschatology), the ministry of the Holy Spirit (pneumatology), and the church (ecclesiology), but precious little about the theology of salvation (soteriology). Most of those which are being written are from a Calvinistic viewpoint. It is astonishing that the theology of salvation is so neglected. After all, salvation for the people of this world is the bottom line of it all.

A major goal towards which end-time prophecy is moving is the salvation of the nations, including both Jews and Gentiles, which includes all the people-groups of the earth. Christ did say that He would be with us until the end of the age, so that we could be His instruments in making disciples of all ethnic peoples (Mt. 28:18-20). Certainly, a major purpose of the church is to be God's instrument in "**taking from among the Gentiles a people for His name**," as James said at the Jerusalem Council (Acts 15:14). It is also abundantly clear that the major reason the Father sent the Holy Spirit on the day of Pentecost was to convict the world of their need of the Savior, to give new birth, and to enable the church to do its work of world evangelization, not just for us to have spiritual highs. At the core of it all is the theology of salvation. If we don't have the message of salvation straight, we are messing up the most significant part of the whole plan of God!

If world evangelization is at the heart of God's plan for this church age (and Christ's last words before His ascension attest to this), then we must investigate the impact of erroneous theologies of salvation upon that program of God. My research for this book has uncovered the extent of the impact of deterministic theology on evangelism and missions, both historically and logically, and the positive impact of a more mediate viewpoint on the restoration of missions. This is addressed in chapter 17.

It is not just within evangelicalism that we find ourselves in disarray in reference to the message of salvation. In relation to non-Evangelicals, we are in confusion. For example, the 1994 *Evangelicals and Catholics Together* compromise of the gospel message by outstanding evangelical leaders swept the Reformation doctrine of justification by faith alone under the rug. There are many other ways in which the purity of the gospel is being eclipsed within evangelical circles. Although this is the special concern of chapter 12, the problem bleeds through all the topics addressed in this book.

My Personal Theological Pilgrimage

This book is the result of a personal theological pilgrimage. When I came to salvation as an engineering student, I was active in an Arminian church. I early became convinced of the doctrine of eternal security. At seminary I accepted the moderate Calvinism I was taught, and in turn taught it for a score of years. However, a dialogue with an extreme Calvinistic colleague and my teaching of the life of Christ and the book of Acts forced me to re-examine my Calvinism. Perhaps a defining moment in my pilgrimage was a question posed to me on a radio call-in program about the relationship of foreknowledge and election. Weeks later, while meditating on this question, I suddenly realized that there are really only two biblical passages on the issue and both give a consistent order (Rom. 8:29-30; I Pet. 1:1-2). This moved me to my present mediate position between Calvinism and Arminianism.

I gave an exploratory paper at the Evangelical Theological Society annual meeting in Toronto in 1981, which drew considerable interest. Since1992 I have presented the results of in-depth research on various subtopics at various ETS meetings. It has been very exciting to see how all the pieces have come together for a mediate theology of salvation. Whether the research be exegetical or historical, I have been constantly astonished at how it all fits together in resolving the supposed contradictions, antinomies, and paradoxes, which have plagued our theologies over the ages. But this really should not surprise us, since all Scripture has one Author, the Holy Spirit, and there should be no real contradictions in our theology. See appendix A for more details of my pilgrimage.

My Most Significant Discoveries

Some of the most significant discoveries I made in the course of my research are well-known facts of which I was ignorant; perhaps many of my readers share my ignorance. Other discoveries are more obscure points of fact that others have already published, but their writings were not accessible to most of us. There are a number of other important facts that I dug out of reference works and primary sources, the significance of which has been missed by most scholars. Since 9/11/01 we have heard about the failure of the FBI to "connect the dots." I believe that I have made some significant and correct connections between the dots of biblical data which have not been connected hitherto. Some of these are surprising, at least they were to me. Some of these exegetical and theological discoveries are:

1. A total lack of inductive evidence for any eternal exhaustive decrees of God–four centuries of useless debate about the order of fictional decrees
2. That mistranslation of a clause in Ephesians 1:11 could be so crucial to determinism's erroneous wall-to-wall decree(s)
3. That, only 26 verses into Genesis, God began a process of self-limitation of the exercise of His sovereignty, a fact so widely ignored.

4. That Augustinian exegesis of Romans 9 totally fails to see the Old Testament background and broader context of Jewish issues.
5. Buswell's exposé of a fundamental philosophical error: that God cannot know that which He has not determined.
6. Although many church fathers saw the significance of the *imago dei* in reference to free will, it is poorly articulated in evangelical theology.
7. The great significance of human trichotomy in biblical anthropology in explaining the fall and regeneration of man
8. The widespread extrapolation of depravity to total inability
9. God's many appeals to sinners to repent, believe, choose life, and seek God (50 times) obscured by mistranslation of Rom. 3:11
10. The total failure of so many interpreters to see the context of John 6:44, 65, the godly remnant of Israel turned over to the Son
11. The negative consequence of continued imprecise use of the Old Testament word 'atonement' in theological discourse, in the light of the contrasting objective/subjective distinction of the Greek words for propitiation, reconciliation, and, especially, the eight words for redemption
12. That despite the clarity of evidence for the substitutionary nature of Christ's sacrifice, so many Evangelicals have denied it.
13. The total lack of linguistic evidence for a pregnant meaning of *proginoskein*
14. That the rare word *proorizein* should have never been translated 'to predestinate,' as in the Vulgate and derived English translations
15. That the pre-NT usage of *eklegomai* and cognates should have such a different connotation from modern translations
16. That the consistent order of 'foreknowledge' and election-/foreordination should be explained away in such a cavalier fashion
17. That the election of Israel and Christ is so little developed in discussion of the election of the church
18. That the possibility of corporate election should have been so little considered, since the corporate entity concept is so foundational to biblical truth.
19. That so many would miss the importance of the conviction of the Spirit and especially the connection of Christ's promise in John 16:8-11 with its Pentecost realization (cf. ch. 9).
20. That so many theologians have constructed an *ordo salutis* without

reference to the convicting work of the Spirit.

21. That so many hold to the priority of regeneration before repentant faith without a shred of inductive basis
22. That the widespread notion of faith as a direct gift of God should have such little real inductive basis
23. The widespread extrapolation of God's calling to the notion of irresistible grace
24. The endemic compromises of the doctrine of justification by faith alone among professed Evangelicals
25. The externalistic misdefinition of repentance, causing widespread confusion of repentance and conversion, aggravated by egregious errors in the theological dictionaries
26. The widespread failure among both Calvinists and Arminians in holding to salvation by discipleship by failing to see Christ's three discipleship passages in their diachronic contexts, especially ignoring the word 'daily' in Luke 9:23
27. The widespread lack of assurance among both Arminians and Calvinists from backloading human performance into ultimate salvation
28. An erroneous presupposition of both Arminians and Calvinists, coupled with failure to see the broader context, which has obscured the true meaning of Hebrews 6:1-9
29. The significant, little understood difference between eternal security and perseverance of the saints
30. In reference to Matthew 16:18, the frequent reference to the Aramaic substructure without any research of the actual Aramaic words
31. The serious consequences of failure to recognize the force of the periphrastic perfect passive participle in Matthew 16:19

My research into missiology and church history has produced other discoveries (see chapter 17 & 18):

1. The widespread practical denial of the paradigm for persuasion evangelism and missions established by Christ and the apostles
2. The theological roots of the "Great Protestant Omission"–two centuries devoid of foreign missions after the Reformation; three, from the English-speaking world
3. The two virtually unknown theological mentors of the modern missionary movement: Andrew Fuller in Great Britain and Edward

3. The two virtually unknown theological mentors of the modern missionary movement: Andrew Fuller in Great Britain and Edward Griffin in America
4. The connection of the neo-Edwardsian New Divinity theology's doctrine of general redemption with the Second Great Awakening and the first American foreign missions
5. That Aurelius Augustine was the first predestinarian church father, and that the pre-Augustinian fathers coined the term 'free will.'
6. That unconditional election and irresistible grace were never voiced among Christians until the later ministry of Augustine (417), that a semi-Augustinian position was affirmed at the Synod of Orange (Aurasio) in 529, and that unconditional election was hardly heard of for a millennium again until resurrected by the Reformers.
7. That limited atonement was never voiced among Christians, including the Reformers, until Calvin's successor, Theodore Beza, and never put into any doctrinal statement until the Canons of Dort (1619).
8. That after the Reformation there were over a dozen significant movements reacting to and modifying the determinism of the Reformers.

The Importance of Details

A major flaw of a deductive approach to any subject, whether it be science, medicine, or theology, is the tendency to make sweeping generalizations without adequate attention to the details of the data. Carl Sagan got plenty of media attention for his sweeping generalizations about evolution in the universe, but when we read the incredible detail of writers, such as Michael Denton and Michael Behe, we see that evolutionists' sweeping generalizations get undermined by a host of details of fact.[2]

The major advantage of an inductive, empirical approach is that it forces us to pay attention to the details of the data. Indeed, in the preface of Behe's *Darwin's Black Box*, this biochemist alerts his readers to the daunting task they will face in reading his book, because of the incredible multiplicity of details he must discuss in order to do justice to the subject. Many of my readers will face the same problem. I have been forced to go into great detail of linguistic, grammatical, syntactical, exegetical, and historical material to do justice to my subject. You will have to bear with me if you really want to get to the bottom of these issues, even if the detail at times gets tedious. There is no other way to get to the whole truth.

---

1. Roger Olson, "Don't Hate Me Because I'm an Arminian!" *Christianity Today*, 43 (Sept. 6, 1999), pp. 87-94.

2. Michael Denton, *Evolution: A Theory in Crisis* (Bethesda, MD: Adler & Adler, 1985) and Michael Behe, *Darwin's Black Box* (NY: Free Press, 1996).

> There is a great danger, when once we have adhered to one particular school of thought or adopted one particular system of theology, of reading the Bible in the light of that school or system and finding its distinctive features in what we read. . . . The remedy for this is to bear resolutely in mind that our systems of doctrine must be based on biblical exegesis, not imposed upon it.
>
> -F. F. Bruce

1

PROLEGOMENA: HOW THEOLOGIANS "DO IN" THEOLOGY

In a doctoral course in Liberation Theology some years ago, my mind was diverted to the cover of one of the textbooks: *Doing Theology in a Revolutionary Situation* by Jose Miguez Bonino.[1] I circled the words "Doing theology in" as an expression of irony, since that is exactly what the Liberation Theology people do. Under a veneer of Bible passages, they hide a core of raw Marxist doctrine—all to the undoing of any legitimate theology.

It is all well and good to use the liberation theology people as whipping boys, but how many evangelical theologians have contributed to the undoing of theology as well? Theology used to be called the 'queen of the sciences.' It has long since been dethroned. Evangelical theology is in a sorry state, and we have only ourselves to blame. Walter Kaiser once said that the proof that evangelical theology is in a crisis is that Dallas Seminary had to hire a noted theologian away from Trinity Evangelical Divinity School.[2] A further indications is seen in the paucity of actual theological articles (about 20%) in the "Journal of the Evangelical **Theological** Society."

What is the cause of this decline? I would suggest that the faulty approaches to theology used by many Evangelicals is to blame! Evangelical theologians of great scholarly credentials have come to radically different conclusions and developed radically contradicting systems of theology. Consequently, the whole theological process is discredited. Let us consider how theology is undone by distorted perspectives, defective attitudes, and unsound methodologies. Examples can be found in different areas of theology. I trust my readers will not be offended if I raise your hackles. My purpose is to challenge your thinking, not to offend you.

APPROACHING THEOLOGY FROM A DISTORTED PERSPECTIVE

We all approach theological study from preconceived perspectives. It is the point from which we are approaching the data. In reading scientific instruments, we may get a wrong reading through lack of attention to parallax error (not 90°). Approaching the data from a skewed angle is even more harmful in theology.

Denial of the inspiration or sufficiency of Scripture

The most serious and fundamental problem comes when we enter into theological discussion with those who have a weak view of Scripture. It will inevitably color the results. Many will insist that their difference from us Evangelicals is hermeneutical or interpretive, when in reality the difference is more basic. Their view of the Bible's inspiration gives them a distorted perspective. They have the liberty to focus on certain passages at the expense of others since they do not believe that "**all Scripture is God-breathed**." As Evangelicals, we must give weight to all of God's revelation in Scripture. A score of years ago, I debated a pastor on capital punishment over the radio. As the debate progressed, I began to sense that we were not on the same page, his view of Scripture was different from mine. After we went off the air, I asked him more directly and got confirmation of my suspicion. There was no basis for coming to agreement since his perspective was skewed.

Another perspective problem arises from denial of the sufficiency of biblical revelation. This takes two forms. One is a reliance upon the historical development of the church as being not only providential but also authoritative. This is not only the Roman Catholic view but has a substantial support among Protestants and even Evangelicals as well. I remember a dialog I once had in print with a British Anglican bishop in Pakistan, who was professedly evangelical in theology. He admitted that hierarchy in church structure was not found in Scripture but was justified because of its historical development in the early church. It could be noted, of course, that the development continued on to the full-blown Roman Catholic system, including the papacy. Why stop with the Anglican episcopate? Carry it to its logical conclusion. In reality, the problem is the denial of the sufficiency of Scripture. This kind of thinking keeps cropping up among non-Anglican Evangelicals as well, in their undue deference to the decisions of church councils, synods, creeds, and the general historical development of churches.

A second form of this practical denial of sufficiency is seen in the tendency of theologians to defer to the views of the church fathers. Again, this is the special emphasis of Roman Catholicism, but is common also among Evangelicals today. I recently came across a work by Jean Daillè, a 17th century Huguenot pastor in Paris, entitled, *A Treatise on the Right Use of the Fathers*, in which he gave seventeen reasons why we cannot develop our theology from the fathers.[3] Although he was especially responding to heavy Romanist dependence upon the fathers, his arguments are just as relevant today. There are many contemporary examples of such dependence. I cite Heth and Wenham's *Jesus and Divorce* as a case in point.[4] They devote the first three chapter to the historical development before giving the biblical discussion, which thus skews the perspective. Even then they do not simply give an inductive exposition of the biblical data, but rather, provide a setting of the various views in contradistinction to each other (not an especially profitable methodology).

I see a number of problems with this tendency and expand upon them in chapter 18. The most serious is that the record of the history of Christianity is very fragmentary. The writings of many early Christian leaders have been lost or, in many cases, intentionally destroyed. Not only were Christians persecuted until AD 313 in the Roman empire, but as the politically dominant hierarchical church gained power, nonconforming Christians were in turn persecuted and their writings destroyed. If that weren't enough, after the fall of Rome, during the medieval period the barbarians destroyed much of the literary heritage of Christendom. I doubt that a good sampling of the viewpoints of early Christians even exists in the surviving writings.

The 'cult of the personality,' usually used in reference to communist leaders, is relevant here also. Origen was a great scholar who had a tremendous impact upon Christian theology. In many regards, however, he was the source of many heresies. Even more significant is the incredible impact of Augustine of Hippo. Much of Roman Catholicism and Protestantism can be traced back to him, for better or for worse. Luther and Calvin are highly reverenced by many Protestants today, but they had feet of clay. Many other denominational founders and church leaders are also more highly revered than they should be. This can only be described as a manifestation of the cult of the personality.

A distorted concept of God

Our concept of God and His attributes should rightly color our whole theology. Calvinists tend to identify holiness as the foremost attribute of God. Arminians (and liberals) tend to focus upon the love of God as primary. Even though I, too, taught one of those positions for many years, I now wonder why we must emphasize any attribute of God as more important than another. Do we not believe that the Lord Jesus was the most perfectly balanced and integrated personality ever? Do we not believe that God's love and holiness are perfectly met in the cross? George W. Peters developed a diagram (a triangle within a circle) which represents all the attributes of God as perfectly balanced in relation to each other.[5] Paul Enns stated this explicitly: "In the study of God's attributes it is important not to exalt one attribute over another; when that is done it presents a caricature of God."[6] I would suggest that this is a better starting point for our study of the theology of salvation than the others.

Substituting personal experience for Scripture

A century ago it could be said that there were three sources of authority usually appealed to in Christendom: Scripture, the traditions of the church, and reason. With the development of existential theology by Karl Barth earlier in the 20th century, existential experience was added as a fourth. Additionally, the pentecostal and charismatic movements also give greater weight to personal experience in the determination of truth. The question is essentially whether we interpret Scripture through our experience or interpret our experience by the plumbline of Scripture. The problem lies in the increased subjectivity of the process, if varying human experiences become our criteria. With the relativism of our contemporary culture, this subjectivity does not seem objectionable to people today.

Curiously, experience seems to be a major factor in the decision-making process of some from vastly differing traditions. Iain Murray tells the story of his conversion from premillennialism to postmillennialism in an account which involved only a passing reference to a few Scripture passages.[7] One would think that such a major theological pilgrimage would be based upon some serious biblical studies rather than just his own flow of experience.

Losing sight of the central themes of the Bible

The great scandal of the Protestant Reformation lays in the fact that Protestants did not send out missionaries for almost two centuries after the reformation. Even then, the first missionaries represented the radical fringe of the reformation rather than its 'mainstream'. This was despite the fact that the greatest theologian of the apostolic church was also its greatest missionary—the Apostle Paul. Somehow, the Reformers, and especially their successors, lost sight of a central theme of God's word: world evangelization. Indeed many learned theologians of the post-reformation period were most ingenious in rationalizing away the force of the missionary mandate.[8] It might be argued whether their theology was the cause or the consequence of this great omission. In any case, it did bleed through to the fabric of their theology. In the same way today, we construct our theologies oblivious of evangelism, missions, and other central biblical themes. We come with our own theological agenda and only perceive a small part of God's agenda.

Cultural overhang

As a missiologist, I would also suspect that much of our Western theological agenda and structure arises from our Greek-philosophy-derived culture and cognitive process, or ways of thinking. The theological agenda tends to be set by the demands of the various cultures in which we live. David Hesselgrave has put it well:

> But in the process of rigorous, biblical theologizing there are incipient dangers also. We can mistake the theology for the revelation. We can go beyond the revelation and insist upon our conclusions even where the Bible does not speak plainly. And—most important for our present consideration—we can communicate our theological systems and communicate in the manner of our theologizing rather than communicate the message of the Bible itself and in the manner of biblical revelation.[9]

Thus we must also admit that our Western theological systems are substantially incomplete because they do not face the agenda demanded of Christians in the Muslim, Hindu, Buddhist, Confucianist, or Animistic worlds. Indeed, have our theologies adequately confronted supernaturalistic cultures, where we confront overt demonic forces (Eph. 6:12)?

Even more important is to appreciate how much our cultural cognitive process differs from that of the Hebrew way of thinking and expressing ideas, which we find in the words of Christ Jesus and of some of the apostles. This is vital in the interpretation of Scripture. Not only must we be aware of the cultural context issue in our interpretation, but also of the cultural shift within the New Testament itself.

APPROACHING THEOLOGY WITH A DEFECTIVE ATTITUDE

There are a number of ways in which defective attitudes surface in our theological enterprise. Let us isolate a few.

A denominational or traditional bias

Frequently Christians' understanding of theology is seriously colored by their own denominational traditional background. We would expect this to be a problem for poorly taught laymen, who may not have the linguistic and hermeneutical background to decide theological issues without referring to their own background. We might even expect it from pastors who, although trained in these disciplines, have let the use of them lapse because of the pressures of pastoral ministry. But we would not expect it to be so rife among teachers and writers of theology. I suspect an emotional bonding to the denominational or theological tradition of our background is far more pervasive than most of us would like to admit.

We must remember that the Lord Jesus explicitly warned about putting the traditions of men before the word of God. He said to the Pharisees that **"you invalidated the word of God for the sake of your tradition"** (Mt. 15:6). The Apostle Paul warned the Colossian Christians about the danger of being taken **"captive through philosophy and empty deception, according to the tradition of men, . . ."** (Col. 2:8). We must be sensitive to this danger.

Indeed, F. F. Bruce, as an "impenitent Augustinian and Calvinist," in his foreword to Forster and Marston's God's *Strategy in Human History,* states:

> There is a great danger, when once we have adhered to one particular school of thought or adopted one particular system of theology, of reading the Bible in the light of that school or system and finding its distinctive features in what we read...The remedy for this is to bear resolutely in mind that our systems of doctrine must be based on biblical exegesis, not imposed upon it. The authors of this work bear this in mind, and make a special point of asking what the Scriptures really say.[10]

One egregious example from a noted scholar comes to mind: "He has commanded in the Old Testament the teaching of the 'whole counsel' of God, which is indeed the Reformed system of theology."[11] Quite apart from whether one is Reformed, Methodist, Baptist, or Pentecostal, it smacks of intellectual and spiritual arrogance to claim that any human system of doctrine can be considered "the whole counsel of God." We humans can only claim, at the most, to have perceived a small part of the whole plan of God. I suspect that few adherents of any of the diverse evangelical theological systems would be willing to claim their own system to be "the whole counsel of God." We have much to learn from Christians of other viewpoints, whether we agree with their systems or not.

The emotional attachment to a tradition also shows up in the flack I have received about statements in my missions textbook about the lack of missionary interest on the part of the Reformers—more emotional reaction than to anything else in my book. One reviewer suggested that, instead of dispelling missionary myths, I have perpetuated the myth that the Reformers were not missionary minded. None of his documentation is at all convincing to me, since the reality is that for two centuries after the Reformation Protestants did precious little to send out missionaries. Upon my discussing this with a missiological statesman of Reformed persuasion, he explained, "Well, that reviewer is T.R., "True Reformed." That spoke volumes!

A missionary friend of mine in Scandinavia once told me that in biblical discussions in Scandinavia, whether among Baptists, Pentecostals, or Mission Covenanters, the question usually is raised, "What did Luther say?" I believe there is a serious danger of giving undue reverence to the Reformers, or for that matter any other human leaders, living or dead, as great as they might be! As towering figures as the Reformers were, we must remember that they were grievously in error in some areas of their beliefs and practices, even though they brought a great return to biblical religion. We should not make them the touchstone of truth. It would seem to me that, as Evangelicals, our spiritual heritage may be more appropriately found in the persecuted evangelical prereformation groups and some of the sounder anabaptists of reformation days rather than in the mainstream of the Reformation. Indeed, American evangelicalism owes far more to the radical fringe of the reformation than to its mainstream.[12]

Emotional reaction to opposing views

As human beings we are emotional creatures and tend to react emotionally to views different from our own. This is one of the major obstacles to complete rationality, since we find so much of mankind caught up in irrational behavior. Christians are not exempt from this. G. C. Berkouwer has put it well:

> Reaction is a phenomenon in Christian thought that has played a large role in the history of the Church and its theology. Reaction from some unbiblically one-sided proposition has often landed theology in another unbiblically one-sided proposition. Theologians attacking a caricatured theology have often created their own caricature of Christian thought. Observing that a given aspect of faith was neglected, Christians have often proceeded to accentuate that aspect so much that it became the be-all of the faith, with a resulting neglect of other aspects.[13]

There are many examples of this. One was the reaction against Arianism, which led to the majority church's reference to Mary as the Mother of God, which in turn brought about the reaction toward Nestorianism. All were overreactions. The Roman Catholic Church reacted to the Protestant Reformation by the extremes of the Council of Trent. The Remonstrants took Arminius's reaction to the scholastic Calvinism of his day and carried it to an extreme. In turn, the scholastic Calvinists reacted by hardening the system to supralapsarianism.[14] Perhaps we could bring it closer to home by saying that some branches of fundamentalism have overreacted to liberalism by developing a rigid legalism and unbiblical militancy (I still call myself a fundamentalist, hopefully, in the best sense of the word). Although the charge of obscurantism has long been unfairly leveled against Evangelicals and Fundamentalists, aberrations, such as the King-James-only movement, are clearly over-reactions. Then Neoevangelicals overreacted to extreme fundamentalism, throwing out the baby with the bath water, in the denial of verbal plenary inspiration and in indulgence in teleological ethics (the end justifies the means). And on it goes!

Scholarship and motivation

Let's face it—most theological writers would like to earn the respect of their peers for their scholarship. Even more praiseworthy for an evangelical scholar would be to gain the respect of liberals. Sometimes these natural desires distort the methodology and color the results. Out of this motivation we end up bowing the knee to the Baal of intellectualism (or should we say, an affected intellectualism). One reputed evangelical scholar rarely quoted his evangelical brethren, but quoted non-evangelical writers many times as often. One wonders if he felt that non-evangelicals were far more enlightened theologically and exegetically than evangelical theologians. He never quoted Erich Sauer's two books in that discipline, which F. F. Bruce commended as the best in that field.[15]

In God's sight, motivation is of primary importance. To give that scholar the benefit of the doubt, let us hope that his motivation was to influence liberals toward a more conservative position. However, it is imperative that we check our motivation before we write theology. Who are we trying to impress?

Failure to honestly understand opposing views

Basic to intelligent and spiritually minded theological discussion of any debated issue is an honest attempt to understand what those who hold the opposing viewpoint are really saying. We must be extremely careful to try to understand their whole viewpoint and not misrepresent them. This means that we should not quote them out of context or draw false inferences from their statements. Not only is this basic scholarly integrity, but, especially for us as Christians, it is imperative not to so sin against our fellow believers. Yet this is a continuing problem in theological discussion.

One of the most disturbing things to me over many years has been the continued insistence of some scholars that dispensationalism teaches more than one way of salvation and is therefore doubtfully evangelical. John Gerstner made this charge in his *Primer on Dispensationalism* back in 1982 and reiterated it again in his full-length book in 1991. In the first, he did not even allude to Charles Ryrie's 1965 definitive work in which he had already responded to that charge. Although by 1991 he documented Ryrie and admitted that all the dispensationalists he had heard or read deny teaching more than one way of salvation, he still insisted that this was a valid criticism. He went on to reaffirm it with this statement: "The sheer persistence of this line of criticism by competent and well-meaning Christian theologians says a great deal about the dispensational lack of success at rebuttal."[16] I would suggest it says more about some theologians' failure to understand what dispensationalists are saying. The significant point that Gerstner had not grasped is that although dispensations are not different ways of salvation, they are distinct 'rules of life' for believers in each distinct age. This is a phrase that Lewis Sperry Chafer used over and over again and is most helpful in understanding what dispensationalism is all about. In neither book did Gerstner explain the logical connection he saw between different dispensations and different ways of salvation. There is no such connection despite Gerstner's (and others') insistence that there must be. Perhaps if he had sat down with Charles Ryrie or some other creditable dispensational spokeman, much of this misrepresentation could have been avoided.

To his great credit, J. O. Buswell, Jr., although not a dispensationalist, was very fair in treating the issue of dispensationalists' statements which seem to imply that people under the law were saved on a meritorious basis. He pointed out that similar statements can be found in Charles Hodge and John Calvin, so to be fair we would have to acknowledge this same lapse in the writings of people of both schools in past generations and not just criticize dispensationalists.[17]

METHODOLOGICAL PROBLEMS

As in everyday life, the method we use to get a job done is exceedingly important to its successful completion. As a student in chemistry lab, I used a wrong method of putting a stopper on a glass condenser and ended up reaming the shard of broken glass into my finger. It seemed like a minor methodological error, but the result was catastrophic. Even worse was my experience in jogging. According to Dr. Kenneth Cooper, failure to wind down properly can have catastrophic consequences. Unfortunately, I had not read his book before that one and only time I failed to wind down. An hour later I had a massive heart attack which came close to killing me. As you can imagine, I am now very meticulous about my methodology when I jog. Methodology is exceedingly important in theology as well. Defective methodology will get us erroneous theology. Let us examine a number of current defective methodologies.

Substituting survey of theologies for real theology

Of great importance in our theological methodology is the survey of the development of doctrine in the history of Christianity and of the contemporary views in a particular area. This is important background for our theological study. But it is just that—background. The history of Christian doctrine is not theology, nor is a survey of contemporary theology. Yet some of our greatest evangelical theologians have been satisfied to publish works which never quite make it into the field of theology, per se. I hope all of my readers have already gotten a solid foundation for their theology in the doctrine of verbal plenary inspiration of Scripture. In this regard, I was greatly helped by the writings of B. B. Warfield. Yet Dr. Warfield wrote a helpful little book entitled *The Plan of Salvation*[18] in which he merely surveyed the various theological views. However, there was little reference to Scripture (only 2 references in 132 pages), exegesis, or actual theology. Presumably it was not intended as a theological work. But it is indicative of a strong tendency among theologians to give overweight to such survey.

The great Princeton theologian, Charles Hodge, devoted 55 pages to a discussion of efficacious grace, with extensive survey of the literature. Of this only seven pages are a discussion of the determinative Scripture passages. Strictly, we would have to call this the "history of Christian thought" rather than theology.

More recently, we have R. C. Sproul's *Willing to Believe,* which surveys nine historical positions on the free will/total inability debate, without any real direct exegesis of Scripture.[19] Of approximately forty Bible references found in this book virtually all arise only in the quotations or allusions from his nine historical personalities. There is no direct exegesis of Scripture. But I will return to this in chapter 4 and appendix B.

When I was a young Christian, my pastor, James Rehnberg, complained about some of the professors under whom he had studied in seminary. He said that they would survey several views on a particular point and say, "May the Holy Spirit show you the best view." He felt that the Holy Spirit should have helped those professors to point the students to the right view based upon solid Scriptural reasons. Survey is not theology. We must make sure that our main emphasis is on scriptural exegesis as the inductive basis for our theology and not upon the closely related disciplines, valuable as they may be.

Neglecting the primacy of inductive methodology

I am part of a generation which began to be influenced by inductive Bible study methodology, as set forth by Robert Traina and his disciples. We were taught to observe, observe, and observe again what the Scripture actually says. Groups such as InterVarsity and the Navigators have emphasized asking the right questions of the text and drawing the answers directly out of the text itself. The last century has evidenced an escalation of the science of hermeneutics and the development of the exegetical tools for arriving at the true meaning of the biblical text. Our problem has been to utilize these insights in developing our theologies. Unfortunately, theologians have yet to catch up by giving priority to inductive methodology in our theologies.

The proper place of induction and deduction. It should be axiomatic, both in science and theology, that inductive, empirical evidence is far more dependable than deductive reasoning. Before proceeding any farther, let us get our definitions clearly understood. Induction is defined as "a bringing forward of separate facts or instances, esp. so as to prove a general statement." In logic, it is "reasoning from particular facts or individual cases to a general conclusion." Deduction is "reasoning from a known principle to an unknown, from the general to the specific, or from a premise to a logical conclusion."[20]

Let me illustrate the difference from medical science. For years the medical consensus was that eggs and nuts in our diet contribute to high blood cholesterol and therefore to heart disease, since they are high in fat and cholesterol. Some years ago I became aware of a contrarian approach to diet, which caught my attention because the Lord Jesus confirmed in Luke 11:11-13 that fish and eggs are good things to give to children. Assuming that the Lord Jesus, the Creator, knew more about diet than doctors today, I adopted this contrarian approach with dramatic results in correcting my blood cholesterol. We recently received a copy of the *Nurses' Health Study Newsletter* about a radical reversal of medical advice on eggs and nuts, which resulted from the many years of the Nurses' Health Study. Dr. Willett explains that the previous advice was based upon "hypothesis and indirect evidence rather than direct data."[21] In other words, it was deductive rather than inductive; it was *a priori* rather than *a posteriori*. And it was dead wrong!

Exegesis of the determining Scripture passages gives us the particular facts, which must be the starting point of all theology. Only after we have exhausted the inductive process may we turn to deduction. Deductive reasoning is valid only in confirming and testing the results of our induction or in filling in the gaps where the inductive data is missing or incomplete. It must never be given priority over induction.

A good example of this would be the discussion on the impeccability of Christ. There is no strong inductive data to prove that Christ could not have sinned. Exegesis of Hebrews 4:15 and other relevant passages allows for this viewpoint and perhaps leans towards it. But in the absence of strong inductive evidence, the deductive process comes into play. The implications of Christ's deity and the union of Christ's human and divine natures lead to the doctrine of impeccability. However, we must always go first to induction and recognize the limitations of the deductive process.

An example in an otherwise good book, of putting deduction before induction, is found in Robert H. Stein's discussion of Hebrews 6:4-6.[22] He argues that this difficult passage must be interpreted in the light of the analogy of Scripture. Since many other passages teach the eternal security of the believer, and since the doctrines of predestination and unconditional election confirm eternal security, this passage cannot contradict this truth and must be interpreted in harmony with it. He admits, however, "As one who has always believed in the doctrine of eternal security, I must confess that this passage does indeed conflict with such a view."[23] Unfortunately he does not come up with a cogent interpretation which is harmonious with such a view and thus leaves the problem unresolved. Although his principle is sound, he should have explored all of the inductive data more carefully before resorting to deduction. This I have sought to do in my discussion of this passage in chapter 15.

Philosophical presuppositions. Another way in which deduction has intruded too early in the theological process is in the area of our philosophical presuppositions. By beginning our theological process with certain philosophical presuppositions we, in effect, give them priority over the inductive, exegetical data. I remember a discussion in a seminary theology class which was greatly colored by the professor's statement that "God cannot know that which He has not willed." This was an unexamined philosophical statement which affected the outcome of the discussion. I, as a philosophically naive engineering graduate, bought the premise and the conclusions. Years later in teaching theology I came across a discussion of that presupposition by another theologian, just as well qualified philosophically as my professor, who argued more cogently against it. Perhaps my philosophical naivete is an advantage. It has made me very suspicious of philosophical presuppositions (as the apostle Paul seems to be in Colossians 2:8). I suppose we all have our philosophical presuppositions. But whatever the reality of the case, of this I am sure: we must not give priority to them. Inductive exegesis must be the starting point.

The place of the Biblical-Theology discipline. Most theological writers seem to see the "Biblical-Theology" discipline as inferior and preliminary to systematic theology. Having taught both disciplines for over a quarter century, I have concluded that this is not the case. Biblical Theology is fully an equal and parallel discipline to systematics.[A] It is only our Greek- influenced, western-cultural way of thinking which has prejudiced us to favor systematics over Biblical Theology. Since the Biblical discipline is tied in more closely to exegesis and predisposes toward a more inductive methodology, it should be given a larger place in evangelical scholarship. But the neglect of Biblical Theology by Evangelicals has worked against a proper emphasis upon inductive exegesis. I am especially impressed with the value of diachronic Biblical Theology over the other methodologies in use, since it brings out the progressive, historical dimension of biblical revelation.[B] I have found a far greater openness to Biblical Theology in non-western cultures.[24] One good recent effort to

---

A. I have capitalized Biblical Theology to distinguish it as a distinct discipline, not just a biblically oriented theology. It may be defined as the study of theology in a historical, progressive framework, that is, studying God's revelation in the same way God gave it, that is, progressively and in human historical contexts. In my view, the best form is the diachronic methodology as exemplified by Erich Sauer and Geerhardus Vos, since its agenda intrinsically forces us to stay closer to exegesis in its historical, chronological, and dispensational context.

B. "The course of salvation thus shows itself as a *richly coloured chain of periods.* A stairway leading upwards, divided into the most manifold articulated parts of a historic organism. . . . The Holy Scripture is plainly not a spiritual-divine-uniform 'block,' but a wonderful articulated historic-prophetic spiritual *organism.* 'It must be read organically, age-wise, according to the Divine ages'." (Erich Sauer, *The Dawn of World Redemption*, p. 193.)

integrate Biblical and systematic theology is rightly titled, *Integrative Theology*, by Lewis and Demarest.[25] I will seek in my work to examine the relevant Scriptures on any subject diachronically, that is, through time so that we see each passage in sequence in its historical context.

Failure to carry out exegesis properly

Once we are committed to the primacy of an inductive methodology, the next problem is the development of a sound exegetical methodology for inductive study of the relevant Scripture texts. One of the best efforts exegetically is that of James Oliver Buswell, Jr.[26] Although we might not always agree with the results of Buswell's exegesis, his work is commendable as a serious attempt to do the exegesis. It is sad to say that this has not been true of theologies historically or even on the contemporary scene. Let us focus on some especially troublesome areas.

Prooftexting. We frequently accuse the cultists of the practice of prooftexting, by which we mean using a barrage of Scripture references, out of context or otherwise misinterpreted. Indeed the Jehovah's Witnesses have a book of prooftexts for their doctrines, which is available only to their workers. Not only is it selective in leaving out references which contradict their position, but it assumes that a superficial reading of these verses out of context will lead to the truth. This approach implies that careful exegesis is not necessary. But even some of the best evangelical theologians fall into doing the same thing.

On one occasion I checked out a whole paragraph of references in a theology which purported to prove that God is **equally** present everywhere. After hours of investigating all of the references, I concluded that they only supported the omnipresence of God. None of them supported the **equal** presence of God everywhere, which is a dubious notion.

Prooftexting is a violation of the old saying that "a text out of context is pretext." Basically, it is failure to do the necessary work of exegesis. Most of all it violates the first law of interpretation which is the law of context. "Context is king" is a helpful aphorism, which needs to be engraved on the hand of every Bible student. But when theologians fail to discuss the context of each passage referred to, they violate this rule, even if the verse is quoted in full. It is not just the adjacent verses to which I am referring, but also the whole chapter and, indeed, the flow of thought of the whole book. We may not even stop there, because the historical and cultural contexts are also of vital importance. To use language from missiology, we must consider the differing cognitive process (ways of thinking) of the Hebrew and Graeco-Roman cultures into which God's revelation came. For example, Christ's avoidance of the first person in his speech is very different from our cultural way of speaking. Each statement of Scripture must first be exegeted in its own integrity before any theological work can be done. But many have failed to exegete the Scriptures adduced, and thus, are guilty of prooftexting.

Failure to check the original. Frequently we do not do our homework in the original languages and build, not only sermons, but also our theology, on an erroneous English translation, especially when most available translations are imprecise or defective. Over the years, I have noted the tendency of translators to get in the rut of following a translational tradition, rather than courageously representing the original in a fresh way.

One very vivid example of this comes to mind. I had invited an amillennial pastor to present his case in a theology course of mine. He gave a tightly reasoned case based upon the premise that Christ inaugurated the "last days" at His first coming, arguing from the English text of Hebrews 1:1-2. After class some students gathered in my office for discussion, and we checked the Greek text. We were surprised to find the words, *ep' eschatou ton hēmerōn toutōn*, which rendered literally becomes, "at the end of these days." Since the Apostle had just referred to the ancient revelation as coming "in many portions and in many ways", it seems clear that he was now referring to the many ages which preceded the first coming of Christ. This is confirmed by his statement in 9:26: ". . . but now once at the consummation of the ages He has been manifested to put away sin by the sacrifice of Himself" (NAS). Thus, the whole premise of this gentlemen's laborious argument proved to be unsupported and insupportable.[27]

Word studies. The value of word studies is under serious discussion today. No doubt word studies were overworked and abused by past generations of scholars. We now recognize that word studies in themselves cannot uncover the meaning of the text. Words are always to be understood in their contexts. However, we must not throw out the baby with the bath water. Word studies do give us the range of meanings to which a word is susceptible so that we may select the correct meaning by considering the context. But in so doing we must be careful to avoid the abuses of this tool. Donald Carson has suggested sixteen word-study fallacies we must avoid.[28]

Ironically, a major hindrance to doing primary word-study research is the availability of excellent lexicons and theological dictionaries. But for serious theological study we cannot trust secondary sources, even Kittel's *Theological Dictionary.* Bromiley in the Translator's Preface warns, "When this is understood, Kittel is safeguarded against the indiscriminate enthusiasm which would make it a sole and absolute authority in lexical and exegetical matters."[29] In my own research on the meaning of *metanoia* (repentance), I found that the articles in both Kittel and Colin Brown's *Dictionary of New Testament Theology* were not only guilty of bias and faulty judgment, but most heinously misstated the basic linguistic data upon which the reader is to make a judgment. This is in reference to the translation of the corresponding Old Testament Hebrew words in the Septuagint and the

New Testament (cf. appendix G for fuller clarification). How is it that such highly reputed works could err in the most elementary data, which can be (and should be) checked by any Greek novice who knows how to use a Greek concordance? The point is that we must not depend upon secondary sources.

Walter Kaiser has made a significant point which I believe was ignored in the above Kittel articles. He speaks of the "Analogy of Antecedent Scripture", by which he means that we must view each context only in the light of **antecedent** contexts. It seems logical that the same should apply to word studies. We should primarily focus upon the usage of a word before the context in question, since later usage may show semantic shift in a different direction.[30]

Another warning is imperative at this point. Even when we have carefully done our grammatical and syntactical study and considered the results of our word studies, we must not forget the primacy of context in drawing our conclusions. The reason for this is, as Buswell said, that language is not mathematics. Carson has emphasized this in his discussion of the flexibility of New Testament Greek grammar.[31]

An example of a too rigid or pedantic concept of grammar and word usage is seen in the accusation made against the apostle John regarding his Greek usage in the book of Revelation. It is claimed that John's grammar is defective in the repeated phrase, *ho ōn kai ho ēn kai ho erchomenos* ("He who was and is and is the coming one" 1:4, 8). Have these critics ever considered the possibility that John intentionally violated normal usage to make the point that Christ is coming back? How frequently preachers today intentionally use colloquial speech to make a point, such as, "It ain't necessarily so!" John was emphasizing the return of the Lord Jesus, and to emphasize his point intentionally used *erchomai* in an abnormal way. Many other examples could be given from contemporary languages of ungrammatical colloquial expressions used for a variety of reasons. Indeed, language is not mathematics!

Another important principle in word studies is to be careful not to confuse the meanings of distinct Greek words derived from the same root. I will have many occasions to allude to this most important statement in Chamberlain's *Exegetical Grammar*: "*The student should learn once and for all that every single letter added to a Greek root adds something to the idea expressed by the root.*"[C]

Years after graduating from seminary I felt the need as a missionary to restudy baptism. It was quite disillusioning to me to find upon investigation that one of my professors had made serious misstatements about the usage

C. William Douglas Chamberlain, *An Exegetical Grammar of the Greek New Testament* (New York: Macmillan, 1952), p. 11. He gives a list of twentdly distinct words derived from the root *dik*, which is most instructive in illustrating the Greek word-building process. Probably something similar has been done or could be done in the Hebrew.

of *baptizein*, disillusioning until I realized that he had confused *baptein* and *baptizein*. Chamberlain's statement helped me to realize that these are two distinct words with two distinct ranges of meaning.

Old Testament quotations in the New. In recent years I have been especially sensitized about the absolute necessity of carefully studying the Old Testament context of quotations in the New. It frequently casts a totally different light upon our understanding of the flow of thought of the author. One of the most significant examples would be the many quotations in Romans 9, as Forster and Marston highlighted.[32] For example, when we examine Paul's use of the potter's wheel symbolism, drawn from Jeremiah 18:1ff, we get a radically different impression of Paul's point from that which many commentators and theologians read into it. Jeremiah's picture is of the nation Israel as a marred vessel on the potter's wheel, which God can remake as He sovereignly pleases before it is fired. Paul's point is the same. The corporate nation was set aside dispensationally for rejecting the Messiah. God has the sovereign right to restore Israel, as Paul confirms in Romans 11 that He will do.

Old Testament background. A related error is failure to examine the Old Testament background of New Testament concepts. A significant example would be the Old Testament background of the usage of rock in Matthew 16:18. Over thirty times in the Old Testament 'rock' is a symbol used for God. It is unthinkable that we should interpret Christ's words to Peter apart from the Old Testament usage. Therefore, neither Peter himself, nor Peter's confession qualify as good interpretive options. I concur with Augustine's final opinion that Christ Himself is the rock (for fuller discussion see chapter 16).

Not considering all the options. Interpreters (and translators) frequently do not consider all the exegetical options in their interpretation. Sometimes it is a failure to not only consult the original language, but also to consider the grammatical, syntactical, or linguistic options which might solve a problem. This assumes, of course, that the interpreter has even recognized the problem (which is not always true). One astounding example to me, as a missiologist, is the case of the problem of Colossians 1:23. It seems as if Paul is saying that the gospel has been preached to all of creation before AD 63. We know that this was not historically true. If we survey the commentaries we find that neither Peake nor Eadie seem aware of the problem. Moule, Maclaren, Lightfoot, Robertson, and Geisler call it hyperbole or rhetorical coloring. Earle Ellis goes so far as to call it "hyperbole inevitable to a 'born' evangelist."[33] However, what none of these commentators have observed is that the verb *keruxthentos* is an aorist participle which frequently has an ingressive force and as a participle reflects continuing action. Thus it makes perfect sense to translate, "the gospel, **which is beginning to be preached** in all creation under the heavens." The difficulty is so simply resolved without putting Paul (and God's word) in a bad light. So we go back to a basic inductive principle: observe, observe, observe!

Related to this would be a cavalier *a priori* dismissal of certain options because they are not thought to be respectable in the academic community due to certain prejudices and biases. I recall reading a response to a reader's question about the meaning of Matthew 24:34 by a faculty member in the *Bulletin* of a prestigious seminary. He gave a number of possible interpretations, but did not even mention the possibility that *genea* might be mistranslated here and elsewhere. Perhaps a suggestion from the *Scofield Reference Bible* notes is not to be take seriously because C. I Scofield was not a part of the evangelical academic establishment. However, the Scofield note here is totally supportable: "Gr. *genea*, the primary definition of which is 'race, kind, family, stock, breed.' (So all lexicons.)"[34] Years ago I wrote a paper on *The Impact of Mistranslation on the Millennial Issue*, in which I surveyed the major lexicons and found that none of them list 'generation' as the primary meaning of the word, and noted that Kittel rules out this meaning at all: "the sense of the totality of those living as contemporaries is not found in Greek, though it must be presupposed in explanation of d."[35] After surveying the usage in Matthew's Gospel as confirmatory, I quoted Bishop Ryle:

> These verses teach us . . . that until Christ returns to this earth, the Jews will always remain a separate people. . . . I see no other interpretation of these controverted words, 'this generation', which is the least satisfactory, and is not open to very serious objections. . . . The view that I have propounded is not new. It is adopted by Bede, Paroeus, Facius Illyricus, Calovius, Jansenius, Due Veil, Adam Clarke, and Stier.[36]

So we see that Scofield had some illustrious, antecedent support for his suggestion, which should not have been ignored.

Getting into an interpretive rut. One of my teaching colleagues used to drill into his students the question, "What is God doing here?" for their inductive Bible study. Frequently we fail to ask the right questions of the text, and thus fail to get the right answers. There is an impressive amount of literature and discussion about the nature of 'tongues' on the day of Pentecost and subsequently. Some years ago, I was very impressed when one of my brighter students pointed up the missionary significance of the gift of 'languages' (as it ought to be translated) on that day. Here were Jews speaking of God's glorious salvation plan in Gentile languages as a foreglimpse of the ultimate missionary outreach of the church to people of every tongue, tribe, and language. How many commentators have missed this key dimension of the Pentecost event?

Another example of how we frequently fail to ask the right questions of the text is seen in the book of Jonah. I am convinced by the events of chapter four that Jonah did not tell the whole message God sent him to tell—he left out repentance and the possibility of deliverance. It was inconceivable that God should send him to proclaim only doom. Yet none of the commentators I have been able to consult even raise the question as to whether Jonah should have or did preach repentance. It seems clear that Jonah's ethnocentrism caused him to drop from his message the possibility of God's withholding judgment. He wanted Nineveh destroyed. Otherwise why did he sit outside of the city waiting for its destruction? It seems that most commentators have missed a major issue in the book.

Defective hermeneutics

It is beyond the scope of this book to discuss hermeneutics (the science of interpretation) in any detail. There are a host of books available today on this. I believe a word is in order about the imperative of literal hermeneutics. Scholars may debate endlessly about the meaning or non-meaning of this term, but I believe it is more perspicuous and clear than they will admit. There is obviously a crass literalism to be avoided, that is, failure to recognize the many common figures of speech, such as metaphor, simile, hyperbole, etc. Roman Catholicism has lapsed into such crass literalism in failing to see the obvious metaphor in Christ's words, "This is my body." But beyond such readily recognizable figures of speech and poetic language, I am convinced that there is no justification for spiritualizing any part of the Bible. This practice injects a subjectivism which makes God's word a nose of wax to be bent in any direction one's presuppositions lead. I believe this does a disservice to the integrity of God's objective word.

TESTING OUR THEOLOGY

Although we must never fall into pragmatism in developing our theology, I believe it is important to test our theology in the real world of human beings. There is a serious tendency to develop an ivory tower theology which has no relevance to real life, or worse yet, contradicts today's realities. If our theology fails these tests, we should go back to the drawing board and reexamine our theology and see where we might have erred.

As a missionary in Pakistan 40 years ago I found it hard to reconcile the Pope's edicts on birth control with the gross overpopulation of the Indian subcontinent. I lived among wall-to-wall people in the Punjab when there were less than 50 million people in West Pakistan. Now the population there is over 140 million. Deafforestation of the foothills of the Himalayas mountains caused by overpopulation was causing devastating annual floods even then. Most Evangelicals would agree that the Pope's view of birth control is based on natural theology, not Scripture. He should have tested his theology in the real world of suffering humans.

Another way to test our theology is to see its ramifications in related disciplines, such as ethics. When I began to teach Christian ethics years ago, I found that some of the extreme statements made by the early dispensationalists had serious ethical ramifications. They seemed to put us in ethical antinomianism (not soteriological antinomianism, as has been wrongly charged). The ethical test forced me to modify my dispensationalism somewhat.

Years ago, I had numerous opportunities to hear one of the greatest expositors of this century from time to time. I'll never forget him making an absurd statement on one occasion: "The children of all true believers will ultimately come to faith in Christ and be saved, even if it is on their deathbed." That statement should have been subjected to the historical test. If it were true, then Christianity would have to show numerical growth in every geographical area, except where most Christians are martyred. This certainly was not the case when the Muslims conquered North Africa. They did not martyr most of the Christians. As they usually do, they put social, cultural, and financial pressure upon the Christians. The population there now is solidly Muslim, and they were not immigrants; they are the descendants of true believers! So that theological statement needed to be re-examined.

Lastly, there is the apologetic test. For example, there is tremendous apologetic value in the chronological prophecy of Daniel 9:24-27. The 69 heptads of years (483 years) from the decree of Artaxerxes Longimanus (444 BC) bring us wonderfully to the crucifixion of Christ about AD 33, as Sir Robert Anderson showed over a century ago in *The Coming Prince* (p. 128). This apologetic is only valuable for those of us who take prophecy in an essentially literal framework. Those who spiritualize this prophecy to fit their system lose its apologetic efficacy. I think that this is a bad trade-off.

CONCLUSION

Theology did not get a good start after the Reformation, considering that Lutherans and Calvinists put much energy into vitriolic debate about Christ's presence in the elements of the Lord's Supper. However, Paul stressed the Lord's absence: ". . . until He comes" (1 Cor. 11:26). This was little better than the pointless discussion of the *filioque* clause centuries earlier. We need a continuing reformation in the church and in theology, especially in theological methodology. We must start by confessing our past failures as sin, and repent of our carnal biases, or worse yet our failure to do serious exegesis, if we are to restore evangelical theology back into its rightful place as the queen of sciences.

---

1. Jose Miguez Bonino, *Doing Theology in a Revolutionary Situation* (Philadelphia: Fortress Press, 1975).
2. Walter C. Kaiser, Jr., in a lecture at Trinity Evangelical Divinity School, July 18, 1979.
3. Jean Daille, *A Treatise on the Right Use of the Fathers* (1631), trans. T. Smith (Philadelphia: Presbyterian Board, 1842).

4. William A. Heth and Gordon J. Wenham, *Jesus and Divorce: The Problem with the Evangelical Consensus* (Nashville: Thomas Nelson, 1985).

5. George W. Peters, *A Biblical Theology of Missions* (Chicago: Moody Press, 1972), p. 56.

6. Paul Enns, *The Moody Handbook of Theology* (Chicago: Moody Press, 1972), p. 188.

7. Iain Murray, *The Puritan Hope* (London: Banner of Truth).

8. C. Gordon Olson, *What in the World Is God Doing? The Essentials of Global Missions* , 4th ed., pp. 113-20.

9. David J. Hesselgrave, *Communicating Christ Cross-Culturally* (GR: Zondervan, 1978), p. 212.

10. F. F. Bruce in Roger T. Forster and V. Paul Marston, *God's Strategy in Human History*, p. vii.

11. John H. Gerstner, *A Primer on Dispensationalism*, p. 15. I have not had opportunity to find any similar statement in his subsequent full-length critique: *Wrongly Dividing the Word of Truth: A Critique of Dispensationalism*.

12. Earl D. Radmacher, *What the Church Is All About: A Biblical and Historical Study*, pp.79-85.

13. G. C. Berkouwer, "Election and Doctrinal Reaction," *Christianity Today,* 5:586.

14. W. Robert Godfrey, "Reformed Thought on the Extent of the Atonement to 1618," *Westminster Theological Journal*, pp. 155-67.

15. Erich Sauer, *The Dawn of World Redemption* and *The Triumph of the Crucified* (GR: Eerdmans, 1951). George Eldon Ladd in *A Theology of the New Testament* (Eerdmans, 1974) documents Rudolph Bultmann 69 times, with similar numbers for Cullman, Dodd, Jeremias, and John A. T. Robinson. He never refers to Sauer, only has 15 references to Geerhardus Vos; Oswald Allis, 1; F. F. Bruce, 27; Lewis Sperry Chafer, 1; Lightfoot, 4; R. N. Longnecker, 16; L. Morris, 28; Alva McClain, 4; John Murray, 5; Charles Ryrie, 2; etc.

16. Gerstner, *Wrongly Dividing* , p. 152.

17. Buswell, II, p. 314-9.

18. Benjamin B. Warfield, *The Plan of Salvation* (Grand Rapids: Eerdmans Publishing Co., 1935).

19. R. C. Sproul, *Willing to Believe: The Controversy over Free Will* (Grand Rapids: Baker, 1997).

20. David B. Guralnick, *Webster's New World Dictionary* (New York: Prentice Hall, 1986).

21. Walter C. Willett, "Old Beliefs Challenged by New Data," in *Nurses' Health Study Newsletter*, vol. 6 (June 1999), p. 5.

22. Robert H. Stein, *Difficult Passages in the New Testament* (Grand Rapids: Baker, 1990), pp. 348-55.

23. Ibid., p. 353.

24. In 1979 I wrote a paper for David J. Hesselgrave setting forth this proposition entitled. "The Utilization of Biblical Theology in the Third World," about which he was very enthusiastic wanting me to develop into a doctoral project. However, I did not succeed in pulling together the diverse disciplines necessary to complete this project.

25. Gordon R. Lewis and Bruce A. Demarest, *Integrative Theology* (Grand Rapids: Zondervan, 1990)

26. James Oliver Buswell, Jr., *A Systematic Theology of the Christian Religion* (Grand Rapids: Zondervan, 1962).

27. He had stated that the argument was derived from Geerhardus Vos, but I have been unable to document it. I have written a paper entitled, "The Impact of Mistranslation on the Millennial Issue."

28. D. A. Carson, *Exegetical Fallacies* (Grand Rapids: Baker, 1984).

29. Gerhard Kittel ed., *Theological Dictionary of the New Testament* (Grand Rapids: Eerdmans, 1964), vol. I, p. ix.

30. Walter C. Kaiser, Jr., *Toward an Old Testament Theology* (GR: Zondervan, 1978), pp. 18-9.

31. D. A. Carson, *Exegetical Fallacies* (Grand Rapids: Baker, 1984), p. 67ff.

32. Roger T. Forster and V. Paul Marston, *God's Strategy in Human History*, pp. 69-99.

33. E. Earle Ellis, "Colossians". *Wycliffe Bible Commentary* (Chicago: Moody, 1962), p. 1139.

34. C. I. Scofield, *The Scofield Reference Bible* (NY: Oxford University Press, 1909), en loc.

35. Friedreich Buchsel in Gerhard Kittel, *Theological Dictionary of the New Testament*, vol. I:662-3.

36. J. C. Ryle, *Expository Thoughts on the Gospels* (NY: Robert Carter, 1875), pp. 323-4.

The full Arminian position is as much open to error as is extreme Calvinism. My aim is to reach beyond the Calvinist-Arminian controversy to a position which is biblical, and which therefore accepts whatever is true in both Calvinism and Arminianism. -I. Howard Marshall

Calvinism emphasizes divine sovereignty and free grace; Arminianism emphasizes human responsibility. The one restricts the saving grace to the elect; the other extends it to all men on the condition of faith. . . . The Bible gives us a theology which is more human than Calvinism, and more divine than Arminianism, and more Christian than either of them. -Philip Schaff

2

WHAT IS MEANT BY A MEDIATE THEOLOGY OF SALVATION?

As far as a theology of salvation is concerned, Evangelicals seem to be divided into two or three polarized camps. Christians get the impression that one must be either a hard-core five-point Calvinist or a rank Arminian, and that there are no other viable options. Indeed, there is a no-man's land between the two, with little communication or interaction on salvation-theology issues. With few exceptions, Calvinists are not reading and responding to Arminian thought regarding salvation-truth, and Arminians are not reading and responding to Calvinistic treatments. After all, the issue was settled almost four centuries ago! And evangelical Lutherans are quite disengaged from the controversy since they are quite confident that Luther settled it in his lifetime, despite the paradoxical nature of Lutheran theology. There is, however, some encouragement in a few recent works from both sides responding to one another, but they are more like volleys from opposing fortresses, with little recognition of any middle ground between.[A]

A. The two volumes Clark Pinnock edited started a new interchange: *Grace Unlimited* (1975) and *The Grace of God, the Will of Man: A Case for Arminianism* (1989). The InterVarsity 'four views' book, *Predestination and Free Will* (1986) sought clarification. The Calvinists responded with their two 1995 volumes: Thomas R. Schreiner & Bruce A. Ware, eds., *The Grace of God, The Bondage of the Will*. They respond to each other but not to a mediate soteriology, which solves most of the problems which they have with each other.

This polarization of positions among Evangelicals is unhealthy and does not foster honest inquiry into what the Bible really teaches. There are many intermediate positions which are not recognized by those at the antipodes. This polarization is harmful to evangelical theology since extremely contradictory positions discredit us in the eyes of non-Evangelicals. I believe that a less polarized, mediate position must be developed by the careful use of a radically fresh inductive study.

My proposal. I proposed a mediate theology of salvation at the annual meeting of the Evangelical Theological Society in Toronto in 1981. I entitled my original paper, "Beyond Calvinism and Arminianism," because I was convinced that we must progress beyond the theological giants of past ages to a more inductive theology of salvation: a mediate soteriology. Indeed, there is significant evidence that John Calvin did not consistently hold to what passes today for Calvinism, especially in his later years, and that Jacob Arminius never really became fully 'Arminian' before his untimely death. Thus, it was their followers who polarized the traditions significantly. It seems that Luther's view was quite paradoxical, virtually self-contradictory, and Lutheranism today reflects that tension.

Be that as it may, rather than persisting in going back to them as the touchstone of truth, as many do, we must go beyond them and their followers' systems and do fresh exegesis of Scripture as the sole foundation for our theology. Only when we have developed our theology of salvation inductively from the word of God may we go back into Christian history to find any confirmation of our conclusions.

I refer to the theology of salvation I am developing as a "Mediate Theology of Salvation" for at least two reasons. It is intermediate to Calvinism and Arminianism. It also emphasizes God's mediate mode of carrying out much of His plan in the present world— through His agents. Historically this view has its roots in a semi-Augustinian view, but since salvation-truth was little developed in Augustine's day (354-430), it would be better to use new terminology. It needs to stand on its own integrity, based upon fresh biblical study.

A neglected legacy. My thesis is that there is a viable middle or mediate position which has been grossly neglected, even repressed. Indeed, among Evangelicals there is a substantial centrist mainstream of Christians who see themselves somewhere in the middle. They might facetiously refer to themselves as 'Calminian.' Many might call themselves Calvinists because they hold to eternal security, but don't accept much of the rest of the Calvinistic system.

There seems to be a great ignorance of a semi-Augustinian position, even among theologically knowledgeable people. During the century after Augustine, the controversy raged over his views of predestination and irresistible grace. At the Synod of Orange (529), a semi-Augustinian consensus was achieved which was the official position of the Western church until the reformation, even though in the main it became increasingly semi-Pelagian in practice.[B]

Although the Reformers reintroduced Augustine's views, I have found at least a dozen distinct movements within three centuries after them which sought to moderate their deterministic views. Some of these could rightly be called semi-Augustinian in essence. There is a gross ignorance, even among theologically knowledgeable people, of the whole spectrum of intermediate positions that have emerged over the centuries since the Reformation. But the fuller historical discussion of these views will be addressed later.

Dispelling the fog. In the light of all this historical data, it is astonishing that reputable scholars can claim that there is no middle ground between Calvinism and Arminianism. Not only opponents of a mediate view, but its advocates also, seem naive of the historical foundations of this position. Samuel Fisk, in defending a middle way, made no reference to the historical antecedents in his two books, although he quoted hundreds of commentators and theologians from the last two centuries who supported such a position.[1] Although I graduated from a seminary (Dallas) which held essentially to Amyraldian Calvinism, I had never heard of the Amyraldian view until I taught systematic theology, and Lewis Sperry Chafer, the founder of that seminary, made no reference to it in his systematic theology.[2]

Years ago B. B. Warfield distinguished six distinct salvation-theology positions among Evangelicals,[3] and in reality there are more. Following his lead, I have been able to distinguish at least eight distinct evangelical views. Warfield, Chafer, Buswell, and Thiessen, all distinguished three kinds of Calvinism, including Amyraldian four-point Calvinism. In addition, the Lutheran, Anglican, and Wesleyan "evangelical Arminian" positions must be distinguished from that of the Remonstrant Arminians and from Arminius himself, whose view is now called "Reformed Arminianism."[4] This still does not distinguish the mediate position I am advocating.

Thiessen's systematic theology in its original edition (1949) espoused conditional election and eternal security, and thus, is the only full theological work holding a mediate theology of salvation. Thiessen didn't develop his position, because he didn't live to complete his *Lectures in Systematic Theology* himself. In more recent years, there have been a few works from a mediate viewpoint. Roy Aldrich questioned faith as a gift of

B. Pelagius was the British monk whose purportedly man-centered view of salvation was vigorously opposed by Augustine. Semi-Pelagianism is the view that man contributes to his own salvation by his own good works. This ignorance of the semi-Augustinian view has led many Calvinists to erroneously label any mediate view as 'semi-Pelagian' and 'synergistic.' Since Pelagius was presumably a heretic, such terms are extremely pejorative and prejudicial. Synergism is a term that came out of reactions to Luther's Augustinian view, which implies that man contributes to his own salvation, which I do not affirm in the least.

God in his germinal article, "The Gift of God" (1965). Samuel Fisk's *Divine Sovereignty and Human Freedom* (1973) and *Calvinistic Paths Retraced* (1985) are significant because he sought to enunciate a mediate position in some detail. Although Fisk quoted hundreds of scholars in support of a mediate view, he didn't develop his own exegetical base for his view. Roger T. Forster and V. Paul Marston's *God's Strategy in Human History* (1973) was a careful exegetical investigation from a mediate perspective. William W. Klein's *The New Chosen People: A Corporate View of Election* (1990) is an in-depth study of one central issue involved. Laurence M. Vance in *The Other Side of Calvinism* (1991, 2nd ed., 1999) has exposed the serious weaknesses of Calvinism from a mediate position with a plethora of quotations from the literature. Michael Eaton in *No Condemnation: a New Theology of Assurance* (1995) was clearly looking for a mediate ground and repudiated both extremes. William Lane Craig's *The Only Wise God: The Compatibility of Divine Foreknowledge and Human Freedom* (1989) provides a philosophical basis in the middle knowledge view he espouses, although he himself is more Arminian. Dave Hunt's exposé of Calvinism, *What Love Is This? Calvinism's Misrepresentation of God* (2002), seems to be in the locus of my position. Although these works address certain aspects of the issue, it seems that no one has written a complete mediate theology of salvation. This is what I am attempting to do, acknowledging the tremendous help I have gotten from the above works.

There are many works from an essentially Amyraldian or moderate Calvinistic viewpoint: Philip Schaff, *History of the Christian Church*, vol. VIII (1892), A. H. Strong, *Systematic Theology* (1907), Lewis Sperry Chafer's unabridged *Systematic Theology* (1948), Robert P. Lightner, *The Death Christ Died*, (1967, 2nd ed. 1999), John F. Walvoord, *Jesus Christ Our Lord* (1969), Norman F. Douty, *The Death of Christ* (1978), R. T. Kendall, *Calvin and English Calvinism to 1649* (1979), Millard J. Erickson, *Christian Theology* (1985), Charles C. Ryrie, *Basic Theology* (1986), Gordon R. Lewis and Bruce A. Demarest, *Integrative Theology*, Alan C. Clifford, *Atonement and Justification* (1990), Norman L. Geisler, *Chosen, but Free* (1999), all defended general redemption.[C] These works are most valuable in moving away from extreme Calvinism.

The polarized views

Philip Schaff has given a helpful contrasting view of Calvinism and Arminianism:

C. Little of Moyse Amyraut's works have been translated into English, but there are three dissertations in English on the Amyraldian movement: Roger Nicole (1966), Brian G. Armstrong, (1969), and Leonard Proctor, (1952). A score of years ago Dr. Nicole gave me the opinion that Amyraut believed in conditional election, but in a recent conversation with him he agreed with Armstrong and Proctor that Amyraut held to unconditional election, but did not emphasize it in his system. Unfortunately, there is great ignorance about the Amyraldian movement.

> Calvinism emphasizes divine sovereignty and free grace; Arminianism emphasizes human responsibility. The one restricts the saving grace to the elect; the other extends it to all men on the condition of faith. Both are right in what they assert; both are wrong in what they deny. If one important truth is pressed to the exclusion of another truth of equal importance, it becomes an error, and loses its hold upon the conscience. The Bible gives us a theology which is more human than Calvinism, and more divine than Arminianism, and more Christian than either of them.[5]

Undoubtedly Calvinism has its good points and bad points. Its emphasis on the sovereignty of God has been a strength, although developed to an extreme. Its view of human depravity has been essentially sound, although also defined in an extreme, unbalanced way. The affirmation of the substitutionary nature of the cross is foundational. The emphasis upon grace and eternal security is vital, although wrongly developed as the perseverance of the saints. Perhaps the greatest strength has been the emphasis upon theology itself.

But many of Calvinism's weaknesses have derived from its tendency to a deductive theology, often colored by Greek philosophy. This is especially evident in conceptions of God's simplicity, impassibility, static immutability, and all-extensive decree(s). Putting regeneration before faith is deductive. Limited atonement and irresistible grace also derive from this deductive and philosophical methodology. God's love for the whole lost world gets lost in the doctrine of unconditional election, which is plagued by its inability to shake the idea of reprobation. Whether admitted or not, there is a determinism among many which tends to undermine human responsibility. Many aspects of Calvinistic doctrine seem to be extrapolations of biblical data. On the experiential level, among extreme Calvinists there is the widespread insecurity of not knowing whether one is among the elect or not, which results in a tendency to introspection and legalism. A weakness in evangelism and global missions has been evident among many Calvinists. Lastly, there is a narrowness of spirit on the part of many extreme Calvinists, by which they write off other Christians as being "barely Christian."

Arminianism also has its strengths and weaknesses. Its emphasis upon general redemption and concomitant universal gospel proclamation is vital. Today, Arminians seem to be way ahead in the use of modern media in world evangelism. God's omniscient foreknowledge is the basis for conditional election. Their emphasis upon human responsibility is biblically important.

The first and foremost weakness of Arminianism has been its denial of eternal security. Generally, its doctrine of sin has been marred by a denial of imputed sin, and its theology of salvation, by a denial of substitution in the cross and affirmation of a governmental approach. Grace and simple faith have been vitiated by a tendency to add continuance in works as a condition for justification, which leads to legalism in both salvation and Christian growth. There is also a strong tendency toward sinless perfectionism. In some Arminian circles, there has long been weakness in the area of inspiration and especially the inerrancy of Scripture, which frequently opens the door toward liberalism. More broadly we could say that there has been a de-emphasis on doctrine and overemphasis on experience as a basis for truth. At times, the truth of God's love is not balanced off with the truth of His justice and holiness.

The above are generalizations and obviously not rigorously true of all Calvinists or all Arminians. Documentation of these points will be given in each chapter. It is my conviction that the resolution of the serious problems that these polarized positions face is to be found in a mediate view. What do I mean by a mediate view?

AN OVERVIEW OF A MEDIATE THEOLOGY OF SALVATION

It is my thesis that a totally distinct, cohesive, and viable system can be derived inductively from Scripture. Even though its historical roots derive more from a semi-Augustinian position, it is not a truncated form of Calvinism, or on the other hand, a form of Arminianism. It stands on its own integrity. Just as Amyraut was accused of Arminianism by some Calvinists and as an inconsistent Calvinist by some Arminians,[6] just so a mediate position will be misunderstood today. For example, the Gerstners saw Billy Graham and Bill Bright as Arminians![7] I suspect this is erroneous. Such categorization is an indication of the failure of many to understand the diversity of viewpoints.

Although I have gotten major help from the mediate writers mentioned above, I am developing a mediate theology of salvation primarily by use of an inductive exegetical methodology. It also finds support from a synthetic, deductive methodology. It finds confirmation in its historical antecedents and its impact upon global evangelism and the spiritual health of the Christian community. Lastly, its logical self-consistency is supportive. I have delineated this position under a number of propositions, which will be developed in detail in subsequent chapters.

God limited the exercise of His sovereignty by creating moral beings and by delegating authority to them.

As we try to understand the attributes of the God who saves us, today we find a polarization of viewpoints even in this basic area. On the one hand, the God of the extreme Calvinists has determined everything that comes to pass in the universe. On the other hand, the 'Open Theists' say that God has determined very little and doesn't even know the whole future. The truth is in the middle.

An inductive study of terms related to the sovereignty of God reveals that the exercise of His sovereignty is not exhaustive in reference to all that transpires in His universe, but that He has delegated significant areas of autonomy to angels and humanity. Satan's revolt against God and humanity's long history of self-determination must be factored into our definition. This is confirmed by the historical narrative of Scripture. Study of terms such as God's kingdom, decrees, counsel, purpose, etc. uncovered no hint of the Calvinistic view of sovereignty. Calvinists speak much about God's decrees, or even a single decree, as all-encompassing. *But no such decree is mentioned in the Old Testament and the word is never used of God's decrees in the New.* Far too much dependence has been put upon one clause of one verse, Ephesians 1:11, which has been made to say far more than the grammar, syntax, and context allow.

Calvinism assumes an exhaustive sovereignty of God based upon an all-inclusive decree of God, which leads to the notion of unconditional election by an *a forteriori* argument. However, when we focus the investigation upon the implications of God's sovereignty for salvation-truth, we find no inductive basis for determinism in salvation either. A careful examination of Romans 9 in the context of the flow of Paul's argument does not support unconditional, individual election to salvation.

On the other hand, we find that open theism, in developing a concept of a God who interacts with man, has come to the indefensible extreme of denying the absolute omniscience of God. My research on these issues is developed in chapter three.

Since the fall did not erase God's image, depravity does not mean total inability to respond to God's initiative.

God created humanity as the noblest of creatures, uniquely made in the image of God Himself, suitable for the ultimate incarnation of the Son of God. Inherent in that creation were moral attributes like God's, a God-conscious human spirit, and a delegated autonomy, which made man responsible for his disobedience in Eden. In the fall that image was marred, but not lost. The human spirit was deadened, which meant spiritual death, alienation from God. Human morality was corrupted, and although now a slave of sin, humanity's God-given autonomy was not withdrawn, but now abused in rebellion against God.

While I affirm Augustine's doctrine of "original sin," with his recognition of Adam's natural headship and imputation of sin to all mankind, as well as personal and transmitted sin, I object to the extrapolation of depravity into total inability of man to respond to God. God and His witnesses consistently expected mankind to exercise their wills in a positive response to both general and special revelation. Indeed, we are commanded to choose and even to seek God. Passages which Calvinists take to teach total inability do not support their view, when seen in their total contexts.

My investigation of the true impact of the fall is developed in chapter three.

Some New Testament terms for Christ's death are general and objective; others are limited and subjective.

Most of the discussion over 'limited' versus 'unlimited atonement' is beside the point, since 'atonement' is not a New Testament word and relates only to the mercy seat in the temple. Chafer and Walvoord have advanced the study by emphasizing the distinction between redemption, propitiation, and reconciliation.[8]

When we focus upon the picture of Christ's death as a **sacrifice**, we find evidence in the prophecy of Isaiah 53, John the Baptizer's announcement, and the epistles of Peter and Paul that His death was substitutionary in nature, and yet, expiatory of the sins of the whole world of sinners. The book of Hebrews develops this picture in emphasizing its once-for-all character, procuring a once-for-all salvation for the believer.

When we focus upon **propitiation**, the objective satisfaction for the sins of the whole world comes into view (1 Jn. 2:2; 4:10). Calvinist attempts to limit the use of the word world (*kosmos*) to the elect do violence both to the context and its usage in the Johannine writings. John uses *kosmos* most often to refer to the hostile world of unregenerate sinners.

The usage of the different Greek terms for redemption point in different directions. Three of the eight words for redemption are used in the objective, universal **ransom** sense (*agorazein*, *lutron, & antilutron*); two of the words (*lutroein & lutrosis*) include both the objective and the subjective; while the other three words (*exagorazein, apolutrosis, & lutrotēs*) relate to the subjective **redemption-liberation** sense, and are limited to believers.

This essential distinction between the two phases of redemption is graphically illustrated by the story of the ransom of newspaper heiress Patty Hearst some years ago. Her father paid the ransom price, but she did not go free because of her own will. We could say that her father bought her *(agorazein)* and paid the ransom *(antilutron)*, but that she did not experience release *(apolutrosis*, etc.). The distinction of *usage* is far more significant than the connection of *etymology*, as linguists emphasize today.

The words for **reconciliation** are used of the subjective reconciliation of sinners to God: *katallassein, katallage, & apokatallassein* all have the idea, 'to change thoroughly so as to bring into harmony, to exchange, to reconcile.' These words are always used of reconciling sinful man to God as a unilateral process, not bilateral (2 Cor. 5:17-21; Rom. 5:8-11; 11:15; Col. 1:20-21). The sequence is clear that Christ has reconciled us believers to God, that in the cross God was in the process of reconciling the world to Himself, and that our message to the world is, "Be reconciled to God."

Thus we may speak of a general propitiation, a ransom price paid for all, a limited redemption-liberation, and a limited reconciliation. The investigation of these New Testament pictures of the cross is developed in chapter five.

Although Christ's death is particularly efficacious for believers, it is potentially available to all humanity.

This question only arises because of the extreme-Calvinistic doctrine of limited atonement. We just noted that some words for Christ's death are objective, general, and universal, while others are subjective and limited to believers. As we examine all scripture, we see that the whole truth is two-sided, and extreme Calvinists are guilty of the reductionist error of trying to force one aspect of the truth into the mold of the other.

The historical background. Limited atonement is the most recent and obviously problematic of the Calvinistic doctrines. None of the church fathers, including Augustine, nor any of the reformers, including Calvin himself, held to it. His successor, Theodore Beza, developed this notion from the logic of unconditional election, as held by Calvin. The problem, as Calvinists have struggled with it, is a logical one. If Christ died as a substitute for a whole world of sinners, then why are all men not saved?

Over the centuries the major response has been that Christ's death is potential, provisional, and conditional in its application. The cross, in and of itself, saves no one, not even the 'elect.' Only those who respond positively to the gospel with repentant faith are saved. The objective, historical dimension of propitiation and the ransom price is only part of the whole, the foundation, but it is not automatically applied to the individual. For that the subjective, personal dimension of liberation-redemption and reconciliation come into play. This duality is expressed in 1 Tim. 4:10: "**. . . the living God, who is the Savior of all men, especially of believers**."

I also suggest that the basis of condemnation has been changed by the cross. It is not now primarily the sins of man, but more significantly, an individual's one sin of unresponsiveness to the gospel. In a sense, there is one sin for which Christ did not die, the sin of unbelief (Jn. 3:18).

The Biblical data. There is no disagreement over the fact that there are numerous references to Christ's death for a limited group of people: the church, the sheep, us believers, etc. However, it is never said explicitly that He died for the elect, per se. On the other hand, there are many passages which give general reference to Christ dying for the world, for whoever believes, the lost, the ungodly, and all mankind. These cannot be explained away, as extreme Calvinists do and as Calvin himself did not do (cf. appendix E).

Problems with a limited view. Some of the problems with limited atonement to be discussed in chapter six are:

- ❑ It restricts the love of God only to the elect.
- ❑ It denies the universal offer of the gospel message. Why does God

invite all to salvation, if Christ did not die for all?

- ❑ It minimizes the necessity for repentant faith on the part of the sinner.
- ❑ It ignores the convicting ministry of the Holy Spirit promised by Christ.
- ❑ It makes it impossible to personalize the gospel.

Election/ foreordination are based upon foreknowledge.

There are only two passages which relate foreknowledge to foreordination and election, and both maintain the same priority of foreknowledge (1 Peter 1:1-2; Rom. 8:28-31). Realization of this simple fact forced me to reexamine the linguistic data upon which the Calvinistic understanding of foreknowledge (*proginoskein*) was built. It is clear that there must be an essential and significant distinction between foreknowledge (*proginoskein*) and foreordination (*prooridzein*). This study convinced me that there is no unambiguous basis for understanding foreknowledge, as having "an active and ordaining force that the Eng. equivalent would not of itself readily suggest."[9] After parroting Berkhof's discussion of the Hebrew and Greek words for years, I began to realize that the mind is a slippery thing, and that if one comes to those same passages without Calvinistic presuppositions, the arguments from the usage of these words evaporate. What was most distressing to my Calvinistic bias was to find that nowhere in classical, Koine, Septuagintal, or New Testament Greek usage does *proginoskein* mean more than "to know beforehand." I discovered that centuries of theological tradition have read into this word a meaning inconsistent with its usage in Greek literature. In Acts 2:23 and 1 Peter 1:20, in reference to Christ, it cannot mean 'to choose beforehand,' since Christ was not one chosen from among many![10]

More recently, I reexamined the meaning of *proorizein* (foreordain). I was astonished to find that it was only used once in classical Greek before the New Testament and rarely after that. Examining *horizein* and *aphorizein* uncovered the fact that the idea of 'destiny' is totally absent from this group of words. Thus, 'predestinate' is a totally inappropriate translation, which was derived from the Latin Vulgate (ca. AD 406).

Examination of Romans 8:28-30 in the light of these word studies and its broader context revealed that Paul was focusing upon the certain glorious future of those who love God and said nothing about unconditional predestination to salvation. Romans 8:29 must be examined in the broader context of the theme of the whole book, which is a righteousness which is **"by faith from first to last"** (1:16-17, NIV). This is confirmed by the 60 times 'faith' and the verb 'to believe' occur in Romans. Therefore, we cannot leave faith out of the plan of salvation (*ordo salutis*) derived from this passage. This study is found in chapter seven.

Even more recently, my investigation of the words for election (*eklegomai, eklektos, eklogē*) uncovered the predominant usage in secular and Septuagintal Greek of 'selection of the best, the choice, excellent.' This meaning is already in translations of Romans 16:13 and 1 Peter 2:4, 6, but also is demanded by the context of Luke 9:35 and Matthew 22:14. Additionally, it makes much better sense in 1 Peter 1:1-2 and many other passages. Christ is the 'choice One,' and we have been made God's 'choice ones' positionally by His work of grace. This doctrine must be understood in the light of the choice of Israel, the revelation of Jesus Christ as the "choice One" of the Father, and the concept of corporate solidarity in the whole Bible.

In the light of these word studies, exegesis of Ephesians 1 reveals that the only election we have is "in Christ," an emphasis repeated twenty times in the first two chapters and that in this church epistle the context militates for corporate, not individual, election.

We would all agree that God's election has to be according to His plan. Since Peter and Paul are consistent in their order, we must not exclude God's omniscience and prescience from His plan. Certainly God does not close His eyes and throw darts! Why should we retreat back into the secret counsels of God to explain the basis of His elective choice?

Election must therefore be seen as conditional and/or corporate, just as salvation is clearly conditioned on faith. An inductive study of the words for chosen and choice and exegesis of Ephesians 1:3-14 in the light of these three word studies is developed in chapter eight.

The conviction of the Spirit mediately prepares sinners for faith.

Lewis Sperry Chafer, by devoting ten pages in his systematic theology to the convicting work of the Spirit, first pointed out the great importance of this doctrine, announced by Christ in John 16:8-11. He saw it as preparing the heart for faith and regeneration by breaking through the spiritual death and blindness which obstruct faith.[11] Buswell, a Calvinist, also saw quite clearly the relation of conviction to the plan of salvation (*ordo salutis*).

Since I show in chapter ten that the Holy Spirit works mediately in reference to faith, the convicting work of the Spirit also seems to be mediate in its operation and, therefore, in its extent. That is, it is as the word of God is preached that the Holy Spirit uses the word and brings men under conviction. We can best understand the ministry of the "other *paraklētos* (helper, encourager, exhorter, advocate)" by noting the parallel with the first *paraklētos*, Christ Himself. He most effectively used the Mosaic Law in the Sermon on the Mount to bring about conviction of sin. He used the Law to bring the rich young ruler under conviction so that he might repent of his failure to love the poor. John Walvoord rightly affirmed that the conviction of the Spirit is neither universal nor limited to the elect, but operates mediately through the word.[12]

A basic and neglected way to understand the ministry of conviction is to examine its historical fulfillment in Acts, since Christ's brief reference to it in John 16 is part of the Upper Room Discourse, a major subject of which is the coming of the Spirit on the day of Pentecost. It follows then that the events on the day of Pentecost in Acts 2 should be the first exemplification of the conviction of the Spirit as promised by Christ. First, the Holy Spirit, the divine Advocate, used Peter to charge the nation with the sin of crucifying Christ. As a result, we are told in 2:37 that they were "**pierced to the heart**" and cried out, "**Brethren, what shall we do?**" Luke uses a unique word, *katannussein*, which means "to strike, or prick violently, to stun."[13] These men were under conviction but had not yet repented as seen in the fact that Peter responded with the imperative, "Repent!" It would seem that the usage of *diaprio* in 5:33 and 7:54 may be negative examples of conviction which did not lead to repentance. These passages reinforce the mediate nature of conviction. This neglected biblical truth is developed in chapter nine.

The new birth is conditioned on repentant faith.

The primacy of faith. The primacy of repentant faith is basic to a mediate theology of salvation. Calvin himself emphasized the primacy of faith but was ambiguous about the order of faith and the new birth. I will follow Calvin's lead in starting with faith rather than election. Extreme Calvinists put the new birth before faith, since they believe that spiritually dead humans cannot exercise faith and, therefore, need to be born again before they can believe. It is revealing that the five points of 'Calvinism' do not even mention as central a concept as faith and thus do not follow Calvin's lead! Since repentance and faith are key words in the apostolic proclamation of the gospel, it is essential to examine the relationship of faith and regeneration inductively.

Related to this is the Calvinistic concept that faith is the immediate gift of God, in other words, the Holy Spirit gives the elect faith like a bolt of lightning. Roy Aldrich raised some serious questions about this which require answers.[14] I would suggest that, if at all, faith is the gift of God, it is given mediately, rather than immediately, indirectly, rather than by the direct activity of the Spirit. It is man who is responsible to exercise repentant faith, not God to give it.

The exegetical flimsiness of using Ephesians 2:8-10 to prove that faith is the gift of God is well known and will be examined carefully. Some proof texts, such as Romans 12:3, Philippians 1:29; 2:13; Acts 5:31; 11:18; 2 Tim. 2:25; and 2 Peter 1:1, have been blatantly pulled out of context to support this misinterpretation.

The priority of repentant faith. If the subject is approached inductively, it is overwhelmingly clear that faith is the condition of the new birth and, therefore, always precedes it. As to *how* those who are spiritually dead can hear, believe, and live, we struggle to understand; but as to the fact, Christ's own words are clear: "**I tell you the truth, a time is coming**

and now has come when the dead will hear the voice of the Son of God and those who hear will live" (John 5:25 NIV). Note that Christ did not say that the regenerated shall hear! They are dead when they hear!

The answer is found, not in regeneration, but in the convicting work of the Holy Spirit, as is discussed in chapter nine. It is the conviction of the Spirit which is the divine initiative, that enables dead men to hear and believe. As a foundation for this investigation in chapter four, I examined the definition of spiritual death and the implications of the fact that the image of God was not totally lost in Eden.

The human factor in faith. Years ago, in teaching the life of Christ and the book of Acts, I kept coming across statements of the Lord Jesus and the apostles which just did not fit with the idea of God directly giving faith to the elect by some work of irresistible grace. In addition, missionary service in the Muslim world and missiological studies forced me to focus upon the process by which sinners come to faith. Although the new birth is an instantaneous work of the Spirit of God, the process by which people come to faith involves heavy human involvement. Many Christians, especially those from a hostile background, can testify to months or years of spiritual struggle in the process of their coming to faith. This is totally harmonious with the case studies found in the New Testament. It should be clarified that faith is not the cause of regeneration; it is the divinely appointed term or condition of salvation. These topics are examined more fully in chapter ten.

God's calling to salvation is not irresistible.

The doctrine of irresistible grace, like the doctrine of unconditional election, was first touted by Augustine about AD 417. Earlier church fathers knew nothing of these two doctrines, and after the Synod of Orange (529), little was heard of them again until the time of the Reformation. The Greek-speaking Eastern churches never accepted these doctrines.

Calvinistic presuppositions. The doctrine of irresistible grace is based upon a number of unstated presuppositions. Foremost is that effectual calling necessarily implies irresistible grace, and that repentant faith is the immediate gift of God. This doctrine is loaded by the doctrine of unconditional election and the notion that regeneration precedes repentant faith.

Problematic proof-texts. John 6:37, 44, and 65 are misused as proof-texts for this by failing to see the context of Christ's statements. He is not saying here that all the elect shall infallibly come to Christ. The context indicates that He is rather speaking about the remnant of regenerate Israelites who belonged to the Father. Now the Son has come, and that remnant is being turned over to Him by the Father and will certainly come to Him. However, most of his hearers were not a part of that godly remnant. Similarly, John 10:16 has also been pulled out of context to support irresistible grace. The Calvinistic interpretation of Acts 13:48 is based upon the usual translations. However, there are a number of alternate renderings which are linguistically and grammatically defensible and do not imply irresistible grace. Acts 16:14 has been given an uncalled-for Calvinistic spin and needs to be balanced off with Acts 17:11-12.

A word study of 'calling.' Upon examining the many occurrences of the Greek words for calling used in an effectual sense, I would suggest the following definition. Calling is God's action in bringing the sinner to salvation, thus commissioning the believer to an exalted position with a new name for service to God. It is used of the process and circumstances of our coming to faith viewed from the divine side, as contrasted with conversion, which is the human side. *The 'called' are those who have responded to the general invitation, and thus, by hindsight, the calling is seen as effectual.*

Contrarian Scriptures. There are a number of passages which stand in direct contradiction to the notion of irresistible grace, which are ignored by Calvinists: Luke 7:30; Acts 7:51, 54; Matthew 13:1-43; 23:47; 1 Corinthians 4:15 & Philemon 10.

Thus it will be seen that the historical and exegetical basis for irresistible grace is absent, especially when the historical context is carefully considered and presuppositions are examined. Chapter eleven is a full investigation of this issue.

God declares sinners to be righteous by repentant faith alone, apart from works.

Ever since Martin Luther trumpeted the watchword of the Reformation, not only did Roman Catholicism vigorously oppose it, but there has been a continuing erosion of this biblical truth among Protestants, and even Evangelicals. Most outrageously, the recent Evangelicals and Catholics Together (ECT) movement has totally compromised this glorious truth by sweeping it under the rug. Arminians have patently added man's continuance in faith as the basis for ultimate salvation. But Calvinists also have subtly added sanctification to repentant faith as a basis for inclusion among the elect and, therefore, for ultimate salvation. This was especially strong in the 'experimental predestinarian' Puritan movement, which sadly undermined their own assurance as badly as that of the Arminians.

In chapter twelve, I update, defend, and develop the Reformation teaching of justification by faith alone. I will seek to clarify the relationship of faith alone (*sola fide*) to repentance, conversion, sanctification, and other terms and concepts which might compromise simple repentant faith. This is necessary, since some of these terms have been grossly misdefined. I will also seek to spell out how the different theological movements have compromised the simplicity of the gospel.

Christ's discipleship teachings are not the way of salvation, but are a challenge to believers.

A serious compromise of justification by faith alone is the tendency of both Arminians and extreme Calvinists to interpret our Lord's discipleship teachings in Matthew 10, 16, and Luke 9, and 14 as conditions of salvation, rather than as He intended them to be, a challenge to believers' lifestyles.

It is especially important to examine these teachings in their contexts in a sequential way. The foundational pattern was set in Matthew 10, where the Lord sent out His regenerate apostles with an extended warning of the persecution which they would face as they proclaim the good news. The exhortation to cross bearing (Mt. 10:37-9) is not a condition for salvation, but rather of being worthy disciples.

The Lord picked up the same theme when He had the apostles alone at Caesarea Philippi (Mt. 16; Lk. 9) to first announce the founding of His church, along with His first announcement of His impending death and resurrection. After inviting in a larger group of dedicated disciples, He repeated the challenge to cross-bearing and added self denial. The crucial word in this discourse is in Luke 9:23, where *daily cross-bearing* is stipulated, which clearly eliminates any consideration of this referring to conditions for salvation.

The third context in Luke 14 expands the teaching to include counting the cost of true discipleship. How muddled is the thinking of those who imagine that in this discourse, Christ is explaining how to get saved. How do they harmonize these rigorous demands with salvation by God's gracious gift?

It is important to also examine Christ's salvation interviews with individuals, such as the Samaritan woman, Nicodemus, Matthew, the man born blind, the rich young ruler, Zaccheus, and Judas Iscariot, especially since this material has been grossly misunderstood.

It is especially important to critique so-called 'lordship salvation,' which I prefer to call 'discipleship salvation' teaching. In this investigation, I examine the question of carnal Christians and fruitless believers, as it relates to the distinction between salvation and rewards. This study is the content of chapter thirteen.

True believers are eternally secure in Christ.

Although I have argued that election is conditioned upon faith, the truly regenerated believer now participates in an unconditional aspect of salvation truth, the assurance of ultimate salvation. The overwhelming plethora of Scripture promises about eternal security seem to be contradicted in the minds of both Arminians and some Calvinists by the warnings of Scripture, especially in the book of Hebrews. An inductive analysis of these passages in no way contradicts eternal security. My own inductive treatment of Hebrews 6 is fresh and heavily drawn from the context of the book. Far too much of the interpretation of these passages has been colored by the Calvinism-Arminianism debate.

It is also significant to distinguish the Calvinistic doctrine of the perseverance of the saints from the biblical teaching of eternal security, since Calvinism has significantly intruded a believer's experiential sanctification into assurance of ultimate salvation. This has led to an introspective mindset, which seriously undermines such assurance and is a serious back-loading of salvation with human performance.

After a brief summary of the positive Scriptural evidence for security, I take up several key issues in chapter fourteen. Chapter fifteen is a discussion of the problem warnings, exhortations, and other problem passages raised by Arminians, focusing on the warnings in Hebrews.

Christ's charge to proclaim salvation on God's terms

Christ's most important instruction at Caesarea Philippi (Mt. 16) has not only been distorted and usurped by the Roman church, but ignored and misunderstood by most Evangelicals. There are a number of significant questions I investigate here. Despite the diversity of opinions about the identity of the Rock upon which the church was built, the evidence for Christ being that Rock is actually quite one-sided.

The victory of the church over the gates of Hades is best understood as a reference to His impending resurrection as the basis for the church's victory. As the Lord gave Peter the awesome responsibility of opening the door of faith to the nation Israel and subsequently to the Gentiles, He also charged him with the responsibility not to bind on earth what God has not already bound in heaven (as the Pharisees were doing), nor to loose on earth what God has not already loosed in heaven (as the Sadducees were doing). This truth is explicit in the periphrastic perfect passive participles, which are poorly translated. Thus, it is an admonition to proclaim the good news on heaven's terms, unadulterated by man's traditions and philosophies. This makes the subject of this passage of the highest priority for all believers, as is emphasized in chapter sixteen.

World evangelism is spawned mostly from movements which reject determinism.

The first test of our theology of salvation should be its harmony, historically and logically, with the implementation of the Great Commission of the Lord Jesus, which is central to God's plan, both in local evangelism and global missions. If our theology seems to be counterproductive to global evangelism, we must re-examine our theology. My study of the history of missions has indicated that the main thrust came from the radical reformation, those movements which began to distance themselves theologically from the determinism of the mainline Reformation. Since global evangelism was central to Christ and His apostles, our obedience to this core value is a valid test. Paul was the church's greatest integrator of missions and theology. Not only is the theological cause for the "Great Protestant Omission" traceable to determinism, but it has been an obstacle to evangelism and revival as well. I have made a fresh study of the theological roots of the modern missionary movement in Great Britain and America and found Andrew Fuller and Edward Griffin to be unsung mentors behind the first missionaries who come out of the Second Great Awakening. This new research is in chapter seventeen.

Christian history is replete with mediate antecedents

Although we must not derive our theology from church history, we should check the results of our exegesis and theological pursuit by the test of history. Even though we recognize the imperfection of the historical record and the progress of the development of Christian doctrine over the centuries, we should find some support and confirmation in the history of Christian thought. I have found significant support for a mediate soteriology in a number of historical realities:

1. For four centuries before Augustine, the church fathers all defended free will. It is widely recognized that Augustine was the first predestinarian and the originator of the doctrines of unconditional election and irresistible grace after AD 417.

2. The Synod of Orange (Aurasio, AD 529) approved Augustine's emphasis upon grace but without his doctrine of predestination and irresistible grace. Its decision was semi-Augustinian, not semi-Pelagian. Little is heard of these doctrines until Martin Luther resuscitated them a millennium later.

3. Luther, Calvin, and the first generation Reformers did not hold to limited atonement, which was not included in any creed until the Synod of Dort (1619). See appendix E for over 30 clear quotations of Calvin on general redemption.

4. There were over a dozen movements in reaction against the Augustinian emphasis of the Reformers. In the main, they were initiated by men who had excellent spiritual and scholarly credentials. Here is a quick list:

a. The Anabaptist movement which broke with Zwingli in Zurich in 1524 and rejected his determinism

b. The Mennonite movement of Menno Simons (1496-1561)

c. Zwingli's successors, Bullinger (1504-1575) and Bibliander, who modified his deterministic views

d. Luther's successor, Philip Melanchthon's (1497-1560) modifications of Luther's view

e. The "free-willers" in the 16th century Anglican church (Bishop John Davenant, et. al.)

f. Jacob Arminius (1560-1609), the Remonstrants, and the Wesleyan movements

g. John Cameron (1580-1625), Moyse Amyraut (1596-1664), and the Amyraldian movement of 17th century Huguenot churches of France, which emphasized general redemption

h. Johannes Cocceius's (1603-1669) attempts to moderate determinism by his form of covenant theology

i. The Pietistic Movement of Phillip Spener (1635-1705) and August Franke (1663-1727) among Lutherans, which rejected determinism and initiated foreign missions

j. The Moravian Movement of Nicholas von Zinzendorf (1700-1760) which influenced the Wesleys and spawned a substantial missions thrust

k. The Marrow men of Scotch Calvinism, who held to the universal offer of the gospel: Thomas Boston (1677-1732), et. al.

l. The neo-Edwardsian New Divinity movement of Samuel Hopkins (1721-1803), Jonathan Edwards, Jr., Edward Griffin (1770-1837), and Joseph Bellamy (1719-1790), which spawned New England's Second Great Awakening of 1785 to 1830 and American foreign missions

m. The Barton W. Stone (1772-1844) and Alexander Campbell (1788-1866) Restorationist movements in the American heartland

See chapter eighteen for the full historical discussion.

The impact of philosophy and logic

After noting the significance of the apostle Paul's warnings about the dangers of Greek philosophy, I have traced a scholasticizing impact upon the church through the ages. This is the root of some of the deterministic misrepresentations of God, from Augustine to the present. Determinism also raises serious problems of non-contradiction in its flight to antinomy, paradox, and mystery in the logical problems it faces. Although I have little enthusiasm for philosophical argument, there are a number of lines of thought which seem supportive of the mediate viewpoint. William Lane Craig has argued most effectively for the concept of middle knowledge. Beyond simple foreknowledge, there is evidence that God also can foreknow the counterfactuals, that is, all the possible events which never take place. Middle knowledge seems to me to be very supportive of a mediate theology.

A common logical error of both Open Theists and Calvinists is to say that God cannot know that which He has not determined. This is to say, nothing can be certain unless it has been determined by God. On this basis, Open Theists say that God's foreknowledge is limited. On this premise, Calvinists say that God has to determine all events that transpire in the universe. Both antipodes are wrong. This is to make an attribute of God contingent upon something which He does, which is totally backward. These issues will be briefly surveyed in appendix L. Since I would not claim to be a philosopher, perhaps I can point readers to fruitful areas of investigation.

THE RESULTANT PLAN OF SALVATION

As relates to the application phase of salvation then the plan of salvation (*ordo salutis)* would be:

A. ***Foreknowledge of repentant believers***
B. ***Election to salvation and service based upon foreknowledge***
C. ***Conviction wrought mediately by the Spirit through human instrumentality***
D. ***Repentance towards God and faith in Christ***
E. ***Justification and regeneration***
F. ***Outward conversion results from regeneration and justification.***
G. ***A truly regenerate and justified believer's salvation is eternal.***
H. ***Sanctification and discipleship are the believer's responsibility by walking in the Spirit. The overcomer will be rewarded in the kingdom.***

CONCLUSIONS

I am thus proposing a distinct mediate theology of salvation, whose historical roots are found in the semi-Augustinianism of the Synod of Orange (529) and a long line of postreformation leaders and theologians who reacted to the determinism of the Reformers. A large number of preachers, commentators, and scholars of the last two centuries have held a mediate position, many without knowing its roots.

It is intermediate between the opposing views of the exercise of God's sovereignty. While affirming God's initiative in salvation, it recognizes God's demand for man's response as a condition for salvation. The mediate view alone is able to avoid compromising justification by repentant faith alone. It alone recognizes the essential place of the convicting work of the Spirit wrought mediately. It alone avoids the confusion of discipleship salvation. It is the soundest way for the believer to experience the full assurance of security in Christ.

In common with Calvinism, it holds to an essentially Augustinian view of the total depravity of man (properly defined), some limited or particular dimensions of the sacrifice of Christ, the substitutionary nature of Christ's death, and the eternal security of the truly born-again believer. In common with Arminianism, it holds to some universal dimensions of the death of Christ without becoming universalist, to conditional election, and to rejection of irresistible grace.

---

1. Samuel Fisk, *Divine Sovereignty and Human Freedom* (Neptune, NJ: Loizeaux Bros., 1973); and *Calvinistic Paths Retraced* (Murphreesboro, TN: Biblical Evangelism Press, 1985).
2. Lewis Sperry Chafer, *Systematic Theology,* 8 vols (Dallas: Dallas Seminary Press, 1947).
3. B. B. Warfield, *The Plan of Salvation* (Eerdmans, 1935), p. 33.
4. Stephen M. Ashby, "Reformed Arminianism," in J. Matthew Pinson, ed., *Four Views on Eternal Security.*
5. Philip Schaff, *History of the Christian Church,* vol. VIII: 815-6.
6. Hugo Grotius quoted by James Nichols, *Calvinism and Arminianism,* I, pp. 220-41.
7. John H. Gerstner and Jonathan Neil Gerstner, "Edwardsean Preparation for Salvation," *Westminster Theological Journal,* 42:5-50.
8. John F. Walvoord, *Jesus Christ, Our Lord* (Chicago: Moody, 1969), pp. 163-90.
9. Ibid., p. 592.
10. The NIV translation is clearly erroneous in 1 Peter 1:20, which reflects a Calvinistic bias.
11. Chafer, VI, pp. 88-99.
12. John F. Walvoord, *The Holy Spirit* (Wheaton, IL: Van Kampen, 1954), p. 111.
13. G. Abbott-Smith, *A Manual Greek Lexicon of the New Testament,* 3d ed. (Edinburgh: T. & T. Clark, 1937), p. 236.
14. Roy L. Aldrich, "The Gift of God," *Bibliotheca Sacra,* 122:487 (July 1965).

BALANCING THE ATTRIBUTES OF GOD[1]

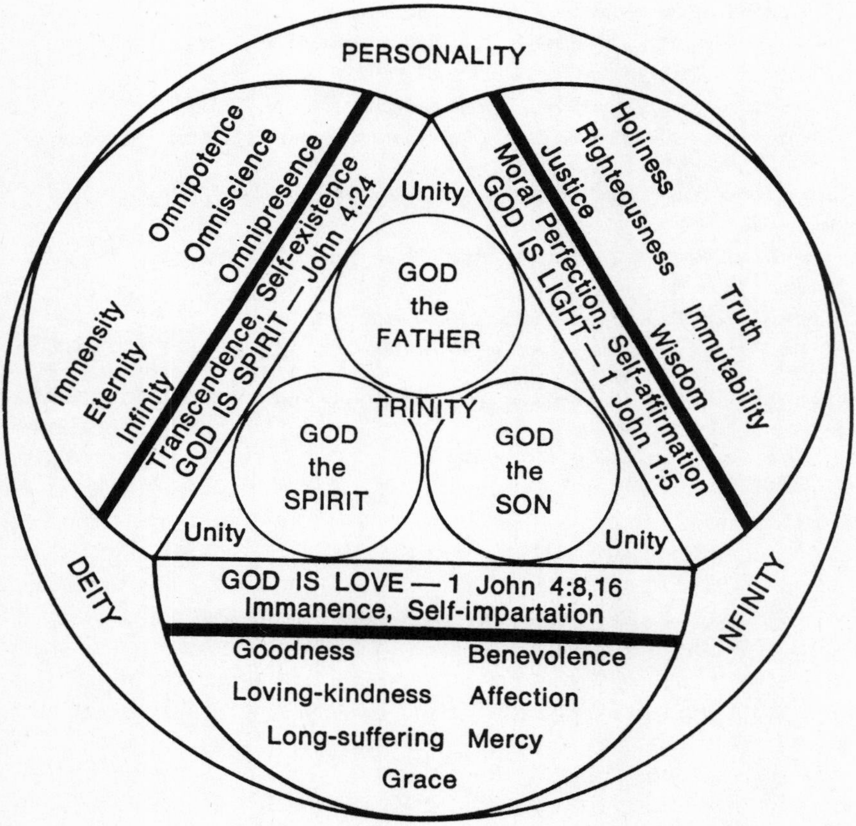

[1] George W. Peters, *A Biblical Theology of Missions*, (Chicago: Moody, 1972) p. 56.

> Evidently we must use greater care in formulating our concept of divine sovereignty than has sometimes been shown among theologians. When we reason without such carefulness (relying on intuition, as it were), ambiguities emerge. . . . The moral seems to be that "sovereignty" is a more complex concept than we often imagine. Use of it requires some careful thinking rather than jumping to conclusions that seem intuitive. What seems intuitive for one theologian will be counterintuitive for another. Intuition misleads us, because generally intuition does not make fine distinctions. Intuitively, we tend to formulate divine sovereignty by excluding anything that looks like it might be a "limitation" on God. -John M. Frame

3

WHAT KIND OF A GOD DO WE HAVE?

Any attempt to develop an inductive theology of salvation must start with the character and attributes of the God who saves sinners. This is foundational. Unfortunately, there has been a serious polarization of evangelical viewpoints in this basic area of theology, perhaps even greater than in the theology of salvation itself. On the one hand, since the days of Augustine there has come into much Christian theology a deterministic concept of God, in which He could almost be called a "control freak." In the major traditions, there is also evidence of the influence of Greek philosophical concepts of God which characterize Him as aloof and uninvolved with humanity. On the other hand, in the last few decades, a new movement has emerged in evangelical theology which, under the influence of liberal process theology, limits the foreknowledge of God to those things which He plans to bring to pass by His power and not to those contingent actions of free moral agents. This has been called open theism or extreme Arminianism.

All sorts of questions are raised by this diversity of viewpoints. Years ago, Doris Day used to sing, "Que Sera, Sera (What will be, will be)." Is this true? Is God the author of sin? Does God actually change His mind? Is God responsible for atrocities, such as the holocaust or nature's calamities? Has God really decreed before creation all that transpires on earth? Does God really answer prayer, or does it just seem that way? If God doesn't control everything, how can the future be certain? Can anybody really get saved, or has God already decided the issue? Who is responsible to live the Christian life, God or me? And so the questions go. The ultimate question is: what kind of a God do we have? Answering this question first will help us to answer all these other questions.

THE DIVERSE VIEWPOINTS

There is a spectrum of at least five different evangelical answers to this foundational question: extreme Calvinism, moderate Calvinism, Mediate theology (set forth here), Arminianism, and the extreme Arminian open view of God. Calvinism's concept of the sovereignty of God is the basis for its doctrines of unconditional election and irresistible grace. Extreme Arminianism ends up with a time-bound God who doesn't know how it will all come out in the end.

Augustinian deterministic Calvinism

I will not try to differentiate the various varieties of Calvinism at this point. The Augustinian notion of God's sovereignty holds to an exhaustive, comprehensive determinism, which is based upon all-inclusive decree(s) of God. Charles Hodge, for example, wrote a heading: "God's decrees relate to all events."[1] Both the Synod of Dort (1618-9) and the Westminister Confession (in the original of 1647-8) explain the sovereignty of God in terms of a single eternal decree of God which encompasses "whatsoever comes to pass." Reformed scholar James Daane argues that these statements are an expression of the "decretal theology" which is a product of the scholastic Calvinism of the late sixteenth and early seventeenth centuries.[2] There is a significant, almost overwhelming, body of recent scholarship which supports Daane's conclusions.[3] As we examine the inductive data for such a concept of sovereignty and decrees, I believe we will see that it is totally baseless, and indeed raises serious problems, such as making God the author of sin

Open Theism or extreme Arminianism

On the other hand, we find those who espouse an "open view of God," the "extreme Arminians." They deny the absolute foreknowledge of God in an effort to explain God's apparently contingent interaction with people in the Old Testament narrative without recourse to anthropomorphisms. They emphasize love as a primary attribute of God and thus find that the traditional doctrine of God's impassibility (He has no passions) untenable. They believe that God actually repents and changes His mind in response to prayer and man's response to Him. Therefore, they question God's immutability and timelessness. Needless to say, they hold to libertarian free will. For a critique of Open Theism see appendix C.

A mediate theological view

Thus, we find a serious polarization of concepts among evangelical scholars concerning who our God really is and how He relates to the human race. It is the burden of this chapter to show that both extreme positions are in serious error, and the truth is in the middle (as it frequently is). These extreme positions in our understanding of God lead to extreme positions on His plan of salvation also, since all of the divisions of theology are interrelated. Therefore, it is absolutely imperative that we develop a correct definition of God's sovereignty in order to grapple with the one-sided theology of salvation proposed by extreme Calvinists and extreme Arminians. Likewise, we must see how the biblical teaching of God's absolute foreknowledge exposes the errors of extreme Arminianism. I suggest that a mediate position resolves the tension in a most satisfying way.

In my own theological pilgrimage, it was providential for a course I taught in 1968-9 that I selected the systematic theology text of J. O. Buswell, Jr. because of his exegetical methodology. Even though he was a five-point Calvinist, he took issue with some of the concepts of God's attributes traditionally held by Augustine and the Reformers. He sensitized me to some of the problems with what has been called the "classic concept of God." He also alerted me to *a fundamental philosophical error in what I had been taught, that is, that God cannot foreknow that which He has not determined.* In reacting to such a notion held by extreme Calvinist Loraine Boettner, Buswell stated:

> But it is presumptuous for man to claim to know what kind of things God could or could not know. There is a mystery in knowledge which will probably never be resolved for us. . . . For men to declare that God could not know a free event in the future seems to me sheer dogmatism.[4]

Buswell's most perceptive statement is a double edged sword, since it also cuts the head off of the extreme Arminian view as well. The biblical evidence for God's infinite omniscience should be clear enough.

There is another closely related error I have detected in the writings of both opposing viewpoints. *A number of writers have confused the certainty of a future event with the determining of that event by God.*[5] Of course, God knows all future events as certain, whether He has determined them or not. His omniscience is unlimited. Both Calvinists and extreme Arminians err in making the certainty of the future contingent upon God's determining it, but with differing outcomes—the Calvinistic future being certain; the extreme Arminian future, partially open and uncertain. I believe both views are in error because God's acts (His decrees) must flow from His attributes (omniscience), not the reverse.

The mediate view I am proposing affirms the essentials of the classic concept of God, as modified by Buswell in the main. I affirm the absolute foreknowledge of God as part of His omniscience, His absolute omnipresence, and His absolute omnipotence, the exercise of which He has chosen to limit in significant ways. The sovereignty of God is affirmed, but it must be defined in the light of that self-limitation. The Greek philosophical concept of the simpleness of God is rejected outright, since God reveals Himself as a Tri-unity, and His works of creation are incredibly complex. The concept of a single all-embracing decree of God must also be rejected, since it derives from the notion of the simpleness of God and is totally without biblical support. Likewise, the impassibility of God (no passions) must be rejected as incompatible with the biblical narrative and is obviously derived from Greek philosophy. God certainly has revealed Himself as emotionally moved by the human condition. Lastly, while affirming the immutability of God, we must recognize His genuine dynamic interaction with humanity, which thus is not a frozen immutability. His attributes are unchanging, but His relationships with mankind are dynamic and changing.

SOVEREIGNTY DEFINED

My research has convinced me that most of the Calvinistic theologies of salvation have been built upon an assumed concept of the sovereignty of God which is not inductively derived from the Scriptures. Indeed, this foundational issue is one of the weakest parts of Calvinism. The word 'sovereignty' is not found in either Testament. In addition, for four centuries theologians have argued endlessly over the order of God's decrees. Yet, the Old Testament says very little about God's decrees, and *there is no reference to them at all in the New.* Furthermore, there is no hint that any of the few decrees mentioned in the Bible were given in eternity past. It is obvious that almost all of this discussion has been deductive in nature, not inductive. This is not to imply in the least that God is not sovereign; nor does lack of inductive evidence *necessarily* prove that those concepts are in error. However, this puts them on much shakier ground, and in the absence of inductive evidence, unless solid deductive evidence is forthcoming, we must conclude that these concepts are derived from certain philosophical notions, not from the Bible.

In reference to a different issue, Reformed theologian John Frame has issued an excellent warning:

> Evidently we must use greater care in formulating our concept of divine sovereignty than has sometimes been shown among theologians. When we reason without such carefulness (relying on intuition, as it were), ambiguities emerge. . . . The moral seems to be that "sovereignty" is a more complex concept than we often imagine. Use of it requires some careful thinking rather than jumping to conclusions that seem intuitive. What seems intuitive for one theologian will be counterintuitive for another. Intuition misleads us, because generally intuition does not make fine distinctions. Intuitively, we tend to formulate divine sovereignty by excluding anything that looks like it might be a "limitation" on God. . . . Only the most extreme nominalists would conceive of

sovereignty in that way.[6]

I am not sure whether Frame, as a Calvinist, might agree with the application of his words to the Augustinian concept of divine sovereignty, but I believe this is appropriate since it is intuitively based upon a philosophical concept of God rather than upon biblical induction.

The Inductive Investigation: Old Testament word studies

Let us immediately go to the inductive investigation of the biblical data. Although modern translations render *YHWH-ELOHIM* as "Sovereign LORD," there is no Hebrew word for sovereignty in the Old Testament,[A] nor is the word sovereignty used in the New. Therefore, as a starting point I checked Louis Berkhof's discussion of the sovereignty of God. He has a list of a couple of dozen references to God's general rulership over creation, the nations of the earth, the pagan gods, the lives of believers, and under the heading "the sovereign will of God," lists for election and reprobation, Romans 9:15-16 and Eph. 1:11; regeneration, James 1:18; and for sanctification, Phil. 2:13. In a careful study of these references, I could find little supportive of the Augustinian view of sovereignty, that is, extending to "all that comes to pass." These New Testament references we will discuss in due course, but we will have to go back and do basic word studies to see if we have overlooked something. Since sovereignty has to do with the political relationship of governance, the terms most directly related to it in the Old Testament are king, kingdom, decrees, and counsel, and in the New, counsel (*boulē*), purpose (*prothēsis*), and will (*thelēma*). Let us seek to understand in what sense God's governance over mankind is spelled out in the Scriptures.

Kingdom. We find four Hebrew terms for kingdom from the same root (*melek*),[7] and concerning divine activity, three major categories: references to the Davidic Covenant promises, prophecies of the Messianic kingdom, and a few references to the general rulership of Yahweh over the nations of the earth (Ps. 103:19; Ps. 145). There are, however, many more references in the Psalms and prophets in which Yahweh is addressed as King, and these are quite instructive. Some are references to the Messiah as King (Ps. 2 & 24), but most stress His mighty acts as ruler of Israel and the nations, as manifested in His works of creation, judgment, deliverance, protection, and cleansing of sin (Ps. 2:7; 5:2; 9:10; 10:16; 20:9; 24:7-10; 44:4; 47:2,6,7; 68:24; 74:12; 84:3; 89:18; 95:3; 98:6; 145:1; Isa. 6:5; 33:22; Jer. 8:19; 10:7, 10). However, there is not a hint in any of these passages of any exhaustive

---

A. We should not be surprised that the abstract term 'sovereignty' is not found in the Hebrew since the cognitive process of the Hebrews has been characterized as "concrete-relational," and they did not even have an abstract term for 'sex,' much less sovereignty.

sovereignty in which Yahweh decreed every event to transpire in the history of the universe.

Indeed, there is a serious question whether the imagery of king and kingdom could possibly communicate this to ancient middle-eastern peoples, unless it were spelled out explicitly in the contexts of the usage. These terms were not only used for the ruler of the great empires, but also for the heads of small cities, and thus, are not really technical terms with a narrow range of meaning conducive to such an idea.[8] Not even the greatest human kings' powers involved direct control of all events in their domain. Of course, their decrees were carried out indirectly by their government functionaries. So it seems highly unlikely that any concept of a direct control of all events by a sovereign could be conveyed by the cultural usage of the words 'king' or 'kingdom.' This is an extrapolation of any possible analogy of human kingly sovereignty: a notion which Augustine and his followers have read or imposed upon these words.

Decrees. Theologians over the centuries have constructed an elaborate theology of decrees. Charles Hodge, for example, in his fifteen-page discussion, which he calls the Augustinian view, never refers to any Scripture in which the word 'decree' appears. There are indeed few such references to God's decrees for him to quote. I could find only eight, which refer to three distinct ideas. Five references refer to God's decrees in relation to His creation (Job 28:26; 38:10; Ps. 148:6; Prov. 8:29; Jer. 5:22). One is the most important decree of Psalm 2:7 referring to the day of the resurrection (cf. Acts 13:33). Lastly, we have an oblique reference to a decree of judgment in the day of Yahweh (Zeph. 2:2) and God's decree that Nebuchadnezzar should be judged with temporary insanity (Dan. 4:24). **Surprisingly, there are absolutely no references to God's decrees in the New Testament.**[B] This data hardly leads one to the all encompassing decrees of the Augustinians. Of course, Hodge quotes other references, the most relevant of which we will discuss subsequently. But most tellingly, his section entitled: "G. The Decrees of God relate to all Events." **contains not one scripture reference**, because there really are none![9]

Counsel. The next word which relates to God's sovereignty is 'counsel,' for which we find more frequent reference in both testaments. The Hebrew *'etsah* is widely used on the human level for counsel or advice. On the divine level there are a score of usages. In Psalm 33:11, in emphasizing the eternality of God's counsel in contrast to that of the nations, it is set in parallelism with "the plans of His heart." Yes, God has an eternal plan. Then the Psalmist looks for guidance from God's counsel (73:24) and rebukes Israel for not waiting for but rather spurning His counsel (106:13;

B. The noun *boulēma* could possibly be translated 'decree' and only occurs in Rom. 9:19, from the mouth of an objector. *Prostagma* does not occur in the New Testament.

107:11). In Proverbs, 'Wisdom' gives her counsel (1:25; 8:14), and the permanence of God's counsel is highlighted (19:21).

The prophets speak of the Messiah's wise, spirit-given counsel (Isa. 11:2) and of the greatness of Yahweh in His counsel and deeds, which are wonderful, omniscient, and abiding (Isa. 28:29; 46:10-11; Jer. 32:19). In Isaiah 46:10 the establishment of his counsel is linked with the accomplishment of His pleasure. However, there is not a hint that this involves any exhaustive efficacious decree in eternity past such as is held by Augustinians. The translators render it as "plan" in contexts which have to do with God's plans of bringing judgment (Isa. 25:1; 46:11; Jer. 49:20; 50:45). Therefore, the most that we can say about the revelation of Yahweh's sovereignty directly revealed in the Old Testament and warranted by our inductive word studies of usage is that our omniscient, omnipotent, omnipresent God sovereignly intervenes in human affairs according to His wise plan as He implements His general rule over the nations and His plan of redemption.

New Testament word studies

Counsel (*Boulē*)

The Greek word *boulē* (and cognates) has as its primary meaning according to the lexicons, 'counsel' or 'purpose.' Arndt and Gingrich also list a secondary meaning, 'resolution' or 'decision,' which tends to be more specific and firm than the primary meaning.[10] Luke uses it five times referring to divine counsel. In His affirmation of John the Baptizer and rebuke of Israel's leadership, the Lord Jesus stated that "**the Pharisees and the lawyers rejected God's purpose for themselves, not having been baptized by John**" (Lk.7:30). Is it not ironic that the very first (and only) connection of this term with God in the Gospels, not only does not imply some exhaustively efficacious implementation of God's eternal plan, but quite the opposite, brings out men's ability to frustrate God's plan for themselves? Apparently God had a plan for the nation Israel, but over the centuries they had failed to conform to that plan, and now their leaders had outright rejected that plan for themselves and the nation.

The Book of Acts. First in Acts we find Peter's extremely relevant charge in his Pentecost sermon: "**. . . this Man, delivered up by the predetermined plan and foreknowledge of God, you nailed to a cross by the hands of godless men and put Him to death**" (Acts 2:23). Peter (as rendered by Luke) uses the strongest possible language to communicate divine sovereignty in the outworking of God's plan for the crucifixion. He uses a participial form of *horizein* (ordain, appoint) to modify *boulē* (counsel). Peter, while acknowledging the outworking of God's pretemporal plan by foreknowledge, placed full responsibility for the crucifixion upon the evil men who did it. Thus, there is no hint of an implication that God forced the will of the Jewish leaders, Judas, Pilate, Herod, or the Roman soldiers. They were doing their own thing in their own sinful way.

For example, Harold Hoehner has shown how the political situation in AD 33 better explains Pilate's motivation than the situation in AD 30.[11] It would be no problem for an omniscient God to orchestrate events by His intensive knowledge of each of the players and circumstances. Indeed, Peter explicitly included God's prescience in the implementation of His plan (Acts 2:23). Since the cross is at the very center of God's plan, it is easy to understand God's most directive involvement in this event. However, we must not extrapolate (see discussion of extrapolation below) the force of Peter's words to other less central events without warrant.

Lewis Sperry Chafer, for example, in discussing the relation of God's foreknowledge to the election of individuals to salvation related this verse to Romans 8:29 and 1 Peter 1:1 and suggested that there is no discernible order.[12] However, we should note that the subject here is different from the other two passages, both of which are presumably speaking of our individual election as preceded by (and conditioned upon) foreknowledge. Here in reference to the cross, not election, Peter seems to put foreknowledge subsequent, since it is the means by which God orchestrated His predetermined plan. However, the Greek idiom of hendiadys may imply that God's counsel is contingent upon His foreknowledge. (For a fuller discussion see chapter 7.)

Later, similar words occur in the disciples' prayer meeting (probably from Peter's lips): **"For truly in this city there were gathered together against Thy holy servant Jesus, whom Thou didst anoint, both Herod and Pontius Pilate, along with the Gentiles and the peoples of Israel, to do whatever Thy hand and Thy purpose foreordained to occur"** (Acts 4:27-8). Here we see 'purpose' (*boulē*) as the subject of 'foreordained' (*proorizein).* This parallels and reinforces the force of Acts 2:23.

In the synagogue of Pisidian Antioch, Paul stated that David served the *boulē* of God in his own generation (13:36), and he reminded the Ephesians elders that he had declared to them the whole counsel (*boulē*) of God (20:27). If the *boulē* of God were all encompassing, how could Paul possibly have declared the whole of it to the Ephesian church in three years? The writer of Hebrews argued that God showed the unchangeableness of his *boulē* by the making of an oath (6:17). So far, there is no hint that this purpose, plan, or counsel of God exhaustively includes every event in the universe, including all the worst recrudescence of Satan's and mankind's evil over the centuries. This leaves just one verse crucial to the Augustinian interpretation.

The crux interpretum. Ephesians 1:9-12 contains the last usage of *boulē* in reference to God's eternal plan and is the crucial proof-text used by Augustinians to support their concept of sovereignty[13]:

> **He made known to us the mystery of His will, according to His kind intention which He purposed in Him with a view to an**

administration suitable to the fulness of the times, that is, the summing up of all thing in Christ, things in the heavens and things upon the earth. In Him also we have obtained an inheritance, having been predestined according to His purpose who works all things after the counsel (*boulē*) of His will, to the end that we who were the first to hope in Christ should be to the praise of His glory.

Here we need a reminder of the *extreme cruciality of context in interpretation*. I had this reinforced recently while viewing a documentary on 'special effects' in film-making, using "Titanic" as a case study. The special effects people have to convince the viewer by the contrived context of their footage that they are now seeing something which happened almost a century ago (augmented by computer graphics and virtual reality). An expert medical doctor in the field made a statement to the effect that *context* is the major factor in fooling the viewer to see what is not actual. Conversely, it is absolutely imperative that we focus on the real context here if we are to understand Paul's words aright.

Has Paul been discussing anything relating to all-encompassing decrees of God in this context? Quite the contrary, Paul is focusing on God's glorious plan of salvation. The word 'decree' is not found here, or for that matter, anywhere in the New Testament of God's decrees. In Ephesians 1:3-6 Paul was focusing on the Father's eternal plan of salvation, and then in 1:7-12 he surveyed the Son's work of redemption past and the inheritance which He purposes for us in the consummation ("the fulness of the times"). Verse 12 is a segue into vv. 12-13 in which the Spirit's work of applying salvation is described. Thus, the total context, before and after verse 11, is salvation oriented.

We must also examine the grammar more closely. Note that the article *ta* with *panta* (all) probably has a demonstrative force, that is, "He works **all these things**."[C] This would make it clear that the "all things" of 1:11 has to do with the 'all **these** things' of the redemptive plan of God just alluded to, not all the rest of human events. Any universalizing of the outworking of God's sovereignty in 'secular' events is totally absent from the context.

In order to verify this interpretation of Ephesians 1:11 it is vital to do a study of the use of the article with the Greek word 'all' (*pas*), found 45 times in the New Testament, usually in the neuter plural (*ta panta*). A careful examination of the context of these usages shows that about 25 times the

---

C. "The article was originally derived from the demonstrative pronoun *ho, hē, to*, and is clearly akin to the relative pronoun *hos, hē, ho*. It always retained some of the demonstrative force. This fact is evidenced by its frequent use in the papyri purely as a demonstrative pronoun" (Dana and Mantey, p. 136). "The article was originally derived from the demonstrative pronoun. That is, its original force was to *point out* something. It has largely kept the force of drawing attention to something" (Daniel Wallace, *Grammar Beyond the Basics*, p. 208). He states that the article intrinsically *conceptualizes*, also *identifies* an object, and at times *definitizes* (pp. 209-10). Cf. A. T. Robertson, *Short Grammar*, p. 68).

article has the demonstrative force mentioned by the grammarians, which restricts its meaning to some referent in the context. About 14 times the demonstrative force is absent, giving a more universal force to the expression. The remaining five are ambiguous or have a textual problem. This leaves the usage of *ta panta* in Ephesians 1:11 as most probably being the demonstrative force, referring back to the outworking of the Father's eternal plan (1:3-6) as implemented by the Beloved Son through the blood-redemption of the cross (1:7-11). All uses of this verse as a proof text for the exhaustive sovereignty of God is isogesis. If there were some antecedent development of such a notion in the usage of the terms, we might be able to excuse such isogesis, but there is not a scintilla of such development in either the Old or the New Testaments!

While we are noting the importance of context, we see the same expression in the preceding verse (1:10), where it is clear that Christ is to head up "all **these** things," that is, all believers in the Church (1:22), whether now in heaven or on earth. Christ is to become the head of the Church universal. Some have misunderstood Paul's use of the neuter gender as referring to the inanimate universe. But the BDF grammar points out that, "The neuter is sometimes used with reference to persons if it is not the individuals but a general quality that is to be emphasized."[14] If the demonstrative force is ignored, universalism results. On what basis do Calvinists universalize it in verse 11?

It is profitable to compare this passage with the parallel context in Paul's companion epistle to the Colossians: "**. . . and through Him to reconcile all things to Himself, having made peace through the blood of the cross; through Him, *I say*, whether things on earth or things in heaven**" (1:20). As translated, this passage seems to teach universalism, and evangelical commentators have struggled with this. However, the simple recognition of the demonstrative force of the article here makes it clear that Paul is referring to those who were rescued from the domain of darkness (1:13) by redemption (1:14) and are now part of the church (1:18), some of whom are on earth and some in heaven (1:20). Failure to recognize this demonstrative use of the article here has led to the heresy of universalism. Failure to recognize this usage in Ephesians 1:11 has led to the serious error of making God a "control freak," who has predetermined every event in the universe.

We should also note that the same Calvinists who insist that the 'all' in 1:11 means all things without exception, are those who argue, in reference to the extent of the "atonement," that 'all' *never*[D] means all without

---

D. Another most instructive usage of this construction is in Romans 11:32, where it occurs twice: "**For God has shut up all in disobedience so that He may show mercy to all.**" Obviously the article does not have a demonstrative force here,and 'all' is to be taken as a universal in the first instance, since all mankind has been shut up in disobedience. By what right do extreme Calvinists limit God's mercy to all in the second instance? Limited atonement restricts God's mercy to the elect by inconsistent exegesis. But this is our subject for chapters 5 and 6.

exception. How inconsistent! It is also worth noting that the verb in verse 11 has nothing to do with decreeing; it is the verb 'works.' The point that the Apostle Paul is making is that God is working out His foreordained plan of salvation according to His wise counsel and will. He says nothing about all other events in human history. He also says nothing about how general or specific His workings are.

It is also very important to note that Paul is referring to the objective work of the Son of God two millenniums ago as the antecedent of "all these things," and that he begins to make reference to the present subjective work of the Holy Spirit in applying salvation *after this* in verse 12-13. The cross was an eternally determined work of God; the same cannot be said about the application phase of the Spirit's work in the life of the individual, at least as far as this passage goes.

Therefore, the heavy weight which Augustinians put upon this one verse, after careful scrutiny leaves their viewpoint in serious doubt. It is irresponsible to build a whole theological system upon a possible, though improbable interpretation of that verse! Although it only takes one verse of Scripture to be a basis for truth, we must be absolutely sure that we have correctly interpreted that one verse; otherwise, we are prone to serious error.

Cognates of *boulē*

This brings us to the verb *boulomai* (to purpose, to will), which is used three times with God as the subject. We have already looked at Hebrews 6:17, which is not significant in this regard. In James 1:18, we have the participle *boulētheis* used adverbially to describe the new birth. Although the translators tend to render it, "Of His own will," more literally it is, "purposefully" or "intentionally" that God gave us new birth. Does this verse clarify whether the new birth is implemented according to an unconditional or a conditional plan of God? Not at all! It is not explicit in that regard.

The third reference is 2 Peter 3:9: "**The Lord is not slow about His promise, as some count slowness, but is patient toward you, not wishing (*boulomai*) for any to perish but for all to come to repentance**." This verse has proved to be a major problem to the Augustinian view. Indeed, it is in harmony with the whole tenor of Scripture that the eternal plan of God is that the gospel of Christ might be made available to every last human being before Christ returns.[15] This purpose of God that all should come to repentance would seem to make the offer of the gospel a bona fide offer. God's motivation is not ambivalent in this regard, lest He be accused of insincerity. God is in no way double-minded.

The last related word is *boulēma*, which only occurs in Romans 9:19. Since there is an extended discussion of this context below, consideration of this word will be postponed to that discussion.

Purpose

The word *prothēsis* occurs five times in reference to God's plan. Arndt and Gingrich give: "plan, purpose, resolve, will, . . . design" as meanings.[16] Three usages have to do with God's plan of salvation (Rom. 8:28; Eph. 1:11; 2 Tim. 1:9) and two have to do with God's plan for the transition from national Israel to the Church in the general outworking of His plan of redemption. (Rom. 9:11; Eph. 3:11). There is no reference to a comprehensive plan for every event in human history. The question is how we come to be included in this salvation plan. In Romans 8:28 Paul first mentions **"those who love God, who are the called according to His *prothēsis*."** Here we see God's salvation plan or design including those who love God. Paul makes it clear throughout the epistle that their calling to love God involves repentant faith. Their justification and glorification is by faith. Faith must also be a prominent factor in his reference to foreknowledge and predestination, since this is part of an unbroken sequence of five steps. In 2 Timothy 1:9, Paul confirms that our salvation and calling is according to His own gracious plan or design. Whether this is worked out conditionally or unconditionally is not stipulated. Romans 9:11 will be discussed as part of the broader discussion of Romans 9-11. Thus, we find no explicit support for the Augustinian view here either.

Will

A study of the usage of *thelēma* is mostly tangential to the concerns of this investigation. It is used about 18 times of the moral will of God in some regard, five times of God's salvation plan in some form, twice of God's guidance of a believer's walk, numerous times of Christ's own desire to fulfill the will of the Father, and a number of other general references. Again, we find no revelation of a comprehensive determinative decree for the universe which is all-encompassing. However, Calvinists take it that "God's decree is synonymous with God's will." This is based upon Beza's statement: "Nothing falls outside of the divine willing, even when certain events are clearly contrary to God's will."[17] Again the inductive data in the use of *thelēma* does not support this notion.

The Self-limitations of God's Sovereignty

Since the Bible opens in Genesis with God limiting Himself, perhaps this is where we should start. Just in the act of creating mankind in His own image as moral beings with free will, God thus limited the exercise of His sovereignty. We know from other Scripture that God had already created Lucifer and the angels as free moral agents. Did God cause Lucifer to rebel and become the Satan who invaded the garden of Eden with the temptation of mankind? To answer in the affirmative is to make God the author of sin, which some extreme Calvinists do not hesitate to do.

A mere 26 verses into Genesis we find God delegating the dominion or rule of the earth to Adam and Eve. **"Then God said, 'Let Us make man in Our image, according to Our likeness; and let them rule over the fish of the sea and over the birds of the sky and over the cattle and over all the earth, and over every creeping thing that creeps on the earth'"** (Gen. 1:26). Immediately after the statement in verse 27 about the creation of humanity, God's command to fill, subdue, and rule over the earth is stated, which is repeated for emphasis. It is incontrovertible that by delegating such authority to mankind, God was by so much limiting the exercise of His own rule as sovereign.

Man to be God's regent over the earth

Satan's success in causing the fall of humanity in the garden is later seen as a usurpation of that rule previously given to man. The book of Job is probably the earliest indication of Satan's evil autonomy and authority. In Job, he was not acting as an agent of the sovereign God, but an accuser working in opposition to God and His people. Again in the book of Daniel, we clearly see the heavenly conflict between God's angels and Satan's, which is manifested in genuine conflict between Satan's people and God's people here on earth.[18] When Satan tested the Second Adam, the Lord Jesus, in the wilderness (Mt. 4:8-11) and offered Him the kingdoms of this world, Christ did not question this authority which Satan exercised. Later He called Satan "the prince of this world" (Jn. 12:31; 14:30; 16:11), and Paul called him "the god of this world" (2 Cor. 4:4) and "the prince of the power of the air" (Eph. 2:2). Very significant and astonishing are the words of Hebrews 2:14 in the NIV: **"Since the children have flesh and blood, he too shared in their humanity so that by his death he might destroy him who holds the power of death—that is, the devil. . ."** Obviously God has chosen to greatly limit the exercise of His own sovereignty thereby. Scripture is unambiguous here, isn't it?

The record before the deluge is of fallen man exercising free will in 'doing his own thing' to such an extent that the vendetta-filled violence brought God's almost total judgment upon mankind. Erich Sauer used the phrase "human self-determination" to describe this period. As Noah's survivor family emerged from the ark, God made a covenant with him, which was intended to repress the murderous violence so prevalent before the flood. He instituted the death penalty upon the murderer: **"Whoever sheds man's blood, by man his blood shall be shed, for in the image of God He made man"** (Gen. 9:6). Here was a further delegation of God's sovereign rule to human magistrates and governments, which centuries later He confirmed and amplified in the Mosaic Law. Later yet, addressing Israel's unjust rulers in Psalm 82:6 God said, "I said, 'You are gods, and all of you are sons of the Most High.'" Thus, it is plain that God had made human rulers to be god-like in exercising the power of life and death, an incredible delegation of His sovereign power and authority.

When the Lord Jesus appeared to Israel as their Messiah-King announcing His impending kingdom, the clear implication was that God was not then exercising His rule over mankind and God's kingdom needed to be inaugurated. Most significantly, in submitting to crucifixion at the hands of the Roman government, the Lord Jesus tacitly recognized its God-given power. The Apostle Paul reaffirmed this explicitly in Romans 13:1-7. Even though evil governments have grossly abused that authority right up to the present, God has never withdrawn that delegation of some of His sovereign authority.

Additional limitations on sovereignty

Furthermore, every promise God made to mankind is an additional limitation of His sovereign freedom. He has thus bound Himself and will not go against His word. As if that isn't enough, He additionally made covenants with mankind, such as, the Noahic, the Abrahamic, the Mosaic, the Davidic, and the New Covenant, which are all really contracts God made with mankind. One is bilateral (the Mosaic); the rest are essentially unilateral (although they have some contingent features). God thereby limited the exercise of His sovereignty even more overtly.

The Bible is full of prophecies about the future kingdom of God and of Christ, by which the coming Messiah would implement righteousness, justice, and peace over all the earth, that is, over all humanity by His personal rule. Since the first coming prophecies were fulfilled literally, we must take these second coming prophecies literally also (the basis of premillennialism). These prophecies clearly imply that God's rule and dominion were not yet manifest on the earth, certainly not before Messiah's advent, and not literally in the two millenniums since then. Does this not strongly imply a limitation in the exercise of His sovereignty at present? Those who tell us that God is now exercising His reign through His church would have to admit that God's reign is in a very sorry state, far short of the prophesied glories of the kingdom. They need to take off their rose-colored glasses and get real. Yes, we are progressing in world evangelization, but the most we can claim is about six percent of the world's population as evangelical Christians. In the West, we are going backward in our impact on society and in the rest of the world, we are facing serious persecution from Muslims, Marxists, Hindus, and others. If God is exercising the fulness of His sovereign rule right now, He apparently is not a very powerful God. *But the real answer is that He has not chosen to exercise the fullness of His sovereign rule now.* This reality must be factored into any definition of God's sovereignty we might develop.[E]

E. As I reviewed this paragraph, I realized that Augustine's view of the millennium was conductive to his extrapolated view of sovereignty. This was also true of Calvin and most of those of reformed tradition today. There is a connection between premillennialism and a mediate soteriology.

Let me make it clear that the issue is not whether God is sovereign over all of creation or not. He can do anything in all of His creation which He purposes to do, in harmony with His attributes and His word. The issue is rather, does He actively exercise His sovereignty in every event in the universe? Or has He chosen to delegate rule and authority to His creatures, angels and humans? Bruce Reichenbach has put it well, "To be sovereign does not mean that everything that occurs accords with the will of the sovereign or that the sovereign can bring about anything he or she wants."[19]

Problems with All-inclusive Decree(s) of God

Not only is there an astounding lack of direct scriptural evidence for the Augustinian notion of a wall-to-wall decree or decrees of God in past eternity, but there is also clear revelation of God's self-limitation of the exercise of His sovereignty. Therefore, there are many extremely serious problems raised by such a concept of sovereignty, which must be faced by our Augustinian friends.

An extreme extrapolation of Biblical data

Extrapolation is a word which is used by scientists and engineers when they make graphs of data. As a former engineer, I recall our attempts to draw smooth curves to connect the dots on graphs. There is a certain amount of guesswork in constructing the line between the points, which we call *interpolation*. Any point on that estimated line is an interpolation, which may or not be an accurate estimate. But an *extrapolation*, on the other hand, is when we go beyond the data, off to the right or left on the graph. This is extremely risky! Once we go beyond the data, we have no idea which way the data might lead the curve. Extrapolation of graphs of stock performance in the financial world is even more risky, since the market can turn on a dime.

Augustinian theology is an extreme extrapolation of the biblical data; it is not only risky but dangerous. Since the Old Testament says so little about God's decrees and the New even less (zero), the decrees of Calvinistic theology are pure speculation. All discussion about the logical or chronological order of God's decrees in eternity past is absolute nonsense. It is worse than the medieval theologians' discussions about the number of angels which can dance on the head of a pin.

The investigation given above of other related terms such as king, kingdom, counsel, will, etc. has yielded nothing which allows us to define God's sovereignty in such a way. Ephesians 1:11 has been grossly pulled out of its context and extrapolated to make it a reference to an all-inclusive decree(s), when the subject at hand is God's gracious plan of salvation, planned by the Father and implemented by the Son of God.

They make God the author of sin.

The most serious other problem of an all-encompassing decree is that it must include all sin, including Satan's original rebellion against God, the fall of Adam and Eve in the garden, and ultimately, all the rest of the sin of mankind throughout the ages. The more extreme writers, such as Gordon Clark, Herman Hoeksema, Cornelius Van Til, and B. B. Warfield are at least consistent in owning up to this incredible admission. Probably most Calvinists would not go this far, and, to that extent, are seriously inconsistent. Either the decree is all-encompassing or it is not! For this reason we find the curious historical anomaly that when the Westminister Confession crossed the Atlantic, American Calvinists changed the wording to "decrees," undoubtedly to resolve this problem.[20] This was so that they could speak about *a decree to permit sin*, in contrast with one absolute decree. This softens the impact somewhat. A single decree does not allow this.

However, this still does not resolve the problem of their interpretation of Ephesians 1:11. If it is all-inclusive, then all sin must be included. If it is not all-inclusive, as I suggested above, then it cannot be used of a *partially* exhaustive concept of sovereignty (excluding sin) and must be explained in its context as I have sought to do. The more moderate Calvinists cannot exclude sin from its scope, and yet, have it include everything else. There must be an exegetical basis for excluding sin from its purview, lest they are drawn in with the most extreme theologians in making God the author of sin. A mediate view does not face this conundrum.

It is not just sin as an abstract concept with which Augustinians must deal, it is especially the worst outbreaks of human sin and depravity as well which must be explained. What about the wicked violence of the pre-deluge society? Did God decree that? It is inconceivable that God had decreed such a sordid history of human depravity. Moses tells us that "**the LORD was sorry that He had made man on the earth, and He was grieved in His heart**" (6:6). Although this may be understood as anthropomorphism, yet there must still be a core truth in this statement which is irreconcilable with a nominalistic concept of God and His supposed decrees. We could trace through the Old Testament to see God's dealings with Israel in their sin and God's judgments as well and find the same tension. Our definition of sovereignty must by all means take this historical record fully into account.

To say that God had exhaustively decreed the sin and rebellion of mankind is to go far beyond anything stated in Scripture. It is solely based upon a philosophic concept of God. Can you imagine the council of the Trinity in eternity past saying, "Let's decree the slaughter of 20 million in World War I, and how about 45 million in World War II, and let's make sure that Hitler gets six million Jews in the holocaust (along with Christians and Poles), Mao his over twenty million Chinese, and Stalin his twelve million white Russians. Let us decree that the Sudanese Muslim government slaughters and enslaves thousands of south Sudanese Christians. And while the Muslims are at it we should have them rampage, rape, burn, slaughter, and terrorize Christians in Nigeria, Pakistan, Indonesia, and wherever. Don't leave out the World Trade Center.[F] And while we are at it before we create the human race let us decree to consign the vast majority of them to Hell without any possibility of them believing." Calvin admitted the problem of the "horrible decree,"[G] but it is a problem of Augustine's own making. I will not attempt to give a philosophical solution to the problem of evil, but I am sure that the Augustinian scenario has no basis inductively but is purely deductive and rationalistic.

Norman Geisler has personalized the issue:

> A well-known conference speaker was explaining how he was unable to come to grips with the tragic death of his son. Leaning on his strong Calvinistic background, he gradually came to the conclusion: *God* killed my son!" He triumphantly informed us that "then, and only then, did I get peace about the matter." A sovereign God killed his son, and therein he found ground for a great spiritual victory, he assured us. I thought to myself, "I wonder what he would say if his daughter had been raped?" Would he not be able to come to grips with the matter until he concluded victoriously that "God raped my daughter!" God forbid! Some views do not need to be refuted; they simply need to be stated.[21]

They obscure God's dealings in history.

Since we have begun to note the problems of sin in history, let us broaden our focus to other historical issues. Reformed scholar James Daane has pointed out how a decree or decrees in past eternity obscures the outworking of God's elective program in human history. He shows that the major biblical doctrine of election focused upon the election of the nation Israel, the election of the Lord Jesus as Messiah, and the election of the church. "When predestination is defined as God's eternal determination of 'whatsoever comes to pass,' the dimension of the historical, which is of the very fabric of Christianity, is lost." He suggests it even ends up with a

---

F. Four days after I arrived back in Pakistan in 1997, 30 thousand Muslims rampaged through the Christian village of Shanti Nagar ("place of peace"), raping the girls, torching houses, a hospital, dispensaries, schools, and farm equipment. This was the worst anti-Christian incident in Pakistan's 50-year history, which left a terrible psychological scar on all Pakistani Christians. I saw the scene eleven days later and talked with the traumatized people. The economic impact has also been devastating. That was only the beginning, as seen in more recent events. Did God really do this? Although God *may* have been using the Muslims to judge American on 9/11, God did not do it! This is the reality of life in this sin-cursed world and bears little relationship to deductive theology.

G. I recognize that to be fair *horibilis* can be translated 'astonishing,' but the usual rendering 'horrible' is not inappropriate!

"deification of the decree."[22]

In addition, we should also note that the historical, biblical covenants are also obscured. Instead of focusing upon the Noahic, Abrahamic, Mosaic, Davidic, and New Covenants explicitly revealed in Scripture, decretal theology (as Daane calls it) focuses upon theological covenants which do not have any explicit biblical support. All speak of a Covenant of Grace as an all-encompassing covenant of God with mankind, but cannot agree as to who the parties are. Is it Abraham, Christ representing the elect, all the elect, etc.? Some also hold to a Covenant of Redemption in eternity past between the Father and the Son, again without any explicit biblical references to support it. But beyond this crucial deficiency, there is the problem of the obscuring of the historical nature of God's plan of redemption. After all, the biblical narrative chronicles in detail the whole progressive outworking and revelation of God's eternal plan. It starts right in Eden, is radically affected by the deluge, progresses with Abraham and the vicissitudes of Israel's history, centers in the historical birth, ministry, death, and resurrection of Jesus of Nazareth, and is perpetuated through world evangelism beginning at Pentecost. But this progressive historical development of God's plan is seriously obscured by decretal theology's a-historical theological covenants.

Daane is also very concerned about the flattening out of the biblical timeline by relegating it all to an eternal decree. No reality in time can affect the immutable and impassible God of the eternal decree. The Covenant of Redemption in eternity past moves God's workings out of time. Daane echoes some of Buswell's concerns about a scholastic concept of God's timelessness and immutability common in decretal theology.

They cannot explain man's free will without recourse to paradox.

For four centuries the church fathers never questioned man's free will. Indeed, they coined the term in response to the fatalism of some Greek philosophies and religions, such as Manicheanism[23]. It wasn't until Augustine, perhaps relapsing back into his Manichean and neo-Platonist past, developed a deterministic concept of God late in his ministry (417-430) that free will was questioned. Today, it is a 'dirty word' in the minds of many Calvinists.

But the question of determinism and free moral agency remains very real and serious for all Calvinists. The more extreme among them tend to see God as the novelist, writing the whole script, and us humans as mere players in the drama. God is the puppet master, and we are the puppets. Moderate Calvinists recognize that we have free moral agency (limited by man's bondage of sin) and seek to harmonize it with God's sovereignty, by recourse to words such as paradox, antinomy, apparent contradiction, anomaly, or mystery. They are fond of resorting to Deuteronomy 29:29 to get them out of an insuperable bind. But this does not really resolve a very real contradiction.

Another response of Calvinists is to speak philosophically of "compatiblism, or soft determinism." I doubt whether any of the biblical examples they give are valid, but even if they were, it is irresponsible to extrapolate a few anecdotal examples into universal compatiblism.

Certainly the biblical narrative portrayed Adam and Eve as free moral agents, whom God held accountable for their actions. Even though in the fall, man became a slave of sin, the continuing narrative portrays mankind as acting freely and still totally responsible for their actions, since God pronounces judgment upon disobedience to His commands and will. Resort to secondary causes, such as environment and heredity, is inadequate since mankind, created in God's image, distinct from the animals, is uniquely responsible to God. It is striking how many of the church fathers refer to the image of God in man in connection with free will, namely, Tertullian, Novatian, Cyril of Jerusalem, Gregory of Nyssa, etc.[24]

Norman Geisler points out that logically there are only three possible views: "self-determinism (self-caused actions), determinism (acts caused by another), and indeterminism (acts with no cause whatsoever)." He shows, I think successfully, that philosophically, the only defensible view is self-determinism, but more importantly, it is the only view which is biblically defensible. This will be discussed more in depth in the next chapter.[25]

Such a God could never respond to mankind conditionally.

One hardly needs to adduce specific Scripture references to show that God responds to mankind conditionally, as seen in the conditional statements of His laws, His will, His judgments, His salvation, and the Christian life. Calvinists and Arminians have been discussing the nature of that conditionality for centuries, but of the abundance of such conditional statements in Scripture there is no room for discussion. Does God actually respond to man's response to His conditional statements? Does He really answer prayer? Are some of His blessings conditioned upon obedience? Does He really spare people from temporal judgments when they repent? Is salvation really conditioned on faith? The extreme Calvinist must see all of this as predetermined and not an actual response to human contingency. If this were true, then mankind could never have a relationship with a personal God who responds to us in any real sense.

If a spouse in marriage does not interact with his/her spouse in any responsive way, no real marriage is possible. I just heard of a woman whose husband never had any serious conversation with her, they never went out for dinner, or the like, over twelve years of marriage. Need I tell you that the marriage ended up in divorce. It was not a personal relationship. In what sense can we call God a personal God if He does not really interact with us?

Such decree(s) must include reprobation.

James Daane has suggested that the problem faced in the preaching of traditional Reformed theology is that "*reprobation is always there.*"[26] Even though the Synod of Dort tried heroically to separate election and reprobation by denying that they operate "in the same manner," seventeenth and eighteenth-century scholastic Reformed theology gave them equal footing. "God was increasingly seen as determining alike the destiny of an amoral sparrow, the unbelief of the reprobate, and the faith of the elect." Ultimately this led to the single decree of the Westminister Confession.[27] But decretal theology with its wall-to-wall decree cannot avoid making election and reprobation coordinate, thus making it unpreachable, unscriptural, and irrational.

Such decree(s) parallel the gross errors of Islam.

It is not surprising that some of the opponents of decretal theology should see a parallel with the fatalism of Islam, but it is amazing that even some of its advocates have made this connection. Having lived in a Muslim country for seven years and having continued involvement in Muslim evangelism right up to the present, this tangency is of extreme concern to me. When people ask me, "Why do Muslim extremists do the things they do, like terrorism, for example?" my response is that the root is in their defective view of the character of God. Indeed, foundational to our ethics is our concept of the character of God. How could the inquisitors in Spain torture people in the name of Christ? They justified the inquisition by quotation from Augustine's writings in which God is portrayed as a coercive God. Such a concept of God encouraged Augustine to persecute the Donatists (cf. ch. 18).

In a parallel way, Allah of the Muslims is a coercive God and a Muslim convert to Christ is to be starved and beaten to return to Islam, and failing that, should be murdered by his closest relatives. Loraine Boettner may have been relatively unfamiliar with Islam when he wrote his defense of extreme Calvinism in 1952,[H] but his words are nevertheless astonishing:

> Then, too, when we stop to consider that among non-Christian religions Mohammedanism [sic.: Islam] has so many millions who believe in some kind of Predestination, that the doctrine of Fatalism has been held in some form or other in several heathen countries, and that the mechanistic and deterministic philosophies have exerted such great influences in England, Germany, and America, we see that this doctrine is at least worthy of careful study.[28]

H. I had a brief correspondence with Dr. Boettner about Augustine in the 1970s when he lived in Rockport, MO. Perhaps he had little exposure to Islam or Muslims and thus was naive of the negative impact of his statement.

Most disturbing is that Boettner did not see fatalism and determinism as negative. Most extreme Calvinists, however, seek to distance themselves from the fatalism of Islam.[29]

However, Brother Andrew of Open Doors fame shared an experience which illustrates this connection in his understanding. He tells of hearing two Christian women discussing a hostage situation and lamenting that there is nothing that we can do about these things. He thought to suggest to them that they ought to become Muslims because they would find such thinking more conducive to Islamic theology, where fatalism reigns. His point is that prayer can and does make a vast difference. He went on to tell how in 1983 his Open Doors ministry issued a call to pray for the Soviet Union and the demise of the Iron Curtain. Within a year, Gorbachev emerged, and within six, the Berlin wall came tumbling down. The rest is history![30]

Perhaps it would help if I illustrate the fatalism of Islam from the narrative of the film, *Lawrence of Arabia*, which was replayed on television recently. While Lawrence and the army of Sheikh Ali were crossing the desert to capture the Turk garrison at Aqaba, one of the men, Ghasim, fell off his camel unnoticed and was left behind in the worst part of the desert called, 'The Sun's Anvil.' When Lawrence proposed going back to rescue him, Sheik Ali said, "Ghasim's time has come, it is written." Lawrence responded, "Nothing is written." This apparently provoked Sheikh Ali to react angrily, "Aqaba, what of Aqaba? You will not be at Aqaba, English! Go back, blasphemer, but you will not be at Aqaba!" Lawrence responded, "I shall be at Aqaba! It is written (pointing to his head) in here," upon which he turned back alone and rescued Ghasim. After the rescue, Sheikh Ali stated, "Truly for some men nothing is written unless they write it." Later, as they invest Lawrence with the robes of a Sharif, someone says, "People for whom nothing is written may write themselves a plan." As history records, they conquered the Turks at Aqaba and changed the course of the Middle East. This is a fascinating vignette into Lawrence's struggle with the fatalism of his Arab Muslim colleagues, which pervades the Islamic mindset.

Norman Geisler has supported this understanding of Islamic thinking from the Qur'an itself: "If We [Allah] had so willed, We could certainly have brought Every soul its true guidance; But the Word from Me Will come true. 'I will Fill Hell with jinn and men all together'" (Surah 32:13). The Persian Muslim poet, Omar Khayyam graphically reinforced this:

> Tis all a chequer-board of night and days
> Where destiny with men for pieces plays;
> Hither and thither moves and mates and slays,
> And one by one back in the closet lays.[31]

I would suggest that this same fatalism about evangelism and world missions has been an albatross on the back of Christ's church since the

Reformation. But then, this is the subject of chapter 17, so I mustn't get ahead of myself.

There is another parallel between Calvinistic and Islamic theology which was just brought to my attention by Jordanian theologian, Imad Shahadeh: "There is no grace in the Qur'an. Actually the concept of God in the Qur'an is that he is so free, so powerful, all the other attributes really stem from his will, rather than from his nature. He is so powerful that he is not even bound to a promise."[32] Calvinists also believe that God cannot know that which He has not decreed, in other words that an attribute of God stems from His will, rather than the reverse. Of course, His will must flow from His attributes, not the reverse.

Richard Bailey is a long-term missionary to Muslims. He recently pointed out that according to Islamic theology Allah has no emotions, he is impassible: ". . . Islam's concept that God is so much greater than us and so different than us that He can have no such emotions. For a Muslim to believe that God is like us in any way is idolatrous blasphemy."[33] Bailey pointed me to the centuries of Muslim theologians wrestling with the relationship of Aristotle and Neo-Platonism to Islamic theology, and the fact that it was the Muslims who reintroduced Aristotle back into medieval Europe in time for Thomas Aquinas and others to incorporate his philosophy into Christian theology. Where did medieval theologians get the absurd notion of the impassibility of God? They got it from Aristotle through the Muslims.[34] It is not surprising that there is a parallel.

Samuel M. Zwemer, the great Reformed pioneer missionary to the Muslims, who was thoroughly committed to reformed doctrine, bluntly made the comparison:

> . . . what might be called ultra-Calvinism has carried the day. The terminology of their teaching is Calvinistic, but its practical effect is pure fatalism. Most Moslem sects 'deny all free-agency in man and say that man is necessarily constrained by the force of God's eternal and immutable decree to act as he does.' God wills both good and evil; there is no escaping from the caprice of His decree. Religion is Islam, i.e., resignation. Fatalism has paralyzed progress; hope perishes under the weight of this iron bondage . . .[35]

Such decree(s) unduly limit God's love.

Don Carson's Griffith-Thomas lectures on *The Difficult Doctrine of the Love of God* point out some of the problems all Evangelicals face in defining and defending the attribute of God's love. He suggests five different ways in which God's love is spoken of in the Bible, the fourth of which is: "*God's particular, effective, selecting love toward his elect.*" In discussing the third, "*God's salvific stance toward his fallen world*", he admits that "God's love for the world cannot be collapsed into his love for the elect,"[36] as extreme Calvinists are wont to do. It impressed me that Jerom Zanchi, one of the originators of limited atonement, in his discussion of the attributes of God, *leaves out His love.* I suspect that Carson's problem is exacerbated by his Calvinism. If God does not desire the salvation of the "non-elect" (not a biblical category), then it can hardly be said that He loves them. However, this is a topic for chapter 6 in connection with the question, "For Whom Did Christ Die?"

GOD'S SOVEREIGNTY IN SALVATION

We should note at this point that it is not necessary for Augustinians to prove this concept of exhaustive sovereignty in order to establish their view of sovereignty in reference to salvation, that is, unconditional election and irresistible grace. They only need to prove that God's decrees in reference to *salvation* are all-inclusive. But instead of seeking to prove the more limited propositions relating to salvation, Augustinians always seem to focus on God's decrees as being all-inclusive in reference to all events in the universe. Why do they do this? It seems to me that this is a type of *a forteriori* argument. That is, if the broader concept of God's decrees is true, then the narrower concept regarding matters of salvation-truth automatically follows; it does not need to be specifically investigated. However, since we have just seen the incredible lack of evidence for the exhaustive exercise of sovereignty, sovereignty in relation to salvation-truth must now be specifically investigated.

James Daane has shown how this developed historically:

> The inclusion of election and reprobation as mere instances of a cosmic, wall-to-wall doctrine of predestination, eased the transfer of election and reprobation back into the first locus of systematic theology, in which the doctrine of God is discussed. Calvin had rescued election and reprobation from there, where scholastic orthodoxy had treated it, and had transferred it to the locus of soteriology, where election and reprobation are discussed in the context of man's sin and God's grace. . . . But Calvin's advance beyond medieval scholasticism was soon squandered. His valuable biblical perspective was negated when Beza his successor, falling back into medieval scholasticism, . . . assigned predestination to the locus of the doctrine of God, and proceeded to develop a decretal theology . . . [37]

Therefore, having sought to show that there is no basis for determinism in the locus of the doctrine of God, we must go to the locus of the doctrine of salvation to see whether there is any basis there either. Arguments for the Augustinian view of God's sovereignty in salvation-truth are usually dependent upon concepts of "predestination," unconditional election, foreknowledge, and irresistible grace. These arguments are supposedly based upon word-studies of the relevant terms and such passages as

Romans 9:6-29 and Ephesians 1:4-13. Careful word-studies of foreknowledge, election, and foreordination will be discussed in chapters 7 and 8, but I get the impression that there is circular reasoning in the Augustinian construct. The treatments of foreknowledge, election, and predestination have as an unstated premise the Augustinian view of universal sovereignty. Without that premise, I believe that the inductive data is not at all supportive of their view of foreknowledge, election, and predestination upon which their view of God's sovereignty in salvation is built. This is why I referred to their approach as an *a forteriori* approach, that is, that universal sovereignty is so strongly held that the other parts of the system fall into place almost automatically. This is why "sovereign grace" is really a catch phrase in Calvinistic circles. In any case, they always depend heavily on their understanding of Romans chapter nine.

Romans chapters 9–11

The ninth chapter of Romans has occasioned much discussion between Calvinists and others, since Calvinists see this as a lynchpin in their case for God's sovereignty manifest in the unconditional election of individuals. I suggest that when we examine this passage in the light of its context, along with careful examination of the many Old Testament passages which Paul quotes in their contexts, there is absolutely no case for the unconditional election of individuals here. As we examine the flow of Paul's thought in the broader context of Romans, we find that the subject is totally other than what Calvinists make it out to be. Careful examination of these contexts is absolutely imperative for an honest dealing with the argument of the text.[38]

Context. First, the broader context of Romans must be considered. I have recently come to realize that there was a Jew/Gentile issue in the churches in Rome which keeps surfacing all through the epistle. This is so pervasive that liberal scholar F. C. Bauer claimed that the epistle was written to Hebrew Christians. His view has never been accepted because it is clearly wrong, but he had a point. Probably the original core of the churches consisted of many Jews and proselytes converted on the day of Pentecost, augmented by converts from Paul's first two missionary journeys who migrated to Rome. However, when Claudius Caesar expelled the Jews from Rome (Acts 18:2), the church naturally became totally Gentile. When the Jews drifted back into Rome under Nero, including Priscilla and Aquila (Rom. 16:3), the Hebrew Christians were no longer running the church and may have felt like second-class members. They felt denigrated in the dispensational transition from Israel to the New Testament church—after all weren't they God's chosen ('choice') people? And now they heard that Paul was calling himself an apostle to the Gentiles, of all things! "Paul, you've abandoned your own people Israel," they must have been complaining. What about two millenniums of promises made to Israel—has the word of

God been negated? Has God also abandoned Israel? Thus, we see Paul addressing all these issues in Romans. Please study the relevance of the following passages: 1:2, 3, 5, 16; 2:11, 17, 24, 25-29; 3:1, 9, 19-20, 21, 29, 31, 4:1, 6, 9, 12, 13-25; 6:14; 7:1-6, 7-25; 8:3-7; ch. 9-11; 14:1-23; 15:8-12, 16-18, 25-27, 31; 16:25-26.[39]

So when we come to the ninth chapter, we must not look only at the context of chapters 9-11, but recognize that this issue of the transition from Israel being God's choice people to its replacement by the body church, composed of both Jew and Gentile, permeates the whole book. Most commentators recognize that the issue in these three chapters is the vindication of God's righteousness or fairness in setting Israel aside in favor of the Church. First, we see that 9:1-29 deals with God's sovereign justice in His dealings with Israel. Then, in 9:30--10:15 Paul focuses upon the proclamation of righteousness by faith to all mankind. In 10:16--11:32 Paul shows how God foreknew and used Israel's fall for world salvation.

I will focus upon the first 29 verses. It is imperative that the reader open the biblical text at this point in order to grasp this discussion. Otherwise, stop reading (unless you have memorized Romans 9)! The major theological issue which we must decide in this passage is whether Paul is discussing the unconditional election of individuals or God's dealings with Israel corporately.

God's dealings with corporate Israel: 9:1-29

In surveying God's just dealings with Israel, Paul shares his burden for the salvation of a people who had been greatly advantaged (9:1-5). Probably some of the Jewish Christians felt that Paul had abandoned his own people, so he uses very strong language to assure them of his great concern for the salvation of Jews. He expands the issue of Israel's advantage begun in 3:1-3 with an impressive list coming down to the giving of the divine Messiah of the Jews.

Then in 9:6-13 he shows how in God's separating out the nation Israel, physical descent did not guarantee being retained in the chosen lineage. Paul makes this point explicitly in 9:6: **"For they are not all Israel who are *descended* from Israel."**[1] There are many who can trace their lineage back to Abraham and Jacob, who are not Jews; they are not "**children of the promise**" (9:7, 8). Then he gave two examples of this. The lineage would be through Isaac, the miracle child procreated in harmony with God's order for the family. He says nothing about Ishmael's salvation or lack thereof. God blessed Ishmael and the impression is that he was a believer: "**God was with the lad . . .**" (Gen. 16:10-12; 21:17-20). The focus is upon the

---

1. I would remind my amillennial readers that Paul says absolutely nothing here about Gentiles becoming part of "spiritual Israel," since that would be a converse of his statement. The rules of logic tell us that the truth or fallacy of a converse of a statement is indeterminate. This is confirmed by careful exegesis of Galatians 6:16.

lineage of the nation.

Then Paul pointed out the choice of Jacob over Esau for the promised lineage of the nation, quoting a part of God's word to Rebekah before their birth (but I must quote the whole): "**Two nations are in your womb; and two peoples shall be separated from your body; and one people shall be stronger than the other; and the older shall serve the younger**" (Gen. 25:23). Is it not obvious that Paul's focus in using this quotation is not on the individuals, but upon the separation of the nation of Israel from the Edomites? Esau as an individual never served Jacob; indeed, the opposite is true in that Jacob served Esau a red lentil stew to induce him to give up his birthright! However, the subjugation of the Edomites to the Israelites began under David, was complete under Solomon, and continued on and off until the Babylonian captivity. Paul then confirmed this by quoting from Malachi 1:2-4, which was written about fifteen centuries later about God's judgment upon the Edomites and His continuing love for Israel (expanded in Obadiah): "**Jacob I loved, but Esau I hated, and I have made his mountains a desolation . . . Though Edom says, . . .**" Is it not obvious that Jacob and Esau are euphemisms for the nations in the brief portion which Paul quoted? Malachi has personalized the nations by using the names of their progenitors. I am confident that the apostle Paul did not intend to wrench these sentences out of their prophetic contexts to make them teach a doctrine of unconditional individual election. Unfortunately, their close juxtaposition in 9:12-13 has allowed careless interpreters to read such a doctrine into them unjustifiably. But this is isogesis, not careful contextual exegesis!

Four examples. Paul went on in 9:14-29 to give four examples of God's sovereign justice in His dealings with the nation Israel, explicitly raising the issue of charges of God's injustice in v. 14. The first is in relation to Moses' experience with his people when they had sinned in worshiping a golden calf. At first, when God said He would destroy Israel and make a new nation from Moses, he interceded for Israel and God heard him (Ex. 32:10-14). Then he pled again for God to forgive Israel, suggesting that God blot out his own name from His book (Ex. 32:32). When God expressed a reluctance to continue His presence in the midst of Israel, Moses interceded again and pled for God to show him His ways (33:1-16). God then favored Moses to see His presence in a special way, and the passage which Paul quoted is in this connection: "**I myself will make all My goodness pass before you, and I will proclaim the name of the Lord before you; and I will be gracious to whom I will be gracious, and will show compassion on whom I will show compassion**" (33:19). The issue here is the continuance of God's gracious and compassionate favor upon the nation Israel in specially favoring their leader, Moses. It is in this regard that Paul argues in v. 16 that "**God's purpose . . . does not depend on the man who wills and the man who runs, but on God who has mercy**" (9:11, 16). The passage in Exodus has nothing to do with individual, unconditional election to salvation. If that were the point which Paul was making, it would be a serious abuse of the Exodus narrative.[J] But thus far there is nothing in the Romans passage to support such an inference. Dave Hunt points out how the Calvinist's treatment of this and other passages puts a negative spin on them, emphasizing reprobation.[40] Note that neither in the Exodus passage, or in Paul's use of it, is there anything about reprobation–it is all about mercy and compassion upon Moses and Israel as a nation. Certainly Moses' salvation is not at issue, since he was the recipient of a unique blessing.

Paul's second example is God's dealings with Pharaoh, the god-king of a grossly idolatrous nation, in hardening him for judgment (9:17-18). It is commonly understood that each of the ten judgments related to the idolatrous religion of Egypt. Judgment came upon the gods of Egypt and their human regent, who himself was worshiped as god. This is a classic example of the principle which Paul had stated in Romans 1:24, 26, 28, that God judgmentally gave the most hardened heathen over to a depraved mind. First of all, God stated His sovereign intention to Moses: "**But I will harden Pharaoh's heart that I may multiply My signs and My wonders in the land of Egypt**" (Ex. 7:3). Then we see seven clear references to Pharaoh's heart being characteristically hard (Ex. 7:13-14, 22; 8:19; 9:7) and even to Pharaoh hardening his own heart (8:15, 32),[K] before God then hardened his heart even further judgmentally (Ex. 9:12; 10:1, 20; 11:10; 14:8).

It was in this connection that the words of God to Pharaoh were spoken (Ex. 9:16), which Paul quoted "**For this very purpose I raised you up, to demonstrate my power in you, and that my name might be proclaimed throughout the whole earth**" (Rom. 9:17). The issue here clearly was God's sovereign purpose to bring Israel out of Egypt and to make a signal demonstration of His judgment upon corrupt idolatrous religion in the process. Pharaoh and his nation were ripe for judgment (cf. Gen. 15:13-16). God was making an example of Pharaoh and his false prophets and priests, who were forerunners of subsequent false prophets, who were singled our for denunciation by the Lord Jesus (Mt. 7:15-23), by Paul (Rom. 1:18-32; 2 Tim. 3:1-9, note reference to Jannes and Jambres), by Peter (2 Pet. 2), and by Jude (4-19). So let me emphasize that this has absolutely nothing to do with God's sovereignty in unconditional election of anybody to salvation or to reprobation. When Paul wrote that "**He hardens whom He desires**"

J. It should be noted that Ex. 33:12, 17 is one of the five passages in which Calvinists claim that *yada'* has an elective pregnant force. However, God is simply expressing His close personal relationship with Moses which has been greatly strengthened by Moses' intercession for Israel. See appendix F.

K. Five times the Qal perfect is used which would be a "characteristic perfect," describing the characteristic state of Pharaoh's heart (J. Wash Watts, *Hebrew Syntax*, p. 24), and twice it is a Hiphil perfect, (causative active) clearly indicating that Pharaoh caused his own heart to be hard (8:15 & 32).

(9:18b), he was not referring to an arbitrary reprobation in eternity past of people yet unborn, but of giving Satan's key representatives over judgmentally to a depraved mind (Rom. 1:24, 26, 28; 2:5). This passage has nothing to do with reprobation of the "non-elect" in eternity past.

Paul drew the third example from Jeremiah's observation of the potter's wheel (Jer. 18:1-11), although he did not quote him directly (9:19-24). He began by responding to a fatalistic person who objects to what he has written thus far: **"You will say to me then, 'Why does He still find fault? For who resists His will?'"** (9:19). Note well that these are not Paul's words but those of an objector. In essence the objector is saying, "If God has already decided to set Israel aside in favor of the Church, how can Israel be blamed, and how can Jews resist the will of a sovereign God in this regard?" Here instead of *boulē*, we find *boulēma*, which with the result ending *ma* might indicate a more formal, crystallized plan or counsel.[41] Perhaps it comes closest to the idea of a 'decree,' which seems to be the way it is used in First Clement (esp. 33:3). Note that the only use of *boulēma* in the whole New Testament is from the lips of a fatalistic objector, not as an expression of God's truth.

Paul's answer to this fatalistic objector comes from the potter's wheel. Let us note that Jeremiah saw the vessel being formed on the wheel being marred, but then remade by the potter since the clay was soft. Its form had not yet been fixed by firing in the kiln. The point that God explains to Jeremiah is that the nation Israel is clay in His hands, and the nation's future is contingent upon their response to His word: **"if that nation against which I have spoken turns from its evil, I will relent concerning the calamity I planned to bring on it. . . So now then, speak to the men of Judah and against the inhabitants of Jerusalem saying, 'Thus says the LORD, "Behold, I am fashioning calamity against you and devising a plan against you. Oh turn back, each of you from his evil way, and reform your ways and your deeds"'"** (18:8, 11). Calvinists ignore the fact that the issues Paul is dealing with and the message of God through Jeremiah both relate to the nation Israel *corporately*. Indeed, the conditional nature of God's dealings with Israel are explicit in the Jeremiah passage. Paul later addressed the cause of Israel's being set aside as their unbelief (9:30-33; 10:16-21). Here he spoke of God's patience with Israel for the years of His entreaty to them through Christ and His apostles (9:22). The key word here is *katērtismena* ("*prepare, make, create*"). The question is whether this is middle or passive? The Arndt and Gingrich lexicon suggests it may be a middle voice: "*having prepared themselves f. destruction* Rom. 9:22."[42] This would harmonize with Jeremiah's context by putting the onus upon Israel.

The point which Paul is making here is that God has the sovereign right as a potter to use Israel for two millennia and then set them aside in favor of the Church. Additionally, in Romans 11 he shows the justice of this decision in the fact that a remnant of Jews are still being saved (11:1-10), and that He will ultimately restore Israel to the place of blessing corporately (11:11-32).

Verses 23-24 are a segue into his later discussion of the Church's becoming vessels of mercy, by a plan prepared beforehand (*proetoimazein*) for glory. God was patient with Israel's unbelief so that He might reveal the glorious riches of the cross to and through the Church, which is being called from both Jew and Gentile. The context gives no basis for individualizing this statement. Thus, this passage also says nothing about unconditional, individual election to salvation.

The fourth proof of God's sovereign justice in His dealings with national Israel is seen in the four prophetic passages Paul quoted in 9:25-29 (Hosea 2:23; 1:10; Isa. 10:23; 1:9). Although the context of Hosea is about the end-time restoration of national Israel (3:4-5), it seems that Paul is drawing out the principle that those who were not God's people can become the people of God, in support of 9:23-24. Be that as it may, the Isaiah quotations clearly refer to the preservation of a remnant of believing Jews, which point Paul reinforced in 11:1-10. In any case, there is nothing said here either about individual, unconditional election to salvation.

A universal gospel: 9:30–10:15

The chapter divisions here and between 10 and 11 are poorly placed, since Paul moved into a new subject at this juncture. He was vindicating the righteousness of God by discussing the proclamation of God's righteousness by faith to all mankind (9:30–10:15), and coming back to Israel's unbelief and failure (10:16–11:32).[L] His emphasis upon the universality of the gospel message in the first section is totally contradictory to any notion of individual, unconditional election in chapter 9: "**'Whoever believes in Him will not be disappointed.' For there is no distinction between Jew and Greek; for the same *Lord* is Lord of all, abounding in riches for all who call upon Him; for 'Whoever will call upon the name of the Lord will be saved' How then shall they call upon Him in whom they have not believed? And how shall they believe in Him whom they have not heard? And how shall they hear without a preacher? And how shall they preach unless they are sent?**" (10:11-15a). How much more clearly could Paul say that the salvation of the lost is contingent upon human instrumentality? In the segue to the next section, Paul's very simple principle must be foundational to our theology of salvation: "**So faith comes from hearing, and hearing by the word of Christ**" (10:17). In my years as a missionary in Pakistan, I never met a Muslim who was converted by irresistible grace apart from human instrumentality. If it is by irresistible grace, why does it take months or years of patient communication of the word of Christ before most Muslims are saved? Human instrumentality is

L. Paul actually comes back to Israel's unbelief and failure in 10:16-21, which is the important context for his reference to God's foreknowledge of Israel's failure in 11:2. This confirms that *proginoskein* has its normative meaning of foreknowledge, as I discuss in chapter 7.

paramount in preparing the lost for faith, but the new birth is totally a work of the Holy Spirit. But these are points I will argue in subsequent chapters.

Since the Old Testament passages which Paul quotes in Romans 9 do not in the least support the Calvinistic interpretation, Calvinists have a serious dilemma. Either Paul is grossly dishonest in his use of these passages and the integrity of Scripture comes into question, or else, Paul is fairly using these passages and has been grossly misunderstood by western, individualistic Christians, who do not think corporately. I much prefer the latter option. Paul's first readers had no problem understanding his references to God's corporate dealings with Israel because of their corporate-cultural way of thinking and because Paul's discussion of Jew/Gentile issues directly answered their concerns. Any issues related to individual, unconditional election would have been farthest from their concerns or Paul's mind (see appendix B for my critique of John Piper, *The Justification of God*, which I believe is a seriously flawed book).

Do I not believe in the sovereignty of God? Absolutely, but not in the sense in which Augustinians believe it. James Daane, Reformed professor and editor, has addressed well the problem of the single decree in decretal theology:

> That is why Reformed theology has traditionally been unable to relate biblical history and theology. That is why Reformed theology has always been weak in biblical theology, in sharp contrast to its genius for systematic theology. . . . **That is why Reformed theology fails to take seriously the historical aspects of Paul's theology of Jew and Gentile in Romans 9-11.** That is why Reformed theology has never as much as attempted to develop an historical doctrine of election, but has remained content with a purely ahistorical doctrine of individual election. Finally, that is why the mystery Paul sees in the election of the Gentiles, of Christ, and of the church is almost totally absent in Reformed thought. (emphasis mine)[43]

OPEN THEISM'S DENIAL

As I mentioned at the beginning of this chapter, the major error of Open Theism is the denial of God's absolute foreknowledge, which would also compromise His omnipotence and omnipresence. This raises serious questions about the sovereignty of God, the shape of the future, and even of the certainty of God's ultimate victory.

Open theists have a number of concerns. They claim that the several references in the Old Testament narrative to God repenting and changing His mind in interacting with His people proves that God could not know the whole future, but only that part of it which He has determined to transpire, such as the cross. Classic Christian theology has always understood those passages as being figurative representations of God and His actions in human terms (anthropomorphisms). This is to say that God accommodates the communication of His dealings with mankind to the limits of human comprehension, that is, in sequential thought processes. For example, this is quite obvious in the case of God's appearing to Abram as one of three men in Genesis 18:23-32. God dialogs with Abram as if He needs to go to Sodom to investigate the situation, when it is obvious that He actually knows the full reality. God is omniscient and omnipresent as a multitude of other Scriptures attest.

Similarly the representations of God's repentance are clarified by a word study of the Hebrew word, *NACHAM*, which should be translated, 'to relent or have compassion upon.' The key idea is that God, in having compassion upon sinners, relents from the judgment which they might ordinarily deserve. The story of the book of Jonah has been especially misunderstood. It is not that God changed His mind about destroying Nineveh. The fact of the matter rather was that Jonah did not include the conditional nature of the message of judgment because of his desire to see Nineveh destroyed. He omitted any reference to repentance from his warning.

Open theists also claim that the traditional view of God has been colored by Greek philosophical concepts from Aristotle or neo-Platonism. Even though there is much truth to their allegation, in the main the classic concept is soundly based in Scripture. I would agree that the concepts of the simplicity and impassibility of God have no biblical support and that we must be careful in defining terms like immutability,[44] but God's omniscient foreknowledge, His omnipresence, and His omnipotence are biblical. On the other hand, the open theists have admittedly derived many of their ideas from contemporary liberal process philosophy or theology. This is a very serious matter.

It seems to me that most of the other concerns which open theists have with traditional Reformed theology would be shared by other Arminians and by those of us who hold a mediate position. This would include issues of the reality of answered prayer, attributing the origin and continuance of evil to God, the doctrine of reprobation, and even the rigid blueprint concept of the will of God for our individual lives. Although we might share some of the same concerns, we cannot at all identify with the extremes of their position. See appendix C for a fuller discussion of open theism.

CONCLUSIONS

Delineating God's sovereignty

I would like to set out some propositions about the sovereignty of God which I believe can be fully justified from the inductive data of Scripture unmixed with *a priori* considerations:

1. God as Creator has the right to rule His universe in any way He sees fit consistent with His own attributes. If He should choose to delegate spheres of autonomy to His creatures, this in no way limits His

sovereignty.

2. He set up the natural laws which govern the universe and by which the universe continues on in its natural course. Yet He continues to actively uphold His creation, and He can overrule or suspend these laws according to His will (which we call miracles).

3. He also set up the moral laws which govern the moral beings He has created, but He is ultimately above His laws and can do as He wishes consistent with His attributes.

4. Like human sovereigns, God exercises His sovereignty by punishing disobedience to His will at what times and in what ways suits His eternal plan.

5. God has continued to delegate authority to humans as He pleases: capital punishment and human government (Gen. 9:6); to priests, judges, and kings in Israel, elders in the church, and husbands in the family. This delegated authority intrinsically implies a limited autonomy.

6. By His omniscient foreknowledge of both eventualities and non-eventual possibilities God orchestrates and arranges those events He chooses without coercing the wills of the moral agents involved. God's foreknowledge cannot be contingent upon His will.

7. Much of God's involvement since He completed creation and rested on the seventh day, He accomplishes mediately, or indirectly, through His agents, and through orchestrating natural and human events.

8. Whenever it pleases Him, God intervenes in the world by supernatural acts such as miracles, the new birth and other ministries of the Holy Spirit. This is implemented in harmony with His eternal plan.

9. There is no biblical basis for the notion that God has exhaustively decreed every last event which transpires in His universe.

10. By the nature of promises, covenants, and prophecies, God limits Himself voluntarily. Of course, God is never the inferior party to any bilateral covenant, which might imply an involuntary element which would compromise His sovereignty.

11. Romans 9 says nothing about the unconditional election of individuals to salvation.

I have sought to do an inductive investigation of the biblical evidence for the Augustinian concept of God's sovereignty, after looking in the standard Calvinistic theologies for clues as to where in the Bible to find such a concept of exhaustive determinism. Those theologies gave no inductive data so I had to survey the key biblical terms. Most astounding was the almost total lack of basis for the Calvinistic concept of either a single comprehensive decree of God in eternity past, or even of a multiplicity of such decrees. Since sovereignty has to do with governance, study of the words related to God as king and His kingdom yielded no impression of God as a totally controlling monarch, who actually and totally manipulates all His subjects in the universe, even those in total rebellion against Him. Rather, right from Genesis 1 onward, we find that God progressively delegates more and more of His rule to His creatures. The one crucial verse adduced endlessly by the Calvinists, Ephesians 1:11, in the light of the context and grammar can be far more plausibly interpreted as relating to the foundation of God's plan of salvation in the work of the Son, rather than as stipulating God's exhaustive and minute determination of "all that comes to pass" in the universe.

It was readily acknowledged that this proves little directly about Calvinistic salvation-truth concepts such as unconditional election and irresistible grace. But there is a heavy indirect connection between the these concepts and exhaustive sovereignty, indeed it is the premise. Although I will take up these issues in the subsequent chapters of this book, the study of Romans chapter 9 was appropriate at this point, since Calvinists build so much upon their understanding of it. Here also the context of Paul's argument, especially in the light of the Old Testament passages he refers to, was not at all supportive of determinism in salvation either.

Less attention was devoted to the opposite error of open theism, since it is a relatively new movement and has relatively few adherents. It is included only because of the great interest it has aroused in the last decade. The reaction has come mostly from Calvinists. Even though I agree with the Calvinists that this is a dangerous movement in presuming to limit what God can or cannot know about the future, it does have something to say to the Calvinists about their philosophically derived distortions of God's character. In an overemphasis upon the transcendence of God, His immanent activity in human history gets somehow lost in the shuffle, or at least minimized.

---

1. Charles Hodge, *Systematic Theology*, I:535.
2. James Daane, *The Freedom of God: A Study of Election and Pulpit*, pp. 34-73.
3. See works by Alan Clifford, R. T. Kendall, Laurence Vance, Norman Geisler, Curt Daniel, Charles Bell, Michael Eaton, Brian Armstrong, and Basil Hall in the bibliography.
4. J. Oliver Buswell, Jr., *A Systematic Theology of the Christian Religion*, vol. I, p. 46.
5. Gregory A. Boyd, *God of the Possible*, p. 32; Norman L. Geisler, *Chosen But Free*, pp. 43, 45.
6. John M. Frame, "The Spirit and the Scriptures," in D. A. Carson and John D. Woodbridge, eds., *Hermeneutics, Authority and Canon* (Academie, 1986), pp. 223-4.
7. Francis Brown, *The New Brown-Driver-Briggs-Gesenius Hebrew and English Lexicon*, pp. 574-5.
8. R. Laird Harris, Gleason L. Archer, Jr., & Bruce K. Waltke, eds., *Theological Wordbook of the Old Testament* (Chicago: Moody, 1980), I:507-9.
9. Hodge, I:535-549.
10. Arndt and Gingrich, *A Greek-English Lexicon* , p. 145.

11. Harold Hoehner, "Chronological Aspects of the Life of Christ: Part V," *Bibliotheca Sacra* 524 (Oct. '74) pp. 340-8 (Also published in book form).

12. Lewis Sperry Chafer, *Systematic Theology* (Dallas Seminary Press, 1948), vol. III, pp. 173-4.

13. John Feinberg is typical in the weight he puts on Eph. 1:11 in David and Randall Basinger, eds. *Predestination and Free Will*, pp. 29-32.

14. Blass, DeBrunner, and Funk, *Grammar*, p. 76. We must remember that the Greek usage of gender is significantly different than our English usage.

15. C. Gordon Olson, *What in the World Is God Doing? The Essentials of Global Missions*, 4th ed., pp. 21-80.

16. Arndt and Gingrich, p. 713.

17. Patrick H. Mell, *A Southern Baptist Looks at Predestination* (Cape Coral: Christian Gospel Foundation, n.d.), p. 53; Theodore Beza, cited by Vance, pp. 479, 481.

18. Forster and Marston, *God's Strategy*, ch. 1.

19. Bruce Reichenbach, in Basinger, p. 105.

20. Daane, pp. 41-42; the original British edition of the Westminister Confession has "decree" in the singular.

21. Norman L. Geisler, *Chosen But Free*, p.133.

22. Daane, pp. 43, 55-56.

23. Geisler, pp. 145-154.

24. Ibid, pp. 147-149.

25. Ibid, pp. 175-180. Although I don't agree with all of his reasoning, I think his essential arguments are sound.

26. Daane, p. 35.

27. Ibid, pp. 38-43.

28. Loraine Boettner, *The Reformed Doctrine of Predestination*, p. 2.

29. Gary North, *Dominion and Common Grace*, p. 231; Talbot and Crampton, p. 4; Coppes, p. 23,cited by Vance, p. 703.

30. Brother Andrew, *And God Changed His Mind . . . Because His people dared to ask* (Tarrytown:Revell, 1990), pp. 11-25.

31. Geisler, pp. 133-34.

32. Imad Shahadeh, "Panel Discussion" at ETS 2000, Nashville, TN, November 2000.

33. Richard Bailey, "Prayer Letter #505," June 2001.

34. John L. Esposito, ed., *The Oxford History of Islam*, (NY: Oxford Univ. Press, 1999), pp. 269-345.

35. Samuel M. Zwemer, *Religions of Mission Fields*, pp. 244-5, as quoted by Fisk, *Calvinistic Paths*, p. 225.

36. D. A. Carson, *The Difficult Doctrine of the Love of God* (Wheaton: Crossway, 2000), pp. 17-19.

37. Daane, p. 38.

38. For additional discussion see Forster and Marston; William W. Klein, *The New Chosen People*; and commentaries by Craig Blomberg and Leon Morris.

39. D. A. Carson, Douglas Moo, and Leon Morris, *An Introduction to the New Testament*, pp. 244-45.

40. Dave Hunt, *What Love Is This?*, pp. 311-2.

41. William Douglas Chamberlain, *An Exegetical Grammar of the Greek New Testament*, pp. 9-12.

42. Arndt and Gingrich, p. 419.

43. Daane, p. 88 (emphasis mine).

44. Bruce Ware, "An Evangelical Reformulation of the Doctrine of the Immutability of God," *Journal of the Evangelical Theological Society*, 29:4, pp. 431-49.

I find, then that man was by God constituted free, master of his own will and power; indicating the presence of God's image and likeness in him by nothing so well as this constitution of his nature. . . . –you will find that when He sets before man good and evil, life and death, that the entire course of discipline is arranged in precepts by God's calling men from sin, and threatening and exhorting them; and this on no other ground than that man is free, with a will either for obedience or resistance.

-Tertullian (AD 155-225)

4

WHATEVER HAPPENED TO THE IMAGE OF GOD IN MAN?

Foundational to a sound theology of salvation is a sound, biblically rigorous view of humanity: his original creation, his fall and depravity, and an evaluation of the extent to which his original nobility was affected by the fall. Distorted conceptions of the impact of the fall have in turn distorted our view of the nature of salvation, especially in regards to how sinners come to saving repentant faith in Christ. The process by which unbelievers become believers is the subject of subsequent chapters of this work. But before we can intelligently deal with this crucial subject, we must go back to the Garden of Eden and start with man's originally created nobility and understand what was involved in the image of God (*imago Dei*).[A] Only then can we appraise, in a balanced way, the consequences of the fall on humanity by affirming depravity but being careful not to exaggerate its impact under the pressure of a theological agenda coming from other loci of theology.

There is a significant historical background to our investigation. At this point, I will only alert you to a few key personalities and reserve the full

A. Theologians love to drop Latin phrases into their discussions. I have a suspicion that this is not in the least helpful to many readers who do not know Latin, and only serves to obfuscate the issue under discussion. This is theological jargon at its worst. However, since *imago Dei* is a terse, easily understood phrase, I will use it.

historical investigation for chapter 18, since I am convinced that the Scripture investigation must come first. At this point, we can only note that the controversy really began with the British monk, Pelagius (350-423), and his weak teaching, probably denial, of human depravity. Before this the church fathers wrote in defense of free will against the deterministic cults and philosophies of their day, indeed, they coined the term 'free will.' Then the North African Bishop, Augustine (354-430), developed his theology of salvation (to the limited extent he did develop it) out of his controversy with Pelagius in the early fifth century. The controversy raged for a century after his death in 430, until a semi-Augustinian consensus was achieved at the Synod of Orange in 529. Although the western church drifted over the centuries towards semi-Pelagianism and the controversy erupted from time to time, the official position was semi-Augustinian. At the time of the Reformation, Luther got into controversy with the reformist Catholic scholar, Erasmus. As an erstwhile Augustinian monk, Luther pressed the full Augustinian position and wrote the *Bondage of the Will* as a refutation of Erasmus's more moderate view. I will seek to show that the truth of Scripture lies between the polarized positions of Augustine and Pelagius, Luther and Erasmus,[1] and as we move into the theology of salvation, Calvin and Arminius. But first we must begin our inductive biblical investigation.

Humanity's Original Nobility

The original image of God in man

Before we can correctly evaluate the impact of the fall on mankind, we must look into the difficult and controversial issue of the image of God in man. Much has been written about it from differing perspectives, but there is enough biblical data to arrive at some firm conclusions. Millard Erickson's extensive discussion provides a helpful summary and evaluation of three prominent views of the meaning of the image of God. He shows the weaknesses of the relational and functional views and rightly suggests that the substantive view must be taken as the primary intent of Scripture. First, let us set Genesis 1:26-7 before us:

> **Then God said, "Let Us make man in Our image, according to Our likeness; and let them rule over the fish of the sea and over the birds of the sky and over the cattle and over all the earth, and over every creeping thing that creeps on the earth." God created man in His own image, in the image of God He created him; male and female He created them.**

The use of the word 'substantive' does not imply any physical or bodily likeness between God and man, such as the Mormons understand.[2] Erickson clarifies the substantive view:

> All of the substantive views we have mentioned, with their widely differing conceptions of the nature of the image of God, agree in

> one particular: the locus of the image. It is located within man; it is a quality or capacity resident in his nature. Although it is God who conferred the image upon man, it resides in man whether or not he recognizes God's existence or his work.[3]

I agree with Erickson's affirmation of Luther's unitary view of the image, that is, that 'image' and 'likeness' in Genesis 1:26-7 are an obvious example of Hebrew parallelism and should not be distinguished as some theologians do.[4] Although Erickson rightly rejects Barth and Brunner's relational view of the image as being based upon their existential philosophy, we do need to recognize an element of validity here. Man was uniquely created to be able to have a personal relationship with God and with other humans such as animals cannot sustain. But this springs from the innate quality within man which God created. The relational implications of the image of God spring from its innate, substantive reality in man's nature.

The functional view is based upon the connection in the Genesis passage between the image and the rule which God delegated to Adam. Its adherents also refer to Psalm 8:5-6: **"Yet You have made him a little lower than God, and You crown him with glory and majesty. You make him to rule over the works of Your hands; You have put all things under his feet."** I believe they rightly see that Psalm 8 is based upon Genesis 1. However, writers like Mowinckel, Snaith, and Verduin erroneously limit the image to the dominion dimension.[5] It makes more sense to see the functional aspect of man's rule over the earth as derived from the substantive reality.

So the adherents of both the relational and the functional views are guilty of reductionist errors. Humanity's relationships with God and with other humans and his ability to exercise dominion over the lower creation, both derive from his constituent nature. So there is truth in all three views, and we must not affirm one to the exclusion of the others. *What man does (relate to God and other people) and is able to do (exercise rule) is dependent upon who he is (the substantive reality).*

So what is that substantive reality as expressed in the image of God? Since the context emphasizes humanity's distinctiveness from the animal creation over which he was given rule, we should expect this aspect of the image to be part of mankind's uniqueness. Geerhardus Vos focused upon man's immortality:

> 'Immortality' in philosophical language may express the persistence of the soul, which, even when the body is dissolved, retains its identity of individual being. In this sense every human being is under all circumstances 'immortal', and so were our first parents created; so were they after the fall. Next, 'immortality' is used in theological terminology for that state of man in which he has nothing in him which would cause death.[6]

This is not a matter of controversy among evangelical theologians, although little notice seems to be taken of Vos's suggestion, so we will move on.

We can validly infer some characteristics of the image of God from the New Testament, which uses this imagery in passages related to the restoration of the image through salvation in Christ. Erickson rightly objects to the tendency of theologians to misuse Colossians 3:10 by overintellectualizing the image.[7] It reads: "**. . . and have put on the new self who is being renewed to a true knowledge according to the image of the One who created him—.**" The context here makes it clear that Paul is not just speaking about the intellectual capacity of man, which is implied by *homo sapiens*, which is a clear uniqueness of mankind (even though evolutionary primatologists are trying to minimize it). Paul's focus goes beyond man's intelligence to his knowledge of God's revealed truth, which needs to be restored in fallen man, through new birth and the ongoing renewal process in the mind of the believer. Indeed, the Old Testament has a lot to say about the cruciality of knowledge of the truth in our relationship with God. The wisdom literature is replete with such references as are the prophetic books. God says through Hosea, "**My people are destroyed for lack of knowledge**" (4:6). Although man can never be omniscient, as God is, certainly the human intellect must be a part of the image of God, especially his ability to know God and His ways.

By the same process of backward extrapolation, we can infer from the parallel passage in Ephesians 4:24 that the moral qualities of righteousness and holiness are also part of the image of God: "**. . . and put on the new self, which in *the likeness of* God has been created in righteousness and holiness of the truth.**" It is widely understood that Adam was created in innocence with the possibility of attaining righteousness and holiness by continued fellowship with and obedience to God. Thus man was created as a moral being faced with moral choices, which animals are incapable of making.

The one other New Testament clue comes in 2 Corinthians 3:18: "**But we all, with unveiled face, beholding as in a mirror the glory of the Lord, are being transformed into the same image from glory to glory, just as from the Lord, the Spirit.**" Can we infer from this that a certain aspect of God's glory was reflected in the epitome of His earthly creation, mankind? This is confirmed in 1 Corinthians 11:7: "**For a man ought not to have his head covered, since he is the image and glory of God; but the woman is the glory of man.**"

We begin to see a pattern emerging from these references. In Theology Proper, we distinguish the communicable (or moral) from the incommunicable (or non-moral) attributes of God as developed from the study of what the Holy Spirit is working to accomplish in the life of the believer. Would this not be a basis for understanding all of the communicable attributes of God as related to the image of God in man, even if a specific attribute is not explicitly referred to in Scripture? Since God is love and explicitly desires

His children to love Him and one another in response, it would seem inordinate to leave the attribute of love out of the original image. Since God is holy, an incipient holiness must have been a part of the original image. Since God is a Spirit, the spiritual nature of unfallen man must have been a part of the image. Thus, just as God is a personal God with intellect, emotions, and will, the image of God in man must involve intellect, emotions, and will. Seeing the manifold dimensions of the image of God in man, I would conclude that far too many treatments of this theme have suffered from the reductionist error— focusing on a part of the truth to the exclusion of the whole. We should include the full spectrum of God's communicable or moral attributes.

Humanity's tripartite nature

This brings us to the age-old controversy over dichotomy versus trichotomy in man's original creation. This issue is significant to our understanding of the nature of spiritual death and of regeneration. The fact that a majority of theologians have opted for dichotomy has obscured these two essential truths. The dichotomous view of mankind's original nature tends to exaggerate the impact of the fall, and it is important to derive a balanced Scriptural view from all that the Bible says. If Adam did not have a human spirit distinct from his soul, then we cannot explain the fall in any literal language but must call "spiritual death" a symbolic expression. In this view, soul and spirit couldn't be affected by sin distinctively, which a trichotomist can affirm. The trichotomist understands the human spirit as the God-conscious part of unfallen man, while the soul is the self-conscious part. In the fall, it was the human spirit which was most affected. God had said, "**. . . for in the day that you eat from it you will surely die**" (Gen. 2:17). Adam and Eve did not die physically or soulishly, since *nephesh* clearly includes the concept of physical life. Dichotomists have to take spiritual death as a figure of speech, since they do not distinguish soul and spirit. Obviously, the soul/spirit did not die, or man would have become less than an animal. Trichotomists argue that the human spirit, the God-conscious part of man, literally died. As I will show later in this chapter, death is essentially a separation from God. Paul confirmed this in his description of the pagan Gentiles, "**. . . excluded from the life of God because of the ignorance that is in them, because of the hardness of their heart**" (Eph. 4:18).

On this basis also, the trichotomist understands the new birth to be a literal resurrection or making alive of the deadened human spirit. On the other hand, the dichotomist is reduced to calling it a figure of speech, a "spiritual resurrection."

Let us revisit this old discussion and seek to clarify the issues. In our discussion, we must not be distracted by the nature of fallen man, which is quite another question. In essence, the major argument for the dichotomy view is the interchangeable use of soul and spirit in much of Scripture. This is not debatable, but it is explainable in harmony with trichotomy. Since most of Scripture is describing the anthropology of fallen man, this is not really direct evidence for the original condition of Adam and Eve.

Over a century ago J. B. Heard suggested that another reason why the Old Testament does not show a distinction between soul and spirit relates to the progress of revelation. Since God did not choose to reveal His triune nature explicitly before the coming of the Messiah, there is a parallelism in His not revealing the tripartite nature of man. "It would be out of harmony with the 'analogy of faith,' if the tripartite nature of man were fully described in those books of the Bible which only contain implied hints of the plurality of persons in the Godhead."[8]

Therefore, the explicit evidence for the human spirit being distinct from the soul is found in four New Testament passages:

> **"Now may the God of peace Himself sanctify you entirely; and may your spirit and soul and body be preserved complete, without blame at the coming of our Lord Jesus Christ"** (1 Thess. 5:23; **"For who among men knows the *thoughts* of a man except the spirit of the man which is in him? Even so the *thoughts* of God no one knows except the Spirit of God. . . . But a natural [soulish] man does not accept the things of the Spirit of God, for they are foolishness to him; and he cannot understand them, because they are spiritually appraised. But he who is spiritual appraises all things, yet he himself is appraised by no one"** (1 Cor. 2:11, 14-15); **". . . it is sown a natural [soulish] body, it is raised a spiritual body. If there is a natural [soulish] body, there is also a spiritual *body*. So also it is written 'The first man, Adam, *became* a living soul.' The last Adam became a life-giving spirit. However, the spiritual is not first, but the natural [soulish]; then the spiritual.** (1 Cor. 15:44-46; in the Greek contrast between *psuchikos* and *pneumatikos* in both passages); **"For the word of God is living and active and sharper than any two-edged sword, and piercing as far as the division of soul and spirit, of both joints and marrow, and able to judge the thoughts and intentions of the heart"** (Heb. 4:12).

The connection of James 3:15 with Jude 19 is also supportive. For a fuller discussion of the arguments for both the dichotomous and the trichotomous views of man's original nature see appendix D, "Humanity's Tripartite Nature."

A majority of theologians have opted for dichotomy, since as the theological center shifted from the Greek world to the Latin locus in Augustine's day, trichotomy fell into disfavor. It was suggested by Heard that this was because the Latin language does not easily cope with the distinction of soul and spirit.[9] In any case, the trichotomous view may have been restored by

Luther, as claimed by F. J. Delitzsch. The advocacy of men like Delitzsch, C. J. Ellicott, Henry Alford (tentatively), H. P. Liddon, R. H. Lightfoot, W. G. T. Shedd, and L. S. Chafer must not be ignored.[10] In any case, the significance of the trichotomous view is that Adam and Eve did have a God-conscious part of their natures, the human spirit, which was most seriously affected in the fall, but not in the sense which some would have us believe. Since animals have *nephesh* or soul-life (Gen. 1:30) and man did not become a mere animal in the fall, there is a more subtle understanding of the fall, which the dichotomists cannot recognize. This understanding relates to the remnant *imago dei* after the fall. Before we look more into the implications of the fall, we should seek to understand Adam's created autonomy.

Humanity's original autonomy

By the very act of creating free moral agents, God limited the exercise of His sovereignty. His command to Adam in Genesis 2:16-17 clearly implies his investing Adam with free moral agency, or free will, as the early church fathers called it: "**From any tree of the garden you may eat freely; but from the tree of the knowledge of good and evil you shall not eat, for in the day that you eat from it you shall surely die**." This injunction was the only limitation on man's autonomy. Although man was dependent upon God for his very existence and for his continued life and blessing, his behavior was not predetermined or forced (even though Luther implied this). Most Evangelicals of all stripes would agree that God **only permitted** the fall. Man was not a mere puppet, else the command becomes farcical. Man was to learn dependence upon God as his fellowship with Him was to grow and deepen. Part of Satan's deception of Eve was to wean her away from dependence upon God and to cause her to doubt His goodness and beneficial care for them by doubting the reason for the one prohibition. Thus, Satan tempted Adam and Eve to abuse the God-given autonomy by disobedience to the only restriction He had put upon their autonomy.

It is very obvious from the rest of the biblical record that mankind did not lose that autonomy, but continued to exercise it in direct disobedience to God and His will. The only limitation on humanity's freedom now was the internal and external consequences of the fall as described in the judgments of Genesis 3 and the spiritual death implied in 2:17. This brings us to the consequences of the fall.

The Fall and Human Depravity

Augustine's doctrine of original sin

There are many aspects of Augustine's doctrine of original sin which can and must be affirmed, although the term 'original sin' may not be the best way of describing it. Chafer rightly distinguished between personal sin, transmitted sin, and imputed sin.[11] The transmission of the sin nature to the whole race hardly needs defense at this juncture, since it is axiomatic (Eph.

2:1-3). Augustine rightly argued for the natural headship of Adam as the basis for his development of the doctrine of imputed sin. This is not a matter of a supposed covenant, since there is no covenant language to be seen in Genesis 2. I believe Augustine's arguments for a seminal headship are convincing.[12] It is also clear that the context of Roman 5:12ff focuses on the idea of the imputation of sin to all mankind, so even if Augustine's exegesis was a bit weak, his conclusion was correct. I will not belabor the issue here.

Human depravity not in dispute

Many Calvinists frequently assume that they are the only Christians who hold a biblical view of depravity. Thus, they insist we must refer to "total depravity," perhaps unaware that the Latin *depravare* is an intensive compound word already signifying "totally corrupt" or "completely crooked."[13] Thus, adding the word 'total' is an indication of a doubly intensified concept of depravity in Calvinism. But knowledgeable Calvinists will admit that Jacob Arminius and John Wesley had a fully biblical view of depravity, even though the Remonstrants and many Arminians have had a weakened and shallow understanding.[14] So the balanced view of depravity advocated in this chapter may not satisfy all Calvinists, but I should not be accused of Arminianism or semi-Pelagianism for seeking to balance the truth.

Geisler suggests that extreme Calvinism has an "intensive" view of depravity, in contrast to a biblical, "extensive" understanding. The intensive view, in effect, holds that the image of God and the human will is essentially destroyed.[15] The extensive view holds that the whole person of humanity was corrupted by sin, but that the image of God and the human will have not been destroyed but rather corrupted. This is essentially the semi-Augustinian view of the Synod of Orange (AD 529), not the semi-Pelagianism of the later Roman church.[B]

While it is beyond the scope of this book to give a full exposition of depravity, Thiessen's summary is helpful:

> . . . it does mean that every sinner is totally destitute of that love to God which is the fundamental requirement of the law (Deut. 6:4, 5; Matt. 22:35-38); that he is supremely given to a preference of himself to God (2 Tim. 3:4); that he has an aversion to God which on occasion becomes active enmity to Him (Rom. 8:7); that his every faculty is disordered and corrupted (Eph. 4:18); that he has no thought, feeling, or deed of which God can fully approve (Rom. 7:18); and that he has entered upon a line of constant progress in

---

B. It is really not honest for scholars like R. C. Sproul and J. I. Packer to accuse other Evangelicals of being "semi-Pelagian" rather than to recognize the distinct semi-Augustinian view, as I have explained in ch.18.

depravity, from which he can in no wise turn away in his own strength . . . .[16]

Does mankind retain any autonomy?

There might well be a question about the use of the term 'free will' as it was used by the church fathers for centuries before Augustine. Since humanity has become enslaved to sin, Satan, and the world-system, a term related to freedom might be questioned. Luther rightly spoke about the "bondage of the will." Perhaps a more appropriate term would be autonomy. Obviously this is a limited autonomy since man is bound by sin, but it is real nevertheless. R. C. Sproul objects to the use of the term: "If God is sovereign, then man cannot be autonomous. Conversely if man is autonomous, then God cannot be sovereign. The two are mutually exclusive concepts."[17] However, this all depends upon our definitions of these terms. If one assumes the Augustinian definition of sovereignty, then Sproul is right. But in the previous chapter, I have shown that the Augustinian concept of sovereignty is totally without scriptural warrant. The reality is that the usage of the term 'autonomous' in secular life rarely implies total autonomy, nor do I claim total autonomy for man. (In geopolitics, an 'autonomous region' in a sovereign country usually has a limited autonomy.) So there is no conflict between a biblical view of divine sovereignty and of human autonomy.

Thus, after the fall man retained some of the God-given autonomy although it is limited by sin. Indeed, in his sin mankind continued increasingly to abuse that autonomy. As we have noted, the period from the fall to the deluge was a period of unrelenting and progressive rebellion against God and His will. Erich Sauer referred to it as a period of "human self-determination."[18] Certainly God had not programmed humanity to play out the violence, concerning which Moses stated that **"The LORD was sorry that He had made man on the earth, and He was grieved in His heart"** (Gen. 6:6). In fact, the history of God's chosen people Israel is hardly more encouraging. Man was 'doing his own thing.' This is not only clear throughout the rest of the Old Testament narrative, but it stands out in boldface. It would be depressing to read of humanity's descent into progressive rebellion if we believed that God had programmed it in eternity past and if we did not believe that God was working behind the scenes to accomplish His purpose in preparing His plan of salvation for lost mankind.

So when we come to the Gospels and see the rapidity with which Israel began to oppose and plot the demise of their Messiah, we must acknowledge that mankind had been consistently and grossly abusing its autonomy. There are two mistranslated and misinterpreted passages in the Gospels which highlight this. Matthew 11:12 reads, **"And from the days of John the Baptist until now the kingdom of heaven suffers violence, and violent men take it by force."** When we compare this with the similar statement of the Lord in Luke 16:16, it becomes clear: **"The Law and the Prophets were proclaimed until John; since then the gospel of the kingdom of God is preached, and everyone is forcing his way into it."** The translators have missed the force of *pas eis autēn biadzetai*. The *eis* should be rendered 'against' not 'into.'[19] Thus: **"everyone is perpetrating violence against it"** makes better sense in the light of Matthew 11:12, where *biastai harpadzousin autēn* should be rendered, **"violent men usurp it."** John had already suffered the ultimate violence of being beheaded, short of that which the Messiah Himself was shortly to suffer in His crucifixion. Thus, the two principal representatives of the kingdom, the King and His herald suffered ultimate violence.

The Lord repeatedly warned His apostles of the opposition they would suffer (Mt. 10:16-42), which began to be fulfilled shortly after the day of Pentecost. The book of Acts is a detailed chronicle of ongoing persecution. Not just in history but also in apostolic prophecy we find testimony to its unmitigated continuance until Christ returns (Mt. 24-25; 1 Tim. 4:1ff; 2 Tim. 3:1ff; 2 Thess. 2:1-12; 2 Pet. 3:1-9). Not only did the church suffer severe persecution under the Romans for three centuries, but especially in recent years severe persecution of true Christians around the world has become common place and is escalating.[C] Certainly this is not the record of man acting out some imagined eternal decree; it is man abusing the autonomy God gave him at creation by becoming Satan's instruments of hostility to God and His kingdom.

The image of God defaced, not erased

One dimension of the fall which has been seriously overlooked by modern theologians is its impact upon the image of God in humanity. However, many of the early church fathers touched on this important issue, and some connected it with free will.[20] It is clear that the image was not totally lost in the fall. There are a number of Scriptures which make this very clear: Genesis 9:6; Acts 17:28; James 3:9; and 1 Corinthians 11:7. Let us examine them.

Genesis 9:6. Moses, inspired by the Spirit, gave us an important clue at this strategic juncture in the history of revelation—immediately after the deluge. Before the flood, violence escalated from a vengeance syndrome bringing on God's judgment of a worldwide deluge. But God, in making the Noahic Covenant with the remnant humanity, affirms in Genesis 8:21 that Adam's sin nature had been transmitted to all mankind: **"I will never again curse the ground on account of man, for the intent of man's heart is evil from his youth; and I will never again destroy every living thing, as**

C. I hardly need give examples of extreme persecution of Christians by Muslims in a score of countries these days.

I have done." Now a new provision for human violence and depravity must be initiated—capital punishment and the attendant civil government necessary to implement it. **"Whoever sheds man's blood, by man his blood shall be shed, for in the image of God He made man"** (9:6). But in so doing God affirms that man still retains the image of God, and thereby, offers some positive hope for mankind's future

Geerhardus Vos discussed which participant in homicide is referred to in Genesis 9:6. The answer is that probably all three parties are in mind.[21] The victim of murder was created in God's image, and thus, murder is an assault upon God's image in man. The perpetrator was also created in God's image and, therefore, is responsible for his actions, and should commensurately be judged by the shedding of his own lifeblood. The magistrate or ruler who must impose the death sentence also retains enough of the image of God to be deemed competent to judge the case. This is confirmed by the language of Psalm 82, which refers to God's judgment of rulers who judge unjustly, with an exhortation to do justice. In 82:6 they are addressed in stunning language: **"I said, 'You are gods, and all of you are sons of the Most High.'"** Since they retain something of God's image, God delegated to them this divine prerogative of taking human life, whether they were regenerate or not.

Centuries later, the Lord Jesus quoted this verse in defense of His claims to be the divine Messiah:

> **Jesus answered them, "Has it not been written in your Law, 'I said you are gods'? If he called them gods, to whom the word of God came (and the Scripture cannot be broken) do you say of Him, who the Father sanctified and sent into the world, 'You are blaspheming,' because I said, 'I am the Son of God'?** (Jn. 10:34-36).

As Buswell explains, in the flow of our Lord's logic He was arguing that since mankind retains the image of God and since rulers were delegated divine prerogative, it is not inordinate for a man (Himself) to claim to be God incarnate. They should not have closed their minds to that possibility, as indeed they had done.[22] Further, we could even say that God created man in His own image in the first place, with a view to the ultimate incarnation of the Son of God.

Acts 17:28. The Apostle Paul in his message on Mars Hill used the words of a Greek poet to reinforce the truth of Genesis:

> **. . . that they should seek God, if perhaps they might grope for Him and find Him, though He is not far from each one of us; for in Him we live and move and exist, as even some of your own poets have said, 'For we also are His offspring.' Being then the offspring of God, we ought not to think that the Divine Nature is like gold or silver or stone, an image formed by the**

art or thought of man.

Paul implies that men are able to seek God based upon the *imago dei,* even though he doesn't use that language to the pagan Greeks. Deterministic theology's concept of depravity does not leave room for man to seek God, despite the dozens of references in Scripture to do just that. This injunction to seek God must be based upon the remnant image of God in man.

James 2:9. **"With it [the tongue] we bless our Lord and Father, and with it we curse men, who have been made in the likeness of God."** This is a straightforward passing reference to the retained image of God in fallen mankind, which serves to reinforce the impressions we have already obtained from the passages above. It really only takes one such statement to establish this fact.

1 Corinthians 11:7. **"For a man ought not to have his head covered, since he is the image and glory of God; but the woman is the glory of man."** Again, we have a passing reference to man having been created in God's image as part of Paul's argument on a related subject, the relationship of men and women in the church.

Although the truth of the remnant *imago dei* is nowhere directly developed in Scripture, it is the underlying presupposition of the apostles' discussions. Therefore, we must be careful to factor this foundational truth into our biblical doctrine of sin. It would seem that, in the main, deterministic theologies of salvation have not taken the *igago dei* into account in order to present the truth in its biblical balance. Although certain functional aspects of the image of God were damaged, it is clear that the ontological reality survived the fall and His image was not lost or erased. This implies that fallen mankind, still in God's image is able to respond to God's entreaties. Depravity does not mean inability!

Spiritual death must be carefully defined.

The fact of spiritual death in Eden and its spread to the whole human race is incontrovertible. The Genesis account strongly implies it, and the apostle Paul is explicit about it. God's word to Adam was clear: "**. . . for in the day that you eat from it you shall surely die**" (2:16). The beginning of the process of physical death is not an adequate explanation of these words; spiritual death must be the reference here, since death was to be immediate. The Lord Jesus implied man's spiritual death with His enigmatic and oft misunderstood words,[D] **"Let the dead bury their own dead"**

D. An understanding of Middle Eastern and Asian cultures makes it clear that the man's father had not yet died, but that as the oldest son, he felt that he must first return to fulfill family responsibilities before following Christ. If his father had just died he would have been arranging his burial before sunset, not stopping to listen to the Lord Jesus.

(Mt. 8:21). It is Paul's doctrinal teaching which is most explicit: "**Therefore, just as through one man sin entered into the world, and death through sin, and so death spread to all men, because all sinned . . .**" (Rom. 5:12); "**And you were dead in your trespasses and sins, . . .**" (Eph. 2:1). The problem is to define spiritual death. Deterministic theologies of salvation are prone to use the illustration of the impossibility of evangelizing a corpse in a funeral parlor as indicative of the reality of spiritual death. How valid is this illustration?

First, we must consider the constituent nature of mankind. If humans are a dichotomy, we would have to understand spiritual death as a figure of speech, since the soul=spirit could not have died literally. Man would not have had a distinct human spirit, which would be especially impacted by the fall. But if we take the trichotomous view of man, spiritual death can be understood literally. If, in fact, the human spirit is distinct, and especially the God-conscious part of man, spiritual death is best explained as the death of the human spirit, and the new birth as the quickening or resurrecting of the human spirit, not just figuratively, but literally.

This is confirmed by the words of Christ Himself in John 5:24-29. In vv. 24-27 He uses the imagery of the new birth as a spiritual resurrection: "**I tell you the truth, a time is coming and has now come when the dead will hear the voice of the son of God and those who hear will live. For as the Father has life in himself, so he has granted the Son to have life in himself**" (NIV). This is set in parallelism with the promise of bodily resurrection in similar language in vv. 28-29: "**Do not be amazed at this, for a time is coming when all who are in their graves will hear his voice, and come out—those who have done good will rise to live, and those who have done evil will rise to be condemned**" (NIV). Since the second is a literal resurrection (of the body), so also must the first be a literal resurrection (of the human spirit). Thus, neither spiritual death nor the new birth are figurative language. The human spirit died literally, and the human spirit is made alive literally.

Here, however, our understanding of this truth is significantly dependent upon our definition of death. A comprehensive definition of death must fit spiritual, physical, and eternal death to be adequate. The common element of all three is separation. Spiritual death is separation from God (Isa. 59:1-2; Eph. 4:18); physical death is separation of the soul and spirit from the body (as well as separation of the person from loved ones); and eternal death is the eternal separation of the person from God (Rev. 19:20; 20:10, 14). Although various cultic theologies try to argue that death is a cessation of conscious existence, Scripture will not allow this. *Thus we may define spiritual death as the rendering of the God-conscious part of man inoperative and, as a consequence, the separation of man from God.* This makes it clear that the illustration of the funeral parlor corpse is invalid and misleading. This is confirmed by our investigation of the residual image of God in man.

Does depravity mean total inability?

Despite the claim of Packer and Johnston that the present-day Evangelical Christian "has semi-Pelagianism in his blood,"[23] depravity in a real sense is affirmed by most evangelical theologians (even though there may be a serious problem of communicating it to their constituency). However, there has been a subtle semantic shift in Calvinistic circles from total depravity to total inability. But the first does not necessarily imply the second.

The biblical testimony is clear that humanity is totally unable to save itself. The new birth is one-hundred percent a work of the Spirit of God, as John 1:12-13 makes clear. Man cannot contribute one iota to his regeneration. But if repentant faith is the required condition of regeneration, as I will show in chapter 12, then the whole question as to whether fallen human beings can exercise repentance and faith must be examined. One would never get the notion from the Old Testament narrative that mankind is totally unable to respond to God's confrontations. It gives a consistent picture of God confronting fallen man and expecting a positive response.

The Old Testament narrative portrays God as taking the initiative from the very beginning in confronting lost mankind. God confronted Adam and Eve in the garden, and it is generally implied from His provision of shed-blood garments to cover their nakedness that they responded positively. The expulsion from the garden, while denying access to the tree of life, had the positive impact of impressing mankind with their alienation and spiritual need. Even before Cain murdered Abel, God confronted Cain with both his unsatisfactory sacrifice and his lack of faith (Gen. 4:5-7; Heb. 11:4). After the murder, God again confronted Cain, but it is clear He got no positive response. Although, in the main, the Cainite descendants degenerated into godlessness, Enosh, the son of Seth, marked the beginning of men calling upon the name of the LORD (4:26). God then confronted mankind through prophets like Enoch and Noah (Jude 14; 2 Pet. 2:5) and in the latter case none responded. One wonders why God would confront persistent rejecters like Cain if the missing element was a repentant faith which God Himself gives based upon His unconditional election? The implication of God's confrontation is that Cain was able to respond positively.

I will also show in chapter 10 that man is responsible to exercise repentant faith; it is not a direct gift of God. I have already touched on this line of thought in the previous chapter, but the main point here is that God does not seem to be operating on the premise that man is totally unable to respond to His confrontation. As we trace the history of Israel, it is abundantly clear that God continued to confront the nation in many different ways, especially through the prophets, as to their need to seek Him, to repent, and to return to Him.

The New Testament record is similar. We can hardly imagine a more confrontational person than John the Baptizer. Upon John's imprisonment, the Lord Jesus Himself began a very confrontational ministry. Beginning at

Pentecost, the apostles, likewise, adopted a very confrontational style, designed to bring about repentant faith in their hearers, indeed, *demanding* repentant faith from their hearers. All of this assumes the possibility of a positive response from their hearers, even though, in the main, the response has been negative right up until the present. But if we follow the apostolic example, we must adopt a confrontational approach to the unregenerate based upon the premise that they can respond positively. Indeed, Paul especially used an apologetic method which appealed to his hearers' whole personality: intellect, emotions, and will (Acts 17:2-4,17; 18:4; 19:8-9; 26:28). So although it is clear that sinners cannot please God by their moral behavior, they are able to respond to the gospel of Christ.

Our Calvinistic friends will argue that since man is spiritually dead, apart from irresistible grace, evangelism is like going into a funeral parlor and preaching to the corpses there. They cannot respond. I would suggest that based upon the biblically accurate definition of spiritual death, such analogies are totally inappropriate. In any case, analogies prove nothing.

Does fallen man retain free will?

The first denial of free will. Free will is a dirty word among Calvinists. I suspect one would get one's mouth washed out with soap for even uttering it.[E] But not so with the church fathers up to the earlier Augustine, who not only coined the term but defended the concept against the determinism of Neo-Platonism, Gnosticism, and Manicheanism. Forster and Marston have given ample citations from the early fathers to document this fact. I am especially intrigued by the way many of them connected the image of God with free will, for example, Tertullian (c. 155-225):

> I find, then, that man was by God constituted free, master of his own will and power; indicating the presence of God's image and likeness in him by nothing so well as by this constitution of his nature ...... —you will find that when He sets before man good and evil, life and death, that the entire course of discipline is arranged in precepts by God's calling men from sin, and threatening and exhorting them; and this on no other ground than that man is free, with a will either for obedience or resistance.[24]

Novatian of Rome (c. 200-258), Cyril of Jerusalem (c. 312-386), and Gregory of Nyssa (c. 335-395), all made an explicit connection between the image of God and man's free will. "Not a single church figure in the first 300 years rejected it [free-will] and most of them stated it in works still extant."[25]

E. In the debate over "open theism" there seems to be considerable confusion about the use of terms as "free-will theism," tending to make it synonymous with "open theism." Whether it is the Calvinists or the "Open Theists" who are making this false identification is not clear to me, but those who argue for free will should not be pejoratively identified with "open theism." (cf. Sproul, *Willing*, pp. 140-43.)

Geisler has augmented their collation by contrasting documentation from Augustine's earlier writings with his later ones to show that by AD 417 his view had radically hardened to a denial of free will. Since the change came while he was seeking to coerce the Donatists back into the Roman church, it seems that there was a non-theological agenda behind his shift.[26] It seems that Luther and Calvin, in countering the semi-Pelagianism of Roman Catholicism, pushed Augustine's denial of the freedom of the will even further.[27]

Who makes us do it?. Comedian Flip Wilson became famous for saying, "The Devil made me do it." Some theologians in trying to explain how Adam with a good nature could perform an evil act, have pushed the problem back to Satan. But since it is clear biblically that God did not create any sinful beings, this only pushes the problem back one step. Martin Luther, having been a good Augustinian monk, pushed the problem back one more step to God and His decrees by including Satan's sin in God's decrees. Extreme Calvinist R. C. Sproul is not willing to go that far, but admits that it is an "excruciating problem."[28] But we saw in the last chapter that the biblical basis for this notion of an all-inclusive decree (including sin) is non-existent, and, even more seriously, it contradicts explicit Scripture (Hab. 1:13; Heb. 6:18; Jas. 1:13)

Moderate Calvinist Norman Geisler has argued quite effectively, both rationally and biblically, that self-caused actions are the best explanation for the origin of evil. It is in the creation of His creatures with free choice that the possibility of evil can best be explained. God created Lucifer as a holy cherub, but Ezekiel addressed him as the evil power behind the wicked king of Tyre: **"You were in Eden, the garden of God; . . . On the day that you were created they were prepared. You were the anointed cherub who covers, and I placed you *there*. . . . You were blameless in your ways from the day you were created, until unrighteousness was found in you"** (Ezek. 28:13-15). Geisler suggests that there are only three options: "My actions are (1) uncaused; (2) caused by someone (or something) else; or (3) caused by my Self. And there are many reasons to support the last view." He goes on to show that extreme Calvinists make a fundamental error in failing to distinguish between self-caused *being*, which is impossible apart from God, and self-caused *action*, which is the only way to explain Lucifer's sin.[29] Clearly, Lucifer's sin was self-caused.

God's judgment of Lucifer for his sin (Ezek. 28:16-19; 1 Tim. 3:6; Rev. 20:10), of fallen angels (Jude 6-7; 2 Pet. 2:4; Rev. 12:4, 9), of Adam and Eve (Gen. 3:1-19) makes it clear that God holds free creatures morally responsible for their free choices. Since God holds all mankind morally responsible for their moral choices, fallen people must have adequate freedom of the will to make moral choices; otherwise, He could not justly judge them for their deeds (Rev. 20:12). One of the most dominant ideas of Scripture, from Genesis to the Revelation, is that God judges the sins of individuals, families, and nations.

Direct Scripture evidence. But there is direct Scriptural evidence for the idea that fallen man continues to exercise his uncoerced will, not only in the ordinary decisions of life, but also in moral decisions relating to God. Moses challenged Israel: **"I call heaven and earth to witness against you today, that I have set before you life and death, the blessing and the curse. So choose life in order that you may live, you and your descendants, by loving the LORD your God, by obeying His voice, and by holding fast to Him;"** (Deut. 30:19-20a). A generation later Joshua made the same challenge: **"And if it is disagreeable in your sight to serve the LORD, choose for yourselves today whom you will serve: . . ."** (Josh. 24:15. Elijah asked a similar question: **How long will you hesitate between two opinions? If the LORD is God, follow Him; but if Baal, follow him"** (1 Kgs 18:21). Isaiah similarly exhorted Israel: **"Come now, and let us reason together, . . .If you consent and obey, . . .But if you refuse and rebel, . . ."** (Isa. 1:18-19). That great Calvinist, Charles Spurgeon, was saved through hearing Isaiah 45:22: **"Turn to Me and be saved, all the ends of the earth; For I am God, and there is no other."** Didn't Moses, Joshua, and the prophets understand the doctrine of total inability and know that man cannot "choose life"? Too bad they never learned from the Calvinists! By the way, 'choose' is another Calvinistic dirty word, which they assume means synergism. Somehow they think it robs God of His sovereignty. Not in the least!

The proclamation of the Lord Jesus was similar: **"Jesus came into Galilee, preaching the gospel of God, and saying, 'The time is fulfilled, and the kingdom of God is at hand; repent and believe in the gospel'"** (Mk. 1:14b-15). He also identified the problem of the Jewish leaders: **"You search the Scriptures because you think that in them you have eternal life; it is these that testify about Me; and you are unwilling to come to me so that you may have life"** (Jn. 5:39-40). Later He gave His universal invitation: **"Come to Me, all who are weary and heavy-laden, and I will give you rest"** (Mt. 11:28). Later, at the Feast, He explained the contingent factor in our coming to the truth: **"If anyone is willing to do His will, he will know of the teaching, whether it is of God or whether I speak from myself"** (Jn. 7:17). Then in similar language He repeated His invitation: **"If anyone is thirsty, let him come to Me and drink. He who believes in Me, as the Scripture said, 'From his innermost being will flow river of living water'"** (Jn. 7:37-8). In His passion week parable of the king's wedding feast (expounded in ch. 8), He again attributed the Jewish leaders' problem to unwillingness (Mt. 22:3). This is capped off with the words of His final lament over Jerusalem: **"Jerusalem, Jerusalem, who kills the prophets and stones those who are sent to her! How often I wanted to gather your children together, the way a hen gathers her chicks under her wings, and you were unwilling. Behold, your house is being left to**

you desolate" (Mt. 23:37-8). Judgment came upon those who were unwilling. It is the will of man, not the will of God which is the problem. So both as to those who positively respond and those who reject, the Lord Jesus made it clear that the issue is the human will.

Peter picked up his Lord's words: "**You must repent—and, as an expression of it, let every one of you be baptized in the name of Jesus Christ—that you may have your sins forgiven; and then you will receive the gift of the Holy Spirit, . . .**" (Acts 2:38, Williams). Paul's words on Mars Hill are built upon man's ability to respond: "**Therefore having overlooked the times of ignorance, God is now declaring to men that all *people* everywhere should repent**" (Acts 17:30). His reminder to the Ephesian elders summarizes his ministry: "**. . . solemnly testifying to both Jews and Greeks of repentance toward God and faith in our Lord Jesus Christ**" (Acts 20:21). In Peter's warning about the end-time mockers, the NASB totally misses the force of *thelontas*, so I quote NIV: "**But they deliberately forget that long ago by God's word the heavens existed and the earth was formed out of water and with water**" (2 Pet. 3:5). Creation and the flood are two key issues that modern man does not want to accept, because then he would have to respond to God's claims.

I suspect that some of my readers are saying, "Gordon, we are familiar with all these basic passages, why quote them?" Sometimes we miss the obvious force of the familiar. Norman Douty's comment is pointed:

> Moreover, in the Apostolic preaching of the Gospel, sinners were spoken to as if expected to act then and there—without any suggestion that, after all they were under some insuperable necessity of doing nothing. It is simply a matter of record that the primitive preachers did not tell their hearers that they had absolutely no ability to do anything in response to God's call, invitation, command and threat.[30]

Philosophically oriented Calvinists will respond with the idea of "compatiblism," which means that although God has determined all things, He works in parallel with the human will to accomplish all things. As discussed in the previous chapter, there is no evidence that God works all things which come to pass, so wall-to-wall compatiblism is unnecessary and unsupportable.

Can man respond to general revelation?

There is another factor, general revelation, which plays into this whole discussion about man's inability. Calvin recognized this in commenting on John 1:9:

> For we know that men have this unique quality above the other animals, that they are endowed with reason and intelligence and that they bear the distinction between right and wrong engraved in

their conscience. Thus there is no man to whom some awareness of the eternal light does not penetrate."[31]

Even the canons of Dort recognized that after the fall mankind retained some benefits of revelation through nature and the human conscience. Pink even suggested correctly that mankind *gained* conscience in the fall.[32] This excerpt from the canons of Dort shows how far today's extreme Calvinists have gone, even beyond Dort:

> There remains, however, in man since the fall, the glimmering of natural light, whereby he retains some knowledge of God, of natural things, and of the differences between good and evil, and discovers some regard for virtue, good order in society, and for maintaining an orderly external deportment.[33]

At least two kinds of general revelation are usually recognized; God's revelation in nature and in human conscience. The latter is easily supportable from the "knowledge of good and evil" ascribed to Adam and Eve in the garden (Gen. 3:22), but also in Romans 2:14-15:

> **For when Gentiles who do not have the Law do instinctively the things of the Law, these, not having the Law, are a law to themselves, in that they show the work of the Law written in their hearts, their conscience bearing witness and their thoughts alternately accusing or else defending them, . . .**

We can understand human ability to seek God as based upon general revelation. The Scriptures are clear about the revelation of God in nature:

> **The heavens are telling of the glory of God; and their expanse is declaring the work of His hands. Day to day pour forth speech, and night to night reveals knowledge. There is no speech, nor are there words; their voice is not heard. Their line [sound] has gone out through all the earth, and their utterances to the end of the world** (Ps. 19:1-4b).

Paul is just as explicit as David:

> **For the wrath of God is revealed from heaven against all ungodliness and unrighteousness of men who suppress the truth in unrighteousness, because that which is known about God is evident within them; for God made it evident to them. For since the creation of the world His invisible attributes, His eternal power and divine nature, have been clearly seen, being understood through what has been made, so that they are without excuse** (Rom. 1:18-20).

Since God holds humanity accountable for their response to general revelation of both kinds, it would seem that people must have some ability to respond to it, otherwise He couldn't hold them accountable.

The best book I read in 1975 was *Daktar: Diplomat in Bangladesh* in which missionary surgeon Viggo Olsen tells of his and his wife's pilgrimage to God, when he was an intern at Long Island College Hospital. As agnostics, Viggo and Joan first struggled with the question, "Is there a God who created the universe?" After considerable investigation and reading of apologetic books, they concluded that a Creator God does indeed exist. Then they followed the classic apologetic sequence by moving on to the question as to whether the Bible or any other holy book gives a credible revelation of Him. After research which dispelled the critical attacks on the Bible they had heard in college, they finally tried to find out whether Jesus was really the Son of God. In the process, they were both converted and became outstanding missionaries for Christ'[34] For them general revelation was a necessary first step toward Christ. I suspect that there are thousands of other Christians who could give similar testimonies.

I have a hard time understanding how some extreme Calvinists can deny the apologetic efficacy of general revelation. In doing so they are reflecting their distorted view of depravity. *Since God expects mankind to be able to respond to general revelation, which is in many cases a necessary starting point, would it not seem incongruous if people were totally unable to respond to special revelation in the gospel?* Indeed, I believe I have given adequate Scriptural testimony that He does expect fallen man to respond to both general revelation and special revelation in the gospel of Christ.

Can mankind seek God?

The only time my extreme Calvinistic colleague, Alvin Baker, ever admitted to any problem with his Calvinism was when he said that Isaiah 55:6 troubled him. However, if he had checked them out, he would have found a host of other passages which totally contradict the notion of inability simply by opening his concordance to "seek." Most extreme Calvinists base their view on the English of Romans 3:10-11: "**There is none righteous, not even one; There is none who understands, There is none who seeks for God.**" In Paul's paraphrase of the Septuagint of Psalm 14, he was careful to use the intensified verb *ekzēteo,* rather than the simple *zēteo*. From its usage in Acts 15:17; Heb. 11:6; 12:17; and 1 Pet. 1:10, it is clear that Paul is not referring to an indifferent seeking, but a 'diligently seeking' for God. (The verb has an even more intensified force in Luke 11:50, where it is rendered 'require.') So Paul was not affirming that no one ever seeks God at all, but rather that **no one diligently seeks God**. It might also be significant that this verb is a present participle, which could be either gnomic or customary. If it is customary, it would refer to a regularly recurring action,[35] and thus, could be rendered, "**no one customarily and diligently seeks God**." Otherwise, if neither of the above were true, Scripture would be in contradiction with itself. *I could only find about fifty verses which contradict a superficial reading of Romans 3:10-11!* Why do extreme Calvinists ignore the fifty and focus on the one? William A. Butler, that "brilliant and profound thinker," probably got it right: "*We hold a few texts so near the eyes that they hide the rest of the Bible.*"[36] In this case, it is just one text!

The context of Psalm 14 is also very important, since Paul is quoting it. David is saying that the atheistic fool, who says in his heart that there is no God, does not diligently seek God. Although Paul expands the application of David's words somewhat, he is giving a generalized statement about the human race as a whole, extending to both Jews and Gentiles, but not intended to be all-inclusive. This becomes clear from the fifty other references, a few of which we will now examine.

Hear God's predictive warning of exile to a disobedient Israel: "**But from there you will seek the LORD your God, and you will find Him if you search for *Him* with all your heart and all your soul**" (Deut. 4:29). Asaph's Psalm: "**Seek the LORD and His strength; Seek His face continually**" (1 Chr. 16:11). David's command to Israel's leaders: "**Now set your heart and your soul to seek the LORD your God;**" (1 Chr. 22:19a). David's exhortation to Solomon: "**If you seek Him, He will let you find Him; but if you forsake Him, He will reject you forever**" (1 Chr. 28:9b). The prophecy of Azariah the son of Oded: "**And if you seek Him, He will let you find Him; but if you forsake Him, He will forsake you** (2 Chr. 15:2b). "**Let the heart of those who seek the LORD be glad. Seek the LORD and His strength; Seek His face continually**" (Ps. 105:3b-4). In Isaiah's wonderful invitation chapter: "**Seek the LORD while He may be found; call upon Him while He is near. Let the wicked forsake his way and the unrighteous man his thoughts; and let him return to the LORD, and He will have compassion on him, and to our God, for He will abundantly pardon**" (Isa. 55:6-7). Jeremiah's prophecy to Israel at the end of exile: "**Then you will call upon Me and come and pray to me, and I will listen to you. You will seek Me and find Me when you search for Me with all your heart**" (Jer. 29:12-13). God's rebuke to apostate Israel: "**I will go away and return to My place until they acknowledge their guilt and seek My face; in their affliction they will earnestly seek Me**" (Hos. 5:15). Amos's double exhortation: "**Seek Me that you may live**" (Amos 5:4, 6). "**Seek the LORD, all you humble of the earth**" (Zeph. 2:3).

If I hear someone muttering, "Sounds like synergism to me," your argument is not with me; it is with the word of the living God. I repudiate that pejorative term, 'synergism.'[F] If someone naively responds that these are

---

F. Synergism is a term applied to the view that God and man work together in salvation. I take the position that faith is not a work (John 6:27-9; Rom. 4:16). Repentant faith is simply acknowledging our bankruptcy and receiving Christ, which we are commanded to do.

all part of the old dispensation, hear Paul, the apostle of monergistic grace on Mars hill: "**. . . and He made from one *man* every nation of mankind to live on all the face of the earth, . . . that they would seek God, if perhaps they might grope for Him and find Him, though He is not far from each one of us; for in Him we live and move and exist . . .**" (Acts 17:26-28a), and "**. . . to those who by perseverance in doing good seek for glory and honor and immortality, eternal life**" (Rom. 2:7). I am tempted to list the remainder of the fifty references here, but you can find them in any concordance.

The prodigal son. We must also consider the parable of the prodigal son in Luke 15:11-32. Some may be ambivalent as to whether it is referring to the restoration of a backslider or the salvation of a sinner. The Lord's language is clear: "**. . . for this son of mine was dead and has come to life again; he was lost and has been found**" (15:24). The father repeats the same language to the older brother in v. 32. He was spiritually dead and lost. Yet the Lord makes the point that "**he came to his senses**" in the far country and repented of his sin and his unworthiness (15:17-19), and he took the initiative to go to the father (15:20). This is in total harmony with the multiplicity of other passages which I have adduced above. This is very hard to reconcile with total inability. What is more, the Lord emphasized, in all three of the parables of the lost things, the great joy in heaven when a sinner repents (15:7, 10, 25, 32)–there is even music and dancing! If sinners are saved by irresistible grace according to unconditional election by God in eternity past, what would be the point of rejoicing in heaven? The salvation of the 'elect' would be so cut and dried, there could be no surprise and rejoicing at what was a foregone conclusion. Do you see why teaching the Gospels caused me to get disillusioned with Calvinism?

Case studies. Let us go beyond our concordance to case studies. Consider Andrew and John, who sought the Lord after hearing the Baptizer's witness. Nathaniel was dubious about Philip's witness but took the trouble to check out Jesus of Nazareth (Jn. 1:35-51). Nicodemus sought out the Lord, albeit by night, and ultimately came to faith in Him (Jn. 3:1-21). The Ethiopian eunuch, although an excluded Gentile, had traveled to Jerusalem to worship and found the Lord through the other Philip on the Gaza road (Acts 8:26-38). The Roman centurion, Cornelius, prayed and worshiped the God of Israel, although yet unsaved. God honored his prayers and alms to Israel with the privilege of becoming the first Gentile convert in the church (Acts 10:1–11:17, esp. 11:14). Consider the noble-minded Berean Jews who examined the Scriptures daily to verify Paul's message and "therefore" believed (Acts 17:10-12).

In the early 60s, the young Maulvi (Mullah) of a mosque in a village in central Pakistan, where there were no Christians, became disillusioned with Islam. He came to the Lahore railway station thinking to inquire about

Christianity or Hinduism, by crossing over to India. He inquired at a tea stall as to whether there were any Christians there and was pointed to a sweeper on the platform, who, although illiterate, was a born-again Christian. The sweeper took Ismail to the leaders of Bethany Assembly, who took him in and worked with him for some time. He attended worship each Lord's day until one day when it was my turn to preach. The message from 1 Corinthians 13 was on love (something Muslims hear little about). Totally oblivious to this Muslim in the congregation, I didn't even give a gospel appeal, as I now habitually do. After half an hour of open prayer time, as the bread was being distributed during the Lord's table, Ismail said out loud, "Give me some!" When one of the stunned elders gave a nod of approval, he was included. He shaved off his beard after the service, was baptized in the canal the next day, and changed his name to Timotheus. He began immediately to join us in witness for Christ. It is probable that he was martyred when he went back to his home. We don't know for sure.

I recently interviewed Chris, an Iranian-American Muslim convert. In his teens in Egypt, Chris kept asking people about the meaning of life, and no one could give him a cogent answer. He began to study the Quran with a mature and knowledgeable Muslim, who actually raised more questions about the Quran than he had answers and thus, disillusioned Chris with Islam. When he came to college in North Carolina, he got into a Bible study with some other international students, and after a year trusted Christ. Although his American father has not yet become a Christian, Chris has now won his Muslim mother and some other relatives to Christ and has been appointed as a missionary to Iranians.

Eugene is another young man I have known for a decade, who went through a five-year search for God before he came to faith in Christ. There were many blind alleys in that search, but he did not give up. According to Calvinism, we should doubt the truth of these personal testimonies. This just can't happen! "No one seeks the Lord," we are told. Or perhaps these individuals sought out the Lord because they were already among the elect, it might be argued. But the Calvinistic doctrine of inability doesn't leave room for even the elect to seek God! The doctrine of irresistible grace portrays the elect as being passive in conversion. But we do have the biblical antecedents and exhortations I have already set out. There must be something wrong with the theology!

This morning I was reminded of the other side of the coin. Marti DeHaan did a special TV program on Samaria and quoted the Lord's words to the Samaritan woman: "**Yet a time is coming and has now come when the true worshipers will worship the Father in spirit and truth, for they are the kind of worshipers the Father seeks**" (Jn. 4:23, NIV). A question came into my mind, which so stunned me that I repeated it three times out loud, "Why should the Father have to seek out those whom He has already unconditionally elected?" If God has already unconditionally elected "the elect," why should he have to seek them out? It doesn't make sense! The Lord Jesus came to seek and to save the lost, not 'the elect.' But this is the subject of chapters 7 and 8, so I mustn't get ahead of myself. But think about it!

Problem Scripture passages

There are a number of Scripture passage upon which Calvinists base their concept of inability. Although some have already been discussed, and others will be discussed subsequently, it is important to examine them at this point.

John 6:44, 65. - **"No one can come to me unless the Father who sent Me draws him; and I will raise him up at the last day. . . . And He was saying, 'For this reason I have said to you, that no one can come to Me unless it has been granted him from the Father."** Calvinists assume that apart from an irresistible drawing of the 'elect,' no one else (the 'non-elect') is allowed to come to Christ for salvation.[G] On the surface, it might seem that they are right. However, this is to ignore the context, which is crucial.

The Lord is addressing those who have seen Him and yet have not believed (6:36), who are set in contrast with the believing remnant of Israelites who belonged to the Father, but now have been committed into His hands. He refers to them in vs. 37 & 39 as **"all that the Father gives Me."** He keeps stressing faith as the distinguishing feature of this remnant (6:35, 40, 47), who were taught by the Father (6:45). He is referring to the early disciples, who had readily responded to Him when they met Him (cf. Jn. 1), because they were regenerate. This becomes clear in His high-priestly prayer in 17:6, 9, & 24, where He clearly identifies them as His early disciples set in contradistinction from those who were to later come to faith through their word (17:20), thus not all the 'elect.' Therefore, from the flow of the context it becomes clear that this has nothing to do with the 'elect,' but rather with the believing remnant, the genuine nucleus.

The broader thrust of the Gospel of John is equally as significant as this immediate contextual consideration of which it is a part. Right from the beginning, John portrays the contrast of the believing remnant of Israel with the hostile Jewish leadership and skeptical majority (1:11-12; 2:23-25; 3:18-20, 36; 4:39-41; 5:18, 37-47,; 6:26-27, 36, 41-43, 60-64; 7:17, 25-27, 31, 47-52; 8:12-30, 47; 9:39, 10:19-21, etc.). The Lord Jesus made it clear that the Father had been trying to teach Israel through His word (5:38), through Abraham (8:56-8), through Moses (5:45-47; 7:19-24), through John the Baptizer (1:6-8, 19-34; 3:25-36; 5:33-35), but in the main they were not willing to believe (5:40). But through all of this sometimes heated dialog with the

---

G. Packer has stated that this is one of five major passages upon which he bases his Calvinistic viewpoint.

Jewish leaders there was a continued flow of those who did profess faith in Him (1:12-13; 35-51; 2:23; 4:1, 39-42; 7:31; 8:30; 10:41-2; 11:45, etc.). But not all came with genuine motives, and the Lord was constantly challenging them, so as to sort out those who came for political or material motives.

Thus it was because some of the professing believers were questioning His heavenly origin and grumbling among themselves, rather than asking Him directly, that the Lord said, "**Do not grumble among yourselves. No one can come to Me unless the Father who sent Me draws him; and I will raise him up on the last day. It is written in the prophets, 'And they shall all be taught of God.' Everyone who has heard and learned from the Father, comes to Me**" (6:6:43b-45). It would seem that some of these Jews had an acute case of "gospel hardening," that is, they had seen the Lord work incredible miracles, especially the feeding of the five (really, fifteen) thousand, heard His marvelous teachings, and yet did not really believe. Because there were serious problems with their mind set, they could not come to Christ. For instance, He had previously challenged them: "**And the Father who sent Me, He has testified of Me. You have neither heard His voice at any time nor seen His form. You do not have His word abiding in you, for you do not believe Him whom He sent. You search the Scriptures because you think that in them you have eternal life; it is these that testify about Me; and you are unwilling to come to Me so that you may have life**" (5:37-40). Here was the root of the problem—they did not have the Scriptures in their hearts and thus were unwilling to trust Him.

Then He targeted another root of their unbelief: "**How can you believe, when you receive glory from one another and you do not seek the glory that is from the *one and* only God?**" (5:44). Lastly, He focused more narrowly on their first mind-set problem: "**For if you believed Moses, you would believe Me, for he wrote about Me, but if you do not believe his writing, how will you believe My words?**" (5:46-7). It wasn't because they were non-elect that they couldn't come to Him, it was because they were unwilling to believe and obey the revelation God had given over two millennia throughout the Old Testament!

Few of the commentators have paid any attention to the passage in Isaiah from which the Lord quoted (54:13). Isaiah is speaking of the glories which await a repentant Israel, saying, "**All your sons will be taught of the LORD.**" Then in the next section he gives that wonderful appeal to come to God for His free grace, to listen that they may live, and to "**seek the LORD while He may be found**" (55:1-7). There is certainly nothing of election in the Isaiah passage Christ quotes. Quite the contrary, the problem was Israel's unbelief in His word, just as in Christ's day–their skeptical mind set.

How does the Father draw people to Christ? Is it an irresistible drawing, as held by Calvinists? This is possible, but certainly not necessary, since Arndt and Gingrich list a second meaning of *helkein*, "fig. of the pull on man's inner life," with a number of references from the classical Greek and two from the Septuagint, which are not at all indicative of any supposed irresistibility. "**I have loved you with an everlasting love; therefore I have drawn you with lovingkindness**" (Jer. 31.3). "**Therefore the maidens love you. Draw me after you and let us run together**" (Songs 1:3-4).[37] Since these references to drawing connects more with the issue of God's effectual calling and the Calvinistic notion of irresistible grace, please see the extended discussion in chapter 11 (p. 136).

Although verse 65 is part of the same general context of the contrast of believers with unbelievers, there are some additional considerations here. **"And He was saying, 'For this reason I have said to you, that no one can come to Me, unless it has been granted him from the Father.'"** Apart from the context, this might seem to imply that apart from irresistible grace, the non-elect are hopelessly reprobated to Hell. Here also the flow of the context is exceedingly important. Many of his professing disciples had just been grumbling at His words (6:61), and then the immediately preceding verse is crucial, "**... 'But there are some of you who do not believe.' For Jesus knew from the beginning who they were who did not believe, and who it was that would betray Him**" (6:64). "**As a result of this many of His disciples withdrew, and were not walking with Him anymore**" (6:66). "**'Did I Myself not choose you, the twelve, and yet one of you is a devil?'**" (6:70).

Thus it is in reference to professing disciples, who had walked with Him for an extensive period of time and sat under His teaching and seen His miracles, especially to Judas Iscariot, that the Lord made the statement in 6:65. They were rejecting the greatest light that anybody could reject. They had professed to believe, but they were counterfeits. These are the ones to whom God was not granting the privilege to come to Him. What is the principle here? Is it the hidden counsel of God to which the Calvinists are so want to flee?

The answer is given by a converted Pharisee many years later who had severely persecuted the church of Christ. He had held the garments of those who stoned Stephen. He had resisted the convicting work of the Holy Spirit, kicking against the ox-goad. And yet God saved him. We need not be ignorant of the reason for he tells us why in 1 Timothy 1:12-13. "**I thank Christ Jesus our Lord, who has strengthened me, because He considered me faithful, putting me into service; even though I was formerly a blasphemer and a persecutor and a violent aggressor. And yet I was shown mercy, because I acted ignorantly in unbelief.**" He had not closed his heart against great light. But Judas and the other counterfeit disciples sinned again the greatest light and thus came under the judgmental blindness so frequently mentioned in Scripture. Not long afterward in a discussion with some Pharisees the Lord said, "'**For judgment I came into this world, that those who do not see may see; and that those who see may become blind.' Those of the Pharisees who were with Him heard these things and said to Him, 'We are not blind too, are we?' Jesus said to**

them, 'If you were blind, you would have no sin; but since you say, 'We see,' your sin remains'" (John 9:39-41). So John 6:65 must be understood in a judgmental sense, and not as having anything to do with election or reprobation in eternity past.

Another similar statement comes in a similar context: **"Why do you not understand what I am saying? It is because you cannot hear My word. You are of your father the devil, and you want to do the desires of your father"** (8:43-44a). This statement cannot be generalized to all unregenerate people, since it is clear that the Lord Jesus is addressing some hard-core unbelievers who were planning to have Him killed. They were the ones who could not hear His word.

This same principle is operative in John 12:39-40: **"For this reason they could not believe, for Isaiah said again, 'He has blinded their eyes and He hardened their heart, so that they would not see with their eyes and perceive with their heart, and be converted and I heal them.'"** The context is the passion week, when the hostility of the rulers was reaching a peak and a hostile crowd had challenged Him (12:34) and was ignoring His miraculous works (12:37). He had spoken of impending judgment (12:31). The Isaiah quotation speaks of judgmental blindness upon those who closed their hearts to great light, which was now being fulfilled especially in Israel's rejection of their Messiah. It has nothing to do with any supposed inability of all mankind to respond to the gospel.

Although Romans 8:7-8 is frequently quoted by Calvinists to support their concept of inability, it affirms the inability of unregenerate man to fulfill the law or please God morally, but it says nothing about mankind's ability or inability to believe the gospel.

Romans 9:15-16 is a favorite proof-text of Calvinists, which we have discussed in the previous chapter. There I pointed to the antecedent of 'it' in v. 16, which is God's sovereign purpose to choose Jacob over Esau as the progenitor of the nation Israel, as mentioned in v. 11. Thus this passage also has nothing to do with human inability to believe the gospel message.

Similarly, 1 Corinthians 2:14-15 has nothing to do with the issue: **"But a natural man does not accept the things of the Spirit of God, for they are foolishness to him; and he cannot understand them, because they are spiritually appraised. But he who is spiritual appraises all thing, yet he himself is appraised by no one."** Here Paul is speaking about the whole process of revelation and inspiration by which the Holy Spirit communicated even the "deep things of God" through the apostles, which were ultimately written down in Scripture. It is in obvious contrast to the "spiritual man" who appraises all these deep truths. Thus he was not speaking of an inability of all the unregenerate to understand and believe the simple gospel message as proclaimed by the apostles.[H] The fact is that we were all 'natural' men once, but we did come to understand the simple demands of the gospel. Subsequent chapters explain how this happens.

CONCLUSIONS

Since the original image of God involved all the communicable attributes of God, and since the Bible is clear that the image was not lost or erased, we find that the residual aspects of the image provide a basis for God confronting sinful man, both directly and mediately, demanding repentance and return to Him. There is no hint anywhere in the Bible that mankind cannot respond to God's initiative.

I have also argued that the tripartite nature of man implies that the human spirit, the God-conscious part of man, became inoperative in unregenerate man, that spiritual death means separation from God (Eph. 4:18), not the total destruction of the spirit. This is also a basis for God's appeal to sinners.

I also argue that God delegated a sphere of limited autonomy to mankind, which, since the fall, man has egregiously abused in his rebellion. This in no way diminishes God's sovereignty. A proper definition of sovereignty is compatible with an understanding of man's limited autonomy without making God the author of sin.

While affirming man's depravity, I reject the extrapolation of depravity to total inability. Yes, man is unable to contribute one iota to his own salvation, but we are held accountable for our response to God's revelation, both general and special, in the gospel. Just as Lucifer and Adam were held responsible for the exercise of their free wills in sin against God, just as really, all humans, although enslaved to sin, are accountable to exercise their wills in repentance and faith. Indeed, we are even commanded to seek God. The difficult Scripture passages upon which Calvinists base their doctrine of total inability, such as John 6:44, 65, have been significantly taken out of context to mean the opposite of our Lord's emphasis upon the imperative of faith and upon judgment for obstinate unbelief.

Thus a mediate theology of salvation can be soundly based upon the residual image of God in fallen humanity, separated from the life of God, but with a human spirit which can respond to the convicting work of the Holy Spirit (cf. ch. 9). A sound doctrine of salvation cannot be built upon a fictitious concept of total inability, supportable only by funeral parlor analogies.

H. I am deeply indebted to Reformed scholars, such as B. B. Warfield, whose discussion of inspiration passages such as this were of great help to me in writing my masters' thesis on the inerrancy of Scripture.

Note: This chapter is based upon a paper presented to the Eastern Regional of the Evangelical Theological Society, March 1999 at Myerstown, PA.

---

1. Dave Hunt, *What Love Is This?*, pp. 165-188. Hunt has two good chapters on the Luther/Erasmus dialog.
2. However, a few evangelical trichotomists would see a parallel between the trinitarian nature of God and man's trichotomy. The analogy is not justified since the Trinity involves three distinct persons in unity, but humanity's trichotomy does not. See Laurence M. Vance, *The Other Side of Calvinism* (2nd ed.), pp. 79ff.
3. Millard J. Erickson, *Christian Theology*, p. 502.
4. Lewis and Demarest give solid exegetical basis for rejecting any such distinction: *Integrative Theology*, II, 134.
5. Erickson, pp. 508-12.
6. Geerhardus Vos, *Biblical Theology*, p. 38. Vos does not explicitly link immortality with the image of God.
7. Erickson, p. 499.
8. J. B. Heard, *The Tripartite Nature of Man: Spirit, Soul, and Body* (Edinburg: T. & T. Clark, 1866), pp. 67-68.
9. Ibid, p. vii.
10. H. D. McDonald, *The Christian View of Man*, p. 76.
11. Lewis Sperry Chafer, *Systematic Theology*, III.
12. Henry C. Thiessen, *Systematic Theology*, pp. 264-66; cf. J. O. Buswell, Jr., *Systematic Theology*, I, 304.
13. Vance, *Calvinism* (2nd ed.), p. 185; D. A. Kidd, *Collins Gem Latin Dictionary*, 2nd ed. (Harper-Collins).
14. Sproul, *Willing to Believel*, p. 126; Cunningham, *Theology*, II:389; Jewett, *Election and Predestination*, p. 17.
15. Geisler, *Chosen But Free*, p. 116; Hoitenga, *John Calvin and the Will*, p. 69-70, 73. See note #23 below.
16. Thiessen, p. 268.
17. Sproul, *Willing to Believe*, p. 27.
18. Erich Sauer, *The Dawn of World Redemption*,
19. Dana and Mantey, *Grammar*, p. 103; A more remote meaning, it is common (Luke 12:10; 15:18; Acts 6:11).
20. Geisler, pp. 145-54; Tertullian, Novation, Cyril of Jerusalem, Gregory of Nyssa. Many others could be found.
21. Vos, *Biblical Theology*,
22. Buswell, *Systematic Theology*, II, pp. 19-20.
23. Packer and Johnston, "Historical and Theological Introduction ," in Luther's *Bondage of the Will*, p. 58.
24. Tertullian, *Against Marcion*, Book II, ch. 5, cited by Forster and Marston, p. 250.
25. Forster and Marston, *God's Strategy*, pp. 244ff.
26. Geisler, *Chosen But Free*, pp. 150-1; 161-72.
27. Hoitenga, *Calvin and the Will*, p. 19: "Augustine, while clearly teaching the bondage of the will and the sovereignty of grace, took great care to preserve man's free will. Calvin was much more polemical in his assertion of human impotence and was reluctant to talk of free will." (Quotation taken from A. S. N. Lane, "Did Calvin Believe in Free Will?") On pp. 69ff Hoitenga argues that Calvin's view involved "nearly the complete destruction" of both the natural and supernatural components of the human will.
28. Sproul, *Chosen by God*, p. 31.
29. Geisler, p. 25, full discussion pp. 19-37.
30. Ibid, p.66.
31. Calvin, *Commentaries*, vol. 4, p. 15.
32. Arthur Pink, *Gleanings in Genesis*, pp. 37-38.
33. *Canons of Dort*, III, IV:4.
34. Viggo B. Olsen, *Daktar: Diplomat in Bangladesh* (Chicago: Moody Press, 1973), pp. 29-57.
35. Daniel B. Wallace, *Greek Grammar Beyond the Basics*, pp. 521-3.
36. Norman F. Douty, *The Death of Christ*, p. 66, quoting the Schaff-Herzog Encyclopedia and a secondary source. His point is well taken with or without primary documentation.
37. W. F. Arndt and W. Gingrich. *A Greek-English Lexicon of the New Testament*, p.251.

One of the most enduring errors, the root fallacy presupposes that *every* word *has* a meaning bound up with its shape or its components. In this view, meaning is determined by etymology; that is, by the root or roots of a word.

-D. A. Carson

The student should learn once and for all that every single letter added to a Greek root adds something to the idea expressed by the root.

-William Douglas Chamberlain

5

MORE THAN ATONEMENT: WORD PICTURES OF HIS CROSS

In the course of the research for this inductive theology of salvation, I encountered such a large number of problems with the definition of terms in standard evangelical works, that I am compelled to seek to rectify the current definitions of these terms as a sound basis for theological development. If we start with erroneous definitions of terminology we will probably end up with erroneous conclusions. It seems to me that a lot of the confusion and tensions in contemporary theology stems from sloppy definitions, some of which have been developing for centuries. Somehow more recent linguistic work, massive as it has been, has not rectified some of these past errors.

The communists early saw the importance of definition of terminology in setting a basis for their ideology. They talked about rectification of terms, but unfortunately they were frequently distorting the meanings to their own nefarious ends. Nevertheless, in theology we must begin by honest and careful definition of the crucial terminology in order to arrive at sound results in our theologizing. We will examine the Old Testament picture of atonement, and in the New Testament, sacrifice, propitiation, ransom-redemption, redemption-liberation, and reconciliation. There are many other terms which have been grossly misinterpreted, which will be examined in subsequent chapters: calling, repentance, faith, conversion, foreknowledge, foreordination and election.

OLD TESTAMENT ATONEMENT

It is common knowledge that there is an anomaly in extant theological literature in regard to the widespread usage of the word 'atonement,' when in fact, this word does not occur in the New Testament (except in the KJV). Its continued usage has been justified on the basis of its almost overwhelming usage in most circles for centuries and the difficulty of changing to some more appropriate terminology at this stage of the game. However, there may also be some theological presuppositions for its continued usage. Many feel that the difference between atonement and the actual Greek New Testament words is so insignificant that it is not worthy of serious consideration. The tendency would be for those of a Covenant Theology persuasion to minimize the differences and for Dispensationalists to bring them into focus.

It should be clear that the three major New Testament terms: redemption, propitiation, and reconciliation, are not synonymous. Indeed, Lewis Sperry Chafer highlighted the distinctions between these terms and showed the relationship to this issue in his systematic theology.[1] John Walvoord and Robert Lightner have clarified the distinctions even more.[2] To press the point even further, we should note that there are eight different Greek words for redemption and, as I shall seek to show, there is a significant difference of meaning between these words. Since this is so, it would seem irresponsible to continue to use a blanket term which obscures all of these distinctions. To continue to call the passion of Christ "the atonement," when in fact the word is never used in the New Testament, is not conducive to the kind of precision for which a science such as theology should be known. Such imprecision would be blameworthy in the physical sciences and ought to be also in the "queen of sciences" as well.

The term atonement is especially objectionable, since it describes the Old Testament sacrifices, which were not a final dealing with sin and only anticipated the saving death of Christ. The anticipation clearly falls far short of the fulfillment, as the writer of Hebrews emphasized in so many contexts (Heb. 7:18-9; 8:6-13; 10:1-14). Therefore it would be helpful to suggest another better term for theological usage which would be both accurate and comprehensive enough to include the many New Testament words. Perhaps sacrifice, cross-work, and/or passion would be more helpful. The benefit of distinguishing the distinct terms is to enable us to investigate the objective/subjective dichotomy so essential to a precise understanding of the cross.

A VICARIOUS EXPIATORY SACRIFICE

Pre-cross predictions. The most basic representation of Christ's death, both in Old Testament prophecy and New Testament fulfillment, is as a substitutionary sacrifice, to take away the sin of all mankind. The prophecies are so explicit that we can develop a basic theology of the cross from them alone. Although Psalm 22 mostly focused upon the physical details of His crucifixion, I am indebted to my tenth-grade English teacher for explaining why Christ cried out from the cross, **"My God, my God, why have You forsaken me?"** Although I was not yet a born-again Christian at the time, I remember her explaining that He was pointing the attention of the onlookers to this marvelous prophecy of His crucifixion. We understand, that because He was bearing the sin of the world, the Father had to hide His face from Him.

In 22:6-8, we see the prediction of Messiah's rejection by His own people, including the words of mockery by the rulers; in vv. 9-10, His trust in the Father from the womb; in vv. 11-18, the mob of enemies surrounding Him, the physical sufferings, and details of the crucifixion; in vv. 19-24, His prayer answered by the resurrection (cf. Heb. 5:7); in vv. 25-31, the consequent global evangelization and kingdom.

But Isaiah 52:13–53:12 gives much more of the significance of His sacrifice, indeed, the word guilt-offering is used in 53:10. Ten times mention is made of His sacrifice being for sin, iniquity, and transgressions. Three times it was said that the LORD did it. The contrast between the reference to "all" in 53:6 and "many" in 53:11 & 12 is most significant. Since the identification of **"all of us like sheep have gone astray, each of us has turned to his own way"** is clearly a reference to the whole human race, or at the least, all of Israel, the use of the same expression must be the same: **"But the LORD has caused the iniquity of us all to fall on Him"** (53:6). Two truths emerge. His death was substitutionary, and He became a substitute for **all** sinners. But in 53:11 we find a limitation: **"By His knowledge the Righteous One, My Servant, will justify the many, as He will bear their iniquities."** Here we find the beginnings of the contrast between the objective, historical aspect and the subjective, personal aspect of His sacrifice.

Centuries later, we have the testimony of the last prophet of the old order, John the Baptizer: **"Behold, the Lamb of God who takes away the sin of the world"** (Jn. 1:29). This allusion to the Passover lamb must have seemed enigmatic to the disciples who heard it, but in the light of subsequent revelation it is loaded with meaning. By the Holy Spirit, John confirmed the emphasis of Isaiah 53:6, that Messiah's death was substitutionary, expiatory, and universal in its availability.

Apostolic testimony. The apostle Peter's testimony is substantial. In addition to reference to redemption in 1:18-19, we find three other descriptions in First Peter: **"And He Himself bore our sins in His body on the cross, that we might die to sin and live to righteousness; for by His wounds you were healed"** (2:24); **"For Christ also died for sins once for all, the just for the unjust, in order that He might bring us to God,**

having been put to death in the flesh, but made alive in the spirit" (3:18); "**since Christ has suffered in the flesh, . . .**" (4:1). Here also the substitutionary aspect is undeniable.

Curiously, the apostle Paul made very little of this picture, probably because he uniquely developed the two other pictures of redemption and reconciliation. His passing reference in 1 Corinthians 5:7 is most significant: "**For Christ our Passover also has been sacrificed.**" This builds upon John the Baptizer's Passover lamb allusion. Reminiscent of Isaiah 53, he wrote, "**He made Him who knew no sin *to be* sin[offering] on our behalf, that we might become the righteousness of God in Him**" (2 Cor. 5:21). As a fulfillment of Levitical animal sacrifices: "**just as Christ also loved you, and gave Himself up for us, an offering and a sacrifice to God as a fragrant aroma**" (Eph. 5:2).

Predictably, the author of Hebrews made the most of this foundational understanding of Messiah's death. In 1:3, he introduced the idea: "**When He had made purification of sins, He sat down at the right hand of the Majesty on high.**" Then in developing the idea of Christ's high priestly office, he contrasted Him with the Levitical high priest: "**who does not need daily, like those high priests, to offer up sacrifices, first for His own sins, and then for the *sins* of the people, because this He did once for all when He offered up Himself**" (7:27). What a remarkable picture of the high priest offering up himself instead of an animal sacrifice!

As he developed the analogy of the symbolism of the Levitical temple and sacrifices, he reinforced the contrast: "**and not through the blood of goats and calves, but through His own blood, He entered the holy place once for all, having obtained eternal redemption. . . . how much more will the blood of Christ, who through the eternal Spirit offered Himself without blemish to God, cleanse your conscience from dead works to serve the living God?**" (9:12, 14). Now the emphasis is upon the power of His blood to obtain eternal redemption by cleansing the conscience of the believer from the sin which the dead works of Judaism could not expiate. If my Arminian friends object to "eternal security," I will be happy to settle for "eternal redemption," which sounds to me about equivalent.

A single sacrifice. After developing the covenantal (or better testamental) nature of salvation as a basis for this (9:15-21), the apostle emphasized the singleness of the sacrifice, which he had brought into the previous passages, but now has highlighted: "**nor was it that He should offer Himself often, as the high priest enters the holy place year by year with blood not his own. Otherwise, He would have needed to suffer often since the foundation of the world; but now once at the consummation of the ages He has been manifested to put away sin by the sacrifice of Himself. . . . so Christ also, having been offered once to bear the sins of many . . .**" (9:25-28). Then the climax of his development is reached: "**By this will we have been sanctified through the offering of the body of**

Jesus Christ once for all. . . . but He, having offered one sacrifice for sins for all time, sat down at the right hand of God, . . . For by one offering He has perfected for all time those who are sanctified" (10:10, 12, 14). Notice the seven times in these passages where He reinforced the once-for-all nature of the sacrifice. The consequence of this single sacrifice of the Savior is a once-for-all salvation for the ones who have been sanctified by it. If there were no other passage in the Bible to teach eternal security, I would think that these passages alone would be adequate. The book of Hebrews has more words for confidence, boldness, and assurance than any other book. Yet it has been so badly misunderstood to deny assurance to so many believers. Chapter 15 of this book has a fresh discussion of the warnings of Hebrews harmonious with this, especially of chapter 6, which was so troubling to Jacob Arminius and to Arminians today.

When the Lord Jesus cried out on the cross, "**It is finished**," He signaled the completion of the objective dimension of His sacrifice, by which a complete salvation is available to all sinners who come by faith.

The basis of substitution. We have already seen that substitution is clear in the Isaiah 53 prophecy. Although denied by most Arminians and liberals (and some Amyraldians), substitution in the cross is unambiguous in the New Testament. The use of the preposition *anti* in Matthew 20:28=Mark 10:45 and in 1 Timothy 2:5-6 should be adequate proof. This makes irrelevant the claim that the preposition *huper* does not mean "instead of" but merely "on behalf of." In any case, the very idea of Christ's death as a ransom price for sinners is undeniably substitutionary. Moreover, some of the clearer passages in which *huper* is used in a substitutionary sense are: Romans 4:25; 8:3; 1 Corinthians 15:3; 2 Corinthians 5:14; Galatians 1:4; 2:20; 3:13. Clearly the Levitical sacrifices and the Passover sacrifices were substitutionary and the book of Hebrews makes it clear that Christ's death was a fulfillment of those sin offerings (cf. 1 Cor. 5:7). Christ died both for our benefit and as a substitutionary sin offering.

PROPITIATION

The New Testament words for propitiation or satisfaction (*hilaskomai, hilastērios, hilasmos*) come from the word for mercy, which is rarely used in the New Testament. Indeed, this whole group of words are used relatively infrequently. The connotation of mercy comes out very clearly in the prayer of the publican in Christ's parable as Luke used the verb *hilaskomai*: "**God, be merciful to me, the sinner**" (Lk. 18:13). This also comes out clearly in the description of the Lord Jesus as a "**merciful and faithful high priest**" (Heb. 2:17).

Hebrews 9:5 is the link to the mercy seat on the Ark of the Covenant in the Levitical system: *hilastērion* is used of the mercy seat. Then the apostle Paul used this same word of Christ's sacrifice: "**. . . being justified by His grace through the redemption which is in Christ Jesus; whom God**

displayed publicly as a propitiation in His blood through faith. *This was* to demonstrate His righteousness, because in the forbearance of God He passed over the sins previously committed" (Rom. 3:24-5).[A] Although Christ's death is thus linked to the Levitical mercy seat, its efficacy goes far beyond it. Paul alluded to this in his reference to God passing over the sins previously committed, ie. of pre-cross saints (cf. Heb. 9:15). Now God has displayed the cross as the new mercy seat by which He declares that He is satisfied with the blood of Christ as a full satisfaction for sin and a basis for justification. This is where He demonstrated His mercy.

The apostle John used the noun *hilasmos* twice: "**And if anyone sins, we have an Advocate with the Father, Jesus Christ the righteous; and He Himself is the propitation for our sins; and not for ours only, but also for *those of* the whole world**" (1 Jn. 2:1-2); "**In this is love, not that we loved God, but that He loved us and sent His Son *to be* the propitiation for our sins**" (1 Jn. 4:10). The discussion around the first context concerns those for whom Christ is the propitiation. Some extreme Calvinists take it that John is first identifying "our sins" as the sins of Jewish Christians, and then the whole world is a reference to Gentiles as well. However, I suspect that there is not a New Testament introduction which would say that First John was written to Hebrew Christians. There is no hint of this in the epistle. It is part of what have been called the "general epistles" since there clearly is a universality to them. It is highly unlikely that John, writing from Ephesus in the 90s would be writing only to Jewish believers. The only other alternative is that he is referring to Christ being the propitiation for the sins of all mankind. This would be harmonious with the truth of Isaiah 53:6, which we just examined. Here we have the objective, historical aspect of Christ's death, which is available to all mankind. Chafer had argued that propitiation is a God-ward work of Christ.[3] How wonderful to know that God is perfectly satisfied with the sacrifice of Christ for the sins of the whole world. God is indeed propitious!

TWO DIMENSIONS OF REDEMPTION

Eight Distinct Words Investigated

The tendency of translators and theologians to lump together the diverse ideas behind the eight Greek words related to redemption obscures significant distinctions. At the very least, these words seem to fall into two categories, one with an emphasis upon the objective, historical payment of the ransom price, and the other, upon the subjective liberation of the individual captive. Some words relate to that objective ransom price which the Lord Jesus paid through His passion; others relate to the subjective liberating consequences of this in the individual Christian's salvation, as effectuated by the Holy Spirit.

A. The NIV has reverted back to the erroneous use of 'atonement' here.

Let us examine the usage of the different words. It should not be assumed that because they are all derived from two roots the usage would necessarily relate to their derivation. Since contemporary linguists emphasize the importance of usage over derivation, we must examine the usage carefully. I would suggest that the usage of *agoradzein, lutron,* and *antilutron* seem most definitely to refer to the objective ransom price which Christ's death paid. On the other hand, it seems that *exagoradzein, lutrotes,* and *apolutrosis* most clearly refer to the subjective liberation of the captive. The verb, *lutroein,* from which four of the nouns are derived, and the noun, *lutrosis*, seem to be general, non-specific words encompassing both concepts. Carson warns us of the danger of the root fallacy: "One of the most enduring of errors, the root fallacy presupposes that every word actually *has* a meaning bound up with its shape or its components. In this view, meaning is determined by etymology; that is, by the root or roots of a word."[4]

Focus on the objective aspect

Lutron. Let us focus on the noun *lutron*. *Lutron* in secular usage meant "price of release, ransom"[5] Buchsel in *TDNT* states that, "In the oldest stratum nouns formed thus denote a means. . . . In post-Homeric constructs the means usually has the sense of payment for something."[6] It was especially used of money paid for prisoners of war or slaves. The Septuagintal usage is the same as the secular, and in Jewish usage, it especially is seen as equivalent to a forfeited life. Thus when we come to Christ's usage in Mk. 10:45 and Mt. 20:28, it is clear that the focus is on the substitutionary ransom price, especially in view of this being one of a dozen predictions of his passion: "**just as the Son of Man did not come to be served, but to serve, and to give His life a ransom for many.**" There is no basis for thinking that the consequent meaning of the release of the prisoner might be in view. This is totally objective and historical.

Antilutron. Paul's usage of *antilutron* in 1 Tim. 2:6 is clearly based upon Christ's ransom statement, except that instead of using the preposition *anti* separately, Paul follows the Hellenic Greek liking for compounds: "**For there is one God, and one mediator also between God and men, the man Christ Jesus, who gave Himself as a ransom for all, the testimony *borne* at the proper time.**" "Materially *antilutron* is the same as *lutron.*"[7] Thus the understanding of the focus being upon the objective payment of the ransom price helps us to understand how this ransom can be for "all". There would be a serious theological problem if the focus were to be on the liberation of the captive, since obviously all have not been liberated. Extreme Calvinists have tried to solve the problem by insisting unconvincingly that "all" does not mean all in this and other contexts. A much simpler solution then is to simply note the objective focus of this word. There is no theological incongruity to the idea that the objective ransom price Christ paid was sufficient for all without exception, even though not all have been liberated.

Agoradzein. Least controversial would be the meaning of the verb *agoradzein* since it has a vast secular usage, "to buy, to purchase."[8] Clearly the overwhelming focus is upon the active purchase, and it is frequently used in this sense in the Gospels. Paul's usage in 1 Corinthians 6:20 and 7:23 mentions the price *(timē)*: **"For you have been bought with a price. . ."** This would help us to understand how Peter could use this word in reference to unregenerate false teachers in 2 Peter 2:1: "**. . . just as there will also be false teachers among you, who will secretly introduce destructive heresies, even denying the Master who bought them, bringing swift destruction upon themselves**." Christ paid the objective price, but Peter does not have the liberation of the captive in view. This is confirmed by his later reference to the false teachers in 2:19 as "slaves of corruption."

The usage in Revelation 5:9 and 14:3, 4 might possibly include the liberation dimension, but makes perfect sense in the context in its basic meaning. On the other hand, Buchsel in Kittel mentions its usage in Delphic inscriptions in reference to the sacral manumission of slave, a fictional price being paid by the Greek god Apollo. There is also a Jewish usage in reference to the freeing of a slave. I would suggest, however, that neither of these usages contradicts the point that the main usage of *agoradzo* in the New Testament emphasizes the purchase and its price, not the liberation.

Both aspects undistinguished

Lutroein. The usage of the verb *lutroein* seems to include both dimensions, the objective and the subjective. Indeed, Arndt and Gingrich list the two separately: "1. *free by paying a ransom, redeem...* 2. gener. *set free, redeem, rescue*". They cite 1 Peter 1:18 under the first and Luke 24:21 and Titus 2:14 under the second.[9] This is confirmed by Buchsel's study of the secular usage. The Septuagint and Jewish usage, however, only minimally have the idea of the ransom price and stress the liberation phase.[10]

Lutrosis. The same would seem to be true of the abstract noun *lutrosis* as well. Again, Arndt and Gingrich list the two phases separately, but list the three scriptural usages (Lk. 1:68; 2:38; Heb. 9:12) under the liberation locus and cite the Didache under the ransom aspect.[11] Buchsel agrees and perhaps makes his point too strongly that even Hebrews 9:12 does not involve any thought of a price, even though the context emphasizes the blood of Christ.[12] It would probably be more balanced to admit that both aspects could be in view.

Focus on the subjective aspect

Apolutrosis. When we come to the abstract compound noun *apolutrosis*, however, there seems to be a clear semantic shift caused by the prefix *apo*, from the ransom price to the release of the captive. Thus Arndt and Gingrich only list "release", both literally and figuratively.[13] Buchsel in TDNT confirms this understanding most explicitly:

> A final question must now be put. How far is the idea of a *lutron*, a ransom or the like, still implied in *apolutrosis*? Are we to assume that whenever *apolutrosis* is used there is also a suggestion of *lutron*? In none of the *apolutrosis* passages is there any express reference to a ransom. In the eschatological verses (Lk. 21:28; R. 8:23; Eph. 1:14; 4:30) it is indeed impossible to append the idea; it lies completely beyond the horizon of these passages. Even the other Pauline verses (R. 3:24; 1 C. 1:30; Col. 1:14; Eph. 1:7) do not have in view an act in virtue of which liberation comes. **They think only of the act of emancipation itself, and of what it implies. . . . The true rendering, then, is "redemption" or "liberation," not "ransom." "Release" is also possible in Hb. 11:35 and "remission" in Hb. 9:15** (emphasis mine).[14]

Thus it is clear that the addition of the prefix *apo* has resulted in a very significant semantic shift from the usage of *lutron*. My own study over the years has convinced me, not only of the truth of, but also the importance of Chamberlain's statement in his grammar, "*The student should learn once and for all that every single letter added to a Greek root adds something to the idea expressed by the root.*"[15] Chamberlain's point is again very relevant.

Lutrotes. The one New Testament usage of the personal noun of agency *lutrotes* (redeemer, liberator) in Acts 7:35 also focuses upon the liberation phase by referring to Moses as the liberator. Moses did not pay any ransom price to liberate Israel from Egypt. It is not used in the secular, and its Septuagintal usage is harmonious with this.[16]

Exagoradzein. Paul's usage of the compound verb *exagoradzein* is harmonious with this. Although it is not used in the Septuagint, it is found in Diodorus Siculus (I BC) in reference to the manumission of a slave. All of the New Testament usages are by Paul. "**Christ redeemed us from the curse of the Law, having become a curse for us . . ." ". . . in order that He might redeem thouse who were under the Law, that we might receive the adoption as sons**" (Gal. 3:13, 4:5). Buchsel rightly emphasizes the broader context of the Galatian epistle in reference to the liberation of the Christian from the slavery of the Mosaic Law.[17] It is clear that Paul had the liberation dimension in mind. Indeed, Buchsel is on target when he says, "The predominance of an objectivising understanding of *exegorasen* has led most of the exegetical and biblico-theological work on the passage astray." He goes on to clarify, "*exagoradzo* also means, in accordance with the sense of the *ek* in many composites, an 'intensive buying,' i.e., a buying which exhausts the possibilities available." He sees the usage in the prison epistles as harmonious with this (Col. 4:5; Eph. 5:16).[18] Thus we conclude that the addition of the prefix *ex* radically shifts the emphasis of the word from the price paid to the liberation of the slave. *Agoradzein* and *exagoradzein* must be seen as two distinct words, with distinct, even contrasting ranges of meaning. Chamberlain's point is equally relevant here also. This then is a subjective, personal term.

Clarification of the contrast

Thus it is clear, not only that the linguistic evidence supports a distinction between the objective ransom phase of Christ's death and the subjective liberation phase in the life of the Christian, but also that such a distinction is of great value exegetically and theologically. It helps us to understand how the ransom price could be connected with unregenerate false teachers (2 Pet. 2:1) and all mankind (1 Tim. 2:5-6), when the liberation has been efficacious for only a limited number. Thus it helps resolve the tension between these two truths. Christ's ransom price was sufficient for all mankind and provisionally available to all, but the liberation has been effectual only for those who believe.

An illustration helps us to understand the importance of the distinction. When heiress Patty Hearst was kidnapped by the Symbionese Liberation Army some years ago, her father paid a ransom price of two million dollars. However, Patty, having been brainwashed into sympathy with her captors, even joined them in a bank robbery and refused to be liberated. The *lutron* (ransom price) had been provided, the act of *agoradzein* (paying the ransom) had been fulfilled, but there was no *apolutrosis* or *exagoradzein* (liberation) effectuated. The objective provision was made, but the subjective release did not occur because of the will of the captive. Just so the objective ransom price for the sins of the whole human race was provided on Calvary, but the subjective release of the majority of the captives has not taken place because of their own willful rejection of the redeemer.

Perhaps another illustration will help to highlight the exceedingly important distinction between the objective, historical foundations of salvation and the subjective application to the individual in a personal way. As the third generation was beginning to be born in the pilgrim fathers' communities in New England, a controversy arose over the christening of the grandchildren of believers whose own parents had not become regenerate. A synod in Branford, Connecticut in 1662 decided to allow it and was termed the "half-way covenant" by the dissenters, who felt that it implied that there is such a thing as a half-way Christian. The dissenters departed to the wilderness of New Jersey and founded New Ark on the banks of the Passaic River, an area recently opened up by the departure of the Dutch. To see the city of Newark today one might never imagine it was founded as a consequence of the theological issue of the objective/subjective distinction in salvation truth. The Robert Treat Hotel bears witness today to one of the founders of the city, who understood that the objective work of Christ, by itself, automatically saves no one and that there must be a subjective application by the conviction, regeneration, and sanctification of the Holy Spirit for a person to be called a Christian. To them this was not a marginal issue.

RECONCILIATION

It was uniquely the apostle Paul who developed the picture of reconciliation through the cross, using three related words in the process: *katallassein, katallagē, & apokatallassein*. There is little controversy about the meaning of the words, the first meaning, "to change, exchange, reconcile," and is used twice in Romans 5:9-11:

> **Much more then, having now been justified by His blood, we shall be saved from the wrath *of God* through Him. For if while we were enemies, we were reconciled to God through the death of His Son, much more, having been reconciled, we shall be saved by His life. And not only this, but we also exult in God through our Lord Jesus Christ, through whom we have now received the reconciliation.**

This basic context makes it clear that reconciliation is directed at man's alienation from God, and that we believers are said to have been reconciled to God, even from a state of total enmity toward Him. Since Paul thus designates our prior state as enemies of God, it is clear that this is subjective and individual rather than objective and historical. This happens in the life and experience of the believer as a part of the conversion process. It is also clear that the idea that God was somehow historically reconciled is not supported here or in any of Paul's other passages. Reconciliation is always manward. We have received this reconciliation.

This passage is also a wonderful basis for the security of the believer, since Paul made it clear that if God was able to reconcile us when we were at enmity, He is even "much more" able to complete that salvation through Christ's resurrected and ascended life now interceding for us at the Father's right hand (Heb. 7:25). Amazingly, he said that our future salvation is even more sure than the present.

The interpretation of Paul's discussion in 2 Corinthians 5:18-20 is not quite so straightforward:

> **Now all *these* things are from God, who reconciled us to Himself through Christ, and gave us the ministry of reconciliation, namely that God was in Christ reconciling the world to Himself, not counting their trespasses against them, and He has committed to us the word of reconciliation. Therefore, we are ambassadors for Christ, as though God were entreating through us; we beg [sic. you] on behalf of Christ, be reconciled to God.**

Paul's use of an aorist participle in 5:18 in reference to the believer's reconciliation as a past event is harmonious with what we saw in Romans 5. But Paul's use of a periphrastic present participle in 5:19 in reference to the reconciliation of the world is more difficult. However, the finite verb 'was' is in the imperfect and together they have an imperfect force.[19] Thus we could fairly say that, in the cross, God was in the process of reconciling the world. It is obvious that the world has not yet been reconciled. But the cross was the foundation of that process of reconciliation, which has been going on since that day, as sinners one by one respond to the good news.[20] This is confirmed by Paul's statement that God gave to us believers a ministry of reconciliation and a word of reconciliation. Then he explained in 5:20 how this works—God entreats the world through us, His ambassadors, as we plead with sinners to be reconciled to God (note that the 'you' in v. 20 is not in the Greek). From this it is clear that the work of reconciliation is subjective, not objective; personal, not historical.

Paul used the stronger compound word *apokatallassein* in Ephesians 2:16, speaking of the goal of the cross to thoroughly reconcile Jew and Gentile together in one body, the Church. Abbott-Smith suggests that the prefix *apo* signifies a more complete and thorough reconciliation.[21] Then in the parallel passage in Colossians 1:20-22, Paul expanded the purview to "all kinds of things" to be thoroughly reconciled in the end time, including the reconciliation of the Colossian believers in their day (cf. discussion on p. 58). This is harmonious with his earlier use of these words.

CONCLUSIONS

With so many distinct Greek words used to portray the cross of Christ, it is fuzzy thinking which perpetuates the use of the Old Testament term 'atonement' in theological literature, especially since it only refers to the prefiguring of the Christ's sacrifice in the Levitical system, which was far short of the reality. However, we found the pre-cross predictions most instructive, coupled with the apostolic references to His death as a substitutionary expiatory sacrifice. The book of Hebrews especially contrasted the Levitical offerings with the ultimate efficacy of Christ's sacrifice, an efficacy which guaranteed eternal redemption to the believer.

We saw in the focus upon the words for propitiation an objective universality, which confirmed our understanding of the picture of sacrifice. The work of propitiation thus was Godward in that Christ's death was a perfect satisfaction to the Father for the sins of the whole world.

We found two dimensions in the broad concept of redemption: ransom-redemption, focusing upon the objective ransom price paid; and liberation-redemption, focusing upon the subjective liberation of the sinner from slavery. Here we found that we must not put stress on etymologies of Greek words, but rather be careful students of word usage. Thus, we find that distinct Greek words may be derived from the same root, but having very distinct meanings. Ransom-redemption, like propitiation, is potentially universal in its intent. However, liberation-redemption consistently is limited in its efficacy to believers, as also is reconciliation. These terms portray a subjective application of the merits of Christ's sacrifice to those who claim it in repentant faith.

For centuries there has been endless debate over limited/unlimited atonement. The whole debate has been beside the point. Atonement is not a New Testament word! Some more exegetically oriented theologians have suggested 'particular redemption' as the preferable terminology. However, it is more biblically exact to talk about an 'unlimited or general ransom price or purchase' and a 'limited or particular liberation'. Hence we conclude that the whole question has arisen because of the failure of many theologians to do the careful word studies needed as the basis for sound theology. We can excuse past generations of theologians because they did not have the linguistic resources that we have. Today, however, there is no excuse for such superficial theologizing. Let us get out of the rut of the past! In the next chapter we shall build upon this linguistic foundation to examine the view of extreme Calvinists that Christ died only for the elect.

---

1. Lewis Sperry Chafer, *Systematic Theology*, III, pp. 86-96, 190-93.
2. Robert P. Lightner, *The Death Christ Died: A Case for Unlimited Atonement*, pp. 73-91; *Sin, the Savior, and Salvation*, pp. 117-27; John F. Walvoord, *Jesus Christ, Our Lord*, pp. 163-90.
3. Chafer, III, 93-96.
4. D. A. Carson, *Exegetical Fallacies*, p. 26.
5. Arndt and Gingrich, *A Greek-English Lexicon*, p. 483.
6. Buchsel in *TDNT*, IV, p. 340.
7. Ibid, p. 349.
8. Arndt & Gingrich, p. 12.
9. Arndt and Gingrich, p. 484.
10. Buchsel, pp. 349-50.
11. Arndt and Gingrich, p. 484.
12. Buchsel, p. 351.
13. Arndt and Gingrich, p. 95.
14. Buchsel, pp. 354-5.
15. William Douglas Chamberlain, *An Exegetical Grammar of the Greek New Testament*, p. 11.
16. Ibid, p. 351.
17. Buchsel TDNT, I, pp. 125-6.
18. Ibid, I, pp. 127-8.
19. Wallace, *Grammar*, pp. 647-48.
20. There is exegetical criticism of the KJV and NAS translation that "God was in Christ" in favor of the NIV that "God was reconciling the world to himself in Christ." However, I don't believe it affects the theological implications I have drawn from the passage.
21. Abbott-Smith, *Lexicon*, en loc.

It is incontestable that Christ came for the expiation of the sins of the whole world. But the solution lies close at hand, that whosoever believes in Him should not perish but should have eternal life (John 3:15). . . . For although there is nothing in the world deserving of God's favour, He nevertheless shows He is favourable to the whole world when He calls all without exception to the faith of Christ, which is indeed an entry into life.

-John Calvin

6

FOR WHOM DID CHRIST DIE? THE EXTENT OF THE CROSS

Problems of "Limited Atonement"

A uniquely held doctrine. Extreme Calvinism alone holds to so-called limited atonement, which means that Christ died only for the elect and not in any real sense for the non-elect. It is immediately clear from their statement of the issue, that it derives from their doctrine of unconditional election, which is its premise, and that the issue would probably never have arisen apart from that doctrine. Limited atonement is peculiarly a view of the extreme Calvinists and is rejected by moderate Calvinists, Arminians, Lutherans, Pietists, and those like myself who hold to a mediate understanding of salvation, in short, all other Christians.

A difficult doctrine. Extreme Calvinists admit that limited atonement is the most controversial and problematic of the five points. Calvinist Duane Spencer called it "the most difficult" of the five, and John DeWitt acknowledged that many consider it to be "the Achilles Heel of Calvinism."[1] At the same time, others like A. A. Hodge saw that denial of limited atonement would make a central principle of Arminianism (and of mediate theology of salvation) true.[2] Unthinkable!

A new doctrine. Although I have already argued that detailed historical study should always come after our biblical research, it is important for the reader to know that the doctrine of limited atonement is relatively recent. It was not clearly taught until Calvin's successor Theodore Beza, and does not appear in any creed until the Canons of Dort (1618-9) (see chapter 18). Neither Augustine (d. 430) nor his disciple Prosper of Aquitaine taught it, nor any of the first generation Reformers. (Please see the thirty unambiguous quotations of Calvin on general redemption in appendix E.) There has been a continual and strong reaction against this teaching among the majority of evangelical Christians since it was first propounded.

Since it is increasingly clear that Calvin himself did not hold to limited atonement, in all honesty, I cannot refer to those who hold it as Calvinists. Many terms have been in use: Ultra-Calvinists, Hyper-Calvinists, Developed Calvinists, Scholastic Calvinists, etc. Perhaps for historical accuracy they should be designated as 'Beza-ites.' My Calvinistic friends may feel all of these are prejudicial and pejorative, and if it seems so, I apologize. Norman Geisler uses the term extreme Calvinists, and I use it without any pejorative intent. Most of my friends, associates, former professors, pastors, and colleagues are Calvinists of one kind or another, and I have no desire to insult them

Two dimensions of salvation truth. I have sought to show in the previous chapter that an inductive study of the various New Testament words referring to Christ's saving work reveals two major dimensions: on the one hand, an objective, historical, and universal aspect, and on the other hand, a subjective, individual, and limited aspect. I believe that the truth is two-sided. Taking one side of the truth and forcing all other Scripture to fit in with that is a reductionist error. We must grasp the truth with both hands. It is not that there is any contradiction, paradox, or antinomy in these two aspects of His work on the cross. Both are perfectly in harmony.

When we examine the teachings of the Lord Jesus, we find that there were a significant number of times when He set forth two-sided truths. For example, coming down from the mount of transfiguration His disciples asked about Elijah's return (Mt. 17). The Lord's answer was definitely two-sided: Elijah will come in the future, and also he had come in the person of John, who was beheaded. Both are true! It is mainly us westerners, with our Greek-derived way of thinking (cognitive process), who so easily fall into the reductionist error.

THE ISSUES STATED

Definition and terminology. Many Calvinists prefer other terminology, such as "definite atonement," "particular atonement," "particular redemption," "effective redemption," or "limited redemption." It doesn't seem that the terminology in any way changes the issue, so I will stick to the most common usage. The best definitions come from the historical data. A sixteenth-century Reformed theologian, Jerom Zanchius (1516-90), one of the first to advocate it, is a good representative:

> As God doth not will that each individual of mankind should be saved, so neither did He will that Christ would properly and immediately die for each individual of mankind, whence it follows that, though the blood of Christ, from its own intrinsic dignity, was sufficient for the redemption of all men, yet, **in consequence of His Father's appointment, He shed it intentionally, and therefore effectually and immediately, for the elect only** (emphasis mine).[3]

Since this doctrine first surfaced in the Synod of Dort (1618-9), let us see the Canons of Dort:

> For this was the sovereign counsel, and most gracious will and purpose of God the Father, that the quickening and saving efficacy of the most precious death of his Son should extend **to all the elect, for bestowing upon them alone the gift of justifying faith**, thereby to bring them infallibly to salvation: that is, it was the will of God, that Christ by the blood of the cross, whereby he confirmed the new covenant, should effectually redeem out of every people, tribe, nation, and language, **all those, and those only, who were from eternity chosen to salvation, and given to him by the Father; that he should confer upon them faith, which together with all the other saving gifts of the Holy Spirit, he purchased them by his death** (emphasis mine);[4]

Attempted clarifications. Over the centuries the catch phrase, "sufficient for all, but efficient only for the elect" has continuously surfaced, but, as many have recognized, it resolves little or nothing. Calvin attributed it to the medieval scholastics and saw it as unhelpful.[5] It is a statement that all can accept, and thus does not clarify the issues between the differing parties. I would respond that, if Christ's death is sufficient for all but has no applicability to all, then its sufficiency for all is meaningless. The sufficiency of the cross for all is only meaningful if all can somehow benefit from it.

Another catch phrase which Calvinists have used is, "Christ died for all without distinction, but not for all without exception." This *does* express the view of extreme Calvinists, but does not do justice to the clear teaching of Scripture, which I will show clearly teaches that Christ died for all without exception, as well as for all without distinction.

A logical problem

The problem, as extreme Calvinists have struggled with it, is a logical one. If Christ died as a substitute for a whole world of sinners, then why are not all men saved? If Christ paid the price for the sins of the non-elect, then isn't God demanding a double price for their sin by sending them to hell? Thus extreme Calvinists insist that the intent of Christ's death was only for the elect, and that His death not only makes their salvation possible, but in and of itself also makes their salvation certain. Although limited atonement is the logical outcome of the Calvinistic system, and extreme Calvinists have felt it an essential part of their system, it has proved to be the most objectionable part and the most difficult to defend. Indeed the strongest opposition has come from moderate four-point Calvinists, especially from the Amyraldian movement and its contemporary representatives.[6] This is not surprising since it seems clear that the moderate Calvinists are only trying to restore Calvin's Calvinism. Indeed, Brian Armstrong argues that Amyraut was the greatest Calvin scholar of the 17th century.[A]

Extreme Calvinists are heavily dependent upon logic for their position, especially since the scriptural support is so weak. I have emphasized from the beginning the deductive nature of their approach. This comes through very clearly in the words of Gordon H. Clark: "All the doctrines of Scripture are logically interdependent. Since the most pertinent doctrines have already been discussed, any further appeal to Scriptural passages is anticlimactic and unnecessary."[7] He did go on, however, to give a brief and perfunctory discussion of only seven passages, only one of which is quoted by his opponents. One wonders if he was ignorant of the dozens of other passages which favor general redemption, or whether his mind-set was so totally deductive that the inductive scriptural data was unimportant to him. This seems to be fairly typical of extreme Calvinists.

Over the years that I have studied and taught theology, the inductive biblical evidence for both the substitutionary nature of Christ's death and its universal dimension seemed so obvious that the supposed logical problem never disturbed me. Indeed, a discriminating inductive study of the distinct Greek terms for the cross, as expounded in the previous chapter, highlighted the two-fold nature of this truth, which resolves any logical difficulties. The tension, I believe, arises solely from a defective overly-deductive methodology.

Particularistic arguments

There are a number of arguments adduced by extreme Calvinists against general redemption. Laurence Vance has given a good summary of their reasoning:[8]

Universalism. The first is that if Christ died for all mankind, then inevitably all mankind must be saved. R. C. Sproul states it briefly, "It seems to follow from the idea of unlimited atonement that salvation is universal."[9] W. J. Seaton is more explicit, "If Christ has paid the debt of sin, has saved, ransomed, given His life for *all* men, then *all* men will be saved."[10] Simply put, Seaton, like other extreme Calvinists, has confused the objective work of Christ on the cross with the subjective application of its merits to the

---

A. Brian G. Armstrong, *Calvinism and the Amyraut Heresy*, p. 187-91; 265. Most astounding is Alan C.Clifford's conclusion in his doctoral dissertation that John Wesley was just as close to John Calvin in his theology as was John Owen. See *Atonement and Justification*, pp. 240-244.

individual sinner by repentant faith. He mixes the two together in his statement. Extreme Calvinists confuse and blend together the merits of Christ's death with the application to the individual sinner.

***Double payment*.** Another major argument they present is the double payment argument. Loraine Boettner is representative:

> For God to have laid the sins of all men on Christ would mean that as regards the lost He would be punishing their sins twice, once in Christ, and then again in them. Certainly that would be unjust. If Christ paid their debt, they are free, and the Holy Spirit would invariably bring them to faith and repentance.[11]

***Ineffectual atonement*.** A third argument is the extreme Calvinists' claim that a universal atonement does not actually save anyone. In one sense their claim is true—the merits of Christ's death must be applied to those who in repentant faith claim His salvation. In and of itself the death of Christ saves no one.

***Parallel imputation*.** A fourth line of reasoning of extreme Calvinists is seen in the parallelism of the imputation of Adam's sin to the whole race in bringing condemnation and the imputation of Christ's righteousness to the elect. Charles Hodge claimed that they must be parallel:

> The sin of Adam did not make the condemnation of all men merely possible; it was the ground of their actual condemnation. So the righteousness of Christ did not make the salvation of men merely possible; it secured the actual salvation of those for whom He wrought.[12]

What Hodge overlooked is that justification did not take place at the cross objectively, but takes place when we believe. According to Genesis 15:6, Abraham's justification took place two millenniums before the cross: "**Abraham believed God and it was counted to him for righteousness.**"

***Owen's conundrum*.** The fifth argument came from John Owen:

> God imposed his wrath due unto, and Christ underwent the pains of hell for, **either all the sins of all men, or all the sins of some men, or some sins of all men.** . . . If the first, why, then, are not all freed from the punishment of all their sins? You will say, "Because of their unbelief; they will not believe." But this unbelief, it is a sin, or not? If not, why should they be punished for it? (emphasis mine)[13]

By this conundrum Owen sought to force us logically to the second option since the third is obviously erroneous and he feels he has also eliminated the first. What he fails to take into account is the unique character of the sin of unrepentant unbelief. God certainly has the sovereign right to make this the only sin which could not possibly be under the blood of Christ, if persisted in. That is just what the Bible explicitly states in John 3:18: **"He who believes in Him is not judged; he who does not believe has been judged already, because he has not believed in the name of the only begotten Son of God."** Unbelief is a unique sin.

A mediate response

I have not responded to all of the above arguments separately. Vance has responded very simply to all of them by focusing on the false premise of all their arguments: "This false premise is making the Atonement and its application the same thing; that is, confounding the *provision* of a Savior with the *applying* of salvation."[14]

There is no question that extreme Calvinists teach that Christ's death in and of itself actually saved all the elect and only the elect, thereby confusing the objective provision of the basis of salvation with its subjective application to individual sinners by repentant faith. Hear John Murray: "What does redemption mean? It does not mean redeemability, that we are placed in a redeemable position. It means that Christ purchased and procured redemption."[15] Hear Arthur Pink:

> To say that everything turns on a sinner's acceptance, is to affirm that Christ did nothing more for those who are saved than He did for those who are lost. It is not faith which gives Divine efficacy to the blood; it was the blood which efficaciously purchased faith.[16]

Hear W. E. Best: "Christ's righteousness was imputed to all the elect when Jesus Christ died."[17]

Vance has given a very perceptive response to this confusion of the 'atonement' and its application, which I will summarize and augment.[18] We must ask, why did Christ's sacrifice not save anybody in and of itself without a distinct work of application by the triune God? Why must we distinguish the objective, historical work of the cross in propitiation and ransom-redemption from the subjective application in reconciliation, redemption-release, justification, and regeneration? The answer is manifold:

1. The inductive data for seeing on the one hand, propitiation and ransom-redemption as objectively wrought for all mankind, and on the other hand, reconciliation, redemption-release, justification, and regeneration as subjectively applied individually to only those who have repentant faith is overwhelming. I have already set out part of this in detail in the previous chapter.

2. Pre-cross believers could not have been saved in any real sense if their salvation had to wait until Christ actually died. It is abundantly clear, however, that Old Testament saints were fully justified (Gen. 15:6), forgiven (Ps. 32, 51), redeemed-liberated from sin, reconciled to God, and regenerated, as Reformed Christians would have to affirm. Some have

resolved their problem by extrapolating it all back to eternity past as part of election, thus moving it all out of time-space history totally. This comes dangerously close to neo-orthodoxy's moving of salvation out of real history. Scripture is clear, however, that Old Testament believers were saved on the credit plan, contingent upon the historical event of the cross (Rom. 3:25-26; Heb.9:15).

3. For those elect who were born after the cross, how could Christ's sacrifice actually and effectually save them if they did not yet exist when Christ died (unless one follows Origen in holding to the pre-existing souls view)?

4. How could saved, redeemed, reconciled, justified, and regenerated post-cross elect be born into the world dead in trespasses and sins, if there is no temporally distinct application phase and the cross in and of itself actually saved these elect?

5. The Passover and its clearly distinct application is an analogy to the cross of Christ with its distinct application phase. The blood of the slain lamb had no efficacy unless and until it was applied to the doorposts of the Jewish dwelling. Paul confirms the validity of the analogy in 1 Corinthians 5:7, and most Reformed commentators would affirm it. John Gerstner, however, berated Lightner for appealing to this analogy,[19] but it is still valid, since Paul validated it.

Over the centuries the major response to extreme Calvinist arguments has been that Christ's death is potential, provisional, and conditional in its application. The cross, in and of itself, saves no one, not even the elect. Only those who respond positively to the gospel with repentant faith are saved. As we saw in the last chapter, the objective, historical dimension of sacrifice, propitiation, and the ransom price is only part of the whole, the foundation. But it is not automatically applied to the individual. For that the subjective, personal dimension of redemption-liberation and reconciliation comes into play. This duality is expressed in 1 Tim. 4:10: ". . . **the living God, who is the Savior of all men, especially of believers.**"

We could also suggest that the basis of condemnation has been changed by the cross. It is not now primarily the sins of man, but more significantly the one sin of unresponsiveness to the gospel. In a sense there is one sin for which Christ did not die, the sin of unbelief (Jn. 3:18).

The root of the issue

Lightner has pointed out: "There is no question about it: the issue between limited and unlimited atonement centers in the design or purpose of the redemptive work of Christ."[20] John Murray stated, "the design must be coextensive with the ultimate result."[21] However, this is the very point at issue, and we do not believe that this is sustainable by Scripture.

It is here that the logical connection of unconditional election with limited atonement becomes clear. Starting with the premise of unconditional election, the only consistent view of atonement is a limited atonement. Vance characteristically has described the extreme Calvinistic view very bluntly: "*Christ made a limited Atonement for the "elect" because he did not want anyone else to be saved*" (emphasis mine).[22] This is what Zanchius and the canons of Dort say. These words may sound offensive to extreme Calvinists, but how else can we understand their system? I have been reading, studying, and even teaching from their books for half a century now and feel that there is no way to avoid Vance's bald conclusion. Unconditional election means that God does not want anybody else to be saved but the 'elect!' Theologians have speculated about God's two wills, but this makes God seem to be double-minded. To trace the problem back even one more step, it goes back to a false concept of God's sovereignty, which I have already discussed in the third chapter.

Some have sought to soften the impact of Calvin's "horrible decree" by denying double predestination while holding to single. They suggest that we must focus upon the positive aspect of God's election of the elect, leaving the rest to die in their reprobate condition without any prejudice to their case. However, God's alleged failure to provide irresistible grace for the non-elect does not mitigate the awfulness of such a concept. Single predestination is illogical, inconsistent, and unbiblical. As James Daane says, ". . . reprobation is always there."[23]

It seems to me that this is an issue that Calvin never resolved in his lifetime. Although there is evidence of general redemption in his *Institutes* and earlier writings (see appendix E), most of the general redemption quotations are from his commentaries, thus indicating that the more he dealt with the Scripture text itself, the more he broadened his view on the 'atonement.' It was for Beza to work out this inconsistency with an explicit doctrine of limited atonement. What a tragic blunder!

Moderate Calvinistic responses. The great Baptist theologian, A. H. Strong, a moderate Calvinist, explained how Christ can in some sense be the Savior of all men (1 Tim. 4:10):[B]

> (a) That the atonement of Christ secures for all men a delay in the execution of the sentence against sin, and a space for repentance, together with a continuance of the common blessings of life which have been forfeited by transgression. . . . .
>
> (b) That the atonement of Christ has made objective provision for

B. It is well to note that Strong's statement that the cross "removed from the divine mind" every obstacle to the pardon and restoration of sinners is contradictory to his belief in unconditional election, which certainly is an obstacle in God's mind to the salvation of the major portion of mankind. Herein is the inconsistency of four-point Calvinism, as recognized by many extreme Calvinists and Arminians.

> the salvation of all, by removing from the divine mind every obstacle to the pardon and restoration of sinners, except their wilful opposition to God and refusal to turn to him. . . . .
>
> (c) That the atonement of Christ has procured for all men the powerful incentives to repentance presented in the Cross, and the combined agency of the Christian church and of the Holy Spirit, by which these incentives are brought to bear upon them.[24]

The key word in Strong's statement is 'provision.' As we saw in the last chapter, the Lord Jesus provided a propitiation for all mankind (1 Jn. 2:2). He paid the ransom price for the sins of all humanity including unregenerate false teachers (Mt. 20:28; 2 Pet.2 :1). His death is provisional, potential, and conditional in its application. In and of itself it saves no one apart from the subjective application phase of redemption-liberation and reconciliation, which is conditioned upon repentant faith. Christ's death fully satisfied (propitiated) the offended holiness of God, upon which basis the Holy Spirit declares through His church that God is propitious. The only obstacle now remaining is man's unresponsiveness to God. The convicting ministry of the Spirit has been given to deal with that (Jn. 16:8-11). This will be investigated further in the chapter 9.

More recently Lewis Sperry Chafer gave a clear statement of the moderate Calvinistic position:

> Certainly Christ's death of itself forgives no sinner, nor does it render unnecessary the regenerating work of the Holy Spirit. Any one of the elect whose salvation is predetermined, and for whom Christ died, may live the major portion of his life in open rebellion against God and, during that time, manifest every feature of depravity and spiritual death. This alone should prove that men are not severally saved by the act of Christ in dying, but rather that they are saved by the divine application of that value when they believe.[25]

While I believe that the moderate Calvinistic answers to extreme Calvinism are most helpful, we are left with the serious tension as to how God could determine the fate of individuals in eternity past and yet genuinely desire and provide for the salvation of all mankind. We must hold off that discussion until the next chapter, however, and get on with a direct inductive study of the relevant Scripture passages.

EXEGESIS OF KEY SCRIPTURES

Passages which restrict the impact of His sacrifice

Neither moderate Calvinists, Arminians, or those in between deny that Scripture frequently focuses the extent of the death of Christ upon believers.

This is in recognition of the duality of truth already alluded to. Having acknowledged this common ground with extreme Calvinists, we should note that even some of the passages usually adduced in favor of limited atonement have some ambiguity. A number of the passages adduced by extreme Calvinists do not specifically mention the death of Christ, and thus are not relevant. I will not discuss such here: Matthew 1:21, John 1:9; 5:21.

We should also note that nowhere does the Bible explicitly say that Christ died for the 'elect' per se. Expressions such as 'sheep,' 'the church,' etc. are used in these passages, but without any restrictive language which would in any way compromise the other more general passages.

Lightner aptly points out, "All men, including the elect, are lost until such time as they individually and personally exercise faith in Christ as their own Savior. There simply is no distinction in the Bible between elect and nonelect sinners in their unregenerate state."[26]

Isaiah 53:4-12. - **"All of us like sheep have gone astray, each of us has turned to his own way; but the LORD has caused the iniquity of us all to fall on Him" (53:6).** - Although the prophet speaks continually in the first person in vv.4-6, which extreme Calvinists might take to refer to the elect, the context might lead us to believe he is referring to the nation Israel as a whole, not just the elect of Israel. Not only does he refer to those who "have gone astray" and "turned to his own way", but also in v. 8 to "my people to whom the stroke was due." However, in vv. 11-12 there is a shift to third person, "He will bear their iniquities . . . He Himself bore the sin of many." This shift may be an early indication of the two-sidedness of Messiah's passion already mentioned above. Calvin, however, comments that 'many' is equivalent to 'all,' contrary to the extreme Calvinistic interpretation.[27]

Matthew 20:28; 26:28; Mark 10:45. - **"just as the Son of Man did not come to be served, but to serve, and to give His life a ransom for many."** - Extreme Calvinists take it that the many for whom He paid the ransom price are the elect. It is clear that Calvin himself did not so interpret it: "'Many' is used, not for a definite number, but for a large number, in that He sets Himself over against all others. And this is its meaning also in Rom. 5:15, where Paul is not talking of a part of mankind but of the whole human race."[28] We must not read into our Lord's words a theological concept of election in limiting its focus.

John 10:11, 15.- **". . . and I lay down my life for the sheep."** - Edwin Palmer is typical of extreme Calvinists who add the word 'alone' to Christ's statement. "He lays down His life for His sheep, and His sheep alone."[29] He assumed that sheep is equivalent to elect, but that equivalency is indefensible. However, the definition of sheep is clarified by our Lord's statement to the Jews in 10:26, "But you do not believe, because you are not of my sheep." Christ did not exclude the possibility that any of the unbelieving Jews He was speaking to would subsequently believe and become His sheep. As a matter of fact, John describes in 10:40-42 how many of these Jews followed Him down to Perea and believed on Him there. At the time that the Lord had made the above declaration they were **not** His sheep, and yet subsequently, became such, and thus are also among the elect of God. Therefore, we could say that at a given point of time those who are His sheep are not all of the elect. These two terms are not equivalent. At a given moment His sheep are a subset of the elect of all ages. So if Christ died for His sheep alone, then He did not die for all the elect. You see the logical tangles one gets into in conceptualizing elect sinners who have not yet come to faith in Christ. The Bible never deals with such a category of people; but the Calvinists must do so constantly in their interpretation of Scripture.

John 17:9. **"I pray for them. I am not praying for the world, but for those you have given me, for they are yours."** (NIV) - Extreme Calvinists affirm that there is a parallel between Christ's refusal to pray for the world and their teaching that Christ did not die for the whole world. However, first we must ask why Christ did not pray for the world. Was it because He did not want the world to be saved and He knew that as the sinless Son, the Father would have to answer His prayer? He wept for unbelieving Israel (Mt. 23:37), so this is hardly possible. Was it because as a matter of principle He did not pray for unbelievers? No, on the cross He did pray for those who were crucifying Him (Lk. 23:34), that at the very least the Father would refrain from immediate judgment upon them.

First, we should note that He did not say, "I pray not for the non-elect." In the world (*kosmos*) of unregenerate sinners for whom He did not pray at this time, was a host of people who subsequently believed and evidently were among the elect, and for whom He *did* pray in v. 20: **"I do not ask on behalf of these alone, but for those also who believe in Me through their word; that they may all be one; . . ."** We should also note that this prayer was not a prayer for the *salvation* of the disciples—they had already been saved. He is praying for the Father to keep them, protect them from Satan, sanctify them, unify them, and glorify them. This would not have been an appropriate prayer for those who had not yet believed in Him. So when we understand the nature of our Lord's motivation and prayer, we see it is not at all parallel to a discussion on the extent of the 'atonement.' *It is virtually irrelevant!*

Acts 20:28. - **"Be on guard for yourselves and for all the flock, among which the Holy Spirit has made you overseers, to shepherd the church of God which He purchased with His own blood."** Paul's words to the Ephesian elders appropriately focus the efficacy of Christ's blood in acquiring (*peripoieein*) His church. Since this verb has a broader connotation, it apparently doesn't speak only of His death, but has both the objective and subjective aspects of the salvation of the corporate church in view. Thus it in no way compromises the truth of general redemption.

Romans 5:15, 19. - **"For if by the transgression of the one the many died, much more did the grace of God and the gift by grace of the one Man, Jesus Christ, abound to the many. . . . For as through the one man's disobedience the many were made sinners, even through the obedience of the One the many will be made righteous."** Extreme Calvinists typically take the word 'many' to be a reference to the elect and not to all mankind. That this is an extreme Calvinistic interpretation is seen in the fact that Calvin himself took the word 'many' to mean all mankind. In his comment on Matthew 20:28, he says, "'Many' is used, not for a definite number, but for a large number, in that He sets Himself over against all others. And this is its meaning also in Rom. 5:15, where Paul is not talking of a part of mankind but of the whole human race."[30]

1 Corinthians 15:3. - **"For I delivered to you as of first importance what I also received, that Christ died for our sins according to the Scriptures, . . ."** Here Paul's focus is presumably upon Christ's death for believers since its ultimate benefit is only realized to believers in the Church, those to whom it has been applied, not just those for whom it was provided. But this statement is in no way restrictive; other passages show its broader potential. He does not stipulate as to whom he has in mind, just believers or all of humanity when he says "our." The concept of election does not enter into Paul's language or thought here.

Galatians 3:13. - **"Christ redeemed us from the curse of the Law, having become a curse for us—for it is written, 'Cursed is every one who hangs on a tree'"** Similarly to the previous passage Paul focused upon believers here, and the context clearly limits his meaning to believers, since the unregenerate are never said to have been released from the Mosaic Law, as have been believers (Rom. 7:6; 2 Cor 3:6-11). Having noted this contextual limitation, we should also note that Paul does not use *agoradzein*, as he does in passages with a more general reference, but he used *exagoradzein*, which focuses on the redemption-release aspect of the cross (as I have already clarified in the previous chapter). This is not contradictory to but rather harmonious with general ransom-redemption taught in other passages. Lightner is helpful here: "If references such as this, in which the writer includes himself in the death of Christ, may be used to prove limited atonement, then when writers of Scripture use similar phraseology in speaking of man's sin, it could be said that they teach limited depravity or sin."[31] Then he references Isaiah 53:6 and 64:6. O, consistency, where art thou?

Ephesians 5:25-6. - **"Husbands, love your wives, just as Christ also loved the church and gave Himself up for her; that He might sanctify her, having cleansed her by the washing of water with the word, . . ."**

Extreme Calvinists assume that the focus of Christ's love and sacrifice upon the church thus excludes all other humans. But in the context it is totally appropriate in discussing marriage for Paul to focus on that special love of Christ for His church. Norman Geisler puts it well:

> There are good reasons why the fact that Christ loves the church does not mean He did not love the world as well. For one thing, the fact that I love my wife does not logically mean that I lack love for other persons. It simply puts special focus on my love for someone who is special in my life."[32]

Need I quote John 3:16 to confirm God's love for a lost world at this point? Not only does God love a lost world, but He has the church join Him in inviting a lost world to come to salvation: "And the Spirit and the bride say, 'Come.' And let the one who hears say, 'Come.' And let the one who is thirsty come; let the one who wishes take the water of life without cost." (Rev. 22:17).

Just as there is a special sense in which Christ loves the church over above the world, just so there is a special sense in which Christ's death is especially for the church without being limited to the elect. Note again that the abstract concept of 'elect' does not occur here or in any of these passages.

1 Peter 3:18. - **"For Christ also died for sins once for all, *the* just for *the* unjust, in order that He might bring us to God, having been put to death in the flesh, but made alive in the spirit."**[C] Since Peter is clearly teaching a substitutionary death, the extreme Calvinists argue that His death could only be a substitute for the elect, lest all men would be saved. They cannot harmonize substitution with general redemption, and indeed some moderate Calvinists historically have had a problem in so doing. Most significantly, we should observe that Peter describes Christ's substitution being for the "unjust." This hardly sounds like a synonym for the 'elect.' It describes the whole human race. The goal of that substitution, Peter informs us, is to "bring us (you) to God." So actually this passage gives both the objective aspect (substitution for the unjust) and the subjective aspect (bringing believers to God) together in one statement, as does 1 Timothy 4:10. Although quoted as a proof text by extreme Calvinists, this passage actually affirms both aspects: the first part is general; the second, limited. No contradiction!

Passages which extend the potential to all

Christ died for the 'whole world.' There are many passages which extend the intent of Christ's death and salvation to the whole world. It is

---

C. We should note a textual variant here. Some of the oldest manuscripts read "you" rather than "us," which the NIV translation follows. The difference is probably inconsequential to our discussion.

significant to note that most of the references are in John's writings, and in all these cases the word used is *kosmos*, for which John followed Christ's consistent usage in the negative sense of the unregenerate, hostile world-system of sinners under Satan's dominion. The Abbott-Smith lexicon is clear: "in the ethical sense, of the ungodly, the world as apart from God and thus evil in its tendency:"[33] The Arndt/Gingrich lexicon is more explicit: "*the world*, and everything that belongs to it, appears as that which is at enmity w. God, i.e. lost in sin, wholly at odds w. anything divine, ruined and depraved."[34] Supporting references given are: Jn. 8:23;12:25, 31; 13:1; 14:30; 16:11; 18:23; 1 Jn. 4:17; 5:19; 1 Cor. 3:19; 5:10. In the following references also, according to John's consistent usage, it must have a similar meaning, certainly not 'elect.' Norman Douty has made an extensive survey of the lexicons, Bible encyclopedias, and dictionaries, and stated that none of them support the convoluted meanings read into the word by extreme Calvinists.[35]

John 1:29. The words of John the Baptizer: **"Behold, the Lamb of God who takes away the sin of the world!"** - Extreme Calvinists implausibly try to divert our attention by stating that *kosmos* has a geographical sense in other contexts, and thus refers to the elect in all the world. Although the lexicons do show other meanings in other contexts in other books, John is very consistent in his usage of the word as listed above. The rule for determining word meaning is always to see how the same author uses the word first before we examine usage elsewhere. They violate this important word-study principle.

John 3:16-19. This most familiar passage in the Bible should need no explanation: **"'For God so loved the world, that He gave His one and only Son, that whoever believes in him shall not perish but have everlasting life. For God did not send his Son into the world to condemn the world, but to save the world through him. Whoever believes in him is not condemned, but whoever does not believe stands condemned already because he has not believed in the name of God's one and only Son'"**(NIV). However, John Owen's outrageous rewording of it: "God so loved the elect throughout the world, that he gave his Son with this intention, that by him believers might be saved."[36] Not only does this passage speak of Christ's death for the whole unregenerate world of mankind, but it also stipulates its meaning by the clarifying phrase "whoever believes," which Owen unconscionably omits. This passage could not be clearer that faith, not election, is the condition of salvation. Since there are many other passages which use 'whoever,' I will discuss them under that heading.

John 4:42; 1 John 4:14. **"They said to the woman, 'We no longer believe just because of what you said; now we have heard for ourselves, and we know that this man really is the Savior of the world.'"**

Although this is a quotation of the Samaritans, the second reference shows that John is quoting it approvingly: **"And we have seen and testify that the Father has sent his Son to be the Savior of the world"** (NIV). - I can't imagine a clearer statement of God's intent in sending the Son into the world. Since extreme Calvinists insist that the issue is God's intent, let them accept John's transparent statement.

John 12:46-47. **"I have come *as* a light into the world, that everyone who believes in Me may not remain in darkness. And if any one hears My sayings, and does not keep them, I do not judge him; for I did not come to judge the world, but to save the world."** - The meaning of 'world' in verse 47 is likely close to its meaning in verse 46. There the picture is of a world of unregenerate humans in spiritual darkness, upon which the light of Christ has begun to shine. This is the same world which He came to save. To put a spin on it and make it the world of the elect, as extreme Calvinists do, is an unconscionable distortion.

1 John 2:2. **"and He Himself is the propitiation for our sins; and not for ours only, but also for *those of* the whole world."** - Extreme Calvinists, such as R. C. Sproul, find the greatest difficulty in explaining this verse: "On the surface this text seems to demolish limited atonement."[37] Arthur Pink gave the usual extreme explanation, which I have also heard Harold Camping give on Family Radio Network: "When John says, 'He is the propitiation for *our* sins' he can only mean for the sins of *Jewish believers*. . . . When John added, 'And not for ours only, but also for *the whole world* he signified that Christ was the propitiation for the sins of *Gentile* believers *too*, for as previously shown, 'the world' is a term *contrasted* from Israel." This is not a minor slip in Pink's thinking, for he claimed that "the above interpretation is confirmed by the fact that no other is consistent or intelligible." Even more outrageously, he stated that "to insist that 'the whole world' in 1 John 2:2 signifies the entire human race is to undermine the very foundation of our faith."[38] Although the majority of extreme Calvinists would probably agree with this *ethnological* view, some take a *geographical* view (the world outside Asia Minor), or even an *eschatological* view (the future world at Christ's return).[39]

I doubt if one New Testament introduction could be found which would say that John was writing his epistles to Jewish Christians. The consensus would identify his recipients as believers, both Jewish and Gentile, and not directed evangelistically to the unregenerate. As a matter of fact, John is quite explicit in 5:13: "**These things I have written to you who believe in the name of the Son of God, in order that you may know that you have eternal life.**" What right do extreme Calvinists have in limiting John's clear declaration to just Jewish believers? It is only their doctrinal bias which forces them into such an extreme measure.

Just a few verses farther John gives us an unambiguous picture of what he means by 'world' (*kosmos*): **"We know that we are of God, and the whole world lies in *the power* of the evil one** "(5:19). Certainly John is not saying that it is only the Gentile world that is in Satan's grip, nor that it is the world outside of Asia Minor. No, it is the world of unregenerate mankind, set in contrast to believers. Thus very simply John affirmed that Christ's death is a propitiation for the sins of believers and also for the sins of a lost world of sinners.

2 Corinthians 5:19. **"namely, that God was in Christ reconciling the world to Himself, not counting their trespasses against them, and He has committed to us the word of reconciliation."** - In the previous chapter I have shown how reconciliation is a subjective, experiential dimension of Christ's cross-work, based upon verse 18. In order to relate verse 19 to this, it is essential to note the differing tenses of the two participles. In verse 18 it is an aorist participle, thus indicating a completed action—God reconciled us to Himself. But in verse 19 it is a present participle, thus indicating an ongoing action—God was in Christ in the process of reconciling the world to Himself. The world has not been reconciled to God, but His sacrifice was beginning of the process of reconciling a world of unregenerate sinners to Himself. This is totally harmonious with the usage in the Gospel of John discussed above.

Christ died for all, the lost, the ungodly

There are a host of references to Christ's death for all mankind or every man. The meaning of general availability of salvation is confirmed by the additional connection of His death for the ungodly and for the lost, with no contextual basis for limiting any of these expressions to the elect in any of these passages. It is freely granted that there are contexts in which according to common Greek usage, the word 'all' does not mean all without exception. For instance, in 1 Timothy 6:10, the NAS translation reads: **"For the love of money is a root of all sorts of evil."** It is obvious that not all evils spring out of the love of money. Additionally, in John 12:32 there is a contextual basis in 12:20 for understanding the Lord's reference to all kinds of men being drawn to Christ, that is, Gentiles as well as Jews. Indeed, the notion that all men without exception are being drawn to Christ makes no sense theologically or experientially.

Having noted this, I hasten to insist that in at least one of the following references, and probably in all of them, the allusion to 'all' must be a reference to all mankind without exception. For instance, the same extreme Calvinists who deny that all ever means all without exception, do interpret the 'all' in Ephesians 1:11 as having an all inclusive meaning: **"who works all things after the counsel of His will."** As I have shown in chapter 3, this all-inclusive, exhaustive interpretation is the sole proof text for their view of the outworking of the sovereignty of God, and ignores the context and grammar. They must insist upon it here, at the very least, even if it were a totally unique usage. But, of course, it is not a unique usage. 'All' must mean all at least occasionally, if words are to have any meaning. This reminds me of a President of the United States, who answered evasively, that it all depends upon what the meaning of 'is' is. I believe our extreme Calvinistic friends are guilty of the same sort of obfuscation. Let us examine each context.

2 Corinthians 5:14, 15. **"For the love of Christ controls us, having concluded this, that one died for all, therefore all died; and He died for all, that they who live should no longer live for themselves, but for Him who died and rose again on their behalf."** - Paul's point here is straightforward in his use of 'all' three times in the universal sense of 'all mankind,' set in contrast with "they who live," the limited group of born-again ones. Only a theological agenda would keep an interpreter from this simple conclusion. There is nothing in the context or the syntax of the Greek to raise any question about the prima facie interpretation. Extreme Calvinists have labored long to limit these three 'all's, and Douty, Lightner, Walvoord, and many others have extensive discussion in refutation, but I will rest my case on a total lack of evidence to the contrary.[40]

Romans 5:18. **"So then as through one transgression there resulted condemnation to all men, even so through one act of righteousness there resulted justification of life to all men."** Written not long after the passage just discussed, the thought here is closely related. In this verse Paul closely parallels Adam's one transgression with its universal consequences and the one sacrifice of Christ with its universal intent. Of course, Paul does not say that all men were justified, but he does say that Christ's sacrifice did have that as a potential goal. This is implied in the use of the preposition *eis* (unto). Perhaps one of the less frequent usages of *eis*, given by Dana and Mantey, makes it even clearer: "*For the purpose of. . .*" [41] Thus, we could rightly translate by slightly improving on the NIV: **"even so the purpose of one act of righteous was justification that brings life for all mankind."** The purpose for which Christ died is to make justification available to all mankind. Although the Greek construction is difficult, Paul's intent is clear–a provision for all mankind. Thus extreme Calvinists overlook Paul's logic, that just as Adam's integral connection with the whole human race condemned all mankind, just so Christ's identification with all mankind as the Son of Man, dying as a man, had as its goal bringing justification of life to all mankind.

1 Timothy 2:1-6. **"First of all, then, I urge that entreaties *and* prayers, petitions *and* thanksgivings, be made on behalf of all men, for kings and all who are in authority, so that we may lead a tranquil and quiet life in all godliness and dignity. This is good and acceptable in the sight of God our Savior, who desires all men to be saved and to come to the knowledge of the truth. For there is one God, *and* one**

mediator also between God and men, *the* man Christ Jesus, who gave Himself as a ransom for all . . ." Paul's use of 'all' three times in this context gives a solid base for taking all three in their normative sense of 'all without exception.' His exhortation to pray for "all men" (*huper pantōn anthropōn*) could not be limited to all without distinction, but must also imply all without exception. No restriction to the 'elect' is possible here since most Calvinists admit we don't know who the 'elect' are. Although Paul desired that we especially pray for those in authority, it is clear that he was concerned about the salvation of all men as well (2:4), all without exception as well as all without distinction. Paul used the same Greek expression in both verses and plural in both. We could have no way to restrict our prayer focus to the 'elect' who are still unregenerate. For that matter, such a category is never mentioned in the Bible. So when we come to the reference to Christ's "**ransom for all**" (2:6), it is inordinate to try to force such a limitation upon Paul's words because of a theological agenda. As I have shown in the previous chapter, *lutron* is used of the objective ransom price and not of the subjective application to the individual, so presumably the same would be true of the unique word *antilutron*. Thus the logical problem that extreme Calvinists struggle with does not exist.

1 Timothy 4:10. "**For it is for this we labor and strive, because we have fixed our hope on the living God, who is the Savior of all men, especially of believers.**" Apart from the last phrase Paul's statement might seem to promote universalism, which would be a problem for all evangelical interpreters. We could take note of the fact that *anthrōpos* is sometimes used generically, that is, "all mankind."[42] This might be adequate, but Paul significantly added the last phrase "especially of believers" so that there might be no misunderstanding. Was this a mental lapse on Paul's part, which he patched up with the last phrase? No, I suspect he could have gotten his scribe to redo the sentence, if he had wanted to. There must be intrinsic truth in the first part of the sentence, that God is the Savior of all mankind in some real sense, that is, in the objective, potential sense. But we can all agree that Paul's clarifying phrase narrows the truth down to the ultimate reality—that only believers will be saved. Here, as frequently, the truth is two-sided. God really is the Savior of all mankind in a significant sense, as Strong put it, that there really is no obstacle in God's mind to the pardon of sinners, except their lack of repentant faith (see quotation, p. 132-3).

Calvin's explanation does not fit the context: ". . . for the word *sotēr* is here a general term, and denotes one who defends and preserves. He means that the kindness of God extends to all men."[43] Granted that the word can mean this, but this would have Paul saying that God is the defender and preserver of all mankind, and this is patently untrue. God has not chosen to preserve the lives of all believers, let alone unbelievers. Calvin is guilty of fuzzy thinking here.

Titus 2:11. **"For the grace of God has appeared, bringing salvation to all men, . . ."** Although the syntax of the sentence is difficult, modern translations have followed De Wette, Huther, Wiesinger, Alford, Ellicott, Lange, Arndt and Gingrich, F. F. Bruce, and Hiebert in departing from the KJV by connecting *sōtērios* ("bringing salvation") with "to all men."[44] Since we have just seen this common Pauline concept in the above two passages in 1 Timothy, we can understand his reference here also generically. Thus there must be a real sense in which Christ died for all mankind.

Hebrews 2:9. **"But we do see Him who was made for a little while lower than the angels, namely, Jesus, because of the suffering of death crowned with glory and honor, so that by the grace of God He might taste death for everyone."** The context of this verse stresses the identification of the Lord Jesus with the whole human race in His incarnation (2:6-8, 14-18), so it is appropriate that His death should be for the whole human race. It is noteworthy that the apostle uses the singular here, and Alford comments: "If it be asked, why *pantos* (each) rather than *pantōn* (all), we may safely say that the singular brings out, far more strongly than the plural would, the applicability of Christ's death to each individual man."[45]

Luke 19:10. **"For the Son of Man has come to seek and to save that which was lost."** I can't think of any better term than 'lost' to describe all mankind without exception. It certainly cannot be narrowed to the elect only. In a sense this clear statement of our Lord Jesus as to the intent of His coming should end all discussion about the meaning of 'all' and 'whoever' in the passages we are considering. Lightner has put his finger on the key issue:

> The question is, "*Is it scripturally and logically sound always to restrict every usage of the words 'all,' 'whosoever' and 'world' when they occur in a salvation context?*" This is precisely what the limited redemptionist always does and must do. **There may not be a single exception if the limited viewpoint is to stand** (bold mine).[46]

Romans 5:6. **"For while we were still helpless, at the right time Christ died for the ungodly."** The apostle Paul is in good company with the Lord Jesus for plain speaking in affirming Christ's death for the ungodly, whom he characterized in 5:10 as "enemies of God.." Did Christ die for just the ungodly 'elect,' whoever they may be? If He didn't die for all the ungodly, why didn't Paul explain this? The integrity of language and of the word of God is at stake. If Christ didn't mean to say that He came to save all the lost, then why didn't He plainly say so? Only a theological agenda can explain why interpreters try to deny the plain meaning of these passages!

Salvation is offered to "whoever." . Appropriate to the fact that Christ died for a whole world of sinners, lost people, ungodly people, that is, all mankind, are the 110 references to the gospel being offered to "whoever" without restriction. The apostolic *kērugma* (preaching) ought to be the best effort of the apostles to announce it unambiguously. Listen to Peter: **"And it shall be that everyone who calls on the name of the Lord will be saved"** (Acts 2:21); **"Of Him all the prophets bear witness that through His name everyone who believes in Him receives forgiveness of sins"** (Acts 10:43). Hear Paul: **". . . and through Him everyone who believes is freed from all things, from which you could not be freed through the Law of Moses"** (Acts 13:39); **". . . for 'Whoever will call on the name of the Lord will be saved"** (Rom. 10:13). Hear John in his penultimate offer: **"And let the one who is thirsty come; let the one who wishes take the water of life without cost"** (Rev. 22:17b). If Christ did not die for all human beings, and if the majority of human beings can never ever respond to these invitations, then they are an absolute mockery!

PROBLEMS WITH A LIMITED VIEW

The omnibenevolence of God

It is significant that Calvinists tend to emphasize the holiness of God as His foremost attribute, while Arminians emphasize His love. It is not at all clear to me on what basis such a judgment is made. Is not God infinite in all His attributes? Why must we pick one attribute above another? Are they not all in perfect consistency and harmony with one another? Was not Jesus Christ, the God-man, the most perfectly balanced and integrated man who has ever walked this planet?

Any attempt to limit the love of God is a gross distortion of His infinite character. However, the doctrine of limited atonement does just that in that it denies that God loves the non-elect, since it was by His choice that they are non-elect. They have been excluded from the pale of God's love since Christ did not die for them. It is significant that Jerom Zanchius, one of the early advocates of limited atonement, introduced his discussion of predestination with a survey of God's attributes. But there is no mention of the love of God among them.[47] R. C. Sproul defends the limitation of God's love only to the elect: "Is there any reason that a righteous God ought to be loving toward a creature who hates him and rebels constantly against his divine authority and holiness?"[48] Would Sproul or any extreme Calvinists never before their conversion have fitted this description? Let's face it, many Christians once were such!

Christ's words in the Sermon on the Mount are an adequate answer to Sproul: **"But I say to you, love your enemies and pray for those who persecute you"** (Mt. 5:44). Does God ask us to do something He Himself is unwilling to do? Some extreme Calvinists have raised questions about the universality of God's love by distributing tracts with titles such as, "Does God Love You?" or "God May Not Love You!" However, if we communicate a picture of a less than gracious and loving God to sinners, we not only present a caricature, but also an additional obstacle to their repentance and faith.

According to 1 John 4:16 love is of the very essence of God, and God's character cannot change (Heb. 1:11-12; Jas. 1:17). Scripture is quite clear that God loves the sinner but hates his sin, and as long as he remains unrepentant the wrath of God is upon him. But God's love through the cross extends potentially to the whole human race. Deuteronomy 7:7 indicates that God loved Israel, even though not all were among the elect, and Mark 10:21 mentions that Christ loved the rich young ruler although he turned away from Him.

Geisler has put it well: "So, whereas there is *nothing in the sinner* to merit God's love, nonetheless, *There is something in God* that prompts Him to love all sinners, namely, God is all-loving (omnibenevolent). *Hence extreme Calvinism is in practice a denial of the omnibenevolence of God.*" Geisler goes on to show that the root of the problem is philosophical:

> Extreme Calvinists hold a voluntaristic view of God's attribute of love: God can will to love whomever He chooses and not love (or hate) those He wishes. But if this is so, then God is neither essentially loving nor all-loving. In extreme Calvinism, an action is right (whether loving or not) simply because God wills it."[49]

This sounds dangerously close to the arbitrary Allah of the Muslims.[D]

The universal offer of the gospel

The universal offer of the gospel is freely admitted by most extreme Calvinists, except John Gill and a few others, and certainly is biblically clear (Acts 17:30; Mt. 28:18-20). Lightner states the problem: "Why does God invite all men if Christ did not provide for all?" He quotes Richards most aptly: "To us, no maxim appears more certain *than that a salvation offered implies a salvation provided*; for God will not tantalize his creature by tendering them with that which is not in his hand to bestow."[50]

Outstanding advocates of limited redemption, such as Thomas Crawford, admit a "great difficulty" and plead paradox. A. A. Hodge's response to the admitted problem is to claim that general redemptionists who believe in unconditional election have the same problem.[51] Of course, this does not resolve the problem at all, but he is partially right. All who believe in unconditional election do have the problem, but the general redemptionists have it to a lesser degree. If extreme Calvinists were totally honest with inquirers, they would have to say, "My friend, unless you are one of the elect, Christ did not die for you, and indeed you cannot exercise saving faith to be saved." If moderate Calvinists were totally honest, they would have to admit, "My friend, Christ died for you, but unless you are one

---

D. I say this advisedly as one who has lived for seven years in a Muslim country and has a thorough knowledge of Islam and its theology. My recent concordance study of the words for love in the Qur'an confirmed the idea that Allah only loves good, submissive Muslims.

of the elect, you cannot exercise saving faith to be saved." A Christian holding a mediate position can honestly say, "Christ died for you, and no matter who you are, if you exercise repentant faith you will definitely be saved." W. Lindsay Alexander put it so aptly over a century ago: "On this supposition [of limited atonement], the general invitations and promises of the Gospel are without an adequate basis, and seems like a mere mockery; an offer, in short, of what has not been provided."[52] This leads us to the related issue of the personalization of the gospel.

The personalization of the gospel

Although Lightner touched on this problem of personalization in the first edition of his book, he added an appendix to the second edition (1998) to expand his discussion. He had noted the tendency of limited redemptionists to advocate presentation of the gospel in general terms. However, he focuses on three essentials that must be included: "(1) something about personal sin; (2) the substitutionary death of Christ for the sinner; and (3) faith or trust in Christ's finished work." In emphasizing that the gospel must be personalized, he makes it clear that the limited redemptionist cannot personalize #2 without misleading a non-elect sinner.[53] As I have mentioned above, I am concerned that none who hold unconditional election can really personalize #3 since it would be misleading to tell a non-elect sinner that if he will only trust Christ he will be surely saved, knowing full well that the "non-elect" cannot trust Christ.

I am personally very sensitive to the issue of the personalization of the gospel, since all through my teen years I believed that Christ died for the sins of the world, but did not know that He died for **my** sin. I have no doubt now that I was spiritually dead and unregenerate in that condition. Fifty-three years ago I put my name into John 5:24 and came out with an assurance of salvation which has never left.

As a missionary to Pakistan, I found untold thousands in the Christian community who believed that Christ died for the sins of the world, but had no personal relationship with Christ. They were orthodox in their doctrine, but unregenerate. They, like I, desperately needed to have the gospel personalized. I am convinced that hundred of millions of professing Christians worldwide are lost because they have never been brought to the place of personalizing the gospel in their own life. This is not a marginal issue!

Lightner shows how J. I. Packer made a deliberate switch from the personalization of the sinner's sin (#1) to an explicit denial of the personalization of His substitutionary death (#2):

> The fact is, the New Testament never calls on any man to repent on the ground that Christ died specifically and particularly for him. The basis on which the New Testament invites sinners to put faith in Christ is simply that they need Him, and that He offers Himself to

> them, and that those who receive Him are promised all the benefits that His death secured for His people.[54]

Lightner questions what Packer's biblical basis is for such a pronounced shift. Why must one be personalized, when the other may not?

A score of years ago, Rona, a Jewish co-worker of my daughter came for a Bible study. Joyce had been witnessing to her about the deity of Christ. When no one else showed up for the study, I began to go through Isaiah 53 with Rona, showing her that "all we like sheep have gone astray" and that "the Lord has laid on Him the iniquity of us all." I will never forget the look on her face when she exclaimed, "Now I see it, Jesus is **my sin-bearer**." She has gone on with the Lord and has won her gentile husband to Christ.

All Evangelicals are absolutely right to insist that there must be a personalization of the sin issue in the life of the individual. Extreme Calvinists must prove from Scripture that the death of Christ may not be personalized, and explain why we can't sincerely assure any and every sinner that, if he or she will trust Christ, salvation will surely result.

I would also suggest that the lack of assurance among so many Calvinists, as described by Michael Eaton,[55] is a result of their lack of personalization of the death of Christ and emphasis on the notion of human inability to believe. Was it relevant that much of the lack of personal assurance of salvation I observed in Pakistan was among Presbyterians, who constituted about two-thirds of the Christian community there? I only raise the question; it is for Calvinists to answer it.

The requirement of faith obviated

Extreme Calvinism, in effect, denies that faith is the required condition for salvation. If "Christ purchased faith for the elect" as many hold, then faith cannot be a required condition for salvation. Indeed, extreme Calvinism holds that faith is a consequence of regeneration, not a condition. Thus, there would be no point in telling the unregenerate to believe, since they cannot do so, according to this notion. Since by irresistible grace God regenerates the elect, faith becomes an afterthought, a mere extraneous appendage. This is confirmed by the omission of any mention of faith in the five points of Calvinistic theology, the TULIP. This was not accidental or inconsequential. It is so serious that I have devoted chapter 10 to this issue. It was this issue which began my decades-long pilgrimage to my present mediate position.

Lightner confirms that this is the most serious problem with the limited view. In pointing up the total lack of Scriptural support for the notion that Christ purchased faith for the elect, he asks, "If the cross applies its own benefits and is God's only saving instrumentality, what place does faith have? When are man's sins forgiven—at the cross, thus before multitudes of men are ever born, or when man believes and thus appropriates what Christ has done?"[56] Dozens, yes, hundreds of references can be given to support the latter, that faith is the condition of justification, regeneration, eternal life, etc. (cf. ch. 10).

Owen complicated the issue even more by suggesting that since unbelief is a sin for which Christ died, then unbelief is no more a hindrance than other sins in partaking of the fruit if his death.[57] Not only does this eliminate the need for us to actively exercise faith in Christ, but it is directly contradictory to all the many appeals for repentant faith in Scripture. It is clear that Owen's premise is wrong; unbelief is a unique sin, one which if persisted in will lead to condemnation (Jn. 3:18). When Christ accused the Pharisees of an "unforgivable sin," the context indicates that it was a form of hard-hearted unbelief to which He was referring. Unbelief must be distinguished from other sins lest the necessity of faith be totally obviated.

Christ's ministry to the 'non-elect'

If Christ only died for the elect, we should expect that there would be no point in Christ bothering to deal personally with the 'non-elect,' whoever they might be. Calvinists say that since we do not know who the elect are, we must deal with all men. However, the Lord Jesus did not suffer that limitation, it would seem. Yet the Lord Jesus did not restrict His personal dealings to those we might think to be among the elect. We think of the interview with the rich young ruler found in all three synoptic Gospels. The Lord Jesus failed to get him to see his sinfulness and put his trust in Him. He went away sorrowful, and there is no indication that he ever came to faith in Christ. Didn't the Lord Jesus know that he was non-elect, or to put it more bluntly, "reprobate?" Why did He patiently deal with him step by step? Even more astonishing is Mark's statement (10:21) that Jesus loved him. Doesn't God hate the 'non-elect?' Other examples from the Gospels could be given.

Some may respond that the incarnate Christ's omniscience was limited so that He didn't know the elect status of people He dealt with. This is highly unlikely, but possible. However, we can go back to Genesis 4 and see God's dealings with Cain as most relevant. Step by step God remonstrated with Cain, first for his defective offering, then again after he murdered Abel. If Christ didn't die for Cain, and if he had been reprobated in eternity past, why did God bother to deal with him at all? God certainly knew his status. Again we see how the issue ties in with "unconditional election."

The Spirit's conviction of the world

Although I have devoted the whole of chapter 9 to this subject, it is important at this point to show its extreme relevance to the issue of the extent of the cross. Christ's definitive teaching is in the Upper Room Discourse of John 16:8-11, given just hours before the cross:

> **And He [*paraklētos*], when He comes, will convict the world concerning sin and righteousness and judgment; concerning sin, because they do not believe in Me; and concerning**

righteousness, because I go to the Father and you no longer see Me; and concerning judgment, because the ruler of this world has been judged.

Since Christ died for the whole world of lost sinners, it is totally consistent that when the Holy Spirit came to indwell the church on the day of Pentecost that He would convict the world of lost sinners through His church. Conversely, if Christ died only for the elect, it would be totally incongruous for the Spirit to convict the world. Extreme Calvinist Arthur Pink, apparently sensing this incongruity, makes this incredible statement in trying to explain away the clear force of the passage:

> John 16:8-11 does not describe the 'mission' of the Spirit, but sets forth the *significance of His presence* here in the world. It treats **not** of His subjective work in sinners, showing them their need of Christ, by searching their consciences and striking terror to their hearts; that we have there is entirely objective. . . . **We repeat, John 16:8-11 make no reference to the *mission* of the Spirit of God in the world, for during this dispensation, the Spirit has no mission and ministry worldward . . .**(bold mine).[58]

One has only to see our Lord's use of the word 'world' (*kosmos*) in verse 11, to see how outrageously Pink reads into this passage his own narrow theology. Since here, as in 12:31 and 14:30, "the prince of this world" is a reference to Satan, the 'world' which the Spirit convicts must be the world of unregenerate sinners under Satan's control. Calvin so understood this passage: "Under the term *world* are, I think, included not only those who would be truly converted to Christ, but hypocrites and reprobates."[59] In chapter 9 I have shown how Christ's teaching and prediction began to be fulfilled at Pentecost in Acts 2:37.

The universality of resurrection

Lightner devotes two pages to showing that since Christ's death and resurrection is the basis of our bodily resurrection, and since the lost will also be raised bodily, therefore, Christ's death and resurrection do have an impact upon the non-elect.[60] This is a significant argument, but I will not try to develop it here.

CONCLUSION

Since the inductive basis for limited atonement is so slim, it is clear that the major support comes from a deductive attempt to press what is perceived as logic. This can clearly be traced back to Theodor Beza and his colleagues who reverted to the scholastic dependence upon Aristotelian philosophy, since he wrote to Ramus, "I am committed to Aristotle." See appendix K for a full discussion of this. Even Calvin did not affirm this notion.

1. Cited by Laurence M. Vance, *The Other Side of Calvinism* (2nd ed.), p. 406.
2. A. A. Hodge, *The Atonement,* p. 348; Roger Nicole expressed the same opinion to me recently in a personal conversation (February 2001).
3. Jerom Zanchius, *The Doctrine of Absolute Predestination*, p. 53.
4. Canons of Dort, II, 8.
5. John Calvin, *Commentaries,* 1 John 2:2 , *en loc.*
6. Vance, *Calvinism*, 2nd ed., (1999), pp. 404-14. Vance's second edition is a vast improvement over the first since it was totally rewritten. Norman Geisler, Robert Lightner, and Norman Douty are good examples of moderate Calvinists who have written excellent books in refutation of limited atonement and/or extreme Calvinism.
7. Gordon H. Clark, *The Atonement*, 2nd ed., p. 138.
8. Vance, pp. 422-25.
9. R. C. Sproul, *Grace Unknown,* p. 65.
10. W. J. Seaton, *The Five Points of Calvinism* , p. 15.
11. Loraine Boettner, *The Reformed Faith*, p. 14.
12. Charles Hodge, *Systematic Theology*, vol 2, pp. 551-2.
13. John Owen, *The Death of Christ*, pp. 173-4.
14. Vance, p. 426.
15. John Murray, *Redemption*, p. 63.
16. Arthur Pink, *Satisfaction*, p. 264-5.
17. W. E. Best, *Justification before God (Not by Faith),* p. 26, cited by Vance, p. 426.
18. Vance, pp. 422-432.
19. John Gerstner, *Wrongly Dividing the Word of Truth*, p. 123.
20. Ibid, p.33.
21. John Murray, *The Atonement*, p. 27.
22. Vance, p. 409.
23. Daane, p. 35.
24. Augustus Hopkins Strong, *Systematic Theology*, 2nd ed., pp. 772-3.
25. Lewis Sperry Chafer, *Systematic Theology,* 3:93. While I am grateful to God for the teaching of Dr. Chafer during my first year in seminary, I now wonder that if salvation is predetermined, why the elect do not respond to irresistible grace when they first hear the gospel? Many do not! I am now convinced that the answer is that salvation is not predetermined and that grace is not irresistible.
26. Robert P. Lightner, *The Death Christ Died: A Case for Unlimited Atonement*, p. 48.
27. Calvin, *Sermons on Isaiah*, en loc.
28. Calvin, *Commentary on John*, en loc.
29. Edwin H. Palmer, *The Five Points of Calvinism*, p. 43.
30. Calvin, *Commentaries.*
31. Lightner, pp. 60-61.
32. Geisler, *Chosen, but Free,* p. 76.
33. G. Abbott-Smith, *Manual Lexicon*, p. 255.
34. William F. Arndt and F. Wilbur Gingrich, *Greek-English Lexicon*, p. 447.
35. Norman F. Douty, *The Death of Christ*, pp. 41-45.
36. Owen, p. 214.
37. Sproul, *Grace Unknown*, p. 176.
38. Pink, *Sovereignty*, p. 259-260.

39. For a good survey see Vance, pp. 439-443.

40. Douty, pp. 94-106; Lightner, pp. 64-6; Leon Morris, *The Cross in the New Testament*, p.220.

41. Dana and Mantey, p. 104.

42. Arndt and Gingrich, p. 67.

43. John Calvin, *Commentaries*, trans. Wm. Pringle, p. 112.

44. John Peter Lange, *Titus*, p. 16; Arndt and Gingrich, p. 809; F. F. Bruce, *The Letters of Paul*, p. 293. Bruce considered himself an Augustinian.

45. Alford, *Greek Testament*, p. 1459.

46. Lightner, p. 69.

47. Zanchius, pp. 44-76. It should be noted that in the next section (Chapter I) he does discuss the love of God, not as an essential attribute of God, but only in reference to the elect.

48. R. C. Sproul, *Chosen by God*, p. 33.

49. Geisler, p. 86-7.

50. James Richards, *Lectures on Mental Philosophy and Theology* (1846), p. 322, cited by Lightner, pp. 114-5.

51. Lightner, pp. 115-6.

52. W. Lindsay Alexander, *A System of Biblical Theology* (1888), II, p. 111.

53. Lightner, 2nd ed., pp. 149-53.

54. J. I. Packer, *Evangelism and the Sovereignty of God*, p. 68.

55. Eaton, *No Condemnation*, pp. 15-25.

56. Lightner, pp. 124-30.

57. John Owen, *The Works of John Owen*, X, p. 174.

58. Arthur W. Pink, *The Sovereignty of God*, pp. 92, 94.

59. John Calvin, *Commentary on the Gospel According to John*, p. 138.

60. Lightner, pp. 143-45.

The election of God will be a fatal labyrinth for anyone who does not follow the clear road of faith. Thus, so that we may be confident of remission of sins, so that our consciences may rest in full confidence of eternal life, so that we may boldly call God our Father, under no circumstances must we begin by asking what God decreed concerning us before the world began.

-John Calvin

7

GOD'S GLORIOUS FOREKNOWN PURPOSE FOR HIS CHURCH

The apostle Peter was an uneducated fisherman who admitted that he struggled to understand some of the difficult teachings in Paul's letters (2 Pet. 3:15-16). Apparently election and foreknowledge were not among those "hard to understand" teachings, since Peter himself referred to election four times (1 Pet. 1:1-2; 2:6, 9; 2 Pet. 1:10) in his epistles and foreknowledge three times (1 Pet. 1:2, 20; 2 Pet. 3:17) and is quoted presumably twice in Acts (2:23, 4:28) touching on these ideas. The thought that the election of Hebrew Christians scattered among the Gentiles in the diaspora was "**according to the foreknowledge of God**" did not seem hidden, mysterious, or hard to understand for Peter. He addressed them as: "**Elect according to the foreknowledge of God the Father, through sanctification of the Spirit, unto obedience and sprinkling of the blood of Jesus Christ:**" (1 Pet. 1:2, KJV). Later, writing to the Romans, Paul confirmed Peter's understanding of the relationship of foreknowledge to the related truth of foreordination (or preappointment): "**Because those whom He knew beforehand He appointed beforehand to share the likeness of his Son, so that He might be the First-born among many brothers**" (Rom. 8:29, New Berkeley Version).

By denying that election and foreordination are conditioned on God's foreknowledge, contrary to the only two passages which relate these ideas (1 Pet. 1:1-2; Rom. 8:29), four centuries later, Aurelius Augustine of Hippo was the one who made it hard to understand and accept. The majority western church struggled with his view of unconditional election for a century until the Synod of Orange set it aside in AD 529. A millennium later the Reformers revived this doctrine, but even Calvin called it "a horrible decree." The problem was of Augustine's own making, but not a problem to Peter or Paul.

Someone may say, "Didn't Peter use a reverse order in the Pentecost sermon when he said, "**this *Man*, delivered over by the predetermined plan and foreknowledge of God, you nailed to a cross by the hands of godless men and put *Him* to death**" (Acts 2:23)? Please note, however, that Peter was not speaking about our individual election, but about God's plan for the crucifixion of the Messiah. There is a massive difference between the two! Additionally, the syntax of the verse demands more careful investigation, as we shall do.

I suspect it is superfluous for me to emphasize how crucial the issue of conditional or unconditional election is to our whole theology of salvation. Unconditional election was the key point of Augustine's system; it was the key issue for Calvin's system; and it is still the key issue for contemporary Calvinists of whatever stripe they may be. Their concept of total inability is mostly the background against which unconditional election operates. Irresistible grace is essentially the means by which unconditional election is implemented. Limited atonement (particular redemption) is the logical consequence of unconditional election. The other points of Calvinism are ancillary to unconditional election. This is widely recognized by Calvinists and non-Calvinists alike.

Outstanding questions

In the light of sixteen centuries of theological controversy over election since Augustine, there are many problems to be resolved and questions to be answered. Crucial in resolving these issues is the definition of the terms used. In chapter 5 we saw the importance of carefully distinguishing the various Greek words used for the saving work of Christ on the cross. Now we must press the investigation to an examination of foreknowledge, foreordination, and election.

How does foreknowledge differ from election? Does it have a pregnant meaning (like pregnant chads)? At issue are the questions as to whether election is conditional or unconditional; whether individual or corporate. Are God's foreknowledge and His omniscience contingent upon His will? Can a future event be certain in the mind of God without Him having determined it? What do the Greek words for election really mean? In what sense was Israel elect? In what sense was the Lord Jesus elect? How does the election of Jesus Christ fit into the overall picture? How does the Old Testament election of Israel relate to the New Testament doctrine of election? Are election and foreordination synonyms, and if not, how do they relate? Who are the elect ones according to Scripture and how did they become such? How does the Hebrew cultural emphasis upon corporate solidarity color the issue? How much emphasis does the Bible put upon election, after all? How do the context and the grammar of key passages, such as Ephesians 1 and Romans 8–11, impact our understanding? Nothing can be assumed as a given. You can see that we really have our work cut out for us in this investigation.

Two of the most crucial passages for our study of predestination and election are found in the heart of Paul's letter to the Romans: 8:28-30 and 9:1-29. We have already examined 9:1-29 in chapter 3. In order to unpack the truth of 8:28-30 there are two very important Greek words we must study in the context of the whole flow of Paul's thinking in this epistle: *proginoskein* ('to foreknow') and *proorizein* ('to foreordain' or 'to pre-appoint'). *Our word study of the first will indicate that it has its normal primary meaning of 'foreknow' in this and all other contexts. On the other hand, the second, which is a very rare word, has been grossly misunderstood and mistranslated and has nothing to do with 'predestination.'*

In this chapter, we shall do word studies of *proginoskein* and *proorizein* and seek to understand them in the context of Romans. Then in the next chapter we shall investigate the meaning of the words for election in the flow of God's election of Israel, of Christ, of the apostles, and of the Church, especially focusing upon Ephesians 1:3-14.

THE MEANING OF THE TERMS

A Word Study of Foreknowledge

Calvinistic claims

A major premise of Calvinistic theology is that the Greek verb for 'to foreknow' (*proginoskein*) and the noun 'foreknowledge, prescience' (*prognosis)* have a pregnant meaning of "making one the object of loving care or elective love."[1] This is based upon their assertion that the Hebrew word 'to know' (*yada'*) also has this pregnant connotation in a few contexts (Gen. 18:19; Ex. 33:12; Jer. 1:5; Amos 3:2; Hos. 13:5). Additionally, they also claim that the simple Greek word 'to know' (ginoskein) has this connotation in a few contexts (1 Cor. 8:3; Gal. 4:9; 2 Tim. 2:19). Thus when they come to the seven usages of *proginoskein* and *prognosis* in the New Testament, they claim that a pregnant meaning is to be understood there as well, although most will admit that it has no such connotation in the secular or Septuagintal Greek. Their agenda in making this claim is to establish a basis for unconditional, individual election and to explain away the simple truth that God's plan is based upon His foreknowledge. I will show that there is no linguistic basis for this notion of a pregnant meaning and that we must take these words in their normative sense, 'to foreknow' and 'foreknowledge.'

Conditionality. If we understand these words with their normative meanings, two key passages clearly confirm the conditionality of God's foreordination and election: 1 Peter 1:1-2 and Romans 8:28-30. If there were a pregnant meaning, then it would be more difficult to make a case for election being conditioned upon the foreknowledge of God since foreknowledge and election would become essentially synonymous, which is what many of them claim. This then undermines the prima facie reading of 1 Peter 1:1-2 and Romans 8:28-30 as making election or foreordination contingent upon God's foreknowledge. It also raises the question as to how Peter can speak of being "elect according to the foreknowledge of God" and how Paul can write, "whom He foreknew, He also foreordained to be conformed to the image of His Son" if indeed these terms are virtually synonymous and redundant. I have asked my Calvinistic theologian friends this question and the response is always a deafening silence. There must be an essential difference between these terms!

Methodology. Thomas Edgar is a Greek scholar who recently gave a paper on the meaning of *proginoskein.* He objects to the procedure of building the meaning of this word upon the meaning of a Hebrew word or even upon a supposed meaning for *ginoskein.* Even though I had gone into considerable detail in a paper I presented years ago in showing that there is no such pregnant meaning in either *yada'* or *ginoskein,* I am sure that Edgar's point is well taken. Thus I have put this detailed material in appendix F for those who care to check it out. But Edgar is absolutely right that this is a highly questionable methodology. Even if *yada'* did have such a pregnant meaning (and it does not), it says little or nothing about the meaning of the Greek words.[2] This is confirmed by Carson's reference to another category of word-study errors: "14. Problems related to the Semitic background of the New Testament." While recognizing that the Septuagint has influenced the meaning of New Testament Greek words to some extent, he goes on to warn: "But it is to say that it is methodologically irresponsible to read the meaning of a Hebrew word into its Greek equivalent without further ado. The case must be argued."[3] And those who read a pregnant meaning into *ginoskein* put heavy dependence upon their spin on *yada'*.[4]

Yada'. It should be emphasized that the Calvinists claim this pregnant meaning in only five out of 944 times *yada'* is used in the Old Testament, when overwhelmingly it has a meaning directly related to 'to know.' It is used of a personal relationship over 90 times, and this is how it is actually used in the five touted references when examined in their contexts (Gen. 18:19; Ex. 33:12; Amos 3:2; Hos. 13:5; Jer. 1:5). The standard Hebrew lexicon, the BDB version of Gesenius, does not list any such pregnant meaning.[5] It is very significant that the Septuagint translation gives no hint of this pregnant meaning of *yada'* in the way it translates it into the Greek. Also, it is always translated in the KJV by a meaning directly related to knowing, never to choosing. The Calvinistic linguistic scholars who wrote and edited another standard Hebrew wordbook made no mention of any such pregnant meaning either.[6] Thus this notion of a pregnant meaning is a concoction of theologians.[A]

Those theologians who make this claim have to demonstrate that this pregnant meaning is an absolute exegetical necessity in order to make sense of these five passages, not just a mere possibility or feasibility, as Edgar points out. This they cannot do, as I have shown in the appendix. We must always give preference to the primary meaning of a word in every context unless the context demands a secondary or tertiary meaning which has been established in other contexts as well. Even if this pregnant meaning could be supported in these five places, there are several problems. Since these are only five out of 944 usages, it seems to fall under the stricture of another exegetical fallacy of what Carson terms: "4. Appeal to unknown or unlikely meanings."[7] In reality there is no such pregnant meaning in the Hebrew to carry over to the Greek *ginoskein.* See appendix F for a fuller discussion of *yada'.*

Ginoskein. As far as the supposed pregnant meaning of the common Greek *ginoskein* ('to know, perceive') is concerned, it is important to remind the reader of the important principle of Greek word study, that usage, not etymology, is determinative in understanding meaning. Carson lists this as the number one fallacy: "the root fallacy."[8] Even if *ginoskein* had such a pregnant meaning in a few contexts (which it does not), this would not prove anything about the usage of *proginoskein.* These are two different words, although related. Chamberlain's point, which I have quoted repeatedly, is exceedingly important, that every letter added to a Greek root changes the meaning, sometimes very significantly.[9]

Ginoskein is used about 223 times in the New Testament and in the KJV is always translated by some word directly related to knowing, never with a connotation of choosing.[10] There is no hint of an elective connotation in secular Greek either. Neither Thayer nor Abbott-Smith lexicons mention any such pregnant meaning. While Bertram in *TDNT* does mention an elective connotation for *ginoskein* in the Septuagint, the seven references he gives do not support his contention in the least. Arndt and Gingrich give two Septuagint references in support of an elective connotation, but *ginoskein* does not even occur in Hos. 12:1 and the context of Amos 3:2 is totally unsupportive.[11]

In all three of the touted New Testament contexts (1 Cor. 8:3; Gal. 4:9; and 2 Tim. 2:19) the idea of knowledge as a personal relationship fully explains the meaning. This connotation of 'knowing' meaning a personal relationship is indeed found in the Hebrew, the Greek, and in the English. When we ask people, "Do you know Christ as your personal Savior?" we are

---

A. Although I am not a great fan of the KJV, the way in which the King James translators rendered a word in the years before 1611 gives a good idea how a word was understood by the translators of the day, before the Calvinistic-Arminian controversy erupted in the years immediately following, as seen in the Synod of Dort (1618-19) and the Westminister Assembly (1647-8). Cf. Young's *Concordance*, App. 52-3.

talking about a relationship. This fully satisfies the Biblical usage as well, without reading 'choice' into it. Here also Carson's stricture #4 about unknown or unlikely meanings is relevant since they claim only three out of 223 usages. Please do check out these passages for yourself and see my full discussion in appendix F.

Proginoskein, prognosis.

This brings us to the words in question, which are the verb, *proginoskein* and the noun, *prognosis.* Let us first focus on the way they are used outside the New Testament. There is no pregnant connotation of elective choice hinted at in the Septuagint, in classical Greek usage, in the Koine Greek as found in the papyrii and inscriptions, in Philo or Josephus, nor in the church fathers before Augustine.[12] The verb simply means, "*to know beforehand, foreknow*" and the noun, "*foreknowledge,*"[13] or 'prescience.' Although sometimes New Testament writers do use Greek words in a unique sense, here the burden of proof is upon those who claim this elective force for *proginoskein*. For a fuller discussion of the classical and Hellenistic Jewish usage see appendix F.

The lexicons. Thus the only argument which they could have left comes from reading this supposedly pregnant meaning into the seven usages in the New Testament. Thayer's lexicon doesn't give any such meaning but does refer to Meyer, Philippi and Van Hengel as opposing it. Neither Liddell-Scott-Jones nor Abbott-Smith's lexicons hint at any such meaning. Arndt and Gingrich do list a secondary meaning, "choose beforehand" but give no linguistic support. They only refer to the two Romans usages and four German theological articles for support[14]. However, theology must be built upon linguistic and exegetical data, not the reverse. As we examine the New Testament usages, we will see that this data is totally lacking. As I have shown in my reference to lexicographers, they too are fallible and have their biases, so we must check out their work at every stage.[B]

The church fathers. It is also very significant as to how the early church fathers understood the word. Clement of Rome used it of God's foreknowledge of all things (2 Clement 9:9). At least three of the early fathers, Justin Martyr (*Apol 1, xliv, xlv & xxviii; Dial cxli*), Origen (*Ag Celsus* Bk. 2, ch. 20), and Jerome (*Ag Pelagius* Bk. 3), argue that God's foreknowledge must not be understood as involving fatal necessity or compulsion by God, but that the events foreknown by God are done by men of their own free choice.[15]

Complete New Testament usage

Some writers only examine the usages where God is the subject. Edgar

---

B. See especially my expose of the outrageous distortions of data in *TDNT* in my word studies of repentance and conversion in appendix G.

shows that this is a defective methodology which implies that a verb changes its meaning dependent upon who the subject is. Other verbs do not change meaning when God is the subject. If this principle is allowed, how can we know when meanings are the same or when they are different? It all becomes subjective. Since God uses human language to reveal Himself, if word meanings change when used of God, all objective communication is lost. Since there are other Greek words which God could have used to communicate that supposed pregnant meaning more explicitly, why would He have chosen to obscure the communication process?[16]

No, all the usages of the verb and noun must be examined, and in Acts 26:5 and 2 Peter 3:17 the verb is used with exactly the same meaning as in the rest of Greek literature. In Acts 26:5 in his testimony before Agrippa, referring to the Jews Paul says: **"since they have known about me for a long time previously . . . that I lived as a Pharisee according to the strictest sect of our religion."** Here the meaning was simply to know something about a person beforehand. In 2 Peter 3:17 Peter uses it to refer to his readers' prior knowledge of the distortions of Scripture by unprincipled men. There is neither the possibility nor the claim in either of these passages that the word means anything other than its primary, well-established meaning.

So as we turn to Peter's use of these words in Acts 2:23, 1 Peter 1:1-2, and 1 Peter 1:20, and Paul's use in Romans 8:29-30 and 11:2, we must first of all seek to find out if this well established primary meaning makes sense in these contexts also. We must not switch to some supposed pregnant secondary meaning for theological reasons. I must admit that for a score of years I had bought into this theological spin on these words. But as I reexamined the evidence, I realized that the mind is a slippery thing and that most of us can easily be persuaded of something which has little or no basis in fact. Edgar points out that none of the commentators on Romans who claim a pregnant meaning give even one example of such usage to support their claim.[17] Let us examine the five contexts where this word refers to God as the subject, starting with the earliest.

God's foreknown plan for the cross. On the day of Pentecost the apostle Peter announced to Israel that the Messiah's death and resurrection were according to God's foreknown plan as prophesied by David:

> **. . . this *Man*, delivered up by the predetermined plan and foreknowledge of God, you nailed to a cross by the hands of godless men and put *Him* to death. And God raised Him up again, putting an end to the agony of death, since it was impossible for Him to be held in its power** (Acts 2:23-4).

The Greek reads: "*Touton tē hōrismenē boulē kai prognosei tou theou ekdoton, . . .*"

We come to Peter's (or Luke's) use of the noun *prognosis* here with the straightforward linguistic procedure in mind, that if the primary meaning fits, we must look for no other. Here Peter's meaning is transparent, that our omniscient God worked out His eternally fixed plan by means of His absolute foreknowledge of all the human factors which went into the crucifixion—the motivations and situations of Judas Iscariot, the Jewish leaders, Herod the Tetrarch, Pontius Pilate, the Roman soldiers, the mob, etc.

Calvinists, such as S. M. Baugh, would like to subvert the simplicity of Peter's statement by claiming that God's "appointed purpose" and His "foreknowledge" are essentially synonymous. He does this by identifying the syntactical construction here as 'hendiadys.' Baugh does not quote any grammar or lexicon to support his interpretation: "By using one article for the two nouns *purpose* and *foreknowledge*, Peter is expressing a close interconnection between the two." In his footnote, in trying to refute Godet's classic exegesis, he goes on: "In point of fact the two nouns are expressly united."[C]

I have found three explanations of the Greek usage of 'hendiadys.' The Blass-Debrunner-Funk grammar has: "The co-ordination of two ideas, one of which is dependent upon the other (hendiadys), serves in the NT to avoid a series of dependent genitives:"[18] Turner in Moulton's classic *Syntax* supports this, and the BAGD lexicon gives examples but no clarification. Although Wallace does not use the term, he has an extended discussion of about 50 impersonal constructions having one article, a noun, *kai*, and a 2nd noun (TSKS), as in Acts 2:23. It seems that hendiadys is such a vague construction with so many variants that it is difficult to make dogmatic generalizations about its significance. Perhaps this is why most other grammarians chose not to discuss this figure of speech. However, following Tom Edgar's cue, I have located 29 clear examples: 12 without any article, 12 with one article, and 5 with two articles. Although Wallace gives Acts 1:25 as the only example of identical meanings of both nouns out of the 50 usages of TSKS he has examined, I question even that one, since Judas's ministry was dependent upon his apostleship. This leaves no clear example of identity, whether with no article, one article or two articles.[D]

Baugh, however tries to make us believe that hendiadys makes foreknowledge in Acts 2:23 "expressly united" or close to identical with God's

---

C. S. M. Baugh, "The Meaning of Foreknowledge," in Schreiner & Ware, *Grace of God, Bondage of the Will*, I, p. 190. Note that Baugh makes a barefaced statement about hendiadys without any reference to grammars, lexicons, or parallel syntactical examples in support of his contention.

D. Of the 29 other uses of hendiadys I checked, 8 are from Luke's writings(Lk. 2:47; 21:12, 15; Acts 1:25; 14:17 do; 20:21; 23:6) and two from Peter's (1 Pet. 4:14; 2 Pet. 1:16), none of which are unambiguously equivalent connotations, manifesting a great diversity of relationships. It should be obvious that Luke's and Peter's usage is most significant. In my tabulation I concluded that 13 out of 29 are distinct but hard to classify as to which is dependent upon or modifies which. Only in 4 examples is the second noun dependent upon or modifies the first. However, in 12 examples the first noun seems to be dependent upon the second. My conclusions on Acts 2:23 differ from Wallace's for the above reasons.

determinate counsel because of the use of one article to govern both nouns (similar to the Granville Sharp rule). Wallace made it very clear, however, that the Granville Sharp rule only applies "to personal, singular, non-proper nouns."[19] Indeed, Baugh's spin on hendiadys directly contradicts both the description in the BDF grammar and the force of the 29 parallel examples I have examined

According to this definition, Baugh may be right that this is an example of hendiadys, but he seriously misunderstands the syntax of it. Wallace lists several possibilities for the usage of *kai* (and), including the ascensive, the contrastive, and the explanatory functions. Dana and Mantey list three uses of *kai*, including the adversative.[20]

Baugh is also mistaken in thinking that the use of a single article is definitive here. Wallace shows that this TSKS construction of two substantives with one article joined by 'and' (*kai*) can either be distinct, identical, or overlap semantically.[E] So the use of the article says nothing about the relationship of the two nouns, only the context can do that. Overall, there are three times as many examples of the first noun being dependent upon or modifying the second than the reverse. If this pattern carries over into Acts 2:23 (and many are significantly from Peter's lips and pen and Luke's pen), the outworking of God's appointed purpose depends upon His foreknowledge. And unless we believe that God coerced Judas, the Jewish leaders, Pilate, etc., to do what they did, the straightforward way for God to work out His appointed purpose was to accomplish it by His omniscient foreknowledge. Thus the *prima facie* understanding of Peter's words is perfectly comprehensible as they stand. Except that the translation could be fine tuned accordingly: **"This man was handed over to you by God's appointed purpose through His foreknowledge."** So the syntax of this verse not only leads us to reaffirm the primary meaning of prescience, but also supports the point I have been making elsewhere that God's foreknowledge cannot be contingent upon His will, but the reverse must be true, lest we end up making God's omniscience a contingent attribute, which is unthinkable. (cf. ch. 3, p. 29, 39)

Elect according to foreknowledge. In 1 Peter 1:1-2 we find the noun *prognosis* used in its primary sense, with absolutely no contextual reason to shift to a disputed secondary meaning, except for a theological bias. **"Peter, an apostle of Jesus Christ, to the elect who are sojourners of the Dispersion in Pontus, Galatia, Cappadocia, Asia, and Bithynia, according to the foreknowledge of God the Father, in sanctification of the**

E. Wallace, *Grammar*, pp. 735, cf. 286-90; Thomas Edgar examined 17 examples of hendiadys given as examples in Robertson, BDF, Turner, and Beekman and Callow. He lists: Jas. 4:2; 5:10; Mt. 4:16; Mk. 6:26=Mt. 14:9; Lk. 2:47; 21:15; Acts 1:25; 14:17; 23:6; Rom. 1:5; Col. 1:28; Tit. 2:13; 2 Tim. 1:10; 4:1; 1 Pet. 4:14; 2 Pet. 1:16. I would add Josephus, Antiquities, 12, 98; Polyb.(do); Mt. 24:36; Lk. 21:12; Acts 14:17 (do); 20:21; Jas. 4:2; 2 Cor. 12:21; Eph. 3:12, 18; Col. 2:22; 2 Th. 2:1; Rev. 1:9; 9:15.

Spirit unto obedience and sprinkling of the blood of Jesus Christ: Grace to you and peace be multiplied" (ASV). Although the phrase, "according to the foreknowledge of God the Father" is separated in the Greek (as best represented by the ASV) from the word 'elect' (*eklektois*) by the geographical location of the dispersed Christians, most commentators take them as connected. It is highly unlikely, as Edgar points out, that the prepositional phrase would qualify both the nominative of the writer and the dative of the addressees. Therefore, the meaning is quite straightforward that Peter is writing to "the elect according to the foreknowledge of God."

One wonders how the meaning could be other than this simple statement, for certainly God's foreknowledge must be the basis for everything He does. God the Father does not turn off His omniscience. We have yet to investigate the contextual meaning of 'elect' and 'election', but whatever they do mean, it makes perfect sense that it is according to His foreknowledge. If I may put it bluntly, God does not close His eyes and throw darts.

There is one philosophical objection to Peter's simple statement. I was taught many years ago that God cannot know that which He has not decreed, which notion I have found stated by both Calvinists and extreme Arminians (and have dealt with in chapter 3). Not only does that notion contradict Peter's simple statement, but it also makes God's omniscience a contingent attribute, subject to the activity of His decretive will. This is a highly objectionable view in that it denies the infiniteness of one of God's essential and necessary attributes. God's actions always flow from His attributes, never the reverse.

There is another attempt by some interpreters to undermine the simplicity of Peter's statement. Some would claim that the Greek preposition *kata* ('according to') with the accusative case can be watered down to mean "in agreement with."[21] But the uses of *kata* with the accusative are common and well understood and explained in the standard lexicons and grammars. The one category which best fits the context as listed by Arndt and Gingrich would be: "5. of the norm . . . *according to, in accordance with, in conformity with, corresponding to.* a. to introduce the norm which governs something–"[22] Thus we must understand God's foreknowledge as the norm or standard[23] which governs His elective work. So the prepositional phrase, "according to the foreknowledge of God," clearly governs the verbal noun *eklektois*. This is simple, straightforward, and clear, that is, as long as we don't come to this verse with a philosophical or theological agenda. (I will discuss the meaning of *eklektois* in the next chapter.)

Those who give *proginoskein* a pregnant, elective force have another serious problem. If 'election' and 'foreknowledge' both have an elective idea, then Peter is merely expressing the redundant tautology that we are elect according to the elective choice of God. Let us not insult Peter and the Holy Spirit with such inanity (pardon my bluntness). But we will look at this passage again in the next chapter in connection with the meaning of 'election.'

God's foreknown plan for His Messiah. Peter's third reference to foreknowledge is in the same context as the previous. He echoes the language of Acts 2:23-4 in speaking first of the sacrifice of Christ and then of the resurrection, according to God's foreknown plan: **"knowing that you were not redeemed with perishable things like silver or gold from your futile way of life inherited from your forefathers, but with precious blood, as of a lamb unblemished and spotless, the *blood of* Christ. For He was foreknown before the foundation of the world, but has appeared in these last times for the sake of you who through Him are believers in God, who raised Him from the dead and gave Him glory, so that your faith and hope are in God"** (1 Pet. 1:18-21).

Since this passage is just a few verses away from the preceding use of the word, it is a fair to say that Peter uses the verb here with the same primary connotation it has consistently had in all Greek usage hitherto. Only if the context should **demand** another pregnant meaning may we stray from this. As we focus on the context we see again that the primary meaning of 'foreknowledge' or 'prescience' makes perfect sense.

Context again is so important. The persecuted Christians to whom Peter was writing needed to know that the salvation-hope of which they had become partakers is rooted in the plan of the omniscient God foreknown from before creation, which therefore will surely be consummated "at the revelation of Jesus Christ" (vv. 7, 13), that it is a "salvation ready to be revealed in the last time" (v. 5), and that the prophets not only predicted the sufferings of Christ, but also "the glories to follow" (v. 11). In other words, our omniscient God, who knows the end from the beginning, had a foreknown plan for His Messiah, which He is working out in the cross (vv. 11, 18-19) and resurrection (vv. 3, 21), and will keep believers by His power (vv. 4-5) until Messiah's return. Although they are suffering, their hope for the future is not in vain. Since the context is focusing upon the death and resurrection of Christ, it is unlikely that Peter is referring to any 'elective choice' of Christ.

Additionally, those who would like to see some elective choice here in Peter's usage, need to face a serious Christological problem their spin raises. If we should try to see some 'forechoice' in this verse,[F] a conflict arises with our concept of who Jesus Christ actually is. He was not one first-century Jewish man chosen by God from among many to be the Messiah. Indeed, as James Daane has pointed out, like Isaac of old, the Lord Jesus was supernaturally brought into being to be the Elect (Choice) One of God. Isaac, the ancestor of God's first chosen people, was supernaturally prepared by a miraculous birth (Isa. 43:1, 6, 7, 20, 21). There was no pre-

---

F. As the NIV renders it, which is clearly in error.

existing nation of Israel, which God then chose from among other nations.[G]

In a parallel way there was no extant man named Jesus of Nazareth whom God chose to be His elect Messiah. Through the virgin birth He was supernaturally prepared to be His Elect (Choice) One. I shall subsequently discuss more in detail what is implied in calling the Lord Jesus the Elect One (Lk. 9:35). But it cannot mean that He was one extant individual chosen from among many to be the Messiah, which notion was the basis of more than one ancient heresy. Therefore, to read some elective choice into 1 Peter 1:20 is to lead to Christological heresy. Far better to simply take the word in its primary meaning. That the Lord Jesus is elsewhere referred to as the Father's Elect Servant (Is. 42) is not at issue; the question is whether this is what Peter is referring to here. And we will have to investigate the meaning of that idea in the next chapter. For now, let us turn to the apostle Paul's usage.

Israel's failure anticipated. In understanding Paul's use of *proginoskein* in Romans 11:1-3 it is absolutely imperative to consider the immediately preceding context: "**I ask then, Did God reject his people? By no means! I am an Israelite myself, a descendant of Abraham, from the tribe of Benjamin. God did not reject his people, whom he foreknew. Don't you know what the Scripture says in the passage about Elijah—how he appealed to God against Israel: 'Lord, they have killed your prophets and torn down your altars; I am the only one left, and they are trying to kill me'?**" This is a major context in which Calvinists see a pregnant meaning in *proginoskein* and a few modern translations (excluding the NIV and the NAS) have translated it that way. Although it is true in a sense that God chose Israel, the urgent question is whether this is the point that Paul is making here. The context shows that it is not!

This is in the broader context of Paul's argument of Romans 9–11, that although God sovereignly chose the nation Israel, He also acted justly and righteously in setting Israel aside temporarily because of their unbelief in the Messiah (9:6-29). They missed the way of faith and now God is turning to the Gentiles as well with a universal message (9:30–10:15). In 10:16-21 Paul makes the point very forcefully that both Moses and the prophets had said that Israel had God's word and rejected it, but that Israel would be set aside in favor of another people. First he quoted Isaiah's prediction (Isa. 53:1) that Israel would not believe the Messiah. Then he quoted Moses' prediction that God would make Israel "jealous by that which is not a nation" (Deut. 32:21). Finally in 10:21 he quoted Isaiah's prediction: "**'I was found by those who**

G. "On the basis of the Old Testament narrative concerning Abraham and the birth of his son, and Paul's New Testament interpretation of this Old Testament narrative, it must be said that the nation of Israel is not viewed as one extant nation among many, which is then selectively chosen by God as his elect people. Rather, Israel as the object of God's election not only does not exist but even has no possibility of existence apart from God's elective and creative action." (James Daane, *The Freedom of God*, p. 101.)

sought me not, I became manifest to those who did not ask for me,' but as for Israel he says, 'All the day long I have stretched out my hands to a disobedient and obstinate people'" (Isa. 65:1-2).

So not only did God foreknow that Israel would fail and be supplanted by other people in His plan, but He had Moses (the Law) and Isaiah (the Prophets) explicitly predict this. So when we cross that artificial divider into chapter 11 and find Paul stating that God foreknew Israel, *we must not depart from the primary meaning of the word without doing violence to this immediate context*. Most commentaries and theologians have totally missed this preceding context.

Someone may respond that Paul did not say that God foreknew something about Israel, but that He foreknew Israel. However, in connection with Romans 8:29, Tom Edgar has pointed us to the parallel syntax of Acts 26:5, where Paul testified to Festus and Agrippa: **"So then, all Jews know my manner of life from my youth up, which from the beginning was spent among my *own* nation and at Jerusalem; since they have known about me for a long time previously, if they are willing to testify, that I lived *as* a Pharisee according to the strictest sect of our religion."**

> The most significant thing is the syntax. The object of the verb *proginosko*, "foreknow," is the personal pronoun, "me," *me*. Paul says, "they knew *me* before from the beginning." The passage is clear. The Apostle Paul says very specifically, *proginoskontes me . . . hoti kata . . . ezesa Pharisaios*, "foreknowing me . . . that I lived according to the strictest sect of our religion, a Pharisee." Thus, *to foreknow a person* means to *know something about that person beforehand.* The personal object implies no so-called personal intimate ramifications. . . . This is common to Greek verbs, although it may be confusing for beginning Greek students. Often, Greek verbs take an object where some prepositional idea such as, "about, or something about," seems to be "built into" the Greek term but must be supplied in English.[24]

Edgar goes on to give Hebrews 6:9 and Matthew 12:33 as other examples of this syntactical usage. Thus in Romans 11:2 the Greek idiom signifies that God knew something about Israel beforehand. It was not some unforeseen event that disrupted God's plan!

Then Paul raised the question as to the permanence and totality of that setting aside and goes on to argue that it is not total (Rom. 11:4-10) and it is not final (11:11-32). If we take *proginoskein* in its primary sense, Paul's argument makes perfect sense in the flow of his thought. God knew ahead of time and predicted that Israel would fail to fulfill His purpose for them, indeed, that they would reject their Messiah and be replaced by another people. But this has not upset His plan and purposes in the least or nullified the word of God (9:6) since He foreknew all along all that would transpire. He foreknew that after the rejection of the Lord Jesus there would be a remnant of true Jewish believers (Rom. 11:4-10). He also foreknew that Gentile wild branches would be grafted onto the root of Abraham (11:11-24). He foreknew and has given His prophets to predict an end-time restoration of Israel (11:23-32). But in the meanwhile God's main thrust is to save Gentiles through the church and the ministry of apostles (missionaries) to the Gentiles like Paul and his colleagues (11:11-24). Since God foreknew the whole future of Israel when He chose them, the word of God has not failed (9:6). So we see that the primary meaning makes perfect sense in the context. This is not to deny that God chose Israel in a sense, but this is not the point in 11:2.

Therefore when we come back to the two theologically sensitive passages, we must in no way try to explain away the obvious conditionality of both passages. Romans 8:28-30 will be carefully examined later in this chapter, and 1 Peter 1:1-2 again in the next. But before we can understand Romans 8, we must carefully study the other key term there.

A Word Study of *Proorizein*

No predestination in the Bible. Through the influence of the Latin Vulgate translation, *proorizein* has been translated mainly as "to predestinate." However, this is a very rare word, and there is a serious question as to how it should actually be translated. It never occurred in the Septuagint Greek translation of the Old Testament. It is found only once in the classical Greek literature before the New Testament (Demosthenes) and a few times in secular Greek from the third to the fifth centuries AD. I would suggest that when we examine its six occurrences in four contexts in the New Testament and the meaning of its cognates *horizein* and *aphorizein*, as well as these rare secular usages, a meaning like 'to preappoint' emerges. *Since the idea of "destiny" is not at all present in this group of words, the translation "to predestinate" is totally inappropriate.* Perhaps Jerome was influenced by Augustine's theology in his Vulgate translation. Albeit, we must break from a clearly erroneous translational tradition. Erasmus said that the "Vulgate swarmed with errors."[25]

Procedure. We face a serious methodological problem in determining the meaning of this word because of its rarity. Although we must be careful to avoid the "root fallacy" that Carson and others have warned about, he points out that in the case of rare words, we really have no other alternative but to check out the root and other related words, as mentioned above.[26] I am astonished that I have found very little serious investigation of *proorizein* in the literature. Amazingly, Schmidt in Kittel's *TDNT* does not even give the secular Greek references, but simply refers to "this comparatively late and rare word."[27] We must do what Schmidt has totally failed to do, examine those references.

Secular usage. Let us start by examining the one pre-Christian classical usage in Demosthenes (IV BC; 31, 4). This is in the context of a court case in which Demosthenes was trying to recover an inherited house from Onetor, who had defrauded him. In court he stated: "To prove that these statements of mine are true, that he [Onetor]even now declares that the land is mortgaged for a talent, but that he **laid claim** to two thousand drachmae more on the house, . . ." The word translated "laid claim" is *prosōrisato*.[28] My immediate reaction was probably that of the reader: "What in the world has this got to do with predestination?" Some time later it occurred to me that it is wonderful to know that God has laid claim to us. But this hardly relates to predestination. Classical scholar Arthur Way took note of Demosthenes' usage in his paraphrased translation of Romans 8:29: **"Long ere this He knew our hearts, long ere this He claimed us (as a man claims property by setting his landmarks thereon) as those whom He should mould into the very likeness of His own Son, . . ."**[29] The noun *proorismos* seems to have been used by Hippocrates of the early determination of a disease (Hp praec. 3). In a romance novel of Egypt by Heliodorus in the third century AD, there is a reference to appointing the day of a wedding beforehand (7, 24, 4). There are a few other fifth- and sixth-century, less-relevant examples I have not yet located, so let us move on.

Cognates. It is most instructive to examine the root word *horizein*, which "means 'to limit,' 'to set the limit,' and then fig. 'to fix,' 'to appoint'" in the secular and in the Septuagint, as well as the eight occurrences in the New Testament, according to *TDNT*. Five of the usages are Christological: Luke 22:22; Acts 2:23; 10:42; 17:31; and Romans 1:4. In each of Luke's usages Christ was **appointed** by the Father to a ministry, either of the cross or as judge. In Romans 1:4 Christ was "**designated** the son of God with power by the resurrection." The compound *aphorizein*, used 10 times in the New Testament, means 'to separate,' and is frequently used of God separating, marking off, or appointing someone for His service (Rom. 1:1; Gal. 1:15; Acts 13:2). Schmidt confirms: "In connection with what was said about *horizo*, it seems that at the heart of the NT we find the principle of God separating, i.e., marking off for His service."[30]

New Testament usage. Thus when we come back to consider the possible impact of these meanings upon the usage of *proorizein* in the New Testament, we should consider that in Acts 4:28 the main idea is that God's power and counsel had **previously appointed** the crucifixion to happen. In 1 Corinthians 2:7 Paul is referring to the wisdom of God in the gospel of the cross, which although previously hidden and now revealed was **previously appointed** for the Church's glory. We should consider that in Romans 8:29-30 the main idea is that God has **previously appointed** those who love God "to be conformed to the image of His Son." In Ephesians 1:5 we see a very similar meaning that God has **previously appointed** His elect Church "to adoption as sons." In Ephesians 1:11 we might consider that the Church has been **previously appointed** to obtain the inheritance which God has planned for us. Thus in all four contexts the connotation harmonious with the root meaning "previously appointed" makes perfect sense. This also fits with the extrabiblical usage. But as mentioned earlier, the idea of destiny is not found in *horizein, aphorizein,* or in the limited secular use of *proorizein,* and therefore it should not be imposed upon the six New Testament usages. I will examine the theologically significant contexts in more detail below.

Versions. Since we have so little primary data to go on to determine the meaning of *proorizein*, there are two other ways to confirm the soundness of our conclusions above. How did the early Christian translations of this word render it and how did the earliest church fathers understand it? One of the earliest versions was the Syriac Peshitta, which Lamsa has translated. Here are his renderings of the Peshitta: "had previously decreed" (Acts 4:28); "But God **ordained** it before the world" (1 Cor. 2:7); "He knew them in advance and He **marked** them with the likeness of the image of His Son, that He might be the first-born among many brethren. Moreover, those whom He marked in advance, He has called, . . ." (Rom. 8:29-30); "And He **marked** us with His love to be His from the beginning, and adopted us to be sons . . ." (Eph. 1:5); "By whom we have been chosen, as He **marked** us from the beginning so He wanted to carry out everything according to the good judgment of His will" (Eph. 1:11).[31] Additional study will have to be done of some of the other early versions to approach certainty, but this will have to suffice for now.

Patristic usage. Lampe has given us over thirty references to *proorizein, proorisis, proorismenos, proorismos, prooristikos* from the early church fathers. John of Damascus (VIII AD) distinguished *proorizein* from *proginoskein.* Paul of Samosata (III AD) wrote of God **preordaining** the incarnation through the virgin. Marcellus's (IV AD) comment on wisdom in Prov. 8:23 is that the dispensations were **preappointed**. Irenaeus (II AD) wrote that "when the number is fulfilled which He has **preappointed** with him, all will be raised [from the dead]." Clement (I-II AD) referred to "the love of God, which He has **preappointed** before the foundation of the world." He also wrote of how [God] of Himself distributed benefit to Greeks and barbarians and to those **preappointed** from among them, having been called according to the seasonal (?) dwelling." Nilus of Sinai (V AD). commented on Mt. 25:34 to the effect that their struggles were **preappointed** and the virtues of those whose approaching struggles were seen (?). Ignatius (I-II AD) addressed his epistle to the Ephesians "to the ancient church which Almighty God had **preappointed.**" Lastly, there is a relevant use of the noun *proorismos* in Origen's (III AD) comment on Rom. 1:3: "To him the beginning of the calling and justification is not a **preappointment**, for if this was the beginning of the order and if those who were stealthily introduced made a powerful persuasion using improper reasoning concerning [his] origin, indeed, the foreknowledge is before the **preappointment**." I take it that in none of the patristic references does the meaning "to predestinate" emerge, and in all of them the rendering 'to preappoint' makes perfect sense.[32] Origen seems also to affirm the point I am making about foreknowledge necessarily preceding preappointment, although translation from Lampe's brief citation is difficult.

Lexicons. Since this exhausts the primary sources, let us check the secondary ones. John Parkhurst's 16th century lexicon does not list 'predestinate' among the meanings: "II. To decree or ordain before-hand, to fore-ordain, fore-appoint."[33] Thayer's lexicon has, "*to predetermine, decide beforehand,* Vulg. [exc. In Acts] *praedestino, . . . to foreordain, appoint beforehand,* Ro. viii.29 sq.; *tina eis ti*, one to obtain a thing. Eph. i.5 . . ." Please note that a century ago, Thayer, although noting the Vulgate rendering, did not list 'predestinate' among the meanings in English. Similarly, the Abbott-Smith lexicon did not include 'predestinate' among the meanings. On the other hand, Arndt and Gingrich, after referencing the limited secular usage, gave, "*decide upon beforehand, predestine* of God" with the biblical references, and they seem not to have investigated the patristic usage, other than an allusion to Ignatius.[34] I will not dignify Schmidt's totally inadequate and biased article in *TDNT* by quoting it. Lastly, it should be noted that Lampe did not give 'predestinate' as a meaning which he found in the church fathers, but rather "predetermine." I believe that the references I have given above suggest that even this word may be too strong, and that "preappoint" would be more appropriate.

Modern translations. It is significant that a number of other modern translations besides Arthur Way have abandoned "predestinate," in breaking free from the precedent of the Vulgate. Reference Romans 8:29 in the New English Bible: "**For God knew His own before ever they were, and also ordained that they should be shaped in the likeness of His Son., . . .**" Charles B. Williams has "**marked off as His own**," J. B. Rotherham "**fore-appointed**," A. T. Robertson has "**pre-appointed**," William F. Beck has "**appointed long ago**," the Berkeley Modern Language Bible, "**appointed beforehand**," and the Revised Version (1886), American Standard Version (1901), James Denney, Alfred Marshall, and F. F. Bruce all have "**fore-ordained**," which is not greatly different from 'preappointed.' Ordained has to do with God's order and appointment to service as did the use of *horizein* in reference to Christ's ministry, where appointment is a more appropriate rendering.

It seems to me that generation after generation of translators should have recognized the extreme theological significance of this word and researched back before the Latin Vulgate to its primary usage. Apparently only the above translators really did their homework on this. The others were in a translational rut or else were so biased theologically that they were not open to other possibilities. This has done great damage to the truth.

Implications. Some might feel that I am making too fine a point of all of this. Let me ask you, Does it matter whether the Bible speaks of being 'predestined to salvation or condemnation' or whether it speaks of being 'preappointed to the image of Christ and His service?' It seem to me that the difference has vast theological and personal significance. The word 'predestination' carries with it strong overtones of Augustine's notion of unconditional election. However, Calvinists and Arminians alike can agree that God has preappointed believers to be conformed to the image of His Son and to His service.

A glorious future for His children

"But we know that for those who love Him, for those called in agreement with His purpose, God makes all things work together for good. Because those whom He knew beforehand He appointed beforehand to share the likeness of His Son, so that He might be the Firstborn among many brothers" (Rom. 8:28-29, New Berkeley Version).[35] Now we have come to the second context in which the meaning of *proginoskein* has vast implications for our theology of salvation. I have chosen to quote a translation, done by predominantly Calvinistic translators, which I believe fairly represents the original of both *proginoskein* and *proorizein*. Here we need to see how the context impacts any possible pregnant meaning of *proginoskein* other than the primary one, 'to foreknow.'

The broader context of Romans. The key verse of Romans is widely recognized to be 1:17: **"For in the gospel a righteousness from God is revealed, a righteousness that is by faith from first to last, just as it is written: 'The righteous will live by faith'" (NIV).** Paul then goes on to show how God makes that righteousness available to mankind which totally lacks it (1:18–3:20) through justification by faith alone (3:21–5:21) and sanctification by faith (6:1–8:39). That it is all "by faith from first to last" is attested by the fact that the words 'faith' and 'to believe' occur a total of 60 times and 'disbelieve' 9 times in this book, punctuating his major arguments. Since Martin Luther recovered the glorious truth of the fourth link in Paul's five-link sequence, which is justification by faith alone, evangelical Christians have sought to emphasize the cruciality of faith in God's whole plan of salvation. This is seen in the rest of Paul's sequence in 8:30 (ASV): **". . . and whom he foreordained, them he also called: and whom he called, them he also justified: and whom he justified, them he also glorified."** Certainly the calling to salvation is by repentant faith (see ch. 11). The final glorification also has to be by faith. Is it possible that we can leave faith out of the foreknowledge which is the "first" of the process? May we understand that in His foreordination (better, 'preappointment') God turns off His omniscient foreknowledge? This seems to me unthinkable![H]

In order to get the full flow of Paul's thinking here, we must also go back ten verses: **"For I consider that the sufferings of this present time are not worthy to be compared with the glory that is to be revealed to us"** (Rom. 8:18). In the rest of this chapter, Paul moves on to focus upon the certainty of the future glory of God's children, which he first mentioned in 8:17-18. In Romans 9–11, he even raises the question of the future for Israel, even though for the while Israel has failed and been set aside. It is with this future focus in mind that Paul speaks the goal of our glorification in 8:30 and the four stages which precede it. We must keep this in mind as we look at this sequence of five steps in God's plan of salvation. It is so striking that theologians have developed an *ordo salutis* (plan of salvation) from these verses.[36] It all starts with God's foreknowing His people, who are identified as those who love God. Next in the sequence is foreordination or more precisely preappointment (*proorizein*), then calling, then justification, and lastly, glorification. There is some discussion as to whether the sequence is logical or chronological, or both. Probably it is both. In any case, it must start with foreknowledge before and distinct from *proorizein*, just as *proorizein* must precede and be distinct from 'calling', and calling distinct from justification, and justification distinct from glorification, which logically and chronologically comes last.

Thus any definition of *proginoskein* which would make it in any way synonymous with *proorizein* would absolutely destroy the logic of Paul's (and the Spirit's) sequence. This would reduce it to a mere redundancy and totally undo the symmetry of the development. I believe this is the final refutation of any pregnant connotation for *proginoskein.*

Additionally, we should note that there is nothing in the context which would say anything about any unconditional decrees in eternity past as to who will be saved and who will be consigned to hell. Paul is starting with God's foreknowledge of us and stating that God has preappointed us to be conformed to the image of His Son, which is glorification. God does work all things together for those who love Him since our future is certain and glorious. God is for us, and nothing can separate us from His love in Christ. The focus is not on any presumed past 'predestination,' but on the certainty of a glorious future. So the Calvinists are half right on this one. Right about eternal security, but wrong on unconditional election.

***Calvinistic response.*.** One of the ways in which Calvinistic writers have dealt with this self-evident contradiction to their system is seen in John Murray, who very subtly omits any reference to foreknowledge in his discussion of Romans 8:28-30:

H. Is it coincidental that the five points of Calvinism do not even refer to as central a factor as faith? Since they believe that God gives the faith, it becomes so automatic that it is extraneous to the system..

> It is not by any means likely that Paul in Rom 8:28-30, in setting forth the outlines of the order followed in the application of redemption, would begin that enumeration with an act of God which is other than the first in order. In other words, it is altogether likely that he would begin with the first, just as he ends with the last. This argument is strengthened by the consideration that he traces salvation to its ultimate source in the election of God. Surely he traces the application of redemption to its beginning when he says, "whom he did predestinate them he also called."[37]

I presume that this very serious omission of the actual first term (foreknowledge) was not intentional dishonesty on Murray's part, but resulted from his assumption that the two terms are synonymous. However, in giving him the benefit of the doubt, I must point out that this is a very serious mishandling of God's word, whether intentional or not!

Another response to conditional election, which I have heard from my Calvinistic colleagues, is that Paul says, "whom He foreknew" not 'what He foreknew about them.' Their point is that if Paul had wanted to allude to God's foreknowledge of the faith of the saved, he would not have used a personal object (*ous*) to the verb. However, I have previously quoted Tom Edgar's observation on the syntax of personal objects with this verb which indicates that this idiom means that something is known about the object.

Thus when we come back to Romans 8:29 we must seriously consider the probability that God's foreknowledge of something about "those who love God" is "built into" the Greek although not obvious in English. *But it is the context, not just in these verses, but the context of the whole book of Romans, which strongly suggests that faith is that which God foreknows about His people, as we have already pointed out.* Since the subject of Romans is "**a righteousness that is by faith from first to last**" and since 'faith' and 'believing' occur sixty times in Romans, it becomes clear the repentant faith is that which God foresees as the basis of His pre-appointment of His saints. He foreknows our faith, pre-appoints those who will believe, calls us by faith, justifies us by faith, and glorifies us by faith. It is a faith process "**from first to last.**" God does not close His eyes and throw darts.

CONCLUSIONS

Now we must pull together the results of these two major word studies and the exegesis of Romans 8. I have shown that there is absolutely no linguistic basis for seeing an elective connotation in God's foreknowledge, or in the Hebrew or Greek words for knowing, even if it were legitimate to try to base it upon them. The secular usage, the Septuagint, and the early church fathers contain no hint of this imagined pregnant meaning. All of the seven usages in the New Testament, examined carefully in their contexts, cannot be forced into supporting it either. The claims all come from theologians, but not one unambiguous, incontestable linguistic example can be given for an elective connotation.

It also seems that very few translators and linguists, and virtually no theologians, have bothered to dig more deeply into the meaning of *proorizein*. The rare secular Greek usage raises overwhelming doubt about the traditional rendering 'to predestinate.' Since the verb from which it is derived, *horizein*, is used of being appointed to service or responsibility, a good case can be made for the rendering of *proorizein* as 'preappointment.' I have shown that this meaning makes better sense in the four New Testament contexts in which it is used, and that this is confirmed by the early translations (versions)and the early church fathers' usage of the word. Although the older lexicons do not even mention 'to predestinate' as a meaning, some of the more recent lexicons and theological works, having been influenced by deductive theological considerations, do list that meaning. Although a majority of the translations have blindly followed the Vulgate rendering, I have identified a dozen translations and Greek commentators who have broken away from this translational rut. **Thus the word 'predestinate' should have never gotten into any Bible translation.** The consequence of this is clear since the word 'predestinate' itself carries strong overtones of unconditional election.

Therefore, there is absolutely no basis for denying the clearly conditional force of both 1 Peter 1:1-2 and Romans 8:28-30, conditioned on what God foreknew about His saints, especially their faith. It is absolutely irresponsible to build the doctrine of absolute predestination upon the dubious rendering of such a rare Greek word! In the next chapter, the words for election and its criteria will be investigated.

Note: This chapter is based upon a paper presented to the Eastern Regional of the Evangelical Theological Society, Langhorne, PA, April 1993.

---

1. Berkhof, *Systematic Theology*, p. 111-2.
2. Thomas R. Edgar, "The Meaning of *PROORIZO*," a paper given at the ETS, March 30, 2001 at Langhorne, PA.
3. D. A. Carson, *Exegetical Fallacies*, pp. 62-64.
4. See Bertram and Bultmann in Kittel, *TDNT*, I, p. 700, text and footnotes.
5. Francis Brown, *The New Brown-Driver-Briggs-Gesenius Hebrew and English Lexicon*, pp 393-5.
6. Harris, Archer, & Waltke, eds., *Theological Wordbook*, I, p. 366-7. There is some ambiguity as to the identity of the author of this article, but it is probably Paul Gilchrist of Covenant College, who is also presumably a Calvinist.
7. Carson, pp. 36-40.
8. Ibid, p. 26; also Daniel B. Wallace, *Greek Grammar Beyond the Basics*, p. 363.
9. Chamberlain, *Exegetical Grammar*, p. 11.
10. Robert Young, *Analytical Concordance to the Bible*, Appendix, p. 72.
11. John Henry Thayer, *Lexicon*, p. 117-8; G. Abbott-Smith, *Lexicon*, p. 92; Bertram, in *TDNT*, I, p. 700; Arndt and Gingrich, *Lexicon*, pp. 159-161. Bertram does not discuss the 7 usages in their contexts.

12. Bultmann in *TDNT*, I, pp. 715-6; also Liddell, Scott, and Jones, *Lexicon,* 9th ed., p. 1473; Moulton and Milligan, *Vocabulary*, p. 538; and G. W. H. Lampe, *A Patristic Greek Lexicon* (Oxford, 1961), p. 1141. I have personally checked the LXX and Josephus usages.

13. G. Abbott-Smith, *Lexicon*, p. 379.

14. Thayer, p. 538; Abbott-Smith, p. 379; Arndt and Gingrich, p. 710.

15. They are quoted in Forster and Marston, *God's Strategy in Human History*, pp. 191-2.

16. Edgar C. James, "Foreknowledge and Foreordination," in *Bibliotheca Sacra* (July 1965), p. 217; S. M. Baugh, "The Meaning of Foreknowledge," in *Still Sovereign*, eds. Thomas R. Schreiner and Bruce Ware, pp. 183-200; Douglas Moo, *Romans*, p. 522. Refutation in Thomas R. Edgar, "The Meaning of *PROORIZO*," a paper given at ETS Eastern Sectional, March 30, 2001 at PBU, p. 2.

17. Thomas Edgar, p. 1. He refers to commentaries by Dunn, Fitzmeyer, Moo, Morris, Murray, and Schreiner.

18. Blass, Debrunner, Funk, *Greek Grammar*, p. 228; Nigel Turner, *Syntax* in James Hope Moulton, III, pp. 335-56. There is no reference to hendiadys in the grammars of Dana and Mantey, Chamberlain, Wallace, or A. T. Robertson's short grammar. He alluded to it in passing in his fuller work but declined to discuss it. The supplement gives one example.

19. Wallace, *Greek Grammar*, pp 286-90, 271.

20. Wallace, pp. 670-4; Dana and Mantey, pp. 249-52.

21. Buswell, II, p. 140.

22. Arndt and Gingrich, p. 408.

23. Wallace, p. 377; William Douglas Chamberlain, *An Exegetical Grammar of the Greek New Testament*, p. 123.

24. Edgar, p. 3.

25. Erasmus, *The Praise of Folly*, cited by Hunt, p. 171.

26. Carson, pp. 31-32.

27. K. L. Schmidt in Kittel, *TDNT*, V, pp. 452-56.

28. Demosthenes, 31,4, *Against Onetor.*

29. Arthur Way, *The Letters of St. Paul* (London: Macmillan, 1926), p. 129

30. Schmidt, p. 452-5.

31. George Lamsa, *The New Testament according to the Peshitta.*

32. G. W. H. Lampe, *A Patristic Greek Lexicon*, p. 1161. I have sought to translate or summarize the brief untranslated Greek citations which Lampe gives, which is difficult because of their brevity and lack of context, and my limited resources and expertise. I challenge any more competent Greek scholar who might question my conclusions to access these passages and give better renderings for us all.

33. John Parkhurst, *A Greek and English Lexicon of the New Testament*, new edition by Hugh James Rose (London: many publishers, 1829), pp. 727-28. Bishop Parkhurst was a refugee in Zurich during the time of the persecution by Queen Mary, and met Zwingli's successor, Bullinger, there.

34. Thayer, p. 541; Abbott-Smith, p. 382; Arndt and Gingrich, p. 716.

35. Gerrit Verkuyl, ed., *The Modern Language Bible: The New Berkeley Version* (rev. 1969). Of 20 scholars on the revision committee only 2 or 3 are not identifiably of Calvinistic tradition.

36. L. Berkhof, *Systematic Theology*, pp. 415-17.

37. John Murray, *Redemption: Accomplished and Applied* (GR: Eerdmans, 1955), p. 94.

What predestination means, in its most elementary form, is that our final destination, heaven or hell, is decided by God, not only before we get there, but before we are even born.

-R. C. Sproul

You will be saved or damned *for* all eternity because you were saved or damned *from* all eternity.

-George Bryson
Guide to understanding Calvinism

8

WHO ARE GOD'S CHOICE PEOPLE?

Having carefully examined the meanings of foreknowledge and foreordination (better preappointment), now we must move on to understand the biblical teaching on election. In order to get an accurate picture, it will be absolutely necessary to trace through the Old Testament context of election, and then do an in-depth word study of the three Greek words which relate to election, since our current translations are deficient in the way these words are rendered. The word studies may seem tedious, but are absolutely necessary. Only then can we hope to understand the key passages which explain election theologically, especially Luke 9:35; Matthew 22:14; 1 Peter 1:1-2; 2 Peter 1:10-11, and Ephesians 1:3-14.

THE ELECTION OF THE PATRIARCHS

The biblical concept of election begins with the calling of the patriarch Abraham, the progenitor of God's ancient 'chosen people,' into the promised land. We don't know the details of his conversion from his idolatrous background in Ur of the Chaldees to faith in the true God. We do know that God called him to settle in the less-populated land of Canaan so that he might begin a separated nation dedicated to the service of the true God, Yahweh. As Abram matured in his faith, God made wonderful promises to him (Gen. 12:1-3) and then sealed them with a covenant of blessing (Gen. 15). This covenant was reiterated and expanded on a number of occasions, culminating in the promise of his ultimate descendant, the Messiah (Gen. 22:16-18).

We understand that Abram was not the only believer of his time, but rather was chosen from among other believers to begin a whole new program of God. His nephew Lot is identified as a believer, as was Melchizedek, who is described as being greater than Abram (Heb. 7). It is very plausible that Job was a believer in the same general time frame, but having no connection with Abram. So there is nothing in Scripture which even implies that God's choice of Abram was unto his salvation, but rather unto the service of God.[1] The same can be said for his descendants. Although Isaac, his legitimate son, was to be the heir and the bearer of the promise, there is no hint in Scripture that Isaac was chosen to salvation and Ishmael reprobated to Hell. Rather God promised Hagar that Ishmael would be blessed (Gen. 16:10-12; 21:17-20). When God told Rebekah that there were two nations in her womb, and that the Edomites would serve the Israelites (Gen. 25:23), it is intriguing how this prophecy was fulfilled by Jacob's cunning and deceit. Although Esau is later characterized as a profane man, this was not by God's choice, even though determinists misinterpret Romans 9 to imply that. God's choice had to do with the *nations* coming from Rebekah's womb and did not determine their salvation: "**Two nations are in your womb; and two peoples shall be separated from your body; and one people shall be stronger than the other; and the older shall serve the younger**."

Indeed, it is transparent that physical descent from Jacob did not guarantee salvation for anyone. This is not only clear in the Old Testament narrative, but in Paul's later explanations in Roman 2 and 9-11. If you missed the point of my discussion of Romans 9 in chapter 3 of this book, let me remind you of the absolute imperative of careful study of the Old Testament texts which Paul quoted there. From this it becomes clear that Paul is not at all referring to an unconditional election of individuals to salvation. So God's choice of Abraham, Isaac, and Jacob did not guarantee salvation to any of them or to any of their descendants. The point of it all is that Israel was to be a witness to the one true God in an idolatrous, polytheistic world. Even when they failed God, they were to be a "crucible nation," as Erich Sauer has suggested (Deut. 4:20).[2] Both the blessings upon them for obedience and the judgments for disobedience were to be a testimony for the truth of Yahweh, as indeed they were over the centuries. Abraham, Isaac, and Jacob's witness was relatively feeble, but Joseph's was outstanding. When God brought Israel out of Egypt under Moses, that witness was exceedingly powerful, as was attested to by the many Psalms which refer to it. We could also mention David, Solomon, Jonah, Daniel, and many others who continued that witness in various ways in diverse circumstances.

A crucial issue related to this is the conditionality of the Abrahamic covenant. Amillennial writers tend to emphasize the conditionality of the covenant; premillennialists have tended to emphasize its unconditionality. However, Dr. Imad Shahadeh, the founder of the Jordan Evangelical Theological Seminary (JETS), a Palestinian who has given wonderful balance to this issue.[3] He has proposed that which I have been teaching for many years, that, as far as its ultimate fulfillment is concerned, it is unconditional. However, for each generation of Israelites and for each individual Jew, the blessings of the covenant were clearly conditional. It is fairly obvious that even before the coming of God's Messiah, most Jews were not enjoying the blessings of the Abrahamic Covenant because of their disobedience to God. It is indisputable that since the cross very few Jews have been receiving the blessings promised to Abraham. All of this is important background for our study of the election of the New Testament church.

The servanthood of Israel comes into particular focus in the latter part of Isaiah's prophecy (Isa. 41:8-9). However, in that context Isaiah sees the ultimate fulfillment of Israel's ministry in the Messiah, Yahweh's Servant (Isa. 42:1-7): "**Behold, My Servant, whom I uphold; my chosen one in whom My soul delights. I have put My Spirit upon Him; He will bring forth justice to the nations. . . . and I will appoint you as a covenant to the people, as a light to the nations, to open blind eyes, . . .**" (42:1, 6b-7a). The noun used here is *bāchir*, 'elect,' which is derived from the verb *bāchar.* It is most important to understand the usage of *bāchar* ('to choose, elect, decide for') in order to get the connotation of *bāchir*. This verb and its derivatives are common, occurring 198 times in the Old Testament. "It is important to note, however, that it always involves a careful, well thought-out choice. . . . In all of these cases serviceability rather than simple arbitrariness is at the heart of the choosing." The derived noun bāchûr, sometimes refers to young men, "in that the picked or chosen men in a military context are usually the young men." The derived adjective *mibhār* means 'chosen,' or 'choice': "As such it is often translated as a superlative."[4] Quell confirms that in the Septuagint translation of the Hebrew, it is rendered, "that which is choice or excellent," "what is desired or costly," "what is costly in the concept of the pure," or "also emphasizes the choice or excellent element . . ."[5]

The point should be clear that the translators should have referred to Him as the "choice One" in harmony with its frequent usage in the Hebrew. Indeed, I will show that Jesus of Nazareth was never *chosen* to be the Messiah. This is exceedingly important for our understanding of election in the New Testament. There is also another very important consideration for our background study.

CORPORATE SOLIDARITY

The concept of corporate solidarity is not an abstract idea in Middle and Far Eastern cultures. During World War II thousands of Japanese pilots were willing to become Kamikaze (divine wind) by crashing their bomb-laden planes on the decks of American aircraft carriers. Even today the Japanese are famous for their loyalty, not only to their extended families, but even to the business corporations to which they devote their lives. More recently, hundreds of thousands of Iranian young men went into battle against Iraq (and Saddam Hussain), with the full expectation that they would become martyrs. Some of this may be explainable in terms of Islamic theology, but, since they were fighting other Muslims, much of it has to relate to ideas of national corporate solidarity. And even more contemporaneously, the Palestinian young men who become suicide bombers in the Intefadeh in Israel must be doing so under some concept of corporate solidarity.[A]

But this is not just a cultural notion. It is a biblical concept rooted in the third chapter of Genesis and in New Testament theology based upon the fall. Certainly the Pauline doctrine of the imputation and transmission of Adam's sin to the whole race (Rom. 5:12ff) establishes the principle of corporate solidarity from the very beginning of the human race. William Klein summarizes R. P. Shedd's Old Testament data for corporate or ethnic solidarity:

> (1) The personality of the group transcended time and space so a family could be identified with its ancestor (Ge 13:15-17; Isa 41:8; Hos 11:1; Mal 1:3-4). (2) Punishment and blessing extended beyond the specific individual responsible. As for punishment see the account of Achan's sin (Jos 7) or Korah's rebellion (Nu 16), as well as the statements in Ex 20:5-6. As for blessing note Ge 12:3 and Ex 32:13. (3) Regarding the covenant Shedd states, "All the members of a covenantal community are subordinate to the whole. To sever oneself from the group is to be cut off from the covenant and thereby from the covenant-making God." (4) The high priests, on the Day of Atonement, sacrificed for the sins of the people (Lev 16:15, 19, 21). The sins of the community, seen as a unity, could be transferred to the scapegoat. (5) Certain prayers expressed the intercessor's sense of corporate guilt (Ne 9:33; Da 9:5-19). . . . In parallel to Shedd's points, any reader notices that the writer of the Old Testament commonly treat the entire people of Israel as a unit (Isa 5:1-7; Jer 12:10).[6]

Klein went on to cite H. Wheeler Robinson as a strong advocate of the idea of "corporate personality" in the Old Testament, and, after alluding to his discussion of 2 Samuel 21:1-14 regarding King Saul's sin of the slaughter of the Gibeonites and David's judgment upon his family as a consequence, quotes Robinson's most apt statement:

> Corporate personality means for us the treatment of the family, the clan, or the nation, as the unit in place of the individual. It does not

---

A Having lived for seven years in Pakistan, I only then began to grasp these ideas of corporate solidarity in that culture.

> mean that no individual life is recognized, but simply that in a number of realms in which we have come to think individualistically, and to treat the single man as the unit, *e.g.*, for punishment or reward, ancient thought envisaged the whole group of which he was part.[7]

A number of other biblical scholars have developed the idea of corporate personality, including C. H. Dodd, A. Nygren, and Herman Ridderbos. More recently missiologists have also seen the extreme importance of our understanding of the diverse cognitive processes or ways of thinking in Asian and African peoples, much of which is characterized by corporate solidarity.

A WORD STUDY OF ELECTION
(*eklegomai, eklektos, eklogē*)

It is surprising that the connotation of 'the choice of the excellent,' which we saw in the Hebrew words and the Greek of the Septuagint, is not adequately carried over into our New Testament translations, especially since this idea is predominant in the secular Greek as well. Our present translations only give it its due in three verses. I will suggest that there are several other New Testament contexts where this connotation is the only acceptable rendering, and a number of others where it could make a significant difference theologically.

Pre-New Testament usage. The verb *eklegomai* has as its basic meaning in the middle voice, "to choose something for oneself," "to make one's choice." According to G. Shrenk in *TDNT*, the secular Greek predominantly evidences the derived connotation of the selection of the best or the choice, such as "the most beautiful of what is to be praised" or "something good from literary treasures." G. Quell confirms that in the Septuagint we see "that which is choice or excellent" or "what is desired, or costly." The adjective *eklektos* generally means 'chosen,' or 'select.' In the secular Greek the predominant meaning is 'choice' or 'selected.' In the Septuagint it has a similar usage: "choice, select, costly, sterling, purified, profitable, best of its kind, of top quality." This is also clearly seen in the New Testament in Romans 16:13 and 1 Peter 2:4, 6. The meaning of the abstract noun *eklogē* in the secular Greek is predominantly 'selection', also having a qualitative connotation. It is not found in the canonical Septuagint, but in the Jewish writings the usage is predominantly of human free choice.[8] *Thus as we come to the New Testament usage of these words, we must be sensitive to this predominant meaning in the secular and Septuagintal Greek.* Indeed, it is most significant.

New Testament Usage

In the New Testament, the verb *eklegomai* ('to choose') is used 21 times, three of which refer to human choice, most to God's choice of Israel,

Christ's choice of the twelve apostles, the end-time elect, God's choice by principle of the poor and weak (1 Cor. 1), etc., and two theologically significant references: Luke 9:35 and Ephesians 1:4. Both of these require detailed consideration below.

The adjective *eklektos* ('chosen,' 'choice,' 'elect') is found in the New Testament 22 times, nine of which are in end-time contexts of tribulation saints. The Lord Jesus used it in the aphorism in the parable of the king's wedding feast (Mt. 22:1-14). It is in the words of Israel's rulers as Christ hangs on the cross (Lk. 23:35), Peter's two references to Christians (1 Pet. 1:1-2 & 2 Pet. 1:10), in his reference to Christ, the 'choice' One of God (1 Pet. 2:4, 6), to the church as the 'elect' of God (1 Pet. 2:9); and the references in 2 John 1, 13, probably to churches. In addition to Paul's reference to the elect angels (1 Tim. 5:21) and **"Rufus, the choice man in the Lord"** (Rom. 16:13), he surprisingly used it theologically only four times (Rom. 8:33; Col. 3:12; 2 Tim. 2:10; and Tit. 1:1), all of which are plural. There is never any reference to a singular 'elect' individual.

Of the seven usages of the abstract noun *eklogē* ('election'), four are Paul's references to Israel in Romans 9-11,[B] and only one to Christians in 1 Thessalonians 1:4. God told Ananias that Saul of Tarsus was His 'chosen' instrument for witness to Gentiles (Acts 9:15). Peter's only use of the word is 2 Peter 1:10.

Christ, the Choice One. We must first consider the three references to the Lord Jesus as the elect of God. The starting point must be the Father's words on the Mount of Transfiguration (Lk. 9:35): **"This is my Son, *My* Chosen One (*ho eklelegmenos*); listen to Him!"** This language identifies Him with God's Elect Servant in the last part of Isaiah (42:1-7), and, as in the Hebrew, the parallel with "beloved Son" in the other Synoptic references (Mt. 17:5=Mk. 9:7) makes it clear that we must understand this as 'Choice One,' since they quote it as: **"This is My beloved Son, with whom I am well pleased; listen to Him!"** Thus 'beloved' equals 'choice.' Luke showed how His being the Elect Messiah was the heart of the issue with the Jewish rulers throughout His ministry, reaching its acme as they mocked Him as He hung on the cross: **"And even the rulers were sneering at Him, saying, 'He saved other; let Him save Himself if this is the Christ of God, His Chosen One"** (23:35).

Peter very explicitly confirmed this understanding in his usage in 1 Peter 2:4, 6: **"And coming to Him as to a living stone, rejected by men, but choice and precious in the sight of God. . . . 'Behold I lay in Zion a choice stone, a precious corner *stone*'."** As we had noted in our discussion of foreknowledge in chapter 7, in reference to 1 Peter 1:20, there is no way here that Jesus of Nazareth is to be considered as chosen by God

---

B Thus 15 out of 51 usages of this group of words probably relate to the Jewish people. Since Israel was God's ancient chosen people, this is understandable and significant.

from among other Jews to be the Messiah. Clearly, the connotation of 'choice' or 'select,' which we saw in the secular and Septuagint usage, is absolutely demanded in both of these contexts, and this is confirmed by the close connection with 'precious.' The Lord Jesus was in no way chosen by God; He is the 'Choice One.' The notion that Jesus of Nazareth was chosen to be the Messiah at His baptism is the heart of two ancient heresies, the Cerinthian form of Gnosticism and the Ebionite heresy.

Nor was He chosen in any other sense. As James Daane pointed out, like the nation Israel, He was formed by a miraculous birth:

> God's election must produce what it elects. And it does. Isaac is a son of miracle. . . . the nation of Israel is not viewed as one extant nation among many, which is then selectively chosen by God as his elect people. Rather, Israel as the object of God's election not only does not exist but even has no possibility of existence apart from God's elective and creative action.[9]

In the same way, through the virgin birth, Jesus of Nazareth was uniquely brought into being to be the 'choice One' of God; He was never chosen. Thus the pre-New Testament usage of these words is not only helpful, but *mandatory* to understand the real meaning of election.

Christ's decisive parable and aphorism. As we examine the few theologically significant passages, we must start with the parable of the king's wedding feast in **Matthew 22:1-14.** Because of its length, I will not quote it in full, but ask you to stop and open your Bible to this passage.[C] Note in 22:3 that those who were invited to the wedding feast **"were unwilling to come."** They even mistreated and killed the messenger slaves (22:6). The king emphasized that those invited **"were not worthy"** (22:8) and sent judgment upon them. Then he had his slaves invite people from the highways indiscriminately, **"both evil and good"** (22:9-10). Even though wedding garments were surely provided for the guests, when a guest was found without them, he was ejected into outer darkness (22:11-13). At that point the Lord Jesus gave this famous and enigmatic aphorism: **"For many are called, but few chosen"** (22:14). If the Lord Jesus were speaking in verse 14 about unconditional election, there would be *a radical disconnect with the parable* to which this aphorism is attached. Some interpreters recognize this and see this as a "non-technical use" of *eklektoi.* However some may try to dismiss the relevance of the parable and aphorism to this issue, we are obliged to interpret the aphorism in harmony with the parable. Otherwise we insult the logical acumen of our Lord Jesus.

I have read this parable for over fifty years and must confess that I was blind to the obvious contradiction the standard translations raise. But when

---

C I am convinced that much theological discussion is wasted if we do not keep the passage under discussion open before us. We must give priority to the word of God in the way we read theology!

we go back to the secular and Septuagintal use of this word and to the usage in Luke 9:35, 1 Peter 2:4, 6, and Romans 16:13, we have an easy solution to an extremely serious interpretive problem. We would then translate: **"Many are invited, but few are choice."** I believe this is an appropriate translation since those who didn't respond to Christ's invitation are described as "**unwilling to come**" and "**not worthy**"—this was not attributed to God's choice. On the other hand, those who ended up in the feast were not chosen either; they had merely responded to the open invitation.

Some will react that this seems to make salvation a matter of human merit. But the answer is clearly found in the fact that in salvation it is God who makes the believer "choice" by His grace. This is the point of the provision of wedding garments for the guests, who would have had no opportunity to procure them on their own. Justification by faith involves God's provision of the wedding garments. This symbolism was anticipated in Isaiah 61:10: "**I will rejoice greatly in the LORD, my soul will exult in my God; for He has clothed me with garments of salvation, He has wrapped me with a robe of righteousness, as a bridegroom decks himself with a garland, and as a bride adorns herself with her jewels.**" The broader New Testament also calls believers "saints," without in any way undermining the gracious character of salvation, since we understand this to be positional truth. Since this also is positional truth, we need not shrink from the appellation "choice."

The broader context of this parable and its aphorism confirms the appropriateness of this translation. It is one of a group of parables the Lord Jesus gave after his triumphal entry at the beginning of passion week, in all of which the Lord declared His own rejection by His own choice people, Israel. In accusing God's choice nation of being unwilling to accept the invitation He had been extending to them for over 3 years, He made it clear that the invitation is going to go out to all, whom the king will then qualify to be His select guests, although their previous condition was both "evil and good." Thus in effect He set in contrast God's ancient choice nation and the new "choice people" to whom the kingdom of God would be given, an idea explicitly declared in the previous context: **"Therefore I say to you, the kingdom of God will be taken away from you, and be given to a nation producing the fruit of it"** (Mt. 21:43). There is strong irony in Christ's aphorism: the choice nation is being set aside and indiscriminate invitees ("evil and good") become choice by God's gracious plan.

The chosen apostles. The Gospel writers also used the verb *eklegomai* a number of times in reference to the Lord's choice of His twelve apostles, which of course included Judas Iscariot (Lk. 6:13; Jn. 6:70; 13:18; 15:16, 19). None of these says anything about a doctrine of election to salvation, since the Eleven were already saved before He chose them as apostles, and Judas was clearly a counterfeit. The Lord even referred to this fact in John 6:70. It is outrageous, therefore, that Calvinists are prone to use John 15:16 as a prooftext for the notion of unconditional election: **"You did not choose Me, but I chose you, and appointed you, that you should go and bear fruit, and that your fruit should remain, . . ."** To extrapolate the address and meaning of this verse to all believers in a doctrinal way is seriously misguided, even though *by application* we can affirm that all believers have been appointed to bear abiding fruit. This brings us to the major context of the doctrinal discussion.

Peter's simple explanation. Now we must come back to the beginning, the simple statement of that philosophically naive fisherman, the apostle Peter, that believers are **"elect (*eklektoi*) according to the foreknowledge of God the Father, by the sanctifying work of the Spirit, that you may obey Jesus Christ and be sprinkled with His blood:"** (1 Pet. 1:1-2). I have already discussed it in the previous chapter in reference to the meaning of *prognosis*. Now we must seek to understand the meaning of *eklektoi.* From the predominant usage in the secular and Septuagintal Greek, we may immediately understand that Peter is addressing the Christians as '**choice ones**,' just as Paul addressed Christians in his letters as '**saints**.' In both cases, this is positional truth: we are such because of God's work of salvation by grace. Indeed, Peter's explanation is that this was accomplished by the "**sanctifying work of the Spirit**," which we understand from the analogy of Scripture took place when we were saved by putting faith in Christ. By no stretch of the imagination did this take place in eternity past, although it was by God's foreknowledge. What God knew in eternity is now being implemented by the Holy Spirit.

Thus if we try to read a pregnant determinative meaning into *prognosis*, we contradict Peter's simple explanation that our becoming God's choice ones is by the sanctifying work of the Spirit. No, Peter was naive of the abstruse and abstract doctrine of unconditional election in eternity past and felt that the truth he was setting forth was not "hard to understand." He affirms that we are choice according to God's foreknowledge of events in time, that is, the outworking of His plan by the preaching of the gospel and the "**sanctifying work of the Spirit.**" This is confirmed by the root idea of sanctify as 'to separate, to set apart.'

It is very significant that after Peter has referred in the next chapter to Christ as the "choice stone" (2:4, 6), he went on to refer to the Church as **"an elect [choice] race, a royal priesthood, a holy nation, a people for *God's* own possession, that you may show forth the excellencies of him who called you out of darkness into his marvelous light: who in time past were no people, but now are the people of God:"** (2:9 ASV). Peter borrowed language used of the nation Israel to refer to the Church, thus indicating that the Church's election, like Israel's, was corporate. So not only did Peter indicate in chapter 1 that election is conditional, but in chapter 2 that it is corporate.

Peter's single use of the noun 'election' is very supportive of this understanding: **"Therefore, my brothers, be all the more eager to make your calling and election [choice] sure. For if you do these things, you will never fall, and you will receive a rich welcome into the eternal kingdom of our Lord and Savior Jesus Christ"** (2 Pet. 1:10-11, NIV). Here no subtleties of exegesis are required. The issue is quite simple: if individual election is unconditional, how can anything which those professing believers do change that eternal reality? Unconditional election means that there is **no condition** which any person can meet in order to become elect or to remain elect. But clearly Peter affirms that they must be "**diligent**" (NAS) to make it sure. Peter is thinking of those counterfeit believers who must not be careless about their spiritual state. This exhortation is in total contradiction to the notion of unconditional individual election foisted upon the church four centuries after Pentecost by Augustine.

Paul's usage

Paul's use of the noun is more complex. In addition to 1 Thessalonians 1:4, he used it four times in the Roman 9-11 discussion of Israel's election. But first in order: **". . . knowing, brethren beloved by God, *His* choice of you; for our gospel did not come to you in word only, but also in power and in the Holy Spirit and with full conviction;"** Here also my point is simple: if this is a reference to individual election, how could Paul know that of every individual in the Thessalonian church? He spoke of the manifest work of God in their corporate conversion, not only, as we remember from Acts, that in just a month or so some Jews and many Gentiles were converted before his untimely departure, but also the radical change in their lifestyle (1:3, 6-10). Since the New Testament consistently warns of counterfeit believers in every church, Paul could not have known this about every individual in the church there. But Paul is convinced that there is an elect company of believers in Thessalonika. Beyond this we cannot confidently go, and there is nothing in the context which requires us to presume individual unconditional election here. He saw that they had met the condition of repentant faith and had come into "**much full assurance**" (*plērophoria pollē*) by the powerful working of the Spirit. As in 1 Peter 1:2, they became God's choice people by the work of the Spirit in conviction, regeneration, and sanctification, not by an eternal decree.

In reference to the Greeks' search for wisdom in philosophy and the revelation of God's wisdom in the gospel of Christ, Paul spoke about God's chosen plan which goes contrary to the things men value.

> **For consider your calling, brethren, that there were not many wise according to the flesh, not many mighty, not many noble; but God has chosen the foolish things of the world to shame the wise, and God has chosen the weak things of the world to shame the things which are strong, and the base things of the**

> **world and the despised, God has chosen, the things that are not, that He might nullify the things that are, that no man should boast before God** (1 Cor. 1:26-29).

This context is perfectly understandable in terms of the general principles which are operative in the way humanity responds to God's calling through the gospel message. The Lord Jesus had explained this principle after dealing with the rich young ruler: "**Truly I say to you, it is hard for a rich man to enter the kingdom of heaven**" (Mt. 19:23). One does not have to be very bright to observe that today it is not the world's intellectuals, power brokers, millionaires, and "beautiful people" who are responding in significant numbers to the gospel. This is fully explainable in terms of human nature and predilections and is hardly based upon some mysterious unconditional election of individuals by God. Indeed, Paul went on to tell how the open secret of God's wisdom has now been revealed through the apostles (2:6-7). Thus I am astonished that J. I. Packer stated that this passage is one of the five major passages upon which the Calvinistic doctrine of election is based.[10] Here is a clear case of reading one's theology into a passage. The principle enunciated here is simple and not mysterious: wealth, power, prestige, and intellectualism are obstacles to people coming to faith in Christ.

Romans. There are five theologically significant passages in Romans: **"He who did not spare His own Son, but delivered Him up for us all, how will He not also with Him freely give us all things? Who will bring a charge against God's elect [choice ones]? God is the one who justifies; who is the one who condemns?"** (Rom. 8:32-34). Here we have the wonderful consequence of the five-linked chain of vv. 28-31. Now that we have been foreknown, pre-appointed to be conformed to the image of Christ, called, justified, and glorified, there can be no condemnation (8:1). Certainly justification and glorification put in a past tense must be understood as positional truth. Since we are also positionally God's *eklektoi*, the idea of God allowing a condemnatory charge against us is unthinkable. Which possible rendering, 'chosen' or 'choice,' makes better sense in the flow of Paul's logic? He had identified us as **"those who love God"** in v. 28. I would suggest that either is possible in this context, but that 'choice' is to be preferred: **"Who will bring a charge against God choice ones?"** It is not because He has chosen us, but because He has positionally called us His choice ones, that no charge can be entertained in His courts. In this case Paul's usage in Romans 16:13 would be the same as here. Remember that the predominant prior usage of *eklektos* is 'choice.'

Paul's reference in Romans 9:11 is to the selection of Jacob over Esau to be the progenitor of the His choice nation. Salvation is not at all the issue here, nor are Jacob and Esau in view as individuals, as I argued in chapter 3 of this book. The context of Romans 9–11 is God's fairness in setting Israel aside dispensationally and turning to the Gentiles. Israel's being God's

…ce people corporately for two millennia did not automatically save any Jew, nor did it rule out salvation for Gentiles. But it gave awesome privileges and responsibilities to the nation Israel (9:1-6).

Paul's other three uses of the abstract noun 'election' or 'choice' in chapter 11 all relate to the same issue. **"In the same way then, there has also come to be at the present time a remnant according to God's gracious choice"** (11:5). In the preceding verses, Paul has referred to God's reserving a remnant of 7000 in the days of Elijah and has made a comparison with the remnant of Jewish believers in his day according to a principle of God's gracious choice. This he explained involved a hardening of unbelieving Israel, as part of that transition from Israel to the Church: **"What then? That which Israel is seeking for, it has not obtained, but the election obtained it, and the rest were hardened"** (11:7 NAS, margin). From the strong corporate context of this passage, it is close to obvious that Paul is not speaking of the selection of individual Jews to be that remnant, but rather a dealing with the Jewish people corporately. In the preceding chapter he had made it abundantly clear that faith is the principle upon which that remnant came into being (9:30–33; 10:2-4, 8-17).

The third use in this context is even more obviously a corporate allusion: **"From the standpoint of the gospel they are enemies for your sake, but from the standpoint of *God's* choice they are beloved for the sake of the fathers;"** (11:28). The clear antecedent of 'they' are the Jews who are enemies of the gospel, and yet, Paul says that corporately they are still God's elect nation, which he had just argued will ultimately be converted in the end time at the return of the Deliverer (11:11-27). Most transparently here, the abstract noun *eklogē* could not refer to individual unconditional election to salvation. Thus there is a consistent corporate usage of this term in these four usages.

Later Pauline references. The context of Colossians 3:12 is also helpful: **"Therefore, as God's chosen people, holy and dearly loved, clothe yourselves with compassion, kindness, humility, gentleness, and patience"** (NIV). Now coming to this verse with the prior usage in mind, let us retranslate accordingly: **"Therefore, as God's choice people, holy and dearly loved, clothe yourselves with compassion, kindness, humility, gentleness, and patience."** Remember that in many of Paul's letters he extensively describes the believer's exalted position in Christ, and then immediately bases his exhortations for godly living upon that position (Rom. 12:1-2; Eph. 4:1; Col. 3:1-3). Since we have been exalted to become God's choice people, holy and dearly loved, how appropriate that these moral qualities should be seen in us. On the other hand, being chosen by God with no revealed conditions would not be nearly as solid a base for moral appeal. Some who see themselves as 'the elect of God' are arrogant, self-righteous, and proud. Certainly the nation Israel, so conscious of their being the chosen people of God, had become arrogant, self-righteous, and proud in

Christ's day. In this light, a strong case can be made for the rende[illegible] "choice ones."

Let us also consider the context of Paul's usage in Titus 1:1: **"Paul, a servant of God and an apostle of Jesus Christ for the faith of God's elect and the knowledge of the truth that leads to godliness—a faith and knowledge resting on the hope of eternal life, which God, who does not lie, promised before the beginning of time"** (NIV). Here Paul writes to Titus, his missionary colleague, for the benefit of God's *eklectoi* with a view to strengthening their faith and enhancing their godliness. This is, of course, his epistle of good works. As in Colossians 3:12, I take it that the appeal to godliness is more harmonious with Paul's usual appeal based upon our exalted position in Christ, God's 'choice ones.' In his other epistles, more frequently, he addresses the recipients as 'saints' (Rom. 1:7; 1 Cor. 1:2; 2 Cor. 1:1; Eph. 1:1; Phil. 1:1; Col. 1:2), but here those to whom Titus is ministering are called 'choice ones.' This rendering, as before, simply takes note of the predominant meaning in the secular and Septuagintal Greek. Here it is worth noting how he links their being elect to their faith. Of course, we cannot separate them.

Paul's reference to the *eklektoi* in 2 Timothy 2:10 brings out an aspect which is reflected in other contexts. **". . . for which I am suffering even to the point of being chained like a criminal. But God's word is not chained. Therefore I endure everything for the sake of the elect [choice ones], that they too may obtain the salvation that is in Christ Jesus, with eternal glory"** (NIV). Again, we must decide whether the traditional rendering 'elect' fits the context, or whether we should go back to the predominant pre-New Testament usage of 'choice.' If God's people have been unconditionally elected to salvation, it escapes my understanding how Paul can say that his suffering in the Mamertine prison in Rome could contribute in any way to their ultimate salvation. On the other hand, Paul's propagation of the word of God even from prison could have a big impact upon the lives of many believers, if they are understood to be God's choice people, not just some privileged class of 'elect.' There is also an overtone of suffering in Christ's frequent reference in His prophetic discourse to the *eklektoi* in the great tribulation (Mt. 24:22, 24, 31; Mk. 13:20, 22, 27; & possibly Lk. 18:7). I would think that suffering saints are far more appropriately described as the 'choice ones,' rather than the 'unconditionally elected ones.'

Other considerations

John's usage. The elder apostle John's use of the adjective twice in 2 John to refer to a church as the "elect lady" and to his own church as the "elect sister" (vv. 1, 13) is euphemism in a time of growing persecution, to obscure his meaning to hostile eyes. Mission agencies working today in restricted countries have developed a similar code to communicate with our "workers." The corporate implications of his usage are quite transparent.

Relationship to legein. There is another underlying question that arises in the study of this group of words. They are derived from the very common verb *legein*, which has over a dozen meanings in the New Testament. Are any of these meanings significant in understanding the meanings of the derivatives? While being careful to avoid the "root fallacy" that Carson warned about, nevertheless, it seems to me that some of these meanings may be worth taking into account. For *legein* Arndt and Gingrich list as II, 1, c. as "*order, command, direct, enjoin*," and for II, 3. "*call, name*."[11] Since God's choice Servant of Isaiah 42 was called to service, His apostles were called to service, and Paul's emphasis is upon our being chosen to a lifestyle commensurate with His service, this linguistic connection to these connotations of *legein* may have some significance. In many of these passages one gets the impression that we are being called and named as His servants, and such a call is really an order or command. Unfortunately, most of humanity has not responded to that call or command.

Slight doctrinal emphasis. Is it not amazing that out of 51 usages of this group of words in the New Testament, only ten could possibly refer to a doctrine of election of individuals, whether conditional or unconditional? Three are in Peter, six in Paul, and the one enigmatic aphorism of Christ. It is also striking that beyond this there is no other theological reference in the four Gospels, Acts, James, Hebrews, Jude or the Johannine writings.[D] When we consider the centrality of unconditional election in Augustine's system and the theological controversies his view has engendered, one wonders whether this is really an adequate base for a whole theological system. We must examine these few contexts very carefully to make sure of our understanding, as I have just done.

In consideration of the clear connotation of "choice of the excellent" noted in the Hebrew, the secular Greek, the Septuagint Greek translation, and also in the New Testament in numerous passages, one wonders how the word 'elect' and 'election' even came into the picture. It would seem that the Greek word *eklektos* is related to the Latin "*electus*, past part. of *eligere* to elect, fr. *e* out + *legere* to choose."[12] The Latin *legere* would be connected with the Greek *legein* 'to call.' In essence, the English 'elect' thus is one stage removed from being a direct transliteration of the Greek, not a translation. The danger of transliterating Greek words into our New Testament is that any meaning that one pleases can thus be imposed upon that transliterated and really coined English word. Other examples of this problem would be *musterion*, which does not mean 'mystery;' *baptisma*, which has a meaning more specific than the coined word 'baptism,' and *apostasia*, which does not necessarily mean 'apostasy.' The point I am making is that the word 'elect' has a connotation in the mind of the

D In chapter 11 I have dealt with the misunderstood passages in John's Gospel where the Lord referred to "those whom the Father has given me."

Calvinists and many other Christians which is not in the Greek word *eklektos.*

Election Exclusively in Christ: Ephesians 1:3-14

Apart from 1 Corinthians 1:26-29, already discussed, Paul used the verb *eklegomai* only once and that in the most theologically significant passage: **"Blessed be the God and Father of our Lord Jesus Christ, who has blessed us with every spiritual blessing in the heavenly *places* in Christ: even as he chose us in him before the foundation of the world, that we should be holy and without blemish before him in love: having foreordained us unto adoption as sons through Jesus Christ unto himself, according to the good pleasure of his will, to the praise of the glory of his grace, which he freely bestowed on us in the Beloved:"** (ASV). I have already emphasized that in the secular Greek and the Septuagint Old Testament, the verb also is frequently used of choosing the choice, excellent, costly, or desirable. The major question is whether this connotation is carried over into this context. This question must be openly discussed since we have seen such clear examples of the adjective *eklektos* and the verb (in Lk. 9:35) having this connotation carried over into the New Testament. Another question which must be raised is whether Paul is speaking about individual selection or God's choice of the corporate church. Even if this is a reference to individual election to salvation, is it conditional or unconditional? Nothing can be assumed!

***Election is in Christ*.** Another consideration to factor in is the truth of the Lord Jesus as the Choice One, as noted above. The nation Israel was God's choice servant, but the latter part of Isaiah parallels the Messiah as God's ultimate elect or choice servant. This then became the issue between the Lord Jesus and the rulers of Israel. Although God attested His election in every possible way, they summarily finalized their rejection of Him as God's elect by mocking Him in those terms on the cross (Lk. 23:35). Now that He has risen and ascended on high, the corporate church is God's choice servant, chosen from the foundation of the world. It is not incidental that Paul wrote that we are chosen **"in Him."** This idea is strongly reinforced by the twenty times in the first two chapters of Ephesians that Paul used the expressions, "in Him," "in Christ," "in Christ Jesus," "in the Beloved One" (1:1, 3, 4, 6, 7, 9, 10 do, 12, 13 do, 15, 20; 2:6, 7, 10, 13, 15, 21, 22). Since He is the elect one, we are left with the very strong impression that the only possible election is "in Him," and there is no election apart from Him. He did not write that we are chosen **to be** in Him, but that we are **chosen in Him**. Our election or chosenness is in Christ. Thus it is only those individuals who are connected to Him by faith who are the elect or chosen ones. He is the corporate head of the Church and only those who have a relationship with Him by faith can in any sense be called the elect. Thus there can be no direct or individual election apart from union with Him. This should be almost axiomatic.

We must also factor in the basis of our election. The fact is that the only two passages which relate election or its related truth of pre-appointment to God's foreknowledge both put foreknowledge first. Peter had made it clear that we are **"elect [choice] according to the foreknowledge of God"** (1 Pet 1:1-2). Then we saw that Paul also gave priority to God's foreknowledge in Romans 8:29: **"Whom He foreknew He preappointed to be conformed to the image of His Son."** To go back to Christ's parable of the wedding feast, God foreknew who would respond to the open invitation given on the highways of life. The conditionality of it based upon our relationship to the Elect One by faith becomes paramount. In a real sense election is both corporate and individual. The foundational truth is the corporate election of the Church "in Christ." Individual election, if we may speak about it at all, is secondary and ancillary; it comes only through a faith-connection with the Head. Therefore, it is conditional, as both Peter and Paul have affirmed so simply and clearly. As far as I can see, the only basis for not accepting this truth is a prior theological commitment.

Relationship to foreordination/preappointment. Ephesians 1 is the only passage in which election is directly connected with foreordination or 'preappointment'. The verb *eklegomai* is in the aorist tense indicative and the verb *proorizein* is an aorist participle. Wallace points out that in this case the action of the participle is probably simultaneous to the action of the main verb and its adverbial function is possibly that of means, manner, or result.[13] Thus foreordination or preappointment is clearly distinct from election, but closely related. The exact relationship is hard to define with certainty. Of the three options Wallace gives for this syntactical relationship, result seems the most likely since it is a preappointment to adoption as sons. Paul's references to adoption are threefold: in Galatians 4:5-7 he uses this cultural illustration of our present liberated sonship; in Romans 8:14-15 he refers to the Spirit of adoption we have received; while in Romans 8:23 he speaks about the future liberation of our bodies from the curse as the final stage of that adoption to sonship. Paul's use of *huiothesia* as the Greco-Roman appointment of a child as the son and heir fits in well with the rendering of *proorizein* as 'preappointment' and confirms this connotation.

Appointment to a future inheritance revealed. Since *proorizein* is used again in 1:11, we must examine that context also: **"... making known to us the mystery of his will, according to his good pleasure which he purposed in him unto a dispensation of the fulness of the times, to sum up all [these] things in Christ, the things in the heavens, and the things upon the earth: in whom also we were made a heritage, having been foreordained according to the purpose of him who works all [these] things after the counsel of his will:"** (1:9-11, ASV). Now the adverbial participle of *proorizein* modifies the aorist of *klēroein*, a verb which occurs only here in the New Testament. Although here the two verbs are in the passive, we have the same syntactical relationship as above. Foerster in *TDNT* says its meaning in the secular Greek and the church fathers is 'to appoint' or 'to apportion.' He states:

> *klēroō* does not denote a pre-temporal act. It is an 'appointment' or 'determination' which affects men in their being. It is also the goal which is assigned to them in their calling. Materially, then, it is related to *eklēthēmen* ['we were called'], but with the nuance, implicit in *klēros* ['a lot'], that the call imparts something to the called, namely, a life's goal."[14]

This connotation is totally supportive of the understanding of *proorizein* which I have been arguing from its total usage, 'to preappoint.' Although the exact meaning of *klēroein* is difficult to verify since it is so rare, Paul's reference twice in the passage (1:14, 18) to our inheritance (*klēronomia*) and to our adoption as sons (1:5) confirms the idea of our being appointed to an inheritance. So the participle of *proorizein* probably explains that this was done by preappointing us according to His purpose or plan.

As noted in my discussion of Ephesians 1:11 in chapter 3, God is the One who works all *these* things (His salvation plan) according to the counsel of His will. It is not a wall-to-wall statement of God's direct involvement in every event which transpires in the whole universe.[E] Rightly understood, this in no way supports interpreting verse 4 as a reference to individual, unconditional election. Paul's statement that God is working out His salvation plan according to His eternal purpose says nothing about how specifically He may or may not have elected individuals. Indeed, Paul is here focusing upon God's intentions and purposes (1:9) for His 'choice ones' in the consummation (1:10) to preappoint them to a guaranteed inheritance (1:11), the seal and pledge of which is the promised Holy Spirit (1:13-14). Notice how this focus on the future continues on in 1:18, in 1:21, and in 2:7 where he refers to God's grace to His saints in the coming ages. In discussing Romans 8:28-30 in the last chapter, I pointed out that same futuristic perspective in Paul's use of *proorizein* there as well. The focus is not upon eternity past, but upon the glorious future for those who are now "in Christ." We had also observed the same futuristic perspective in 1 Peter 1 in connection with *eklektois*. All three of these definitive Scripture passages are in harmony in focusing on the future glory of God's choice church, with only the passing allusion to its beginning before creation. Notice the balance.

E The demonstrative use of the article in *ta panta* has been overlooked in most translations, and refers back to God's plan of salvation, not all things which transpire in the universe, as commonly understood by Augustinians. See the discussion in chapter 3.

The open secret of election

A key theme of Paul's theology, referred to in Ephesians 1:9 and initiated by the Lord Jesus in Matthew 13, is the truth of the "**mysteries of the kingdom of God.**" It is important, first off, to understand that *mustērion* should never have been merely transliterated as "mystery." From Paul's consistent usage in passages such as, Romans 16:25-6; Ephesians 3:4-5; and Colossians 1:26-7, it clearly has the connotation of "open secret," as Williams has rendered it.[15] The *mustērion* was hidden from past ages, but now has been revealed. This open secret is a complex of truths related to the Church, the body of Christ: the union of Jew and Gentile in the Church (Eph. 3:4-5), the organic body nature of the Church itself (Col. 1:24-26); the indwelling Christ as the riches of the open secret (Col. 1:27); and the transformation of our bodies at the rapture of the Church (1 Cor. 15:50-54).

This is relevant to our discussion of the nature of election in two regards. First, it is clear that the basis of God's election is not a mystery today, but has been revealed. As I will show in the next section, the Lord Jesus *did reveal* the human criteria by which God elects His choice ones. Deuteronomy 29:29 should not be quoted as proof that God's criteria are hidden or mysterious or arbitrary or capricious. Second, since Paul keeps connecting these open secrets relating to the church with God's choice of His people through the gospel, there is substantiation that Paul has in mind a corporate election in Ephesians 1:4. Let us look into both of these ideas.

The criteria of God's choice

Since God has revealed the open secret of the basis upon which people can be saved, we should not have to search very far into the New Testament to find out the criteria which contribute to people coming to repentant faith in Christ. Indeed, the Lord Jesus had a lot to say about these criteria.

God's secret will? The basis of God's foreordination is held to be part of God's secret counsel by our Calvinistic friends, frequently quoting Deuteronomy 29:29: **"The secret things belong to the Lord our God, but the things revealed belong to us and to our sons forever, that we may observe all the words of the law."** However, God really **has revealed** the basis of His foreordination and calling to salvation. Since the Lord Jesus explained its basis on a number of occasions, no one need be ignorant as to the basis of God's foreordination.

Christ the revealer. In the Sermon on the Mount He made it very clear that it was not the arrogant and self-righteous, but "the poor in spirit" who would be blessed to possess the kingdom of God (Mt. 5:3), those who recognize their spiritual poverty and need. After reproaching the towns of Israel which had sinned against such great light in rejecting Him (Mt. 11:20-24), He said, **"I praise Thee, O Father, Lord of heaven and earth, that Thou didst hide these things from the wise and intelligent and didst**

reveal them to babes. Yes, Father for thus it was well-pleasing in Thy sight" (11:25-26). The next verse (11:27) is a favorite proof text of those who believe in a hidden and arbitrary sovereign election. However, from the context we see that the "babes" can be identified as the **"anyone to whom the Son wills to reveal *Him*,"** and He followed this up immediately with His universal invitation: **"Come to Me, all who are weary and heavy-laden, and I will give you rest"** (11:28). Need I explain the connection of the "poor in spirit" to the "babes?"

Then the cruciality of the parable of the four soils is seen not only in its repetition in all three Synoptic Gospels, but also in the interpretation supplied by the Lord Himself. Luke's record comes down to a main point in 8:15: **"And the *seed* in the good soil, these are the ones who have heard the word in an honest and good heart, and hold it fast, and bear fruit with perseverance."** Apparently a person who has a heart which is honestly open to the truth is the one who responds to the gospel message. No mystery here! There are many occasions on which the Lord commended those who had faith and rebuked those who had closed their hearts in unbelief. I have given many more examples in chapter 10.

The apostolic revelation. The apostle Paul also had considerable to say about the basis of foreordination. Consider1Corinthians 1:26-29, which I have just quoted above. In expanding on the teaching of the Lord Jesus, Paul reminded the arrogant Corinthian Christians, proud of their sophisticated Greek philosophical knowledge and their liberated lifestyle, of the broad principles which have governed the selective process by which people come to faith in Christ. It is the common people, the poor, the ignorant, the marginalized and weak, who recognize their spiritual need and are more open to respond to the gospel message. He is not speaking of an unconditional decision made by God in eternity about individuals. Quite the contrary, this passage shows that the basis for election *has been revealed*.

There are many other clear human factors which enter in prominently, which I have identified in chapter 11. One of those factors which Paul identifies as operative in his own conversion was ignorance: **"I thank Christ Jesus our Lord, who has strengthened me, because He considered me faithful, putting me into service; even though I was formerly a blasphemer and a persecutor and a violent aggressor. And yet I was shown mercy, because I acted ignorantly in unbelief"** (1 Tim. 1:12-13). Paul has taken us into the supposedly secret counsels of God to identify the factor of *ignorance* as a basis upon which God showed him mercy.

In 2 Thessalonians 2:9-11 he contrasts this with the basis upon which in the end time God will close the door of salvation in a judgmental delusion: **". . . *that is*, the one whose coming is in accord with the activity of Satan, with all power and signs and false wonders, and with all the deception of wickedness for those who perish, <u>because they did not receive the love of the truth</u> so as to be saved. And for this reason God will send**

upon them a deluding influence so that they might believe what is false, . . .". His reference to **"those who did not receive the love of the truth"** seems to be the converse of the good soil of Christ's parable and the language of Paul's colleague Luke in Acts 17:11-12, in reference to the Berean Jews: **"Now these were more nobleminded than those in Thessalonika, for they received the word with great eagerness, examining the Scriptures daily, *to see* whether these things were so. Many of them therefore believed, along with a number of prominent Greek women and men."** Please note the extreme significance of Luke's "therefore" in verse 12. The Bereans were those who had "honest hearts" (Lk. 8:15) to check out Paul's message in the Scriptures. So there really is some revealed basis for God's election and calling. It is not mysterious and unconditional, certainly not arbitrary or capricious!

Thus there are significant examples of the analogy of Scripture to identify faith in Romans 8:29 as that which God foreknew in His elect people. My Calvinistic friends will cry out in holy horror that this sounds like meritorious works and synergism (a pejorative term). I respond with Paul's answer in Romans 4:16: **"For this reason *it is* by faith that *it might be* in accordance with grace, in order that the promise may be certain to all the descendants, not only to those who are of the Law, but also to those who are of the faith of Abraham, who is the father of us all."** There is nothing meritorious in repentant faith since it is simply acknowledging our bankruptcy and reaching out to receive God's free gift of eternal life. But all of us, Calvinists, Arminians, and those of us in the middle alike, must find the essential harmony between a doctrine of election, the teachings of Christ, and the other anecdotal evidence I have given. We cannot ignore a part of the evidence because it does not fit our system.

The new choice people of God. It should be noted that Ephesians is pre-eminently Paul's epistle of the church, the body of Christ. Other than reference to Tychicus, the bearer of the letter, there are no personal references in the letter. Because the phrase "in Ephesus" is not found in the oldest manuscripts, it is taken by many scholars that this was a circular letter for the churches of the province of Asia, and went first to Ephesus, the founding church. The key issue of the oneness of both Jew and Gentile in the one body is a major theme. Klein and others have argued for the corporate nature of election. A number of cogent arguments can be given:

1. Israel's election by God was clearly corporate and did not guarantee salvation to anybody; it was for service.

2. The concept of corporate solidarity is not only essential to the cultures into which the Old Testament came, but is an essential component of the Old Testament itself. Corporate solidarity is still today integral to Asian and African cultures. With our strong emphasis upon individualism, this has been lost in our western cultures. It is not

surprising that the notion of individual election to salvation arose in the western, Latin church and is totally absent from eastern Christianity. The Greek churches, which presumably understood Greek better, have no concept of individual election.

3. Peter unequivocally confirmed the corporate nature of election in 1 Peter 2:9, as we have seen. Paul's heavy corporate-solidarity emphasis in Romans 5 and 9–11, strongly colors the rest of his epistles. The idea of Adam, as corporate head of the human race, affecting the whole race by one sin (Rom. 5:12ff.), both transmitted and imputed, is hard for westerners to grasp. We more easily accept that Christ was our representative head, suffering for our sins. That Israel should corporately be set aside and cut off from the root of Abraham is another major issue in Romans. The references to churches in 2 John is further confirmatory.

4. There are many New Testament symbols of the church which have strong corporate overtones: the vine, the body, the temple of God, the flock, the bride, and the people (nation) of God.

5. The ordinances of the church are ultimately corporate in nature. The Lord's table is more obvious, but when we relate water baptism to spirit-baptism putting us into the corporate church, its corporate dimension is also clear.

6. Election (chosenness) is functional. Israel was chosen to be God's servant nation. The twelve apostles were chosen to be messengers to Israel, and this did not guarantee their salvation (i.e. Judas).

7. The use of the adjective 'elect' is always in the plural, except in Rom. 16:13 and 2 John, where the references were not to individuals as elect.[16]

When we take these considerations into account, we can see how Paul could well be referring to the corporate church as that which God chose in eternity past to become His choice people.

The Significance of Election

Our understanding of Christian election must be founded upon the election of Israel and of Christ. In neither case was there an unconditional election to salvation. The Church succeeded Israel as the choice people of God in this present age of grace, and it only exists because of its connection by faith with its Head, Jesus Christ, the Choice One of the Father. We have seen that the predominant meaning of 'choice' and 'choice of the best' in secular Greek and the Septuagint does carry over into the New Testament very significantly, and incredibly opens up the meaning of key passages such as Luke 9:35, Matthew 22:14, and 1 Peter 1:1-2, and had already been recognized in 1 Peter 2:4, 6. Although the traditional translations are meaningful in most other passages, it is clear that the translators have not given adequate consideration to the predominant usage before the New Testament.

In considering all the theologically relevant passages, I have concluded that there is no basis for a doctrine of individual unconditional election. The corporate nature of election is so clear in enough contexts to lead to the probability that all should be taken corporately. I grant that this is difficult to prove or disprove with absolute certainty. I have also suggested that there are significant number of contexts in which conditional election is clear. Conversely there is no clear, unambiguous evidence of unconditional election in any of the contexts. Therefore, we must not read unconditional election into those contexts which could be taken either way. The presumption in those cases is in favor of a consistent picture of election being conditioned upon the sinner's response to the gospel message in repentant faith.

Is election corporate or is it conditional? I suspect that it is both, and that, whichever way you slice it, unconditional individual election is in error. At the very least, I trust I have raised enough doubts about Augustine's novel doctrine to cause my Calvinistic friends to stop building their whole theology of salvation upon it.

---

1. Sauer, The Dawn of World Redemption:, pp. 89-90.

2. Ibid, pp. 108-120.

3. Imad Shahadeh, Panel Discussion, Evangelical Theological Society Annual Meeting, Nashville, TN, November, 2000. As one of very few Arab premillennial Christians, he affirms that God will restore Israel in the land in His time, but that the present generation of Jews, who are there in unbelief in the gospel, have no real right to the land. The previous panel discussion of Hebrew Christian leaders that afternoon brought out the fact that 85% of the Jews in Israel are non-religious and that very few are Christians. So the primary issue for Christians today is to be even-handed in emphasizing even-handed justice and fairness for both Israelis and Palestinians.

4. John N. Oswalt in Harris, Archer, Waltke, *Theological Wordbook of the Old Testament*, pp. 100-101.

5. G. Quell, in *Theological Dictionary of the New Testament*, IV, p. 145.

6. William W. Klein, *The New Chosen People*, p. 37, referencing R. P. Shedd, *Man in Community*, pp. 3-41.

7. H. Wheeler Robinson, as cited by Klein, p. 39.

8. G. Schrenk and G. Quell in *TDNT*, IV, p. 144-5; 176-182; Arndt and Gingrich, pp. 241-242.

9. James Daane, *The Freedom of God*, p. 101.

10. From the debate between Clark Pinnock and J. I. Packer on Calvinism and Arminianism.

11. Arndt and Gingrich, *Lexicon*, p. 470-1.

12. *Webster's Collegiate Dictionary*, 5th ed., p. 320.

13. Wallace, *Grammar*, pp. 624-6. Note chart #82 on p. 626.

14. Werner Foerster in *TDNT*, III, pp. 764-5. Foerster's reference to 'being called' seems to be of a textual variant.

15. Charles B. Williams, *The New Testament*, p. 445. Curiously Williams has only used this rendering in Colossians and not in the parallel passages in Ephesians. He should have been consistent.

16. Klein; *Chosen People*; Daane, *Freedom of God*; Forster and Marston, *Strategy*. Ideas drawn from many sources.

I know not how the Spirit moves
Convincing men of sin,
Revealing Jesus through the word,
Creating faith in Him.
But I know whom I have believed,
And am persuaded that He is able
To keep that which I've committed
Unto Him against that day.
-Daniel W. Whittle

9

HOW CAN DEAD MEN BELIEVE? THE CONVICTION OF THE SPIRIT

It would seem that all evangelical Christians desire to retain the divine initiative in their understanding of the plan of salvation. Since mankind is spiritually dead, we need some explanation as to how spiritually dead sinners can come to faith in Christ. Calvinists hark back to Augustine's doctrine of irresistible grace which involves regeneration preceding faith, which will specifically be addressed in subsequent chapters. Arminians, on the other hand, have a doctrine of universal prevenient grace, which enables all fallen men to respond to God's message of grace. Those of us in the middle do not find either solution satisfying, because neither is inductively derived. We find the answer in the explicit teaching of the Lord Jesus in the upper room, just before the cross and preparatory to the Pentecost event. We believe that this is the neglected key to the problem.

The neglected key

The tragedy is that in most of the discussion around these issues a vital key to its resolution has been overlooked, even though clearly predicted in the Upper Room Discourse (Jn. 16:7-11) and exemplified on the day of Pentecost and many times subsequently in the Acts and the Epistles. The only theologians I can find who have given serious attention to the doctrine of the convicting work of the Spirit are Lewis Sperry Chafer and James Oliver Buswell, Jr. Chafer devoted eleven pages to conviction in his Pneumatology, three pages in his doctrinal summarization, and made other incidental references to it. Buswell devoted eight pages to his discussion, and additionally made a number of other references to it. Few of the other theologians I was able to consult gave more than a passing notice to this doctrine, if at all. In 1948 Chafer wrote, "Within the whole divine enterprise of winning the lost, there is no factor more vital than the work of the Holy Spirit in which He convinces or reproves the *cosmos* world respecting sin, righteousness, and judgment."[1] In 1962 Buswell wrote: "The convicting work of the Holy Spirit is, in my opinion, a neglected subject, the careful contemplation of which would clarify several important obscurities in theological discussions."[2] He further expanded:

> The doctrine of conviction as a work of the Holy Spirit prior to either regeneration or faith, it seems to me, solves this problem.... Prior to either regeneration or faith, the Holy Spirit does convict the lost *sufficiently* so that those who reject God's grace are wholly to blame for their lost condition, and *effectively* in the elect, so that those who are saved must acknowledge that their faith is wholly a gift of God.[3]

Although Buswell was a five-point Calvinist, his discussion of conviction seems very moderate, even Arminian.

The core of the issue is how spiritually dead people can hear the gospel, believe, and be saved. In order to solve the problem, starting from their concept of total inability, extreme Calvinists have reversed the biblical order and put regeneration before faith (which Calvin did not do, cf. ch. 10). On the other hand, Arminians and evangelical Lutherans have not been very successful in answering the charge of synergism, thus compromising the gracious nature of salvation. An inductive study of the convicting or convincing work of the Spirit will lead to a mediate solution to the problem and is a vital key to resolving the centuries-old controversy between the Calvinists and the Arminians.

Calvinists put a great stress upon objective truth: the objective decrees of God in eternity and objective realities in redemption history. But they struggle in the subjective realm. That is, how can one be included among the elect, and how can one know if one is among the elect? What can unregenerate people do while waiting for God's irresistible grace? Edwardsian preparationism was a bad solution to an intractable problem. It was the Anabaptists, Moravians and pietistic Lutherans who began to try to balance off the strong objectivism with a more personal experiential and subjective approach. Arminians and moderate Calvinists have sought to balance the objective and subjective dimensions of salvation. Today the Pentecostal and charismatic movements have overemphasized the subjective aspect. Albeit, pietistic subjectivism is an important dimension of mainstream evangelicalism today. My thesis is that the restoration of the doctrine of the conviction of the Spirit provides the necessary balance and is the key to this whole conundrum.

In making this proposal I would like to make a vital distinction which has not been adequately recognized in the soteriological literature. This is the distinction between the means by which people come to saving faith in Christ, which is a process having heavy human involvement, and on the other hand, the new birth itself, which is one-hundred per cent the work of the Holy Spirit, accomplished instantaneously without any human participation. Thus we have a process in which the Holy Spirit works mediately through human instrumentality to bring the sinner under conviction leading to faith, which then triggers the Spirit's work of regeneration. This is an extremely simple distinction, but it seems to have been almost totally overlooked.

THE HISTORY OF THE DOCTRINE

There is no discussion of John 16:7-11 or of the doctrine of conviction in Calvin's *Institutes.* In his commentaries there is some discussion, but he referred to the "obscurity of the passage" and did not relate it to any theological principle. He stated, "Christ does not speak of secret revelations, but of the power of the Spirit, which appears in the outward doctrine of the Gospel, and in the voice of men."[4] He held that conviction extends both to the truly converted and also to hypocrites and reprobates: "Some are moved in good earnest . . . others do not sincerely yield." He alluded to 1 Corinthians 14:23 as an example of conviction. Buswell claims William Ames (1576-1633) as ascribing conviction as preparatory to salvation.[5]

Charles Hodge saw the conviction of sin as an aspect of common grace, which is necessitated by human depravity. He referred to "an influence of the Spirit on the minds distinct from and accessary to the power of the truth." In his extended discussion of this aspect of common grace, he twice alludes to the language of John 16 but never quoted it or exegeted it as a determinative scripture for this doctrine, nor indeed called it a distinct doctrine.[6]

Similarly W. G. T. Shedd discussed the "work of conviction which is preparatory or antecedent to regeneration." He discussed this under the rubric of Edwardsian preparationism. Curiously, he never specifically alluded to or referred to John 16:7-11. "The sinner cannot co-operate in the work of regeneration, but he can in the work of conviction."[7]

A. H. Strong did not have any treatment of the convicting work of the Spirit or any discussion of John 16:7-11, only using this passage as a proof text for other issues. In discussing the means of regeneration he referred to the truth (word) and the Spirit and tended to follow Melanchthon in including the will of man.[8]

L. Berkhof had no discussion of the conviction of the Spirit and minimal passing references to John 16:8ff. He apparently did not see it as preparatory to regeneration, for he referred to the Holy Spirit pleading "the cause of believers against the world (John 16:8), . . ." In another context on the external call, he referenced John 16:8, 9 also in a negative sense. Apparently the doctrine of conviction found no place in relation to his view of irresistible grace.[9]

Extreme Calvinists have a serious problem with this passage because it does not fit into their pat system. Most outrageously, Arthur W. Pink goes to the extent of denying the truth of the passage:

> But, it may be said, is not the present mission of the Holy Spirit to 'convict *the world* of sin'? And we answer, It is not. The *mission* of the Spirit is threefold; to glorify Christ, to vivify the elect, to edify the saints. John 16:8-11 does not describe the 'mission' of the Spirit, but sets forth the *significance of His presence* here in the world. It treats not of His subjective work in sinners, showing them their need of Christ, by searching their consciences and striking terror to their hearts; what we have there is entirely objective.

How ironic that in the very act of denying its patent truth, Pink explains most aptly that which he rejects. He reaffirmed that denial even more explicitly farther along: ". . . during this dispensation, the Spirit has no mission and ministry worldward. . . ."[10]

From a more contemporary Arminian theologian, Orton Wiley, we get a good brief introductory statement, quoting John 16:8-11. In the next chapter he had a two-page explanation, again quoting John 16:8. In a subsequent discussion of prevenient grace he seemed to see it as distinct from the conviction of the Spirit, since he made no further reference to conviction of the Spirit.[11]

EXEGESIS OF THE DETERMINING SCRIPTURES

The context of John 16:7-11

First we must get the passage before us:

> **But I tell you the truth, it is to your advantage that I go away; for if I do not go away, the Helper [*Paraklētos*] will not come to you; but if I go, I will send Him to you. And He when He comes, will convict the world of sin and righteousness and judgment; concerning sin, because they do not believe in Me; and concerning righteousness, because I go to the Father and you no longer see Me; and concerning judgment, because the ruler of this world has been judged.**

Calvin's reference to the obscurity of the passage is only understandable in the light of the medieval scholastic mindset against which he was struggling. He was having to be a pioneer in hermeneutics and had not yet focused on the lucid context of our determining Scripture. The watchword,

"Context is king!" is totally appropriate here. One of the main themes of the Upper Room Discourse is the prophecy by our Lord of the coming of the Holy Spirit, which was to be fulfilled about fifty days forward on the day of Pentecost. Not only did Christ state this explicitly in John 14:16-17 but reaffirmed it in many different ways:

> **And I will ask the Father and He will give you another Helper, that He may be with you forever, that is the Spirit of truth, whom the world cannot receive, because it does not behold Him or know Him, but you know Him because He abides with you, and will be in you.**

Then He identified a specific day in which the Spirit would be **given** (14:20), which is obviously Pentecost. In the subsequent chapters, He keeps weaving this idea into the rest of the discourse. In 14:26 and again in 15:26, He spoke of the Father **sending** the Spirit. There He also spoke about the Spirit **coming** from the Father, which word He used again in 16:7, 8, & 13. In 15:26 He also spoke of the Spirit **proceeding** from the Father in the present tense, which reference has occasioned the controversial and dubious notion of the eternal procession of the Spirit.[A] However, it seems likely in the context that this is a futuristic use of the present tense, thus reinforcing the other statements. Lastly, in 16:7 He reiterated the verb 'send.' Thus 'give' is used once, 'send' three times, 'come' four times, and 'proceed' once. It is clear that the Lord Jesus is predicting Pentecost as an advent of the Holy Spirit equally as earth-shaking as His own at Bethlehem. Frank Bottome was not in the least off target in penning the hymn, "The Comforter Has Come."

Of course, we all believe in the omnipresence of the Holy Spirit and might wonder how Christ could predict the advent of an omnipresent Person. However, although the Son of God Himself shares the omnipresence of the Trinity, yet He had an advent through incarnation. Thus Ryrie's clarification that the Holy Spirit came to reside in the newborn church is very cogent.[12] In any case it is clear from the context that the Holy Spirit was to begin His special ministry of conviction on the day of Pentecost. Thus it is astonishing to me that few, if any, theologians or commentators have made the connection between the convicting work of the Spirit and the events recorded in Acts 2. We will come back to this presently. First we must carefully examine the meaning of the key words.

The meaning of *elegchein* (to convict, convince)

In the Greek philosophers *elegchein* and its cognates are mostly used in the intellectual realm of the controverting of propositions. Epictetus, howev-

---

A. The controversy between the Eastern Orthodox and Western Catholic churches over the eternal procession of the Spirit, which ostensibly caused the split, was totally beside the point since Jn. 15:26 says nothing about an eternal procession.

er, used it in an ethical sense, of the cure of souls. In the Septuagint it is used to translate Hebrew words meaning, 'to rebuke,' 'to shame,' 'to punish,' 'condemn,' 'convict,' 'to test,' and 'to examine.' Buchsel in *TDNT* concluded that:

> . . . it denotes the disciplining and educating of man by God as a result of His judicial activity. This embraces all aspects of education from the conviction of the sinner to chastisement and punishment, from the instruction of the righteous by severe tests to his direction by teaching and admonition.

It is used seventeen times in the New Testament and means "to show someone his sin and to summon him to repentance." The means used to bring this about are: the prophet, conscience, the self-revelation of light, divine instruction, and the Law. *Elegchos* has the sense of 'proof,' 'convincing,' 'refutation,' 'investigation,' and 'account.' The abstract noun *elegsis* means 'persuasion,' 'refutation.'[13]

Arndt and Gingrich list four New Testament meanings: "1. *bring to light, expose, set forth. . . . 2. convict or convince someone of someth., point someth. out to someone. . . .* 3. *reprove, correct. . . .* 4. heightened, *punish, discipline. . . .*"[14] (A number of current English dictionaries indicate that today the older usage of 'convict' has been replaced by 'convince' except in the legal sphere.)

Most of the New Testament usages have to do with confronting and reproving moral error, whether in an unbeliever (Lk. 3:19) or believers (most). Paul used it twice to encourage Titus to refute and correct the doctrinal errors of professing Christians (1:9, 13). Only in 1 Corinthians 14:24 is it used in the sense of John 16 to refer to convicting or convincing an unbeliever to repent and believe the gospel. Jude used it of the return of Christ in final judgment upon the godless (15). The abstract noun *elegchos* is used in Hebrews 11:1 of faith as a conviction of the unseen, which I see in a subjective sense.

The meaning of *paraklētos*

The Lord's new term used the fourth time here in this discourse of the coming Holy Spirit casts significant light on the nature of this anticipated ministry. The translators have struggled to come up with one English word to communicate this multifaceted term. Arndt and Gingrich list among its meanings: 'mediator,' 'intercessor,' and 'helper.' The abstract noun *paraklēsis* and the verb from which they are derived, *parakalein*, have the connotations of 'encouragement,' 'exhortation,' and 'comfort.'[15] Perhaps most relevant to the conviction ministry of Christ which the Spirit was to assume at Pentecost, is the connotation of '**exhortation**.'

The meaning of *kosmos* (world)

It should go without saying that John's usage of *kosmos*, which is so replete at about a hundred times, must be determinative as to our Lord's meaning here. Abbott-Smith lists four connected usages:

> 1. *order* . . . 2. *ornament, adornment* . . . 3. Later, the *world* or *universe,* as an ordered system . . . 4. In late writers only, *the world, i.e. the earth*; . . . hence by meton., (a) of the human inhabitants of the world . . . (b) of worldly affairs or possessions . . .; (c) in ethical sense, of the ungodly, the world as apart from God and thus evil in its tendency. . .[16]

John overwhelmingly uses it in the fourth sense, especially 4.(c). This is not a matter of controversy, and thus in our exegesis of the passage, we must focus on the Holy Spirit's ministry to the unregenerate people of this evil world-system, who need salvation. This is made even more striking by Christ's reference to Satan as the "prince of this world" in 12:31, and again even more significantly in our passage (16:11).

The development of Christ's thought

Christ, the *Parakletos*. Thus when the Lord Jesus promised the coming of the Holy Spirit into the world on the day of Pentecost, one of His significant ministries was to be the convicting, convincing, exposing, and reproving of unregenerate mankind in regard to the three areas He stipulated. The verb is a simple future which would imply that this ministry of the Spirit had not yet begun, and thus that Pentecost was to be the initiation of this particular ministry. Indeed, there is no reference to any such activity of the Spirit in the Old Testament or Gospel accounts. Christ himself was the first *Parakletos*, who while He was in the world sought to bring people under the conviction of sin, righteousness, and judgment.

There are many examples. Certainly the Sermon on the Mount was His use of the Mosaic Law to bring Pharisaic Jews under the conviction of their sin and recognition of their need of His righteousness. We think of how His sinless character and supernatural works brought conviction to the apostles, such as in Luke 5:8. His interview with the rich young ruler is another striking example of our Lord's use of the Law to bring the conviction of sin (Mt. 19:16-26). Here, however, even He did not succeed in getting this rich man to realize that he did not love his neighbor as himself, thus recognizing his need of the Messiah. But now as He was to depart and His personal ministry of conviction must necessarily end, He promised the Holy Spirit as another *Paraklētos*. The Spirit would begin to take the responsibility for this important ministry and He was not limited to a human body.

Christ's clarification. Contrary to Calvin's appraisal of the passage as being obscure, the Lord Jesus gave an explanation of the threefold convicting ministry of the Spirit. It is granted that His explanation in John

16:8-11 is not transparent. But by drawing upon the broader context of Scripture the meaning does become clear. In 16:9 He explained that the conviction of sin relates to the world's unbelief in Him: "**. . . concerning sin, because they do not believe in Me.**" A starting point would be John's earlier references to mankind's sin as the key issue with which Christ had to deal (John 1:5, 29) and also the main obstacle to people coming to Christ (1:5, 10-11, 3:19-21). More specifically He focused upon the one sin which is the central issue in order to be saved—rejection of the Messiah Himself (3:18, 36). This highlights the uniqueness of unbelief as the only unforgivable sin. People need to be convinced that they are sinners, but especially of the seriousness of unbelief in Christ.

Chafer focused upon the imperative of the convicting work of the Spirit in the plan of salvation by referring to the spiritual blindness of mankind.[17] John used this symbolism repeatedly in his Gospel. Christ is the light come into the world, and men were so spiritually blind that God had to send John the Baptizer to point people to the light (1:6-9).[B] The apostle Paul confirms the spiritual blindness of the unregenerate as not just being a natural problem of man's sin, but also a satanic blindness as well. "**But even if our gospel is veiled, it is veiled to those who are perishing, in whose case the god of this world has blinded the minds of the unbelieving, that they might not see the light of the gospel of the glory of Christ, who is the image of God**" (2 Cor. 4:3-4).

The necessity occasioned by the spiritual death of mankind raises a significant issue. The extreme Calvinistic scenario is that since man is spiritually dead and unable to believe, therefore the unregenerate must be born again in order to believe. Although I address the unscriptural nature of this reversed sequence in chapter 10, let me alert you to the words of Christ in John 5:25 in reference to the new birth: "**Truly, truly, I say to you, an hour is coming and now is, when the dead shall hear the voice of the Son of God; and those who hear shall live.**" He did not say that the regenerate shall hear, but that the **dead** shall hear and come to life spiritually. I believe that the convicting, convincing work of the Spirit is the key as to how this can happen.

The second focus of conviction is explained in verse 10, "**. . . and concerning righteousness, because I go to the Father, and you no longer behold Me.**" While He was in the world, the Lord Jesus brought conviction of righteousness. He was the perfect example of absolute righteousness. Just the fact of His sinless person brought conviction about the source of true righteousness. He was full of grace and truth. Additionally, we should consider that He went back to the Father by way of

---

B. It should be noted that John 1:9 does not make the enlightenment of Christ's advent universal, as held by the Quakers, but rather general. It is strange that few, if any, commentators have recognized that *panta anthropon* can easily be rendered "all mankind," that is, that Christ's enlightenment reaches out to all mankind, not just Jews.

the cross and resurrection, thus providing the basis for sinners to be declared righteous. Therefore, based upon Christ's going to the Father in this way, Paul could expound this doctrine of justification in the epistle to the Romans, the theme of which is the righteousness of God, or more exactly, a righteousness from God. Christ thus is the ultimate source of righteousness for unrighteous mankind (Rom. 10:4). This is the heart of the gospel about which the Spirit came to convince mankind and is discussed in my chapter 12.

The third focus of conviction is explained in verse 11, "**. . . and concerning judgment, because the ruler of this world has been judged**." Again the connection is not transparent. This is a reference to Satan's judgment in the cross. This connects with John 12:31-32: "**Now judgment is upon this world; now the ruler of this world shall be cast out, and I, if I be lifted up from the earth, will draw all men to Myself**." Satan's doom was sealed in the cross, even though he is now a usurper, at large, prowling about like a roaring lion (1 Pet. 5:8). Most relevant to the unregenerate people of this world-system is the fact that their doom has also been sealed, as long as they are not liberated from Satan's power. The Lord Jesus thus made this logical connection of the judgment of Satan through the cross and His drawing all mankind unto Himself in faith. I suggest that the convicting work of the Spirit is the means by which He is drawing all mankind unto Himself. Satan's power was broken in the cross as Paul later affirmed in Colossians 2:15: "**When He had disarmed the rulers and authorities, He made public display of them, having triumphed over them through Him.**" Satan's condemnation makes it imperative that those who are under his sway claim the Messiah's finished work to experience redemption-liberation. This is the third area of truth about which the Spirit has come to convince the unregenerate of this satanic world-system. Since the Spirit's ministry focuses on these three area, our witness for Christ must be brought into harmony with the Spirit's strategy in pointing people to Christ.

ITS HISTORICAL ACTUALIZATION

Pentecost

With the crystal-clear context of the Upper Room Discourse and His promise to send the Spirit in mind, it now seems obvious that we should move to the fulfillment of that promise in the events of Acts chapter two. Indeed, the Lord himself confirmed this fulfillment a week before Pentecost:

> **Gathering them together, He commanded them not to leave Jerusalem, but to wait for what the Father had promised, 'Which,'** ***He said*****, 'you heard of from Me; for John baptized with water, but you will be baptized with the Holy Spirit not many days from now.' . . . but you will receive power when the Holy Spirit has come upon you; and you shall be My witnesses . . .'**

(Acts 1:4-5, 8).

What is totally astonishing is that few commentators or theologians, if any, make this connection. Let us hope that many preachers and evangelists over the centuries have done better than the theologians and commentators. As we examine the inspired record, verse 37 stands out. Peter has completed his sermon, boldly proclaiming the risen Messiah and charging Israel with His death. At that point we read, "**Now when they heard *this*, they were pierced to the heart, and said to Peter and the rest of the apostles, 'Brethren, what shall we do?'**" Here we have thousands of Jews who are evidently under the conviction of the Spirit, but they were not yet saved. Essentially they are asking the apostles how they can be saved. The verb *katanussein,* which is used here is a *hapax legomenon* (occurring only once) and means, "1. *to strike or prick violently.* 2. *to stun.* 3. of strong emotion, pass., *to be smitten: tēn kardian*, Ac 2[37]."[18]

Then in verse 38 we have Peter's answer: "**And Peter *said* to them, 'Repent, and let each of you be baptized in the name of Jesus Christ for the forgiveness of your sins, and you shall receive the gift of the Holy Spirit.'**" They needed to repent as a condition of receiving the Holy Spirit. Thus in the brief time between v. 37 and their actual repentance they were the recipients of the Spirit's convicting ministry, but not yet of His regenerating work. Conviction precedes repentance, which precedes the gift of the Spirit's indwelling and regeneration. It seems clear that the Spirit used the supernatural gift of languages and Peter's sermon as the means of bringing them under conviction. Conviction is apparently a mediate or indirect ministry of the Spirit, as contrasted with the work of regeneration, which is immediate and direct.

We are not told whether the three thousand who were saved were the only ones who had come under conviction. Presumably many more came under conviction who did not repent at this time. Perhaps many of them were among the thousands who were saved subsequently. Perhaps many never came to repentance and faith. We are not told. We shall have to discuss this issue of the extent of conviction in short order.

Other examples

Positive examples. The book of Acts is replete with other accounts which relate to this ministry of conviction. We see some very explicit statements of a positive response to the Spirit's working. However, every time we see people being saved we can understand the Spirit's convicting work is involved, whether Luke explicitly alluded to it or not. In connection with the healing of the lame man outside the temple gate, Peter and John's witness caused thousands more to believe (3:11–4:4). Luke consistently connected their being Spirit-filled with their boldness and the resulting fruitfulness of their witness (4:8, 31, 33; 5:32; 6:10; 7:55; 9:17; 11:24; 13:9, 52; etc.). Mostly the result was positive, but as in Stephen's martyrdom there was a negative response. In Samaria Philip saw multitudes come to Christ (8:5-8).

Even when Saul of Tarsus was persecuting Christians, the Holy Spirit was convicting him through the witness of Stephen and other Christians' testimonies as he dragged them into court. The risen Lord said to him, "**It is hard for you to kick against the goads**" (26:9-14). Up to that point he had been resisting the conviction of the Spirit. But after his conversion and subsequent filling with the Spirit, he immediately proclaimed Christ boldly in Damascus (9:17-22). Peter's ministry in Lydda, Sharon, and Joppa got a massive response (9:35, 42), which was connected with outstanding miraculous signs by the Holy Spirit.

Cornelius and his household were not saved people before Peter preached to them (11:14), but the Spirit must have been working in their lives before they heard the gospel from Peter. Then the outstanding follow-up of the conversion of these first Gentiles took place in Antioch of Syria, where a large number of Gentiles were saved through Jewish believers from Cyprus and Cyrene, and later through the Spirit-filled ministry of Barnabas (11:19-26). The Holy Spirit continued working there as Saul/ Paul and Barnabas were sent out as the first cross-cultural missionaries among the Gentiles (13:1-3).

On their first stop in Cyprus Barnabas and Paul were the instruments of the Spirit in persuading the proconsul, Sergius Paulus, who had summoned them to share the gospel. In Antioch of Pisidia after Paul's sermon in the synagogue, we find a striking account: "**And as Paul and Barnabas were going out, the people kept begging that these things might be spoken to them the next Sabbath**" (Acts 13:42). It would seem clear that many were under conviction and from the next verse that some were being saved. Possibly many were convicted but not yet saved. Responding to the Jewish opposition, the apostles announced: "**It was necessary that the word of God should be spoken to you first; since you repudiate it and judge yourselves unworthy of eternal life, behold, we are turning to the Gentiles**" (13:46). Many of those convicted Gentiles rejoiced at the opportunity and believed (13:48). This verse has been a major Calvinistic prooftext, but I will show in chapter 11 that the translation needs to be corrected to: "**And as many as had been devoting themselves to eternal life were believing.**"

On Paul's second missionary journey we have the account of Lydia's conversion: "**. . . and the Lord opened her heart to respond to the things spoken by Paul**" (Acts 16:14). Although Calvinists are inclined to see this as an example of irresistible grace, it can equally be understood as a reference to the convincing, enlightening work of the Spirit. As we shall see presently, it is our responsibility to be the instruments of the Spirit in opening sinners' eyes to the truth (Acts 26:18). Subsequently, the Philippian jailer also was most certainly under the convicting ministry of the Spirit to have cried out,

"Sirs, what must I do to be saved?" (Acts 16:30). He had heard the testimony of Paul and Silas in prison and being overwhelmed by the extraordinary circumstances, he recognized his own need of eternal salvation. Paul's response was very similar to that of Peter on the day of Pentecost, except that he used the imperative "believe" instead of "repent."

The language Luke used to describe Paul's witness at Thessalonica ('reasoned,' 'explaining,' 'giving evidence') indicates that he sought to be the Spirit's instrument in persuading the Jews and devout Gentiles in the synagogue, which resulted in a great multitude of conversions (17:1-4). This is harmonious with the meaning of *elegchein* seen above. Again at Athens and Corinth Luke used similar words related to convincing and persuading, i.e., 'reasoning,' 'trying to persuade' (17:17; 18:4). Especially at Corinth this convincing ministry of the Spirit through Paul was effective in the conversion of two synagogue rulers, Crispus and Sosthenes, in his eighteen-month ministry there, as well as many other Jews and Gentiles (18:8, 17). Certainly the example Calvin gave from 1 Corinthians 14:24-25 is relevant: **"But if all prophesy, and an unbeliever or an ungifted man enters, he is convicted by all, he is called to account by all; the secrets of his heart are disclosed; and so he will fall on his face and worship God, declaring that God is certainly among you."**

Negative reactions. There are also some accounts which might be understood as a negative reaction to the Spirit's conviction. After the second arrest of the apostles and Peter's defense, we see a negative reaction in Acts 5:33: **"But when they heard this they were cut to the quick and were intending to slay them."** Similarly after Stephen's defense and charge we see a similar reaction using the same word *diaprіein*: **"Now when they heard this they were cut to the quick, and they began gnashing their teeth at him"** (Acts 7:54). Were they under the conviction of the Holy Spirit? We cannot be sure. But Stephen had just accused them of always resisting the Holy Spirit (7:51). If so, it would indicate that not all who are convicted come to faith. Related to this might be the account of Felix ,the governor's, reaction to Paul's forthright witness in which he was possibly under conviction: **"And as he was discussing righteousness, self-control and the judgment to come, Felix became frightened and said, 'Go away for the present, and when I find time, I will summon you'"** (Acts 24:25).

Human instrumentality. Since the cognates of *elegchein* have the sense of 'proof', 'refutation', and 'persuasion', it might be relevant to consider accounts where the Holy Spirit was using the apostles in related activity. We are told in Acts 14:1: **"And it came about that in Iconium they entered the synagogue of the Jews together, and spoke <u>in such a manner</u> that a great multitude believed, both of Jews and Greeks."** In Acts 18:28 we see a similar emphasis upon the human instrumentality in reference to Apollos's witness: **". . . for he powerfully refuted the Jews in public, demonstrating by the Scriptures that Jesus was the Christ."** And there are a number of allusions to Paul's use of reasoning and persuasion in his evangelism, such as 18:4: "**And he was reasoning in the synagogue every Sabbath and trying to persuade Jews and Gentiles.**" Human instrumentality comes through very clearly in Paul's testimony about Christ's apostolic charge to him: "**. . . to open their eyes so that they may turn from darkness to light and from the dominion of Satan to God, in order that they may receive forgiveness of sins and an inheritance among those who have been sanctified by faith in Me**" (Acts 26:18). It is clear that the above enumerated things are the work of the Holy Spirit, but Christ mandated Paul to do them. It is of interest that Berkhof mentions that Lutherans use this passage in constructing an *ordo salutis*, but as a Calvinist he apparently did not feel comfortable in doing so.[19] I believe the issue is the Holy Spirit's use of human instrumentality in His ministry of conviction. Calvinists tend to see all of the Spirit's ministries function directly and immediately.[20]

The epistles. The epistles also shed some light on this ministry of the Spirit. "**And it is the Spirit who bears witness, because the Spirit is the truth. For there are three that bear witness, the Spirit and the water and the blood; and the three are in agreement**" (1 John 5:7-8). Here it seems that the focus is on objective witnesses to the gospel message by his reference to the water and the blood. Thus at least we can say that the Spirit uses objective witnesses in His work of conviction. Hebrews 10:29 also seems relevant in reference to those who are convicted but never really come to repentance and faith, the counterfeit believers: "**How much severer punishment do you think he will deserve who has trampled under foot the Son of God, and has regarded as unclean the blood of the covenant by which he was sanctified, and has insulted the Spirit of grace?**" Since these counterfeits had never been regenerated, apparently they were convicted by the Spirit and in failing to believe had insulted the Holy Spirit by rejecting so much light (see the fuller exposition in chapter 15). Jude (15) also speaks of Christ in His coming convicting the ungodly, but it will be too late for repentance.

THE EXTENT OF THE MINISTRY OF CONVICTION

One question that has been minimally discussed by the theologians is the extent of the Spirit's ministry of conviction. Is it universal, is it general, or is it limited only to the elect? The answers to this question from Chafer and Buswell are puzzling and inconsistent. Chafer, as a moderate Calvinist, held that it is limited to the elect. "Though reference is made to the *cosmos* world as the objective toward which the Holy Spirit's work is directed, the conviction that the Spirit accomplishes is of necessity individual and, according to all related Scriptures, is restricted to those whom 'the Lord our

God shall call'."[21] The inconsistency here is that Chafer had always stressed the world-system of the unregenerate as hostile to God. He also taught general redemption. Here, however, his Calvinistic leanings bleed through. On the other hand, Buswell, as a five-point Calvinist, posited a universal ministry of conviction: "By its universality I mean that, although I cannot cogently prove it from the Scripture, I postulate that the convicting work of the Holy Spirit is absolutely universal to the entire human race in all ages and in all areas."[22] He arrived at this through misunderstanding of John 1:9 (previously discussed) and his belief that the witness of nature is part of the witness used by the Spirit in conviction. His conclusion, however, is more consistent with Arminian theology. Much more satisfying to me, after studying the biblical examples of conviction noted above, is the view of John F. Walvoord: "The fact is that the Spirit of God brings conviction and understanding to many who never believe, who turn from the gospel even after the way of salvation is made plain to them."[23] The data I have assembled above, it seems to me, confirms Walvoord's statement. This is in harmony with the mediate nature of many of God's workings in relation to world evangelization. This is also in harmony with Calvin's understanding: "Under the term *world* are, I think, included not only those who would be truly converted to Christ, but hypocrites and reprobates.."[24]

THE NATURE OF CONVICTION

One outstanding question then is whether conviction is objective or subjective, external or internal. From the evidence adduced above, I would take it that conviction is both internal and external. The secular and Septuagintal usage of *elegchein* was more objective, but the New Testament balances both aspects. Since the Holy Spirit came to indwell the Church, it follows that He works through the members of Christ's body as they proclaim the word of God. This is the clear pattern of the book of Acts. In one sense He works internally through His disciples using the objective truth they proclaim. Additionally, we see a more direct, internal ministry in a number of the examples: the day of Pentecost events and the case of Lydia might be most convincing. So I would suggest both and internal and external aspect of the Holy Spirit's ministry.

CONCLUSIONS

In making the distinction between the means that the Holy Spirit uses in bringing spiritually dead sinners to saving faith and the direct work of the Spirit in regeneration, I believe we have the key as to how the spiritually dead can believe prior to regeneration. A general ministry of the Spirit's conviction of the sinner through human instrumentality of the ministry of the word of God, best explains all the Scriptural data. Since we are to be the instrumentality the Holy Spirit uses to bring conviction, we must follow the apostolic example by focusing on the three areas which Christ emphasized.

Limiting it to the elect moves the focus back to a deterministic view of God's decrees. Universalizing it to all men at all times does not do justice to Christ's use of the future tense and the rest of New Testament evidence. Although Calvin's references to it are harmonious with this, it does not fit into the system of extreme Calvinism, especially their doctrine of irresistible grace. This is an issue to be discussed in the next chapter.

Note: This chapter is based upon a paper given at the Annual Meeting of the Evangelical Theological Society, Jackson, MS, November, 1996.

---

1. Lewis Sperry Chafer, *Systematic Theology* (Dallas: Dallas Seminary Press, 1948), VI, p. 88.
2. James Oliver Buswell, Jr., *A Systematic Theology of the Christian Religion*, II, p. 157.
3. Buswell, II, p. 163.
4. John Calvin, *Commentary on the Gospel according to John*, trans. William Pringle II, pp. 137-8.
5. Buswell, II, p. 162.
6. Charles Hodge, *Systematic Theology* (GR: Eerdmanns, 1968 reprint), II, pp. 660; cf. 654-6, 660-675.
7. W. G. T. Shedd, *Dogmatic Theology* (Nashville: Thomas Nelson, 1980 reprint), II, pp. 515; cf. 511-528
8. Augustus Hopkins Strong, *Systematic Theology* (Philadelphia: Judson Press, 1906), p. 822
9. L. Berkhof, *Systematic Theology* (GR: Eerdmanns, 1953), pp. 401, 459.
10. Arthur W. Pink, *The Sovereignty of God*, p. 92., 94
11. H. Orton Wiley, *Christian Theology* (Kansas City, MO: Beacon Hill, 1952), II, pp. 331-2, 340-357.
12. Although I am sure that I heard this point made by Dr. Ryrie in class, there is undoubtedly documentation somewhere in his many books.
13. Friedrich Buchsel in Gerhard Kittel, *Theological Dictionary of the New Testament*, II, pp. 473-476.
14. William F. Arndt and F. Wilbur Gingrich, *A Greek-English Lexicon of the New Testament*, pp. 248-9.
15. Arndt and Gingrich, pp. 622-24.
16. G. Abbott-Smith, *A Manual Greek Lexicon of the New Testament* (Edinburgh: T. & T. Clark, 1937), p. 255.
17. Chafer, VI, p. 90.
18. Abbott-Smith, p. 237.
19. Berkhof, p. 416.
20. Charles Hodge, II, p. 663.
21. Chafer, VI, p. 94.
22. Buswell, II, p. 160.
23. John F. Walvoord, *The Holy Spirit*, p. 111; also Ryrie, *Basic Theology*, pp. 324-5.
24. John Calvin, *Commentary on the Gospel According to John*, p. 138; see also *Institutes.*, 3.24.8.

His grace has planned it all,
'Tis mine but to believe,
And recognize His work of love
and Christ receive.
For me He died,
For me He lives,
And everlasting life and light
He freely gives.

-Norman J. Clayton

10

THE PRIORITY OF REPENTANT FAITH

One of the most egregious examples of the tendency of many theologians to favor a deductive rationalistic approach to theology over an inductive, exegetically based methodology is seen in the question as to whether faith is a prior condition or a consequence of the new birth. In the prolegomena I have warned of the erroneous methodology which fails to give inductive exegesis of the Scriptural data priority over a rationalistic, deductive methodology. I believe that this warning is especially called for in this pivotal salvation issue.

As I have interacted with extreme Calvinism over the years, I have concluded that this is a major crucial issue, and yet it is rarely discussed or confronted by either Calvinists or Arminians. In the 1970s when an extreme Calvinistic colleague emphasized its importance to Calvinistic theology, my theological pilgrimage really began. It is a major presupposition of the Calvinistic system that because man is spiritually dead, he must be regenerated before he can repent and believe. I was shocked to hear this since the inductive data is so clearly opposite. This is a presupposition which has rarely been discussed and certainly not argued in detail by Calvinistic writers to my knowledge. Possibly non-Calvinists do not focus upon it because they may not be aware of how central the issue is to the Calvinistic system. The only significant treatment I can find is a brief chapter by Samuel Fisk in his lesser known book, *Calvinistic Paths Retraced* and more recently Norman Geisler has two appendices on it in *Chosen But Free*.[1] I will survey the historical background of the discussion, the inductive Scriptural data, the consequences and implications of the

Calvinistic view, and then propose a solution.

FAITH PRIOR TO THE NEW BIRTH

The historical background

John Calvin. Calvin struggled with the problem of the order of faith and regeneration. In his commentary on John 1:12-13 (which passage presents a serious problem to the Calvinistic view), in arguing a different issue against the Catholic interpretation, he put it one way: "But if faith regenerates us, so that we are *the sons of God,* and if God breathes faith into us from heaven, it plainly appears that not by possibility only, but actually—as we say—is the grace of adoption offered to us by Christ."[2] Then he reversed himself, "The contradiction appears still more glaring from what immediately follows. The Evangelist says that those who *believe* are already *born of God.*"[3] Later on he directly addressed the problem:

> It may be thought that the Evangelist reverses the natural order by making regeneration to precede faith, whereas, on the contrary, it is an effect of faith, and therefore ought to be placed later. I reply, that both statements perfectly agree; because by faith we receive the *incorruptible seed,* (1 Pet. i.23) by which we are born again to a new and divine life. And yet faith itself is a work of the Holy Spirit, who dwells in none but the children of God. So then, in various respects, faith is a part of our regeneration, and an entrance into the kingdom of God, that he may reckon us among his children. The illumination of our minds by the Holy Spirit belongs to our renewal, and thus faith flows from regeneration as its source; but since it is by the same faith that we receive Christ, who sanctifies us by his Spirit, on that account it is said to be the beginning of our adoption.[4]

In subsequent clarification it seems to me that he indicated that one is an objective fact, while the reverse is our subjective perception of the truth.

Calvinistic theologians. It seems that Calvin's successors are far less aware of the problem and tend to just refer to the "Calvinistic order" of regeneration prior to faith. Charles Hodge had separate chapters on regeneration and faith, but did not discuss the order other than by the implication of placing the chapter on regeneration before the chapter on faith and in the following statement: "The Scriptures therefore recognize the Holy Spirit as the immediate author of regeneration, of repentance, of faith, and of all holy exercises."[5] The key word is 'immediate' for all of these things. Note as well as his order in the sequence. Loraine Boettner was more explicit: "If any person believes, it is because God has quickened him; and if any person fails to believe, it is because God has withheld that grace which He was under no obligation to bestow." He offered no Scriptural support for his order, and continued, ". . . so the soul dead in sin is first transferred to spiritual life and then exercises faith and repentance and does good works."[6]

Berkhof did not directly come to grips with the issue. In an extensive wrestling with the nature of regeneration, he seemed to indirectly imply that the solution is found in the distinction between the begetting (male) and birth (female) analogy to human birth which is found in contemporary Reformed theology. In an extensive discussion of the order of calling and regeneration, he did not explicitly mention faith (although implied in calling). Later he sought to show that regeneration is not mediated by the word of God, but is a direct work of the Spirit, which argument clearly excludes faith in the word of God as a condition for regeneration. He failed to consider the possibility that although regeneration itself is the direct work of the Spirit, the means of people coming to faith could be mediate through the word of God.[7] In the subsequent chapter on faith, he was more explicit: "This faith is not first of all an activity of man, but a potentiality wrought by God in the heart of the sinner. The seed of faith is implanted in man in regeneration."[8]

John Murray also raised the distinction between the human birth analogy of procreating and bearing, but did not press its implication in his discussion. He was, however, very explicit about the order: "It should be specially noted that even faith that Jesus is the Christ is the effect of regeneration. This is, of course, a clear implication of John 3:3-8. . . . We are not born again by faith or repentance or conversion; we repent and believe because we have been regenerated."[9] He did not explain how he saw that implication in this passage.

James Boice is if anything even more explicit about the order: "We know from Paul's teaching elsewhere that justification presupposes faith (Rom. 5:1), so we can insert faith before justification, but after regeneration."[10] Thus Boice has more overtly than his predecessors opened up the can of worms of having us regenerated logically (and chronologically?) before being justified. Reformed theology has rightly long objected to the Roman Catholic concept of putting infused grace prior to justification. Boice and his predecessors seem to have done in reality the very thing they have been opposing in Romanism! Is it possible in the *ordo salutis* to be regenerated and not yet be justified? R. C. Sproul is one among many contemporary extreme Calvinists who affirms the maxim that "Regeneration precedes faith" is "a cardinal point of Reformed theology."[11]

Direct scriptural data

Years ago I surveyed the two most basic New Testament soteriological books, the Gospel of John and the book of Acts, and felt that the inductive data was more than adequate to refute this extreme Calvinistic presupposition. Now upon expanding my study to the rest of the New Testament, I am absolutely astonished at how developed Calvinism flies in the face of the overwhelming consistency of Scripture in placing repentant faith before regeneration as a condition. At least Calvin himself seemed to wrestle with what seemed to him as the ambiguities of the situation. It was actually a tension between the inductive data and deductive reasoning from his theological system. His successors in general seem to have totally overlooked the plethora of inductive data contradicting their deductive presuppositions. The pioneers of inductive Bible study methodology hammered home this prime rule, "**Observe, observe, observe!**" Somehow this basic hermeneutical axiom has not filtered over into the theological realm. Words absolutely fail me in expressing the irony of the situation. Let us hasten to the data.

Can the dead believe? First off, the question arises as to the seeming impossibility of unregenerate sinners, who are spiritually dead, ever responding to the word of God in faith. If we start with John's Gospel the answer comes early in the words of the Lord Jesus, "**Truly, truly, I say to you, an hour is coming and now is, when the dead shall hear the voice of the Son of God, and those who hear shall live**" (John 5:25). There is no debate among evangelical interpreters that this is a reference to sinners being born again. Notice that Christ did not say that the regenerate shall hear His voice, but that the *dead* shall hear his voice and come to life. They are dead when they hear! As to **how** those who are spiritually dead can hear, believe, and be born again, there may be some discussion, but as to the fact, Christ's own words are clear. In chapter 4, I suggested that a balanced biblical understanding of depravity and spiritual death does not contradict the exercise of repentant faith on the part of sinful mankind. In chapter 9, I have suggested that the convicting, convincing ministry of the Spirit totally removes any obstacle. Let us examine the inductive data.

The Gospel of John. As we trace through the New Testament inductively, we see that the new birth and those truths inseparably related to it are repeatedly conditioned on repentant faith. Let us start with John's Gospel. "**Yet to all who received him, to those who believed in his name, he gave the right to become the children of God—. . .**" (Jn. 1:12, NIV). Notice that it is those who receive Him (even those who believe on His name) who are given the right (*exousia*) to become the children of God. Faith first; then new birth. The NIV rendering of the aorist verb 'received' makes the sequence even clearer. The relationship of believing on His name to receiving Christ is obscured in the KJV and NAS since it is tacked onto the end of the sentence in common Greek word order. But *tois pisteuousin* is clearly an attributive participle and in the NIV it rightly is put immediately after those who received Christ, with an appositional force.[12] Thus receiving is synonymous with believing, and both describe the condition upon which God gives the right (*exousia*) to become the children of God. The intervention of the word *exousia* before the description of new birth (becoming children of God) makes it impossible to reverse the order here. Thus we have, believing/receiving—> given the right to become —> children of God. Calvinists sometimes point out that the verb for believing is a present participle, which might indicate continued action of believing. However, the word 'received' (*elabon*) is an aorist, which is usually described as non-durative, usually in past time, and the present participle with the article characterizes such people as believers.

Unfortunately the NIV takes liberties with 1:13 in rendering *oude ek thelēmatos sarkos* as "nor of human decision," which reveals a decided Calvinistic bias. They may call it "dynamic equivalence" but it really is a paraphrase, not translation. Here the KJV and the NAS are more literal and leave the interpretation up to the reader, as they ought: "**. . . who were born, not of blood, nor of the will of the flesh nor of the will of man, but of God**" (1:13, NAS). We would all agree that we cannot will ourselves to be born again; it is totally a work of the Spirit of God. But in John's sequence, just noted, faith is the clear condition upon which God gives sinners the right or authority. Here the analogy with human procreation and birth breaks down. Sinners, created in God's image, can claim that right by faith to be born into God's family! How astonishing! Nevertheless, whatever spin we may try to put on this passage, faith comes first.

The most famous verse of the Bible is only a little less clear. In John 3:16 it is those who believe who get eternal life, not the reverse. I suspect few would like to argue that having eternal life does not imply regeneration since the result of regeneration is by definition the impartation of new, eternal, divine life into the heart of the sinner dead in sin. The verb 'believing' is a substantival participle which is "both gnomic and continual."[13] In any case, this does not in any way affect John's sequence since the verb 'have' (*echēi*) is subjunctive. The beginning of the believing must precede the having of eternal life.

"**. . . but whoever drinks of the water that I will give him shall never thirst; but the water that I will give him will become in him a well of water springing up to eternal life**" (Jn. 4:14). The Lord Jesus told the Samaritan woman first to drink (by faith); then she would have a well of water (the Holy Spirit) springing up to eternal life. The order is the same. Throughout the Gospel of John, drinking is symbolic of the initial act of faith. In this symbolism, drinking obviously has to precede the water springing up in the individual to eternal life by the Holy Spirit. There is no ambiguity in the Greek tenses here. It is the sinner who drinks or exercises faith.

A similar symbolism is used in the bread of life discourse. "**Jesus said to them, 'I am the bread of life; he who comes to Me shall not hunger, and he who believes in me shall never thirst. . . . For this is the will of My Father, that everyone who beholds the Son and believes in Him, may have eternal life; . . . he who eats this bread shall live forever**" (6:35, 40, 58). Although the symbolism of v. 35 should be adequately clear, the future tense of verses 40 and 58 shows that the believing is antecedent to the possession of eternal life. I mention this because some have contended that the order is not clear in statements like verse 47 and that the possession of eternal life presupposes the believing. This is not possible in the above verses.

The same symbolism is found in the dramatic tabernacles feast claim of our Lord:

> **Now on the last day, the great day of the feast, Jesus stood and cried out, saying, "If any man is thirsty, let him come to me and drink. He who believes in Me, as the Scripture said, 'From his innermost being shall flow rivers of living water.'" But this He spoke of the Spirit, whom those who believed in Him were to receive; for the Spirit was not yet give, because Jesus was not yet glorified** (7:37-9).

The Lord Jesus clearly set believing as a condition of receiving the Spirit, as further clarified by John's comment in v. 39, where the substantival participle is in the aorist tense. Although John usually uses the present participle,[14] the aorist here confirms the priority of the disciples' faith, since the indwelling Spirit was not yet received until John 20 or Acts 2 (as variously understood).

Although this sampling of this Gospel should be adequate, allusion to the key verse should cap it off nicely: "**. . . but these have been written that you may believe that Jesus is the Christ, the Son of God; and that believing you may have life in His name**" (20:31). Here clearly John used an instrumental participle 'believing', which modifies the action of the main verb, 'to have' life. The instrumental force of the participle could be better translated, "**and that <u>by</u> believing you may have life.**" First faith, then life.

Acts. We would expect that the apostolic preaching (*kērugma)* of the early church as recorded in Acts would give us crystal clear data on this sequence. Such is the case. In Acts 2:37-38 we see the fulfillment of Christ's prediction about the Spirit's convicting work (Jn. 16:8-11). "**Now when they heard this, they were pierced to the heart, and said to Peter and the rest of the apostles, 'Brethren, what shall we do?' And Peter said to them, 'Repent, . . . for the forgiveness of your sins, and you shall receive the gift of the Holy Spirit'**" (Acts 2:37-38). First they were convicted ("pierced to the heart") and said, "What shall we do?" Peter told them to repent, apparently on the presupposition that the conviction of the Spirit enabled them to do so. Only then would they receive the gift of the Holy Spirit—what could be clearer?

Subsequently, in replying to the Jewish leaders, Peter said that God gives the Holy Spirit "**to those who obey** (*peitharcheo*='to obey authority,''to be persuaded') **Him**" (5:32). A positive response must precede the giving of the Holy Spirit and regeneration. In Philip's ministry in Samaria the sequence is undeniable.

"**But when they believed Philip preaching the good news about the**

kingdom of God and the name of Jesus Christ, they were being baptized, men and women alike. . . . they sent them Peter and John, who came down and prayed for them that they might receive the Holy Spirit. For He had not yet fallen upon any of them." (8:12, 14b-16a). We note that the Samaritans believed and were baptized but did not receive the Spirit until days later. Although the delay here is exceptional, the sequence is normative.

In Peter's brief to the Jerusalem Christians about the conversion of Cornelius and his household, we note: "**if God gave them the same gift [the Spirit] as He gave us, who believed in the Lord Jesus Christ . . .**" (11:17). Note that here *pisteusasin* is an aorist participle with instrumental or temporal usage, most probably expressing the means by which the apostles and the Gentiles received the gift of the Spirit, thus: "**. . . by believing in the Lord Jesus.**"

Likewise in the Jerusalem Council Peter maintained the same sequence: "**cleansing their hearts by faith**" (15:9). Similarly Paul conditioned another ministry of the Holy Spirit upon faith in 26:18: "**sanctified by faith.**" Thus every relevant context indicates the same sequence: first faith, then regeneration or a related ministry of the Spirit. See also Acts 10:43 and 13:39.

The epistle to the Romans. Although the Apostle Paul makes little reference to regeneration in this great theological treatise, since Luther's time there has been little dispute among Evangelicals that faith is the condition for justification. The centrality of faith in salvation is seen in the key verse: "**For in it [the gospel] the righteousness of God is revealed from faith to faith; as it is written, 'But the righteous man shall live by faith'**" (1:17). The NIV renders *ek pisteōs eis pistin* even more forcefully: "**For in the gospel a righteousness from God is revealed, a righteousness that is by faith from first to last.**" Faith cannot be made an appendage to our theological system; it is at the core. *It is ironic that faith is not even mentioned in the five points of Calvinism, especially since justification by faith had become the governing principle of the Protestant reformation.* I should not need to expound the consistent order in Romans of justification conditioned on faith. I will simply list the plethora of references: 3:22, 25, 26, 28, 30; 4:3, 5, 9, 16, 24; & 5:1, 2 (18 in total). If my reader has missed the significance of 4:16, allow me to reinforce its significance: "**For this reason it is by faith, in order that it may be in accordance with grace, so that the promise will be guaranteed to all the descendants.**" Faith is not in any way meritorious or to be thought of as a work. That faith should be understood as a *condition* of salvation (justification, regeneration, etc.) in no way undermines the gracious nature of salvation. The last passage also requires special comment: "**. . . through whom also we have obtained our introduction by faith into this grace in which we stand**" (5:1-2). If regeneration precedes faith, how can Paul say that faith was the means of our introduction into God's grace. By Calvinistic lights regeneration is that which introduces us into God's grace.

Later in discussing the circumstances of Israel's being set aside dispensationally, Paul came back to his theme:

> **What shall we say then? That Gentiles, who did not pursue righteousness, attained righteousness, even the righteousness which is by faith; but Israel, pursuing a law of righteousness, did not arrive at that law. Why? Because they did not pursue it by faith, but as though it were by works** (9:30-32).

Then he amplified the instrumentality of faith: "**. . . righteousness based on faith . . .**" (10:6); "**. . . believe in your heart that God raised Him from the dead, you shall be saved; for with the heart man believes, resulting in righteousness. . .** " (10:9,10); "**So faith comes from hearing, and hearing by the word of Christ**" (10:17).

If regeneration precedes faith, we have the incongruent sequence, which Boice affirmed, of regeneration—> faith —> justification and salvation. This would certainly imply that logically it is possible to be born again without justification. We should also note here that it is man who does the believing in his heart. God does not believe for us, nor does he even say that God puts the faith in our hearts. Berkhof was clearly wrong in denying the mediacy of the word of God in regeneration. Again let me stress my understanding that calling (the circumstances by which we come to faith) is mediate through the word of God, but that regeneration itself is immediately and directly one hundred percent the work of the Spirit. This crucial distinction seems to have been lost in the discussion.

The epistles to the Galatians and Ephesians. It is probable that Paul's epistle to the Galatians set out justification by faith even before Romans. But in chapter three there is the additional dimension of his discussion in that he was more explicit about the relationship of faith to the receiving of the Spirit: "**. . . did you receive the Spirit by the works of the Law, or by hearing with faith?**" (Gal. 3:2); "**Does He then, who provides you with the Spirit and works miracles among you, do it by the works of the Law, or by hearing with faith?**" (3:5); "**. . . so that we might receive the promise of the Spirit through faith**" (3:14); "**For you are all sons of God through faith in Christ Jesus**" (3:26). There are no subtleties of exegesis needed here since the sequence is self-explanatory. In understanding how Paul's sequence is possible, it is important to distinguish the convicting ministry of the Spirit (which precedes faith) from the indwelling and regenerating works of the Spirit, which are subsequent to faith (cf. chapter 10). But in any case the sequence in Paul's thought is consistent throughout and absolutely clear.

By the time of the first Roman imprisonment, Paul had not changed his mind: "**In Him, you also, after listening to the message of truth, the**

gospel of your salvation—having also believed, you were sealed in Him with the Holy Spirit of promise, . . ." (Eph. 1:13). Here again we have an aorist participle, *pisteusantes*, ('having believed') modifying the main verb *esphragisthēte*, ('you were sealed') by the Spirit. It could be either a temporal or an instrumental participle. Both options establish my point that faith precedes and is instrumental in the sealing ministry of the Spirit. Might it be viable to say that regeneration precedes the faith and sealing? This is highly improbable and virtually impossible.

Passages on the relationship of faith and the word of God. The Lord Jesus, early in His parable of the four soils, established the priority of the word of God in the process of people coming to faith and salvation. The Lord attributed the differing responses to His word to differences in the soil, not to any sovereign work of irresistible grace. The devil also gets into the picture: "**When anyone hears the word of the kingdom, and does not understand it, the evil one comes and snatches away what has been sown in his heart**" (Mt. 13:19). Luke adds: "**. . . so that they might not believe and be saved**" (Lk. 8:12). The sequence here is clear: hearing the word of God —> believing —> being saved. It is hard to imagine how it might be possible for the new birth to precede "being saved." Christ does not even intimate that a differentiating factor between the soils is God's elective choice. There is an intrinsic difference between the soils themselves. The second category of soil is explained thus: "**. . . yet he has no firm root in himself, but is only temporary, . . .**" (Mt. 13:21). There is a difference in the soil. The fourth category is described: "**And the seed in the good soil, these are the ones who have heard the word in an honest and good heart, and hold it fast, and bear fruit with perseverance**" (Lk. 8:15). There is apparently a difference in the soil here also. The Lord Jesus attributes the difference to a mindset of the heart. We find that many individuals have their hearts closed to the gospel by their religious or irreligious background. Certainly those of us who have worked in the Muslim world find most people's hearts have been poisoned against the gospel by the brainwashing of Islamic teaching. In our own society we increasingly find people brainwashed with relativistic and evolutionary dogmas, which close their minds to the gospel. I would suggest that the universal spiritual blindness of the whole human race is overcome by the convicting work of the Spirit as diverse antecedent factors in the individual's life come into play. Here the pattern is set by our Lord that it is faith in the word of God which is prior to being saved.

Calvinists would tend to react to the above by saying, "Doesn't this attribute salvation to human merit?" However, a mindset is not something meritorious, and remember, the Lord Jesus taught it; our job is to adjust our theology to His clear teaching.

Peter seemed to have understood the words of our Lord in this way: "**. . . obtaining as the outcome of your faith the salvation of your souls**" (1

Pet. 1:9). Then in the same context he linked faith in the word of God in the same order: "**. . . for you have been born again not of seed which is perishable but imperishable, that is, through the living and abiding word of God**" (1:23). Although Martin Luther tended to see the word of God as working through its own intrinsic power, Reformed theologians have focused more on the ministry of the Spirit in its working. In any case, it is as people believe the word of God that they are born again. The word of God does not become operative by itself. The issue is faith in the word of God. The extreme Calvinistic scenario separates faith from the word of God thus: the word of God proclaimed —> regeneration —> faith. But faith must be in the word of God before regeneration can possibly take place.

The writer of Hebrews also made the direct link between the word of God and faith: "**For indeed we have had good news preached to us, just as they also; but the word they heard did not profit them, because it was not united by faith in those who heard. For we who have believed enter that [salvation] rest,**" (Heb. 4:2-3a). We must not insert regeneration in between the word of God and faith. No, it is conviction which prepares the sinful heart for faith.

WHAT IS THE SOURCE OF FAITH?

Is faith the gift of God?

Part of the extreme Calvinistic reversal of faith and the new birth is their supposition that repentance and faith are the direct gift of God, an immediate or direct work of the Holy Spirit in the human heart. I remind you of the Hodge quotation earlier in this chapter, which is very explicit. This is another unexamined presupposition of Calvinistic theology.

Roy Aldrich, in a germinal article entitled, "The Gift of God," objected to the Calvinistic reversal, not only because of its lack of Scriptural support, but also because, although this viewpoint intends to maintain the purity of grace, it actually undermines it. Since the sinner cannot believe until he becomes the object of irresistible grace, Shedd, for example, instructs the sinner to 1) read and hear the divine Word; 2) give serious application of the mind to the truth; and 3) pray for the gift of the Holy Spirit for conviction and regeneration.[15] Aldrich continues:

> A doctrine of total depravity that excluded the possibility of faith must also exclude the possibilities of "hearing the word," "giving serious application to divine truth," and "praying for the Holy Spirit for conviction and regeneration." The extreme Calvinist deals with a rather lively spiritual corpse after all.[16]

Jonathan Edwards actually listed thirteen steps of preparation. The issue of preparationism in Reformed theology is a self-induced conundrum. It is not a problem for non-Calvinists. Thus it is clear that another pivotal issue is the question of the source of faith. Is faith directly the gift of God? Or is it developed in the sinners heart mediately? Or, when we come down to cases, is it in any real sense the gift of God?

Misused proof-texts

Ephesians 2:8-9. Calvinists have a ready arsenal of proof-texts for the idea that faith is the direct, immediate gift of God. By far the most frequently referred to is Ephesians 2:8-9 (need I quote it?). The exegetical flimsiness of using this passage in this way should be common knowledge. Apparently it is not. Chrysostom, Theodoret, Theophylact, Calvin, Calovius, Olshausen, Meyer, Chandler, Adam Clarke, Ellicot, Alford, Salmond in EGT, Eadie, Vincent, A. T. Robertson, Wuest, F. F. Bruce ("an impenitent Augustinian and Calvinist"), and even extreme Calvinist Homer Hoeksema are among the host who reject such isogesis since they recognized that the relative pronoun *touto* (this) is neuter and *pistis* (faith) is feminine and cannot serve as its antecedent.[17] Although Calvin doesn't explain the grammar, he is very explicit about this error:

> And here we must advert to a very common error in the interpretation of this passage. Many persons restrict the word *gift* to faith alone. But Paul is only repeating in other words the former sentiment. His meaning is, **not that faith is the gift of God**, but that salvation is given to us by God, or, that we obtain it by the gift of God (emphasis mine).[18]

Thus it is clear that the demonstrative *touto* refers to the whole concept of salvation by grace. Gregory Sapaugh reinforces this by noting that "This position is further supported by the parallelism between *ouk hymon* ('and this not of yourselves') in 2:8 and *ouk ex ergon* ('not of works') in 2:9. The latter phrase would not be meaningful if it referred to *pisteos* ('faith'). Instead, it clearly means salvation is 'not of works.'"[19] This is exactly what Paul affirmed in Romans 6:23: "**. . . but the free gift of God is eternal life in Christ Jesus our Lord.**" Vance makes a most important point here: "But by its very nature a gift has to be received or rejected. There is no such thing as an irresistible gift."[20] Is there any question that all those who continue to ignore the unambiguous grammar and scholarly opinion of even Calvin himself are rightly called extreme or hyper-Calvinists. R. C. Sproul is entrenched in his deductive dogmatism when he says: "This passage should seal the matter forever. The faith by which we are saved is a gift of God."[21]

Acts. In a number of cases, such as Acts 5:31 ("**. . . to grant repentance to Israel, . . .**") and 11:18 ("**. . . Well then, God has granted to the Gentiles also the repentance *that leads* to life.**") the context indicates that God is giving the opportunity for repentant faith to a class of people, not that God is giving faith directly on an individual basis. Acts 5:31 obviously cannot be an irresistible gift of repentance to individuals since in the main

Israel did not repent. Acts 11:18, when seen in its context, clearly is a reference to the dispensational opportunity now being offered to the Gentiles based upon the conversion of Cornelius and his household, not to God giving repentance to individuals as a direct gift. The other apostles and the Judean church had not yet understood that Gentiles could be saved directly, so this response to Peter's defense of his actions obviously is a reference to *the opportunity to repent*.

Three other proof texts in Acts are referenced by Calvinists. Acts 13:48 and 16:14 say nothing directly about repentant faith being the gift of God. Starting with Calvinistic presuppositions, these verses might seem to support their case, but I have discussed both elsewhere in this volume, Acts 13:48 in the next chapter and 16:14 in the previous. However, Acts 18:27 requires comment here: "**. . . he [Apollos] greatly helped those who had believed through grace.**" Calvinists read into this, "believed through irresistible grace." Of course, non-Calvinists believe that it is through God's grace that we have opportunity to believe in Christ. Indeed, when we exercise repentant faith we are affirming the gracious nature of salvation, the harmony of which Paul emphasized in Romans 4:16, already noted: "**For this reason *it is* by faith, in order that it *may be* in accordance with grace, . . .**" As discussed in the previous chapter, the convicting work of the Spirit further assures that salvation is all of grace, without assuming that faith is a direct gift of God.

Other Pauline proof-texts. Although the language of 2 Timothy 2:25 ("**. . . with gentleness correcting those who are in opposition, if perhaps God may grant them repentance leading to the knowledge of the truth, . . .**") does not so obviously exclude repentance as the immediate gift of God, it is clear from the context that God uses means in correcting those in opposition, specifically Timothy's gentle and patient correction. The broader context refers to heretical teachers (2:17-18, 23), not to ordinary unsaved people. Timothy is to be kind in trying to teach them the truth, in the hope that they will repent of their doctrinal error and cease being the devil's tool in disrupting the churches.[A]

Calvinists also use Philippians 1:29 ("**For to you it has been granted for Christ's sake, not only to believe in Him, but also to suffer for His sake, . . .**") to prove their point, but it is clear that we are given faith only in the same sense in which we are given suffering, that is, mediately through circumstances. No one would argue that suffering is an immediate and irresistible work of grace. As in the two Acts passages above, Paul is referring to the privilege and opportunity given to the Philippian Christians to believe, while alerting them to the fact that suffering for Christ comes with that

A. I am convinced that an additional major means to deal with both argumentative unbelievers and backslidden believers is praying that God will bring other witnesses into their lives to reinforce our teaching so as to bring them to the truth. I have seen remarkable answers to such prayer.

privilege.

Some proof-texts like Romans 12:3 (“**. . . as God has allotted to each a measure of faith.**”), 1 Corinthians 12:8-9 (“**For to one is given the word of wisdom through the Spirit, . . . to another faith by the same Spirit, . . .** ”), 1 Corinthians 4:7 (“**What do you have that you did not receive?**”), and Philippians 2:13 (“**. . . for it is God who is at work in you, both to will and to work for *His* good pleasure.**”) are blatantly pulled out of context, having to do with the spiritual gift of 'faith' or the ongoing work of the Holy Spirit in the life of the believer rather than saving faith for the sinner. None of these contexts has anything to do with how sinners believe and are saved.

Two other Pauline passages seem relevant only to those who study the KJV alone: Galatians 2:20 and Philippians 3:9 have the “faith of Christ," which some Calvinists assume is a reference to faith which Christ gives. However, these are obviously objective genitives and should be translated "faith in Christ,” as rendered by most of the modern translations, supported by the mass of commentaries. Christ is to be the object of our faith.

There are a number of other Pauline passages referred to by Calvinists which apart from Calvinistic presuppositions seem totally irrelevant to the issue at hand. They are: 1 Thessalonians 1:4-6; 1 Corinthians 2:4-5; 7:25 (adduced by Augustine); 2 Corinthians 4:6; Romans 10:17 (affirms the opposite); and Ephesians 1:17-18. The connection of all these passages to faith as a gift from God is so obscure that I can’t imagine how to try to respond. This is the worst form of prooftexting.

Petrine proof-texts. Two Petrine passages are adduced by Calvinists. The first is easily clarified: “**. . . who through Him [Christ] are believers in God, . . .**” (1 Pet. 1:21). For the Christian it is a axiomatic that it is through Christ that we really became believers in the true God in a real sense. Even if they had been religious Jews, as were many of the recipients of this letter, in the main they did not really know God until they trusted in Christ.

In 2 Peter 1:1 the believers addressed are said to have obtained (*lachousin*) a like precious faith: “**To those who have obtained a faith of equal standing with ours, . . .**” (RSV). Since the verb (*lachousin*) is an aorist *active* participle, it should be translated as per the KJV, RSV, and Williams, ‘obtained’ rather than ‘received,’ which would be passive.[22] The point is that faith must be actively exercised by people, not passively received as a gift from God. Thus careful examination of the grammar has turned a Calvinistic proof text against their view. Additionally, the use of the adjective *isotimon* (‘of the same kind’) would militate for the objective connotation of the faith (*pistis*), that is, the body of truths which we believe, rather than our subjective, individual faith. If this is true, this passage proves to be irrelevant to the issue. In any case, Peter does not explain how they obtained that faith, which is the point under discussion, except that he used the active voice.

Johannine proof-texts. Three references in the bread of life discourse (John 6:37, 44-45, 65) are also misused in this connection and say nothing directly about faith as a gift of God. Calvinists read into them the idea of irresistible grace. However, Christ is not saying in 6:37 that all the elect shall infallibly come to Christ, but the context indicates that He is rather speaking about the remnant of regenerate Israelites who had belonged to the Father. Now the Son has come, and that remnant is being turned over to Him by the Father and will certainly come to Him. But most in that multitude were not a part of that remnant. For a fuller discussion of these verses please see chapters 4 and 11.

Thus careful consideration of these proof-text passages in their contexts shows that there is no inductive basis for seeing faith as a direct gift from God. It is salvation which is the gift of God, and faith is simply the means by which we receive it.

Faith develops mediately in human hearts.

Since God is never represented in Scripture as striking people with faith as a direct gift, where then does faith come from? A number of Scriptural observations are relevant to this important question:

Faith comes mediately through the propagation of the word of God. The instrumentality of the word of God in producing faith in the human heart is clear according to Romans 10:17: "**So faith comes from hearing, and hearing by the word of Christ**." D. L. Moody wrote, "I used to think that faith would strike me like a lightning bolt, but then somebody showed me Rom. 10:17. I turned to the word of God, and faith came and has been growing ever since."[23]

The conviction of the Spirit prepares the heart for faith. The solution to the conundrum faced by extreme Calvinists is found in the convicting or convincing ministry of the Spirit (Jn. 16:8-11). Clearly Acts 2:37ff was the first fulfillment and a graphic case study among the many examples in the book of Acts. The Spirit works through human instrumentality to convict sinners of the sin of unbelief, man's total lack of righteousness, and God's sure judgment upon sin. Conviction is neither universal or limited to the elect.

Faith is always ascribed to man, not God. It is not incidental to the Gospel record that the Lord Jesus commented on the faith of individuals in such a way that it is clear that faith is a human phenomenon. There are nine different individuals, as recorded in 14 different Gospel passages, whose faith is highlighted. Christ responded to the faith of the palsied man and his bearers (Mt. 9:2; Mk. 2:5; Lk. 5:20) by healing him. He told many like the immoral woman, "**Your faith has saved you**" (Lk. 7:50). The woman with the flow of blood was told, "**Your faith has made you well**" (Mt. 9:22; Mk. 5:29,34; Lk. 8:48). The two blind men who received their sight were told, **"It shall be done to you according to your faith"** (Mt. 9:28-29). The synagogue ruler, whose daughter was raised from the dead was told, **"Only believe, and she will be made well"** (Lk. 8:50). The one cleansed leper who returned to thank the Lord was told, **"Your faith has made you well"** (Lk. 17:19). Bartimaeus and his companion were told, **"Receive your sight; your faith has made you well"** (Mk. 10:52; Lk. 18:42, probably distinct from Matthew's account).

Paul says that the faith of the ungodly is reckoned as righteousness (Rom. 4:5). This is out of sequence if man has no participation in faith! The noun *pistis* ('faith') and the verb *pisteuein* ('to trust') occur 60 times in Romans, the theme of which is a righteousness by faith **"from first to last"** (1:17, NIV). Calvin himself recognized this truth:

> The next question is, in what way do men receive that salvation which is offered to them by the hand of God? The answer is, *by faith*; and hence he concludes that nothing connected with it is our own. If on the part of God, it is by grace alone, and **if we bring nothing but faith,** which strips us of all commendation, it follows that salvation does not come from us. . . . When, **on the part of man**, the act of receiving salvation is made to consist in faith alone, **all other means**, on which men are accustomed to rely, are discarded. Faith, then, bring a man empty to God, that he may be filled with the blessings of Christ (bold mine).[24]

Note that Calvin is not reticent about calling faith a means.

Christ constantly pointed up the faith of those individuals who possessed it. If faith is solely and immediately the gift of God, it would not have been consistent or appropriate for Christ to commend the Centurion and the Syrophoenician woman for the greatness of their faith (Mt. 8:10, 13; Lk. 7:9; Mt. 15:28).

The conversion of some people is attributed to antecedent conditions. The parable of the four soils does seem to indicate some antecedent differences in the soils of peoples' hearts which account for their coming to faith (Lk. 8:11-15). Cornelius' prayer (and his alms) are mentioned by the angel in reference to the opportunity given him to hear the message of faith (Acts 10:4). Lest anyone say that he was already regenerate, remember Peter's recitation of the angel's words to Cornelius that **"he [Peter] shall speak words to you by which you will be saved**," (Acts 11:14). Luke records that the noble-minded Bereans examined the Scriptures daily and that **"many of them <u>therefore</u> believed**," (Acts 17:12). Luke's "therefore" does not fit Calvinistic theology. The Apostle Paul stated that although he was the chief of sinners, he was shown mercy **because** he acted ignorantly in unbelief (1 Tim. 1:13-16). Calvinistic theology says that the basis of God's saving mercy is an unrevealed mystery.

God uses people to bring unbelievers to faith. Examples should be unnecessary. The Lord Jesus commanded His disciples to become "fishers of men." In the Great Commission He commanded them to "make disciples." When He commissioned Paul, He sent him to the Gentiles "**to open their eyes so that they may turn from darkness unto light and from the dominion of Satan to God,**" (Acts 26:17-18). The Holy Spirit normally works mediately through His servants. This is axiomatic.

The oft-repeated command to repent and believe presupposes the possibility of response. Not only so, but Paul stated that the command is to all men everywhere (Acts 17:30-31). The "all" here must refer to all without exception since the "everywhere" implies all without distinction.

Why are people commanded to seek God? Was Isaiah also ignorant of the Calvinistic doctrine that men are spiritual corpses and cannot seek God in any way (Isa. 55:6)? See full discussion in chapter 4.

It is clear that God gives people opportunity to believe in answer to our prayer and witness. In 1 Tim. 2:1-6 Paul links our prayers for "**all men**" (v. 1) with the desire of God that "**all men**" might be saved (v. 4), and the fact that Christ "**gave Himself as a ransom for all**" (v. 6). Frequently God uses the witness of other Christians unknown to us in answer to our prayers. As an example, some years ago Northeastern Bible College students especially prayed one night for the salvation of a student's brother on the west coast. He was saved the very next day through other Christians' witness to him. Frequently God uses human instrumentality in answering our prayers.

Problems with a direct gift of faith

If faith is the immediate gift of God, why did Christ bother to witness, argue, and persuade the non-elect? He would certainly know that they were non-elect and would not come to faith. This is clearest in His dealings with individuals like the rich young ruler. (Mark records that Christ loved him.)

Why should Paul bother to use persuasion at all? Luke highlighted the fact so frequently in Acts (17:3-4,17; 18:4; 19:8-9) that Paul used a confrontative and persuasive approach. One would think that the elect would believe upon hearing the gospel merely stated. Indeed, why should the elect not believe the first time that they hear the gospel? Buswell cited Calvinistic missionaries who would preach only once in each village under that supposition.[25] Apparently the human element of persistence and persuasion are important factors in people coming to faith in Christ. To press this line of thought one step further, one could raise the question about the validity of any sort of human methodology at all in preaching the gospel, if indeed faith is the immediate gift of God. Some extreme Calvinists pursue this to its logical conclusion and deny any use of means. But most acknowledge the validity of means and resort to paradox or antinomy to explain the inconsistency. Some object to more direct use of means, such as a public invitation. However, on the day of Pentecost, the apostles must have had some means to separate out the inquirers so that they could baptize them and incorporate them into the new-born church.

Why did Christ marvel at unbelief? If faith is the immediate gift of God, Christ should not have been astonished at the unbelief of the inhabitants of Nazareth. Didn't Christ know what every good Calvinist knows—that they were spiritually dead and could do no other than disbelieve?

How can unbelief be judged? The late great Donald Grey Barnhouse once raised the question as to how God could judge unbelief as sin, if indeed faith is the gift of God? If it is God who has withheld the gift of faith, unbelief cannot be called a sin.

How can we explain degrees of unbelief being judged more sorely? If it is God who chooses not to give the non-elect the gift of faith, how can God justly judge some more severely than others? (cf. Mt. 11:20ff.)

How can demonic activity hinder a direct work of the Spirit? In the parable of the soils the Lord Jesus made it clear that Satan can intervene in the process of sinners coming to faith: "**And those beside the road are those who have heard; then the devil comes and takes away the word from their heart, so that they may not believe and be saved**" (Lk. 8:12; also 2 Cor. 4:4). If Satan had the power to intervene in a direct, irresistible work of the Holy Spirit, then he would be more powerful than the Spirit.

Why are some classes of people harder to win than others? Paul identifies the Cretans as a problem people (Titus 1:12-13), and we could identify Muslims and upper-caste Hindus today as such. Natural factors and the extent of Satan's activity need to be taken into account. If the Spirit immediately produces faith in the heart of the elect, cannot the Spirit break through a Muslim's heart with equal ease as with an American nominal Christian? Since the church growth initiative of Donald A. McGavran beginning in the 50s, missiologists have been engaged in very fruitful study of the human factors (religious, sociological, anthropological, etc.) which contribute to people coming to faith in significant numbers. There was a negative response from Calvinists at first, but Calvinistic missiologists have had to ignore the theological problems and get involved in this research and implementation.

Why does God give the gift of faith to so many Americans and to so few Libyans, Mongolians, Tibetans, Afghans, Tunisians, Turks, etc.? If one starts with extreme Calvinistic premises, one is forced to the conclusion that God is partial and loves Americans more than others.

Coming to faith is a process.

While the new birth itself is an instantaneous work of the Holy Spirit in which man has no participation, the process by which humans come to faith may take years and involve spiritual struggles. Indeed, Satan's agents try their worst to sidetrack the inquirer to keep him from coming to faith. Ignorance of the real nature of the gospel is a major hindrance, as are all the smokescreens the godless world-system raises. And of course, the sinful nature and depravity of the inquirer is a major obstacle. The Spirit keeps on using Christian witness to break down these obstacles until the person comes to genuine repentant faith. But the process must be clearly distinguished from the new birth itself, otherwise confusion results. This simple distinction does not fit in with Calvinistic doctrine at all.

Faith is not meritorious.

Nothing stated under these headings is profound; these points should be obvious to all. Yet they directly contradict the deterministic theology which sees the Holy Spirit as immediately and irresistibly 'zapping' the elect with faith and leaving the non-elect in reprobation. They may plead paradox and antinomy, but the conflict and contradiction goes far beyond antimony.

I will be accused of synergism by my Calvinistic friends, but even that term is pejorative and begs the question. Its derivation from *ergeo* implies that we believe in works (man working with God). However, faith is not a work! Christ told a works-oriented multitude to believe in the Son: **"This is the work of God, that you believe in Him whom He has sent**" (Jn. 6:29). Certainly all would agree that Christ is not calling faith a meritorious work. It is simply responding to God's gift. Otherwise Christ would contradict Paul's argument in Romans 4:16 "**that it is by faith that it might be by grace**."

CONCLUSIONS

This study leads me to the following conclusions:

1) Contemporary Calvinists have gone far beyond Calvin in this area and show a serious lapse into a scholastic deductionism rather than giving preference to direct Scriptural inductive study.

2) The inductive data is overwhelmingly consistent in showing that faith precedes and is the condition for regeneration.

3) Faith is not the immediate, direct gift of God, but comes mediately through the proclamation of the word of God and human instrumentality.

4) We must distinguish the means of coming to faith in Christ, which is a mediate process, from regeneration itself, which is a direct, immediate, and instantaneous work of God.

5) The key to solving the problem of how spiritually dead sinners can repent and believe is found in the convicting ministry of the Spirit.

Note: This chapter is based on a paper given at the Eastern Sectional of the Evangelical Theological Society at Lanham, MD, March 1996.

---

1. Samuel Fisk, *Calvinistic Paths Retraced*; Norman Geisler, *Chosen But Free*, appendices 5 and 10.
2. Calvin, *Commentary on the Gospel according to John,* trans. Wm Pringle (GR: Baker, 1979), en loc, p. 41.
3. Ibid., p. 42.
4. Ibid., p. 44.
5. Charles Hodge, *Systematic Theology* (GR: Eerdmans, 1968 (1873)), II, p. 663.
6. Loraine Boettner, *The Reformed Doctrine of Predestination,* 5th ed. (GR: Eerdmans, 1941), pp. 166-7.
7. L. Berkhof, *Systematic Theology* (GR: Eerdmans, 1941), pp. 467-76.
8. Ibid, p. 503.
9. John Murray, *Redemption: Accomplished and Applied* (GR: Eerdmans, 1955), pp. 98, 103.
10. James Montgomery Boice, *Awakening to God*, p. 53.
11. R. C. Sproul, *Chosen by God*, p. 72.
12. Daniel B. Wallace, *Greek Grammar: Beyond the Basics* (GR: Zondervan, 1996), pp. 617-9.
13. Ibid, p. 620.
14. Wallace, p. 621, footnote.
15. W. G. T. Shedd, *Dogmatic Theology* (Nashville: Thomas Nelson, 1980), II, p. 472ff.
16. Aldrich, "The Gift of God," *Bibliotheca Sacra,* vol. 122: p. 248.
17. Henry Alford, *The Greek Testament* (Chicago: Moody, 1958), III, p. 94.
18. John Calvin, *Commentaries,* trans. Pringle, vol. XXI, pp. 228-9.
19. Gregory Sapaugh, "Is Faith a Gift? A study of Ephesians 2:8, " *Journal of the Grace Evangelical Society* 7, no. 12 (Spring 1994), pp. 39-40.
20. Laurence M. Vance, *The Other Side of Calvinism*, pp. 516-7.
21. Sproul, *Chosen by God*, p. 119.
22. A. T. Robertson, *Word Pictures*, VI, p. 147; Cleon L. Rogers, Jr., and Cleon L. Rogers, III, *Linguistic and Exegetical Key to the New Testament* (Zondervan, 1998), p. 581.
23. D. L. Moody, paraphrased since exact reference unavailable.
24. Calvin, *Commentaries on the Epistles of Paul to the Galatians and Ephesians*, trans. Wm. Pringle (GR: Baker, 1979 reprint), XXI:227 (see also footnote by Bloomfield, pp. 227-8).
25. James Oliver Buswell, Jr., *A Systematic Theology of the Christian Religion*, II, p. 132ff.

> The Irresistible and the Indisputable are two weapons which the very nature of His [God's] scheme forbids Him to use. Merely to override a human will . . . would be for Him useless. He cannot ravish. He can only woo. . . .
>
> There are only two kinds of people in the end: those who say to God, "Thy will be done," and those to whom God says, in the end, "Thy will be done." All that are in Hell, choose it. Without that selfchoice there could be no Hell.
>
> -C. S. Lewis

11

HOW DOES GOD CALL SINNERS?

THE BACKGROUND OF THE STUDY

The biblical idea of 'calling' is a broad term to describe the process of how sinners come to repentant faith in Christ. God invites, yes, summons a lost human race to receive salvation in Christ and to appointment to service for Him. All are obligated to respond to that summons, but the fact is that most do not. Why do some respond to the proclamation of the gospel while others do not? Bishop Augustine of Hippo answered that ultimately only the elect respond because they are the only ones whom God draws to Himself with irresistible grace. Although in the early fifth century he was the first to tout this notion, the majority Roman church wrestled with it in the Synod of Orange (AD 529) and omitted irresistible grace from the 25 canons of their concluding resolution. Calvin essentially revived this doctrine as a part of his tightly knit theology of salvation and all Calvinists would affirm irresistible grace, which is of course one of the five points of Calvinism.

In the process of reviewing the standard Calvinistic works on this subject, I was impressed with the widespread relapse into proof-texting and the absence of exegesis in the sections on irresistible grace. Some of the key passages which purportedly support irresistible grace are taken out of their historical context and used in a cavalier fashion without so much as a look at the context. Believing firmly that context and philology are the foundations of exegesis, I felt it imperative to press the linguistic and contextual considerations relevant to this issue. First, I will do a word study of the Greek words for calling, examine the presuppositions of irresistible grace, and then examine in context all of the Scriptures adduced.

A WORD STUDY OF CALLING (*KALEEIN, KLĒSIS, KLĒTOS*)

A survey of the usages of these words indicates that in the Gospels they are used frequently in three of Christ's parables in the sense of an invitation to a feast (Mt. 22:1-14; Lk. 14:7-14, 15-24). Two of the parables are the basis for the idea of a general 'call' or invitation to all mankind to salvation in the kingdom. So when the Lord Jesus capped the parable of the king's wedding feast with the aphorism, **"For many are called, but few are chosen"** (Mt. 22:14), most recognize the meaning 'invited,' as in the margin of the NAS translation and in the text of the NIV. One other statement of the Lord Jesus, found in all three synoptic Gospels, would also be a reference to that general invitation: **"I have not come to call the righteous but sinners to repentance"** (Lk.5:32=Mt. 9:13=Mk. 2:17). It is obvious that the invitation to all sinners precedes the repentance.

Then over fifty times in the epistles, mostly in Paul's letters, these words are used in a more technical sense of the completed process in the life of believers by which they came to Christ and therefore is usually referred to as an effectual calling. How that calling became effectual is the point of dispute between Calvinists and others. Is it an irresistible calling, or is it described as having been already effectuated because it is indeed a *fait accompli*, an accomplished fact? I would argue that the apostles used it in a narrower technical sense especially of those who have responded to the general call or gospel invitation and are thus referred by hindsight as the 'called.' To use the analogy of the parables of the Lord Jesus, it is as if the king at the banquet refers to those in the banquet hall as the 'invitees,' even though many others were invited but refused to come. It was an effectual calling (invitation) since those present had responded to the invitation and are referred to as the invited ones in a narrower, technical sense. Those who refused to attend, although invited, are now irrelevant to the purpose of the invitation and thus not designated as invitees, the 'called.' This is all brought out so clearly in Christ's parable of the king's wedding feast in Matthew 22, already examined in detail in chapter 8 (p. 180-1). This parable is totally at odds with irresistible grace. However, there are many other shades of meaning in this group of words which must be examined.

From the secular and Septuagintal usage, we find a prominent idea of commissioning someone. Coenen in his article in *DNTT* pointed out: "... in later chapters of Isaiah, . . . we have the profoundest use of *kaleo* in the sense of service and dedication, linked with an exceptionally frequent appearance of *eklegomai,* choose." In Isa. 42:6; 43:1; 45:3,4 it is used of the calling of Israel, Cyrus, the Messiah (Isa. 41:2): 'calling him in righteousness to his service.'[1] There are about ten usages of *kaleo* in Isaiah 42-55, and in every case it is the translation of the Hebrew *qara'*. In this regard, the BDB Gesenius lexicon lists the fifth meaning as "*summon*" and under that "**e.** *call and commission, appoint* . . . **f.** *call and endow* (with privilege)"[2]

Therefore, it is appropriate to consider whether this connotation carries over to *kaleo* in the New Testament, which is confirmed by Paul's usage: "**called *as* an apostle**" (Rom. 1:1; 1 Cor. 1:1; also Gal. 1:15). Is this then an aspect of the calling of all believers, that we are appointed or commissioned to His service? This seems to be what Paul affirms in Ephesians 4:1: "**Therefore I, the prisoner of the Lord, implore you to walk in a manner worthy of the calling with which you have been called . . .**" From Martin Luther's exposition onward the issue of 'vocation' has been discussed here. From this I take it that all believers were privileged to be commissioned or appointed as God's servants at the point of conversion. There is also a unique usage in 1 Corinthians 7:20 which seems to support the use of *klēsis* as calling or vocation in a more secular sense: "**Let each man remain in that condition in which he was called.**" Based upon parallel secular Greek usage Arndt and Gingrich list as a second meaning "2. *Station* in life, *position, vocation*"[3] Thus the Christian life itself is seen as a calling or vocation.

Further observations on the connotation of 'to summon' are in order. This meaning is clear in the Gospels and Acts (Mt. 2:7; 20:8; 25:14; Lk. 19:13; Acts 4:18; 24:2). Schmidt in *TDNT* comments: "That God calls with a view to man obeying finds a human par[allel] in P. Hamb., I, 29, 3 (89 A.D.) . . . The existence of such a par[allel] in the human sphere make it clear that the God of the Bible is a person confronting persons . . ."[4] I have previously emphasized in chapter 4 (p. 99-106) God's consistent confrontation of humanity in their sin, with the concomitant implication of man's ability to respond.

In the Septuagint and in the Gospels the verb also has the sense of 'to name,' which seems to be confirmed by Paul in Romans 1:7 and 1 Corinthians 1:2: "**called saints**," or possibly, "named saints."

In consideration of the many aspects of this group of words, Schmidt is undoubtedly correct in saying that "in the NT *kalein* is a technical term for the process of salvation."[5] Upon examining the many occurrences used in an effectual sense, I would suggest the following definition. *Calling is God's action in bringing the sinner to salvation, thus commissioning the believer to an exalted position with a new name for service to God.* It is used of the process and circumstances of our coming to faith viewed from the divine side, as contrasted with conversion, which is the human side.

Perhaps Cremer overstated the case: "Nowhere do we find the conjunction with *eis or en,* which would give *kalein* the meaning of effectual calling, or which would involve the call having been already accepted. In fact this is foreign to the word, which always points exclusively to the origins of one's status as a Christian."[6] It is frequently used by Paul of the circumstances and process by which we came to faith (esp. 1 Cor. 7:15, 17-24). It implies that we have responded to the general invitation and thus by hindsight appears to be effectual.

Additional observations on key passages

2 Thessalonians 2:14 is an early significant usage: "**And it was for this He called you through our gospel, that you may gain the glory of our Lord Jesus Christ.**" My observation is simple—that the calling was accomplished by means of the preaching of the gospel by Paul. Thus calling is accomplished mediately, not immediately (which might imply irresistible grace). As we unpack Paul's thought, we should note that in the preceding verse (as discussed in chapter 8) their salvation came "**through sanctification by the Spirit and faith in the truth.**" Allusion to a conditional element (faith in the truth) would seem to eliminate a direct work of irresistible grace. Of course, our interpretation will be strongly colored by our preunderstanding of the relation of repentant faith to the new birth, already discussed in the previous chapter.

Another significant observation from 1 Corinthians 1:26ff should be noted. He stated that not many wise, mighty, or noble are called to salvation. Does God sovereignly discriminate against such people, or are there human factors involved in the sparseness of their response to the general calling of the gospel? It would seem reasonable and common to human experience that pride would be a major human factor which hinders the intelligencia, the nobility, and the powerful from putting faith in Christ. Although Paul's usage of these words emphasizes God's initiative in salvation, this seems to be a counter indication to reading into the biblical concept of calling an irresistible, direct 'zapping' of the sinner by the Spirit. Indeed, we must go back to the parable of the king's wedding feast, which Schmidt called the *crux interpretum*, to see that those in the feast are those who responded to the general invitation.[7]

Later we have Paul's most theological reference to calling: "**But we know that for those who love Him, for those called in agreement with His purpose, God makes all things work together for good. Because those whom He knew beforehand He appointed beforehand to share the likeness of His Son, so that He might be the First-born among many brothers**" (Rom. 8:28-29, New Berkeley Version). First we note Paul's emphasis upon believers as "**those who love Him,**" which comes first in the emphatic position in the Greek sentence (as retained in the NBV). Then in apposition crux this we are designated as "**those called in agreement with His purpose.**" As discussed in chapter 3, there are three usages of *prothesis* in reference to God's plan of salvation, as confirmed by the BAGD listing: "plan, purpose, resolve, will, . . . design." Paul stressed the purpose of the calling to be that we should "**share the likeness of His Son.**" In other passages he expanded that purpose to include: called to freedom (Gal. 5:13), to hope (Eph. 1:18; 4:4), to peace in one body (Col. 3:15), not to impurity but in sanctification (1 Thess. 4:7), to suffering (1 Pet. 2:21), and to be a blessing (1 Pet. 3:9). Thus God has many purposes in commissioning us and calling us saints. The means of implementing that plan are explained in Romans 8:29-30, which I have discussed in detail in chapter 7 (p. 169-71) in reference to foreknowledge and preappointment. That discussion makes it clear that there is no basis here for an irresistible force in God's calling us to salvation.

Although Paul's use of calling in Romans 11:28-29 is not a reference to our individual salvation, but rather to God's ultimate plan for the nation Israel, nevertheless there is an applicable principle here: "**. . . for the gifts and the calling of God are irrevocable.**" There is no hint in this context that the calling of Israel, in regard to their ultimate restoration back to the place of blessing, is irresistible. However, not only is God's plan for Israel irrevocable, but the true Christian's salvation is also irrevocable. This is the glorious truth of eternal security. *Thus the calling to salvation is irrevocable, but not irresistible!*

One other theologically significant context comes from Peter's pen: "**Therefore, brethren, be all the more diligent to make certain about His calling and choosing you; for as long as you practice these things, you will never stumble**" (2 Pet. 1:10). The first question to address is whether Peter is referring to the individual's objective calling, or whether it is our subjective perception of it? The context from his previous use of the term 'calling' in 1:3 speaks of the virtues or qualities we should be diligent to manifest in the Christian life. It is failure to focus on one's purification from the former sins which elicits Peter's exhortation. Thus it seems to be the believer's subjective perception, remembrance, and awareness of his calling about which Peter is concerned, as a basis for a useful and fruitful Christian life (1:8). This then says little about the irresistibility of the calling, pro or con. Nor does it undermine the irrevocability of the calling, as Arminians might claim.

PRESUPPOSITIONS OF IRRESISTIBLE GRACE

In reviewing the major Calvinistic works, I have been greatly impressed with the major part that significant presuppositions play in their discussion. Some of these discussions seem almost irrelevant to the subject at hand apart from some unstated presuppositions. It is only when the non-Calvinistic reader reminds himself of the unstated presuppositions in their minds that he can even see the relevancy of the discussion.[8] This is because this topic is very deductive. In his chapter on effective call, Sproul does not give even one Scripture reference (except the ones in his quotation of Zane Hodges), apart from using the raising of Lazarus as an illustration.[9] Therefore, before it is possible to exegete the relevant Scriptures, it is imperative for me to list some of the presuppositions which I have discerned in their writings.

Effectual calling necessarily implies irresistible grace.

Most writers rightly distinguish between the general call (or invitation) of the gospel to all mankind and the effectual calling, which is related only to the saved. However, Calvinists seem to assume that this necessarily implies the idea of irresistible grace. This is not at all a necessary implication, but an extrapolation of the data.

Irresistible grace presupposes unconditional election.

Perhaps the main source of the first presupposition is this second one. Starting with the premise of unconditional election, the doctrine of effectual calling is automatically converted into irresistible grace. The interrelatedness of the five points of Calvinism is emphasized by most Calvinists and is most obvious at this point. Bruce Ware states that Calvinism's irresistible understanding of effectual calling and grace "is a necessary complement to its doctrine of unconditional election, each of which entails and is entailed by the other, and both of which are necessary to its soteriology."[10] Palmer, in his chapter on irresistible grace, discusses some Scripture passage relating to others of the five points, but gives only two direct proof texts without any significant discussion. From this it is clear that his thinking is almost completely deductive, not inductive.[11] Predestination is discussed in chapter 7 and election in chapter 8, in which careful study of the key words reveals no basis for unconditional election or predestination.

Irresistible grace follows from an all-inclusive decree.

Since Calvinists believe that their concept of God's sovereignty requires an eternal decree of God by which He has determined "all that comes to pass," His work of salvation must be irresistible. Duane Spencer wrote, "God is not omnipotent if he can be resisted and rejected."[12] In chapter 3, I have already dealt with the lack of inductive support for such a divine decree, which is based upon a gross extrapolation of Ephesians 1:11.

Irresistible grace is necessitated by man's total inability.

There is a strong logical connection between the Calvinistic notion of man's total inability, already discussed in chapter 4, and their doctrine of irresistible grace. Non-Calvinists also believe that man is totally unable to save himself, but we reject the idea that man is totally unable to repent and believe in Christ. Arminians have solved the problem with their doctrine of prevenient (preparing) grace, which does not have any inductive basis. In chapter 9, I have emphasized the importance of the convicting work of the Spirit as the key. In any case, Scripture is clear that man is responsible to repent and believe, thus implying ability to do so. In no case is irresistible grace a necessary or viable answer. It is a solution to a problem which does not exist!

Regeneration precedes repentance and faith.

Calvinists assume that since man is spiritually dead, he cannot believe and must be regenerated in order to believe. This assumption is rarely (if ever) discussed or defended in their writings and is a clear reversal of the scriptural order. Boettner focused most of his discussion of efficacious grace upon the monergism of regeneration, that is, the direct bestowal of new birth upon the elect.[13] This minimizes the place of human instrumentality in the process of coming to repentant faith. Christ said that the dead, not the regenerate shall hear the voice of the Son of God and live (John 5:24,25). This is made possible by the convicting work of the Spirit, not by regeneration. I have discussed this deductive reversal at length in the previous chapter (10).

Conditional salvation would be contrary to grace.

Calvinists insist that if God's calling is not irresistible, it would undermine monergistic grace. Those who do not hold to irresistible grace are pejoratively called "synergists." However, those of us who believe that repentant faith is the condition of salvation and that it is not meritorious can hold to monergistic grace in regeneration just as consistently as extreme Calvinists. I have also discussed this in the preceding chapter (10).

Irresistible grace is effectuated by a direct gift of faith.

Integral to the notion of irresistible grace is the idea that repentance and faith are the immediate or direct gift of God. God gives repentant faith to the elect and withholds it from the non-elect. Storms' statement is typical: "The Bible portrays faith and repentance as God's gifts to his elect."[14] A contextual study of all the Calvinistic proof texts in chapter 10 indicated a total lack of inductive evidence for such a notion. If it can be said at all (and this is doubtful) that faith is the gift of God, it must be understood mediately, not immediately or directly.

CALVINISTIC PROOF-TEXTS EXAMINED

As I have examined the treatments of irresistible grace by Calvinists, I am absolutely amazed at the lack of serious exegetical discussion by most, especially a failure to see each passage in its context. Many writers do not even bother to quote the passages, let alone focus on the all-important context.

Ezekiel 37:1-14

Gordon Clark claimed that the prophecy of the dry bones in the valley is a proof of irresistible grace, as well as all the other points of the TULIP.[15] Clearly in making that claim, he has departed far from any literal interpretation of the passage and has ignored the Spirit-given interpretation in vv. 11-14: **"Son of man, these bones are the whole house of Israel . . . I will bring you into the land of Israel."** This comes in the context of many prophecies of the end-time restoration of Israel to the promised land and cannot be lightly spiritualized, as those of amillennial viewpoint tend to do. Without getting into a discussion of the millennial issue, let me say that it is irresponsible to build one's theology of salvation upon a spiritualized interpretation of this passage, which holds that Israel means the church. In short my response is that if we can spiritualize this and other Old Testament prophecies, then we can spiritualize away the literal force of the first-coming Messianic prophecies as well, which would undermine the apologetic significance of these prophecies.

Psalm 65:4

Clark also sees irresistible grace here, but he does not quote or refer to the context,[16] which I shall do: **"To You all men come. Iniquities prevail against me; As for our transgressions, You forgive them. How blessed is the one whom You choose and bring near *to You* to dwell in Your courts. We will be satisfied with the goodness of Your house, Your holy temple. . . . You who are the trust of all the ends of the earth and of the farthest sea"** (Ps. 65:2-5, underlining mine). Vance rightly faults Clark for not even quoting the whole verse thus omitting the purpose of the choosing and bringing near, that is, to dwell in God's temple in Jerusalem.[17] Notice that the words "to you" are not in the Hebrew original. This Psalm must be understood in the context of the worship of ancient Israel, centered in the temple. David preceded this verse with very universalistic language (65:2) and followed it with even more obvious reference to the Gentiles scattered over the earth (65:5). This hardly serves the particularistic ends to which Clark wants to use half of a verse, wrenched out of its context. Yes, God did choose Israel as His choice people, greatly privileged to worship God in the temple, a privilege which in the main the Gentiles did not enjoy. But to make this a proof of unconditional election and irresistible grace is baseless. God chose the Aaronic priests to "dwell in His courts," and David as Israel's king found worship in His tabernacle a great privilege. The issue here is of God's special favor to the nation Israel. But as we have noted in chapter 8, this privilege did not automatically save any Israelites. Clark's technical discussion of the grammar apart from the context is a discredit to his brilliance.[18] His treatment of other Old Testament passages is similarly cavalier, and to respond to others would be too tedious for my readers. Let us move on to the New.

Luke 14:15-24

Since Bishop Augustine of Hippo innovated the notion of irresistible grace, let us see his basis for it in the parable of the great dinner invitation. Since those invited made irrational excuses, the host had his slaves not only bring in the handicapped, but also recruit others from the public thoroughfares. Augustine put the strongest spin on the word *anagkazein* by interpreting it in the sense of physical compulsion or coercion. In writing to

Vincentius, a non-conformist who advocated freedom of conscience: "You are of the opinion that no one should be compelled to follow righteousness, and yet you read that the householder said to his servants, 'Whomever you shall find, compel them to come in.'"[19] Although he misused Lk. 14:23 in connection with the church coercing people (the Donatists) into the Catholic Church, the connection of this to God's coercion in irresistible grace is obvious. It is curious that none of the contemporary Calvinists I could check dare to try to use this reference in support, except for Pink: ". . . the Greek *anagkazō* genuinely has the idea of 'forceful' constraint," for which he references Grundman [sic] in *TDNT*.[20] However, when we examine Grundmann's article, we find a broad spectrum of meanings: "*anagkazō* is to cause or compel someone in all the varying degrees from friendly pressure to forceful compulsion (On the individual meanings, cf. the lexicons.)." He lists the usage in the Septuagint and Josephus, which indicates circumstantial "constraint." Since his summary of the New Testament usage is so brief, we must check the lexicons, as he suggested.[21]

Arndt and Gingrich list two meanings: "**1.** *compel, force*, of inner and outer compulsion. . . . **2.** weakened *invite (urgently), urge (strongly)*. . ."[22] It is most significant that of the other eight usages of this verb in the New Testament only one refers to any sort of physical force (Acts 26:11). All the rest have to do with some personal (Mt. 14:22=Mk. 6:45), socio-religious (Gal. 2:3, 14; 6:12), or circumstantial (Acts 28:19; 2 Cor. 12:11) pressure to act. So Augustine's interpretation is extremely improbable.

But this still leaves open the possible use of this for irresistible grace. The only possible context the Calvinists might use is this parable, since God is never the subject of this verb anywhere else. First we must determine what actually happened in the parable itself—did the slaves actually force the people to come with physical force? The host in the parable is not identified as a king or anyone who might be able to use or get away with the use of force. So Arndt and Gingrich's second meaning of an urgent invitation is really required. Otherwise we would have to agree with Augustine's misuse of the parable for human coercion to faith. Since this is obviously a violation of the evangelical conscience, there can be absolutely no basis for the use of this parable for irresistible grace either. It doesn't work either way! Pink has not thought through the consequences of his use of this verse for irresistible grace. Apparently other Calvinists have rightly seen the inconsistency and have declined to reference it.

John 6:37, 44, 65

Calvinists see in Christ's statement that, **"All that the Father gives Me shall come to Me"** a reference to the elect, who will irresistibly be drawn to Christ. They feel this is confirmed by the converse in v. 44, **"No one can come to Me, unless the Father who sent Me draws him."** There is no consideration of any alternate interpretation which might be suggested by the context. But rather than assuming that the Lord Jesus is referring to all the elect, we should seek to understand the expression in the light of the historical contextual flow.

Context. In the Bread of Life Discourse the Lord has been having a rather animated dialogue with a somewhat skeptical inquiring multitude (vv. 24ff). He had just stated that although they had seen Him, they still have not believed (6:36). Then in contrast he refers to the truly believing disciples in the multitude as "**all that the Father gives Me**," who are inevitably coming to Him. The key issue all the way through the dialogue is faith or its lack (6:29, 35, 40, 47, 64), and he symbolizes faith as appropriation by eating and drinking Him (6:35, 51, 53-58). A little later He emphasized the human response factor: "**If anyone is willing to do His will, he will know of the teaching, whether it is of God or whether I speak from Myself**" (7:17).

Identification. In order to understand this passage aright, we must first identify who these people are whom Christ identified as, "**all that the Father gives Me.**" Since He used this phrase at least four other times we must examine those contexts also. "**This is the will of Him who sent Me, that of all that He has given Me I lose nothing, but raise it up on the last day**" (6:39). "**. . . that the Son may glorify You, even as You gave Him authority over all flesh, that to all whom You have given Him, He may give eternal life**" (17:1-2). "**I manifested Your name to the men whom You gave Me out of the world. They were Yours and You gave them to Me, and they have kept Your word**" (17:6). "**I ask on their behalf; I do not ask on behalf of the world, but of those whom You hast given Me; for they are Yours**" (17:9). From this context of the Lord's high priestly prayer, it becomes clear that He is referring to the living disciples, whom the Father had given Him, especially to the eleven apostles. This could not be a reference to that abstract concept of the elect of all ages for a number of reasons. We see first in 17:6 that the Lord Jesus had shown the Father to them personally. This could not be true of the elect of past ages, and the past tense He used (aorist) would not likely include the elect of future ages. The clause, "**they have kept Your word**" also eliminates believers of other ages, since it is obvious that this could not be said about future generations. Additionally, He later clarifies that those who in turn believe through their word are distinct from those whom the Father had given him: "**I do not ask on behalf of these alone, but for those also who believe in Me through their word . . .**" (17:20). So the idea is clear in both contexts that the Father is turning the godly Jewish remnant over to the Son during His earthly ministry. These are the believing ones who inevitably come to Him. Thus this passage has nothing to do with irresistible grace upon unbelievers, since these were already sincere believers.

The believing remnant. Throughout the previous ages, the Old Testament saints had put their trust in the Father as Yahweh. Now that the Son has begun His ministry, that believing remnant is being given to the Son by the Father. This included many converts of John the Baptizer, as the apostle John had described in chapter 1, including himself, James, Peter, Andrew, Nathaniel, and others. Previously they had "**heard and learned from the Father**" (John 6:45). Now they are transferring their faith to the Son, that is, they are coming to Him. Our Lord's quotation from Isaiah 54:13 in John 6:45 is strong confirmation of this: "**It is written in the prophets, '*And they shall all be taught of GOD.*' Everyone who has heard and learned from the Father comes to Me**" (6:45). It becomes increasingly clear that those contemporary disciples who were under His ministry and were really open to the Father's teaching from the Old Testament, were the ones who came to Him in faith. A clear example is Christ's comment at Caesarea Philippi after Peter's confession of His deity: "**Blessed are you, Simon Barjona, because flesh and blood did not reveal *this* to you, but My Father who is in heaven** " (Mt. 16:17).

Drawing. The 'drawing' of John 6:44 requires further consideration, however: "**No one can come to Me, unless the Father who sent Me draws him; and I will raise him up on the last day.**" Augustinians see this as an irresistible drawing. This is possible, but certainly not necessary, since the BAGD lexicon lists a second meaning for *helkuo*, "to draw a pers. in the direction of values for inner life, *draw, attract, an extended fig. use of mng.*" Then a dozen references from the secular Greek and the Septuagint are given in support of this in connection with the two references from the Gospel of John. None of these are at all indicative of any supposed irresistibility: "**I have loved you with an everlasting love; therefore I have drawn you with lovingkindness**" (Jer. 31.3). "**Therefore the maidens love you. Draw me after you and let us run together**" (Songs 1:3-4).[23] Additionally the LSJ lexicon lists among many meanings: "8. *Draw to oneself, attract. . .*" Half a dozen references additional to those in BAGD are listed in support. *Note that the primary literal meaning of the verb 'to draw, to drag' has reference to physical objects, whereas the figurative usage in reference to the inner life of a person is appropriately not coercive*.

The Lord Jesus used the same word, *elkuo,* again in John 12:32: "**'And I, if I be lifted up from the earth, will draw all men to Myself'.**" In the context, especially of 12:20, it is clear that He is referring to Gentiles as well as Jews when He speaks of 'all men', which we know can be translated as 'all kinds of men.' Therefore, I would not claim this passage as a proof of general redemption. But neither can it be adduced as a proof of irresistible grace.

Secondary meaning. It should be clear that the primary meaning, "pull, drag, draw,' in reference to physical objects is inappropriate here. It certainly does not fit our two contexts: "No one can come to Me unless the

Father who sent Me drags him" and "I . . . will drag all men to Myself." I am astonished that Boettner even highlights that meaning in his discussion.[24] Sproul prefers "compel," for which he claims that *TDNT* "defines it to mean to compel by irresistible superiority. Linguistically and lexicographically, the word means 'to compel.'"[25] The truth is that Oepke in *TDNT* gives no such definition, and by his statement Sproul shows that he does not understand the difference between a theological dictionary and a lexicon. Oepke has written an article on *helkuein* in which there is a paragraph listing many secular and biblical usages. Sproul found the meaning "compel" in two papyri in reference to some sort of physical compulsion. But then Oepke went on to say: "More comparable with the Johannine usage is that of Porphyr. Marc., 16. . . Cf. Also Corp. Herm., X, 6." Both references support the second meaning given in BAGD above, that is, a figurative meaning having to do with the inner life. Then in the more definitive large print paragraph, Oepke concludes: "The word is used of mother love in 4 Macc. 14:13; 15:11. We find a beneficent 'drawing' of God in `*Ier.* 38:3 [31:3]: . . . The original refers more to patience. The LXX is thinking, not so much of drawing out in deliverance . . . but of drawing to oneself in love. This usage is distinctively developed by Jn, . . ."[26] Sproul badly misuses this *TDNT* article (cf. endnote). Do we really want to believe that God drags us kicking and screaming to salvation? Is our God really a coercive God? I should hope that most Calvinists would not want to go along with Boettner in this use of the primary, non-figurative connotation.[27] Thus it seems to me that the secondary, figurative meaning is absolutely required.

So how are people drawn to Christ? The context of John 6:44 makes clear that they were drawn by the testimony of Abraham, Moses, and the prophets of the Old Testament Scriptures, as contemporary Jews checked out the supernatural credentials of Jesus of Nazareth and concluded with Nathaniel, **"Rabbi, You are the Son of God; You are the King of Israel"** (Jn. 1:49). Now since Pentecost, God has used the apostolic message and ministry, working mediately through Christian witnesses. It is as simple as that. Dean Henry Alford, that master exegete, confirms this:

> That this 'drawing ' is not irresistible grace, is confessed even by Augustine himself, the great upholder of the doctrines of grace. "If a man . . . come unwillingly, he does not believe; if he does not believe, he does not come. For we do not run to Christ on our feet, but by faith; not with the movement of the body, but with the free will of the heart." . . . The Greek expositors take the view which I have adopted above. . . . This *drawing* now is being exerted on all the world—in accordance with the Lord's prophecy (12:32) and His command (Matthew 28:19-20).[28]

Transition. Vance points out another significant observation, that in John 6:44 it is *the Father* who has been drawing people to Christ, since the

Father has been putting the believing remnant of Jews into the charge of the Son (“**all who the Father gives Me**”). However, in 12:32 the Lord Jesus stated that after the cross, *He Himself* would draw all kinds of people to Himself.[29] This obvious contrast with 6:44 confirms that the issue is the believing Jewish remnant in contrast to a diversity of Gentiles, neither of which says anything about irresistible grace. Calvinists have ignored the context.

John 6:65. Although 6:65 is part of the same general context of the contrast of believers with unbelievers, there are some additional considerations here. “**And He was saying, ‘For this reason I have said to you, that no one can come to Me, unless it has been granted him from the Father’.**” Apart from the context this might seem to imply that apart from irresistible grace, the non-elect are hopelessly reprobated to Hell. Here also the flow of the context is exceedingly important. Many of his professing disciples had just been grumbling at His words (6:61), and then the immediately preceding verse is crucial, “**... ‘But there are some of you who do not believe.’ For Jesus knew from the beginning who they were who did not believe, and who it was that would betray Him**” (6:64). “**As a result of this many of His disciples withdrew, and were not walking with Him anymore**” (6:66). “**‘Did I Myself not choose you, the twelve, and yet one of you is a devil?’**” (6:70).

Rejecting great light. Thus it is in reference to professed disciples who had walked with Him for an extensive period of time, sat under His teaching, and seen His miracles, especially to Judas Iscariot, that the Lord made this statement. They were rejecting the greatest light that anybody could reject. They had professed to believe but were counterfeits. These are the ones to whom God was not granting the privilege to come to Him. What is the principle here? Is it the hidden counsel of God to which the Calvinists are so want to flee? Or is it God’s judgment upon the rejection of great light? I would suggest that the answer is given by a converted Pharisee many years later who had severely persecuted the church of Christ. He had held the garments of those who stoned Stephen. He had resisted the convicting work of the Holy Spirit, kicking against the oxgoad (Acts 26:14). And yet God saved him. We need not be ignorant of the reason for he tells us why in 1 Timothy 1:12-13. “**I thank Christ Jesus our Lord, who has strengthened me, because He considered me faithful, putting me into service; even though I was formerly a blasphemer and a persecutor and a violent aggressor. And yet I was shown mercy, because I acted ignorantly in unbelief.**” He had not closed his heart against great light. But Judas and the other counterfeit disciples sinned against the greatest light possible, and thus came under the judgmental blindness so frequently mentioned in Scripture.

Judgment. Not long afterward in a discussion with some Pharisees the Lord said, "'**For judgment I came into this world, that those who do not see may see; and that those who see may become blind.' Those of the Pharisees who were with Him heard these things and said to Him, 'We are not blind too, are we?' Jesus said to them, 'If you were blind, you would have no sin; but since you say, 'We see,' your sin remains**'" (John 9:39-41). So John 6:65 must be understood in a judgmental sense and not as having anything to do with election or reprobation in eternity past.

This same principle is operative in John 12:37-48, which has been pulled out of its context to show that there are non-elect who cannot believe and be saved. This passage also speaks of judgmental blindness upon those who closed their hearts to such great light: "**But though He had performed so many signs before them, *yet* they were not believing in Him; . . . He who rejects Me, and does not receive My sayings, has one who judges him; the word I spoke is what will judge him at the last day**" (Jn. 12:37, 48).

John 10:16

Calvinists assume that the "**other sheep, which are not of this fold**," is a reference to as yet unsaved elect who must be saved and brought into Christ's flock. Edwin Palmer obscured this verse by misquoting it, substituting the word 'flock' for 'fold.[30] But the difference is significant, for Christ speaks of "**this fold**", which implies another fold. What two folds could He be referring to? All His disciples were Jews. The day was coming in which that great missionary purpose of God would be fulfilled when He would bring Samaritans, proselytes, and Gentiles into the one flock with one shepherd. Actually He already had a fold of Samaritan believers, which Phillip later brought into the flock of the church. We just noted that He again raised the same Jew/Gentile dichotomy later in 12:32. This is a much more context-sensitive exegesis than reading into the text of a theological concept, which is isogesis.

Acts 9:1-19; 22:1-21; 26:1-20

Many Calvinists would use the conversion of Saul of Tarsus as an example of irresistible grace, as does Custance. "Did those who tried to rationalize Election in this way not remember that Paul was coerced by the sovereign grace of God? . . . Paul was turned about with violence because he 'kicked against the pricks' of the goad of God's grace (Acts 9:5, sic)."[31] Custance is prey to the idea that Saul was coerced to faith by Christ. I would insist that there is nothing in the narrative or Paul's letters to support that idea. Certainly Saul went through a long spiritual struggle from the time he witnessed the martyrdom of Stephen, exacerbated by hearing the repeated testimonies of the Christians he persecuted (Acts 26:10-11; 1 Tim. 1:12-16), until the very moment that he heard the words of the risen Lord Jesus, "**I am Jesus whom you are persecuting.**" Instantaneously he realized that he had been tragically and absolutely wrong. He had thought sincerely that he was serving the true God of Israel, when in reality he was persecuting God's Messiah and His true people. It is very possible that as he heard the truth from the lips of Christians, that he struggled with doubts about his own position. Certainly the Holy Spirit had been convicting him through their words, since that is the obvious meaning of the oxgoad the Lord referred to (26:14). At that point he had a choice to deny the truth or to face the new reality with which he was confronted. Granted the facts that he now faced were overwhelming, still God did not force his will. I have already referenced his analysis in 1 Timothy 1:12-16, that he had acted "ignorantly in unbelief." We must understand him in the light of Christ's explanation of the good soil of the parable of the soils, who respond to the word with **"an honest heart"** (Lk. 8:15). Instantaneously he faced the facts, repented (a change of mind or attitude) and believed on Christ. The narrative is totally comprehensible without irresistible grace.

Acts 13:48

Another favorite Calvinistic proof text is in Luke's comment on the turning of Paul and Barnabas to the Gentiles after the strong Jewish opposition at Antioch of Pisidia: "**And when the Gentiles heard this, they began rejoicing and glorifying the word of the Lord; and as many as had been appointed to eternal life believed.**" A survey of translations indicates an overwhelming agreement with the NAS quoted above and seems supportive of the Calvinistic viewpoint. Knowing the tendency of translators to follow a tradition, even to the point of getting into a rut, I felt this passage demands extremely careful philological and contextual study. I could only find Rotherham ("as many as had become disposed for . . .") and Alfred Marshall's Interlinear ("having been disposed") to have broken from the rut. My conclusion is that most translators have overlooked important data.

Three issues. There are three issues which must be faced: the context, the meaning of *tassein*, and whether this is a middle or passive verb. The BAGD lexicon gives as a primary meaning of *tassein*:

> "1. to bring about an order of things by arranging, *arrange, put in place* . . . b. of a pers. put into a specific position, used with a prep.. . . *tassein tina eis - assign someone to a (certain) classification* . . . pass. *belong to, be classed among those possessing - hosoi ēsan tetagmenoi eis zōēn aiōnion* **Ac 13:48.**— *tassein heauton eis diakonian - devote oneself to a service* [2 secular Greek examples] **1 Cor 16:15.**"[32]

Although I have not found any source which considered the fact that *tetagmenoi*, being a perfect participle in form, can be either middle or passive, this is of great significance in our exegesis.[A] Additionally, we can identify this as a periphrastic pluperfect construction, which tends to show action antecedent (cause or condition) to the main verb, *episteusan*.[33] The use of a neuter plural subject with a plural verb tends to emphasize the individuality of each subject.[34] The middle voice, being reflexive, could be rendered, **"as many as had devoted themselves to eternal life believed"** or **"as many as had arranged (positioned) themselves toward eternal life believed."** The first rendering is suggested by the usage in 1 Cor. 16:15: **"The household of Stephanas . . . have devoted themselves for the ministry to the saints."** The second rendering is suggested by the first meaning listed in BAGD and the strong military use of the word in secular Greek according to the LSJ lexicon: "*—draw up in order of battle, form, array, marshal,* . . . Med., *fall in, form in order of battle* . . . 2. *post, station* . . . III. c. acc. rei, *place in a certain order or relative position*."[35] Gerhard Delling in *TDNT* concurs with that general understanding in reference to Acts 13:48: "The idea that God's will to save is accomplished in Christians with their conversion is obviously not connected with the thought of predestination (IV, 192, 1ff.), but rather with that of conferring status (–>31, 20ff.); cf. *ouk axious* Ac 13:46."[36] Delling here is pointing to a contextual argument, so let us move on to examine the context.

Context. First we must examine the narrower context. When the Jews began to contradict and blaspheme, the apostles said, "**It was necessary that the word of God should be spoken to you first; since you repudiate it, and judge yourselves unworthy of eternal life, behold, we are turning to the Gentiles**" (Acts 13:46). The contrast Luke makes between these words of the apostles and his own statement in 13:48 is clear. Since the Jews had **put themselves** in a position hostile to eternal life, the apostles were very explicit by the use of the reflexive pronoun ('yourselves') to attribute the cause to their attitude Then Luke in explaining the opposite response of the Gentiles would be most likely intending a reflexive middle voice, rather than a passive, in attributing the cause of the Gentile's faith to their attitude, which in 13:42 was evidenced in their pleading with the apostles to come back on a second Sabbath to give the word of God. The parallel is striking.

Then we must examine the broader context of Luke's statements here in Acts. We have a close parallel in Iconium: "**. . . they entered the syna-**

A. Bagster's *Analytical Greek Lexicon*, p. xx, "The middle voice has only two tenses peculiar to itself, the future and the aorist. As to the other tenses, the passive form is used to indicate reflexive action: . . ." I am astonished that this important grammatical point is given so little mention in the lexicons, grammars, and commentaries, nor was I taught it in four years of Greek studies. The tools only mention the passive and do not alert the student to the possibility of the middle voice in the other tenses.

gogue of the Jews together, and spoke in such a manner that a great multitude believed, both of Jews and of Greeks" (14:1). Here also Luke gives an explanation of a human cause for many coming to faith; he does not attribute it to irresistible grace or predestination. There is another close parallel in Berea: "**Now these were more nobleminded than those in Thessalonica, for they received the word with great eagerness, examining the Scriptures daily,** ***to see*** **whether these things were so. Many of them therefore believed, along with a number of prominent Greek women and men**" (17:11-12). Since Luke's theological perspective, presumably derived from Paul, allowed him to attribute the faith of the converts in two other cities to human factors, we must be open to that probability in Antioch of Pisidia as well. I believe the semantics, grammar, and syntax as explained above cogently lead to that conclusion.

My exegesis is not new or novel. This was proposed by Dean Henry Alford a century and a half ago:

> The Jews had *judged themselves unworthy of eternal life:* the Gentiles, as many as were disposed to eternal life, believed. . . . but to find *in this text* pre-ordination to life asserted, is to force both the word and the context to a meaning which they do not contain. . . . Wordsworth well observes that it would be interesting to enquire what influence such renderings as this of *praeordinati* in the Vulgate version had on the minds of men like St. Augustine and his followers in the Western Church in treating the great questions of free will, election, reprobation, and final perseverance. . . . The tendency of the Eastern Fathers, who read the original Greek, was, he remarks, in a different direction from that of the Western School.[37]

He references Bengel and DeWette as supporting his view and Mede and Schottg. as taking the military sense I have alluded to above. Of course, we have far vaster Greek resources upon which to base our exegesis than they had centuries ago.

Acts 16:14

"**A woman named Lydia, . . . a worshiper of God, was listening; and the Lord opened her heart to respond to the things spoken by Paul.**" Augustinians assume that Luke's statement that the Lord opened Lydia's heart to respond to the things spoken by the apostles, is a proof of irresistible grace. I do not question the Holy Spirit's initiative in opening the sinner's heart to the gospel message, but believe that it is by the conviction of the Holy Spirit (Jn. 16:8-11), which is neither irresistible nor immediate. Over the years of Biblical study, I have been increasingly impressed with how much of God's work is mediate rather than immediate. Yes, clearly the new birth is 100% immediate and directly the work of the Spirit. But there is strong evidence that the convicting work of the Spirit is accomplished mediately through human means. See chapter 9 for the historical examples of conviction, which came through human instrumentality. The same is true with Lydia since Luke emphasizes that she was listening to the things spoken by Paul. There is also an important antecedent factor mentioned by Luke which has been overlooked, that she was "a worshiper of God." Whether she was Jewish, a devout Gentile, or a proselyte, is not clear. But it is clear that she had been exposed to the Old Testament in her association with the Jewish women who had gathered for prayer on the Sabbath (16:13). To foist the notion of irresistible grace upon this passage is theological, not exegetical and contextual.

I have just pointed out that Luke balances off this perspective of God's initiative in Acts 17:11-12, where he attributed the faith of the noble minded Bereans to their mindset. Then in Acts 26:17-18 we find that God charged Paul in his ministry to the Gentiles, **"to whom I am sending you, to open their eyes so that they may turn from darkness to light and from the dominion of Satan to God, that they may receive forgiveness of sins and an inheritance among those who have been sanctified by faith in Me."** This is not exclusively the work of the Holy Spirit. He uses human instrumentality in bringing sinners to faith, although when they believe, the Spirit directly and without human involvement regenerates them.

Romans 8:28-30

Augustinians seem to resort to this passage most consistently to prove irresistible grace so we must revisit it. Because 'calling' is found third in a sequence connected presumably with predestination, Calvinists interpret the calling irresistibly. In chapter 7 I have already shown that there is no linguistic basis for the idea that foreknowledge has a deterministic connotation and that *proorizein* does not have anything to do with destiny, but should be translated 'to preappoint.' That preappointment is clearly conditioned upon God's foreknowledge, as confirmed by Peter in 1 Peter 1:1-2. The notion of irresistible grace would never have been connected with this passage apart from this serious mistranslation.

We also saw the importance of its broader context of the major theme of Romans, a righteousness from God appropriated by faith. *Pisteuo* and *pistis* occur 60 times in the epistle. **"For in the gospel a righteousness from God is revealed, a righteousness that is by faith from first to last"** (Rom. 1:17 NIV). The whole plan of salvation is by faith from foreknowledge to preappointment to calling to justification to glorification. There is no idea of unconditional election or of irresistible grace here.

Romans 9:1-29

Romans 9 is a major camping ground of Calvinists, who especially focus upon 9:19-22. I have discussed this in considerable detail in chapter

3, pointing out how the passage has nothing to do with the unconditional election of individuals and therefore with irresistible grace. The context is totally about the choice of the nation Israel as a channel of blessing and salvation for the whole world, and then God's justice in setting Israel aside when they rejected His Messiah. This becomes absolutely clear when one examines the Old Testament passages which Paul quoted in their own contexts. Please see the exposition at the end of my third chapter and a critique of John Piper's book in appendix B.

Miscellaneous proof-texts

There are a number of proof texts referred to by Calvinists, usually in a list without any exegetical support. Vance complains: "No exegesis is ever attempted, and little comment is made beside the standard Calvinistic cliches."[38] Although I have not surveyed all the Calvinistic works as extensively as Vance has, I would have to agree with him. Some of the passages which seem irrelevant to the issue if taken literally are Ps. 110:3, John 5:21, and Phil. 2:12-13. James 1:18 is significant and I have discussed it previously (cf. p. 59).

PASSAGES WHICH REFUTE IRRESISTIBLE GRACE

There are a number of passages which stand in direct contradiction to the doctrine of irresistible grace, which are ignored by determinists. Let us examine them in their contexts.

Matthew 13:1-43=Mark 4:1-20=Luke 8:4-15

When we search for an explanation as to why some people get saved and why others who hear the word of God remain unsaved, Christ's two important parables here give us an answer. We must not flee to some mysterious elective decree of God worked out by irresistible grace. In the parable of the soils the Lord attributed the differing response to factors related to the soils themselves. The first soil had been packed down by the feet of bypassers and was not open to the seed. The second had a rocky pan which made the soil shallow. The third had not been properly weeded, and although it germinated and grew, it did not bear fruit. **"But the *seed* in the good soil, these are the ones who have heard the word in an honest and good heart, and hold it fast, and bear fruit with perseverance"** (Lk. 8:15). The Lord Jesus attributed the response to an attitude of heart in the individual, not to irresistible grace. This is not meritorious, for that would contradict Paul's later teaching of grace, but rather points to a responsive heart. Both the parable of the four soils and of the wheat and the counterfeit tares also attribute rejection of the message to demonic influence (Mt. 13:19, 38-39). This is clearly seen in Satan's use of diverse religious prejudices (ie. Islam), cults, anti-biblical ideologies, etc. to hinder and confuse the process of bringing people to faith in Christ. Although the Lord

Jesus constantly attributed faith or unbelief to individuals (Mt. 8:10, 9:2, 22, 29), this does not thereby make faith meritorious. Indeed, Paul is very explicit in making faith and merit contrary principles (Rom. 4:16). Most significantly, Christ does not in any way attribute the difference to irresistible grace.

Some might raise the issue of Christ's quotation of Isaiah 6 in verses 10-15, especially, "**but to them it has not been granted**" (Mt. 13:11). However, we should understand all of these parables as judgmental in nature, occasioned in Matthew's sequence of events by the strong rejections of Messiah in chapter twelve.[39] This is not the outworking of a decree of reprobation, but rather a response to Israel's rejection of Him.

Matthew 23:37

After over three years of ministering to "this nation (genea)" of Israel and rebuking their unbelief, the Messiah cries out, "**O Jerusalem, Jerusalem, who kills the prophets and stones those who are sent to her! How often I wanted to gather your children together, the way a hen gathers her chicks under her wings, and you were unwilling.**" Although I believe we could make a good case for Israel's rejection of the Messiah as being part of God's eternal plan, yet the Lord attributes it to Israel's unwillingness. The cause of Israel's unbelief was not some lack of irresistible grace arising from a decree of reprobation which passed them by. No, Christ attributed it to Israel's willfulness.

Luke 7:30

Luke (or Christ) singled out the religious leaders of Israel as those who were resisting God's purpose: "**But the Pharisees and the lawyers rejected God's purpose for themselves, not having been baptized by John.**" This statement would seem by itself to be simple and straightforward, that men can reject and thwart God's purpose for themselves. It is only a deterministic interpretation of "irresistible grace" which would seem to deny that fact. The fact that men are unsaved and going to Hell is attributed to their own self will, not to some mysterious elective purpose of God worked out in irresistible grace.

Acts 7:51

Stephen's accusation against the Jews who were about to kill him is most significant. "**You men who are stiff-necked and uncircumcised in heart and ears are always resisting the Holy Spirit; you are doing just as your fathers did.**" From this statement it seems difficult to avoid the conclusion that the Holy Spirit can be resisted. The implication is that the Holy Spirit had been seeking to convict them through Stephen's message, but they were resisting that convicting work. This is in harmony with Christ's reference in John 16:8 that the Spirit was to convict the world *(kosmos) of* unregenerate sinners. In the Gospel of John *kosmos* is uniformly used of the world of godless sinners under Satan's control. But Acts 7:54 records their negative reaction to that convicting work: "**Now when they heard this, they were cut to the quick, and they began gnashing their teeth at him.**" So conviction is not limited to the elect, nor is it irresistible.

1 Corinthians 4:15 and Philemon 10

In both of these passages, Paul speaks metaphorically of his having begotten the Corinthian Christians and Onesimus into Christian faith. It almost sounds as if he is taking credit for their new birth, and we know that this could not be the case. The new birth itself must be one hundred percent the work of the Holy Spirit. Although Paul did not literally contribute to their actual regeneration per se, he used this figurative language to emphasize the point that he did have a lot to do with the circumstances which led them up to faith in Christ. There would have been no Corinthian church if he hadn't obeyed the Greatest Commission of Matthew 28:18-20.[40] But in any case Calvinists have failed to distinguish the human element in the ministry and circumstances of bringing people to faith, from the new birth itself, which is a distinct issue.

Calvinistic responses

Most Calvinistic writers do not see the serious problems raised to their view by the above passages and therefore do not try to address them. Some like Boettner and Custance are ambivalent about the use of the word 'irresistible' since they acknowledge that the Holy Spirit can be and is usually resisted by most who hear the word of God.[41] Essentially they hold that grace is resistible up to the point when it is God's will for the elect to be efficaciously regenerated; then it becomes irresistible. Of course, they have no inductive biblical data to support their scenario. So we are back to a deductive argument, which is really arguing in circles. Geisler suggests that all of the above passages teach that "God's grace is not irresistible on those who are unwilling."[42] I heartily agree!

PROBLEMS OF COHERENCE

The insincerity of the general call

George Bryson has described the bottom line of the message of extreme Calvinism very tersely and bluntly: **"You will be saved or damned *for* all eternity because you were saved or damned *from* all eternity."**[43] Such a blunt statement will make many Calvinists angry, but it certainly represents the view of R. C. Sproul, among many others: "What predestination means, in its most elementary form, is that our final destination, heaven or hell, is decided by God not only before we get there, but before we are even born."[44] I cannot understand how anybody who believes in unconditional election and irresistible grace can escape from the force of this characterization. This leaves the sincerity of the general call to salvation in a totally incoherent position.

If all mankind is totally unable to respond to the general call, and only those unconditionally elected by God will be the recipients of irresistible grace, then there is no way that we can maintain the sincerity of that general invitation of the gospel. What about Paul's response to the Philippian jailor's question, "What must I do to be saved?" Paul's answer was not sincere, if Calvinism is true. To tell him the whole truth he should have said, "If you are among the elect, you will not be able to resist the Spirit's irresistible grace and you will necessarily believe on the Lord Jesus Christ and be saved. However, if you are not among the elect, you cannot do anything to be saved and will go to Hell. Tough rocks!"

Calvinists will say that people can reject Christ of their own free will, but they cannot accept Him of their own free will. John Wesley bluntly stated that the doctrine of predestination "represents our Lord as a hypocrite, a deceiver of the people, a man void of common sincerity, as mocking his helpless creatures by offering what he never intends to give, by saying one thing and meaning another."[45] While I am not an Arminian or Wesleyan, I must agree with Wesley's coherence argument. The Calvinistic gospel mocks the 'non-elect,' and is not "good news."

Is the God of the Bible coercive?

As we have already observed, some Calvinists are willing to use words like 'coerce,' 'compel,' or 'constraint' to describe what is involved in irresistible grace. This raises the question we started out with in chapter 3, "What kind of a God do we have?" Is He a coercive God? There is no evidence either in the biblical narrative or in the didactic books that God works coercively. Indeed, the age-long problem of the silence of God is a far greater mystery, that is, why does God seem so reticent to intervene in human affairs, especially when godless forces seem to be winning the day? Even today we struggle with this question. Why did God not intervene in the World Trade Center terrorism? The answer has to be that although God retains His ultimate sovereign power, He has chosen not to directly use it for His own reasons.

Why restrict irresistible grace to the elect?

R. C. Sproul recognizes the seriousness of this problem: "The nasty problem for the Calvinist is seen in the [question]. If God can and does choose to insure the salvation of some, why then does he not insure the salvation of all?"[46] While claiming that this is not a problem for only Calvinists, he does not seem to be aware that it is the Calvinistic presuppositions which cause the problem. Since non-Calvinists do not accept the premise that God saves by irresistible power, we do not have the problem. Yes, we agree that God has the power to insure the salvation of everyone, but since

He hasn't chosen to implement the plan of salvation by irresistible power, He refrains from exercising it. Sproul thinks the non-Calvinist is concerned about God violating man's freedom, and that is probably the tenor of many Arminian arguments. However, those of us in the middle are more impressed with the way in which from Eden onward God has delegated responsibility to mankind, as I have spelled out in considerable detail in chapter 3 and 4.

Yes, all Christians have a problem explaining why all of mankind do not have equal opportunity to hear and respond to the gospel message, but at least non-Calvinists don't have to explain why God directly consigns 'non-elect' to Hell without any possibility of response and salvation. It is not so much that we "choose Christ," but that we respond in repentant faith when confronted with the message of reconciliation. This is not meritorious and contrary to grace, as Calvinists seem to think.

Preparationism

One of the strangest anomalies of Calvinism, which goes back at least to Jonathan Edwards, is the issue of preparationism. If we believe in irresistible grace, and people are totally passive in regeneration, what can spiritually dead people do to prepare themselves for God's irresistible grace? The consistent answer would be, nothing! But this was not a satisfying answer to the Christian conscience, so Calvinists discussed various specific steps to prepare for regeneration, whenever God should sovereignly choose to give it. To me it seems so absurd that it would be laughable if it were not so tragic. Coherent Calvinism cannot advocate any sort of preparationism. As Roy Aldrich put it:

> A doctrine of total depravity that excluded the possibility of faith must also exclude the possibilities of "hearing the word," "giving serious application to divine truth," and "praying for the Holy Spirit for conviction and regeneration." The extreme Calvinist deals with a rather lively spiritual corpse after all.[47]

Word magic

Norman Geisler feels that extreme Calvinists are "using word magic in an attempt to hide the fact that they believe God forces the unwilling against their will." I have already noted Sproul's objection to the representation that they believe that people come to salvation kicking and screaming, since first the desire is planted in their hearts so that they come willingly. But Geisler exposes the "euphemistic language" they use by including the implied words in brackets in Sproul's statements: "If God gives us a[n irresistible] desire for Christ we will [irresistibly] act according to that desire." "Once that desire is [irresistibly] planted, those who come to Christ do not come kicking and screaming against their wills."[48] The true intent of the Calvinistic doctrine of irresistible grace cannot be hidden by word magic.

CONCLUSIONS

In conclusion, I would suggest that the doctrine of irresistible grace has been derived by Augustinians through a deductive process from the other points of the TULIP, rather than through a careful inductive exegetical study of all the relevant Scripture. The historical context of the favorite proof texts needs to be given weightier consideration, the presuppositions ought to be brought out into the open and examined thoroughly, and more careful word study of the usage of the term 'calling' needs to be done. I trust that I have challenged my Calvinistic friends to do these things.

Note: This chapter is based upon a paper presented at the ETS Annual Meeting, Philadelphia, March, 1994.

---

1. L. Coenen in Colin Brown, ed. *Dictionary of New Testament Theology*. I. 271ff.
2. Francis Brown, *The New Brown-Driver-Briggs-Gesenius Hebrew and English Lexicon*, pp. 895-6.
3. Arndt and Gingrich, p. 437.
4. K. L. Schmidt in Kittel, *Theological Dictionary of the New Testament*, III, p. 490.
5. Ibid, p. 489.
6. Hermann Cremer, *Biblico-Theological Lexicon of the New Testament Greek (J. & J.* Clark. 1883), p. 330f.
7. Schmidt, p. 494.
8. For example, Charles Hodge, *Systematic Theology* (GR: Eerdmans, 1968), II, pp. 687-714.
9. R. C. Sproul, *Grace Unknown: the Heart of Reformed Theology*, pp. 179-96. I fear that the kind of irresistible grace he advocates is indeed unknown in the Scriptures, at least to judge by the total lack of direct Scriptural evidence in his chapter.
10. Bruce A. Ware, "The Place of Effectual Calling and Grace in a Calvinistic Soteriology," in Thomas R. Schreiner and Bruce A. Ware, eds., *The Grace of God; The Bondage of the Will*, II:345.
11. Edwin H. Palmer, *The Five Points of Calvinism: a Study Guide*, pp. 56-67. He references John 6:37, 44 and Acts 16:14, but doesn't even quote them.
12. Duane Edward Spencer, *TULIP: The Five Points of Calvinism in the Light of Scripture*, p. 48.
13. Loraine Boettner, *Predestination*, 5th ed., pp. 162-181. Berkhof shows the close identification of effectual calling and regeneration in 17th century Reformed theology, and although he distinguished the two, he made no reference to faith in reference to regeneration; L. Berkhof, *Systematic Theology*, rev. ed., pp. 469-476.
14. C. Samuel Storms, *Chosen for Life* (GR: Baker, 1987), p. 46, as quoted by Vance, p. 513.
15. Gordon H. Clark, *Predestination*, pp. 198-200.
16. Ibid, p. 174.
17. Vance, *The Other Side of Calvinism* (rev. ed.), p. 502.
18. Clark goes into some detail in identifying the verb form as a piel, which he admits is not quite causative, but emphatic, and then totally ignores the context, which really should be our primary consideration in exegesis.
19. Aurelius Augustine, "Letter to Vincentius," 2, 5. Also "Vincentius," 5 (AD 408); *Corr. Don.*, 21, 23; "Letter to Donatus," 3 (AD 416), as quoted and referenced by Forster and Marston, pp. 284, 292. Augustines's advocacy of the use of the physical force of the Roman government to coerce the Donatists back into the Catholic Church has been the basis of the use of physical force in the inquisition and in the consistent persecution of other Christian groups by the Roman church over the centuries. How much did it influence those good Augustinians, Luther and

Calvin, in their persecution and execution of Anabaptists and Servetus is an issue I do not have time to resolve. See Forster and Marston, pp. 257-95.

20. Arthur C. Custance, *The Sovereignty of Grace*, p. 185.

21. Walter Grundmann in *TDNT*, I: 344-7. Grundmann doesn't use the adjective 'circumstantial' of "constraint," but all of the references he adduces in the Septuagint and Josephus lead to that conclusion. See Ps. 107:13 (Gk. 106:13) for an example.

22. Arndt and Gingrich, p. 51.

23. Bagster- Arndt-Gingrich-Danker, *A Greek-English Lexicon of the New Testament,* p.318.

24. L. Boettner, *Reformed Faith*, p. 11.

25. R. C. Sproul, *Chosen by God*, p. 69.

26. Albrecht Oepke in *TDNT*, II:503. What Sproul has done here is to pick out of many diverse usages, the one obscure usage which suits his theology, ignoring all the rest, both of Oepke's explicit opinion in reference to the Johannine usage, and the three definitions given by BAGD and the many definitions given in LSJ. The phrase Sproul used, "to compel by irresistible superiority" is not found in *TDNT* or in any of the lexicons. The only time the word 'irresistible' is used in the Oepke article is in reference to a Hebrew word, which may or may not have anything to do with *helkuein*, probably not. Either Sproul is naive of the proper use of a theological dictionary or he has not been honest in its use and is guilty of partial pleading.

27. Sproul, pp. 122-3; Although Sproul repudiates the idea of God dragging us kicking and screaming, his use of the word 'compel' certainly communicates that meaning.

28. Henry Alford, *The New Testament for English Readers: John*, p. 521. The Augustine quotation was probably from his early writings.

29. Vance, p. 511.

30. Edwin H. Palmer, *The Five Points of Calvinism* (GR: Guardian Press. 1972). p.62.

31. Custance, p. 66. (The best texts do not have the goad in Acts 9:5, but rather 26:14.)

32. Bagster-Arndt-Gingrich-Danker Lexicon, p. 991.

33. Wallace, *Grammar Beyond Basics*, pp. 649, 626.

34. Ibid, p. 400f.

35. Liddell-Scott-Jones Lexicon, pp. 1759-60.

36. Gerhard Delling in *TDNT*, VIII, pp. 28-9.

37. Henry Alford, *The Greek Testament*, II, 153-4.

38. Vance, p. 503.

39. Alva J. McClain, *The Greatness of the Kingdom* (Chicago: Moody, 1959), pp. 322-3.

40. C. Gordon Olson, "The Missiological Implications of Sotenology." a paper presented to the Evangelical Missiological Society, Eastern Section, May 1,1992 at Phoenixville, PA; cf. chapter 17 for updated research.

41. Custance, pp. 175-6; Boettner, pp. 168, 178; Sproul, *Grace Unknown*, p. 189..

42. Geisler, *Chosen*, pp. 94-96.

43. George L. Bryson, *The Five Points of Calvinism: "Weighed and Found Wanting," p. 121.* Reformed professor, Douglas Wilson, says, "George Bryson is a very unusual non-Calvinist. He is able to describe the doctrinal position of Calvinism without putting any extra eggs in the pudding. His descriptions are fair and accurate, and he clearly knows his subject" (Quoted on the cover).

44. Sproul, *Chosen*, p. 22.

45. John Wesley, "Sermon on Free Grace" in *Sermons*, I: 482ff, as quoted by Philip Schaff, *History*, 8: 566.

46. Sproul, p. 35.

47. Roy L. Aldrich, "The Gift of God," *Bibliotheca Sacra*, vol. 122, p. 248.

48. Geisler, pp. 96-7. Geisler is quoting from Sproul, pp. 120-123.

Then I grasped that the justice of God is that righteousness by which through grace and sheer mercy God justifies us through faith. Thereupon I felt myself to be reborn and to have gone through open doors into paradise. The whole of Scripture took on a new meaning, and whereas before the justice of God had filled me with hate, now it became to me inexpressibly sweet in greater love. -Martin Luther

12

WHATEVER HAPPENED TO JUSTIFICATION BY FAITH ALONE?

One might think that for evangelical Christians justification by faith alone would be a 'slam dunk,' a universally acknowledged doctrine. I had not even thought it necessary to include a chapter on it until recent events like the *Evangelicals and Catholics Together* (*ECT*) and the document signed in Augsburg on Reformation Day, 1999 between Lutherans and Catholics caused me to reconsider. Upon further reflection I realized that there are many other compromises of this glorious truth, which make it clear that the gospel is not just under eclipse but also under siege as well. Therefore, this chapter is absolutely imperative. According to surveys of George Barna, James Hunter, and others, 77% of Evangelicals say that mankind is basically good by nature and 87% say that in salvation God helps those who help themselves.[1]

This is not unimportant or marginal truth. The Apostle Paul saw the compromises of this truth by the legalism in the Galatian churches as a major threat to the gospel of Christ. He accused them of deserting Christ for another gospel and twice repeated the warning that anyone who preaches a contrary gospel is accursed (Gal.1:6-9). Paul made very clear to them that we can neither be justified by law-works or be matured in the Christian life by them. Even Peter's compromise in breaking table fellowship with Gentile Christians was a nullification of God's grace and a reversal of the cross of Christ (2:21). Paul feared that he had labored over them in vain because of their legalistic reversion to mere observances (4:9-

11). He told the legalists that they had cut themselves off from Christ and had moved outside of the pale of His grace (5:4).

Later as Paul wrote his more reflective and theological expansion of this truth in his letter to the Roman church, he emphasized that the righteousness which comes from God in the gospel is available to sinful man only "**by faith from first to last**" (1:16-17 NIV). He went on to expound that glorious truth of justification by faith alone, which was the watchword of the Reformation.

The Reformers' concerns. Martin Luther said it is the "article upon which the church stands or falls."[2] It has been described as the material principle of the Reformation, because it was the essential difference between the Romanist concept of salvation in which Luther had been steeped and the great biblical doctrine which he rediscovered in Galatians and Romans. He found the legalisms into which the Galatians had fallen closely akin to the legalisms of the Roman church.

Although it was the grossness of the sale of indulgences which triggered Luther's 95 theses against Roman Catholic errors, the heart of his concern was with their denial of justification by faith alone. Not only did they have an erroneous definition of justification as 'to make righteous,' and a serious confusion of justification and sanctification, but the whole Roman system itself was a denial of the faith-alone principle, which he saw in Galatians and Romans. Their understanding of the sacraments as the means by which merit is distributed to the faithful from the church's treasury of merit was totally opposed to the biblical doctrine.

John Calvin stated that justification by faith alone is "the principal ground on which religion must be supported."[3] The Reformers saw this as the essence of the gospel of Christ. If we want to claim the title 'Evangelical' we must recognize that it comes from the Greek word for gospel, *euangelion*. Although since the modernist-fundamentalist controversy began, we have used this word to describe those who hold to the verbal plenary inspiration of Scripture, we do so because the essence of the gospel is dependent upon the trustworthiness of the Bible. Too frequently the word Evangelical is used merely as a synonym for Protestant (such as in "Evangelical Lutheran Church"), but it is clear that most Protestants no longer hold to the trustworthiness of the Scripture or the essence of the gospel– justification by grace through faith alone.

The Reformers saw Roman Catholicism as an eclipse of the true gospel. Sproul explains, "An eclipse of the sun does not destroy the sun. An eclipse *obscures* the light of the sun. It brings darkness where there was light. The Reformation sought to remove the eclipse so that the light of the gospel could once again shine in its full brilliance, being perceived with clarity."[4]

Since the Reformation, a number of movements have also eclipsed the gospel: dead orthodoxy's mere objectivizing, modernism's outright denial, neo-orthodoxy's philosophical word-juggling, postmodernism's relativizing, and the cults' superimposing extrabiblical authorities upon God's word. Even within the evangelical community there are a number of theological movements which I believe compromise the purity of justification by grace through faith alone. I will address them in short order.

Justification defined

A major problem in the dialog between Catholics and Evangelicals over the centuries has been the definition of terms. In the *ECT* dialogue, this is obviously a major sticking point. Chuck Colson admitted to R. C. Sproul in a private conversation that the two sides do not always agree in the meaning of statements in *ECT*.[5] So it is imperative to focus upon the definition of terms used in the discussion.

The truth of justification has been obscured by our perpetuation of the old Latin-originated words in our theological and biblical discussions. This goes back to the dominant use of the Latin Vulgate for over a millennium, both by Catholics and Protestants. To exacerbate the situation, Augustine of Hippo relied primarily upon the Latin in writing his theology, which has dominated both Catholic and Protestant theology ever since. I would suggest that there are many errors which have come down to us from this faulty translation and its influence.

Since the Greek word which the New Testament uses (*dikaioein*) means "to declare righteous," it would have been clearer if the translators had simply translated it this way.[A] But translators and theologians have stuck to the more obscure and ambiguous word, 'to justify.' The Greek word clearly has a forensic, legal connotation and is in the language of the courts. Thus the Apostle Paul set out the truth of God's declaration of the sinner as righteous in His sight based on faith alone, without any works of any kind. Following Paul's teaching, the Reformers stressed that it was an alien righteousness, that is, alien to the sinner before conversion. Romanism stubbornly clung to the error of a prior, infused righteousness, that is, that God declares the righteous to be righteous. In this they were just following Augustine, who saw justification as involving an inherent rather than imputed righteousness.[6] They objected to the 'legal fiction' of the evangelical doctrine. But Evangelicals have understood justification as an early step in the process of transforming a godless sinner into a saint, the last phase of which is our transformation by the resurrection at Christ's return.

Thus we must emphasize that, although God's plan of salvation has many aspects, which include conversion, regeneration, sanctification, and

A. George Abbott-Smith, *A Manual Lexicon*, p. 116: "cl. to deem right, to do one justice; . . . in NT, as LXX (1) to show to be righteous, (2) to declare, pronounce righteous."; Arndt and Gingrich, *Lexicon* , p. 196: "2. To justify, vindicate, treat as just; . . . 3a. Be acquitted, be pronounced and treated as righteous."

ultimately glorification, God's declaration of repentant sinners to be righteous is distinct from, and not to be confused with, these other aspects. It is important to get the force of Paul's phrase, "the righteousness of God." It could be the attribute of God which Paul has in mind, if he is using the genitive case. However, in the Greek the same form is also used for the ablative case, which would be translated, "**a righteousness from God**," as in the NIV translation. Thus Paul would not be speaking about God's attribute, but rather a righteousness which God makes available to sinful men. As we study the development of Paul's thought in the whole of Romans, we realize that this is exactly the main theme: a righteousness of which mankind is totally devoid (1:18–3:23); a righteousness which God reckons to sinners by faith (3:24–5:21); a righteousness which God works in the life of the believer through the Holy Spirit (6:1–8:39); a righteousness which Israel missed and which is available to all humanity by faith (9:1–11:36); a righteousness which is worked out in human relationships (12:1–15:13); and a righteousness which is to be made known to the nations (15:14–16:27).

Luther struggled with the righteousness of God as an attribute of God since it seemed to mock him in his great sense of sinfulness. But when through his study of Romans he grasped for the first time that God makes righteousness available to the sinner by justification, he was born again and began to love God.[B]

It is not just the meaning of the Greek word, but the whole flow of Paul's thinking in Romans that makes this abundantly clear. Understandably, the Catholic Douay translation by translating *dikaiosune* as the "justice of God" obscured the truth. The King James Version and subsequent translations helped some by translating it "the righteousness of God." But it was for the New International Version to properly render the phrase "**a righteousness from God**" (1:17; 3:21-22). The correctness of this translation is confirmed by Paul's whole explanation in chapter 4 as to how justification involves God counting sinners like Abraham and David to be righteous by faith. Paul builds upon Genesis 15:6: "**And Abraham**

B. Luther's own words: "I greatly longed to understand Paul's Epistle to the Romans and nothing stood in the way but that one expression, 'the justice of God,' because I took it to mean that justice whereby God is just and deals justly in punishing the unjust. My situation was that, although an impeccable monk, I stood before God as a sinner troubled in conscience, and I had no confidence that my merit would assuage him. Therefore I did not love a just and angry God, but rather hated and murmured against him. Yet I clung to the dear Paul and had a great yearning to know what he meant.

Night and day I pondered until I saw the connection between the justice of God and the statement that "the just shall live by his faith." Then I grasped that the justice of God is that righteousness by which through grace and sheer mercy God justifies us through faith. Thereupon I felt myself to be reborn and to have gone through open doors into paradise. The whole of Scripture took on a new meaning, and whereas before the 'justice of God had filled me with hate, now it became to me inexpressibly sweet in greater love. This passage of Paul became to me a gate to heaven'" (Roland Bainton, *Here I Stand*, pp. 49-50).

believed God, and it was reckoned to him as righteousness" (Rom. 4:3), and upon Psalm 32:1-2: "**Blessed is the man whose sin the Lord will not take into account**" (Rom. 4:8).

This truth of imputation becomes even clearer when we consider some of the appropriate synonyms, as 'reckon, count, account, or charge.' Paul talks about a two-fold imputation: of our sin to Christ the sin-bearer, and of Christ's righteousness to believing sinners. Thus not only are all our sins charged to Christ's account when He bore them on the cross, but also His perfect righteousness is accounted to us to give us perfect standing with God. The whole argument of the letter to the Romans is based upon this foundation.

Based on faith alone

When we consider the justification of men like Abraham and David, as Paul develops it, it is obvious that they were not consistently righteous in their conduct. Neither were most of the other Old Testament saints like Lot, Moses, Solomon, Jehoshaphat, or Manasseh, for that matter. Even New Testament saints like Peter and the Corinthian Christians manifested considerable inconsistency problems, which would destroy salvation, if it were not based upon faith alone.

During the Reformation, the Roman Catholic church objected that the Apostle Paul did not use the word 'alone' in his discussion of justification. This is technically true, but when we see the flow of his thought, it is obvious that his meaning is 'by faith **alone**,' since he contrasted faith with law-works, with circumcision, and with works of righteousness in general.

See how straightforward Paul is in his statements in Romans:

> "**. . . being justified as a gift by His grace through the redemption which is in Christ Jesus**" (3:24); "**For we maintain that a man is justified by faith apart from the works of the Law**" (3:28); "**But to the one who does not work, but believes in Him who justifies the ungodly, his faith is reckoned as righteousness**" (4:5); "**But the free gift is not like the transgression. For if by the transgression of the one the many died, much more did the grace of God and the gift by the grace of the one Man, Jesus Christ, abound to the many**" (5:15); "**For the wages of sin is death, but the free gift of God is eternal life in Christ Jesus our Lord**" (6:23).

When we survey Paul's other letters, we find the same clarity: Galatians 2:16; 3:2-14; Ephesians 2:8-10; Titus 3:5, etc. Paul arrived at that clarity, humanly speaking, in moving out of the Pharisaic legalism of his pre-conversion life in Judaism, although he made it very clear in Galatians that it was by direct revelation of God that he got the gospel message in its clarity.

Not uniquely Paul's doctrine. Some have claimed that this was Paul's own spin on the gospel, which stands in contradiction to the message of the Lord Jesus and the other apostles, especially James. However, when we turn to the Synoptic Gospels, we find that the strong emphasis upon repentance and faith started right with John the Baptizer (Mt. 3:2) and was constantly reiterated by the Lord Jesus Himself (Mt. 4:17; 8:10, 13; 9:12-13, 22; 11:28-30; 18:3; 19:25-26; 20:28; 21:31-32; Mk. 1:15; 6:12; Lk. 5:20, 31-32; 13:3; 23:42-43; 24:45-49). The Lord Jesus did not choose to explicate the doctrine of justification by faith, since during His ministry the key issue was Himself and the chosen nation's relationship to Him. Many years after Christ's resurrection and ascension, the apostle John was led by the Spirit to write a fourth Gospel to focus on the necessity of believing on and receiving Him. This is why we find the verb 'to believe' 94 times in this Gospel, with much teaching about the nature of that faith. In addition, all four Gospels record the Lord's consistent opposition to Judaism's traditionalism, externalism, and legalism, which is the basis upon which Paul built his theology. Lastly, we can study the apostolic preaching, (*kērugma*) summarized in the book of Acts, to confirm that Paul's doctrine was in total harmony (2:28; 3:16; 5:31; 10:43; 11:17-18; 13:38-9; 15:11; 16:31; 17:11-12, 30; 20:21; 22:16; 24:24; & 26:18-20).

Harmony with James. The major problem in the minds of many opponents to this truth is the apostle James' teaching in chapter 2 of his epistle: "**You see that a man is justified by works, and not by faith alone**" (2:24). This does require clarification. It is clear that James did not write to contradict Paul, since it is generally acknowledged that James wrote much before Paul. Contrariwise, it is highly unlikely that Paul was writing to contradict James, since Paul wrote much about the importance of good works in the life of the believer (cf. Titus). He was not an antinomian in denying absolutes of morality, since he wrote about being under "the law of Christ," among other such teachings. Luther wrongly resolved it by denigrating James' epistle.

The first clarification comes from the proper translation of 'to justify' to which we have already alluded: 'to declare righteous.' The difference between Paul and James is clarified if we consider who is the subject of this verb. In Paul's writings it is God who declares the sinner righteous by faith alone. James, however, is concerned about how people view the professing believer, and the necessity of showing our faith to others so that they will declare us righteous: "**But someone may well say, 'You have faith, and I have works; show me your faith without the works, and I will show you my faith by my works'**" (2:18). In that case people are the subject of the verb 'to declare righteous.'

A second consideration is the differing usage of the verb 'to believe' by Paul and James. Paul is obviously referring to genuine faith or trust in Christ, whereas James is using it in the sense of a mere profession of faith.

This is clear from 2:19: **"You believe that God is one. You do well; the demons also believe, and shudder."** Here believing means intellectual assent to the truth, rather than trust in Christ as Savior. Other examples of such usage can be given: John 2:23-25; 6:64-66; 8:32 and Acts 8:13, 18-24.

Thirdly, we must recognize the differing definitions of 'works,' as Paul and James use the same word but have two different terms in mind. By works Paul has in mind the law-works or any other works by which people are trying to earn merit before God. This is clear from the whole development of his thought. James, on the other hand, means the fruit of true faith in the life of the believer. We are justified in the sight of men by the consistent life we lead.

It is most interesting that both Paul and James use Abraham as an example to make their differing points. Paul refers to Genesis 15:6 from nearly the beginning of Abram's life of faith, even before his name was changed. James refers to the triumphant acme of his life of faith about forty years later, when he offered up Isaac on Mount Moriah. It is significant that upward of half of the human race today believes that he offered up his son there (even though Muslims believe it was Ishmael). So Abram was declared righteous by God based on his faith alone, as attested by Genesis 15, but he was declared righteous by people based upon the fruit of his faith in the offering of his son.

So Luther should not have denigrated the book of James in order to maintain the purity of Pauline doctrine. Indeed, it would seem that Luther was so overwhelmed about the rediscovery of this marvelous Pauline truth that he reacted too far in the opposite direction by making the dichotomy between faith and works too sharp.

The harmony of grace and faith

Paul, as the great advocate of a gracious salvation, makes a special point of the perfect harmony of a by-faith salvation with the principle of grace: "**For this reason it is by faith, that *it might be* in accordance with grace, in order that the promise may be certain to all the descendants, not only to those who are of the Law, but also to those who are of the faith of Abraham, who is the father of us all . . .**" (Rom. 4:16). This is especially important because of the misconceptions as to the meaning of the word 'grace.' It is clear from Paul's usage that he means 'the unmerited favor of God,' because of the way he sets faith and works in contradistinction. He sets faith in opposition to law-works (Rom. 3:19-31; 4:13-15), to confidence in circumcision (4:9-12), and ultimately to any works of righteousness (Rom. 4:1-8; Eph. 2:8-9; Tit. 3:5).

The human race is so bent on self-salvation that even religions which parrot the word grace don't have a clue to its real meaning. Adherents of the Sikh religion use the word for grace (*pershad*) a lot, but their religion is a works-oriented religion. The same can be said for Roman Catholicism, which abundantly uses the word grace, but seems clueless as to its biblical meaning. They endlessly quote the erroneous translation, "Hail, Mary, full of grace," and then go about trying to establish their own righteousness by their own works, including devotions to Mary, which is pagan.

I imagine this was true of the Pharisees in Christ's day as well (Rom. 9:30-32). The crowd of works-oriented Jews who had followed the Lord Jesus across the lake of Galilee asked, **"What shall we do, that we may work the works of God?"** His answer was instructive, **"This is the work of God, that you believe in Him whom He has sent"** (John 6:28-29). Some have mistakenly thought He was saying that faith is a work. Nothing could be farther from the truth! Rather, He was seeking to wean them away from their works-obsessed mindset. Faith is to be set in contradistinction to works in order to maintain the grace principle of salvation (Rom. 4:16).

Justification and sanctification

One of the most significant issues over the centuries has been the relationship of justification and sanctification. This was an issue between the Catholic church and the Reformers, between the Reformers and other Protestants, between Evangelicals with differing views of salvation truth, and even among Calvinists. Again, fuzziness of definition contributes significantly to the confusion. So let us focus on definitions and relationships.

Definitions. Since justification is a declaration by God that the believing sinner is counted righteous in His sight, it must be a once-for-all declaration of God, not a continuing process (Rom. 4:5). Justification must be distinct from, but simultaneous with regeneration (the new birth), since both are conditioned upon faith (demonstrated in chapter 10). We are justified by faith and born again by faith. Both are instantaneous and initial.

Sanctification, however, is used in two tenses in the New Testament. It is used in the past tense of positional sanctification and in the present tense of our progressive growth in holiness. Again we find that the translation into English is somewhat confusing, although not at all controversial. Both the Hebrew and Greek words have to do with being 'separated from, set apart unto something', and in that sense becoming holy or sanctified. Holy is the Anglo-Saxon word; sanctified is Latin-derived.

Believers are called "saints" 61 times in the New Testament, reflecting the truth that at the point of initial faith, we were positionally set apart for God. This term was used irrespective of the degree of holiness attained in their lifestyle. Paul said that the Corinthian believers **"had been sanctified"** (1 Cor. 6:11), even though some of them were **"yet carnal"** (3:3), and there were serious moral problems in the church there.

On the other hand, the apostles continually exhorted believers to progress in the ongoing process of experiential sanctification. For example, Paul's exhortation in 2 Corinthians 7:1 uses the word holiness: **"Therefore,**

having these promises, beloved, let us cleanse ourselves from all defilement of flesh and spirit, perfecting holiness in the fear of God." Many other terms and images communicate the same idea throughout Scripture. Theologically, this is the way the term sanctification is most commonly used, but positional sanctification must also be recognized and distinguished. It is appropriate to use the dichotomy, position versus condition; standing versus state.

Relationships. Thus while positional sanctification, like regeneration, is simultaneous with, yet distinct from justification, progressive sanctification must be kept far more distinct in our thinking. The new birth and positional sanctification begin the lifelong process of progressive sanctification. Although it is called 'progressive,' it is not always continuously up hill in the lives of all believers. Indeed, we all stumble and fall from time to time. But God's goal is that we should be continuously separated from the world, the flesh, and Satan's forces, and set apart for the things of God.

The question that has troubled Christians over the ages is, does lack of progressive sanctification in the life of a believer in any way condition or cancel one's justification? Since justification is a declaration by God, we must answer with a resounding, NO! Lack of holiness in the life of a professing believer may raise serious questions in the minds of other Christians, but ultimately only God has the final answer as to the status of the individual. We have the right to challenge and question the fruitless believer, but we have no right to write them off, as many tend to do.

Many would object to the above by quoting the words of the Lord Jesus, "**You will know them by their fruits**" (Mt. 7:16). Here, as always, it is absolutely imperative to check the context. In the whole context He is warning about false prophets who come "**in sheep's clothing, but inwardly are ravenous wolves.**" These we can and must discern by their fruits, but there is not a verse of Scripture which states or implies that we can know for sure about a professing Christian who does not manifest the kind of fruit we would like to see. Peter used a whole chapter of his second epistle to alert us to deal with false teachers. But we have neither example nor exhortation to write off fruitless or problem believers.

They may be disciplined and/or excommunicated for some of the more serious sins. But we must not assume that they were and are not justified saints. God disciplined Ananias and Sapphira (Acts 5), and the Corinthian church was to excommunicate the unrepentant immoral man (1 Cor. 5), but we must not assume, as many do, that they were not true believers. On the other hand, Peter discerned from the words of Simon, the baptized magician, that he was not a real believer (Acts 8:20-23). When some of the Galatians fell into denial of justification by faith alone, Paul began to have doubts about their salvation and challenged them (Gal. 4:9-11). But we must avoid any doctrinal understanding which backloads the doctrine of justification by faith alone with a particular legalistic standard of progressive sanctification which we might like to adopt. Does not God know ahead the outcome of each individual's life? He could not possibly justify a sinner and then later change His mind based upon lack of sanctification.

It is true that the New Testament does challenge us with tests of eternal life (as in 1 John), by which we can examine our own lives to see those lifestyle problems which seriously raise questions about our salvation. But I am concerned about the way that legalistic Christians write off problem believers and the way that some legalistic Christians fall back into extreme introspection which seriously undermines their own assurance.[7]

Repentance, faith, and conversion

There has been a long-standing confusion about the relationship and definitions of repentance, faith, and conversion. Perhaps it started with the Roman Catholic mistranslation in the Douay-Rheims Version of repentance (*metanoia*) as 'penance,' which implies some works on the part of man. Although this had been corrected by Martin Luther, in the Protestant versions, and even in the contemporary Catholic versions, there still are a number of serious misconceptions about these key words and their relationships.

Repentance and conversion. Perhaps the most persistent error arises from the confusion of repentance and conversion since they are frequently linked together in Scripture. Many theology books discuss repentance and faith under the heading of conversion. Although this has some validity in that repentance and faith are the necessary conditions for conversion, it should be recognized that conversion goes far beyond initial repentance and faith. *Simply put, repentance is a change of mind or attitude, whereas conversion is a change of direction.* Before a person can change the direction of life, there must first be a change of mind or attitude. This can be illustrated by driving down an interstate highway in the wrong direction (not the wrong lane). First, there must be the realization that I am headed in the wrong direction, which is repentance. Only then can one look for the first exit to make a U-turn and get going in the right direction, which is conversion.

The danger of confusing the two is that conversion is not always, or even usually, overnight. It frequently involves **a process**, first of coming to repentant faith and then, after being born again, through regeneration and progressive sanctification the lifestyle begins to turn around. In some cases it is sudden and radical, but in others it is slow and gradual. For example, the latter was the case with Abraham, Jacob, and many other saints in both testaments.

Let us briefly look at the linguistic data (cf. appendix G for more detail):

1. The Hebrew word which comes closest to repentance is *nachām*, and the Septuagint Greek Old Testament translated it 14 times by the equivalent Greek term, *metanoeein* and at times as *metamelomai* (to feel remorse). No verse with *nachām* in it is quoted in the New Testament.

2. The Hebrew word which comes closest to conversion is *shub*, which means "to turn round, return (qal), bring back, restore (hiph),"[8] and in the Greek Septuagint is translated in most of the 1040 occurrences as some compound of *strephein* (to turn) and in the New Testament is so translated 4 times.

3. *Shub* is never rendered as *metanoeein* either in the Septuagint or in the New Testament, so we see total consistency between the Hebrew and Greek with no confusion of these two distinct ideas.

4. The secular Greek usage of *metanoeein* is clear: "to change one's mind, . . . To change one's resolve or purpose, . . . to come to a different opinion, to change one's view, . . . If the change of mind derives from recognition that the earlier view was foolish, improper or evil, there arises the sense 'to regret,' 'to feel remorse,' 'to rue.'"[9]

5. In later Jewish and Christian Greek literature there is some confusion between repentance and conversion, but this is irrelevant to the New Testament usage, especially since Christ and the apostles emphasized the necessity of an internal change of heart and mind in opposition to the Pharisaic tendency toward externalism. It is unthinkable that the Lord Jesus and His apostles would have had an externalistic concept of repentance.

Since there is considerable confusion in the lexicons, theological dictionaries, and theologies, those who have any doubt about the accuracy of the above must examine the careful word studies in appendix G. Unfortunately there is not just confusion but also critical misstatements of fact, which I have sought to rectify.

Contributing to the confusion is the assumption on the part of many that since these two terms are frequently coordinated by connecting them with a conjunction, they must be synonymous, such as, "repent and return." Undoubtedly, many examples could be given in both testaments. However, just because two terms are so associated does not imply that they are synonyms. This is as illogical as saying that apples and oranges means that apples equals oranges. Indeed, there is a logical progression of thought, as I have already explained, from repentance (a change of mind or attitude) forward to conversion (a turning around of the lifestyle). It is worth noting that many of the scholars who are guilty of this false assumption are part of a more legalistic, sacramental wing of Christendom. No, the Lord Jesus would have spoken out bluntly against any such confusion of internal change of heart with mere external change. Indeed, He frequently did so in excoriating the Pharisees.

There is also some confusion in John Calvin's writings on this important distinction. This can be traced down through Calvinistic writing to the present. They tend to define repentance as "a turning from all sin." This is totally without linguistic foundation in the way the word is used in Greek literature up to New Testament times. Let us face up to reality. If this definition is correct, then no one will get to heaven, because no one has turned from all sin. Even conversion cannot be so defined without serious implications.

Repentance and remorse. Another area of confusion in the minds of many today is failure to distinguish repentance from remorse. The first is the consistently correct rendering of *metanoia*; the second comes from the usage of *metamelomai*. The distinction can be best illustrated by contrasting Peter and Judas. After Peter denied the Lord, he repented and was restored into fellowship with Him. After Judas' betrayal of the Lord did not work out the way he intended (He apparently hoped that the Lord would slip through the hands of His arrestors, as He had many times before), he went out, returned the money (Mt. 27:3), and committed suicide. This was remorse. Paul made the distinction clear in 2 Corinthians 7:10: "**. . . For the sorrow that is according to *the will of* God produces a repentance without regret, *leading* to salvation; but the sorrow of the world produces death**." Although the usage of *metamelomai* is not always consistent, Thayer says that *metanoia/metanoeein* is the "fuller and nobler term."[10]

Repentance and faith. Another question is the relationship of repentance and faith. It is very striking how much the emphasis in the Synoptic Gospels and in the early chapters of Acts is upon repentance. Quite in contrast we find that repentance is never mentioned in the Gospel of John but 'believe' occurs 94 times. We also note in the book of Acts that as the gospel went out into the Gentile world the emphasis shifts from repentance to faith and believing. This continues into the epistles. Perhaps the best key is Paul's statement to the Ephesian elders in Acts 20:21: "**solemnly testifying to both Jews and Greeks of repentance toward God and faith in our Lord Jesus Christ**." This is not a new connection, since Mark's record of the first preaching of the Lord Jesus was the same: "**The time is fulfilled, and the kingdom of God is at hand; repent and believe the gospel**" (1:15).

From this it becomes clear that repentance and faith are two sides of the same coin: repentance is the tails, the negative side, and faith is the heads, the positive side. Before a person can believe, he must change his mind about God, Christ, and himself, and only then can he put his trust in Christ for salvation. When the message came to the nation Israel with their apostate religion, they needed to repent and recognize their own sinfulness and need of the Savior Messiah. As the gospel went out into the Gentile world, the apostles contextualized the message in terms more meaningful to their hearers by emphasizing the need to "**believe on the Lord Jesus Christ, and you shall be saved**" (Acts. 16:31). Thus there is only one condition for salvation, not two, three, or four. Charles Ryrie has used the expression 'repentant faith,' which is most apt, and you will notice that I have adopted it.

The compromises of faith alone

The Roman Catholic compromise. We have already noted the Roman Catholic compromise of biblical doctrine. The Council of Trent (1547-8) unfortunately hardened their opposition to the Protestant position by hurling anathemas at those who affirmed the Reformation view. Rome has never retracted those anathemas, despite the unofficial agreements of the *Evangelicals and Catholics Together* (1994) and the more recent document of the Lutherans and Catholics (1999). Ironically *ECT* did not make any reference to the teaching of justification by faith *alone*, either in the points agreed upon or in the points of disagreement for further study. **Thus they swept it under the rug!** It is clear that the sacramental system of salvation totally contradicts a by-grace-through-faith-alone salvation. No matter what word games such signatories play, Rome would have to scrap its whole merit system to be consistent with a gracious conception of salvation. This involves the notion of a treasury of merit which Christ bestowed on the Catholic Church for it to distribute to its people in a piecemeal fashion by means of the five relevant sacraments and the other merit-earning devotions advocated by the Church. Sproul rightly says that the contradiction is foundational and systemic.[11] It implies that the sacrifice of Christ was not sufficient for our salvation, but that we must add to it.

To make the situation even worse, the fact is that now since Vatican Council II (1962-65) many Catholics do not hold to traditional Catholicism any more. There is a major liberal element in the Roman church, which holds to the evolutionary philosophy of Father Tielhard de Chardin. They retain Catholic symbolism, but the teaching is radically liberal and therefore rejects the evangelical gospel as well.

The Arminian compromise. It is not clear as to what extent Jacob Arminius compromised the grace principle, but contemporary Arminianism does tend to do so by its denial of the eternal security of true believers. Since in their view the believer's future salvation is contingent upon his own perseverence in faith and good works, there is a significant compromise of the by-grace-through-faith-alone principle. I learned this very dramatically as a new believer in an Arminian church. When the pastor asked me to substitute for him in leading the midweek prayer meeting, I naively chose eternal security as my subject. I began the study by asking the question,

"When you get to heaven to what will you be able to attribute your final salvation?" All present (20-25) responded in the same vein, "Because of my faith in Christ and my persistence in living a Christian life." It was faith plus! I believe that this would be a good representation of the theology and preaching in most Arminian churches.

The Puritan back-loading of the gospel. Recent studies, mostly coming out of Great Britain, reveal a strong tendency among the Puritans or developed Calvinists to back-load experiential sanctification into the salvation message. Michael Eaton observed a strong pattern of introspection and legalism, which he found unsettles the believer's assurance of final salvation. Given the Calvinist's doctrine of unconditional election, the burning question continues on through life, "How do I know whether I am among the elect, or not?" This causes them to look inward to their sanctification rather than Christward. Indeed, some great Puritan preachers went to their deathbed unsure of their elect status.[12]

This has been perpetuated to the present as manifest in the confusion of salvation and discipleship in the writings of Reformed Baptists, such as, Walter Chantry's *Today's Gospel: Authentic or Synthetic?* They tend to highly question the salvation of anyone who does not achieve a high degree of sanctification according to their legalistic standards.

Less acute is the "lordship salvation" teaching of John MacArthur, which also fails to distinguish salvation from discipleship.[13] In this sense it also backloads the gospel with the works of sanctification. But I will focus upon this issue in the next chapter.

The sacramental compromise. There are hundreds of millions of Protestants who hold to a sacramental concept of salvation, which compromises the purity of gracious salvation. This would start with the doctrine of baptismal regeneration, that is, the idea that in some way baptism has efficacy in moving us to salvation (cf. appendix H). The sacramental concept of the Lord's supper augments this, that is, the notion that in some magical way grace is communicated to the participant through the elements. This has strong roots in the later church fathers, including Augustine and was perpetuated by the Roman Catholic Church. Then it was carried over into Protestantism and is found especially among Lutherans, Anglicans (Episcopalians), and others.

The liberal denial. Since the end of the last century there has been a modernistic takeover of the major denominations in the western world. Kenneth Kantzer once stated that in 1890 all of the Protestant theological seminaries in the USA were evangelical except Harvard. By 1920 they had all become liberal, some more and some less. The control of these denominations fell into the hands of the liberals. (More recently the Southern Baptists alone have succeeded in reversing that trend by the evangelicals regaining control of their institutions.)

The point is that liberalism, which denies the inspiration of Scripture, almost inevitably also denies the gospel of Christ. Back in the 30s the "social gospel" replaced the salvation message in those denominations. Since then various forms of neo-orthodoxy, modernism, and now post-modernism have been in vogue in those denominations, all of which tend to undermine the gracious nature of salvation.

The charismatic de-emphasis. There is also a great danger in the charismatic movement (and to some extent in Pentecostalism as well) shifting the emphasis away from the reformation doctrine of justification by faith alone and the finished work of Christ to the present subjective experience of the believer. Charismatic experiences are the focus, not the cross of Christ and the Pauline theology of the cross.

CONCLUSION

From all of this it is plain that the gospel of Christ is under siege in this present day. The human tendency to want to earn salvation has seriously compromised the gospel, even among professing evangelical believers.

1. As quoted by R. C. Sproul, *Faith Alone: The Evangelical Doctrine of Justification*, p. 12.
2. Martin Luther, as quoted by R. C. Sproul, *Faith Alone*, p. 18.
3. John Calvin, *Institutes*, 3.11.1
4. Sproul, p. 19.
5. Ibid, p. 37.
6. Alister E. McGrath, *Institia Dei: A History of the Christian Doctrine of Justification*, I:31.
7. Michael Eaton, *No Condemnation: A New Theology of Assurance*, pp. 23-25.
8. J. Goetzmann in Colin Brown, ed., *The New International Dictionary of New Testament Theology*, I, 357.
9. Johannes Behm in Kittel, IV, 978-9.
10. Joseph Henry Thayer, *A Greek-English Lexicon of the New Testament*, p, 405.
11. Sproul, p. 68.
12. Michael Eaton, *No Condemnation: A New Theology of Assurance*, p. 4.
13. John F. MacArthur, *The Gospel According to Jesus.*

Absolutely free! Yes, it is absolutely free.
God's grace has made salvation
Absolutely free!
Tell again the story
Of His wondrous love to me,
How God has made His great salvation,
Absolutely free.
-Author Unknown

13

ARE WE SAVED BY DISCIPLESHIP?

As a new Christian half a century ago, I struggled with the passages in the Synoptic Gospels which recorded the Lord Jesus' most rigorous teaching about discipleship (Mt. 10:32-39; Mt. 16:13-28=Mk. 8:31-37=Lk. 9:22-25; Lk. 14:25-35). I knew for sure that I had been saved by grace through faith alone, based upon wonderful Pauline passages, such as Ephesians 2:8-9, which I had memorized. But as I read His demands for discipleship, I sensed a serious tension, indeed apparent contradiction between the two. I struggled with this until I learned the distinction between salvation and discipleship from some book or teacher. This seemed immediately to clear up the problem, and in subsequent years of study I have found this distinction not only helpful, but also essential and foundational to our whole theology of salvation. I suspect that failure to understand this distinction may be one thing which has caused the modernists to claim that Paul's gospel is different from that of the Lord Jesus. Of more immediate concern, however, is the absolute confusion caused among Evangelicals, whether Calvinistic or Arminian, who don't recognize this simple distinction.

In short, the Lord Jesus seemed to be saying that it would cost us something to become saved, while the Apostle Paul made clear that it is by His unmerited favor through faith alone. If the Lord were speaking about salvation, then we could identify a number of essential conditions for becoming saved: take up one's cross and follow Him to martyrdom, self-denial, severance from one's family, counting a significant cost (and presumably having to pay it), selling all our possessions and giving them to the poor, and following Christ wholeheartedly. Indeed, this is the way that many evangelical Christians understand Christ's words. If this is correct, extremely few people will be saved! Probably very few of my readers will make it. Indeed, I doubt if I myself would make it, despite half a century in vocational Christian ministry at some considerable sacrifice financially, healthwise, and in many other ways. (To quote a fictional TV western character, "Fact, not brag.") I am sure that there are legions who have sacrificed far more, who by this standard will not make it either. Obviously, something doesn't compute! Our mission in this chapter then (if we should choose to accept it) is to examine the validity of the distinction between salvation and discipleship. I would suggest that this is not at all a mission impossible.

It is amazing how writers at opposite ends of the spectrum of viewpoints on the theology of salvation ignore this fundamental distinction. Arminian Robert Shank has as a premise of his whole discussion against eternal security that in these passages Christ is telling us how to be saved.[1] At the opposite end we find the neo-Puritans, such as Walter Chantry and Harold Camping, for example. Camping wrote, "A true saving faith in the Lord Jesus Christ involves the act of self denial."[2] Chantry, in decrying the easy-believism and "cheap grace" of contemporary evangelical doctrine and evangelism, states, "It is an essential demand of the gospel that he [the rich young ruler] forsake his wealth." He goes on to say that we "have to sell all in obedience to Christ."[3] John MacArthur's view has been termed "lordship salvation," but because he bases his understanding upon a denial of the distinction between salvation and discipleship, I would suggest that 'discipleship salvation' is a better appellation.[4] He stated, ". . . no distinction has done so much to undermine the authority of Jesus' message."[5] On the other hand, Charles Ryrie has stated, "No distinction is more vital to theology, more basic to a correct understanding of the New Testament, or more relevant to every believer's life and witness."[6] So we must look at the teaching of the Lord Jesus and see how it relates to that of the apostles.

CHRIST'S DISCIPLESHIP TEACHINGS

Before we can turn to the three key discipleship discourses, we must first pay attention to the meaning of the word 'disciple' (*mathētēs*): "*learner, pupil, disciple.* 1. gener. *Pupil, apprentice* (in contrast to the teacher)."[7] We become disciples through coming to Him in repentant faith (John 6:35) and begin to learn of Him. This is the symbolism of that great gospel invitation of Matthew 11:28-30: **"Come to Me, all who are weary and heavy-laden, and I will give you rest. Take My yoke upon you, and learn from Me, for I am gentle and humble in heart; and <u>you shall find rest for your souls. For My yoke is easy and my load is light</u>."** In the culture of the day, the disciple sat at the feet of the teacher (rabbi) to learn from his instruction and also to live with Him and learn from his lifestyle. To 'take up a yoke of discipleship' was an expression reflecting this culture (also reflected in the

Sanskrit based cultures of northern India: *guru/shagird*). It is not simplistic to suggest that Christ's first command is to **come to Him**; only then is it possible to **come after Him** (Mt. 16:24). We are not saved by walking on the narrow road with Him. In the Sermon on the Mount He commanded people to **"enter by the narrow gate"** (Mt. 7:13), which is, of course, Himself (Jn. 10:9), in order to get onto the narrow road. It is only a legalistic mindset which ignores these simple distinctions, to the utter eclipsing of the simple gospel message.

If you will allow me to pursue the implications of the previous chapters at this point, the Lord Jesus did not say, "Come to me you unconditionally elected ones, who by irresistible grace and prior regeneration are enabled to come to me, and I will give you rest." His invitation was to **all** who labor and are heavy-laden, which sounds like a good description of all unregenerate people. If the invitation is not bona fide to all, He mocks the "non-elect," whoever they may be. (I've never found that expression in the Bible.)

Some months later in the Bread of Life discourse, the Lord used the symbolism of eating and drinking to picture coming to Him and believing on Him: **"I am the bread of life; he who comes to Me shall not hunger, and he who believes in Me shall never thirst"** (Jn. 6:35). In short, coming to Him in faith make us His disciples. So as we turn to the Lord's discipleship teachings, to avoid confusion it is imperative to examine the contexts, especially in reference to development in time and the dynamics of His ministry.[A]

Sending out twelve ambassadors

The first passage chronologically is found in Matthew 10:32-39, in connection with the sending out of the Twelve to the towns and cities of the nation Israel at the end of the second full year of His ministry. (Mark and Luke record the sending out of the Twelve, but do not include the discourse.) After the immediate brief instructions for the venture at hand, He launched into an extended discourse about the persecution His ambassadors will experience right on to the end of the age (10:16-37). He spoke about their being delivered up to courts, being scourged, brought before rulers, family members betraying them, being hated for His sake, not fearing those who kill the body, bringing a sword, not peace, and loving Him more than family. Against this background He charged, **"And he who does not take his cross and follow after Me is not worthy of Me. He who has found his life shall lose it, and he who has lost his life for My sake shall find it"** (10:38-39). Then He went on to speak about the reward which comes to those who go out to serve in His name (10:40-42).

A. The discipline of Biblical Theology teaches us that it is imperative to understand God's revelation in its historical context, taking into full account the progressive nature of His revelation. Systematic theologians don't always pay adequate attention to this important principle.

A few observations about this passage are in order. Please note that He said nothing about being saved or becoming His disciple here. Rather, He spoke about being worthy of Him (37, 38). It would have been inordinate for Him to charge His twelve apostles with the need for salvation at this point since most of them had been his disciples for over two years (cf. John 1), and had been selected from among a much larger band of disciples to be His apostles. So now in giving them a charge to go out to the people of Israel to confront them with the message of repentance (Mk. 6:12), He warned them in no uncertain terms of the persecution that would attend their representing Him as His apostles (sent ones). After charging them regarding cross-bearing, He alluded to the rewards for their worthy service (10:40-42). Thus to read into His words a message of salvation would be to ignore what He actually said and the context in which He said it.

Rather, the context demands that we understand the Lord to be telling His born-again apostles (except for Judas) that to be worthy of Him as they represent Him (10:40), they will have to be ready to face persecution, even death. The key phrase is: **"he who has lost his life for My sake."** They are going to have to give their lives over to the Lord, and that is the only way they will really find a true purpose in life and thus really "find" it. The word translated 'life' is *psuchē*, which is never used of the eternal life (*zoē*) which we receive in salvation. The apostles already had eternal life; now they needed to find the meaningful life in the center of God's will. The exhortation here is for true disciples to follow after Christ in order to be worthy of Him. Salvation is not at all an issue; indeed it is rewards He is speaking about, and salvation is not a reward; it is a free gift, not a matter of worthiness.

Facing His passion

The next context is some months later, well into the final year of His ministry, as the Lord retreated north to Caesarea Philippi at the headwaters of the east branch of the Jordan with His apostles. There He elicited Peter's famous confession of His deity and announced a new direction for the remaining months of His ministry—Jerusalem and the cross (Mt. 16:13-28=Mk. 8:31-37=Lk. 9:22-25). This is the occasion for the first of a dozen prophecies of His impending passion which the Lord made over these last approximately nine months of His ministry. This was also the first intimation to His apostles of the church, which He was now planning to build, based upon that predicted passion. (See chapter 16 for a fuller exposition of this passage.) After Peter's seriously misguided attempt to dissuade the Lord, Mark's Gospel indicates that the Lord summoned a crowd of other disciples and gave the second of His discipleship discourses in words similar to the first occasion:

> **If anyone wishes to come after Me, let him deny himself, and take up his cross, and follow Me. For whoever wishes to save**

> **his life shall lose it; but whoever loses his life for My sake shall find it. For what will a man be profited, if he gains the whole world, and forfeits his soul? Or what will a man give in exchange for his soul? For the Son of Man is going to come in the glory of His Father with His angels; and will then recompense every man according to his deeds** (Mt. 16:24-27).

From the previous discourse, the apostles should have understood that now that the divine Messiah is committed to go up to Jerusalem to die, their lives would be at risk, and at the least the persecution which He had already intimated would undoubtedly follow. It is in the light of this then that He emphasized self-denial and a willingness to take up their crosses to follow Him to death.

Thus, even though the Lord had summoned a crowd of other disciples who had apparently followed Him there (cf. Mark), there is no more basis for assuming that He is giving salvation truth here than in the previous context. That this crowd had followed Him way up to Caesarea Philippi in Gentile territory would indicate that they were in the main strongly motivated disciples. They, along with the apostles, needed to hear this discipleship challenge of the Lord. Those in the crowd who had less sincere, perhaps political, motivations needed to be alerted to the fact that a cross, not a throne, was in the offing. So any assumption that the presence of the crowd would imply that the Lord must be speaking about salvation is gratuitous. There is no invitation here to *come to Him*, but rather an exhortation to *follow after Him* to possible death in Jerusalem. *This simple distinction is not simplistic.*

Luke added one word to his record which makes a salvation interpretation totally absurd: **"'If anyone wishes to come after Me, let him deny himself, and take up his cross <u>daily</u>, and follow Me'"** (9:23). It is the little word "daily" which totally destroys the Arminian and neo-Puritan interpretations. We are to take up our cross **daily.** If salvation were the subject, we would have to get saved daily, and salvation would become the piecemeal dispensing of merit a little at a time based on works, as Roman Catholicism advocates. The Epistle to the Hebrews totally eradicates this possibility by emphasizing that Jesus Christ died once for all that we might be saved once for all (Heb. 7:25-27; 9:12, 24-26; 10:10-14). **This one word is the *crux interpretum* of this passage and must on no account be overlooked.** But I note that John MacArthur makes only passing reference to Luke 9:23 in his *Gospel According to Jesus* and does not recognize the significance of this very important word.[8]

The rest of the passage (Mt. 16:25-27) has also been widely misunderstood as referring to eternal salvation. Some of the ambiguity comes from the use of the word *psuchē*, which can be translated either as 'soul' or 'life,' but is never used of eternal life (*zoē*). The context makes it clear that it should be consistently translated here as 'life.' The verb, 'to save,' (*sōdzein)* is used in secular Greek of salvation "from peril, injury, or suffering."[9] We can immediately see the relevance to the immediate context as the Lord warned His disciples of the cost of following Him to His passion in Jerusalem. So He was really warning them that if they try to save their lives from peril, injury, or suffering, they will in reality lose their lives, which then would count for nothing in the light of eternity. Then He reinforced this with the next clause of 16:25, **"Indeed, whoever should lose his life for My sake, he will find it"** (Olson rendering).[B] From the world's point of view they are losing their lives, but in reality they will find life's true significance. Like the previous context (Mt.10), this has to do with discipleship, not salvation. In verse 26, He reinforced this truth one step farther, by emphasizing the absolute profitlessness of gaining even the whole world (of money, fame, and power) and forfeiting one's own life. Such a life is a total waste in God's sight.

The issue here relates to salvaging our lives for Christ's sake. If we believers try to save our lives for ourselves by clinging to them and using them for our own agenda, they will be lost or wasted as far as the program of Christ is concerned. On the other hand, if we lose our life in the sense of giving it up to Christ, only then will we really salvage it.

As in Matthew 10, the Lord Jesus concluded by promising to reward faithful service when He returns (16:27-28) and to judge the believer's works (cf. 1 Cor. 3:10-15; 2 Cor. 5:9-11). The issue is not salvation but true discipleship. Mark and Luke use almost identical words in their accounts, and the slight differences are of minimal significance (except for the word 'daily'). Need I reiterate that salvation is not a reward; it is the free gift of God?

In Perea shortly before His passion

Luke alone recorded this third significant discipleship discourse given to a great crowd of His followers as His ministry comes to a close (Luke 14:25-35). This is in Perea across the Jordan in the last stage of His final trip up to Jerusalem to be crucified. It is fair to assume that a significant part of the crowd following along with Him had come to believe in His messiahship. In a few weeks many of them would be welcoming Him to Jerusalem with shouts of Hosanna. Their presence does not necessarily imply that He would be explaining the way of salvation to them at this point. He could just as well have been seeking to clarify to genuine believers the rigorous demands of discipleship and to thin out the ranks of those who had other, perhaps political, motivations.

As we examine the account in Luke 14, we find that only one verse closely parallels the other discipleship passages, verse 27: **"Whoever does not carry his own cross and come after Me cannot be My disciple."** And

B. Dana and Mantey point out that the particle *de* at times is emphatic or intensive, 'indeed,' p. 244.

verse 26 is similar to Matthew 10:37, but is put more bluntly, using hyperbole: **"If anyone comes to Me, and does not hate his own father and mother and wife and children and brother and sisters, yes, and even his own life, he cannot be my disciple."** Comparing this with the Matthew 10 statement helps us to recognize the hyperbole of His figurative language. But the next section on the cost of discipleship being likened to counting the cost of building a tower or of winning a battle is a new emphasis. Again, as in Matthew 10 and 16, we must understand Him to be talking about being a **worthy** disciple in the face of persecution, a disciple in the fullest sense of the word. Additionally, He is warning His insincere followers that they need to anticipate persecution and a high cost of discipleship and to settle the issue beforehand. He may well have intended to sort out the true from the false, but this is quite different from setting out a cost as a precondition for salvation.

If He had been speaking about how to become saved, the rigorous demands He made would be absolutely out of the question for any spiritually dead person to fulfill. If Christ were expecting the unregenerate to respond to this rigorous demand, He would have, as Aldrich had said, "a very lively corpse indeed." In demanding that an inquirer count a cost (which he would subsequently have to pay), He would have been totally contradicting any offer of salvation as a free gift. The two are totally incompatible. To cap it off, the Lord required that His disciples give up all their own possessions (Lk. 14:33). If this is a precondition for salvation, there would be extremely few Christians in the world, and it is transparent that salvation would cost us financially and materially. In that case salvation could hardly be a gift of His unmerited favor, could it?

CHRIST'S SALVATION WITNESS

Now that we have distinguished salvation from discipleship in our Lord's most explicit teachings to His disciples, let us see how this understanding is confirmed in the way he dealt with individuals. Did He use discipleship language in dealing with unregenerate inquirers or not? Let us look first at the example or paradigm of His earliest disciples.

The progressive discipleship of His first disciples

John tells the story of the Messiah's recruiting of the first four of His disciples from among the disciples of John the Baptizer (Jn. 1:35-51). He only identifies Andrew as one of the two who heard John give testimony to Jesus being the Lamb of God, but both tradition and literary style incline us to understand that John himself was the second. They promptly switched their allegiance to the Lord Jesus and indicated their interest in becoming His disciples. Since they were John's disciples, we can understand that they had already repented and been baptized. Thus we can understand them to be regenerate Israelites. The same would be true of Simon, Philip, and

Nathaniel. Clearly the Lord attested the regenerate state of Nathaniel, as his own declaration of Jesus' deity and messiahship confirms. His message to them is to follow Him as disciples (1:43). His words, "follow me" are clearly not an invitation to be saved. Christ did not have to invite them to come **to Him** since they had already done that. Apparently they were joined subsequently by a larger number of believing disciples, who followed the Lord on a more casual, intermittent basis.

It was some months later that the Lord recruited the four fishermen, Peter, Andrew, James, and John as *full-time disciples*, causing them to leave their family fishing business to fish for people (Mt. 4:18-22; Mk. 1:16-20; Lk. 5:1-11). This was the second stage in their progressive commitment to His person and program. Then it was well over a year later that He commissioned the twelve to be His apostles (Mt. 10:1-15; Mk. 6:7-11; Lk. 9:1-5), as the third stage. Thus there is no basis here for understanding His discipleship language as being an invitation to come to Him for salvation. They made a progressively deeper commitment to him after their conversion. *Please note that all of the above discipleship teaching (Mt. 10, 16; Lk. 9, 14) came long after this.*

Nicodemus, the distinguished teacher of Israel

Even as early as the first passover of our Lord's ministry He was reluctant to entrust Himself to some of His early converts (Jn. 2:23-25). This passage is most instructive of the range of meanings to which the verb *pisteuo* is susceptible. In 2:22 it is used of those who professed Him about whom He had doubts. Yet the very same word is used to describe His reluctance to entrust (commit) Himself to them, "**for He Himself knew what was in man**."

Earlier in his Gospel, John had used 'believe' as a synonym for 'receiving Christ' (Jn. 1:12-13). From this we understand that saving faith is an appropriation of Christ Himself. Some might hesitate to use the word 'commitment' as a synonym.[10] Certainly the idea of appropriation is confirmed by the symbolism of eating and drinking used in subsequent chapters (4:14; 6:35; 7:37-39). This introduces us to Nicodemus, whom Christ confronted quite abruptly.

In any case, it is clear from this that Nicodemus had not yet made any significant commitment to the Lord Jesus, although he sincerely acknowledged the Lord's teaching ministry as from God. So the Lord immediately exposed the ignorance of Nicodemus as the distinguished teacher of Israel, who had no clue as to the Old Testament teaching of the necessity of a new birth (Ezek. 36:25-27). God had spoken about cleansing Israel from their sin with clean water and putting His Spirit within them to enable them to do His will. MacArthur says that the Savior's demand for a new birth was "shocking to Nicodemus (John 3:9). Don't miss that point or minimize Jesus' challenge to this man. Our Lord's strategy in witnessing was to go for the throat, and He established His direct, confrontal approach in this first encounter."[11] The legalism and externalism of Pharisaic rabbinic teaching had blinded him as to the heart of God's previous revelation.[C] After pointing Nicodemus to Himself (Jn. 3:10-13), the Lord used the symbolism of the brass snake which Moses erected in the wilderness as a picture of His coming crucifixion. It was also a reminder of the rebellious sin of Israel and God's judgment which occasioned this incident. Even though the word 'repentance' is not used here, it would take a vast change of mind or attitude for Nicodemus to take this look of faith to the Messiah, who was instructing him so bluntly. Apparently he did not do so at this point in time, but when he saw the Lord Jesus being lifted up in crucifixion over three years later, he summoned up the courage to commit himself by helping to embalm the Lord's body (Jn. 19:39). He must have remembered the Lord's words of John 3:14.

MacArthur, however, extrapolates the implications of this account by focusing upon the word 'obedience' in John 3:36: "Real faith results in obedience."[12] There is a serious issue of the translation of *apeitheein* here and elsewhere. Although it usually means "to disobey, be disobedient" Arndt and Gingrich state:

> . . . since, in the view of the early Christians, the supreme disobedience was a refusal to believe their gospel, ἀ. may be restricted in some passages to the mng. *disbelieve, be an unbeliever.* This sense, though greatly disputed (it is not found outside our lit.), seems most probable in Jn. 3:36; Ac14:2; 19:9; Ro 15:31, and only slightly less prob. in Ro 2:8; 1 Pt 2:8; 3:1, perh. also vs. 20; 4:17; 1 Mg. 8:2.[13]

Since the positive verb *peitheein* has the meaning, "*convince, persuade*, etc." and since John sets *apeitheein* in opposition to *pisteuein*, it seems clear that this is John's meaning.[14] It seems to me that to read obedience into this word is an unjustified legalistic spin. How much obedience must result from genuine faith? How immediately must that obedience begin? It sounds to me like front-loading obedience into the definition of faith.

An immoral Samaritan woman (John 4)

There seems to be nothing supportive of discipleship salvation in the Lord's witness to the Samaritan woman. However, MacArthur suggests that His invitation to her to drink of the living water conveys commitment as well as appropriation. By quoting Matthew 20:22 (**"Are you able to drink the cup that I am about to drink?"**) and John 18:11 (**"The cup which the**

C. Although there are many interpretations of the water of 3:5, it is simplest and best to understand it as a symbol of the Holy Spirit, and it can be translated, "water, even the Spirit." This is confirmed by the same symbolism in Jn. 4:14 and 7:37-39. It certainly does not refer to baptism, which only symbolizes Spirit baptism and cleansing from sin.

Father has given Me, shall I not drink it?") he seems to have made his point. However, in moving beyond commitment to obedience again, he seems to have gone beyond the data by pushing a dubious translation of *apeitheein*, as discussed above.[15] Commitment and obedience are two different things.

A turncoat tax-collector

A major issue related to discipleship salvation in the account of Matthew's conversion is the issue of the new convert's sense of sinfulness (Mt. 9:9-13; Mk. 2:13-17; Lk. 5:27-32). MacArthur is on target in emphasizing the importance of an inquirer having a sense of sin in coming to Christ. Matthew as a tax-collector was indeed a despicable sinner in the eyes of the Jews and in the eyes of God. After Matthew had left his tax office to follow the Lord and invited other notorious sinners to meet the Lord Jesus at a banquet, the Lord responded to the Pharisaic criticism with the most significant statement: **"I have not come to call the righteous but sinners to repentance"** (Lk. 9:32). The self-righteous Pharisees did not recognize their sin; Matthew certainly had. The question must be raised as to how immediate and deep must be that sense of sin for a person to be genuinely saved? May we extrapolate Matthew's story as a notorious sinner as a paradigm for all conversions, even of children raised in a Christian home? Probably not!

MacArthur seems to do so: "It is impossible to suggest that a person can encounter the holy God of Scripture and be saved without also coming to grips with the heinousness of his own sin and consequently longing to turn from it."[16] He then gives examples of Peter, Paul, Job, and Isaiah coming to a deep sense of their own sinfulness (Lk.5:8; 1 Tim. 1:15; Job 42:6; Isaiah 6:5). The major problem with this is that none of these examples express the heart condition of these men at the point of their conversion, indeed, for some it was after years of God's dealings with them. Furthermore we don't know the actual point of Matthew's conversion. When the Lord Jesus walked by his tax-office and called him in two words to "**Follow Me**," was this the first contact they had made? It is highly unlikely! Matthew wouldn't have even known who he was. There were no pictures of the Lord in the newspaper or television for him to recognize Him. What clue did he have as to His claims or message? Almost certainly Matthew had been in the crowd hearing our Lord's teaching at least once before. Was he converted on one of those occasions? Probably, but we just don't know. So this account says nothing about Matthew's sense of sinfulness at the point of his conversion. This usually grows as we grow in the Lord, and Christians ought to have a strong sense of repugnance for sin in their lives.

MacArthur is rightly concerned about the lack of such concern and repugnance among many Christians. But I fear that his discipleship salvation view has given him a hypercritical view of evangelical churches: "Even the most conservative churches are *teeming with people* who, claiming to be born again, live like pagans" (emphasis mine).[17] I hope he is wrong in this, and in my own experience in preaching in hundreds of evangelical churches and having been in leadership in a number I cannot verify his impression.[D] I do know there are compromising churches which tolerate blatant sin in their midst. I am sure that there are legions of churches, whose evangelical credentials are suspect, which may fit his appraisal. I, too, decry the widespread lack of church discipline, which contributes to the sad state of evangelical churches. I would agree that our churches are full of mediocre Christians, who are not out and out for Christ. But this is not the same as churches teeming with people living "like pagans." In any case, I doubt very seriously that making the terms or conditions of salvation harder will help at all. According to Matthew 16:19, it will just make us more pharisaic rather than genuinely holy: **". . . And whatever you bind on earth must have already been bound in heaven"** (Amplified Version). Making the conditions of salvation harder than genuine repentant faith is to bind on earth what God has not already bound in heaven. See my full exposition in chapter 16.

A man blind from birth (John 9)

The most significant issue related to the conversion of the man blind from birth is how much doctrinal and moral understanding must the new convert have to be saved? At the point of conversion many new believers have only a dim understanding of the person and work of Christ. The man born blind, whose physical and spiritual sight was restored by the Lord Jesus, had very limited understanding, but he made a significant commitment to Him, which resulted in his excommunication from the synagogue (9:24-34). At this point the Lord revealed His messiahship to him, and he worshiped Him (9:35-38). How much he understood of His deity or of His moral teachings at this point is speculation.

Is this man's story a paradigm which can be extrapolated to all conversions? Certainly the unique miracle of his sight having been restored gave him some theological understanding without his having received any oral teaching from the Lord (9:30-33). He knew that Jesus had come from God and argued that point with his inquisitors. Geerhardus Vos has referred to this kind of revelation as act-revelation as contrasted with word-revelation.[18]

The danger of demanding a radical and immediate transformation of all converts' understanding at the point of conversion is to revert to a legalistic judging of people by an artificial idealistic standard. When a professing believer does not show an adequate doctrinal or ethical transformation, there is a danger of writing him off as an unbeliever too hastily. A missionary

---

D. My ministry has been mostly in centrist (moderately Calvinistic) Baptist, Independent, and Evangelical Free churches, not in Arminian or Reformed churches.

friend told me about a Muslim convert who was struggling to get victory in his Christian life a decade after his conversion. He found that the root of the man's problem, because of his Muslim background, was that he was still having problems with the deity of Christ. Was he a sincere believer? Probably so. Other sincere believers have moral problems from their old life. Should we write them off as unbelievers? I believe that we must challenge them to examine themselves according to 2 Corinthians 13:5, etc., but that we must not be hasty in writing them off, as some are inclined to do.

Thomas Constable has articulated a caution: "But not everyone who believes the gospel realizes that the Savior has the right to be sovereign over his life. . . . All that is required for salvation is believing the gospel message."[19] However, we should make it clear to the new believer that the Lord Jesus does have this right, and that the major focus of his life should be to understand the implications of His lordship for himself.

A self-righteous synagogue ruler

Not too long after the discipleship discourse of Luke 14, a works-oriented synagogue ruler came to the Lord with his revealing question, as all three Synoptics record it: "Teacher, what good thing shall I do that I may obtain eternal life?" (Mt. 19:16-26=Mk. 10:17-27=Lk. 18:18-27). This passage has also been misused by those who put a legalistic spin on salvation, since they have missed the main point of the story.[20] The Lord Jesus was seeking to wean him step by step away from this mindset. First, He pointed him to the Mosaic Law, which Paul later explained was to bring people under the guilt of sin (Rom. 3:19-20; 1 Tim. 1:8-11). This must have been Christ's motivation also, but the man supposed that keeping part of the Law was adequate, since he asked, "Which ones?" The Lord pointed him to the Leviticus 17:18 summary of the second tablet of the Law: **"You shall love your neighbor as yourself"** (Mt. 19:19). This was to get him to see, as a rich man, that he did not love his neighbor as himself. In his self-righteousness, however, he responded, **"Teacher, I have kept all these things from my youth up; what am I still lacking?"** (Mk. 10:20; Mt. 19:20). In order to bring this young man into an awareness of his own sinfulness, the Lord instructed him to sell his possessions, give to the poor, and come and follow Him. This was the ultimate test of whether he had kept the intent of the Law. He didn't get the point apparently, since he went away sorrowful. *The Lord was trying to get him to see that he didn't love his neighbor as himself and therefore that he hadn't really kept the Law.*

The truth of this understanding is confirmed by the following dialogue with His disciples. After pointing out the obstacle which riches present to people in getting saved (which Paul confirmed in 1 Cor. 1:26-28), the Lord resorted to hyperbole to emphasize His point. Legions of legalistic commentators have tried to make a camel's passage through the eye of a needle a human possibility by the supposition that the eye of the needle is a reference to some postern gate, which a camel could conceivably negotiate. This is not only without a scintilla of evidence, but also totally at odds with the point the Lord made in the next interchange. The disciples understood the incredibility of His hyperbole in crying out in astonishment, **"Then who can be saved?"** His answer is clear: **"With men this is impossible, but with God all things are possible."** When will legalists learn that, humanly speaking, salvation is an impossibility? Salvation must be a work of God's unmerited favor, else no one would be saved. But since the contemporary Jewish view was that riches are a sign of God's favor, Christ's point was astonishing to the disciples: that riches predispose people away from the gospel.

We should note in passing a point I have made elsewhere, that there are many other human factors which predispose people either toward or against the gospel (pre-eminently Islam and evolutionary humanism). This hardly fits with unconditional election. We should also note that Mark recorded the observation, **"And looking at him, Jesus felt a love for him, . . ."** (10:21). We wonder, does God love the non-elect? We don't know whether this man ever came to faith in the Messiah. It might seem that such questions were irrelevant to the Lord Jesus and only occur to those who have been predisposed to Augustinian theology. (Many Calvinists teach that God does not love the non-elect.)

When the issue of the cost of salvation is raised it should be obvious to any evangelical Christian that the only cost is that which Christ paid, as Peter expressed it so clearly, **". . . knowing that you were not redeemed with perishable things like silver or gold from your futile way of life inherited from your forefathers, but with precious blood, as of a lamb unblemished and spotless, *the blood* of Christ"** (1 Pet. 1:18-19).

So we must not take our Lord's words to this self-righteous religious ruler as a basis for saying that an inquirer has to sell his property and give to the poor in order to be saved. Walter Chantry has built most of his case for discipleship salvation upon his misunderstanding of this passage. I venture to say that Chantry himself did not forsake his wealth in order to be saved. I suspect that like the rest of us he simply established a personal relationship with Christ by faith in Him and His gospel. When Chantry says that we "have to sell all in obedience to Christ," I suspect he does not mean this to be taken literally. But he does not clarify.

John MacArthur also, although much of his discussion about this ruler is helpful, misses this key point: After wrongly connecting this with the discipleship teaching of Luke 14:33, he states: "Our Lord gave this young man a test. He had to choose between his possessions and Jesus Christ. He failed the test. No matter what he believed, since he was unwilling to forsake all, he could not be a disciple of Christ. Salvation is for those who are willing to forsake everything."[21] If this dialogue is to be so understood as a paradigm for the salvation of all people, then this is the only place in

Scripture that an unbeliever was challenged with this option. I wonder if Pastor MacArthur himself was willing to forsake everything at the time of his conversion? Does he lay this demand upon all the inquirers he seeks to lead to Christ? Does he require this of all prospective church members? Let's be real. If salvation is a matter of passing or failing such a test, the gospel is not a gospel of grace, as MacArthur has sought to proclaim in harmony with his Calvinism, the name of his church, and of his radio program, "Grace to You." In that case, it would be a thoroughly legalistic corruption of the gospel.

The subsequent clarification by the Lord to His apostles of His intent in Matthew 19:23-26 is significantly not expounded by MacArthur, except in passing in the next chapter. As I noted above, the Lord is making it clear that if salvation depends upon man, it is an absolute impossibility; it is possible only with God. I suspect that he would agree with this statement, but his exposition contradicts it.

The very least I would insist upon is that this case study should not be extrapolated to be a general rule for all, since this man's self-righteousness was uniquely hardcore. This was not the case with the next example.

Zaccheus, the crooked tax-collector

The account of the conversion of Zaccheus is quite terse and concluded with one main point which the Lord stated: **"The Son of Man has come to seek and to save that which was lost"** (Lk. 19:1-10). As with Matthew, we don't know how much prior teaching of the Lord he had heard. Once the Lord Jesus came into his house we don't know what He told him about being saved. We can only reconstruct a hint of the extortionate methods of his practices from his admission of fraud and his ready willingness to give half (not all) of his goods to the poor. We do well to understand this, as most do, as the fruit of his conversion, certainly not the condition, as MacArthur recognizes.[22] Thus this example proves very little for or against discipleship salvation.

Judas Iscariot, the counterfeit believer

Judas is the classic case study of a counterfeit believer, a condition that the broader New Testament warns us against. Arminians might feel that he was a true believer who lost his salvation, but the Lord was fully aware as much as a year before the cross that Judas was a counterfeit, and that others of His professing believers were not genuine. After the bread of life discourse when some professing believers grumbled about the difficulty of His teaching, He said, **"'But there are some of you who do not believe.' For Jesus knew from the beginning who they were who did not believe, and who it was that would betray Him. . . . 'Did I Myself not choose you, the twelve, and yet one of you is a devil?'"** (Jn. 6:64, 70). It isn't that their faith would fail; they never had it. As a result many stopped following Him.

The best explanation of Judas' true character I have ever come across

I heard from an evangelist named Carl Olson (no relation) half a century ago. He suggested that Judas may have been quite sincere in getting caught up in the expectation of Jesus' messiahship and kingdom and the excitement of being a part of it. But being unregenerate his greed was the weak point Satan used (see Jn. 12:4-6). Judas had seen the Lord escape from His would-be captors so many times before, that he rationalized that he could get his thirty pieces of silver, and then the Lord would slip through His captors hands again. He could have his cake and eat it too! But when it did not turn out as expected, in remorse he returned the money and went out and hanged himself (Mt. 27:3-10).

When we contrast Judas with Peter, we can see the difference between remorse (*metamelomai*) and true repentance (*metanoeein*). Years later Paul explained: **"For the sorrow that is according to the will of God produces a repentance without regret, *leading* to salvation; but the sorrow of the world produces death"** (2 Cor. 7:10).

John made very clear that when counterfeit believers depart they prove that they were counterfeits: **"They went out from us, but they were not *really* of us; for if they had been of us, they would have remained with us; but *they went out*, in order that it might be shown that they all are not of us"** (1 Jn. 2:19). True believers will persevere. Thus we find a number of confirmatory passages regarding counterfeit believers: the parables of the four soils and of the wheat and the tares; Hebrews 3:12; 10:26-31; Galatians 4:11; and the warnings of 2 Corinthians 13:5 and 2 Peter 1:10.

John MacArthur takes Zane Hodges and R. B. Thieme to task for failing to give due recognition to the existence of counterfeits among professing believers and holding that "genuine believers may indeed succumb to apostasy." We recognize that true believers can fall into temporary denial, like Peter did, but apostasy is too strong a word. True believers do backslide, and some are in a backslidden state when they die. Whatever our view, most would agree with MacArthur's statement: "We can't always see whose faith is genuine and whose is a sham, but the Lord knows."[23] This is based upon 2 Timothy 2:19: **"Nevertheless, the firm foundation of God stands, having this seal, 'The Lord knows those who are His,' and, 'Let everyone who names the name of the Lord abstain from wickedness.'"** The problem with discipleship salvation is that it writes off many true believers in a legalistic way.

Two significant parables.

Two of the ten parables of the kingdom which the Lord Jesus gave us are most relevant to this: **"The kingdom of heaven is like a treasure hidden in the field, which a man found and hid; and from joy over it he goes and sells all that he has, and buys that field. Again, the kingdom of heaven is like a merchant seeking fine pearls, and upon finding one**

pearl of great value, he went and sold all that he had, and bought it" (Mt. 13:44-46). Parables are the most difficult part of our Lord's teaching to interpret, especially when there is no introductory explanation, as here. We must interpret parables in the light of Christ's clear teaching elsewhere. Probably a majority of interpreters take it that the sinner is represented by the man who sells all to buy either the treasure or the pearl. However, it is imperative to ask, who has sold all that he had to buy something of great value? The answer should be obvious. The Lord Jesus sold all that He had to redeem us from sin. The basic word for redemption is the ordinary word 'to buy.' Christ purchased us with His own blood. What could be clearer? Can we purchase salvation? Absolutely not! We are bankrupt; we don't have anything to sell by which we might purchase it, even if it were for sale. It is God's gift of free grace (Rom. 3:24; 6:23; Eph. 2:8-9). How then can all these interpreters say that we have to sell all in order to be saved? I believe this shows the depth to which a legalistic concept of salvation has penetrated the Protestant world since the Reformation.

One might wonder about the identity of the treasure and the pearl in these parables. This is not central to my point. But Israel is represented as God's treasure, and in a parallel way we can see the church as the pearl of great value.

THE ISSUES OF DISCIPLESHIP SALVATION

The historical background

It would seem that the background of the issue began about the time of World War I when Lewis Sperry Chafer wrote two books: *He That Is Spiritual* and *Grace: The Glorious Theme.* The first of these seemed to set up a dichotomy between the spiritual Christian and the carnal Christian as if these were two distinct states or levels of the Christian life. This is the way that B. B. Warfield understood it in reacting to Chafer's teaching. It might not have come to much if Chafer had not founded Dallas Theological Seminary, since this gave his teaching a greater impetus. I myself was privileged to take Chafer's course on the spiritual life shortly before he died, and I did not understand him to be teaching two distinct states or levels. However, some of his students and students of students have extrapolated his teaching to suggest that there is little difference between the lifestyle of a carnal Christian and the unregenerate. Indeed, some of Chafer's own statements might give that impression. Some from the reformed tradition like Warfield reacted strongly against this line of teaching.[24]

Chafer's dispensational teaching in *Grace* and subsequently in his *Systematic Theology* sought to counter the legalisms he saw especially in the reformed tradition, but also in Arminianism and other traditions. As an evangelist turned Bible teacher, he was concerned about the legalism in salvation preaching which added other conditions to the simple command to **"believe on the Lord Jesus Christ, and you shall be saved"** (Acts

16:31). Many have added baptism, confession, and repentance as separate conditions, and even various forms of good works to simple faith. He also saw grace as the essence of the rule of life for believers in this age and was concerned about the sabbatarianism and other legalisms found among evangelical Christians. Early dispensationalists found a number of very helpful dichotomies in the Scriptures, which were conducive to clarifying God's truth in a number of areas. C. I Scofield had expounded a number of simple contrasts in his little booklet, *Rightly Dividing the Word of Truth*: salvation and rewards, law and grace, the gospel of the kingdom and the gospel of grace, etc. In his zeal to correct the muddied teaching of Covenant Theology, it seems that Chafer overdrew some of these contrasts. I believe that these contrasts are essentially true to Scripture, but the overdrawn expression of them taught by a number of dispensationalists has brought a strong reaction, especially from the reformed tradition. Zane Hodges' two books, *The Hungry Inherit, The Gospel under Siege*, and *Absolutely Free* have drawn a strong reaction. Charles Ryrie's *Balancing the Christian Life* and *So Great Salvation* have drawn fire. It is not expedient to discuss these contrasting views at this point.

Frank Graham wrote a little booklet in the '60s in which he denied the possibility of there being any carnal Christians. Walter Chantry's book, *Today's Gospel: Authentic or Synthetic?* (1970) was an early critique of shallow evangelicalism. John MacArthur's *The Gospel According to Jesus* (1988) was an expansion of Chantry's critique focusing upon Hodges' and Ryrie's views, from a professed dispensationalist. His view has been termed "lordship salvation" although he is not happy with this label. Since MacArthur is also very explicit in denying the distinction between salvation and discipleship, I think it would be more appropriate to call it "discipleship salvation." Since MacArthur has been the major advocate of this view, I will seek to evaluate his position rather than Chantry's, which is indefensibly extreme.

I keep coming back to Christ's charge to Peter in Matthew 16:19 not to bind on earth what God has not bound in heaven, as the Pharisees were doing, and not to loose on earth what God has not loosed in heaven, as the Sadducees were doing. We must in no way make the terms of salvation harder or easier than Christ and the apostles proclaimed them. Otherwise we fall into the legalism of the Pharisees or the rationalism of the Sadducees. Both extremes were in serious error. (For a fuller discussion see ch. 16.)

The key issues in the discussion

John MacArthur was right in sensing that lordship is not the key issue. He makes very clear that he has never taught that an inquirer must understand all the implications of the lordship of Christ to be saved.[25] The issue really is, are we to be saved through the demands of discipleship discussed above? As I have already made clear, the answer is a resounding 'no.' In the main MacArthur has not grasped the implications of the word "daily" in Luke 9:23.

However, I believe that some of MacArthur's critique of evangelicalism is valid. Unfortunately, his solution to the problem of the shallowness of contemporary Evangelicalism is unbiblical and legalistic. It seems to me that MacArthur's cure is worse than the disease. The solution is not to make salvation harder to obtain by adding unbiblical, additional conditions to faith alone, but to emphasize Christ's discipleship demands to professing believers. MacArthur has joined the Pharisees in binding on earth what God has not already bound in heaven by defining faith in a legalistic way. There is the opposite danger of other Evangelicals joining the Sadducees in making salvation too easy by a superficial definition of repentant faith. They are loosing on earth what God has not already loosed in heaven. Faith has to be more than mere profession, more than intellectual assent to certain propositions about the gospel. It is the appropriation or receiving of Christ into the life, which means trust in the person and work of the divine Messiah (Jn. 1:12). The essence of Evangelicalism is a personal relationship with the Lord Jesus. Nothing less will do.

Dispensational considerations. In my own teaching over the years, although I still hold essentially to Ryrie's form of dispensationalism, I have had to back off from some of Chafer's overdrawn dichotomies. In teaching Christian ethics I concluded that we must hold absolutes of morality, indeed Paul says we are under the law of Christ (1 Cor. 9:22ff). So although we are not under the Mosaic Law **as a system**, law as a principle is still to be operative in evangelism, the Christian life, and society. There was grace operating in the age of the Mosaic Law and there is to be the law of Christ operative in this church age of grace. In emphasizing this as preeminently the age of grace, there is a danger of minimizing the importance of properly using the Mosaic Law as the major means of getting enquirers, not only to recognize their sin, but also that they are under the judgment of God for their sin (Rom. 3:19-20; 1 Tim. 1:8-11). This is what the Lord Jesus consistently did.

Chafer's overdrawn emphasis upon the distinction between the gospel of the kingdom and the gospel of grace becomes a factor here. I hold this distinction to be essentially correct. However, there is a common core of salvation truth which is found in the gospel, regardless of the form in which it is presented in its various contexts. Thus when John the Baptizer, the Lord Himself, and His apostles announced the impending kingdom, they preached repentant faith as the necessary condition of salvation (Mk. 1:15). The focus was upon the necessity for Israel to repent of the "dead works" (Heb. 6:2) of their apostate religion and put their faith in the divine Messiah, who was presenting Himself to "His own people" (Jn. 1:11-12). Christ's teachings are not to be in any way relegated to the future kingdom age, but were immediately relevant to His own presentation of Himself as Israel's Messiah-king.

Thus in the Sermon on the Mount, the Lord expounded the true interpretation of the Mosaic Law, in contrast to the externalistic rabbinic interpretations, in order to get the Jewish nation to see themselves as sinners under God's judgment. This became clear to me years ago as a missionary in Muslim Pakistan in trying to get self-righteous, externalistic, legalistic Muslims to see themselves as sinners. The Sermon on the Mount was the ideal tool for this. Additionally, the principles of ethics in the Sermon are still operative for Christian morality today. However, Ryrie is essentially right that the primary and full interpretation of the Sermon was not intended for this age of grace.[26] But when we come down to the bottom line, there is only one paragraph of the Sermon with which we struggle as to its direct application today, which is Matthew 5:38-42. The rest understood in its context may be directly *applied* today, although not directly *addressed* to the church, per se.

We can easily understand the shift of emphasis from 'repentance' in the Synoptic Gospels and early Acts to 'believing' in the Gospel of John and later Acts and the epistles as a part of the shift from Israel to the Gentiles. In the Jewish context the message was 'repent;' to the Gentiles, 'believe.' This is both a dispensational issue and one of contextualization. (See the excursis at the end of this chapter.)

Even though I have rejected the major premise of MacArthur's whole book, I must hasten to emphasize that some of his critique of contemporary evangelicalism is valid. Some have watered down of the essence of saving faith in a way that falls short of the Scriptural definition. As I have shared in my pilgrimage story, all through my teen years I was an unregenerate but creditable professing Christian. I never questioned that Christ died for the sins of the world. But a personal relationship with Christ was missing until I was born again. I met so many orthodox Christians in Pakistan who had little clue about a personal relationship or being born again. And certainly the statistic that one-third of Americans claim to be born again raises serious questions, especially since so many Protestant churches are not even evangelical.

Reformed/Calvinistic presuppositions. It is not accidental that the advocates of discipleship salvation are extreme Calvinists. I have detected significant Calvinistic presuppositions in their arguments, which significantly influence the outcome.

The first is the confusion of repentance and conversion, which involves a misdefinition of repentance. I have already presented my reasons for distinguishing repentance and conversion, although they are closely related in Scripture (cf. app. G). The problem is if repentance means a turning from sin, then to what extent must the inquirer turn from sin before he is saved? Repentance is an internal issue of the heart, as is faith. But conversion is an external change of lifestyle, which can only be said to issue from and connect with repentant faith. Otherwise, we would be making an external succession of acts by the individual the condition for true salvation, and this would be the legalism which Chafer was rightly seeking to refute.

A second presupposition which keeps coming up is that repentant faith is the direct gift of God. This first came to my attention when MacArthur's associate, James Rosscup, was presenting a paper on repentance at the 1992 meeting of the Evangelical Theological Society. One of the respondents objected that his view sounded like a works-oriented way of salvation, to which Rosscup responded to the effect that since repentance is the gift of God the whole thing has to be by His grace anyway. I have found the same rationalization several places in MacArthur's book as well. Indeed, he uses Ephesians 2:8-9 as a proof text, well aware that the relative pronoun does not correspond to the noun faith.[27] (I have discussed this at length in ch. 10).

A third presupposition is that faith involves obedience. I have already discussed this, but in essence it comes from a mistranslation of the Greek word *peitheein* and drawing a false connotation from *hupakuein*.

A fourth presupposition is that justification and sanctification are integrally connected. There has been a strong tendency to overemphasize the connection between justification and progressive sanctification. Michael Eaton, who is a theologian and pastor in Reformed circles, has identified this tendency among the Puritans and their successors, which has resulted in extreme introspection, legalism, and weakness of assurance.[28]

Salvation and rewards. One of the distinctions, which Scofield made and which dispensationalists have usually emphasized, is that between salvation and rewards. On the other hand, I sense a strong reticence on the part of some from the Reformed tradition to acknowledge this distinction. For example, Harold Camping of Family Radio seems to feel that any acknowledgment of God's rewarding of the faithful service of believers would be to undermine the gracious character of salvation. I can't imagine why he would conclude this, since there is no logical contradiction between the two, and there is so much Scripture to support both truths. Part of the problem for Camping may be his failure to distinguish between the judgment seat of Christ and the great white throne judgment of the lost (Rev. 20:15), which is a consequence of his amillennialism.[29] Perhaps the clearest passage here is 1 Corinthians 3:10-15, which pictures Christians building the church upon the rock Christ Jesus. Paul is very explicit that if our work for Christ survives the fire of the day of Christ, we shall receive a reward. On the other hand, concerning the one whose work is burned up as being wood, hay, or stubble, **"he himself shall be saved, yet so as through fire"** (3:15). Clearly the judgment seat (*bēma*) of Christ is an examination of a believer's works, which could hardly be a description of the issue salvation by grace through faith alone.

Are there carnal Christians and fruitless believers?. It is useless to try to deny that carnal Christians existed in the Corinthian church or for that matter today, as Frank Graham and many others have done. Paul was very explicit in 1 Corinthians 3:1-3 in contrasting spiritual Christians from two other varieties: "**And I, brethren, could not speak to you as to spiritual men, but as to men of the flesh, as to babes in Christ. I gave you milk to drink, not solid food; for you were not yet able *to receive it*. Indeed, even now you are not yet able, for you are still fleshly. For since there is jealousy and strife among you, are you not fleshly, and are you not walking like mere men?**"

Some fleshly believers (*sarkinos*) were identified as babes in Christ, new Christians who have not yet grown (1 Cor. 3:1). But he directly confronted others as being more acutely fleshly (*sarkikos*) in behaving as the unregenerate in regard to party politics in the church (3:2-4). This is not to say that they were totally given over to a pagan lifestyle. However, later when Paul addressed the problem of the incestuous man in the church, the discipline he counseled was so **"that his spirit may be saved in the day of the Lord Jesus"** (1 Cor. 5:5). Even though Paul had some very positive things to say about the Corinthian church (1:4-9), there were many other evidences of carnality among them. Much as some would like to legislate carnal Christians out of existence by insisting that such people are not really Christians, this is a legalistic solution to the problem. One form of legalism I have observed over the years is the desire to legislate the ideal among God's people. This is an erroneous solution.

What was this discipline of the incestuous professing believer **"to deliver such a one to Satan for the destruction of the flesh, . . ."** (1 Cor. 5:5)? Of the two major interpretations, the most viable is that the church should excommunicate him, if unrepentant, and pray for his premature physical death. This is confirmed by the parallel situation of those abusing the Lord's table: "**For this reason many among you are weak and sick, and a number sleep**" (1 Cor. 11:30), which he described as a disciplinary judgment on those believers, so that they **"may not be condemned along with the world"** (11:32).

We already have the striking example made of Ananias and Sapphira, who although they were willing to make a substantial gift to the church, lied about it (Acts 5:1-11). There is absolutely no basis for questioning the reality of their salvation. John confirmed this principle in 1 John 5:16-17 in speaking about a sin of a brother unto death. Although Arminians have the 'luxury' of saying this is the loss of salvation, more calvinistically minded interpreters would have to lean to it being premature physical death. I am also convinced that this was also a danger for some of the Hebrew Christians addressed in Hebrews 6:1-9 (see full exposition in chapter 15). It is also possible that Romans 8:13 is a reference to the same truth, but you will have to check out the Greek to verify this opinion.

Whenever, we raise the specter of there being such a thing as a fruitless

Christian, we hear the protest misquoted from Matthew 7:16, **"You will know them by their fruits."** Apparently the protestors never bother to look at the context, which is about the false prophets, the ravenous wolves in sheep's clothing, whom we can identify by their fruits. But the fact is that it is sometimes hard to tell the difference between a carnal Christian and a counterfeit believer. Paul was not always sure. But we can see the evil fruits of that liberal preacher who denies the salvation message or that legalistic priest who is distributing piecemeal salvation by human merit.

I have just suggested that some of the problem-Christians described in Hebrews 6:8 were bearing "thorns and thistles" rather than good fruit. Then we have the curious fact that in the parable of the soils, since the Lord Jesus referred to four kinds of soil, not three, He apparently had four distinct types of people in mind (Mt. 13:3-9, 18-23). His interpretation of the third category raises a question: **"And the one on whom seed was sown among the thorns, this is the man who hears the word, and the worry of the world, and the deceitfulness of riches choke the word, and it becomes unfruitful."** Most Calvinistic interpreters agree that the second category describes counterfeit believers, but why would he make a distinct, third category in the parable to also refer to counterfeits? Did He not really mean to delineate four types of people? To interpret categories two and three as the same is to imply that there was a slippage in our Lord's thinking! Perish the thought! The analogy of Scripture indicates that these are true believers in whose life the word of God is not allowed to bear fruit. There is no hint, as in the second category, that the plant dies or never grew at all. When weeds choke out crop plants, they don't usually die, but they can't bear any significant produce. Luke's record is: **". . . and as they go on their way they are choked with worries and riches and pleasures of this life, and bring no fruit to maturity"** (Lk. 8:14). This implies that the plant is alive and bears immature, useless fruit. Unfortunately, this does describe many Christians today. We cannot be dogmatic about the interpretation of parables, but certainly this option is worthy of serious consideration.

This is not to condone the lifestyle of believers described in these many passages. Each of us will have to give account at the judgment seat of Christ. There are also temporal consequences for our sins and failure to do the full will of God. But the Scriptures are very realistic in portraying life as it is, not as we might idealize it.

Is there a higher Christian life? Warfield objected to Chafer's teaching as an echo of "the jargon of Higher Life teachers." He mistook it to be an expression of a "second blessing," or a "second work of grace" type of teaching.[30] Those who are familiar with Chafer's teaching know that nothing could be further from the truth. On the other hand, Christian experience is not monolithic. There is a continuum of levels of Christian living which can be distinguished. Chafer distinguished salvation and fellowship with God. Every Christian will have to admit that our walk in fellowship with God is not an unbroken, totally level experience. Indeed, Chafer taught that the slightest sin breaks that fellowship so that it needs to be restored by confession (1 Jn. 1:9).

CONCLUSIONS

As we have examined the three major discipleship teachings of the Lord Jesus in chronological sequence and context, we have seen clearly that He is not explaining the way of salvation but is putting demands of discipleship upon those who had already been converted. *The word 'daily' in Luke 9:23 is crucial.* Then in examining the Lord's salvation witness to a number of unbelieving individuals we observed that He did not lay discipleship teaching upon them. This includes the rich young ruler, which dialogue has been grossly misunderstood in a legalistic way.

I have suggested that the so-called 'lordship salvation' issue would be better recognized as a 'discipleship salvation' issue. There are strong Calvinistic presuppositions underlying this view. At bottom the distinction between salvation and discipleship is clear and important in order to avoid legalism, even if the legalism be promoted under the name of 'grace.'

Excursis on the Difference between the Synoptics and the Gospel of John

It may be well at this point to raise the question as to why we find so little explanation of salvation truth in the Synoptic Gospels, as compared with the Gospel of John. We should consider that the primary issue up to this point was His own person—is He the Messiah? In reality much of the Gospel of Matthew is an exposition of the meaning of repentance, the things which Israel needed to repent of in view of the King's arrival in their midst. The Sermon on the Mount spelled out the major spiritual problems extant in the nation: their misinterpretations of the Law, their externalism and ostentation, their materialism, etc. Other discourses pointed up their hypocrisy, legalism, unbelief, etc. So if they became convinced of His messiahship, these are the things they would need to change their minds about. Since His claims to be the Messiah were absolutely clear, they either needed to believe in Him or reject Him. Thus the message of John the Baptizer, the Lord Himself, and His apostles, focused upon repentance. They would need to change their minds about their spiritual condition, their apostate religion, and who He was, in order to put their faith in Him. The issue was clear and needed no other clarification.

However, many years later in the 90s the apostle John was in Ephesus trying to communicate the gospel in the Gentile world. The issues they faced were very different from those faced by the Jewish nation half a century earlier. John realized that he needed to contextualize the Gospel account and clarify the issue of faith/believing. As he thought back about incidents and discourses which the Synoptic writers had not recorded, he realized that the interview with Nicodemus, the Samaritan woman, the Bread of Life discourse, some of Christ's other dialogues with the Jewish leaders, the incident at the feast of Tabernacles, the Upper Room Discourse, and many other things would help to contextualize the message for those Gentiles in Ephesus. This is why we find 'to believe' 94 times in his Gospel record, but no reference to repentance.

Note: This chapter is based upon a paper given at the Eastern Section of the Evangelical theological Society, Langhorne, PA, March 2001.

---

1. Robert Shank, *Life in the Son*, p. 18.
2. Harold Camping, in *Family Radio News.*
3. Walter Chantry, *Today's Gospel: Authentic or Synthetic?*, p. 47.
4. Charles Ryrie refers to it as "so-called lordship/discipleship/mastery salvation." in *So Great Salvation*, p. 29.
5. John F. MacArthur, Jr., *The Gospel According to Jesus*, p. 30
6. Charles C. Ryrie in the foreword to Zane C. Hodges, *The Hungry Inherit*, p. 7.
7. Arndt and Gingrich, *Greek-English Lexicon*, p. 486.
8. MacArthur, p. 202.
9. Abbot-Smith, p. 436.
10. G. Michael Cocoris, *Lordship Salvation—Is It Biblical?*, p. 13.
11. MacArthur, pp. 37-47, esp. 39; his treatment here is quite helpful.
12. Ibid, pp. 46-47.
13. Arndt and Gingrich, p. 82.
14. Ibid, pp. 644-5.
15. MacArthur, pp. 52-53.
16. Ibid, p. 60.
17. Ibid, p. 59.
18. Geerhardus Vos, *Biblical Theology*, pp. 6-7.
19. Thomas L. Constable, "The Gospel Message" in *Walvoord: A Tribute*, pp. 203-4.
20. I am greatly indebted to Alan A. McRae, the founder of Biblical Theological Seminary, for the main ideas of this exposition, which he gave in a popular lecture in Dallas, attendant to his Griffith-Thomas Memorial Lectureship at Dallas Seminary in the early 50s.
21. MacArthur, p. 78.
22. Ibid, p. 95.
23. Ibid, p. 97-9, see John Witmer's critique of Hodges' view in footnote 3; Thieme quote on p. 98; Hodges quote in footnote 7.
24. Ibid, p. 24, see footnote 6 for discussion of B. B. Warfield's review in *The Princeton Theological Review* (April 1919), pp. 322-27.
25. Ibid, pp. 29-30, 196, see also p. 202 for his discussion of Lk. 9:23.
26. Charles C. Ryrie, *Dispensationalism Today*, p. 109.
27. MacArthur, p. 33, 183, and pp. 172-3 on Eph. 2:8-9.
28. Michael Eaton, *No Condemnation: A New Theology of Assurance* (Downers' Grove: IVP, 1995).
29. I recognize that Harold Camping is not a trained theologian, but as a most vocal spokesman for his extreme form of Reformed theology, it is appropriate to reference him. Since such statements are repeatedly aired on Family Radio, it is extraneous to try to document an exact quotation.
30. Warfield, p. 322.

. . . unless one understands and accepts the doctrine of eternal security, one *can not* accept without a great deal of reservation the doctrines of the grace of God. *The whole body of grace truth loses very much of its meaning to those who reject the doctrine of eternal security.*

-J. F. Strombeck

14

WHY BOTH ARMINIANS AND CALVINISTS STRUGGLE WITH ETERNAL SECURITY

As a new believer in an Arminian church, the first doctrinal issue with which I wrestled was the security of the believer. My childhood buddy Herb Hage, through whom I came to the Lord, and I began to look up every relevant passage and check key word usage in a concordance. We were also greatly helped by John F. Strombeck's fine book, *Shall Never Perish*.[1] Within some months we both became strongly convinced that salvation is eternal, not probationary. Half a century of study has confirmed the correctness of that conclusion.

Although James Arminius never did deny eternal security, his Remonstrant followers did, as did the Wesleyan movement. Thus it is commonly thought that the dividing line between Calvinism and Arminianism is the teaching of eternal security. But even in this area of eternal security, it seems clear that we must go "beyond Arminianism and Calvinism" to get at the whole truth, since there is a tendency in both camps to intrude human performance into the ultimate salvation of the believer. I should clarify that it is only the extreme Calvinists who reject 'eternal security.' I had thought that this would be an easy section to write, but as I researched further, I found a lot of confusion of definition and interpretation of relevant Scripture, which requires two chapters at the least.

Here I will focus on an accurate definition, the significance, and some implications of the doctrine. I will summarize some of the positive biblical rationale, but in the next chapter I shall go into some detail in dealing with the so-called problem passages, foremost of which is Hebrews 6. During the decade I served as a Bible answerman on radio station WFME, the most frequent question I got related to this section. It was the most troubling to Arminius and to most Arminians (and Calvinists for that matter). I believe I have a unique contribution to make in this area.

CLARIFICATION OF THE DOCTRINE

There are so many misunderstandings as to what the doctrine of eternal security is that it is imperative to define it clearly: **Whoever once truly trusts Christ's finished sacrifice and resurrection for eternal life and is born again can never be lost, no matter what work (or lack of work) may accompany that faith.**[2]

First, I should clarify that the truth of eternal security in Christ is not identical to the traditional Calvinistic doctrine of the **perseverance** of the saints. I much prefer the **preservation** of the saints, because the emphasis is upon the work of the triune God, not upon the works of man. This is not just a semantic difference; there is a significant conceptual difference as well. Many Calvinistic writers recognize this and reject the term eternal security and the phrase, "once saved, always saved." The nub of the difference is that Calvinists have generally put the onus upon the saints to persevere, while a biblical concept of eternal security puts the responsibility upon God to preserve the saved. This means that in the final analysis the extreme Calvinistic view is that the good works of the saints are necessary to ultimate salvation. Laurence Vance has made a careful study of this issue and has given extensive documentation, some of which I will quote. He says: "But by confounding God's *preservation* of the believer with the believer's *perseverance* in the faith, Calvinists have contradicted their entire system of theology."[3] John Murray is a good representative: "But let us appreciate the doctrine of the perseverance of the saints and recognize that we may entertain the faith of our security in Christ only as we persevere in faith and holiness to the end."[4] Pink is even more explicit: "Those who persevere not in faith and holiness, love and obedience, will assuredly perish."[5] Although Calvinists admit that true believers can fall temporarily, they are unanimous in holding that a true believer will come back to Christ before death. However, Charles Hodge, in commenting on Paul's words in 1 Corinthians 9:27, wrote, ". . . this devoted apostle considered himself as engaged in a lifestruggle of his salvation."[6]

John Calvin's doctrine of temporary faith is an enigma, inconsistent with his other doctrines. He spoke of a "false work of grace" and in like manner Sproul says that "we may think that we have faith when in fact we have no faith." A. A. Hodge wrote, "*Perseverance in holiness*, therefore, in opposition to all weakness and temptations, is the *only sure evidence* of the genuineness of past experience, of the validity of our confidence as to our future salvation."[7] Over the centuries, Calvinists have consistently believed that those who do not persevere until the end of life were never really saved in the first place. How could Charles Hodge, as a core Calvinistic theological authority, even entertain the idea that Paul had to struggle to keep himself saved and might not succeed (become a castaway)? He could hardly say that Paul was not saved in the first place, could he?

Most serious is the common Calvinistic notion that one cannot know whether one is among the elect or not. This affected much of Puritan thinking and is still rife among the Reformed. Asahel Nettleton, a powerful 19th century evangelical preacher represents the problem: "The most that I have ventured to say respecting myself is, that I think it possible I may get to heaven."[8] Michael Eaton describes another serious consequence of this kind of theology from personal experience: ". . . an ossified legalism, a crippling introspection, and a harshness of spirit that seemed nothing like the Jesus of the Bible."[9]

Eaton has chronicled the contemporary seriousness of the problem and shows how serious a matter it has been for what he calls "Developed Calvinism," as well as for Arminianism. Speaking from experience as a long-term high-Calvinist pastor, he states: "Is it not a fact of history that the Calvinist has tended to have less assurance of salvation than the Arminian? The Arminian is at least sure of his present salvation. As a result of the high Calvinist doctrine the Calvinist often doubts his present salvation and thus has a less contented frame of mind than his evangelical Arminian friend."[10]

Parallels between Arminianism and extreme Calvinism

This then seems to be very similar to the Arminian view. Robert Shank is a good representative: "There is no saving faith apart from obedience. . . . There is no valid assurance of election and final salvation for any man, apart from deliberate perseverance in faith."[11] Michael Eaton has demonstrated the irony of the weak assurance of "developed Calvinists" and Arminians alike. He compares Calvinistic preacher Asahel Nettleton with John Fletcher, a friend of John Wesley, and shows that neither had any assurance of ultimate salvation:

> These great men exemplify a theological problem that has troubled evangelical churches and preachers since the 17th century, if not before. On the one hand, Nettleton's doubts relate to the *genuineness* of salvation. On the other hand, Fletcher said no Christian could be absolutely sure about the *permanence* of their salvation. Nettleton's teaching has been popularly summarized in the phrase 'Once saved, always saved' - but he was not quite sure that he was even once saved! John Fletcher taught 'Once saved, maybe lost'! I find neither doctrine very encouraging. In fact, both seem rather terrifying. . . For the Evangelical Arminianism and the kind of Calvinism that developed in English-

> speaking evangelicalism after the end of the 16th century have, I believe, both been legalistic. Developed Calvinism has also exhibited, I suggest, strongly introspective tendencies.[12]

The point is, that as long as human performance intrudes into the issue of ultimate salvation, there can be no "full assurance of faith" (Heb. 10:22) or full assurance of any kind, it matters not whether one calls oneself a Calvinist or an Arminian. In this regard there is a remarkable parallel between Arminians and extreme Calvinists: both in effect make human performance until the end of life an essential condition of ultimate salvation.

Some years ago I noticed that Robert Shank's defense of Arminian conditional security had as a premise the understanding that Christ's major discipleship passages (Mt. 10; 16; Lk. 9; 14) are salvation truth.[13] About that time I was interacting with Calvinist John MacArthur's "lordship salvation" position in which he does the same thing, so much so that in my discussion in chapter 13, I suggest it should be called "discipleship salvation." I believe I have shown in that chapter that both are tragically wrong.

I have observed another striking parallel between extreme Calvinists and Arminians. Both assume that there is no such thing as fruitless or carnal believers. Arminians would say that any Christian who is fruitless or carnal has lost his salvation; extreme Calvinists would say that such a person was never really saved in the first place. But Scripture is very explicit in recognizing and accounting for carnal and fruitless believers (1 Cor. 3:1-3, 15; 5:1-13; 11:17-34; Mt. 13:22; Heb. 6:7-8; 2 Pet. 2:7). I have already examined this issue in chapter 13.

The parallels go even farther. Both make fear of ultimate perdition a major motivation for moral behavior. Arminians generally say that sin can cause a Christian to lose salvation, and this is why we all must fear falling into sin. Extreme Calvinists would say that a sinful lifestyle is proof that a professing Christian is not among the elect. Indeed, the only proof that one is among the elect is perseverence in holiness until the end. But fear of ultimate condemnation is the motivation for holiness here also. Stanley aptly comments, "Fear and love do not mingle well. One will always dilute the other. Furthermore, fear spills over into worry. Let's be realistic for a moment. If my salvation is not a settled issue, how can I be anxious for nothing (see Phil. 4:6)?"[14] Now it is true that fear of loss of rewards at the judgment seat of Christ is a biblical motivation for godliness, but not fear of hell.

I have also observed another parallel connected with that. There is a fuzziness in both circles in distinguishing salvation and rewards. The Lord Jesus and the apostles clearly taught that there are rewards in the kingdom for godly service for Christ, which are over and above simply being saved. Some extreme Calvinists deny this outright. My impression is that most Arminians do also. Words like rewards, crowns, inheritance, etc. are sprinkled throughout the New Testament and need to be given adequate consideration.

Vance also points out another striking parallel. He finds that both extreme Calvinistic and Arminian commentators come up with the same erroneous misinterpretations of some key passages of Scripture (i.e.,1 Tim. 4:16; Mt. 24:13), Both kinds of interpretations deny the eternal security of the Christian based on faith in Christ alone. Both intrude human performance as a condition of ultimate salvation into their comments.[15]

Understanding Arminian thinking

I have never really been an Arminian, since after my conversion, I quickly distanced myself from conditional security. However, Charles Stanley was a convinced (and probably convincing) Arminian for a decade, until as a seminary student he restudied the issue from scratch. He attributes his shift of viewpoint to two factors:

> First, I was guilty of ignoring the context of many verses I quoted to defend my view. As I began digging deeper into the events and discussions surrounding these passages, they took on a different meaning. Second, I discovered through my study that the concept of salvation through faith alone cannot be reconciled with the belief that one can forfeit his or her salvation. If I must do or not do something to keep from losing my salvation, salvation would be by faith and works.

Early on I learned the truth of Stanley's appraisal. My Arminian pastor asked me to lead the mid-week Bible study and prayer meeting in his absence. As a 20-year-old college student, I naively selected eternal security as my subject. I began by asking the group of 20 to 25 believers, "When you get to heaven, on what basis will you be able to say that you got there?" Everyone responded in a similar vein, that it will be by faith in Christ plus faithfulness and obedience to Him. There were different ways of expressing it, *but not one said it was by faith in Christ alone*! This was a vivid lesson for me.

Stanley describes how when he first began to grasp security, it was as if a light came on and he was freed from prison. He had the awesome thought, "I had been eternally secure since the day as a twelve-year-old when I prayed, asking Jesus to save me." As a consequence he began to experience the true meaning of unconditional love. Words like 'grace,' 'peace,' and 'joy' took on new meaning in his experience. There was a new intimacy with Christ as he felt secure in love and acceptance. He felt release from the bondage of guilt and fear that had dominated for a decade (Jn. 8:32).

He also explains that essentially there are two Arminian scenarios as to how a Christian can lose salvation. Some say it is only through apostasy, quoting Heb. 6:4-6, the parable of the four soils, and "falling from grace" (Gal. 5:4). Others focus on the illogic of a holy God allowing sinful behavior in a

Christian's life with impunity. The latter say, "God is merciful, but not a fool!" "It would be unfair for God to give equal salvation to faithless and faithful Christians alike." " Eternal security is just a license to sin." "There must be a point of no return in the life of the sinful Christian."[16]

R. T. Kendall was a fervent Arminian for even longer than Charles Stanley was and thought eternal security was a devilish doctrine. However, one day in 1955, driving from his student pastorate in an Arminian church to his Arminian college, the Holy Spirit gave him a unique experience which caused him to know that he was eternally and unconditionally saved. This experience opened up the Scriptures to him in such a way as to see that actually all truly born-again believers are eternally secure, not just himself! The irony is that all true believers are eternally secure, whether or not they believe it. And indeed some Calvinists also do not have the assurance that they are really saved and secure in Christ.

Earl Radmacher was also taught in his youth that eternal security was a doctrine of the devil. What so confused him was the conflicting counsel as to how to get saved: "hang onto God," "let go and let God," "pray through," or "surrender to God." After he was saved at age fourteen, because he was untaught in the truths of the grace of God, he was on a spiritual roller coaster until he came to the truth of eternal security.[17]

Let it be absolutely clear that I am not advocating the eternal security of all professing Christians, no matter how orthodox or evangelical they might seem to be in their doctrine. The New Testament is very clear that there are counterfeit Christians who make a false, superficial profession of faith in Christ, but have never been genuinely born again. It is also clear that there are backslidden, carnal Christians, whose lifestyle is not glorifying to God. They will be deprived of reward at the judgment seat of Christ, but they themselves will be saved "so as by fire" (1 Cor. 3:15). Sometimes it is hard for us to distinguish the counterfeits from the backslidden. But the Lord knows their hearts and He is the ultimate judge.

Thus the challenge for us is to develop a position on security which maintains the Pauline doctrine of justification by faith alone without lapsing into the legalistic addition of works found both in Arminianism and extreme Calvinism. Approaching it inductively from the mediate position I have been espousing will avoid the confusion of the extreme views.

WHAT IS AT STAKE? WHY BELIEVE IT?

I have believed in eternal security for over half a century for one simple reason: God says it in His word. I have mentioned my early research while I was studying chemical engineering, before I learned Greek and Hebrew in seminary. Since then I have learned many reasons why that early concordance study could have been defective. However, my continued study, teaching, preaching, and interacting with other Christians (whether on my radio call-in program or in meetings of the Evangelical Theological Society, etc.) have only confirmed the conclusions of that early study.

Many renowned scholars, both Calvinistic and Arminian, have confessed to a very real tension between the positive promises of the Bible and the exhortations, warnings, and problem passages. Howard Marshall, an outstanding Arminian scholar, has confessed that the tension has to be left unresolved.[18] Robert Stein, as one who holds to eternal security, confessed that he had no satisfying exegesis of Hebrews 6. However, I am convinced that the tension is resolvable, indeed, for believers in the inerrancy of Scripture, *it must be resolvable*. Moderate Calvinistic and mediate writers have made substantial progress in resolving that tension.

The second reason for believing in eternal security is its integral connection with the great Pauline doctrine of justification by grace through faith alone, so important to the Reformation. This was a significant factor in Charles Stanley's "conversion." Years earlier Strombeck had written, "*The whole body of grace truth loses very much of its meaning to those who reject the doctrine of eternal security*" (italics his)[19] Somewhere in his four excellent books, Strombeck used the illustration as to how the color printed on one side of a fabric "bleeds through" to the other side. In a similar way, denial of security bleeds through all the other teachings of the those who deny it, whether Arminian or extreme Calvinist. The full forgiveness of the cross and the unconditional love of God for His children are compromised with human performance by denial of security.

Kendall points out another issue at stake in the denial of eternal security. He suggests that many Arminians are really hedging their bets. "Their view is that, even if the doctrine of once saved, always saved is true, they still prefer to play it safe and live the Christian life as though this doctrine might not be true. After all, if it is true, they will be saved anyway—if it is not true, they hope to be sure they have enough good works to cushion their security." It is like people who lift their feet as the jetplane takes off to help it along, rather than fully trust the plane. It is like the man who got baptized thirteen times, by every conceivable mode, just to hedge his bets. Kendall urges such people to "go for broke"—stake your whole case on the finished work of Christ alone.[20]

Furthermore, I can confirm Kendall's experience that coming to believe in security opened up the Scriptures in a new way for me. Although, unlike Kendall, I did not have the erroneous theological baggage to clear out of my thinking, I did begin to sense a wonderful harmony of Scripture, both as I first wrestled with the issue and in my studies over these years. Indeed, as already mentioned, I would think the unresolved tension perceived by many honest interpreters like Marshall would be a great obstacle to belief in the inerrancy of Scripture. Perhaps this explains why many evangelical Arminian denominations do not have any traditional belief in the inerrancy of Scripture.[21] Appreciation for the wonderful doctrinal harmony of the Bible is a great reinforcement of faith in the verbal, plenary inspiration of Scripture.

The last reason I mention relates to the quality of our fellowship with the Lord and the motivations for godly Christian living. Shortly after coming to understanding of security I was greatly blessed by Strombeck's second book, *Disciplined by Grace*. There I learned for the first time the implications of Paul's words to Titus: "**For the grace of God has appeared, bringing salvation to all men, instructing us to deny ungodliness and worldy desire and to live sensibly, righteously and godly in the present age, . . .**" (2:11-12). How thrilling it was to see, as he took us through Paul's epistles, how all of his appeals for godly living were based, not on the Mosaic Law, but upon the gracious salvation God has freely given us (Rom. 12:1-2; Eph. 4:1-3; Col. 3:1-4, etc.).

Both Kendall and Stanley have described the frustrating legalism they experienced among those who deny security, and Michael Eaton has described the legalism he experienced in "developed Calvinism" and found in the writings of the Puritans. The point of these writers is to show that intruding human performance into the issue of our ultimate salvation, not only compromises the clear biblical teaching of salvation by grace alone, through faith alone, by Christ alone, but it compromises the biblical basis for a godly Christian life under the gracious hand of a loving God. We who are parents understand the importance of showing unconditional love to our children as a basis for a healthy, positive relationship. "If abandoning the faith or falling into sin short-circuits salvation, I have the ability to demonstrate unconditional love to a greater extent than God."[22] How can we trust a heavenly Father whose love for us is conditioned upon our performance until the last breath of life? How can we experience true fellowship with such a God? How can we have peace in our Christian life if there is always uncertainty about where we *really* stand with Him? How can we live a stable Christian life if we constantly fear that God will ultimately disown us? Kendall goes so far as to say that legalistic morality is not true biblical godliness. When we understand Christ's constant exposing of the legalism of the Pharisees' morality, we would have to agree with Kendall.

THE POSITIVE BIBLICAL BASIS

The positive biblical evidence for the eternal security of the believer is so overwhelming, that I am amazed that Christians who struggle with security don't seek more assiduously to resolve the tension with the so-called problem passages. This I will seek to do in the next chapter. First, we must get clearly fixed in mind the positive biblical rationale for security. Chafer suggested a simple outline for discussion which is hard to improve on: there are substantial and extensive Scriptures which relate security to each of the members of the Trinity, Father, Son, and Holy Spirit. I can only give a brief overview of a few.

The Father's Preservation of His Choice People

The age-spanning purpose of God

Although I have departed from the Calvinistic understanding of predestination, this in no way weakens the force of Paul's chain of logic in Romans 8:28-30. Paul starts with a wonderfully assuring promise to believers, which many Christians have found a great encouragement in times of contrary circumstances: "**And we know that God causes all things to work together for good to those who love God, to those who are called according to *His* purpose** (8:28). If a true believer could lose salvation and go to hell, this promise is meaningless. Paul does not set up loving God as a condition, but rather a description of those who are called by God to salvation. Then he gives the reason that verse 28 is true:

> **For God knew his own before ever they were, and also ordained that they should be shaped to the likeness of his Son, that he might be the eldest among a large family of brothers; and it is these, so fore-ordained, whom he has also called. And those whom he called he has justified, and to those whom he justified he has also given his splendour** (New English Bible–a more accurate translation here, cf. ch. 7).

There is an unbreakable chain of five links in this promise. It starts with God's foreknowledge and finishes with glorification. If anyone should become lost along the way, Paul's logic and the faithfulness of God to His promises are destroyed. 'Calling' is that work by which a sinner comes to faith in Christ by responding to the universal invitation of the gospel. Those who are called are those who love God, in other words, true Christians. Paul is very explicit that God has pre-appointed them to be conformed to the likeness of His Son, and not only declares them to be righteous in His sight, but has already counted them to be glorified (aorist, not future tense). Then in 8:31-35, Paul asks seven unanswerable questions. Paul's mind is boggled by God's overwhelming grace in that God is now for us, that He will freely give us all things with Christ, that no one can lay any charge against God's elect since God is the one who declares us righteous and Christ now intercedes for us, and that no one or no thing can separate us from God's love. One hundred percent of those whom God foreknew He will glorify by conforming them to Christ's image. This is outrageously true whether or not those who want to intrude human performance into the sequence can believe it.

Over half a century ago, I claimed Christ's simple promise of John 5:24 (shame on you if you can't quote it from memory) and have been convinced that He will fulfill this promise and that of Roman 8, not only in my case, but also for all who are truly born again. Although I may not accept all of the Calvinism of my first theology professor Lewis Sperry Chafer, his statement exposes the universe-shaking issue at stake:

> The failure of one soul to be saved and to reach glory whom God has ordained to that end means the disruption of the whole actuality of divine sovereignty. If God could fail in anything, He ceases to be God and the universe is drifting to a destiny about which God Himself could know nothing.[23]

Those who hold to conditional security must assume that there is an implicit condition here of continued human performance, which would stand in total contradiction to the gracious, unmerited nature of salvation expressed in Romans 4:16: "**For this reason *it is* by faith, in order that *it may be* in accordance with grace, so that the promise will be guaranteed to all the descendants, not only to those who are of the Law, but also to those who are of the faith of Abraham, who is the father of us all.**"

God's unbounded love provides a much-more salvation.

The apostle Paul amplified the statement of Christ in John 3:16 regarding the greatness of God's saving love:

> **. . . the love of God has been poured out within our hearts through the Holy Spirit who was given to us. For while we were still helpless, at the right time Christ died for the ungodly. . . . But God demonstrates His own love toward us, in that while we were yet sinners, Christ died for us. Much more then, having now been justified by His blood, we shall be saved from the wrath *of God* through Him. For if while we were enemies we were reconciled to God through the death of His Son, much more, having been reconciled, we shall be saved by His life** (Rom. 5:5-10).

Paul's Spirit-inspired logic here is inexorable. If God could love us and reconcile us to Himself when we were in hostility to Him, now that He has already reconciled us to Himself through the death of Christ, is it not even more sure that He will complete this work of salvation? Paul turns the tables on human logic by saying that our future salvation is even more sure than our present salvation. Is it not easier for God to complete the saving of saints than it was to save us from His wrath in the first place when we were sinners? The answer is a resounding 'yes' because of the saving life of Christ–His present intercession for us at the Father's right hand, which he refers to again in 8:34, and is confirmed in Hebrews 7:25 and in 1 John 2:2. If that were not enough, Paul lists every entity in the universe which might be able to separate us from the love of God, and affirms that none of them can do so (Rom. 8:38-39). This certainly must include Satan, the demons, the world-system, and our own sinful flesh. This is how Paul can affirm that "**God causes all things to work together for good**" for His saints. Thus there is a synergism between the Father and the Son since Christ's intercessory work contributes to our security.

God's infinite power to keep us saved

Actually attempting to separate the works of the members of the Trinity in this regard is impossible, since the Lord Jesus mentioned another synergism of the members of the Trinity in His promise in John 10:27-29: "**My sheep hear My voice, and I know them, and they follow Me; and I give eternal life to them, and they will never perish; and no one will snatch them out of My hand. My Father, who has given *them* to Me, is greater than all; and no one is able to snatch *them* out of the Father's hand.**" As a new Christian fifty years ago, I got a book which treated this passage. I couldn't believe how the writer inserted conditional 'ifs' into Christ's unconditioned promise: "**If** My sheep hear my voice," and "**If** they follow Me." The Lord makes six parallel statements about His sheep, and to insert a condition in two of them to suit our theology or our predilections is to violate the word of God. This is a simple case of tampering with Scripture. Once we become His sheep through the new birth, these six things are characteristic of His sheep. And the promise He makes to His sheep is a promise of absolute protection.

Some Arminians rationalize that we can wriggle out of His hand and lose salvation, but the burden of proof is upon them to show that this is possible. The fact is that sheep will stray. I believe the Lord chose this symbolism intentionally to communicate that He will keep sheep who are prone to stray. He reinforced this promise by stating that His omnipotent Father will protect His sheep. Not only do all the other positive promises contradict the possibility of wriggling out of His hand, but I will show in the next chapter that the warnings they consider to be warnings of hell given to sheep are not really such. His sheep need not fear ever going to hell. Writing to those who have been born again, Peter reaffirmed this truth which he heard from the lips of the Lord: "**. . . to *obtain* an inheritance *which is* imperishable and undefiled and will not fade away, reserved in heaven for you, who are protected by the power of God through faith for a salvation ready to be revealed in the last time**" (1 Pet. 1:4-5). It is clear that Peter understood Christ's promise in absolute terms.

Although Paul did not hear Christ's words directly, he appropriated the truth to himself: "**. . . for I know who I have believed and I am convinced that He is able to guard what I have entrusted to Him until that day**" (2 Tim. 1:12). Paul believed this, not just for himself, but for all those who have responded to God's call, as we saw in Romans 8, and based upon Abraham's conviction of omnipotence, that "**being fully assured that what God had promised, He was able also to perform**" (Rom. 4:21). The Lord's brother had the same conviction: "**Now to Him who is able to keep you from stumbling, and to make you stand in the presence of His glory blameless with great joy,**" (Jude 24).

The Son's Preservation of His Sheep

His great and precious promises

I have already shared how it was Christ's promise in John 5:24 which was most instrumental in bringing me into assurance of eternal life. I said, "Lord, I have heard Your word and believed on You and Your Father, and you said that I have eternal life and will not come into condemnation, but have already passed from death to life. I take You at Your word that this life really is eternal, not temporary, and that you mean what you say." I 'went for broke' on the cross and word of Christ. Moreover, the promises in the bread of life discourse (Jn. 6:35-40) are even more explicit:

> **Jesus said to them, "I am the bread of life; he who come to me will not hunger, and he who believes in Me will never thirst. . . . All that the Father gives Me will come to Me, and the one who comes to Me I will certainly not cast out. . . . This is the will of Him who sent Me, that of all that He has given Me I lose nothing, but raise it up on the last day. For this is the will of My Father, that everyone who beholds the Son and believes in Him will have eternal life, and I Myself will raise him up on the last day."**

If one who came to Christ and believed on Him could ever again spiritually hunger and thirst in hell, then Christ misled us! To avoid any ambiguity, not only did He assert that a new believer will not be rejected upon coming to Him, but that He will not reject such a one at any future time. This understanding of 6:37 is supported by the assurance of future protection and resurrection in 6:39-40. I can't grasp how the Lord Jesus could have made it any more explicit than He did. Thus the promise of John 10:27-29 must likewise be understood in absolute terms.

His intercessory prayers

Calvinists have long pointed to the impossibility that the Father should not respond to the prayers of the Son since He was sinless and in total harmony with the will of the Father. Christ's prayer for Peter (Lk. 22:32) was efficacious. We must believe that His high-priestly prayer in the garden will be efficacious: "**I am no longer in the world; and *yet* they themselves are in the world, and I come to You. Holy Father, keep them in Your name, *the name* which You have given Me, that they may be one even as We *are***" (Jn. 17:11). This prayer was not just for the Eleven but for all subsequent believers: "**I do not ask on behalf of these alone, but for those also who believe in Me through their word**" (17:20). The loss of one sheep would imply that Christ's prayer went unanswered. Unthinkable! This is even more unthinkable because of Hebrews 7:25, Romans 5:10; 8:34, already discussed, and 1 John 2:1-2: "**And if anyone sins, we have an Advocate (Intercessor) with the Father, Jesus Christ the righteous; and**

He Himself is the propitiation for our sins . . ." As discussed in chapter 5, propitiation means a total satisfaction for the Father's offended holiness by the cross of Christ. This then is the basis of Christ's high-priestly ministry for His children at the Father's right hand. For the children of God the sin issue was totally settled on the cross when He cried, "**It is finished.**"

His completed propitiation, redemption, and reconciliation

Paul clearly showed how the justification of the ungodly is based upon the propitiation of Christ's shed blood on the cross in Romans 3:24-25, already discussed in chapter 5. There we saw that one phase of His redemptive work, better called ransom-redemption, like propitiation, was the objective basis for forgiveness for any who claims it by faith. He paid the ransom price for the sins of all mankind. However, some of the Greek words for redemption focus on the liberation of the captive, both the present possession and the future liberation of the body: "**In Him we have redemption through His blood, the forgiveness of our trespasses, according to the riches of His grace**" (Eph. 1:7); "**In Him, you also, after listening to the message of truth, the gospel of your salvation–having also believed, you were sealed in Him with the Holy Spirit of promise, who is given as a pledge of our inheritance, with a view to the redemption of *God's own* possession, to the praise of His glory**" (Eph. 1:14). We now have redemption as a present possession, but await the final liberation of our bodies. Since the Lord Jesus fully paid for all our sins, if a Christian should go to hell, God would be getting double payment for our sins, first from Christ, and then from that condemned Christian. But our just God would never do such a thing! Paul tied redemption in with the sealing work of the Spirit, to which we must now turn.

The Spirit's Preservation of His Saints

The sealing and earnest of the Spirit

Paul's connection of the certainty of the future redemption of the body with the sealing and earnest of the Spirit provides a segue into all the relevant ministries of the Spirit. His earlier reference to the sealing and earnest (pledge) in 2 Corinthians 1:21-22 does not make that connection, although he does connect it with the anointing of the Spirit: "**Now He who establishes us with you in Christ and anointed us is God, who also sealed us and gave *us* the Spirit in our hearts as a pledge (earnest).**" There is a common misconception (especially in Pentecostal circles) that God specially anoints a few for ministry. But Paul made it clear that all believers have been anointed since we have all been set aside for ministry, which John confirmed in 1 John 2:20, 27. I cannot elaborate here on the Graeco-Roman cultural concept of the sealing of a purchase until the day of redemption and of the giving of earnest money as a down payment until making full payment on that day. The Holy Spirit is God's seal and earnest pledge that the transaction of salvation which He began at our conversion will be consummated on that day. God's integrity as an 'honest dealer' is at stake. With apology to native Americans, we could say that God is not an 'Indian giver.'[A] This is the basis of Paul's later exhortation in Ephesians 4:30: **"Do not grieve the Holy Spirit of God, by whom you were sealed for the day of redemption."**

Irreversibly born again by the Spirit

If we were to treat the Spirit's ministries diachronically, we should have started with our Lord's words to Nicodemus in John 3:1-15 about the new birth and John's reference to it in his prologue (Jn. 1:12-13): **"But as many as received Him, to them He gave the right to become children of God, *even* to those who believe in His name, who were born, not of blood nor of the will of the flesh nor of the will of man, but of God."** From this it is clear that it is by the new birth that we become children in the family of God. The new birth is a supernatural and irreversible work of the Spirit, not just a reformation or turning over a new leaf. Not only did Peter understand that God **"has caused us to be born again to a living hope through the resurrection of Jesus Christ from the dead"** (1 Pet. 1:3), but also that **"you have been born again not of seed which is perishable but imperishable, *that is,* through the living and enduring word of God"** (2:23). Paul's unique use of the word regeneration (*palingenesia*) in Titus 3:5 is reminiscent of Christ's use of it in Matthew 19:28 to refer to that end time transformation of all of creation. That certainly will be an irreversible transformation as well.

I hope my experience growing up in an Arminian church is not typical, but I do not believe I heard the new birth ever preached. After I was born again, I listened for it carefully for two years and still didn't hear it. It seemed to me at the time that my pastor's concept of salvation was more a work of man, and thus was reversible. I trust that most Arminians believe and preach the new birth and have a deeper understanding than he had.

I remember when Jimmy Carter was elected President and said that he was a born-again Christian, the media people, who had never heard of it, went scrambling to supposed authorities, such as Prof. Henlee Barnett to get a definition. I was not shocked that his definition was so fuzzy and man-centered, because I had been using his Christian ethics textbook and found it to be a strange mixture of evangelistic Southern Baptist language with much of the old social-gospel liberalism. However, the biblical portrayal of the new birth as the impartation of divine life by the Spirit into the spiritually dead sinner, thus constituting him as a new creation in Christ (2 Cor. 5:17), would seem to imply the irreversibility of this work of God, not of man.

A. Some of my younger readers may not be familiar with this expression common among children in my childhood, when one child gives something to another, and then changes his mind and takes it back. Perhaps the colonists saw native Americans as fickle, since they did not have the same concept of property in their culture.

Permanently indwelt by the Spirit

One of the major subjects of the Upper Room Discourse is the promise of the giving, sending, and coming of the Holy Spirit on the day of Pentecost and its implications. Although the Lord had alluded to the opportunity to pray for the Holy Spirit in Luke 11:13, there is no indication that any of the apostles did so. In the light of their failure to do so His words in John 14:16-17 are more meaningful: **"I will ask the Father, and He will give you another Helper, that He may be with you forever; *that is* the Spirit of truth, whom the world cannot receive, because it does not see Him or know Him, *but* you know Him because He abides with you and will be in you."** A study of the Hebrew text of the whole Old Testament reveals an almost total absence of the preposition 'in' in reference to the Holy Spirit and believers. Thus David could pray, **"Do not cast me away from Your presence and do not take Your Holy Spirit from me"** (Ps. 51:11). Christ's clear implication was that the Holy Spirit abode **with** pre-Pentecost saints, not **in them.** David was not afraid of losing his salvation, but of losing the presence of God in the person of the Spirit **with him.** Accordingly he prayed: **"Restore to me the joy of Your salvation"** (52:12a). But now the Lord promised His apostles that **"in that day"** (14:20) the Spirit **"will be in you."** I find Ryrie's explanation most satisfying that on the day of Pentecost the omnipresent Holy Spirit came to dwell in the Church, both individually and corporately.[24] He was not only to regenerate believers as He had done previously, but also to indwell them permanently: **". . . that He may be with you forever."**

In this discourse the Lord continued to emphasize the new order which would be inaugurated in the age of the Holy Spirit: **"But the Helper, the Holy Spirit, whom the Father will send in My name, He will teach you all things, and bring to your remembrance all that I said to you"** (14:26). **"When the Helper comes, whom I will send to you from the Father, *that is* the Spirit of truth who proceeds[B] from the Father, He will testify about Me"** (15:26). **"But I tell you the truth, it is to your advantage that I go away; for if I do not go away, the Helper will not come to you; but if I go, I will send Him to you. And He, when He comes will convict the world concerning sin and righteousness and judgment;"** (16:7-8). **"But when He, the Spirit of truth, comes, He will guide you into all the truth . . ."** (16:13a). It totally escapes me how some theologians, because of their commitment to a theological system, can deny that the Holy Spirit came on the day of Pentecost to inaugurate a number of new ministries, and that there are essential differences between His ministries before Pentecost and after. Paul later affirmed this new reality of the indwelling Spirit in 1 Corinthians 6:19-20 and Romans 8:9-11 as essential to being a Christian. He

B. This is most likely a futuristic use of the present tense and like the other future tenses the Lord used, a reference to Pentecost. How tragic that the Roman and Eastern churches made controversy about some imagined on-going present procession of the Spirit the excuse for the division a millennium ago.

thus assured the Roman Christians that "**He who raised Christ Jesus from the dead will also give life to your mortal bodies through His Spirit who dwells in you.**" The present permanently indwelling Spirit is the guarantee of our final salvation.

Immersed in/ identified with Christ's body by the Spirit

Having become convinced that *baptizein* refers to immersion and identification, I wonder if the usual transliteration as 'to baptize' (and 'baptism') has obscured the truth, rather than helped it. In any case, just before His ascension, the Lord promised that the disciples would "**be baptized with the Holy Spirit not many days from now**" (Acts 1:5). One does not need a Ph.D. in mathematics to see this also as a reference to the Pentecost event of the next chapter. Although the word *baptisma* is not used in Acts 2 in reference to the Spirit (only water), Peter so understood it when he gave testimony about the first Gentile conversions: "**And as I began to speak, the Holy Spirit fell upon them just as *He did* upon us at the beginning. And I remembered the word of the Lord, how He used to say, 'John baptized with water, but you will be baptized with the Holy Spirit**" (Acts 11:15-16).

Thus Paul's later doctrinal clarification is most important: "**For by one Spirit we were all baptized into one body, whether Jews or Greeks, whether slaves or free, and we were all made to drink of one Spirit**" (1 Cor. 12:13). Since the context is all about the church as the body of Christ, Paul had no hesitation in affirming that even those carnal Corinthians had been immersed into the Church, the body of Christ by this ministry of the Spirit. It is that ministry which constitutes the Church. By his use of the word 'all' Paul made it clear that even the most backslidden believer in Corinth was still indwelt by the Spirit and part of the body of Christ. Thus there is not one warning of the loss of the Spirit in the New Testament after Pentecost. Rather Paul's exhortations to Christians are positively to "**keep in step with the Spirit**" (Gal. 5:16, NIV); "**ever be filled with the Spirit**" (Eph. 5:18, Williams); "**Do not quench the Spirit**" (1 Thess. 5:19); and "**Do not grieve the Holy Spirit of God**" (Eph. 4:30). These should be the concern of the Christian today, not the fear of losing the Holy Spirit and eternal life with Him.

CAN SIN NEGATE SALVATION?

Some people who reject eternal security feel that they themselves are secure in Christ, but they suspect that not all true Christians are. What about the converted drug addict, the alcoholic, the homosexual, the sexually promiscuous, etc.? They are dubious about them. It is clear that there is more than a little self-righteousness about this line of reasoning. No, either all true Christians are eternally secure or none are. However, others turn the issue upon themselves. They will say, "My sin is so great that I have lost my salvation." What they have really lost is the assurance of salvation. Let us try to get to the bottom of this confusion.

What about sins committed after conversion?

A root error of multitudes of Christians over the centuries has been to think that salvation only provides forgiveness for sins committed before conversion. Some of the church fathers fell prey to this kind of erroneous thinking, and the case of the emperor Constantine is a classic example. He postponed his baptism until just before his death in the hopes that there would be few or no post-baptismal sins for which he would have to personally answer. This kind of thinking is still endemic in the Roman Catholic system. To press the issue back one more step, we could say that it springs from the error of baptismal regeneration—that baptism actually does wash away our sins. (I have dealt with this error in appendix J.)

All sin forgiven. The notion that only pre-conversion sins were forgiven through the sacrifice of Christ is so clearly unbiblical that I call it a root error. It is the source of incredible confusion. Partial forgiveness is totally foreign to the Bible; there is no hint of any time limitations in the biblical declarations of forgiveness. We will start with King Hezekiah's prayer after God extended his life by fifteen years, "**It is You who has kept my soul from the pit of nothingness, for You have cast all my sins behind Your back**" (Isa. 38:17). King David did not think it presumptuous to pray, "**And forgive all my sins**" (Ps. 25:18). Micah had the same conviction about the nation Israel: "**Yes, You will cast all their sins into the depths of the sea**" (Mic. 7:19).

Thus when we come to the ministry of the Lord Jesus, we are not astonished to find Him using such all-inclusive language, with one exception: "**Truly I say to you, all sins shall be forgiven the sons of men, and whatever blasphemies they utter; but whoever blasphemes against the Holy Spirit never has forgiveness, but is guilty of an eternal sin**" (Mk. 3:28-9). The context makes it clear that this was a very specific form of acute unbelief in attributing Christ's miracles to the devil. Even the blasphemies of Saul of Tarsus were forgiven (Act. 9:1; 1 Tim. 1:12-15). Paul's own doctrinal statement is unambiguous: "**. . . He made you alive together with Him, having forgiven us all our transgressions, having canceled out the certificate of debt consisting of decrees against us, which was hostile to us; and He has take it out of the way, having nailed it to the cross**" (Col. 2:13-14). We should also note the many references to "sin" as a totality concept, which includes Adam's sin imputed to us (Rom. 5:12ff), the sin nature inherent in us (Eph. 3:1-3), as well as individual personal sins. The singular "sin" refers to all three aspects of sin, all of which were dealt with at the cross.

It might be helpful to point out that when Christ paid for our sins, all of our sins were yet future. When Christ died for the sins of Old Testament saints, all of their sins were past and only temporarily covered until He should provide the redemption price. This is the point of Paul's statement in Romans 3:24-25: "**. . . being justified as a gift by His grace through the redemption which is in Christ Jesus; whom God displayed publicly as a propitiation in His blood through faith. *This was* to demonstrate His righteousness, because in the forbearance of God He passed over the sins previously committed.**" Some have erroneously thought that this was a reference to the sins they committed before they were converted, but this is not the case. As discussed in chapter 5 (and confirmed in Hebrews), the Levitical sacrifices and sprinkling of blood on the mercy seat only provided a temporary covering for the sins of pre-cross saints. Nothing in the context of Romans 3 or the rest of the New Testament would support this misinterpretation.

I must emphasize that eternal life is not temporal probation, as some cultists teach. When God says "eternal life" He means **eternal** life, not probationary life. The book of Hebrews speaks about "**eternal salvation**" (5:9), "**eternal redemption**" (9:12), and an "**eternal inheritance**" (9:15).

Three aspects of forgiveness. One other point is essential to recognize. There are at least three different dimensions or aspects of forgiveness in the Bible. Basic is the salvation-forgiveness through trust in Christ's finished work. It is total. The second is the fellowship-forgiveness which John referred to in 1 John 1:1-10. The issue is the believer's fellowship with God and fellow believers. This, he makes clear, is contingent upon our walking in the light (1:7) and confessing our sins to the Lord (1:9). Lewis Sperry Chafer used to use this illustration: Salvation is like a steel band connecting the believer to Christ; fellowship with Christ is like a thin thread, broken so easily by sin, but restored so easily by confession. The third dimension is, of course, the horizontal—our fellowship with other believers being contingent upon keeping short accounts with them (Mt. 5:23-24;18:15). Failure to distinguish these distinct aspects has caused untold confusion.

Is full forgiveness a license to sin?

One of the major reasons people reject eternal security is they feel that it is a license to sin. Some years ago I preached on the warning of Hebrews 6 (as expounded in ch. 15) in a church where a friend from my Arminian home church was active. After the message with great agitation, he said, "Gordon, you are just preaching a license to sin!" I responded, "Brother, I believe you are living the Christian life for the same reason that I am—because of your gratitude for His free gift of salvation and your love for God in response. Neither of us is living for God because He threatens us with hell if we don't shape up." This ended the discussion, as I believe it should have. Just as my Arminian friend thought grace to be a license to sin, so also Paul's opponents in Rome misunderstood his message of grace: "**What shall we say then? Are we to continue in sin so that grace may increase?**" (Rom. 6:1). Paul went on to show that our union with Christ makes that unthinkable. But a similar reaction from opponents of eternal security shows that we have got the gospel of grace straight.

Motivation. However, this raises a most important question: what is the true motivation for living a godly life? There is not one passage in the New Testament, rightly understood, which threatens a true believer with hell, if he does not shape up. God doesn't hold a club over our heads, threatening to squash us if we don't get in line. No, the Bible is full of many other higher motivations for obedience. Most parents are smart enough to use positive motivations in the lives of their children before they resort to spanking and negative reinforcement (the board of education on the seat of learning). However, they would never threaten to disavow their child's sonship, except under the most extreme conditions. I take it that God knows far better how to motivate His own children. There are many positive as well as negative motivations which God sets before us.

The highest clearly is gratitude for the gift of eternal life. "**For the love of Christ controls us, having concluded this, that one died for all, therefore all died; and He died for all, so that they who live might no longer live for themselves, but for Him who died and rose again on their behalf**" (2 Cor. 5:14-15). Our love for Christ in response to His love for us is the ultimate motivation for living for Christ. In the same context, Paul had just mentioned another positive reinforcement in the rewards of the judgment seat of Christ: "**For we must all appear at the judgment seat of Christ, so that each one may be recompensed for his deeds in the body, according to what he has done, whether good or bad**" (5:10). This clearly is the reward seat (*bēma*) described in 1 Corinthians 3:11-15 and Romans 14:1-12, not the great white throne judgment of the unsaved dead (Rev. 20:11-15). The different crowns promised to faithful believers are clear examples of such rewards (Jas. 1:12; 1 Thess. 2:19; 1 Pet. 5:4; 1 Cor. 9:24-27; 2 Tim. 4:6-8; Rev. 2:9). Concomitant with this is the fear of loss of rewards which Paul mentions in this connection: "**Therefore, knowing the fear of the Lord, we persuade men, but we are made manifest to God; and I hope that we are made manifest also in your consciences**" (5:11). Although *phobos* is frequently a strong word for fear, the context shows it should not be rendered "terror" as in the KJV. I should hasten to add that Paul built this teaching upon the clear statements of the Lord Jesus (Mt. 16:27; 19:27-30).

Even more serious are the warnings to believers of the temporal consequences of a sinful lifestyle. There are many examples of God's chastisement in Israel's history, such as King David's sin and explicit New Testament references as well (Heb. 12:3-13). Paul uses very strong language about those who destroy the church (the temple of God in 1 Cor. 3:16-17), and his language in 1 Corinthians 5:5 & 11:27-32 is the doctrinal explanation of the premature death of Christians like Ananias and Sapphira (Acts 5:1-11), which truth the apostle John described as the "sin unto death" (1 Jn. 5:16-17). There is no hint in the text that they lost their salvation. There are also a number of other incentives which God uses in our lives. Some extreme Calvinists deny rewards, somehow thinking that it compromises the doctrines of grace. Unfortunately some of our Arminian friends do not seem to have been able to distinguish salvation and rewards either. Failure to make this important distinction has led to untold confusion in the interpretation of Scripture.

Denial of security colors our view of sin and holiness.

There is much confusion about the meaning of holiness and sanctification, which causes both Arminians and Calvinists alike to insist that a holy lifestyle is a condition for ultimate salvation. Passages such as Hebrews 12:14 have been grossly misunderstood: "**Pursue peace with all men, and the sanctification without which no one will see the Lord. See to it that no one comes short of the grace of God; . . .**" The misinterpretation arises because of failure to understand that the core meaning of sanctification (*hagiosmos*, used only here in Hebrews) derives from its verb "1. *to dedicate, separate, set apart for God*; . . . 2. *to purify*, make conformable in character to such dedication: forensically, to free from guilt."[25] There are five uses of the verb in this sense in Hebrews (2:11; 10:10, 14, 29; 13:12), which make it clear that the apostle is using the verb *hagiozein* and the noun *hagiosmos* in the sense of *positional* sanctification, not *experiential* holiness. Paul's usage, however, is quite different. Although he uses *hagiazein* and related nouns (*hagiosmos, hagiosunē, hagiotēs*) in both the positional sense (1 Cor. 6:11; Eph. 5:26) and in the experiential sense (2 Cor. 7:1), he usually uses the word 'justification' to refer to our forensic or legal position in Christ. Since the writer of Hebrews does not use this group of words in the experiential sense, we must not import Paul's quite different usage into Hebrews.[C] Of course, most Evangelicals recognize that the use of the word 'saint' (*hagios*) is consistently positional all through the New Testament. Although the Roman Catholic failure to recognize the positional nature of the usage of 'saints' is the most extreme error and is really semi-Pelagianism, any other attempt to intrude human holiness into our ultimate salvation also seriously compromises salvation by grace alone through faith alone in Christ alone. The legalistic, pumped-up human holiness of Romanism is bankrupt, witness the pedophile priest scandal, as is any other legalistic attempt, whether it be in the Galatian church or any church today.

What degree of human holiness is necessary to guarantee our ultimate salvation? If we were to accept the premise that some human holiness is necessary, then the answer would have to be, "total holiness." Unless we lapse back into the Muslim mindset or that of street philosophers, who hold that God weighs our good deeds against our bad works and judges on this basis, there is no other answer! Does God have some sort of a sliding scale

C. This is one of many indications that Paul is not the author of Hebrews. I have a dozen compelling reasons why Paul could not be the author of Hebrews, but space does not allow elaboration.

with a cut-off point? Romanism has at least attempted to classify mortal and venial sins. Not only do Catholics give fuzzy answers to which sins and how much fall into each category, but James totally contradicts such thinking: **"For whoever keeps the whole law and yet stumbles in one *point*, he has become guilty of all"** (2:10). Paul is just as clear in seeking to relieve the legalistic Galatians of such muddled thinking: **"For as many as are of the works of the Law are under a curse; for it is written, 'Cursed is everyone who does not abide by all things written in the book of the law, to perform them'"** (Gal. 3:10). Since Paul affirms that Christians are under the law of Christ (1 Cor. 9:21), this principle would apply to all Christians as well. Any man-made sliding scale would in reality become a slippery slope which would dump every last one of us into the lake of fire. None of this kind of thinking has the least biblical basis.

What degree of human sinfulness will nullify a Christian's salvation? I believe that those who deny eternal security, whether from an Arminian or an extreme Calvinist perspective, have a poorly developed doctrine of sin. I learned this early in my Christian life when I gave a testimony in a youth meeting at my church, thanking God for victory over a particular sin, which I had confessed to the Lord by claiming 1 John 1:9. Afterward my Arminian pastor got me aside and told me that this was not a sin, it was a mistake! His theology informed him that if it had been a sin, I would have lost my salvation.

I am not clear as to how the Wesleys developed their doctrine of sinless perfection, but I suspect it was overhang from their pre-conversion background in a very legalistic, ascetic, and mystical form of Anglicanism.[26] But their Arminianism has been described as "evangelical Arminianism" in contrast to the Arminianism of the Remonstrant followers of Arminius, over a century earlier. Most intriguingly, one doctoral dissertation argues that Wesley was so influenced by Calvin that his theology was as close to that of Calvin as was that of the Puritan, John Owen, if not closer.[27] In any case, despite Wesley's denial of security and affirmation of sinless perfectionism, the fact that untold multitudes came into assurance of salvation through him shows how many other things he got right. Calvinists the world over are blessed by singing the great hymns of the Wesley brothers. Nevertheless, sinless perfectionism and denial of eternal security were twin errors of the Wesleyan movement which have far reaching consequences.[28]

The sentiment that "real Christians don't sin" is expressed in various forms in both Arminian and extreme Calvinistic circles. It shouldn't take much study of Scripture to see how simplistic and false it is. The biblical narrative is full of believers who sinned, sometimes egregiously.[D] Even if we set aside sins of commission for a moment and consider sins of omission, it becomes obvious that all Christians continuously sin. The apostle James was

D. e.g. Abraham, Lot, Jacob and his sons, Saul, David, Solomon, Amaziah, Uzziah, Peter, Ananias/Sapphira, 1 Cor. 3, 5, & 11 and many others.

so down-to-earth realistic: **"Therefore, to one who knows *the* right thing to do and does not do it, to him it is sin"** (3:17). Most Christians throughout the centuries have been guilty of the sin of failing to fulfill the great commission, at the very least, and it should be unnecessary to enumerate the many sins of omission of which most Christians are guilty. R. T. Kendall, as pastor of a major London church, gives a list of sins common among Christians which is over a page in length, and he affirms that the list is "ridiculously long."[29] For any Christian to say that he has never committed such sins since his conversion is absurd. Just ask his/her spouse! Even when we don't sin overtly, sin is frequently in the motives and thoughts of the heart, as the Lord Jesus emphasized in the Sermon on the Mount (Mt. 5).

CAN FAILURE OF FAITH NEGATE SALVATION?

Another major concern of Arminians is that those who stop believing in Christ must necessarily lose their salvation. They argue that the verb 'to believe,' when used in reference to salvation, is mostly used in the present tense or in a durative or linear usage of the aorist.[30] Although it is true that the verb is frequently used in the present tense, there are a multitude of usages in the aorist and perfect tenses which relate to salvation. Although John uses the present tense of *pisteuein* about three-quarters of the time, and Luke about half the time in Acts, Paul uses the present sparingly in his epistles. Most strikingly, when Paul told the Philippian jailor how to be saved, he used the aorist imperative (Acts 16:31). So the whole foundation of this argument is false. Furthermore, Stanley points out that there are two diverse uses of the present tense, the present habitual and the present continuous. The use of the present does not always imply continuous action.[E] Indeed, we find that there are clear biblical examples of true believers who did not continuously believe and confess Christ. We should hardly have to mention Peter's name to bring recall of his triple denial of Christ at His trial. Did he lose his salvation at that point? The burden of proof is on Arminians to show that he did. No, when the Lord restored him to fellowship, Peter's lack of faith or salvation was not an issue. Indeed, the Lord had assured Peter: **"But I have prayed for you, that your faith may not fail; and you, when once you have turned again, strengthen your brothers"** (Lk. 22:32).

On the other hand, few readers might think to suggest that we examine the account of John the Baptizer in prison (Mt. 11:1-15): **"Now when John, while imprisoned, heard of the works of Christ, he sent *word* by his disciples and said to Him, 'Are You the Expected One, or shall we look for someone else?"** Zane Hodges makes a significant point here:

It is hard to believe one's eyes when this passage is first

E. In the Sanskrit-derived sister languages to Greek of North India (such as Hindi), there actually are different forms for the present habitual and present continuous tenses.

> encountered. Here is the great prophet and forerunner of God's Christ calling into question the very person to whom he had once given bold testimony. . . . Clearly then, this great servant of God is asking a question he presumable had settled decisively long ago. His inquiry is manifestly an expression of doubt about the very truth by which men and women are saved.[31]

There is no question that John was a believer, for the angel told his father that he would be "filled with the Spirit from his mother's womb" (Lk. 1:15). Yet now he is having second thoughts about who Jesus is; his faith seems very weak, virtually extinguished.[F] However, rather than rebuking his lack of faith, the Lord gives him commendation in the strongest terms imaginable: **"Truly I say to you, among those born of women there has not arisen *anyone* greater than John the Baptist!"** Certainly his salvation was not in jeopardy. From these two examples it becomes crystal clear that continuous faith is not a condition of ultimate salvation. What if Peter or John had died in that state of denial or unbelief? Would they have gone to hell? Unthinkable!

The Lord's promise to pray that Peter's faith would not fail raises a significant point. Can a true believer's faith fail in the ultimate sense of apostasy from the faith? Was Peter unique in this regard? Later he testified that the believers to whom he wrote were kept (protected) by the power of God (1 Pet. 1:5). Did not the Lord Jesus pray the same prayer in Gethsemane for the rest of the Eleven and also for those who should believe through their word (Jn. 17:11-12, 20-21)? Is He not right now at the Father's right hand interceding for all believers, by which **"He is able also to save forever those who draw near to God through Him"** (Heb. 7:25)?

Peter himself provided the key as to how God sustains the faith of true believers: **"for you have been born again not of seed which is perishable but imperishable, *that is*, through the living and enduring word of God"** (1 Pet. 1:23). The Lord Jesus had used the symbolism of drinking with the Samaritan woman to communicate the act of believing: **"but whoever drinks of the water that I will give him shall never thirst; but the water that I will give him will become in him a well of water springing up to eternal life"** (Jn. 4:14). First, we should note that the verb 'drinks' is an aorist subjunctive, not a present tense. Second, the promise that those who drink will never thirst again, which is as explicit a promise of eternal security as I can imagine, which He reinforced in the bread of life discourse (Jn. 6:35). Third, the "well of water" is an obvious reference to the Holy Spirit, which is confirmed by His further reference at the feast of Tabernacles, when He cried out, **"If anyone is thirsty, let him come to Me and drink. He who**

F. John's disillusionment is easily explainable in terms of his Spirit-given expectation of Messiah's coming in judgment to deliver and reign over Israel (Mt. 3:1-12). We now know what John did not, that this had to come after passion and death.

believes in Me, as the Scripture said, 'from his innermost being will flow rivers of living water.' But this He spoke of the Spirit, whom those who believed [aorist tense] in Him were to receive; for the Spirit was not yet *given*, because Jesus was not yet glorified" (Jn. 7:37-9).

This is the foundation of His promise of the permanent indwelling of the Spirit to all believers: "**I will ask the Father, and He will give you another Helper, that He may be with you forever; *that is* the Spirit of truth, . . . *but* you know Him because He abides with you and will be in you**" (Jn. 14:16-17). The Lord's express affirmation of the permanence of the Holy Spirit's indwelling is reinforced by Paul's three references to the earnest and sealing of the Holy Spirit (2 Cor. 1:21-22; Eph. 1:13-14; 4:30). The Holy Spirit is an ever-flowing well springing up to eternal life, who keeps true believers in faith. The irreversible nature of the new birth also needs to be emphasized in this connection. True believers may be extremely weak in their faith at any point in the Christian life without jeopardizing their ultimate salvation.

Even John Calvin, through a misunderstanding of Hebrews 6:4-6, taught a doctrine of temporary faith: "Experience shows that the reprobate are sometimes affected in a way so similar to the elect, that even in their own judgment there is no difference between them. Hence it is not strange, that by the Apostle a taste of heavenly gifts, and by Christ Himself a temporary faith, is ascribed to them." He also spoke of an "ineffectual calling" and an "inferior operation of the Spirit."[32]

Many might so misunderstand a number of references to believers who stop believing as a cessation of genuine saving faith. In the parable of the four soils the Lord Jesus explained the second category: "**The one on whom seed was sown on the rocky places, this is the man who hears the word and immediately receives it with joy; yet he has no *firm* root in himself, but is *only* temporary, and when affliction or persecution arises because of the word, immediately he falls away**" (Mt. 13:20-21). Note well that the word of God did not have a firm root in the person himself. It did not involve the whole personality: intellect, emotions, and will. There are examples in John 6:64-66; 8:31; Acts 8:13ff; and James 2:19 of those whose faith was not genuine. Perhaps it did not meet the criterion which Paul stipulated in Romans 10:9, to "**believe in your heart that God raised Him from the dead**." I always liked the tract entitled, "Missing Heaven by 18 Inches," because all through my teen years people thought I was a Christian, but there was no personal heart trust in Christ's finished work. Since I have already shown that it is people who have to do the trusting, we need not blame counterfeit faith on an "inferior work of the Spirit," as Calvin does. The Spirit neither strikes people with genuine or inferior faith for that matter.

Is security based upon the Calvinistic notion of election?

Since I have already repudiated the Calvinistic concept of unconditional, individual election, does that undermine the case for eternal security? Most

Calvinists depend heavily upon their doctrine of election as a basis for "perseverance of the saints." But since this argument is totally deductive, and we have a far stronger inductive basis for eternal security in the direct statements of Scripture, my confidence in eternal security has not been weakened one iota by my strong rejection of unconditional election. (Please refer to chapter 1 for the discussion of the most important distinction between inductive and deductive argumentation, and to chapters 7 and 8 for the meanings of "predestination" and "election" in the original Greek.)

Is saving faith always accompanied by assurance?

One very important question which keeps coming up is whether saving faith is the same as assurance and therefore, should always be manifest in assurance of salvation. Those who argue an equivalency usually reference Hebrews 11:1: **"Now faith is the assurance of *things* hoped for, the conviction of things not seen."** Although this might seem like a definition of faith, the context of the rest of chapter 11, the great "faith chapter," speaks not of saving faith, but of faith in the life of the believer and of the rewards which come from a life of faith: **"And without faith it is impossible to please *Him*, for he who comes to God must believe that He is, and *that* He is a rewarder of those who [diligently] seek Him"** (11:6). I have already noted the cases of Peter and John the Baptizer as believers with saving faith whose assurance was undoubtedly at least temporarily weak. And as Eaton has emphasized, both Arminians and extreme Calvinists, whose salvation is not questioned, had and still have a problem with assurance of future salvation. There are many factors which weaken the assurance of true believers, foremost among which is sin, especially besetting sins. Ignorance of God's promises and doctrinal confusion also contribute to weak assurance. From John's disillusionment in prison we can see how negative circumstances can undermine a believer's assurance. John had expected the Lord to immediately inaugurate His kingdom, and it wasn't happening. Many believers' assurance is unsettled by life's various calamities.

God's purpose is that all believers should quickly come into full assurance (*plērophoria*) as did the Thessalonians (1:5). Unfortunately the force of this Greek word is not well represented in all our translations: "**the full assurance of understanding**" (Col. 2:2); "**the full assurance of hope**" (Heb. 6:11); and "**the full assurance of faith**" (Heb. 10:22). My major concern in this chapter is the doctrinal confusion which undermines assurance.

Why have so many struggled with assurance?

In reference to this doctrinal confusion, it was a shocking experience recently to read Archibald Alexander's *Thoughts on Religious Experience*. It consists mostly of case studies of conversion experiences from the 18th and early 19th centuries as collected by this early Princeton theologian. What was so distressing was to read page after page of people's struggles to come into the assurance of eternal life, with so little clear biblical guidance given them, it would seem. It reminded me of the long struggle John Wesley, although an Anglican priest, had to come to salvation and its assurance.[G] Alexander's anecdotes are probably from among his own Reformed tradition, but he makes some reference to the "Enthusiasts," presumably the Arminians. I don't get the impression from his narratives that either had much of a clue as to how to lead a distressed soul into the assurance of salvation. If many of the Reformed preachers of the day had as little assurance as Asahel Nettleton, it is no wonder that lay people were in confusion. As I discussed this book with the pastor (of Calvinistic convictions) who had lent it to me, we wondered together whether it was D. L. Moody (1837-1899)[H] here in America and C. H. Spurgeon (1834-1892) in Great Britain who set evangelicalism on a better course in the last half of the 19th century. Since that conversation, my research has indicated that it was Andrew Fuller (1754-1815) in Great Britain and the New Divinity theologians of the Second Great Awakening who laid the foundation for Spurgeon and Moody (cf. chapter 17).

Alexander went back in his narrative to the about 300 conversions in Northampton under the ministry of Jonathan Edwards in the 1740s. Edwards narrated how, although almost everyone in town was anxious concerning eternity, some came into assurance rather quickly, but others found it ten times more difficult to come into assurance, going through soul agony for extended periods of time. Edwards struggled to balance the implications of his Calvinism with what he perceived was the inquirers' necessity to acknowledge their own total depravity, against the need to actively help them to come to faith. On the one hand, irresistible grace implies that they should "lie at God's feet and *wait His time.*" On the other hand, he saw their extended agonies and developed the idea of preparationism, which were steps sinners could take to prepare themselves for regeneration. This prompted Roy Aldrich's observation that Edwards had a very lively spiritual corpse, after all.

Alexander's anecdotes from the early 19th century don't seem to get any better. There seemed to be such ignorance of the simple gospel message and such a prevalence of legalism in both the Calvinistic and Arminian camps that so many people struggled for years to come into assurance of salvation. Alexander gives a general impression: "It is a lamentable fact that in this land of churches and of Bibles there are many who know little more

---

G. Wesley was heavily into aceticism, mysticism, legalism, & Platonic philosophy in the many years of his struggle. See Robert G. Tuttle, Jr., *John Wesley: His Life and Theology*, pp. 143-155.

H. "No man has ever done more for the Christian cause in his generation. He had recruited for Christ many who were leaders in the next." (J. C. Pollock in Woodbridge, ed. *Great Leaders of the Christian Church*).

of the doctrines of Christianity that the pagans themselves."[33] I suspect that Fuller, the New Divinity preachers, Moody and Spurgeon may really be key figures in moving Protestants back to a more simple gospel presentation.

FALSE PRESUPPOSITIONS OF DENIAL

As I try to understand why both Arminians and extreme Calvinists struggle to accept the simplicity of eternal security and its concomitant assurance of ultimate salvation, I have discerned a number of presuppositions in their thinking which hinder taking Scripture testimony at face value. Some of these will be dealt with in detail in the next chapter.

All warnings imply loss of salvation.

It is a presumption on the part of so many that whenever they come to a warning in Scripture, that warning is a threat of loss of salvation unless the believer toes the line. This is not only gratuitous, but totally false. Yes, there are warnings to inquirers and counterfeit believers of ultimate condemnation unless they come to Christ in reality. There are also warnings to believers relating to consequences temporally and at the judgment seat of Christ for spiritual failure, but not of loss of salvation.

All exhortations imply that failure results in loss of salvation.

Many also presume that failure to respond properly to all exhortations in Scripture may result in loss of salvation. Exhortations are addressed to a diversity of spiritual conditions, none of which imply that believers who fail to respond may condition their ultimate salvation.

All conditional statements imply continued performance is a necessary condition for ultimate salvation.

Guy Duty is representative of this type of thinking as he traces all the conditional statements from Genesis to Revelation and argues that, even after our conversion, continuance in meeting all those conditions is necessary for ultimate salvation. I agree with Duty that salvation is conditional, but with just one condition at one point in time. Once we have been born again through "**repentance toward God and faith in our Lord Jesus Christ**" (Acts 20:21), all other conditions relate to temporal blessing or rewards at the judgment seat of Christ. Salvation is conditional in its initiation, but unconditional in its continuation since God has promised to preserve true believers.

---

1. John F. Strombeck, *Shall Never Perish* (Moline, IL: Strombeck Agency, 1936). Excellent books have been written by Charles Stanley, R. T. Kendall, Robert Gromacki, Joseph Dillow, Harry Ironside, and others.

2. R. T. Kendall, *Once Saved, Always Saved*, p. 19. Kendall's definition was helpful in formulating mine.

3. Vance has documented Mathison, Gerstner, Pink, Rose, Hoekema, and Talbot and Crampton as Calvinists who object to these terms, p. 562; quotation, p. 566.

4. Murray, *Redemption*, p.155.

5. Pink, *Eternal Security*, p. 28.

6. Charles Hodge, *Commentary on First Corinthians*, p. 169.

7. Calvin, *Institutes*, 3.2; R. C. Sproul, *Chosen by God*, 165-66; A. A. Hodge, *Outlines of Theology*, pp. 544-5.

8. B. Tyler and A. A. Bennett, *The Life and Labours of Asahel Nettleton* (Banner of Truth, repr. 1975), p. 30, quoted by Michael Eaton, *No Condemnation: A New Theology of Assurance*, p. 3.

9. Michael Eaton, *No Condemnation: A New Theology of Assurance* (Downers Grove: IVP, 1995), p. 6.

10. Ibid, p. 20..

11. Robert L. Shank, *Life in the Son* (Springfield, MO: Westcott, 1960), 2nd ed., p. 219, 293.

12. Eaton, pp. 3-4, 9.

13. Shank, p. 18.

14. Charles Stanley, *Eternal Security: Can You Be Sure?* pp. 9-11.

15. Vance, pp. 569-573.

16. Stanley, pp. 4-5, 16-22.

17. Earl D. Radmacher, *Salvation* (Nashville: Word, 2000), pp. 188-9.

18. I. Howard Marshall, *Kept by the Power of God*, 3rd ed. (Carlisle, UK: Paternoster, 1995), p. 278; Robert H. Stein, *Difficult Passages in the New Testament* (GR: Baker, 1990), p. 353.

19. Strombeck, p. 7.

20. Kendall, p. 61-2.

21. This is true of the Evangelical Mission Covenant Church, in which I was raised. Indeed, this has been a significant issue at North Park Theological Seminary over the years. A former colleague of mine, who graduated from a Nazarene seminary, informed me that the Church of the Nazarene does not have any tradition or affirmation of inerrancy. More recently I visited the campus of a college of the Church of God (Anderson, IN), and found no such commitment to inerrancy by their faculty.

22. Stanley, p. 11.

23. Chafter, *ST*, 6:316.

24. Charles C. Ryrie, *Basic Theology*, pp. 362-5; There are other more explicit passages I cannot locate at present.

25. Abbott-Smith, p. 5.

26. Robert G. Tuttle, Jr., *John Wesley: His Life and Theology* (GR: Zondervan, 1978), pp. 143-55.

27. S. Lewis Johnson, Jr. made this statement in tapes on "Particular Redemption" made at Believer's Chapel in Dallas, TX, to which I do not have present access or information. Alan C. Clifford published his dissertation as *Atonement and Justification* (Oxford: Clarendon, 1990).

28. Harry Ironside dealt very effectively with this error from his early years in the Salvation Army and scripture: *Holiness: the False and the True* (Neptune, NJ: Loizeaux Bros).

29. Kendall, pp. 149-50.

30. Robert Shank, *Life in the Son*, 2nd ed. (Springfield, MO: Westcott, 1960), pp. 75-82. Stanley, in referencing Shank's argument, oversimplifies it, p. 73. Shank, however, limits his discussion to a few contexts in John.

31. Zane Hodges, *Absolutely Free*, p. 105.

32. John Calvin, *Institutes of the Christian Religion*, 3.2.11-12; *Commentary*, Lk. 17:13.

33. Archibald Alexander (1772-1851), *Thoughts on Religious Experience*, pp. 67-71, 28.

Through this process two things became apparent. First, I was guilty of ignoring the context of many verses I quoted to defend my view. As I began digging deeper into the events and discussion surrounding these passage, they took on a different meaning. Second, I discovered through my study that the concept of salvation through faith alone cannot be reconciled with the belief that one can forfeit his or her salvation. If I must do or not do something to keep from losing my salvation, salvation would be by faith *and works*. -Charles Stanley

15

IS THE BIBLE AMBIGUOUS ABOUT ETERNAL SECURITY?

I remember a seminary chapel message fifty years ago by Wally Howard, a well-known youth evangelist, who suggested that eternal security was a paradoxical truth, that although the Bible's promises of eternal security are clear, the warnings and our experiences of true Christians losing their salvation must be held in tension. As discussed in the last chapter, there are both Calvinistic and Arminian scholars who would agree. I suggest that this is most definitely an unnecessary concession to contradiction in the biblical text since both sides of the tension cannot possibly be true. Either God's promises of security are true and all true Christians are eternally secure, or else all of the promises have some unstated conditions implied, as Arminians believe. If we believe in the inerrancy and integrity of Scripture, there cannot be any real contradiction. Those who hold to such a serious paradoxical tension must explain how this is logically possible, and they cannot.

In this chapter, I will show that those passages which are perceived by many as 'problem passages' are in total harmony with the promises of security, if each passage is approached inductively in its own integrity and context, and if the faulty presuppositions mentioned in the previous chapter are expunged. We must start with two foundational parables which show that the Lord Jesus distinguished more types of human response to the word of God than many interpreters are willing to admit. Then I will take the book of Hebrews as a paradigm of how best to deal with the problem. Most of the 'problem passages' relate to examples, exhortations, and warnings to true believers relating to the quality of their Christian lives and the consequences, both temporally and for rewards at the judgment seat of Christ. Another group of 'problem passages' relate to superficial professors of faith, counterfeit Christians, or in a most acute form, those who apostatize into rank denial and corruption of the faith. A few passages are best understood as relating to corporate Israel or the Church. Finally, some in the Olivet Discourse are prophetic of the unique Great Tribulation and thus are dispensationally misunderstood by many.

TWO FOUNDATIONAL PARABLES

Parables are notoriously difficult to interpret. Many Christians suppose that the Lord Jesus used parables uniformly throughout His ministry to simplify and clarify the truth. But when we examine His first use of parables in Matthew 13, we find the apostles questioning why He was beginning to use parables (13:10). Since this was in the last half of His ministry, the implication is that He had not used parables previously. His answer was that the parables were given to hide the truth from those who were rejecting His person and message: "**Jesus answered them, 'To you it has been granted to know the mysteries of the kingdom of heaven, but to them it has not been granted. . . . Therefore I speak to them in parables; because while seeing they do not see, and while hearing they do not hear, nor do they understand'**" (13:11, 13). I would suggest that through cavalier use of parables many Christians have jumped to conclusions about the truth which the Lord was communicating. We must be extremely careful in the interpretation of parables.

The parable of the sower and the four soils

This parable is foundational, both because it occurs in all three Synoptic Gospels, and because the Lord Himself gave us its interpretation. The first soil is not controversial: it is those who do not respond at all to the gospel. Arminians presume that the second soil refers to believers who have lost their salvation. This is a possible but not necessary interpretation. Let us examine the explanation: "**The one on whom seed was sown on the rocky places, this is the man who hears the word and immediately receives it with joy; <u>yet he has no *firm* root in himself</u>, but is *only* temporary, and when affliction or persecution arises because of the word, immediately he falls away**" (13:20-21). Note that the word of God had not taken root in this individual's heart. There was a thin layer of soil on a rocky pan, which kept any root from developing ("**no root**" 13:6). It is a presumption that this describes a truly saved individual.

On the other hand, the third type of soil is misunderstood by many Calvinists as well: "**And the one on whom seed was sown among the thorns, this is the man who hears the word, and the worry of the world and the deceitfulness of wealth choke the word, and it becomes unfruitful**" (13:22); "**. . . bring no fruit to maturity**" (Lk. 8:14). In this case the plant did grow up and survive ("**. . . and the thorns <u>grew up with it</u>, and**

choked it out" (Lk. 8:7). There may have even been some stunted fruit, which would be useless since it did not mature. For example, a corn stalk may grow a few feet and produce an ear of corn with no edible kernels. Few interpreters have considered the option that this represents the fruitless Christian. Otherwise, if both refer to counterfeits, there would be little difference between soils number two and three. In that case the Lord Jesus would have been illustrating only three kinds of soil in the parable, not the four as He presented it. I am convinced that the Lord intended us to distinguish **four** types of responses, not three. Many will glibly quote Matthew 7:20, "**by their fruits you will know them**," failing to recognize that in that context the Lord is speaking about false prophets, not about ordinary believers. Yes, there are many true Christians who are leading fruitless lives, whether it fits our theology or not.

The fourth category clearly represents the fruitful Christian: "**And the seed in the good soil, these are the ones who have heard the word in an honest and good heart, and hold it fast, and bear fruit with perseverance**" (Lk. 8:15). Those who believe that the only saved people in this parable are those in the fourth category have a serious theological dilemma. If that were true, Christ would seem to be ascribing their salvation to having "**an honest and good heart.**" This would seem to be a problem for the doctrine of total depravity. However, if the Lord is describing the difference between two different categories of believers due to the difference in their mindset and heart attitude, as I hold, there would be no contradiction to doctrine of depravity before conversion. The Lord is explaining why some believers "**bear fruit, thirty, sixty, and a hundredfold,**" while other equally saved people "**bring no fruit to maturity.**" Interpreters who deny the reality of fruitless Christians are not dealing fairly with all Scripture testimony and observation in biblical churches. Paul called them carnal (1 Cor. 3:3), and Christ identified them clearly in the second foundational parable to which we now turn.[A]

The parable of faithful and faithless trustees

If someone objects to the idea of distinguishing two categories of believers in the previous parable, let them consider a badly neglected parable in Luke 12:41-48, after the Lord's parable teaching of readiness for the His return:

> **Peter said, "Lord, are You addressing this parable to us, or to everyone *else* as well?" And the Lord said, "Who then is the faithful and sensible steward, whom his master will put in charge of his servants, to give them their rations at the proper time? Blessed is that slave whom his master finds so doing when he comes. Truly I say to you that he will put him in charge of all**

A. I wonder whether God's eternal decrees consigned all of us to one of these four categories!

> **his possessions. But if that slave says in his heart, 'My master will be a long time in coming,' and begins to beat the slaves, *both* men and women, and to eat and drink and get drunk; the master of that slave will come on a day when he does not expect *him* and at an hour he does not know, and will cut him in pieces, and assign him a place with the unbelievers. And that slave who knew his master's will and did not get ready or act in accord with his will, will receive many lashes, but the one who did not know *it*, and committed deeds worthy of a flogging, will receive but few. From everyone who has been given much, much will be required; and to whom they entrusted much, of him they will ask all the more.**

Notice Peter's great question. We must identify clearly the kinds of people to whom the Lord is referring. There are four in this parable also. Here the fruitful believers come first (12:42-44) and the counterfeits second ("**assign him a place with the unbelievers**" 12:45-6). Thirdly, we have a disobedient believer, who will suffer loss at the judgment seat of Christ (12:47; cf. 1 Cor. 3:15), and the fourth is the carelessly ignorant believer, whose loss will not be as great (12:48). It is absolutely imperative in our interpretation that we accurately identify the answer to Peter's question, and thus carefully distinguish counterfeits from these three categories of believers. This is what we must seek to do in examining all the so-called problem passages.

The most problematic are found in the Epistle to the Hebrews. Although Arminius never did reject eternal security, he did confess a serious problem with the warnings of Hebrews, especially chapter 6. This is the number one passage with which both Calvinists and Arminians struggle. In a decade as Bible answer-man on radio station WFME in the New York metro area, the most frequent question I got was about Hebrews 6. I would suggest that a careful inductive study of these warnings should be a paradigm or model of how to approach the other 'problem passages.'

THE REAL THRUST OF HEBREWS

Certainly a major obstacle to belief in eternal security is the apparent force of the five warnings in the book of Hebrews (2:1-4; 3:12--4:13; 6:1-9; 10:26-39; 12:25-29). Arminians assume that they are all addressed to born-again Christians and declare their ultimate eternal lostness. On the other hand, Calvinists tend to see all five as addressed to counterfeit Christians. These assumptions need to be examined most carefully in the various contexts. I could not resolve the problems of these warnings as long as I assumed that they were all addressed to the same kind of people.

I suggest that the apostle is addressing at least **three different kinds of people** in those Hebrew Christian congregations, the same kinds of people we find attending church today: inquirers who have not yet professed faith, false professing Christians, and genuinely born-again Christians, some of whom have a serious spiritual problem. Each possibility must be considered in each context. We must not force these five warnings into the same mold based upon certain presuppositions. This would be a lapse into a deductive methodology which is based on our theology, rather than using an inductive approach, which must have priority.

In this connection we must also be aware of the apostle's use of the term "people of God." Just as Old Testament Israel was the "people of God" without every individual being a true believer, just so the apostle refers to the "people of God" in a general professing sense. As a matter of fact, there is nothing in the address of the letter which states it was written to churches. It is a message "to Hebrews" pure and simple, whatever their spiritual state. But when he addresses them as "brethren," we must not imply that they are necessarily true believers (cf. Rom. 9:3). The main burden of the author is that every individual in the Hebrew Christian community, whether an interested inquirer, a counterfeit Christian, or a genuine believer, come into a mature Christian life with assured faith as its basis.

He emphasizes the finally revealed reality (1:1-2) that the divine high priest of the new testament (covenant) offered Himself once-for-all on the cross to provide a once-for-all salvation for those who trust Him. To this end he demonstrates that because the Lord Jesus is fully God and fully man (ch. 1 & 2), he is perfectly qualified for a high priestly ministry far superior to the Aaronic priesthood of the obsolete Mosaic covenant (4:14–5:10; 7:1-8:13), which could not finally and perfectly deal with sin and its guilt (9:1–10:18).

Some of the Jews had not personally appropriated this full forgiveness and assurance of faith: inquirers were in danger of drifting away from this message (2:1-4), and counterfeit believers with an evil heart of unbelief were in danger of apostasy by reverting back to Judaism (3:6–4:12; 10:26-31), thus refusing this final message of God from heaven (12:14-29). Some of the true believers were spiritually immature because of a poor grasp on these central truths of the new testament message of grace (5:11–6:2). Indeed, a few were so confused by the overhang of Judaism's multiple sacrifices that they thought that whenever they backslid into sin they needed to get saved all over again, and thus they were making a shambles of the Christian life and were not only fruitless, but in danger of premature physical death as the most extreme form of spiritual discipline (6:3-8). Thus the writer's many exhortations and warnings are targeted to individuals with diverse spiritual needs and problems, just as we find in any congregation today.

Far from undermining the eternal security of the true believer in Christ, this epistle is freighted with many words, expressions, and concepts designed to affirm this truth in no uncertain terms, as well as to encourage all in the community to personally enter into its full reality. The great irony of these misinterpretations of Hebrews is that this book has more words like confidence/boldness (*parresian* 4t), assurance (*plerophoria 2t, hupostaseos 4t*), confirmation (*bebaios* 8t), access (3t), promises (*epangelia* 17t), hope

(6t), etc. than any other Bible book. The apostle not only speaks of Christ's eternal redemption (9:12), eternal salvation (5:9), eternal inheritance (9:15), but furthermore that He saves us forever (7:25), and that we are perfected for all time (10:14). In sum, He was sacrificed once-for-all that we might be saved once-for-all (7:25-27; 9:12, 25-6; 10:10-14).

He not only wants all to enter into full assurance of hope (6:11) and faith (10:22), but speaks much of the true believer having confidence (3:6; 4:16;10:19, 35), boldness, and perfect access into the very throne of God through a new and living way (7:19; 10:19-22). He speaks of God's promises being confirmed by an oath (6:16), a new testament contract sealed by Christ's blood (9:15-22), providing salvation rest (4:1-11), a strong encouragement (6:18), a hope which is the anchor of the soul because of the unchangeableness of His purpose (6:19), the guarantee of a superior covenant (7:22), and the faithfulness of God to His promises (6:13-17). He caps it off by saying that faith is the assurance of things hoped for (11:1). The believer can live in the reality of a totally cleansed conscience (9:14; 10:22) and a firm hope (3:6; 6:11, 18, 19; 7:19; 10:23).

There is no tension between the absoluteness of these positive statements and the severity of his warnings, if they are rightly understood. Most commentators, both Calvinistic and Arminian, have struggled with a perceived tension by trying to force all of the warnings into the same mold, that is, addressed to the same kind of people. This is the root of their problems in understanding this wonderful epistle aright. **The apostle wrote it to give assurance, not to undermine it.** Let us examine each of these warnings in its own integrity.

The first exhortation/warning (2:1-3)

"For this reason we must pay much closer attention to what we have heard, so that we do not drift away *from it*. For if the word spoken through angels proved unalterable, and every transgression and disobedience received a just penalty, how will we escape if we neglect so great a salvation?" When we examine the first warning (2:1-3), we find no hint that the people addressed have even made a profession of faith. They have heard the message (2:1) and were in danger of drifting away from it and neglecting it. How many times do we see inquirers get very interested and then drift away? This warning reminds them that this message is the word of the living God (1:1f), spoken by the divine Messiah (he had just proved His deity in chapter 1), and confirmed through the apostles by signs and wonders. *Thus there is no escape for inquirers who neglect the message.* This exhortation is relevant to counterfeit Christians as well.

The second exhortation/warning (3:12–4:13)

"Take care, brethren, that there not be in any one of you an evil, unbelieving heart that falls away from the living God. But encourage

[exhort] one another day after day, as long as it is *still* called "Today," so that none of you will be hardened by the deceitfulness of sin. For we have become partakers of Christ, if we hold fast the beginning of our assurance firm until the end" (3:12-14).

The context of the second warning is quite different, so please study the force of the whole context. In 3:1-6 we have a comparison between Moses' house (the nation Israel) and Christ's house (the professing church). In 3:7-11 the apostle quotes extensively from Psalm 95, which deals with the problem of the unregenerate Israelites in the wilderness, who, the Lord said, "**did not know My ways**" (3:10). Against this background he warns his readers, "**lest there should be in any one of you an evil, unbelieving heart, in falling away from the living God**" (3:12). Note that he nowhere implies that they had faith now and might lose it. He is concerned about those who *now* have evil, unbelieving hearts. Although he calls them "brethren" since they are professing believers, just as with the Hebrews of 1500 years earlier, this does not guarantee that they are true believers. In 3:14 we see a conditional statement describing true believers set in contrast to the preceding: "**For we have become partakers of Christ, if we hold fast the beginning of our assurance firm until the end, . . .**" [B] Indeed, in 4:1-2 he is concerned lest having the promises of salvation any of them should come short in the sense that the word of God "**was not united by faith in those who heard.**" Then positively he affirms, "**For we who have believed do enter that [salvation] rest**" (4:3). Then he speaks about the Sabbath rest available for the "people of God" (4:9-10), and that those who rest from their self-effort do enter this salvation rest.[C] Just as Paul warns about the Pharisees who were trying to establish their own righteousness by their works in Romans 9:30--10:4, just so, the author of Hebrews makes a similar point. Note that he uses an aorist tense in 4:3 to refer to their believing, which normally would be punctiliar or non-durative action, as contrasted to the continued action of a present tense. It is those who have already come to true faith who do enter salvation rest. *So the exhortation is for those who have not yet really exercised saving faith to do so and enter in* (4:11). Thus careful examination of the passage in its context makes it clear that it is a warning to counterfeit Christians to make sure of the genuineness of their faith.

The third exhortation/warning (5:11–6:9)

The **context** of the third warning is different yet from the previous two

---

B. Dillow argues that "partakers" is not a reference to all true believers, but only to those who overcome (*Reign*, pp. 585-605). However, I take it that true believers do persevere in faith, whatever the state of their obedience may be at the end.

C. Although many interpreters understand "rest" to be a reference to higher level of victorious Christian living, there are many reasons to understand it to be the rest of salvation. The context is all salvation-oriented. The passage itself contains much salvation language, but no clear reference to victorious living. The writer fears that the Hebrews will fail to enter that salvation-rest. Space does not permit elaboration.

and extremely significant, so don't read on without turning to the passage in your own Bible. The section from 5:11–6:2 is an exhortation to genuine Christians who are spiritually immature to go beyond elementary gospel teaching and "**press on to maturity**" (6:1). Although they had been Christians for some time, they were still babes in Christ and needed to grow to maturity (5:11-14). However, there was a hindrance to their spiritual growth. This is seen in the negative qualifier of 6:2, the danger of trying to relay the foundation: "**. . . not laying again a foundation . . .**" A key interpretive element is to decide the identity of this foundation which some were trying to relay. Many interpreters have identified it as Judaism. *However, when we examine the six characteristics of the foundation, it becomes clear that the foundation is salvation. Their problem was that they were not making progress in the Christian life because they were trying to lay salvation's foundation all over again (which is impossible).* One cannot successfully build the superstructure if one is absorbed in relaying the foundation. A Christian who thinks he needs to get saved repeatedly will not make progress in growth.

The foundation (6:1-2). Note the description of the foundation: 1) "**Repentance from dead works**": Notice that it does not say that the foundation *is* dead works, but rather *repentance from* dead works. This means that when they heard the gospel they repented from the dead works of the apostate and obsolete Jewish religion and trusted Christ.[D] 2) "**Faith toward God**": Before their conversion to Christ, most of the Hebrew Christians did not have a genuine faith in the true God. It was only through Christ that they came to know and believe in the true God. Throughout Israel's history it seems clear that a majority of Jews did not have saving faith. When Christ came, Israel was at a spiritual low point of demonism and unbelief. The Apostle Peter confirms this in writing to Hebrew Christians: "**who through Him are believers in God, who raised Him from the dead, and gave Him glory, so that your faith and hope are in God**" (1 Pet. 1:21). It was through *faith in Christ* that they first became believers in God. 3) "**of instruction about baptisms**": The word baptism is in the plural since there are two baptisms in the New Testament, water and Spirit-baptism. Both relate to salvation truth. Spirit-baptism is coincident with salvation (1 Cor. 12:13), and water baptism is to follow immediately as a public witness of salvation. 4) "**laying on of hands**": To the Jews the laying on of hands meant identification. They identified with the sacrifice upon which they laid their hands. In the early church new converts had hands laid upon them to show identification with the church (Acts 8:12-17; 9:17; 19:1-7). This aspect of the foundation was also salvation-related. Hands were also laid upon the first missionaries to show identification with them in their ministry (Acts 13:1-3),

D. Not that the Old Testament set out a religion of dead works, but that the Judaism of the first century had become an apostate, externalistic, and legalistic religion of the traditions of men (Mt. 15; 23).

but this is not the issue here. 5) "**the resurrection of the dead**": This is also foundational to the Christian and not to the Israelite. The Sadducees rejected resurrection outright (Acts 23:8), and other Jews did not accept the most important resurrection—that of Jesus Christ. Although resurrection is seen in the Old Testament, it was not a significant part of the Judaism of New Testament times, nor of today. 6) "**eternal judgment**": Although eternal judgment is also seen in the Old Testament, Jews then, just like Jews today, focus on this present life, not on judgment and eternal life.[1] Obviously eternal judgment relates to salvation truth. Thus we conclude that the foundation is not Judaism but salvation in Christ. The issue here is for true believers to build their lives upon that foundation.

Some not permitted to go on to maturity (6:3-5). The apostle then makes the devastating statement: **And this we shall do <u>if</u> God permits**" (6:3). This implies that God does not permit some to go on to maturity (probably if they keep trying to relay salvation's foundation). Then he switches from the first person 'we' to the third person 'they'. Clearly we have here a smaller category of people with a serious problem. When we think about it, we can identify a number of cases where God did not allow believers to go on to maturity. Ananias and Sapphira are a dramatic example of this (Acts 5:1-11). We must not assume that they went to hell because of their sin. We can find other examples in Paul's letters of believers who were dying prematurely because of certain sins (1 Cor. 11:28-34; 5:1-8; Rom. 8:13 Gk), and John speaks about "a sin unto death" (1 Jn. 5:15-17). We must not assume he is referring to eternal death. The analogy of faith from these other references would lead us to understand physical death as the issue.

Were these people really believers? Although Calvinists tend to see them as counterfeit Christians, one commentator has said that, if the apostle had wanted to describe genuine believers, he could hardly have found a clearer way to do it (Heb. 6:4-5). They have "**once for all been enlightened**" (6:4). This is the same word (*photizein*) which the apostle Paul used in 2 Cor. 4:3-6 to describe the enlightenment of the gospel as it breaks through the Satanic blindness of the perishing: God "**is the One who has shone in our hearts to give the light of the knowledge of the glory of God in the face of Christ**." He also used it in Eph. 1:18 and the same symbolism in Eph. 5:8-11. Then they are said to "**have tasted of the heavenly gift**" and "**have tasted the good word of God and the powers of the age to come**." The force of the word 'taste' (*geuomai*) is obviously crucial here. The force of the English is much weaker than the Greek. It frequently means 'to eat' or metaphorically, 'to experience.' This becomes clear by comparing its closest usage in 2:9: "**. . . Jesus, because of the suffering of death crowned with glory and honor, that by the grace of God He might taste (*geuo*) death for everyone.**" Christ actually experienced death to the full, and He himself actually used this verb four times of tasting death. He didn't merely sample its flavor, as the English word might imply. A millennium earlier David wrote,

"O taste and see that the Lord is good" (Ps. 34:8), and Peter also used it in this sense (1 Pet. 2:3). Thus these people had really experienced the heavenly gift, the good word of God, and the powers of the coming age. They were also said to **"have been made partakers (*metochoi*) of the Holy Spirit"**. Although some commentators try to weaken the force of this word, its contextual usage will not allow that. It is used five times in Hebrews, three of which (beside 6:4) are used in a vital and deep sense. Just turning back to 3:14 we find, **"For we have become partakers (*metochoi*) of Christ, if we hold fast the beginning of our assurance firm until the end."** This is clearly referring to true believers; so also must 6:4 be. They were really saved! Robert Stein has put it well: "With regard to Hebrews 6:4-6 it is clear that any one of the six characteristics found in these verses can be interpreted as referring to someone who is not a true Christian, but when all six are grouped together, such an interpretation becomes much more difficult, if not impossible."[2] But what happened to these genuine Christians to justify such strong language as we find in 6:6?

Falling away (6:6). They are said to have **"fallen away"** (6:6). We should first notice that there is no 'if' in the Greek, but that *parapesontas* is a participle, as were the preceding verbs. Does this mean a fall from salvation? We must examine the meaning of the word *parapipto.* This is made somewhat more difficult because it does not occur anywhere else in the New Testament (a *hapax legomenon*). Etymologically speaking, it is a compound of the preposition *para* ('beside') and the common verb *pipto* ('to fall'). Williams translated it, "fallen by the wayside" with the footnote, "Picture of runners falling beside the race track."[3] We can also discern its meaning in another way. Although we cannot see its usage in other contexts, we can look at the noun derived from this verb. *Paraptoma* occurs a score of times in the New Testament and means, "Ethically, a *misdeed, trespass* (LXX)"[4] Thus it is the picture of a Christian falling into a trespass. There is no hint of any falling away from salvation in the meaning of this word. Indeed, this picture and the rest of the sentence clarify the whole meaning of the passage. Upon falling into a sin, these Christians thought they had to go back to the starting line of the race and get saved all over again. When runners in a race stumble and fall by the wayside, they would never think of going back to the starting line, but just get back on the track and keep running. Donald Barnhouse used to say that when you stumble in the Christian life, the place to get back on the track is by dealing with the sin that caused the stumbling, alluding to 1 John 1:9. The probability is that these Hebrew Christians had never heard of 1 John 1:9, mainly because it hadn't yet been written. So the apostle warns them that **"it is impossible to renew them [all over again] to [the first, salvation] repentance (6:1), since [by so doing] they again crucify to themselves the Son of God and put Him to open shame"** (6:6). By trying to get saved all over again, they were in effect recrucifying Christ. Notice the emphasis upon repetition in the passage as contrasted with the once-for-all (*hapax*) death of Christ: **"not laying again (*palin*) a foundation"** (6:1); **"renew them again unto repentance, crucifying again"** (*palin anakainizein eis metanoian anastaurountas*, 6:6).

Why would a Christian want to get saved repeatedly? These Hebrew Christians came out of a background in which every time they sinned they had to bring a new sacrifice. From childhood the principle of multiple sacrifices had been etched on their minds. Now as Christians they didn't understand that Christ died once-for-all that we might be saved once-for-all. Since this is the major theme of the next four chapters, it is imperative to examine the following passages: 7:25-27; 9:11-12; 9:24-28; 10:1-4; 10:10-14. For example:

> **Therefore He is able also to save forever those who draw near to God through Him, since He always lives to make intercession for them. For it was fitting for us to have such a high priest, holy, innocent, undefiled, separated from sinners and exalted above the heavens; who does not need daily, like those high priests, to offer up sacrifices, first for His own sins and then for the sins of the people, because this He did once for all when He offered up Himself. . . . But when Christ appeared as a high priest of the good things to come, He entered through the greater and more perfect tabernacle, not made with hands, that is to say, not of this creation; and not through the blood of goats and calves, but through His own blood, He entered the holy place once for all, having obtained eternal redemption. . . . By this will we have been sanctified through the offering of the body of Jesus Christ once for all. And every priest stands daily ministering and offering time after time the same sacrifices, which can never take away sins; but He, having offered one sacrifice for sins for all time, sat down at the right hand of God, . . . For by one offering He has perfected for all time those who are sanctified.**

What could be clearer than that *Jesus Christ died once for all that we might be saved once for all*? This was the glorious truth which these Jewish believers had not really grasped, failure of which was the cause of their lack of spiritual growth. They thought that we must be born again, and again, and again. But the new birth is a once-for-all work of the Holy Spirit of God.

Actually, the main point that the apostle affirms here is that it is impossible to get saved all over again. The inconsistency of the Arminian interpretation has been pointed out by many Calvinistic interpreters. That is, if this is speaking about losing salvation, then Arminians ought never to invite people to be re-saved. Thus this would become a message of absolute despair. Indeed, I have counseled those who thought that they had lost it for good and were in despair. However, when a Christian sins, we are to claim

1 John 1:9 and have our fellowship restored. Loss of salvation cannot be the issue because "**there is therefore now no condemnation for those who are in Christ Jesus**" (Rom. 8:1).

The illustration (6:7-8). Some might object that the illustration of the field does not fit the above interpretation. However, upon closer examination it is most appropriate and harmonious. The ground which yields thorns and thistles is said to be "worthless", "rejected", "disapproved", "disqualified," etc., depending upon which translation you read. The Greek word *adokimos* is the negative of *dokimos* and five other related words, all of which have to do with trial, test, proving, and the result which is approval. Thus *dokimē* is used in this sense in Rom. 5:4; 2 Cor. 2:9; 13:3; Phil. 2:22. *Dokimos* is used in the sense of 'tested', 'accepted', 'approved', in Rom. 14:18; 16:10; 1 Cor. 11:19; 2 Cor. 10:18; 13:7; 2 Tim. 2:15; and Jas. 1:12. Thus the essential idea of the negative is 'disapproval'.

This is also the case in 1 Corinthians 9:27 where the apostle Paul expresses concern lest through indiscipline he should become "disapproved" after having preached to others. Certainly the KJV is wrong in translating "castaway" there, and the NIV is far superior: "disqualified". The issue is not salvation, but approval at the judgment seat of Christ when our service for the Lord will be judged.

The references to "cursed" and "burned" trouble some people. However, there is a vast difference between actually being cursed and being "**close to being cursed.**" One can be close to being killed in an accident and yet be 100 percent alive. Actually, the apostle Paul used the same symbolism in 1 Corinthians 3:11-15, when he wrote that the works of those who build with wood, hay, or straw will be burned up at the day of Christ. "**If any man's work is burned up, he shall suffer loss, but he himself shall be saved, yet so as through fire**." M. R. DeHaan understood this as the sin unto death, that is premature physical death, which will be discussed shortly.

The reassurance (6:9). How do the apostle's words of reassurance to the majority of the Hebrew Christians relate to the preceding? The apostle was convinced of better things about most of them, and that they manifest the appropriate accompaniments of salvation, even though he is giving such a strong warning. He goes on in subsequent verses to describe those accompaniments. However, those who have been living a roller coaster Christian life by trying to get saved repeatedly will inevitably not manifest the "**things that accompany salvation**." Let's face it, not all genuine Christians manifest the appropriate fruit, the accompaniments.[5]

Thus, we conclude that this warning is to truly born-again Hebrew Christians who, because of their upbringing in a religion of multiple sacrifices for sins, thought that whenever they fell into sin they had to get saved all over again. Although there are no Hebrew Christians in exactly the same circumstance today, there are many professing Christians who fall into the same erroneous way of thinking. Roman Catholics do not know that Jesus Christ died once for all that we might be saved once for all. Roman Catholics and Arminian Christians do not believe that we are saved once for all. Sometimes children do not understand that we only need to accept Christ once. Some Christians with besetting sins keep post-dating their time of conversion to put their last fall into sin before their conversion (in their own thinking). Thus, in effect, they are trying to get saved over and over again. This is not some theory. It is sad to report that I had a close friend and colleague who suddenly died young. I alone knew the serious deceit problem in his life, and upon further investigation I concluded that his story fit the pattern described above. But the Lord Jesus died once for all that we might be saved once for all![6]

The fourth exhortation/warning (10:26-39)

This context is much like that of the second warning. Here the apostle is concerned about those who have forsaken meeting with other Christians, and the apostle is concerned lest they be counterfeit Christians. As in chapter 3, he uses the "we" to refer to all professing Hebrew Christians. He is here concerned lest they return to Judaism with its colorful pageantry, and begin again to offer up animal sacrifices for sin. Thus he warns that if they turn away from the sacrifice of Christ, **"there no longer remains a sacrifice for sin**" (10:26). In the plan of God the sacrifice of Christ has replaced the whole Mosaic system.

Much has been made by Arminian interpreters of the use of *epignosis* (knowledge) as if the prepositional prefix requires the meaning 'full knowledge'. However, usage rather than etymology is much more significant in determining meaning of words, and the usage does not bear this out. It is used 20 times in the New Testament and sometimes does mean 'full knowledge', but a number of times it is equivalent to *gnosis* (Rom. 1:28; 1 Tim. 2:4; 2 Tim 2:25; 3:7; 2 Pet. 2:20 - the last passage is exactly parallel). Arndt and Gingrich list "knowledge, recognition" as the meaning. The verb *epiginosko* from which this noun is derived is important. While Arndt and Gingrich list many instances in which "1. with the preposition making its influence felt--a. know exactly, completely, through and through" they also list, "2. with no emphasis on the prep., essentially = *ginoskein*...a. know...b. learn, find out. . . c. notice, perceive, learn of. . . d. understand, know. . . e. learn to know."[7] Thus these professing Christians could well have had a merely intellectual knowledge of Christ and the gospel without being genuinely born again.

The use of the word 'sanctified' in 10:29 also seems to contradict this. However, it must be remembered what the root meaning of the word *hagiazo* is (and of the Hebrew *qodesh*): 'to set apart.' Inanimate objects were 'set apart' for God's use. Clearly Paul uses the word of the unbelieving spouse and children of a mixed marriage in 1 Corinthians 7:15. Professing

Christians were 'set apart' at their baptism, whether they were genuinely saved or not.

I found the expression **"His people"** (10:30) puzzling for many years until I realized that the apostle, in paralleling Israel and the church and quoting from the Old Testament passages about Israel, is referring to God's professing people corporately, without specifying whether they have genuine faith or not. Thus he can speak in most severe language of the fate of those of "His people" who come under the judgment of God: **"a certain terrifying expectation of judgment and the fury of a fire which will consume the adversaries"** (10:27); **"vengeance"** (10:30); **"it is a terrifying thing to fall into the hands of the living God"** (10:31). These people are clearly going to Hell.

The language of 10:29 also is much too severe to be describing a backslidden Christian: **"trampled under foot the Son of God, and has regarded as unclean the blood of the covenant by which he was sanctified, and has insulted the Spirit of grace."** Thus the evidence is all consistent that the apostle has counterfeit Christians in mind in this passage.

The fifth exhortation/warning (12:25-29)

In this passage the address shifts back to that of the first warning, inquirers into the faith. There is nothing in the context which implies that the addressees had even made a profession of faith. And the language of the warning is reminiscent of the first one. The danger was of refusing Him who is speaking from heaven, of turning away from Him. This is the picture of those who had been hearing the message, but were now in danger of turning away from it. Of course, it is equally relevant to counterfeit Christians within the church. Thus there is nothing in the last warning which in any way conditions the eternal security of the truly born-again believer in Jesus Christ.

Conclusion

Thus we conclude that there are at least three different spiritual conditions represented in these passages, conditions which are common in churches today. We have seen that of the five warnings only the third (5:11--6:9) is referring to truly born-again Christians, and it in no way compromises their eternal security in Christ. Indeed, the book of Hebrews was intended to give assurance to true believers, while unsettling counterfeit Christians and complacent inquirers.

ISSUES RELATING TO TRUE BELIEVERS

Hebrews 6 is not the only exhortation and warning to true believers which is unrelated to any notion of loss of salvation. There are also a number of examples of true believers who had a serious problem or concern. I have already alluded to Peter's denial of His Lord and John the Baptizer's doubt and disillusionment in prison. The apostle Paul had a serious concern expressed in 1 Corinthians 9:24-27: "**. . . but I discipline my body and make it my slave, so that, after I have preached to others, I myself will not be disqualified**" (9:27). Arminians have fastened on the rendering 'castaway' in the KJV.[8] Here we have the word *adokimos*, which I discussed in reference to Hebrews 6:8, confirming the accuracy of the NAS and the NIV, "disqualified." Neither Arminians nor Calvinist Charles Hodge (cf. pp. 295-6) have exercised due diligence in their word studies in thinking that Paul had a lifelong struggle for his salvation.

John Mark and Demas were both drop-out missionaries (Acts 13:13; 2 Tim. 4:10), but we have no basis for assuming that they lost their salvation because of missionary failure. Indeed, the Holy Spirit afterward used John Mark to be the author of our second Gospel. John Mark was a 'kosher Jerusalem boy' who found the idolatrous pagan culture of Perga too much for him. I suspect he was the first missionary to experience culture shock. It seems that Demas backslid badly, but there is no hint that he lost his salvation because of this. The world in many different ways presses into the life of far too many true Christians today as well.

Early in the history of the church, Luke gave us a striking account of extreme divine discipline, the story of Ananias and Sapphira (Acts 5:1-11). It is gratuitous to assume that they were believers who lost their salvation, just because they were struck dead physically. There was some evidence of dedication to Christ in giving part of their estate to the church. But Peter confronted them for lying to the Holy Spirit. There is an Old Testament precedent in the death of Uzzah, who reached out his hand to steady the ark of the covenant and was struck dead (2 Sam. 6:6-8). It is just as presumptuous to assume that Uzzah lost his salvation. Neither the chronicler nor Luke have provided an explanation so we must go to the epistles.

There are two parallels in the church of Corinth. Paul exhorted the church to excommunicate an immoral man in extreme language: "***I have decided* to deliver such a one to Satan for the destruction of his flesh, so that his spirit may be saved in the day of the Lord Jesus**" (1 Cor. 5:5). The most straightforward understanding is that 'flesh' refers to his body and thus, like Ananias and Sapphira, to premature physical death. The only significant alternate exegesis is to take the 'flesh' as his sin nature. This is hardly cogent, since it is hard to visualize Satan helping a Christian deal with his sin nature. Paul probably intended more than mere excommunication from the church by the use of such strong language, but it is clear that he did not question the genuineness of his ultimate salvation. In the second epistle it seems that the man had repented, and Paul encouraged the church to restore and forgive him (2 Cor. 2:5-11).[E]

Paul's second concern relates to those who were desecrating the observance of the Lord's table, concerning whom he wrote: "**For he who**

E. Those who deny the existence of carnal Christians, not only fly in the face of 1 Cor. 3:1-3, but also 5:5 and 11:27ff.

eats and drinks, eats and drinks judgment to himself if he does not judge the body rightly. For this reason many among you are weak and sick, and a number sleep. . . . But when we are judged, we are disciplined by the Lord so that we will not be condemned along with the world" (1 Cor. 11:29-32). I hardly need to argue that sleep is a euphemism for physical death or that Paul is not concerned about their ultimate salvation since he is quite explicit. Both of these passages help us to understand the Ananias and Sapphira account.

Somewhat later Paul made an enigmatic statement in his letter to the Romans: "**So then, brethren, we are under obligation, not to the flesh, to live according to the flesh—for if you are living according to the flesh, you must die; but if by the Spirit you are putting to death the deeds of the body, you will live**" (8:12-13). Arminians conclude from this that carnal Christians, who are living according to the flesh, will lose their salvation.[9] There are a number of problems with this. I have just given two examples from Corinth of Christians who were living according to the flesh, concerning whom Paul does not deny their ultimate salvation, even though premature physical death was an issue. There is also a serious translational problem here. Most translations do not take into account the word *mellein* in 8:13, for which Arndt and Gingrich list its primary meaning when used with a present infinitive as: "*be about to, be on the point of*."[10] Rotherham translates it, "ye are about to die;" Moffatt, "you are on the road to death;" Weymouth, "If you so live you are on your way to death;" F. F. Bruce, "you are bound to die;" Knox, "you are marked out for death." I have long puzzled as to why the major translations virtually ignore the word, although I grant that *mellein* is frequently used as a periphrasis for the future tense of the verb. Why not render it according to its first listed usage since it avoids both a serious interpretive and a theological problem? Thus I am suggesting that here also Paul is referring to premature physical death as God's extreme discipline of some carnal Christians. They were in imminent danger of physical death.

The apostle John gave us the last clarification: "**If anyone sees his brother commit a sin that does not lead to death, he should pray and God will give him life. I refer to those whose sin does not lead to death. There is a sin that leads to death. I am not saying that he should pray about that. All wrongdoing is sin, and there is sin that does not lead to death**" (1 Jn. 5:16-17, NIV). The main issue here is whether the death is physical or spiritual. Arminians opt for spiritual and eternal death, but then they have the problem of finding a scriptural stipulation as to which are the venial and which are the mortal sins. There is no such biblical legislation. On the other hand, the clear pattern seen in Corinth should inform our interpretation of this passage. John also is concerned about premature physical death. To this we must also add the force of Hebrews 6:7-8. None of this conditions the eternal security of the true believer.

Exhortations and warnings to true Christians

Discipleship exhortations. In chapter 13 I sought to show that the Lord's three main discipleship exhortation contexts are not related to the salvation issue, but rather to worthy discipleship (Mt. 10:34-39; 16:24-28=Lk. 9:22-27; Lk. 14:25ff). Both Arminians and extreme Calvinists have failed to observe the contexts and the word 'daily' in Luke 9:23 and have assumed that we must deny self and take up our cross in order to be saved: "**If anyone wishes to come after Me, he must deny himself and take up his cross daily and follow Me**." If Christ was talking about a literal cross and execution, then the only way to be sure of salvation would be to become a martyr. This sounds dangerously close to the view of most Muslims today. Even more objectionable is the fact that it would end up being a human-performance salvation, in total contradiction to a by-grace-alone salvation.

The unforgiving slave. The parable of the unforgiving slave, which the Lord told in response to Peter's question about how many times to forgive our brother, poses some difficulty of interpretation (Mt. 18:21-35). Since Christ spoke about the lord of the slave handing him "**over to the torturers until he should repay all that was owed him**," many think that it speaks about believers losing salvation and going to hell. However, with parables we must be careful not to make what we might call too literal a transfer of detail in the parable to real life. Just as in the parable of Luke 12 where the lashes are probably representative of pain, so in this parable the reference to the torturers probably speaks of pain in the life of the unforgiving Christian. The fact is that the unforgiving Christian really tortures himself emotionally and spiritually and will face anguish at the judgment seat of Christ. Salvation is not the issue here.

The fruit-bearing vine. The Lord's extended metaphor of the fruit-bearing branches of the vine in the Upper Room Discourse (Jn. 15:1-16) needs careful examination in this light. Verses 2 and 6 are taken by Arminians to show loss of salvation by Christians, represented as branches in Christ, the true vine: "**Every branch in Me that does not bear fruit, He takes away; and every *branch* that bears fruit, He prunes it so that it may bear more fruit**" (15:2). Here there are two pressing questions: What does the Lord mean by "every branch in Me" and "He takes away?" Dillow has an excellent discussion of "in Me" in which he suggests that, in Christ's usage in the Gospel of John, it refers to a close personal relationship. "A review of the sixteen usages in John seem to suggest, that when He used this phrase, the Lord referred to a life of fellowship, a unity of purpose rather than organic connection. It should be noted that this is somewhat different from Paul's usage. While Paul did use the phrase 'in Christ' in this way, he often used it in a forensic (legal) sense referring to our position in Christ or to our organic membership in His body (e.g., 1 Cor. 12:13). John never does this."[11] He then shows how this is especially clear in John 10:38; 14:20, 30; 16:33; and 17:21-

23. Thus when the Lord spoke about abiding (remaining) in Him (15:4, 5, 6, 7, 8, 9), he meant that believers must remain in fellowship with Him in order to bear fruit. This helps us to understand that salvation (or loss of it) is not the issue in this passage, but our Lord's concern is that we maintain continual fellowship with Him so that we can be fruit-bearing Christians (15:2, 4, 5, 8, 16). Christians who are backslidden and out of fellowship with Him cannot bear fruit. On the other hand, just remaining in union with Christ positionally does not guarantee fruitfulness. As we saw in the parable of the sower, there are genuine Christians who don't bear fruit to maturity. Also in our paradigmatic passage in Hebrews 6, the ultimate issue was the fruitfulness of true believers (6:7-8).

Restorative husbandry. This understanding of the whole passage is confirmed by a closer examination of the verb *airein* used in the clause, **"He takes away."** Although 'take away' is a possible rendering since it is listed third in our two best lexicons, both Abbott-Smith and Arndt/Gingrich list the **first meaning** as, "*lift up, take up, pick up*"; "*to raise, take up, lift or draw up.*"[12] Those who are familiar with grapevine husbandry tell us that it is a regular practice to lift up a marginal branch or a fallen vine off the ground with meticulous care to allow it to heal. Dillow references R. K. Harrison and his own experience in Austria in this regard. Harrison further shows that *airein* has this meaning in 10 out of 24 usages in the Gospel of John.[13] Translators should give this first consideration and thus the NIV rendering "cuts off" is probably unjustified. Does it not make sense that first the Lord should speak of His restorative dealings with His branches before mentioning His more stringent dealings? This leaves the Arminian interpretation on shaky ground.

Stringent husbandry. However, our Arminian friends then hasten to verse 6: **"If anyone does not abide in Me, he is thrown away as a branch and dries up; and they gather them, and cast them into the fire and they are burned."** If the issue in the passage relates to remaining (abiding) in fellowship with Christ, as we are arguing, then we need to understand the symbolism in that light since this is an extended metaphor. Calvinists like Chafer have long suggested that this is a case of extreme divine discipline of the backslidden believer. It is not God who throws the branches into the fire, but men.[14] The passage seems to parallel Hebrews 6:8 and 1 Corinthians 3:11-15. A classic illustration from recent memory is Jim Bakker of the infamous PTL. Since I had viewed very little of this TV program, when the scandal erupted I assumed that Jim was a counterfeit Christian. But when I read his book, *I Was Wrong*, I gradually changed my opinion. In prison as he re-examined the tragic events, he realized that his life and ministry had been all wrong. The world trashed his life and testimony big-time. He was cast out as a branch and thrown into the fire of severe chastisement. I presume his theology was Arminian, but there was no mention of loss of salvation, even though he lost everything else.[15] An illustration proves nothing, but it does help us to understand the severity of Christ's language.

Fruitless faith. Some may question my inclusion of discussion of James 2:15-26 under this heading relating to true believers, but I believe that the broader context of the whole book demands this. James is writing about the behavioral problems of true Christians, and we can search this epistle from beginning to end and not find any other context in which he exhorts or warns counterfeits or apostates.

First off, I should hope my readers have already grasped the harmonization of this passage with Paul's teaching of justification by faith alone (Rom. 4). The subject of the verb *dikaioein* (to declare righteous) is different in these two writers' epistles. Paul is writing about God declaring the sinner righteous by faith alone; James is concerned about the world declaring Christians to be righteous by the good works they can see. Paul is using the word 'works' in a different sense from James. He is referring to law-works by which self-righteous people are trying to get into God's kingdom; James is referring to those good works which are the fruits of genuine faith in the life of the believer. The issue for James is showing our faith to a skeptical world by our good works. Even the allusions to Abraham are different. Paul has in mind Abraham's being justified in God's sight at the beginning of his life of faith; James alludes to his triumphal sacrifice on Mount Moriah over forty years later as a proof of his faith.

James is concerned about the fruitless believer referred to in some of the other passages we have just examined. Certainly James is not saying that a believer who can't back up his faith with good works will go to hell. This again would be a denial of the grace-gift salvation Paul affirms. James talks about the uselessness of such a Christian life (2:20), it is lifeless. Unless we are willing to intrude human performance into our ultimate salvation, there is nothing here which contradicts eternal security.

Ensuring election. The apostle Peter gave an exhortation which is the solution to the assurance problems of both Calvinists and Arminians, as identified by Michael Eaton. It is the solution to extreme Calvinists' hesitancy to affirm that we can be sure that we are among the elect, and to the Arminians notion that human performance can affect our ultimate salvation. **"Therefore, brethren, be all the more diligent to make certain about His calling and choosing you; for as long as you practice these things, you will never stumble; for in this way the entrance into the eternal kingdom of our Lord and Savior Jesus Christ will be abundantly supplied to you"** (2 Pet. 1:10-11). Peter's first concern is that every believer enter into assured certainty about ultimate salvation. Then there are two consequences of diligence in gaining an assured Christian life: we shall never stumble in our walk, and our entrance into the kingdom will be abundant. His reference to 'stumbling' is not a reference to losing salvation, but to those falls and stumbles common to all Christians. He is not referring to mere entrance into the kingdom, which is by God's grace, but to *abundant entrance* as we are rewarded for faithfulness at the judgment seat of Christ.

Arminian Guy Duty understands Peter to be speaking about the objective fact of election being conditioned by our diligence in the ways described. He has not considered the possibility that Peter is alluding to the subjective experiential assurance that is so foundational to a stable Christian life.[16] However, this is the option which is most consonant with the context and the rest of biblical truth. I might be tempted to agree with Duty in order to strengthen my case for conditional election in chapter 8, but honest consideration of the context does not allow this. On the other hand, extreme Calvinists need to recognize that Peter's exhortation implies that Christians can and must do what they can to gain full assurance of present salvation. There is absolutely no need for them to live in uncertainty as to whether or not they are among the 'elect'. Asahel Nettleton was not just a historical oddity. There are many in Reformed churches today who do not believe it is possible to know whether one is among the elect or not.[17]

Working out salvation. It should be superfluous to discuss Paul's exhortation in Philippians 2:12-13, but some Arminians get hung up on it: "**So then, my beloved, just as you have always obeyed, not as in my presence only, but now much more in my absence, work out your salvation with fear and trembling; for it is God who is at work in you, both to will and to work for *His* good pleasure**." Obviously Paul is not exhorting them to work for their salvation. They were already saved, and Paul had great confidence in the Christians at Philippi, for there was neither heresy nor immorality among them, and the whole epistle is exceedingly positive. He is addressing "my beloved," who have always obeyed. The reference to "fear and trembling" is not a reference to hell, but to our life and service being examined at the judgment seat of Christ. Notice how Paul connects the reverential fear of the Lord with that judgment seat in 2 Corinthians 5:10-11. Yes, God was at work in the lives of those Philippian believers so there was no question about their ultimate salvation.

The overcomers. Christ's letters to the seven churches of Asia in Revelation 2 and 3 are not so straightforward to interpret. Years ago I was impressed by Lehman Strauss's argument that all true believers are the 'overcomers' whom the Lord is addressing.[18] But Dillow's arguments for identifying the overcomers as faithful Christians who will be especially rewarded in the kingdom has caused me to change my mind. Arminians take it that these are the true Christians who persevere to the end, the rest losing salvation.[19] Extreme Calvinists see them as the true Christians who persevere to the end, the rest being counterfeits. Dillow argues that the issue is not salvation but promises of reward for faithful believers.[20] Again, we must not argue from a theological position, but seek to examine these letters in their own integrity and context. Although I agree with Dillow, this is a broader issue than I have space to develop here. I will simply take up the 'problem verses.'

Warnings to Asia's churches. In the letter to the church in Ephesus the Lord threatens to remove their lampstand unless they repent (2:6). This must be understood corporately of the church, not a threat to individuals. In the Smyrna letter the Lord Jesus promises those who remain faithful under persecution "**a crown of life**" (2:10). I have previously shown the importance of the distinction between salvation and rewards, and the various crowns promised to the faithful are an important part of these promises. In the letter to the Pergamum church Christ's promise to judge the Nicolaitans within the church does not relate to eternal security (2:14-16). Whatever the exact nature of the Nicolaitan apostasy, such apostates were never true Christians. But the Lord has a charge against the corporate church.

The warnings to the corrupt Thyatira church are quite severe, especially to the Jezebel figure and her children. The Old Testament antecedent of Jezebel would not indicate a true believer (2:20-23). The promises to the faithful remnant in that church (2:24-28) are rewards over and above salvation, as Dillow argues extensively. He shows very convincingly that entrance into the kingdom and reigning with Christ in the kingdom are distinct, the latter a privilege given only to the faithful Christian.[21] Likewise to the Sardis church, it is only the worthy believers, who have not soiled their garments, who are promised reward (3:4-5). Special comment is necessary regarding the promise "**I will not erase his name from the book of life**" (3:5). It is a basic law of logic, often violated by interpreters, that the converse of a true statement may or may not be true (not necessarily true or false, thus undetermined). Christ affirms that he will not erase their names, with no implication that he does or does not erase anybody else's name. Any such implication is to put something into Christ's words which He did not say. Believers in the more faithful Philadelphia church are exhorted not to lose their crown, with no reference to loss of salvation. Lastly, to the true believers in the apostate Laodicea the risen Lord speaks of church discipline and rewards (3:19-21). A warning comes to the church corporately that since it nauseates Him, Christ will spit this church out of His mouth (3:16), with no reference to individual true believers.

I have tried to touch on the key passages of exhortation to true believers, but now must move on to distinct warnings to counterfeits and apostates.

ISSUES RELATING TO APOSTATES AND COUNTERFEITS

While examining the question of whether a true Christian can lose salvation, it is imperative to factor in the reality of counterfeits in the church into the discussion. Counterfeits then become apostates to the faith. We are not at all talking about the eternal security of professing Christians. Judas Iscariot is the classic example of a plausible counterfeit. None of the apostles suspected that Judas was a counterfeit even after Christ's overt identification of him by giving him the choice morsel of food (Jn. 13:23-30). The Lord knew all along that he was a counterfeit—not that he was a true believer who lost his salvation (Jn. 6:64-71; 12:4; 13:2). Judas was one of a number of counterfeit disciples to whom the Lord alluded: "**'But there are some of you who do not believe.' For Jesus knew from the beginning who they were who did not believe, and who it was that would betray Him**" (6:64). I had noted in an earlier chapter that it is in reference to them that He said, "**For this reason I have said to you, that no one can come to Me unless it has granted him from the Father**" (6:65). Judas and those professing disciples had been bathed in the greatest light of God's truth that any humans had ever experienced, and yet were rejecting Christ. He knew that their minds and hearts were so set against the truth, that even His personal ministry could not penetrate. It is not that God reprobated them from eternity past, nor that they had been saved and lost it.

Another less clear example is that of Simon the sorcerer (Acts 8:9-24). Even though Luke says that he believed and was baptized, we find a number of other contexts where *pisteuein* (to believe) is used of something less than saving faith (Jn. 2:23-24; 8:31). Apparently Simon had not really repented of his sorcery and magic and was wanting to use the Holy Spirit for his own ends, perhaps supposing that the Holy Spirit was an impersonal force.[F] Peter discerned him to be an unregenerate person, for he said, "**'May your silver <u>perish with you</u>, because you thought you could obtain the gift of God with money! You have <u>no part</u> or portion in this matter, for <u>your heart is not right</u> before God. Therefore repent of this wickedness of yours, and pray the Lord that, if possible, the intention of your heart may be forgiven you. For I see that you are in the gall of bitterness and in the bondage of iniquity'**" (Acts 8:20-23). Peter understood that he would perish, that he had no part in the work of the Spirit, and that forgiveness was improbable. If Simon had only stumbled, Peter could not have said any of this. Even worse was his response to Peter's exhortation to repent by asking Peter to pray for him. This sounds pious, but *he himself* needed to pray a prayer of repentance, which he apparently did not. So Luke gave us another paradigm of a counterfeit believer.

An egregious contemporary example is Chuck Templeton, who was an early associate and friend of Billy Graham. In 1949 Templeton began to share his intellectual doubts about the veracity of the Bible with Graham, causing him to go through a spiritual crisis. They moved in opposite directions, Graham to full commitment to the Bible as the word of God, and

---

F. Since the Holy Spirit is a person, He can use us, but it is unthinkable that we can use Him. This is the error of many today who abuse the gifts of the Holy Spirit.

then to his worldwide evangelistic ministry, while Templeton moved into skepticism, claiming that Graham had committed intellectual suicide. In that timeframe I heard Templeton preach on Absalom, a very eloquent and dramatic sermon. I don't remember any gospel in it or even what the main point was. Today he is a forthright atheist in Toronto. Lee Strobel interviewed him in connection with Templeton's book, *Farewell to God: My Reasons for Rejecting the Christian Faith* and Strobel's own response, *The Case for Faith.*[22] Reading the account of his conversion and having heard just one sermon, I have no difficulty taking him to have been a counterfeit who became an apostate. John was clear in his analysis of anti-Christian apostates: **"They went out from us, but they were not *really* of us; for if they had been of us, they would have remained with us; but *they went out*, so that it would be shown that they all are not of us"** (1 Jn. 2:19).

Exhortations and warnings to counterfeits and apostates

I have already discussed the warnings of Hebrews, four of which are addressed to inquirers into the faith and/or counterfeit, superficial professors of faith. Just because those Jews were addressed as 'brethren' and the 'people of God,' this does not imply individual, personal faith any more than it did for national Israel before Pentecost. But there are a number of other exhortations and warnings addressed to counterfeits, which we must examine.

Corinthian syncretism. At several points in his epistles, the apostle Paul expressed doubts about the genuineness of some of the people in churches he had founded. Hearing that some of the Corinthians Christians were influenced by Greek philosophy to question the bodily resurrection, he wrote: **"Now I make known to you, brethren, the gospel which I preached to you, which also you received, in which also you stand, by which also you are saved, if you hold fast the word which I preached to you, <u>unless you believed in vain</u>"** (1 Cor. 15:1-2). By the use of the conditional 'if' Paul is entertaining some doubt about the genuineness of the salvation of some because he saw the bodily resurrection of Christ as an essential part of the gospel, as expounded in the rest of the chapter and later in Romans 10:9: **"that if you confess with your mouth Jesus *as* Lord, and believe in your heart that God raised Him from the dead, you will be saved."**

Guy Duty wrote a book arguing that all of the conditional statements in Scripture show that salvation is conditional until consummated in glory.[23] I agree that the initial reception of salvation is conditional, but disagree in that in the ongoing Christian life it is no longer conditional. The new birth, the sealing and earnest of the Spirit, and God's keeping power have put the believer in a radically different position from the inquirer or counterfeit professor of faith. Thus Paul is not expressing doubt that some of the true Corinthian Christians would persevere, but rather that some of them were not genuine. This is presumably the same concern he expressed later in 2

Corinthians 13:5: "**Test yourselves *to see* if you are in the faith; examine yourselves! Or do you not recognize this about yourselves, that Jesus Christ is in you—unless indeed you fail the test?**" He is concerned about their present state, not some future contingency.

Galatian legalism. This may also be his concern for the some of the Galatian Christians who had reverted back to "**the weak and worthless elemental things**" of legalism: "**I fear for you, that perhaps I have labored over you in vain**" (Gal. 4:11). That a favorite Arminian prooftext has been pulled out of context is clear when we see that concern in 5:4 as well: "**You have been severed from Christ, you who are seeking to be justified by law; you have fallen from grace.**" Here he is addressing hard-core legalists who are not just trying to be sanctified by legalism, but justified as well. By putting themselves outside of the pale of God's saving grace, any connection they might have had with Christ was nullified. Allow me to turn the tables at this point. Those who deny eternal security are intruding human performance into salvation and are in danger of being described in Paul's terminology as "fallen from grace." Paul is not talking about those whose faith is wavering or who are being overcome by sins, but rather about legalists, and this is a subtle form of legalism. I do not imply, by any means, that all Arminians are fallen from grace, but I am only seeking to develop Paul's implications.

During the decade I was privileged to be a Bible answerman on a radio call-in program, we were inundated with questions on the sabbath by sabbatarian legalists, who would even lie to push their point of view on the air. During extended conversations with many, both on the air and off, I became convinced that a great many of them didn't have a clue about salvation by grace through faith in Christ alone. They were trusting in their sabbatarianism and indeed were "fallen from grace."

Colossian heresy. The Colossian church was threatened by an incipient Gnostic heresy and Paul hastens to include such a conditional warning early in his epistle: "**. . . yet He has now reconciled you in His fleshly body through death, in order to present you before Him holy and blameless and beyond reproach— <u>if indeed you continue in the faith</u> firmly established and steadfast, and not moved away from the hope of the gospel that you have heard**" (Col. 1:22-23a). It seems that some of those in the church in Colossae were falling prey to a denial of the incarnation, so after reminding them that the Lord had a fully human body which actually died to provide salvation, he warns them not to move away from this essential salvation truth. Although he does not clarify the spiritual status of those who were in danger of moving away from the hope of the gospel, the most likely candidates would be the counterfeits. It is an unjustified assumption of the Arminians that a true Christian could do so.

Prophetic warnings. Paul's warning to the Ephesian elders was given in a similar vein, but as a prediction: **"I know that after my departure savage wolves will come in among you, not sparing the flock; and from among your own selves men will arise, speaking perverse things, to draw away the disciples after them"** (Acts 2:29-30). Although the context does not clarify the spiritual state of these false teachers before their apostasy, the Lord Jesus had clarified this years earlier. After using similar language in the Sermon on the Mount to describe the false prophets (Mt. 7:15-21), the Lord explained: **"Many will say to Me on that day, 'Lord, Lord, did we not prophesy in Your name, and in your name cast out demons, and in Your name perform many miracles?' And then I will declare to them, 'I never knew you; depart from Me, you who practice lawlessness'"** (7:22-23). The Lord will not say, "I knew you, but you departed from Me;" He said, **"I never knew you."** They were never true believers! This is undoubtedly true of other prophecies of end time apostates in 1 Timothy 4:1-3 and 2 Peter 2:1-22, where Peter's concluding words are confirmatory: **"It has happened to them according to the true proverb, 'a dog returns to its own vomit,' and, 'A sow, after washing, *returns* to wallowing in the mire'"** (2:22). Peter does not say that sheep can regress into becoming dogs or pigs.

As I write this section I am struck for the first time with the fact that all these passages focus upon professing Christians who depart into heresy, false teaching, and denial of the gospel. None of them speak about true Christians losing salvation because they lose their faith or are overwhelmed with sins. There are no such passages to which Arminians can point us! Yet these are the usual Arminian scenarios as to how true Christians can lose their salvation.

Issues Relating to Corporate Israel or the Church

One of the pitfalls Arminians fall into is individualizing a passage intended to refer to a corporate entity, such as the nation Israel or the Church. The parable of the demon-possessed man (Mt. 12:43-45) is additionally difficult because it is a parable, as I have already noted. Even if it refers to an individual, it really says nothing about eternal security since exorcizing a demon is not necessarily to gain salvation. But the context shows that it is an analogy of the nation Israel. In the exile the demon of idolatry was exorcized only to have Phariseeism, Sadduceeism, and other corrupt teachings come into the nation. The use of the word *genea* in 12:39 & 45, when correctly translated as 'race, stock, or nation' makes the national analogy clear (cf. p. 24). Christ's contrasting Israel with Gentiles in 12:41-42 confirms this.

Paul's extended metaphor of the branches of the olive tree in Romans 11:17-24 is more relevant to the issue. If he had individuals in mind, it might be helpful to the Arminian cause. However, as I have shown in chapter 3, Romans 9–11 is a section which deals with the dispensational transition of God's dealings with the nation Israel to His dealings with the corporate Church. Is God just in His dealings with national Israel? Paul's main point is that God was fair in cutting off the natural branches from the olive tree of blessing and in grafting in the Gentiles. Similarly God can be fair in grafting in the natural branches of Israel again. None of this implies that individual Jewish or Gentile Christians have been, or ever will be cut off. This passage has nothing to do with eternal security.

Similarly when we come to the letters to the seven churches of Revelation 2–3 we must understand that some expressions are to the whole church. This is especially relevant for the letter to Laodicea (3:14-22). Warner Salman's beautiful painting of Christ knocking at the heart's door notwithstanding, this church is so apostate that Christ is knocking at the door of the church to gain entrance and to have fellowship with individuals in the church. Thus when He says in 3:16, "**I will spit you out of My mouth**," He is not referring to individuals but to the church corporately. This is a church which nauseates the Lord Jesus! Christ would never spit a true believer out of His mouth (Jn. 6:37).

Passages Pulled out of Dispensational Context

The issue of dispensational context arises mostly in the Olivet Discourse. As a dispensationalist, I find Christ's prophetic discourse has a very Jewish tone, which He connected with the unique, future great tribulation period before He returns to earth to reign. I believe this help us to understand Matthew 24:13 and the parables of the ten virgins and the talents as not contradicting the teaching of eternal security. However, since many of my readers may not be dispensationalists, I will address the issue from a broader perspective.

In any case, all would have to recognize the importance of context here in this prophetic sermon of the end times connected to a unique great tribulation period (24:21) and the glorious return of Christ to earth (24:29-31). Throughout the passage the Lord is talking about such difficult times that physical survival is tenuous (vv. 9, 16-20, 28). Thus when He said: "**But the one who endures to the end, he will be saved**" (24:13), it must be considered whether he is referring to physical deliverance or to spiritual salvation since it is well known that *sozein* frequently refers to physical deliverance. In any case this could not refer to the hundreds of millions of Christians who have already died before the return of Christ since the 'end' He refers to is the end of the great tribulation and the return of Christ to earth. Thus if one takes Christ's teaching at all literally (and we must), this verse says nothing about the eternal security of most Christians in past centuries. Then why should end-time believers' eternal security be more jeopardized than that of believers throughout the ages just because the times will be perilous?

Even though I would prefer to focus on the unique great tribulation context of the parable of the ten virgins (25:1-13), let us put that aside and examine the parable itself. First off we note that all were virgins, none prostitutes, or for that matter none even married. They all had oil. It doesn't sound like these were counterfeit believers or apostates, does it? The only problem was that some did not have the foresight to bring extra oil. Arminians assume here that oil is a symbol of the Holy Spirit, and that they lost the Holy Spirit and eternal life. But these are all gratuitous assumptions. When we think back to the foundational parable of the faithful and unfaithful trustees in Luke 12, we remember that the third and fourth type of slaves were believers who were punished for failing to be ready for the Master's return. Some of the virgins had the same problem, lack of preparedness for the Lord's return. Yes, they were excluded from the wedding feast, but it is an assumption that this means exclusion from the kingdom itself. Dillow makes a major case for the idea that while all true believers will be in the kingdom, only faithful ones will receive rewards, such as symbolized in this parable as a wedding feast. It is highly irresponsible to build one's theological system upon the interpretation of very difficult parables set in a unique end-time context.

The same can be said for the parable of the talents. (Mt. 25:14-30). The main point is the rewards Christ will give to his slaves. There are three categories of slaves (servants) distinguished here. The first two are rewarded for faithfulness when the Master returns. The third was characterized as wicked and lazy and not only did he miss out on reward, but was thrown into outer darkness, where there will be weeping and gnashing of teeth. Dillow argues that the outer darkness outside of the wedding feast is not to be assumed to be hell for unbelievers, but could be a place of temporary anguish during the feast. Many believers will experience extreme anguish at the judgment seat of Christ for their lazy unpreparedness for His return and will be deprived of the rewards which are given to the faithful.[24] Perhaps the severity of Christ's language can be taken as hyperbolic emphasis. But even if Dillow is wrong and the third category represents counterfeits, there is nothing in the parable which says that a true Christian loses eternal life. Parables are indeed difficult!

CONCLUSIONS

I trust I have shown to the reader's satisfaction that the principle of distinguishing different categories of people is vitally important in biblical interpretation, especially of parables. Distinguishing the warning of Hebrews 6 from the other warnings in Hebrews is crucial. This gives us the key for the major distinction of other examples, exhortations, and warnings addressed to true believers related to blessings and rewards, from those addressed to counterfeits and apostates. Not only does the letter to the Hebrews provide a paradigm for approaching other biblical material, but it is loaded with positive language to encourage the true believer to enjoy full assurance based on the finished work of Christ alone. Nothing in these passages has undermined the eternal security of the truly born-again believer. Although in the brief bounds of this chapter I could not discuss all passages of concern to Arminians, I trust I have addressed the most difficult and problematic and given a helpful approach to problem passages.

Note: This chapter is based upon a paper given at the Eastern Section of the Evangelical Theological Society at Lanham, MD in April 1992.

---

1. Jakob Jocz, "Judaism," in Howard F. Vos, *Religions in A Changing World* (Chicago: Moody, 1959), p. 53.
2. Stein, Ibid, p. 353.
3. Charles B. Williams, *The New Testament* (Chicago: Moody Press, 1958), p. 489.
4. G. Abbott-Smith, *A Manual Greek Lexicon of the New Testament* (Edinburgh: T. & T. Clark, 1937), 3rd Ed., p. 342.
5. Many will respond by quoting Christ's words from the Sermon on the Mount, "You will know them by their fruits" (Mt. 7:16). However, it should be noted that this is in the context of a warning about the false prophets, the wolves in sheep's clothing. It has nothing to do with discerning in general who is a saved person.
6. The view expounded above is a minority interpretation, to which I was first introduced 45 years ago by a seminary classmate, the late Dr. Phillip R. Williams, who pointed out to me his observations in the Greek text. Over the years I have developed this approach more rigorously. Of previous commentators I could only find out one who hints in this direction, M. R. DeHaan, who in his commentary refers to the sin unto death. More recently Walter A. Henrichsen, *After the Sacrifice* (Zondervan, 1979), pp. 76-81, took a similar position to mine.
7. Arndt and Gingrich, *A Greek-English Lexicon of the New Testament* pp. 290-1.
8. Guy Duty, *If Ye Continue: A Study of the Conditional Aspects of Salvation*, 1966), pp. 103-8.
9. Ibid, p. 101. Duty refers to Rom. 8:13 only in passing and does not discuss the passage.
10. Arndt and Gingrich, pp. 501-2.
11. Joseph C. Dillow, *The Reign of the Servant Kings* (Miami Springs: Schoettle Pub., 1992), pp. 402-3.
12. Arndt and Gingrich, p. 23-4; Abbott-Smith, p. 13.
13. Dillow, p. 409; R. K. Harrison, "Vine" in *NISBE*, 4:986.
14. Lewis Sperry Chafer, *Systematic Theology*, III:298-300; VII:4.
15. Jim Bakker, *I Was Wrong* (Nashville: Thomas Nelson, 1996).
16. Duty, p. 139.
17. Some years ago a reporter from the Newark Star-Ledger interviewed the leaders of a Dutch Reformed church in Bergen County, NJ, all of whom said that they did not know whether or not they were among the 'elect.' Historically this has been a major problem in the Reformed tradition. D. L. Moody found the problem to be rife in Scotland when he ministered there in the 19th century.
18. Lehman Strauss, *The Book of the Revelation* (Neptune, NJ: Loizeaux Bos., 1964), pp. 107-24.
19. Ibid, pp. 146-56.
20. Dillow, pp. 469-86.
21. Ibid.
22. Charles Templeton, *Farewell to God* (Toronto: McClelland and Stewart, 1996); Lee Strobel, *The Case for Faith* (GR: Zondervan, 2000), pp. 9-23.
23. Duty, *If Ye Continue.*
24. Dillow, pp. 389-96.

My hope is built on nothing less
Than Jesus' blood and righteousness
I dare not trust the sweetest frame,
But wholly lean on Jesus' name.

His oath, His covenant, His blood
Support me in the whelming flood;
When all around my soul gives way
He then is all my hope and stay.

On Christ the solid Rock I stand;
All other ground is sinking sand,

-Edward Mote (1834)

16

GOSPEL PROCLAMATION ON GOD'S TERMS

One of the most misunderstood, misused, abused, neglected, and yet vital portions of Scripture is the dialogue of the Lord Jesus with His apostles as He got them apart at Caesarea Philippi for teaching, as recorded in Matthew 16 and more briefly in the parallel synoptic accounts. Many vital issues arise from this passage since it not only included Peter's divinely revealed confession of the Messiah's deity, but also the first mention of the church and its foundation, the investing of Peter with the keys, the binding and loosing, and the first of a dozen predictions of His passion and resurrection. Not only has Romanism sought to usurp this passage as the basis for its cultic heresy, but Protestants seem in the main to have only dimly grasped its monumental significance. Additionally, a large portion of the commentators seem to have fallen into pedantic sophisms in dealing with the key issues, one of which shows intellectual irresponsibility.

My thesis is that the evidence is one-sided that the Lord Jesus taught that He Himself is the rock upon which the church was to be built, certainly not upon Peter. Furthermore, the symbolism of the gates of Hades refers to the Messiah's victory over death and the church's subsequent offensive attack against Satan's grip on the human race moving on the broad road to eternal death. Peter was commissioned by the giving of the keys to lead the charge against Satan's domain by opening the door of faith to the Jews, the Samaritans, and the Gentiles. He was to do this by proclaiming forgiveness on heaven's terms, not on the legalistic terms of the Pharisees, nor the rationalistic terms of the Sadducees, but only upon God's word which is settled forever in heaven. Lastly, the building of the church was to be based upon His predicted passion, the first of a dozen such predictions until they were fulfilled less than a year later. Perhaps my main contribution will be the investigation of the Aramaic issue and outworking of our Lord's words in salvation history.

CHRIST HIMSELF, THE BEDROCK

The first area of gross misinterpretation by many scholars is the identity of the rock upon which Christ was to build His church: "**But I also say to you that you are Peter, and upon this rock I will build My church; and the gates of Hades will not overpower it**" (Mt. 16:18). This is a case where the hymnologists are correct, and the majority of scholars are egregiously wrong. "On Christ the solid rock I stand, all other ground is sinking sand," "Jesus is the rock of our salvation, His banner over us is love," "Rock of ages cleft for me," etc., we sing. But many of the scholars don't believe it! Although the most popular Protestant view identifies Peter's confession of Messiah's deity or his faith as the rock, many scholars ironically join with Roman Catholics in identifying Peter himself (although without all the Romanist implications and pretensions). Some would use Ephesians 2:20 as a basis for associating all the apostles with Peter as the foundation-rock of the church.

In 1997 I was sharing a series of meetings in Pakistan with a British brethren scholar. The last breakfast before we parted he asked me what I had preached on the previous evening. When I told him, he replied incredulously, "Gordon, you don't really believe that Jesus is the rock, do you?" (as if, how could I be so naive?). He referred to the 'Aramaic problem,' of which I was quite aware. Unfortunately there was no time to respond before I had to leave, but that dialogue forced me to dig deeper into the evidence. I was astonished at what I found.

The Old Testament background

It is unthinkable that we could claim to interpret this passage without researching the Old Testament symbolism of the rock (which few commentators do) and do a word study of the Hebrew and Aramaic words related to this (which *virtually none* of the commentators have done!). The symbolism of God as Israel's rock is pervasive in the Old Testament, starting from the repeated allusions in the song of Moses (Deut. 32), right on through.

Two Hebrew words are mainly used in this connection: צור (*tsur*) is used of God 33 times and in reference to the incident of Moses getting water from the rock, seven times. Brown, Driver, and Briggs lexicon gives this definition: "n.m. rock, cliff—1.a. rocky wall, cliff. . . b. rock with flat surface. . . c. a block of stone, boulder. . . d. rock with specific name. 2.a. fig. of God (33t.) as support and defense of his people. . . b. of a heathen god. . . ."[1] Also we see one reference in Is. 51:1 to Israel as if quarried out of Abraham as the founder of the nation. The second word, סלע (*sela'*) is used six times of God and six times in Numbers 20 of the water from the rock, among others.

There are two other relevant words: אבן (*eben*) is used frequently as stone, or weight. Tregelles-Gesenius gives a helpful general definition: "a stone of any kind, whether rough or polished, very large or very small."[2] The one other word is the one most usually connected to Matthew 16: כף (*kaiph*), which is used only twice, both times in the plural. Brown, Driver, Briggs suggest that it might be a loan word from the Aramaic. Jastrow's Aramaic lexicon suggests that it has the same meaning in Hebrew as in the later Aramaic, "rock, stone, ball." Then he lists some other usages in the Targums and Talmud: pearls, jewels, hail-stones, rocks (corals), precious stones, jewelry, shore, border, etc., which are mostly small detached stones. Its two Old Testament usages in Job 30:6 and Jer. 4:29 are consistent with this in indicating the reference to a plurality of detached stones.[3] This is exceedingly important to our understanding of the Messiah's usage in Matthew 16.

Most intriguing is a passage in the Aramaic portion of the Old Testament in Daniel 2:34-5, 45. Nebuchadnezzar's dream of the stone cut without hands (*eben*) smashing the successive world kingdoms and becoming a great mountain which filled the earth uses the Aramaic equivalent of צור (*tsur*) to refer to the mountain, that is, טור(*tur*). Jastrow confirms subsequent Aramaic usage with the same meaning.[4] This is supportive of the understanding that both the related Hebrew and Aramaic terms have reference to the solid bedrock, cliff, or mountain in contrast with the words *eben* and *kaiph*, which refer to detached stones of various sizes, but in later usage shifting to smaller stones like jewels, pearls, hailstones, and balance weights.

There is also another possibility in the Aramaic, שועא (*shu'ah)*, which is used in the targums of Proverbs 30:19 and Ez. 26:4 of a smooth, flat bedrock.[5] It is also the most common rendering of πέτρα (*petra)* in the Syriac versions, whereas πέτρος (*petros*) is never rendered by *shu'ah*.[6]

It is also clear that the overwhelming symbolism of rock is portraying God, the two words (*tsur* and *sela'*) being used 39 times of the true God and once of false gods. This establishes a background for understanding the two different Greek words which the Lord Jesus used in Matthew 16. Incredibly, many commentators pontificate about the Aramaic substratum, but I could find no commentary which mentioned the Hebrew/ Aramaic words *tsur/tur* or *shu'ah*, and few noted the dominant symbolism of God as the Rock in the Old Testament.

The passage and its context

The geographical context of this passage is dramatic. Caesarea Philippi is at the headwater of the eastern branch of the Jordan River where the water gushes out of the side of a cliff. So when the Lord Jesus had elicited the confession of His deity from Peter and then said, "**You are Πέτρος (*Petros*), and upon this πέτρα (*petra*) I will build My church**" (Mt. 16:18), the distinction between these two Greek words cannot be overlooked. More significantly the Old Testament symbolism cannot be ignored in this most Jewish Gospel in which we find record of our Jewish Messiah instructing His twelve Jewish apostles to the Jewish nation (Mt. 10:5-8) based upon the Old Testament kingdom promises. Chrys Caragounis's analysis of the context shows that it occurs in a section of text in which the Lord is "increasingly rejected by all strata of Jewish society, and that the confession pericope [passage]has Jesus' person and mission at its center."[7]

My Greek professor, S. Lewis Johnson, Jr., suggested in class that Matthew used the contrast of these two Greek words to indicate what he saw with his eyes, that is, the Lord's gesture with His hand toward His own chest when He uttered the word πέτρα (*petra*), thus indicating that He Himself is the rock upon which the church was to be built. Matthew did not have a camera or a video cam to record that gesture. He was limited to the use of words to communicate the whole picture to us, and this he did using the genius of the Greek language to its fullest advantage. The sequence of ideas is consistent since Peter had just affirmed the Lord Jesus as deity. Therefore, the divine Messiah alone is qualified to be the foundation of the church. What is the contextual and linguistic basis for Johnson's suggestion?

Johnson once told us that Abbott-Smith's lexicon is worth its weight in gold. Over the years I have found this to be true. His definition of πέτρα (*petra*) is quite pointed:

> [in LXX chiefly for סלע, צור;] ***a rock*** **, i.e. a mass of live rock as distinct from πέτρος, a detached stone or boulder**. . . .; of a hollow rock, *a cave*, ... Metaph., Mt 16[18] . . . (emphasis mine)[8]

Arndt and Gingrich's lexicon is helpful:

> 1. *rock*—a. lit., of the rock in which a tomb is hewn . . . *rocky grotto* . . .*rocky ground* . . . . It forms a suitable foundation for the building of a house . . . . The rock at various places in the desert fr. which Moses drew water by striking it . . . . b. in a play on words w. the name Πέτρος; . . .[9]

One can sense the bias in Cullmann's higher critically oriented treatment in Kittel/Friedrich, *TDNT*. At first he admits that πέτρα (*petra*) is "predominantly used in secular Gk. for a large and solid 'rock.' It may denote equally well the individual cliff or a stony and rocky mountain chain" and that πέτρος (*petros*) "is used for more isolated rocks or small stones, including flints and pebbles for slings." He continues: "Since there is such a great difference in content, the emphasis should be noted, **though in practice one cannot differentiate too strictly between πέτρα and πέτρος**; they are often used interchangeably." (emphasis mine)[10] He only documents interchangeability in the older classical Greek, however, especially since *petros* is never used in the canonical Septuagint. He correctly notes that πέτρα (*petra*) is a rendering of *tsur* and *sela'*, while *eben* is almost always rendered as λίθος (*lithos*). He then obscures this data in a seriously misleading footnote and in subsequent discussion.[A] There is a real question whether that touted interchangeability was perpetuated beyond the classical period since he gives no evidence for it. Then he comments on the usage in our passage:

> The obvious pun which has made its way into the Gk. text as well suggests a material identity between πέτρα and Πέτρος, the more so as **it is impossible to differentiate strictly** between the meanings of the two words. On the other hand, only the **fairly assured Aramaic original** of the saying enables us to assert with confidence the formal and material identity between πέτρα and Πέτρος: πέτρα = כיפא= Πέτρος. Elsewhere in the NT the individual Christian is never called πέτρα, though he is λίθος in the spiritual building, the body of Christ (1 Pt. 2:5). Rightly understood, Christ alone is πέτρα. (emphasis mine)[11]

Cullman goes on to press his irrational denial of the distinction without explaining why it is so impossible to differentiate, when in fact the Aramaic and Greek usage almost totally makes this differentiation. What is this "fairly assured Aramaic original" to which he refers? He and many others refer to the "obvious pun" which they never explain. Play on words, yes; but pun, no! Would the Messiah at this most critical point in His ministry have made a light pun? Certainly not. Caragounis has shown that a wordplay would not be dependent upon the Greek alone since there are many examples in our literature using two distinct words.[12] Cullman's problem is theological and based on his higher critical view, not linguistic. And yet he goes on to make a statement contradictory to that preceding, that "rightly understood, Christ alone is πέτρα (*petra*)." Lewis Johnson's suggestion makes the distinction totally cogent and defensible by a fair-minded word study.

Some may object to making a difference since the difference is just a matter of gender between the two words. However, as we have already seen, the usage of the two words is in contrast. There is also the principle in the Greek word-building process which Chamberlain emphasized: "The student should learn once and for all that every single letter added to a Greek root adds something to the idea expressed by the root."[13] I believe a

---

A. Cullman's footnote #9 says, "The LXX does not usually have *petra* for *tsur* but replaces the fig. word by terms which give the meaning of the image, . . ." The word "usually" is objectionable because *petra* is by far the most common rendering of *tsur* (at least 32 times), and the interpretive rendering *theos* is second (about 20 times). No other word for stone is significant. On p. 96 he goes on to say, ". . . it follows that *kaipha* embraces both the originally more specific meanings of *petra* and *petros (lithos)*." This claim is not at all borne out by the data.

very strong case can be made for a difference in gender having significant impact upon connotation as well. Actually these are two distinct and different words. In addition we have the Messiah's usage in the Sermon on the Mount (Mt. 7:25) of rock foundation upon which a building can be permanently erected. Here it clearly does not mean stone, or even boulder, but the bedrock.

A grammatic-syntactical consideration. It should be noted well that Matthew used a demonstrative with attributive force with the articular noun πέτρα, thus indicating that He is pointing to something. The construction is: ἐπὶ ταῦτῃ τῇ πέτρᾳ (*epi tautē tē petra*). Wallace gives Matthew 16:18 as an example and a list of parallel passages of the same usage, but does not really explain the significance. However, examination of the parallel usage of the same construction indicates to me that there is a strong emphasis indicated in all: Mk. 1:9; 15:39; Lk. 7:44; Jn. 4:15; Acts 1:11; 1 Cor. 11:25; Tit. 1:13; 2 Pet. 1:18; Jude 4; Rev. 11:10.[14] It comes out only in the translation of Acts 1:11: "This **same** Jesus shall come" (AV, NIV, Amplified). But the context of all the other usages confirm this that the words 'same' or 'very' could well be used in every case to bring out the full meaning. Robertson and Davis explain that the article in the Ionic and Attic originally was a demonstrative pronoun and is common in the New Testament as such, and then they refer to Broadus's statement that the Greek article is a pointer in three ways, and that the most common of these is to distinguish one individual from other individuals.[15] Thus we essentially have here a double demonstrative, that is, an actual demonstrative plus the article which still retains some of that force. So the question is whether the Lord is pointing to Simon Peter to identify him, or whether He is pointing to Himself? This does seem to eliminate the 'confession' explanation. This is confirmed by Blass and DeBrunner, who state that the article with nouns tend to designate persons, while the article is usually lacking with abstract nouns.[16] So *petra* is not to be seen as an abstract noun since it has an article. This point further militates again the common Protestant 'confession' view. Subsequently I will show how the cultural context confirms this. We could well paraphrase, "**You, Simon are a stone; but upon this very bedrock [pointing to Himself] I will build my church**."

The Aramaic question. Some evangelical commentators deny that the Lord Jesus is the Rock,[B] as does Cullmann, based upon the supposed Aramaic original. I say 'supposed' because we have no assurance that the Lord was speaking Aramaic here. Greek was widely spoken and used by

---

B. For example, Don Carson refers to a H. Clavier article in German to support the statement that, ". . . the Aramaic *kaipha*, which underlies the Greek, means "(massive) rock" (cf. H. Clavier, "*Petros kai petra*," *Neutestamentliche Studien*, ed. W. Eltester, pp. 101-3). Unless Jastrow's treatment is grossly inadequate, there is not a scintilla of proof for that statement. D. A. Carson, *The Expositors Bible Commentary*, ed. Frank E. Gaebelein, vol 8 (GR: Zondervan, 1984), pp. 367-8.

first-century Jews along with Aramaic and Latin.[17] However, even if He were speaking Aramaic, the argument is pointless. There is no language on the face of the earth which cannot distinguish between bedrock or a cliff and a detached stone, even if the speaker has to use some adjectives or other device. However, in Aramaic, as in Hebrew, the distinct words were readily at hand. *Kaipha (Cephas)* is the name the Lord Himself gave to Simon and it never refers to a boulder, bedrock, cliff or mountain. It consistently refers to smaller stones. Quite in contrast, *tsur* in Hebrew and its Aramaic equivalent (*tur*) consistently refer to mountains, bedrock, cliffs, etc. and *shu'ah* refers to smooth bedrock. So this objection is patently specious. Remember that we do not have the Aramaic of Matthew, if it ever existed, and after all, it is the Greek autographa which are the inspired word of God.

The analogy of Scripture. Since the apostle Peter was the one being addressed, it is important to ask how Peter understood the Lord's words. In Peter's first witness before the Sanhedrin, he quoted Psalm 118:22 in reference to Christ being the stone which they the builders had rejected and who is the unique way of salvation (Acts 4:11-2). Peter used *lithos* since that is the word used in the Septuagint.

Years later in his first epistle he quoted Isaiah 28:16, Psalm 118, and Isaiah 8:14 in reference to Christ:

> **And coming to Him as to a living stone which has been rejected by men, but is choice and precious in the sight of God, you also as living stones, are being build up as a spiritual house for a holy priesthood, to offer up spiritual sacrifices acceptable to God through Jesus Christ. For *this* is contained in Scripture: "Behold, I lay in Zion a choice stone, a precious cornerstone, and he who believes in Him will not be disappointed." This precious value, then, is for you who believe; but for those who disbelieve, "The stone which the builders rejected, this became the very corner stone," and, "A stone of stumbling and a rock of offense";** (1 Pet. 2:4-8).

Again Peter mostly used λίθος (*lithos*) as in the Septuagint. But notably he used πέτρα σκανδάλου (*petra skandalou*) in the Isaiah 8:14 quote as did the Septuagint in rendering *tsur*. It should be well noted that the first two quotations use the symbolism of Messiah as the foundation cornerstone of the church, the spiritual temple of God. These are Messianic prophecies in their own context, and Peter so confirms this. Although the Isaiah 8:14 symbolism is different, the reference is also clearly Messianic, and significantly Peter quotes the Septuagint rendering of *tsur* as πέτρα (*petra*). I take it that Peter gives us an unambiguous inspired commentary on our Lord's words. In no way did he see himself or his confession as the rock.

Although the apostle Paul was not present at Caesarea Philippi, his words in 1 Corinthians 3:10-15 confirm the symbolism of the divine Messiah Himself as the rock. Although Paul is not referring to the church universal, he makes it clear that the foundation for the Corinthian church, which he laid, is the divine Messiah: "**For no man can lay a foundation other than the one which is laid, which is Jesus Christ.**" He picks up the symbolism again in 10:1-4: "**and all drank the same spiritual drink, for they were drinking from a spiritual rock which followed; and the rock was Christ**"[C] At this point it is important to clarify that Moses did not strike a small stone or even a boulder, but undoubtedly it was a cliff rock face from which the water gushed. This is clear from the usage of the two Hebrew words used there.

Paul contributed one other reference to the discussion. Opposing views depend heavily upon one interpretation of Ephesians 2:20 without recognizing a viable alternative view: "**. . . having been built on the foundation of the apostles and prophets, Christ Jesus Himself being the corner *stone*, . . .**" Those who hold that it was Peter and the apostles would base this idea on a possible interpretation of this verse. However, it involves a grammatically ambiguous genitive: "*tō themeliō tōn apostolōn kai prophētōn.*" It is possibly a genitive of apposition or possibly a subjective genitive.[18] Wallace lists this genitive under the grammatically debatable ones. But since Paul is referring in the context to the building of the church, which is God's temple, upon the foundation, the question logically arises as to who the subject of the action is. A subjective genitive would supply the answer: the apostles and prophets.

In the following context he emphasizes his own unique involvement in that process and that of the other apostles and prophets (Eph. 3:1-10). This is in total harmony with his earlier statement to the Corinthians that he had laid the foundation of their church, and others were building upon it. As we have already noted, he then makes an unambiguous statement of Christ as the foundation (1 Cor. 3:10-11). The presumption is that Paul is consistent in his symbolism. We know that Peter was privileged to lay the foundation of the Jerusalem church. He could not be the foundation and also lay it, unless he were God. Only the divine Messiah could be both the foundation and the builder as well. Contrariwise, Carson argues that mixed symbolism is common in the New Testament, but his examples are not convincing.[D]

C. I have omitted the word 'them' from the NAS since it is not in the Greek. The rock did not follow the Israelites, but rather it followed in the biblical account. cf. J. Sidlow Baxter, *Studies in Problem Texts* (GR: Zondervan, 1960), pp. 27-8.

D. Carson, p. 368. He contrasts Christ as the builder here with Paul's 1 Cor. 3:11 reference to Christ as foundation and then assumes the common exegesis of Eph. 2:20 discussed above and other references to Christ as cornerstone. As we have noted, only a divine Messiah can fill all these roles. In Hebrews 9 Messiah is both high priest and sacrifice. This is not a mixed metaphor, but rather a recognition of the Lord's unique person and work which so transcends the Levitical priesthood. There is no mixed metaphor in Carson's keys allusion since the keys Christ gave to Peter are different from the keys He Himself holds in Rev. 1:18; 3:7. The light of the world tension is clarified by the fact that Christ is the light of the world while He is in the world, but upon his ascension we become lights in the world (Jn. 9:5).

The cultural gap factor. The average western Christian struggles with the question: "If the Lord intended to say that He Himself is the rock, then why did He not come out and say directly, 'I am the Rock'?" Some of the commentators also seem to be hung-up on this. Such a question reveals the cultural gap between us as twentieth-century westerners and the Lord Jesus as a first-century Jew of middle-eastern culture. Perusal of the Synoptic Gospels shows that the Lord Jesus rarely used the first person. He normally referred to Himself in a third person manner with the expression 'the son of man.' Even His question in our passage in the AV ("Whom do men say that I, the Son of man, am?" 16:13) has to be corrected to: **"Who do people say that the Son of Man is?"** (NAS). We can well understand Mark and Luke's use of 'I' as a cultural contextualization of our Lord's words for their Greco-Roman readers, but Matthew probably preserves Christ's actual words.[19]

Most relevant is our Lord's dialogue with the Jerusalem leaders in Matthew 21:41-44. After quoting the Psalm 118:22 passage, He said, **"And he who falls on this stone will be broken to pieces; but on whomever it falls, it will scatter him like dust.**" Note the off-handed third person way in which He refers to Himself. It also becomes clear how Peter got the idea of quoting Psalm 118 in 1 Peter 2. I suspect that contemporary Americans have the most 'up front' culture in human history in that we unabashedly use the big 'I' so frequently. First-century Jews did not. Certainly the Lord Jesus did not. So we should not expect Him to talk like a contemporary American.[E]

There is another cultural consideration relevant to this passage. David Hesselgrave has made a most significant contribution to understanding the nature of this cultural gap by focusing upon the various types of cognitive process in different cultures. One of the cultural categories which he focuses upon is "concrete relational thinkers." He shows how animistic tribal peoples and Chinese culture can be identified with this category, and how much in the Old Testament is compatible with it.[20] We can also see Jewish culture in the Old Testament and the Synoptic Gospels as 'concrete relational thinking.' This is to be contrasted with our own culture in which cognitive process is conceptual and abstract. The common Protestant interpretation, that it is Peter's confession which is the rock, is an excellent example of this abstract, conceptual way of thinking. It is highly unlikely that the Jewish Messiah would be referring to so abstract a concept as a confession by the symbolism of a rock. Remember, this is a culture which did not even have an abstract word for 'sex.' It is always concretized and made relational, i.e., "Adam knew his wife." We Americans couldn't communicate without an abstract word like 'sex.' This interpretation is highly improbable on that basis alone.

E. Having lived eight years in a culture greatly influenced by middle-eastern Arab and Persian cultures has sensitized me to the different cognitive process of various cultures. I continue to come across linguistic and cultural connections with the Aramaic and Hebrew OT.

Was Peter rock-like? One other question must be asked in reference to the views that it was Peter or his confession or faith which is the rock. What was rock-like about Peter? As we have seen, *Kaipha* in the Aramaic does not mean 'rock'. 'Stone' is a much more accurate rendering. He was one of the first living stones to be incorporated into the temple of God. But his character was hardly rock-like. He is the only one of the eleven who denied the Lord overtly, even though the others deserted Him. He failed to initiate the mission to the Samaritans, as commissioned by the Lord in Acts 1:8, and after Phillip's successful initiative Peter and John had to hurry down to Samaria to make it official. God had to use two striking visions to convince him to bridge the cultural gap to the Gentiles (Acts 10), and even then he struggled with the integration of Gentiles into the church (Gal. 2). We have no record of his being involved in fulfilling the last part of the Greatest Commission in pioneer evangelism among the Gentiles. Indeed, Paul's statement in Galatians 2:8-9 indicates that Peter continued to see himself as an apostle to the Jewish nation.

The church fathers. Frankly I have never been overly concerned to try to find a consensus of the church fathers, especially since the records we have today are most probably distorted and fragmentary. Nevertheless, it is of some interest to examine their views. Dr. Lannoy of the Sorbonne in Paris has tabulated that of the seventy-seven most authorized fathers and doctors of the church who have commented on this verse, only seventeen interpret it as of Peter, forty-four see it as Peter's confession (including Justin, Cyril, Hilary, Chrysostom, Ambrose, etc.), and sixteen affirm it as Christ Himself (Athanasius, Jerome, Augustine, etc.).[21] So although there is no agreement, a significant number of major fathers confirm our thesis. It is in no way a modern, Protestant, or obscurantist interpretation, as some claim.[22]

The commentaries. In pursuing an inductive approach to this passage, I have sought to do all of my primary research before checking the view of the commentators. Some interaction at this juncture would be profitable.

A. B. Bruce is representative of those who try to make the rock abstract and conceptual: "Personal in form, the sense of this famous logion can be expressed in abstract terms without reference to Peter's personality."[23] H. L. Ellison is a good example of a more contemporary British scholar who dismisses the Greek wordplay in a cavalier fashion without looking for other Aramaic options: "Once it was grasped that the name bestowed was the Aram. *Kepha* . . . it was clear that the alleged pun had to be abandoned, **for it was impossible in Aram.**" (emphasis mine)[24] Although Robert Gundry concludes that the rock is Christ's teaching, he states:

> Nevertheless, the two Greek words provide a wordplay that is good enough to obviate the need of an Aramaic substratum. They share the same stem. No longer shackled by the need to suppose an Aramaic substratum, we can see that Πέτρος [*Petros*] is not the πέτρα [*petra*]

on which Jesus will build his church.[25]

Carson makes the most detailed attempt to support the 'Peter' view. He rejects P. Lampe's argument that both *kepha* and *petros* originally referred to a small stone, not a rock, in favor of H. Clavier's contrary argument.[26] I have already given the linguistic data which supports Lampe and responded to Carson's main points, which are unconvincing.

BUILDING THE CHURCH

Our Lord's dialogue with His apostles at Caesarea Philippi came almost three years into His ministry and less than a year before His passion. For almost three years, John the Baptizer, the Lord Himself, the twelve apostles, and then the seventy-two (or 70) disciples had been proclaiming the impending Messianic kingdom. However, now that His enemies are set on His death, He announces a radically new program, but related to the old, that is, His *ekklesia*, His assembly. Its uniqueness is signaled by this first reference and the simple future of *oikodomeo*, **"I will build my church (assembly)."** It is not coincidental that this context also contains the first explicit reference to His upcoming passion, the first of a dozen such predictions which come in those few months before their fulfillment: **"From that time Jesus began to show His disciples that He must go to Jerusalem, and suffer many things from the elders and chief priests and scribes, and be killed, and be raised up on the third day"** (Mt. 16:21).[F] There were two veiled symbolic allusions to His passion prior to this, nothing explicit (John 2 & the Jonah allusion). But there could be no *ekklesia* until He should first die and rise to provide the basis for the church. So there is no logical reason to depart from the normal understanding of a simple future, that the church was not yet in existence and would not be until after His passion. Indeed, the foundational bedrock had not yet been laid to be able to start construction. Furthermore there could be no church (assembly) until He had gained victory over death and Hades. How was this to be accomplished?

THE GATES OF HADES

Most Christians visualize the word picture which the Lord Jesus gave us here in a reverse way: they somehow see the church as under demonic attack and somehow resisting and triumphing. We often have a fortress mentality. But the Lord said nothing about the gates of the church, nor about Satanic attack. The symbolism is straightforward and needs no sophisticated discussion. The gates of hades cannot uproot themselves and

---

F. See 2) Mt. 17:9; 3) 17:22-3; Lk. 9:43-45; 4) Jn. 10:1-21; 5) Lk. 13:31-4; 6) Lk. 17:25; 7) Mt. 20:17-9, Lk. 18:31-2; 8) Mt. 20:28, Mk. 10:45; 9) Mt. 26:2; 10) Mt. 26:12, Mk. 14:8, Jn. 12:7; 11) Jn. 12:20-36; 12) Mt. 26:26-9. I have never come across any such tabulation in the literature.

attack the church. Gates are always defensive.

So what are the gates of Hades? Hades is of course a transliteration of ᾅδης, which is almost always a rendering of *sheol* in the Septuagint, and before the resurrection of Christ refers consistently to the abode of the dead, both in pagan and Scriptural conception. King Hezekiah wrote about his experience of being spared from entering the gates of Sheol (Isa. 38:10), and the idea of death's association with Hades is virtually a given among interpreters. Its use in the story of the rich man and Lazarus is not clear as to whether Abraham was in a different part of Hades or in a distinct place. In any case, the post-resurrection conception is clear that Hades is the temporary prison of the unsaved dead and that the saved are in "everlasting habitations" (Lk. 16:9), in Paradise (23:43), with the Lord (2 Cor. 5:8), united with Christ (Phil. 1:23), in the heavenly Jerusalem (Heb. 12:22), etc. J. Jeremias commented:

> In virtue of the promise of Jesus His community knows that it is secure from the powers of Hades (Mt. 16:18) because by faith in Him it has access to the kingdom of God. . . . The Christian community also knows, however, that Jesus is the Lord of Hades.[27]

Since Satan is to be cast into the lake of fire at the end of the millennium (Rev. 20:10), it seems he has no direct connection with Hades. But the indirect connection is to the unsaved, who are under his sway and are on the broad road to death (Mt. 7:13-14), Hades (Mt. 11:23; Lk. 10:15; 16:19-31), and ultimately the lake of fire (Rev. 20:13-5).

Thus, the battle between Satan and the church is for the eternal souls of mankind, and that as we win the lost to Christ's salvation, they are snatched from entering the gates of Hades as 'brands from the fire.' It is interesting that this symbolism from Zechariah 3:1-2 involves Satan's accusation against Joshua the high priest as God cleanses his iniquity. So it seems clear that the issue in this passage is not Satan's attack against the church, but rather Christ through His church snatching the souls of mankind from eternal death, Hades, and the lake of fire.

The way that *katischusousin* is usually rendered as 'prevail, overcome' raises a problem. It does seem to imply that the gates of Hades is on the attack. The problem is the translation of the verb *katischuein* since in the secular literature it is usually intransitive, "be strong, powerful, gain the ascendancy."[28] The two New Testament usages in Luke do not help us significantly. I would suggest that our context logically requires the rendering 'withstand' to fit the obvious symbolism. Perhaps Louis Barbieri's suggestion is the most cogent of all. He points out that since the Lord's passion is mentioned subsequently in the context, the Lord "Jesus was thus telling the disciples His death would not prevent His work of building the church."[29] His resurrection was the ultimate victory over the gates of Hades, and assures the believer's victory over death as well. As Peter and the apostles were to proclaim this victory, the gates of Hades would not be able to withstand the attacks of the church as lost people are delivered from Satan's grip and eternal death.

THE KEYS OF THE KINGDOM

The Lord Jesus then seemed to link the gates with keys: **"I will give you the keys of the kingdom of heaven; and whatever you bind on earth shall have been bound in heaven, and whatever you loose on earth shall have been loosed in heaven"** (Mt. 16:19). We should not need to clarify the Roman-Catholic-generated misconception that Peter was given the keys of heaven, an error perpetuated in the plethora of jokes about Peter at heaven's gates deciding admission criteria. This sort of thinking assumes that Peter is here given papal authority with the powers of absolution, inherent in the keys and the binding and loosing. This springs from the simple observational error that overlooks that it is the keys of the *kingdom*, not of heaven itself.

The issue is complicated by the fact that the keys are not to open the gates of Hades, so there is a metaphor shift here. Keys have a twofold significance: they open or shut doors, and they are symbols of authority. The Lord Jesus used keys in the first sense in Luke 11:52 that the scribes had taken away the key of knowledge, not entering in themselves and hindering those entering in. In a similar context of Matthew 23:13 the Lord used the verb from which *kleis* (key) is derived *kleiō* to make a similar accusation: **"you shut off the kingdom of heaven from men; for you do not enter in yourselves, nor do you allow those who are entering to go in."** The second meaning relates to the first and seems evident in Revelation 1:18 and 3:7-8, where Christ has the keys of death and Hades, and since He has the key of David, when He opens no one can shut, and when He shuts, no one can open. Furthermore He sets before the Philadelphia church an open door, presumably of evangelism.

It becomes clear that syntax, word study, and even context alone cannot elucidate our Lord's meaning here. We must see how the progressive fulfillment in the book of Acts clarifies His meaning. The most viable scenario which fulfills all the data was suggested by Alford in the 19th century:

> Another personal promise to Peter, remarkably fulfilled in his being the first to admit both Jews and Gentiles into the Church; thus using the power of the keys to open the door of salvation.[30]

It was Peter who preached the Pentecost sermon through which three thousand Jews were saved. He had the keys to open the door of faith for the nation Israel to enter into the kingdom of God (and more explicitly the church). The Lord Jesus had commanded the apostles to be witnesses to Samaria also (Acts 1:8), but Peter failed to take the initiative, which caused a dilemma. Phillip's preaching resulted in converts and baptisms. But the converts could not receive the Spirit in the normative way (at the time of exercising faith) because Peter had not officially opened the door of faith to the Samaritans. The belated receiving of the Spirit through the laying on of the hands of Peter and John was an anomaly caused by Peter's failure. God made sure that it was Peter who opened the door of faith to the Gentiles by giving visions both to him and to Cornelius to make it happen. Peter thus is pictured as a trustee (*oikonomos*) fulfilling a temporary trusteeship until he completed the task.

It is noteworthy that the gift of languages (tongues) was a supernatural sign probably given on all three occasions to attest this official opening of the doors of faith to the nation Israel. (Although not explicitly mentioned in Samaria, there was undoubtedly some external divine phenomenon to attest the gift of the Spirit.) Later as Paul and Barnabas followed through on that opening out into the Gentile world, Luke used that very language: "**how He had opened a door of faith to the Gentiles**" (Acts 14:27). And in the Jerusalem Council Peter testified on that exact point: "**Brethren, you know that in the early days God made a choice among you, that by my mouth the Gentiles should hear the word of the gospel and believe. And God, who knows the heart, bore witness to them, giving them the Holy Spirit, just as He also did to us**" (Acts 15:7). Thus we conclude that Peter used the authority he had been given on three occasions to open doors of faith. Having fully utilized the keys to open doors of faith to all humanity, he relinquished any related authority. Thus we see no continuing primacy or even leadership in the subsequent New Testament.[G] But the question of the content of Peter's preaching needed to be addressed, and I believe that this is the subject of the rest of Matthew 16:19.

PROCLAMATION ON GOD'S TERMS

It took me many years of wrestling with this text to pick up the major neglected factor, the context of preceding events going back to the beginning of Matthew 16. On the other side of the sea of Galilee He had had a confrontation with the Pharisees and Sadducees. Then follows His warning about the leaven of the Pharisees and Sadducees, their false doctrines (Mt. 16:11-12). Then as they enter Caesarea Philippi we have this pericope. Since the language of the binding and loosing is widely recognized as rabbinic language, the relevance of the context comes into focus. Because later in Matthew 23, Christ essentially accused the Pharisees and scribes of binding on earth what God had not bound in heaven, we can see the relevance (esp. 23:4 & 13). We know that the Sadducees were the rationalists of Judaism, who loosed on earth what God had not loosed in heaven. Robertson affirmed: "Rabbis of the school of Hillel 'loosed' many things that

G. After Acts 11 we see no real leadership or primacy by Peter, or for that matter by James. Many assume that James was the unique pastor of the Jerusalem church. This is based upon unwarranted inferences as well.

the school of Schammai 'bound'."[31] Gundry also noted the "leavenlike teaching of the Pharisees and Sadducees in v. 12."[32] Lange clarified the binding and loosing:

> The object of this binding and loosing is stated only in general terms. No doubt it combined all three elements of the power of the keys, as the non-remission or remission of sins (Chrysostom and many others), —viz.: 1. The principle of admission or non-admission into the church, or the announcement of grace and of judgment (the kingdom of heaven is closed to unbelievers, opened to believers). 2. Personal decision as to the admission of catechumens (Acts viii). 3. The exercise of discipline, . . .[33]

So when we come to the syntax of 16:19, we find significance in the periphrastic future perfect passives in this statement. The problem is exacerbated by the failure of most translators to represent its full force in English. Williams put emphasis upon bringing out the full force of verb tenses into his translation: "**and whatever you forbid on earth must be what is already forbidden in heaven, and whatever you permit on earth must be what is already permitted in heaven.**"[34] The Amplified Version followed his lead, as did the first and last editions of the New American Standard Version. Although the NAS committee waffled in between (1971), they ultimately realized the strong grammatical evidence and corrected the 1995 edition. Chamberlain's grammar states:

> There are a few future perfect periphrastics: *estai dedemenon* and *estai lelumenon* (Mt. 16:19). This is wrongly translated 'shall be bound' and 'shall be loosed,' seeming to make Jesus teach that the apostles' acts will determine the policies of heaven. (Moulton, *Prolegomena*, p. 149f.) They should be translated 'shall have been bound' and 'shall have been loosed.' . . . Cf. Mt. 18:18. This incorrect translation has given expositors and theologians a great deal of trouble.[35]

Robertson's brief comment is in agreement: "All this assumes, of course, that Peter's use of the keys will be in accord with the teaching and mind of Christ. . . . Every preacher uses the keys of the kingdom when he proclaims the terms of salvation in Christ."[36] This is a rare construction in the New Testament, which implies that Matthew must have had a clear intent to use it. Blass and DeBrunner state: "Periphrasis occasionally provides a rhetorically more forceful expression."[37] Gundry's comment gives further confirmation:

> The passives "will have been bound" and "will have been loosed" imply divine action. "In heaven" is a reverential substitute for God's name and also implies divine action. The periphrastic future perfect tense does not mean "will be . . . ," but "will have been . . ." (see J. R. Mantey in *JETS* 16 [1973] 129-38). Thus God will not ratify at the last judgment what Peter does in the present age, but Peter does in the

> present age what God has already determined. In other words, Peter has received direction from God for his scribal activity. This direction consists in Jesus' teaching.[38]

One wonders why the translators have been so timid in giving full force to this rare construction. We can understand why the Authorized Version translators, many of whom were just one step out of Rome, would give a connotation supportive of the Anglo-Catholic contingent, who dominated the translation process.[39] But why do contemporary translators fall into the rut of past poor translations, when doctrinally it is so harmful?

We are told in Psalm 119:89: "**Forever, O LORD, Thy word is settled in heaven**." This is the standard which Peter and the apostles were to use in proclaiming the terms of entrance into the church. They had been taught by the Lord Jesus Himself, but did not yet understand His death, burial, and resurrection and its implications (16:21ff., cf. Lk. 9:44). So the Holy Spirit had to give the apostles further revelation as to its meaning for accurate proclamation, as was fulfilled in the apostolic preaching (*kerugma*). So really the Lord Jesus was charging Peter and the apostles to make sure they did not fall into Pharisaic legalism in proclaiming the message, that is, making salvation's terms harder than heaven's standard. Nor were they to fall into Sadducean rationalization, that is, making salvation too easy and the door too broad. They must 'tell it like it is.'

CONCLUSIONS AND IMPLICATIONS

Conclusions. My most significant conclusion is that the evidence is one-sided that the Lord Jesus the Messiah indicated that He would build His assembly upon His own divine personage. The Old Testament background symbolism of God as the Rock, the availability of several Hebrew and Aramaic words for Him to have used in the wordplay (if indeed He was speaking Aramaic), the substantial distinction of usage of Πέτρος (*petros)* and πέτρα (*petra)*, the wordplay parallels in the literature, Peter's own understanding, the cultural context, the broader context, and the analogy of Scripture—all militate toward this conclusion. The most shocking aspect of this is the absolute failure of virtually all commentators to seriously check out the other Aramaic options before pontificating against this view.

The Lord further ensures the victory of the church over the gates of Hades by His own entering into death and His victorious resurrection, assuring likewise the church's victory over death.

He then delegates to Peter the responsibility to open the door of faith by proclaiming the message of this victory, first to their own nation, then to the Samaritans, and then to the Gentiles. With this He gave a charge that Peter and the church must proclaim it on God's revealed terms, not corrupting the message by legalism or rationalization.

Finally, He gave the first of a dozen explicit predictions of His soon-to-transpire death, burial, and resurrection as the only basis for that church and its victory.

Implications. We should not draw our conclusions motivated by trying to arrive at certain implications. However, we must not shrink from declaring bluntly the clear implications of these conclusions. Exegesis and theology must have their "so what?"

In this day of rapproachment between Evangelicals and Roman Catholics, the 'Peter' view facilitates these dangerous compromises. I believe it is very difficult to hold this view without in some way magnifying Peter and denigrating the Messiah Himself, despite the insistence of its evangelical advocates. The 'confession' view at least does not have that objection, and yet the focus is still too much upon a man, not the divine Messiah Himself. The 'Peter and the apostles' view, with slim Scriptural basis, also opens the door for compromise with Rome.

The common connection of the gates of Hades with Satanic attack on the church has led to a fortress mentality, by which we have failed to see that we are to be on the offensive, not in a defensive posture.

Recognizing the unique, but temporary nature of Peter's stewardship of the keys is significant again in avoiding Roman Catholic pretensions. It also helps to clarify the anomaly of the belated reception of the Samaritan believers in Acts 8.

Recognizing the normative force of the future periphrastic perfect passive participles in the binding and loosing is additionally significant in avoiding compromise with Rome and also in avoiding making salvation's terms either too hard by legalisms or too easy by modernistic rationalizations. It also helps us to understand the charge of Matt. 18:18 for the church's ethical standards also to avoid legalism and permissive rationalizations.

Finally, recognition of the integral connection of this first reference to the church with the first of a dozen explicit predictions of His passion, helps us to grasp the uniqueness of the church as set in contrast to the kingdom offer to Israel.

Note: This chapter is based upon a paper presented at the annual meeting of the Evangelical Theological Society, Santa Clara, CA, November, 1997.

---

1. Brown, Driver, and Briggs, *The New Brown-Driver-Briggs-Gesenius Hebrew and English Lexicon* , p. 849.
2. Samuel P. Tregelles, *Gesenius' Hebrew and Chaldee Lexicon of the Old Testament Scriptures* , p. 8.
3. Marcus Jastrow, *Dictionary of the Targumim, Talmud Babli, Yerushalmi and Midrashic Literature* (N.Y.: Judaica Press, 1982), pp. 634-5.
4. Ibid, p. 526.
5. Jastrow, p. 1538.
6. Chrys C. Caragounis, *Peter and the Rock* (Berlin: DeGruyter, 1990), pp. 32-3.
7. Ibid, p. 118.
8. G. Abbott-Smith, *A Manual Greek Lexicon of the New Testament* (Edinburgh, T. & T. Clark, 1937), p. 359.

9. William F. Arndt and F. Wilbur Gingrich, *A Greek-English Lexicon of the New Testament and Other Early Christian Literature*, p. 660. They go on to suggest only the Roman Catholic and the most common Protestant view of Peter's confession as options, referencing a mass of German literature, mostly higher critical in nature.
10. Cullmann in Gerhard Friedrich, ed., *Theological Dictionary of the New Testament*, trans. Bromiley, VI: 95.
11. Ibid, pp. 98-9.
12. Caragounis, pp. 44-57, 117.
13. William Douglas Chamberlain, *An Exegetical Grammar of the Greek New Testament*, p. 11.
14. Daniel B. Wallace, *Greek Grammar Beyond the Basics* (GR: Zondervan, 1996), pp. 241-2.
15. Robertson and Davis, *A New Short Grammar of the Greek Testament*, 10th ed., p. 275. Wallace agrees.
16. Blass and DeBrunner, *A Greek Grammar*, trans. Robert W. Funk, pp. 133-4.
17. Robert H. Gundry, "The Language Milieu of First-Century Palestine." *Journal of Biblical Literature* 83 (1964): 404-08.
18. Wallace, p. 100.
19. D. A. Carson, *The Expositors Bible Commentary* ed. Frank E. Gaebelein, vol 8, 1984), p. 365.
20. David J. Hesselgrave, *Communicating Christ Cross-Culturally* (GR: Zondervan, 1978), pp. 223-34.
21. Luis Padrosa, "The Roman Catholic Church" in Howard F. Vos, *Religions in a Changing World* (Chicago: Moody, 1959), p. 376. It seems that Augustine changed his view later in life to the view that Christ is the rock, which reference Padrosa quotes. For this shift of view on Augustine's part see John Peter Lange, *The Gospel According to Matthew*, trans. Philip Schaff, 6th ed., p. 296, footnote.
22. Carson, p. 368.
23. A. B. Bruce in W. Robertson Nichol, ed., *The Expositor's Greek Testament* (GR: Eerdmans, 1961), p. 224.
24. H. L. Ellison in G. D. C. Howley, ed., *A New Testament Commentary* (GR: Zondervan, 1969), p. 159.
25. Robert H. Gundry, *Matthew: A Commentary on his Literary and Theological Art*, pp. 333-4.
26. Carson, pp. 367-8.
27. Joachim Jeremias in Gerhard Kittel, ed., *Theological Dictionary of the New Testament*, I: 148-9.
28. Arndt & Gingrich, p. 425.
29. Louis A. Barbieri, Jr. in John F. Walvoord and Roy B. Zuck, eds., *The Bible Knowledge Commentary*, pp. 57-8.
30. Henry Alford, *The Greek Testament*, originally 4 vols. (Chicago: Moody, 1958 [1849]), I: 173-4.
31. A. T. Robertson, *Word Pictures in the New Testament*, 6 vols. (Nashville: Broadman, 1930), I:134.
32. Gundry, *Matthew*, p. 334.
33. Lange, p. 299.
34. Charles B. Williams, *The New Testament in the Language of the People* (Chicago: Moody, 1963 [1937]).
35. Chamberlain, p. 80.
36. Robertson, I: 134. See also his *A Grammar in the Light of Historical Research*, pp. 826, 878f, 887-889, 906.
37. BDF, p. 179.
38. Gundry, p. 335.
39. Gustavus S. Paine, *The Men Behind the King James Version* (GR: Baker, 1977).

To Sardis: "I know your deeds, that you have a name that you are alive, but you are dead. Wake up, and strengthen the things which remain, which were about to die; for I have not found your deed completed in the sight of My God."

To Philadelphia: "I know your deeds. Behold, I have set before you an open door which no one can shut, because you have a little power, and have kept My word, and have not denied My name."

-The Lord Jesus Christ to His churches

17

THE CONFIRMATION OF GLOBAL EVANGELISM

There are three significant tests of any theological system which we must consider: two have been given undue priority in many theological works: the historical testimony and the philosophic tests, but the test of global evangelism has been ignored in the main.

Thus I am suggesting a test of our theology's impact upon evangelism and missions, both historically and contemporaneously. As we examine the main thrust of Scripture inductively, we find that evangelism and missions are axiomatic. Then we must examine our theology in the light of this established axiom to see its harmony and compatibility with local and cross-cultural evangelism, and since this then becomes a deductive process, I will only call it a test or confirmation of our theologies.

The apostle Paul was both the greatest missionary and theologian of the early church. All his epistles were written in the course of his missionary ministry, either to churches planted by his missionary team or to members of his missionary team. Although Paul did not plant the church in Rome, his epistle has a strong missionary evangelism thrust in its key verses (1:14-17), that great missionary chapter (10), and his shared burden to go to unreached peoples (15:18-21). How strange that much theology has developed since the Reformation without any reference to God's global missionary program, indeed, a significant segment of theology has not been conducive to world evangelization, but even hostile to it. In actuality, theology ought to be the handmaiden of worldwide missions implementation.

It has been my privilege to teach both missions and theology for thirty-five years. A major benefit has been the cross-pollenization between the disciplines. My major for the Th.M. degree was theology and for my doctorate, missiology. This chapter will seek to give some of the fruit of this integration. In teaching theology I wrestled with the lack of inductive methodology in much theological enterprise and the missiological problems raised by such deductive theology. In writing the historical section of my missions textbook in the mid 1980s, I realized the deadening impact of such deductive theology upon the missionary enterprise. Indeed, the great scandal of Protestantism was the "Great Protestant Omission," the two centuries in which Protestants did virtually nothing about world evangelization, with another century of inaction in the English-speaking world. We must face the theological roots of that paralysis. In order to do this we must start with a survey of that which should be elementary. I believe it is a strong confirmation of the soundness of the mediate theology I have been espousing.

EVANGELISM AND MISSIONS ARE AXIOMATIC

It should not be necessary for me to remind my readers of the clear priority, imperative, and urgency of indigenous and global evangelism in the New Testament. Unfortunately, theological static has obscured the reception of this clear testimony and forced me to start here. Evangelism and missions are biblically axiomatic and therefore foundational to all sound theology, but not in the minds of many evangelical Christians, including pastors, scholars, and theologians.

The evangelistic foundation

The forerunner of the Messiah, John the Baptizer, was a very confrontational and effective evangelist. Although he started with a small, godly remnant of true Jewish believers, he must have won many others, as evidenced by the great stir his ministry caused in the nation (Jn. 1:19-28), his early arrest by King Herod (Mt. 4:12), his early martyrdom under Herod, Herod's notion that the Lord Jesus was a resurrected John (Mt. 14:1-12), and Christ's attestation of his greatness as an Elijah-like, confrontational witness to the truth (Mt. 11: 1-19).

Certainly the Lord Jesus also was a confrontational evangelist, a personal soul-winner, and at times a cross-cultural missionary. At first He was sent primarily to His own people Israel. In His early Judean ministry He recruited the first of His disciples from among John's disciples (Jn. 1:35-51), but the rest came from His broader evangelistic ministry, which began as soon as John was imprisoned (Mt. 4:12, 17). His witness started with a top Jewish religious leader and teacher, Nicodemus; then crossed a cultural/religious boundary to a sinful Samaritan woman and through her to the people of the Samaritan town of Sychar. He continuously preached to great crowds and gave witness to many individuals. Undoubtedly the four Gospel writers have given us only a small sampling of the total scope of His ministry (Jn. 21:25).

When the Lord Jesus recruited His early disciples to follow Him full-time, He invited them to "**follow Me, and I will make you fishers of men**" (Mt. 4:19). He did not call them to be identifiers of the elect. Every disciple of Christ is to be a fisher of men, whether with a broad net as Peter used on the day of Pentecost, or in a more targeted way as Philip the evangelist won the Ethiopian official. But first the Twelve were sent as ambassadors to their own nation Israel exclusively (Mt. 10:5-15). This confrontational type of ministry would bring tremendous opportunities and commensurate opposition (Mt. 10:16-39), and although the marching orders were later reversed just before the cross (Lk. 22:35-38), the essential mission was the same, to be fishers of men. If fish are to be caught, the fishermen must go to where they are and actively and diligently use the best skills possible. Fish do not usually jump into the boat, even if the fishermen invite them in.

The Lord's ministry was not exclusively to His own people Israel. There were a number of Gentiles, such as the Roman centurion (Mt. 8:5-13), who came under His ministry. Beyond the Samaritans, He moved into fringe areas such as Decapolis or even Tyre and Sidon, which were Gentile. Additionally, He alluded to the ultimate gospel outreach to Gentiles (Jn. 10:16; 12:20-24) before giving the Great Commission after His resurrection. Thus His ministry had a clear cross-cultural dimension.

The greatest decree of the Sovereign

During the forty days after His resurrection in which He appeared to the disciples, He charged them in five different ways to evangelize the whole world, which are half of all His recorded words during that period. As recorded in all four Gospels and Acts, this command has been called "the Great Commission." I would suggest that it has been misnamed; it is the Greatest Decree of the King of the Universe.[A] I presume that it is superfluous for me to give the references, but George Barna surveys of Christians have revealed a gross ignorance of the Great Commission. They are: Matthew 28:18-20; Mark 16:15; Luke 24:45-49; John 20:21; and Acts 1:8. These are the last words He gave to His disciples before His ascension and must not be ignored, soft-pedaled, rationalized, or obfuscated. They are unambiguous and crystal clear: our job is to go and make disciples of "all the ethnic groups" "in all the world" "all the days" before He returns because He has "all authority" in the universe. The only finite imperative in Matthew's record of the commandment of Christ is *mathēteuo*, "**you must all imperatively make disciples**." This is what we, feeble human beings, are responsible to do. Just before His ascension He made it clear that the Holy Spirit will work in and through His witnesses to accomplish world evangelization.

A. For four centuries many theologians have argued about some presumed decrees in past eternity, when in reality the most important decree was explicitly and fully stated by the LORD of the universe during the most dramatic and central days of human history, the 40 after the resurrection.

Cross-cultural extension

Since most of Christ's ministry was focused upon the Jewish nation, the reticence of many Christians to obey this Greatest Commission belies some deep down questions about its genuineness, its significance, its uniqueness, or its priority. I have addressed these issues in detail in chapter 3 of my missions book, *What in the World Is God Doing?* In summary let me state that the Lord Jesus gave many prior indications of the global purpose of His ministry, which were to be fulfilled through His Church after Pentecost. For example, His early ministry to the Samaritan woman (Jn. 4) anticipated the ultimate evangelization of the Samaritans by Phillip the evangelist. The missionary implication of the gift of languages on the day of Pentecost is usually overlooked. The Jewish apostles were proclaiming the mighty works of God to the Jewish nation in at least fifteen Gentile languages, which the diaspora Jews well understood (Acts 2:4-11). Most of those diaspora converts must have returned to their homes in Gentile lands to plant churches there.

Although the ministry focused upon the Jewish nation for a whole decade, Pentecost was anticipatory of the conversion of Gentile Cornelius, the missionary ministry of the apostle Paul and his missionary teams, and the work of global missions right until the end of the age. The giving of the Holy Spirit to the new-born Church on that day was adequate empowerment for what seemed to the apostles a "mission impossible" and even today seems overwhelming to most Christians. Accordingly, the Spirit-filled early disciples gave a bold, confrontational witness to the leaders of their nation, which resulted in persecution and martyrdom. Luke characterized them after being flogged and released: "**So they went on their way from the presence of the Council, rejoicing that they had been considered worthy to suffer shame for His name. And every day, in the temple and from house to house, they kept right on teaching and preaching Jesus as the Christ**" (Acts 5:41-42). Even though God had to use Philip's biculturalism to bridge the gap into the Samaritan community (8:4-8), it was really Peter's responsibility to use the keys to open the door of faith to the Gentiles, and that took a decade and two special visions to bring about (10:1-11:18).

The procrastination of the Jewish apostles in following up the conversion of Gentile Cornelius may have prompted the calling of that unique apostle to the Gentiles by a unique confrontation on the Damascus road. God formed Saul's bi-cultural, choleric personality into the premier missionary and theologian of the apostolic church. This not only teaches us that antecedent human factors are very significant in God's molding of the clay to make the vessel He needs, but also that theology and world evangelism are intended, may I say, predestined to go together. How tragic it is that this great missionary's epistles have been especially distorted to contradict the missionary burden which was at the core of his ministry. All of his epistles were *missionary epistles*, and yet his last missionary epistles to individual missionaries have been misdesignated as "pastoral epistles" in most of the literature of the past century or more. Romans is undoubtedly his greatest theological treatise, but evangelism and missions pulse from beginning (1:14-17) to end (15:18-21), with a whole chapter along the way (10):

> **I am under obligation both to Greeks and to barbarians, both to the wise and to the foolish. So, for my part I am eager to preach the gospel to you also who are in Rome. For I am not ashamed of the gospel, for it is the power of God for salvation to everyone who believes, to the Jew first and also to the Greek.**

All the rest of his epistles were written in the course of his missionary ministry of three extensive tours and as a prisoner in connection with that cross-cultural ministry to the multicultural churches which he had planted on those tours. Indeed, the only history we have of the apostolic church came from a Gentile convert and companion of his. Somehow the missionary dimension of all of this has faded from the mind of the modern church which claims to be proclaiming its theology. But a sound theology cannot be developed apart from this evangelistic and missionary foundation.

We know less about the other apostolic figures. Although John Mark was a missionary dropout, probably resulting from the culture shock of a 'kosher Jerusalem boy' struggling with the idolatrous culture of Perga, God used him to write one of our four Gospels, the one contextualized for the Roman mindset. Similarly, the apostle John's background in Galilee may not have made him a likely candidate for cross-cultural ministry, but as we read his Gospel we can see how years in the Gentile world enabled him to contextualize the message for Gentiles. Others like Matthew, James, and Peter continued to evangelize and disciple their own Jewish people in the main, it would seem.

The confrontational paradigm

The dilemma faced by all determinists is the place of persuasion in ministry and witness. There were many of reformed tradition in past generations who were opposed to any use of means in proclaiming the gospel message. Of course, that would make preaching itself an oxymoron since preaching is a human means. What they mean is that any sort of appeal, invitation, or persuasion of sinners to repent and believe the gospel would somehow deprive God of the glory of their conversion. The real issue is not the use of means, but *which* means are biblically valid? However the solution to this dilemma is not to be found in deductive implications from deductive theology, but rather in examining the model, the paradigm, the example of the Lord Jesus Himself and of His apostles, which we have done above in general terms. But now let us look more finely at the issue of the place of persuasion. This could be called a study in 'elenctics,' which ought to be a category in the study of systematic theology, or at the very least in the study of practical theology.

The contemporary debate has centered around the three 'p's': *presence evangelism, proclamation evangelism, or persuasion evangelism.* Writers of a more liberal stamp are satisfied with mere 'presence evangelism.' This is what I observed in the mission institutions of the 'old-line' churches of Pakistan during my years of missionary service. Most evangelicals would affirm 'proclamation evangelism.' Those of a more Calvinistic bent would be reluctant to go further to 'persuasion evangelism.'

Christ's example. What is the New Testament evidence? Certainly the King's herald had a confrontational ministry. The Lord Jesus Himself seemed to have provoked many confrontations with the people and their leaders, especially according to the testimony of Matthew and John (Jn. 5:16-47; 6:26-66; 7:14-52; 8:12-59; 9:39-41; 10:22-42; 12:44-50; Mt. 21:12-13, 23-46; 22:1-46; 23:1-39). As I scan these references, I realize that 'confrontation' is much too weak a word. The Lord Jesus was certainly a controversialist and the word 'persuasion' is also much too weak. These chapters are filled with argumentation of a very polemic and apologetic nature, which was very effective (Jn. 8:30; 10:42; 12:42, etc.). If we are to follow His example (WWJD?), the Lord Jesus would not be satisfied with anything less than 'persuasion evangelism.'

The apostles' model. The ministry of Peter and the other apostles on the day of Pentecost was certainly argumentative, apologetic, confrontational, and controversial. It is clear that Peter must have given some sort of an overt "invitation" to the crowd since the apostles separated out the 3000 who were to be baptized. Luke doesn't tell us how they did it, but it had to have been something quite overt and directive. Succeeding days only intensified these aspects of their ministry, provoking arrest, intimidation, threats, imprisonment, etc. and resulting in incredible fruit of thousands converted. As the good news began to go out to the Gentiles through the ministry of Paul, Barnabas, and then Silas, Timothy, and many others whom Paul co-opted, the confrontational and persuasive dimension hardly diminished. Luke describes how immediately after Paul's conversion, in Damascus he *proclaimed* Christ by *confounding* the Jews in *proving* that Jesus was the Messiah (Acts 9:20-22). Back in Jerusalem he was "**speaking out boldly in the name of the Lord**" by "**talking and arguing with the Hellenistic *Jews***" (9:28-29). This is just the beginning of the whole pattern of New Testament ministry.

The terms used. David Hesselgrave has given an excellent analysis of the words used and suggests that most writers are guilty of reductionism since there are a score of words to be studied and few are mentioned in the literature. Not only does *euangelizein* occur 54 times and *euangelion*, 76 times, but *kērussein* (herald, proclaim) and its nouns *kērugma* and *kērux* over 60 times more, and *martureein* (bear witness) and its derived nouns well over one hundred times more. This is only the beginning since we find *sungcheein* (confound), *sumbibazein* (prove), *diegeomai* (declare), *suzeteein* (dispute), *laleein* (speak), *dialegomai* (reason with), *peitheein* (persuade), *noutheteein* (admonish, warn), *katechein* (inform, instruct), *deomai*, (beg, beseech), *elengchein* (reprove), *epitimaein* (rebuke), and *parakaleein* (exhort, urge) as well. It is clear that superficial treatments do not do justice to the full range of these aspects of apostolic ministry and therefore lead to a truncated theology of how sinners come to faith in Christ.

Hesselgrave has quoted J. I. Packer extensively to show that he "does not overlook these references, but nevertheless concludes that these various verbs having to do with missionary communication can be best summed up in the word 'teach'."[1] Hesselgrave suggests that terms like 'dispute,' 'reason,' 'persuade,' 'reprove,' 'rebuke,' or 'exhort' can hardly be subsumed under the activity of 'teaching.' Knowing Packer's Calvinism, we can see his agenda in soft-pedalling the confrontational dimension of evangelism. This is just one example of a mindset which could be exemplified a thousand fold.

OBSTACLES TO GLOBAL EVANGELISM

I think that most moderate Calvinists would have to agree that the determinism of 'extreme Calvinism' hinders global evangelism. But I will go a step farther and state that Calvinism in general tends to be a hindrance to the kind of global evangelism stipulated in the New Testament and surveyed above, that is, persuasion evangelism and missions. I believe I can show both a historical connection and a logical, theological connection as well.

The "Great Protestant Omission"

In my missions survey text I devoted a brief chapter to a survey of the paucity of missionary effort for two centuries after the Protestant Reformation until the beginning of the Danish-Halle mission in 1705 (three centuries in the English-speaking world). The Roman Catholics were sending out Jesuit, Dominican, Franciscan, and Augustinian missionaries all over the world, who are said to have gained more converts than were lost to Protestantism. But Protestants during this period were hostile to missions. In these two centuries there are less than a dozen incidents in which any issue of missions arose and most of these involved strong reactions from the Protestant establishment to any such outrageous notion as world evangelism. In the few cases where there was positive action it came from the fringes of Protestantism, not from the Lutheran or Reformed core. For instance, Verceslaus Budovetz went on his own to Istanbul in 1577 and won one Muslim in five years. In 1590 Hadrian Saravia wrote a chapter on missions in a book, which was disputed by Theodore Beza, Calvin's successor in Geneva. Beza insisted that the Great Commission was binding only on the apostles, not on the church today.

The two next items are positive. By 1595 the Dutch Calvinists were sending chaplains out with the colonialists to the East Indies and Ceylon. They translated the Bible into the Malay language and baptized many converts, a substantial Reformed community in Indonesia being the result. Here in the new world in 1644 non-conformist pastor John Eliot became burdened for the nearby Algonquin Indians of Massachusetts and began to learn their language so as to preach the gospel to them. This resulted in over a thousand converts and the publication of the Algonquin Bible by 1663. Eliot's initiative started a sequence of continuing efforts to reach American Indians right to the present.

The next episodes unfortunately are quite negative. In 1651 a Lutheran nobleman, Count Truchsess, challenged the theological faculty of Wittenberg as to why Lutherans were not sending out missionaries in obedience to the Great Commission. Their response is a sad testimony to the thinking of Protestant leaders in that day. They echoed Beza's notion that it was only given to the apostles and was fulfilled by them. Then they said that if the heathen are lost, it is their own fault since they rejected God's word from Noah on down to the Apostles, who evangelized the whole human race. They also argued that it is the responsibility of the government, not the church, to provide for preaching to the heathen.

In 1661 George Fox, the non-conformist founder of the Society of Friends (Quakers), sent three missionaries to China, but tragically they were never heard of again. Three years later an Austrian Lutheran nobleman named Justinian Von Welz began to advocate the cause of foreign missions. When Baron Von Welz's sharp admonitions to Lutheran church authorities fell on deaf ears, he "proceeded to Holland, were he abandoned his baronial title. Following ordination as an 'apostle to the Gentiles,' he sailed for Dutch Guiana (Surinam), where he died an early death before he could reap a harvest."[2] An official refutation of Von Welz's views had been given by Johann Ursinus, a Lutheran theologian, citing the difficulty of the missionary task and of recruiting missionaries, the deep depravity of the heathen making conversion next to impossible, the great need at home, and the responsibility of Christians already living in heathen lands to make the gospel known. Gustav Warneck's comment on this viewpoint is apt: "Where there are Christians, missions are superfluous; and where there are no Christians, they are hopeless.[3]

The Explanations

How can we account for this shocking fact—this great omission? If we visualize the Reformation as a full-fledged restoration of apostolic Christianity, then the facts are unexplainable. But if we realize that the Protestant Reformation was a complex movement involving political, economic, social, cultural, and spiritual factors, it then becomes more comprehensible, though no less reprehensible. There is a vast literature on the connection of the secular Renaissance to the religious Reformation. Certainly the invention of the printing press half a century earlier paved the way for the Protestant movement, especially since it was based upon a return to Scripture and the necessity to disseminate the truth. But for the most part the Reformation did not go far enough in the recovery of God's truth, with the result that a number of theological, circumstantial, and spiritual obstacles remained to the restoration among Protestants of God's program of worldwide evangelism. Let us seek to understand the reasons.

The difficult circumstances of the Protestants

Although the Protestant movement grew very rapidly, it was always a minority in Europe and had to fight for its very existence for centuries. Although it flourished in parts of Germany, Scandinavia, the Low Countries, Switzerland, and ultimately England and Scotland, the struggle in France continued until 1685 when the St. Bartholomew's Day Massacre and the revocation of the Edict of Nantes devastated the Protestant Huguenots. Most survivors fled the country. The Roman Catholic Church did not take the Reformation lying down, but organized a Counter Reformation religiously, economically, politically, and organizationally. Europe was wracked with a series of religious wars in which the Protestants struggled for survival.

To make matters worse, the Protestants quibbled among themselves theologically and in no way presented a united front against the Catholics. Not only did the Lutherans and the Calvinists hurl anathemas against each other, but they persecuted the Anabaptists and Mennonites, who rightly believed in the need for a more radical reformation of the church.

Arising out of the circumstances of the Reformation was the fact that the Protestant countries were geographically more isolated from Africa and Asia and got involved in colonial enterprises more belatedly. While this factor was clearly present, it does not excuse the Protestant slowness, for even after the Dutch, Scandinavians, and English had begun to establish colonies around the world, they still did little to evangelize the non-Christians there. Indeed, the trading companies which they set up hindered the spread of the gospel in most cases.

Common rationalizations

It is also very clear that some of the same rationalization found among Christians today were in vogue at that time. How many have used the expression "charity begins at home" to justify unconcern for missions? Over three centuries ago Ursinus used the argument that the many Jews and heathen at home should be reached before going to pagans in far-off lands. It sounds very familiar. The truth is that we can never totally reach our own homeland, so the time will never come when we will send out missionaries on that basis. We have already noted Ursinus's argument of the responsibility of Christians already in pagan lands to do the work of evangelization. He saw no room for sending missionaries at all. The most serious rationalization was that the heathen are too depraved to respond to the gospel. Ursinus misinterpreted Matthew 7:6: "The holy things of God are not to be cast before such dogs and swine."[4] Christ here is not referring to the heathen but to the false prophets and religious teachers (cf. Matt. 7:15-23; 2 Pet. 2:22). Clearly Ursinus did not understand that the doctrine of depravity involves all men including Europeans, not just the heathen. He seems not to have understood the power of the Holy Spirit to convict and convince men of the truth of the gospel. Of course, centuries of successful missions have put the lie to his pessimism.

The theology of the Reformers

There is considerable controversy over the missionary perspective of the great sixteenth-century Reformers--Luther, Calvin, and Zwingli. It is generally agreed that by the second generation of the reformation, leaders like Beza and Melancthon rationalized away Christian responsibility. But what about Luther and Calvin? A number of writers have sought to defend the essential harmony of their viewpoint with missions to the heathen.[5] Not only are the argument unconvincing, but the embarrassing fact remains: for two centuries Protestant leaders did virtually nothing to advance the cause of world evangelization. The best that can be said is that there was a concern for home missions within Europe. What was the source of the distorted perspective which the second generation leaders evince? They surely didn't get it from the Bible! There are a number of distinct theological problems.

We have already noted the view that the missionary mandate was only given to the Apostles, that they fulfilled it in their generation, and that since there are no apostles today, the commission is not binding on us today. Although this view cannot be attributed directly to Luther or Calvin, Coates admits that:

> It cannot be gainsaid, however, that Luther's expositions of great missionary passages as Matt. 28:19-20 and Mark 16:15 are usually devoid of any missionary emphasis. Moreover, there is a good deal of validity to the contention that Luther's concept of "mission" dealt primarily with the correction of unchristian conditions prevailing within Christendom at his time.[6]

The idea that the Apostles evangelized the heathen world in their own generation is so absurd historically to us today that we are amazed that they could make such statements.

It is true that most translations of Colossians 1:23 might give that impression. But the ingressive aorist participle should be translated "**the gospel that you have heard, which is beginning to be proclaimed in all**

creation under heaven." So neither the Bible nor church history support this absurd notion. Most evangelicals today would agree with the reformers that technically the office of apostle is no longer operative. However, since the missionary takes up part of the responsibility of the apostles and since the same Holy Spirit who was given at Pentecost is working through the church today, we are not thereby excused from obedience to the missionary mandate.

Another weakness inherent in the Reformers' theology was in their concept of the relationship of church and government. The Anabaptists, like most evangelicals today, held to separation of church and state. Unfortunately the Reformers did not see a sharp separation. Indeed, the prevailing view was of a *Landeskirche*, a territorial church. This is still common in Europe. Since all citizens in a territory are baptized into the territorial church, whether Roman Catholic, Lutheran, Anglican, etc., a close relationship exists between the government and the dominant church. (Other churches were viewed as illegal.) Luther and many of the Reformers clearly believed that it was the responsibility of the government to send out the missionaries. Although there was some government involvement in missions, for the most part governments can't be expected to do the work of the church.

The Reformers also seem to have had a distorted understanding of the implications of God's sovereignty. Luther, for example, did have a concern for Jews and Turks: "I do hope that our Gospel, now shining forth with a light so great, will before Judgment Day make an attack also on that abominable prophet Mohammed. May our Lord Jesus Christ do this soon."[7] Note that Luther seems to leave the responsibility with God to bring about the conversion of the Muslims. The same seems to be the case with Calvin. Harry Boer faults all of the reformers but Bucer in this regard.[8] Certainly Theodor Beza's development of the notion of limited atonement did not help. Although many defend the Calvinistic view of sovereignty as compatible with missions, the fact is that many Christians right on down to William Carey's senior associate, John Ryland, have either misused the doctrine of God's sovereignty or else they have a distorted view of His sovereignty. The responsibility to fulfill the Great Commission is ours, not God's.

Finally we note that the Reformers' view of prophetic truth affected their view of missions. Apparently, most of the Reformers believed that the end of the world was near. There was no time for world evangelization before the end. This despite the clear statement of Christ that no one could know the time of His coming (Matt. 24:36).

A limited concept of missions

The Reformers did not seem to have developed a biblical concept of missions. Luther had the idea that missions involved the church merely growing at its boundaries with heathen lands, using the illustration of ever-broadening ripples caused by a stone tossed into the water.[9] It is clear that this concept would have been very unsatisfying to the Apostle Paul (and to the Holy Spirit), since he leapfrogged the area of Asia Minor on his second journey to be moved on by the Spirit to Greece. Another common misconception in that day (and ours) is that one needs a direct commission or call from God to become a missionary. In my missions book I have argued that there is little Scriptural support for the notion of a direct missionary call as normative. Therefore, the lack of a 'call' should not keep missionaries from reaching a lost world of billions.

The spiritual weakness of the Reformation

Although we have identified many different reasons for the Great Omission, ultimately there is only one reason, and it a spiritual one. The Protestant Reformation did not have deep enough spiritual roots. The Reformation was not a great revival in which tens of millions of people were born again. Probably there were only a minority of Protestants who really came to the saving knowledge of Jesus Christ. The rest were swept along with the tide. With the territorial church arrangement of Europe it was not hard to be a Protestant without being born again. It is important to understand that there was much confusion among Protestants about the nature of regeneration or the new birth. Much reliance was placed upon baptism and communion, which were seen as 'sacraments'. Luther himself saw the problem:

> If one considers rightly how the people now act who wish to be Protestant (by profession), and who know how to talk much about Christ, there is nothing behind it. Thus the more part deceive themselves. Tenfold more were they who made a beginning with us, and who had serious pleasure in our teaching, but now not a tenth part of them remain steadfast. . . . .
> If I were now to begin to preach the gospel I would act differently. The great rude masses I would leave under the rule of the Pope. They do not advance the gospel, but only abuse its freedom.[10]

The more we learn about the spiritual state of the reformation churches, the more it seems like Christ's words to the Sardis church in Revelation 3:1 apply, "I know your deeds; you have a reputation of being alive, but you are dead."[11] Before there could be world evangelism, there had to be spiritual renewal. That was two centuries in coming.

THE THEOLOGICAL BASIS OF MODERN MISSIONS

It is imperative to examine the movements, personalities, and theologies out of which the modern missions movement arose. There were two sources of early missions from the European continent: the Pietistic movement in the Lutheran churches and the Moravian church, both of which were at the fringe of Protestantism. The pietistic movement was started by Philip Spener (1635-1705) and developed by August Franke (1663-1727), the founder of the University of Halle. The two pietistic missionaries recruited from the University of Halle by pietistic King Frederick IV of Denmark went out to India in 1705 and were followed by others from the Pietistic movement. But they were far exceeded by the first generation of Moravian church missionaries, 226 of whom entered ten countries between 1732 and 1760. This small persecuted movement sent out more missionaries than all the other Protestants combined. Neither of these movements followed the deterministic theologies of the Reformers. The rest of the Protestants did virtually nothing!

Origins in the English-speaking world

The father of modern missions. William Carey (1761-1834) is rightly considered the father of the modern missionary movement in the English-speaking world and major implementer of missions. To understand how this came about we must inquire as to the environment and influences which gave him impetus. Herbert Kane sketched out the curious background in the 18th century:

> Even before Carey's time there were stirrings of missionary interest in England. In 1719 Isaac Watts wrote his great missionary hymn, "Jesus Shall Reign Where'er the Sun." Several of Charles Wesley's compositions also bear a missionary theme. In 1723 Robert Millar of Paisley wrote A *History of the Propagation of Christianity and the Overthrow of Paganism*, in which he advocated intercession as the primary means of converting the heathen. The idea soon caught on. Twenty years later prayer groups were to be found all over the British Isles. Their chief petition was for the conversion of the heathen world.
>
> In 1746 a memorial was sent to Boston inviting the Christians of the New World to enter into a seven-year "Concert of Prayer" for missionary work. The memorial evoked a ready response from Jonathan Edwards, who the following year issued a call to all believers to engage in intercessory prayer for the spread of the gospel throughout the world.[12]

The irony is that Christians sang and wrote and prayed about missions, but it took several generations before an Englishman **actually did** anything about it! It seems clear that overemphasis on God's sovereignty and underemphasis upon man's responsibility was the major factor in their inaction. The story of William Carey confirms this since as a non-conformist Baptist he was hardly a mainstream Protestant either. Although he was essentially a Calvinist, he struggled with the passivistic impact of determinism among the Calvinistic Baptists.[13] Baptist historian Underwood described the influence of rigid predestinarian views upon the early Particular Baptists:

> Such a theology had a paralysing effect upon the preacher. The notion that for multitudes of men no salvation was either intended or provided in Christ, devitalized evangelistic preaching and effort, depriving men of any feeling of responsibility for extending the Kingdom of God. As early as 1611 Thomas Helwys had put his finger exactly on the spot when he wrote of Calvinism that it "makes some despair utterly as thinking there is no grace for them and that God hath decreed their destruction. And it makes others desperately careless, holding that if God have decreed they shall be saved then they shall be saved, and if God have decreed they shall be damned they shall be damned." . . . But early in the eighteenth century a change came over them. They preached according to what Ivimey calls the "non-invitation scheme" and contented themselves with expounding doctrine. If Christ died not for all but only for the elect, it was useless to invite all to repent and believe in Him. . . . He [one of their leading preachers, John Skepp] made no attempt to awaken the consciences of the unconverted lest he should despoil God of the sole glory of their conversion.[14]

The Baptists were by no means alone in their hostility to missions. In 1796 the General Assembly of the Church of Scotland passed the following statement: "To spread abroad among barbarians and heathen natives the knowledge of the Gospel seems to be highly preposterous, in so far as it anticipates, nay even reverses the order of Nature."[15]

Carey's mentor. The theological roots of Carey's missionary burden must be examined. Samuel Fisk has shown the impact of Andrew Fuller (1754-1815) on the Particular Baptists in England and therefore on Carey and his other associates. Although he gives impressive secondary documentation to support his point, in looking for primary sources I was astonished to find three different editions (one British and two American) of the complete works of Andrew Fuller, study of which totally supports Fisk's thesis.[16] Obviously, Fuller was widely read and appreciated in the end of the 18th and beginning of the 19th centuries on both sides of the Atlantic. He was the mentor, as well as the major backer of the first Baptist missionaries. He was a one-man home office and traveling secretary of the fledgling mission, all the while pastoring a church and writing apologetic and polemic theology. His extensive preaching tours all over England, Scotland, and Ireland on behalf of the mission not only funded the mission, but put him in touch and sometimes in the middle of the theological issues of the day, which stimulated much of his writing. His refutation of Socinianism made him quite famous outside of Baptist circles. The College of New Jersey (Princeton) had offered him a doctorate, which he refused, but some years later Dr. Timothy Dwight of Yale just simply sent him the honorary doctorate, which he could not refuse once awarded. But let us go back to the beginning.

Fuller was raised in a rural, high-Calvinist Baptist church, where the pastor, Mr. Eve, had little or nothing to say to the unconverted. Although Andrew had a spiritual crisis at the age of thirteen, he was almost sixteen before he cast himself upon Christ. "I now found rest for my troubled soul; and I reckon that I should have found it sooner, if I had not entertained the notion of my having no warrant to come to Christ without some previous qualification." As a new Christian he precipitated a controversy in his church by confronting a drunken member and telling him that he could keep himself from sin, to which the sinning Christian, being a hyper-Calvinist replied, "I am not my own keeper." Although the man was excommunicated, and pastor Eve supported Fuller's actions, it started a big discussion as to whether, because of depravity, Christians really can do anything to gain victory over sin. The pastor was forced out, and this began Fuller's struggle with high-Calvinistic doctrine.[17] By age twenty he had preached a few times with some fruit and the church encouraged him to go into ministry. In a year of self-study before they called him as pastor, he began to read widely from his limited resources. He explained:

> With respect to the system of doctrine which I had been used to hear from my youth, it was in the high Calvinistic, or rather hyperCalvinistic strain, admitting nothing spiritually good to be the duty of the unregenerate, and nothing to be addressed to them by way of exhortation, excepting what related to external obedience. . . . But nothing was said to them from the pulpit, in the way of warning them to flee from the wrath to come, or inviting them to apply to Christ for salvation. . .

He compared extreme Calvinist, John Gill's writings with the 16th and 17th century writers like John Bunyan, who "all dealt in free invitation to sinners, to come to Christ and be saved; the consistency of which, with personal election, I could not understand."

Germinal in his search was a pamphlet by Dr. Abraham Taylor, which surveyed the appeals of John the Baptist, the Lord Himself, and His apostles to sinners to repent and believe. By 1777 he was reading Jonathan Edwards, David Brainerd, and Joseph Bellamy, all of which caused him to question the false Calvinism he had been taught. He was undoubtedly influenced by the Wesleyan revivals and the First Great Awakening. By 1781 he wrote *The Gospel Worthy of All Acceptation*, which, when published in 1784, caused a firestorm of controversy. I would suggest that this was one of the most important books written since the Reformation since it provided the theological basis for Carey's mission. Fuller was accused of being an Arminian, although he considered himself a "strict Calvinist."[18] By 1782 the Northamptonshire Baptist Ministers Association had already been influenced by the writings of Edwards and Brainerd to pray monthly for worldwide gospel extension. Although Fuller's memoirs do not mention Carey in this time frame, Carey (7 years his junior) became pastor in nearby Leicester during this period and they must have been in close contact. When in 1792 Carey proposed implementation of global evangelism, it was Fuller and their associates Ryland, Sutcliffe, and Pearce who agreed to "hold the ropes" and became the Baptist mission board members.[19]

In this connection Carey published an eighty-seven page book, *An Enquiry into the Obligation of Christians to Use Means for the Conversion of the Heathens.*[20] In it he answered the prevailing misconceptions about missions and proposed that Christians should form mission societies (agencies) to implement the missionary mandate. The reference to "means" in the title reflects the strong predestinarian views of his day, which opposed use of human means to accomplish God's work. Carey recognized that human means are clearly commanded and exemplified in the Bible. When he later presented the same challenge at the Baptist Ministers' Association at Northamptonshire, his senior colleague, John Ryland, squelched him with the words, "Young man, sit down. When God pleases to convert the heathen, He will do it without your aid or mine."[21] Since Ryland must have been a part of those prayer meetings, it seems clear that he wasn't opposed to the conversion of the unevangelized, but that he thought that our responsibility was limited to prayer. Like most Calvinists of that period, he hadn't considered the implication of Matthew 9:38 that laborers are needed in the harvest field: **"Therefore beseech the Lord of the harvest to send out workers into His harvest."** Carey proved Ryland to be wrong, and to his credit he also became a supporter of the missionary endeavor. But the theological basis had been provided by Fuller, and for the rest of his life he was the mainstay of the Baptist mission. As to William Carey's own theology, a recent study of his extensive correspondence indicated that although he frequently referred to God's providence, he never once explicitly referred to the doctrine of election.[22] Like Fuller he believed in confronting unbelievers with the gospel and in their responsibility and ability to respond.

Another serious obstacle which Carey addressed was the view that it was impossible to convert the heathen. Here it seems clear that the key obstacle was lack of faith in the power of God. Carey simply showed that Eliot, Brainerd, and the Moravian missionaries had had success in winning the heathen and we must "Expect great things from God; attempt great things for God." By October 2, 1792, they formed the Particular Baptist Society for Propagating the Gospel among the Heathen. Although it was a small beginning with a dozen poor Baptist pastors, within a quarter century almost another dozen mission boards had been formed out of this impetus: four in Great Britain, three in America, and some others on continental Europe.

The unheralded mentors of American missions

Samuel Mills' mentor. Just as few Christians today are familiar with Andrew Fuller, similarly far fewer have ever heard of Edward Dorr Griffin (1770-1837). In a similar way he was a key mentor of the whole first generation of American foreign missionaries, and there is an even clearer theological issue involved. Samuel Mills, Jr., the instigator of the famous Haystack Prayer Meeting in 1806, had been converted under the early ministry of

Griffin in Torringford, Connecticut, and had gone to the meeting of the General Assembly in Philadelphia in 1805 to hear him give a stirring missionary message, "The Kingdom of Christ." It so radicalized Mills that he distributed copies on the campus of Williams College in the northwestern corner of Massachusetts, where he was a student. A number of students began to join with him regularly in prayer for the conversion of the heathen. It was in August 1806 that five prayed in the lee of a haystack after a thunderstorm and concluded that God could use them as missionaries. On September 7, 1808 Mills covenanted with four students to form a missionary group, called "The Society of the Brethren," including James Richards of the original group and joined by Luther Rice, both of whom ultimately became foreign missionaries. Foreign missions was thought of as so absurd a notion among Calvinists at that time that the students kept their organization secret and their records in code.

The Andover missionaries. In September of 1808 Adoniram Judson, Jr. had returned to his father's parsonage in Plymouth, Massachusetts greatly concerned about his soul's salvation since his deistic classmate had died in the next room of the inn where he had recently stopped off. Pastor Edward Griffin and Prof. Moses Stuart were visiting his father and counseled the younger Judson to come to the newly formed Andover Seminary as an incidental student to help resolve his questions about the truth of the Christian faith. Someone (was it Griffin?) gave him a copy of Thomas Boston's *Human Nature in its Fourfold State* (cf. ch. 18 re: Boston). He declined their offer and went instead to the city of Boston for a teaching job. There he read this book, which convinced him that he should go to Andover and get the issue settled, which he promptly did. By November he had assurance of salvation and on December 2nd he committed his life to Christ.

In June 1809 Dr. Griffin was installed as the first professor of homiletics at Andover, coming from a very fruitful pastoral ministry in Newark, New Jersey. In September someone (not a student, possibly Griffin) gave him a copy of a missionary sermon by a chaplain for the East India Company, Claudius Buchanan, entitled, "The Star of the East" (pub. 1808/09). Reading this sermon convinced Judson that he must consider foreign missions, and he shared his views on campus with little response. At this point Samuel Nott, Jr. from Union College, who had also been considering foreign missions, came on campus. That winter (1809/1810) Richards, Robbins, and Mills of the Haystack group, arrived from Williams College, bringing the Brethren records with them to reorganize on the new campus. By February 1810 Judson was committed to missions and recruited Gordon Hall, also from Williams, who was in pastoral ministry and had been considering a call to his church. Samuel Newell of Harvard also joined the group.

The missionary-minded students consulted the faculty, "particularly Dr. Griffin," who suggested contacting the London Missionary Society, which Judson did in April. He also suggested that they meet with some pastors at Prof. Moses Stuart's house for consultation, which happened in June 1810.

As a consequence, shortly thereafter Mills, Judson, Nott, and Newell walked six miles to meet with the General Association of Congregational Ministers in Bradford to share their burden for the formation of a mission-sending board, which was inaugurated the following September. When the first five missionaries were ordained in Salem in September 1812, Edward Griffin, by now pastor of the newly formed Park Street Church in Boston, gave the invocation. Out of this came not only the American Board of Commissioners of Foreign Missions, but also the American Baptist Foreign Mission, and in quick succession a host of other denominational mission boards.

A productive collaboration. The key man, Samuel Mills, deferred to Gordon Hall a place among the first five missionaries sent out, feeling that he was better qualified. He then made two extensive home missionary journeys to the West. After return to New York City, he connected again with Dr. Griffin, who by then was in another fruitful pastoral ministry in Newark, across the rivers. In collaboration with Mills in 1814 Griffin proposed the formation of the American Bible Society. By 1816 they again partnered in instigating the formation of The United Foreign Mission Society. They also started an African school under the synod of New York and New Jersey. The close connection of Griffin with the origin of American missions is clear, but what was the theological substratum?

Edward Griffin had graduated from Yale in 1790 with the highest honor and then started an academy at Derby, Connecticut. His parents were not religious, but his uncle was a pastor, and he understood the contemporary Calvinism. He was interested in "religion" but said that since "God had not changed my heart, I said to myself, 'Why should I wait for the Lord any longer?' and devoted myself to law." In 1791 during an illness he came under conviction of sin and within a few months came into the assurance of salvation. He quickly began to win his siblings and parents to Christ. His struggle about entering ministry ended in a few months and he studied under Dr. Jonathan Edwards, Jr. at New Haven. His early ministry resulted in hundreds of conversions in various towns in Connecticut. After marriage in 1796, he was forced by his wife's poor health to relocate to the milder climate of Newark, New Jersey, and upon the death of his senior colleague at First Presbyterian Church, revival broke out in that Griffin saw about 375 come to Christ in two years. It was while in that pastorate that he was called upon to preach to the Presbyterian General Assembly in 1805, and then in 1809 he was called to teach homiletics at Andover Seminary, where Leonard Woods was professor of theology. By 1811 he accepted a call to be pastor of the newly formed Park Street church in Boston, where he helped stem the tide of Unitarianism, which had gripped almost all the churches of the city. His Park Street lectures given during the winter of 1812/13 in defense of evangelical theology were published and read on both sides of the Atlantic.

The "New Divinity" movement

The theological underpinnings of the American missionary movement seem to be little understood. Griffin was a part of the Second Great Awakening and a neo-Edwardsian movement. His mentor, Dr. Jonathan Edwards, Jr., had moved toward a more moderate Calvinism than his father, clearly affirming general redemption. This was the view of a couple of generations of men who succeeded President Edwards, including Leonard Woods, Samuel Spring, John Smalley, Nathaniel Emmons, Adoniram Judson, Sr., Samuel Mills, Sr., Ebenezer Fitch, and later, Edwards A. Park. This view was called the 'New Divinity' and might be better called 'neo-Edwardsian' theology. Park suggested that President Edwards' teaching, both directly and indirectly led to this theology and that men like Joseph Bellamy (1719-1790), Samuel Hopkins (1721-1803), and Stephen West (1735-1818) also in a similar way paved the way for its acceptance. Albeit, Griffin's view is clear since in 1817/19 he published a 300-page book advocating the doctrine of general redemption, which was an integral part of the New Divinity.[23] I would suggest that Griffin's conviction that Christ died for the sins of all mankind, without exception as well as without distinction, made it feasible for him to take the radical step of preaching missions to the General Assembly in a day when it was thought to be an absurd notion.

Their theology. There seems to be considerable confusion as to what the theological position of these neo-Edwardsians really was. They were called 'Consistent Calvinists,' and by their opponents the 'New Divinity.' Although they were not all totally homogeneous theologically, with few exceptions they held to a Calvinistic view of human depravity. This was the Edwards' legacy although Edwards junior seems to be one exception. They were Calvinistic in regard to election also. However, the major unifying factor, which many of the writers have missed, is their view of general redemption, as proved by the anthology of essays edited by Edwards A. Park. Unfortunately in their desire to affirm general redemption some seem to have denied substitution in the cross and moved to the governmental theory more conducive to Arminianism.[B] My analysis of Greek words for the cross in chapters 5 and 6 shows that this was an unnecessary exigency. It is fair to appraise the New Divinity "As a *via media* between Puritan Calvinism and eighteenth century Arminianism."[24]

It is also significant to note a further modification of President Edwards' theology by his grandson, Timothy Dwight (1752-1817), the President of Yale and his protege Nathaniel Taylor (1786-1858), who stressed human free will, the "power to the contrary." This is sometimes referred to as the 'New Haven' theology. They were seeking to respond to the Unitarian charge that determinism promotes immorality by denying human freedoms. This seems to have influenced some of the revivalists of the Second Great Awakening to emphasize the ability which God has bestowed on all people to come to Christ. Evangelist Charles G. Finney (1792-1875) popularized Taylor's views in his revivals in the 1840s and 50s.[25]

B. Professor Leonard Woods at Andover was one who did hold to the substitution.

Moreover, the plot thickens as we dig into the impact of the new divinity movement. We observe that Adoniram Judson's father was one of the new divinity pastors who studied under Bellamy. Samuel Mills, Sr. and Ebenezer Fitch, the first President of Williams College were also new divinity adherents. *Thus it becomes clear that the American missions movement arose out of the new divinity movement, both at Williams College and Andover Seminary.*[26]

Revival connections. There is a strong connection between revival, evangelism, and missions. This can be clearly seen in the Second Great Awakening, which took place from 1785 to 1830. The revival and its attendant conversions mostly happened in the churches of the new divinity pastors, although some historians have tried to minimize the connection by caricaturizing them as dry, heavily theological preachers. However, Bellamy and Emmons were great preachers, who personally trained a host of the new divinity pastors to preach in a popular, extemporaneous style. As early as 1780 Chandler Robbins began to see revival at Plymouth, Mass. and nearby towns. In the mid 80s it spread to other new divinity churches, among which Stephen West and Nathaniel Emmons especially reported abundant conversions. Nathan Strong saw recurring revival at Hartford from 1794 to 1815. By 1799 Samuel Hopkins wrote John Ryland in England of 100 towns in New England and eastern New York state which were experiencing awakening, "mostly if not wholly under preachers of [neo-]Edwardean divinity." The result was that most of the candidates for the ministry were new divinity adherents and the number of such pastors expanded rapidly, by 1792 there were 58 in Connecticut and by 1808, 170 in Massachusetts.[27]

When Timothy Dwight became president of Yale College in 1795 he faced widespread skepticism in the student body influenced by French deism and he confronted it head on. He turned the tide on campus and by 1802 "a student revival at Yale witnessed the conversion of one-third of the student body (75 out of 225 students). It touched off a series of awakenings which revived eastern colleges periodically during the next fifty years."[28]

Hopkins' missionary initiative. Just as Joseph Bellamy was a key man in personally training pastors, Samuel Hopkins was key in developing its theology and missionary burden. As early as 1771 Hopkins drafted a proposal to send freed black slaves back to Africa as missionaries, and he had two eager volunteers in his church at Newport, R.I. Despite opposition from more liberal pastors he sent out a circular to raise support for liberating them and sending them back to Guinea, but the Revolutionary War not only squelched the response, but prospective missionary, John Quamine, was killed in the war. After the war Hopkins renewed his efforts with three surviving candidates, but unfortunately he linked his plans with efforts to colonize freed slaves to Africa, which lost him the support of the Quaker abolitionists. He persisted in his efforts until his death but without success. Following the example of William Carey's Baptist mission, new divinity pastors took the lead in the first home missionary society in Connecticut in

1798 and in Massachusetts in 1799. Hopkins himself became the first president of the Missionary Society of Rhode Island in 1801. In 1808 Andover Theological Seminary was founded mostly by new divinity men.[29]

Missionary recruiter. But the story does not end here. In 1821 Edward Griffin turned down other offers to become a college president to become the President of Williams College, which was struggling with a threat of competition from Amherst. He not only proved to be a 'white knight' in saving the college, but began to mentor another generation of missionaries who went out from Williams College. Eleven men from the class of 1826 were influenced by Griffin toward missions, including Hollis Read who sailed for Calcutta with Hervey and Ramsey. At the Baccalaureate in 1827, Griffin said, "I long to see every class go forth in the spirit of a Mills, Richards, and Robbins, determined to make their influence felt on the other side of the globe." Nathan Brown and ten of his classmates responded. Brown wrote a missionary hymn under Griffin's influence. That outflow continued for many years, both under Griffin through his retirement in 1836, and his successor, Mark Hopkins (1802-1872).[30]

American Baptists' backdoor entrance into missions

Although the first five missionaries were Congregationalists when they embarked for India, Adoniram Judson and Luther Rice on board separate ships, having time to study the issue, came to baptistic convictions. After the missionary team was denied entry into India by the British East India Company, it was decided that Luther Rice should go back to America to stir up support from the Baptists, while the Judsons went on to Burma. "Largely through his efforts, they formed the General Missionary Convention of the Baptist Denomination in the United States. There was stout resistance to the project. Some objected on theological grounds, the old hyper-Calvinism maintaining that such efforts were blasphemous, since God would save those whom he chose, and the others could not be saved in any event."[31] Luther Rice influenced John M. Peck to take leadership in Baptist outreach in the expanding nation and around the world. He too found strong opposition, especially from the Primitive Baptists, to the idea of any use of means in the work of God, whether at home or abroad. Dan O. Shelton tells of Peck's struggles:

> He met pastors who strongly opposed missions. They were obstinate and did not recognize individual responsibility. In consequence of their views they were prayerless, objected to the use of means in the conversion of men, and denied the necessity of sending the Gospel to the destitute. At one meeting they passed a resolution debarring from a seat any one who was a member of a missionary society.[32]

American church historian Sweet confirms: "The doctrinal basis of antimissionism was hyper-Calvinistic. It stated that God in His sovereign power did not need any human means to bring His elect to repentance."[33]

The legacy of missions to American Indians

I had alluded to the early colonists' missions to the American Indians as a significant foundation for both British and American foreign missions. R. Pierce Beaver has made some of the ordination sermons and charges to the first missionaries accessible to us. As I peruse these documents, I sense that American Christians were not so much opposed to missions in the 18th century as they were absorbed with ministry to the native Americans. The 17th century missionaries were first of all pastors, like John Eliot, who were not ordained to Indian work. Thus the first record Beaver gives us was of the ordination of three missionaries of the Scottish S. P. C. K. in 1733. The sermon by Joseph Sewall, pastor of the Old South Church in Boston, was an excellent exposition of Acts 26:16-19, in which he emphasized human responsibility and obedience to God in fulfilling the Great Commission and going **"to open their eyes."** He makes the very point I have made throughout this work: "And though the work itself is truly Divine, (it is the Work of the Holy Spirit savingly to enlighten and change the Heart, and turn Sinners from the power of Satan to God,) yet is our glorious Lord pleased to put honour upon his Ministers in using them as Instruments in his Hand, in this wonderful Work."[34] I sense that just as Calvinism in Great Britain was becoming more rigid in the 18th century, the same was happening in the colonies. However, there was a wonderful cross-pollenization across the Atlantic. Fuller and Carey were reading Edwards, Brainerd, and Bellamy. The Americans were reading Fuller's *The Gospel Worthy of All Acceptation*.[35] Judson read the sermon of Claudius Buchanan, a chaplain of the East India Company, which so affected him. That wonderful interchange of biblical thinking opened the minds of Christians on both sides of the Atlantic to human responsibility to evangelize and fulfill the Great Commission.

Theological crosscurrents in contemporary missiology

One of the major advances in missiology in the last half century had been the 'church growth movement' initiated by the writings of Donald A. McGavran, starting with *The Bridges of God* in 1955. McGavran insisted that we must research how and why some people groups turn to Christ in significant numbers while others are resistant. His suggestion that we should get the statistics of "people-movement conversions" and try to understand the sociological and anthropological factors influencing such mass conversions ran into significant opposition from determinists at first.[36] Such emphasis upon the human factors did not harmonize well with doctrines of unconditional election and irresistible grace. McGavran, having been raised in a missionary family in India in the Restorationist movement, was not bothered by such problems in the least. He had seen the "mass movements" out of untouchability in India and sought to analyze them intelligently. I came into the Punjab of Pakistan in 1956 to find that most of the million in the Christian community had come out of untouchable Hindu background over the previous seventy years, the majority of whom were Presbyterians. Apparently the early Presbyterian missionaries, like David Martin, saw it as a work of the Spirit of God working through family web relationships, but they didn't stop to analyze it as McGavran did. In missions it is obvious that various human factors are important in the way in which various people groups come to Christ. Missionaries began to realize that a number of cultural, linguistic, and religious barriers between different people groups hinder the progress of the gospel and that we need to bridge those gaps. I suspect that by now most Calvinistic missionaries have been forced to go along with the obvious realities of this way of thinking. However, it seems to me that it adds another area of tension for Calvinistic theology since unconditional election and irresistible grace leave little room for such heavy human factors.

DETERMINISM INCONSISTENT WITH EVANGELISM

Since global persuasion evangelism should be axiomatic for the biblical Christian, and since we have seen some serious historical tensions with deterministic theology, let us focus on the theological and logical tensions.

Determinism undermines motivation for evangelism.

If the issue of who will be saved and who will go to hell was settled in eternity past, then there is nothing which any human being can do to change that, whether it be the sinner or the Christian witness. Moderate Calvinists insist that God has decreed the means as well as the end result, but if I refuse to witness for Christ or become a missionary, it follows that this also had been decreed by God and nothing I could do could change it. I can rationalize *ad infinitum* that God did not decree for me to be a witness for Christ or to become a missionary and assume no blame for inaction. We already have enough rationalizations which keep most Christians from a significant witness for Christ without another specious one! Not only do we have rationalizations, but we all face serious natural, spiritual, and circumstantial obstacles which keep us from indigenous and global evangelism. Unless we have a clear and strong motivation to overcome these hindrances, the job will never get done.

This is true of all ministry as well. If I had not had strong motivation, this book would never have been written. Since I began to write it, I have had four major health crises, any one of which could have been fatal, or at the least kept me from pressing on. I am now wondering how much of this has been satanic opposition to prevent this book from seeing the light of day. But in all of this, God's miraculous providence has overruled and, along with the miracles of modern medicine, has kept me alive and functional (I think). I usually don't enjoy getting out there to exercise three times a week to rebuild my badly damaged heart, but I know I would not be alive if I weren't doing it. Motivation is so important.

In this connection that great evangelistic pastor, Charles Spurgeon remarked, "But there are some people so selfish that, provided they go to heaven, it is enough they are in the covenant. They are dear enough people of God. . . ." "They say it is equal whether God ordains a man's life or death. They would sit still to hear men damned. . . . They seem to have no feeling for anyone but themselves. They have dried the heart out of them by some cunning slight of hand." He went on to comment about the father of British extreme Calvinism: "During the pastorate of my venerated predecessor, Dr. Gill, this Church, instead of increasing, gradually decreased. . . . . But mark this, from the day when Fuller, Carey, Sutcliffe, and others, met together to send out missionaries to India, the sun began to dawn of a gracious revival which is not over yet." He added, "The system of theology with which many identify his [Gill's] name has chilled many churches to their very soul, for it has led them to omit the free invitations of the gospel, and to deny that it is the duty of sinners to believe in Jesus."[37]

I do not question that Fuller and Spurgeon were Calvinists. However, as I read Fuller, I sense that he was ambivalent about general versus particular redemption. Scholars quote Spurgeon on both sides of the issue. As can be seen clearly from the citations in appendix E, Calvin himself held to general redemption, as did Moyse Amyraut (see next chapter). I have sat under the ministry of three five-point Calvinists who believed in and practiced evangelism and missions, so I can understand them quite well, although I believe them to be totally inconsistent. However, I notice that they never preach their Calvinism from the pulpit. Indeed, as that professor of homiletics, James Daane, has pointed out, the doctrine of unconditional election is unpreachable.[38]

Total inability promotes pessimism about salvation.

The extrapolation of the biblical doctrine of human depravity into the notion of total inability (cf. ch. 4) has spread a pall of pessimism regarding the possibility of salvation both among the unregenerate under Calvinistic teaching and the Christians who should be confronting them and explaining the simple plan of salvation to them. This was very clear from reading Archibald Alexander's many conversion stories (ch. 14, pp. 318-9) and the testimonies of men like Andrew Fuller and Edward Griffin, as well as the opposition from theologians like Beza and Ursinus. The logic of it is inexorable. If mankind is totally unable to respond to the gospel and must wait for God's irresistible grace based upon an eternal decree, why bother to try to get saved or to win a sinner to Christ? It is all set in concrete. Even worse, if you will pardon the worldly expression, it is a 'stacked deck.'

Determinism leads to lack of persistence in evangelism.

Very few Christians have been saved the first time they heard the gospel of Christ. This is true of those coming out of nominally Christian cultures, but even more striking of those who come from Muslim or Hindu backgrounds. In my lifelong involvement with missionaries to Muslims and Hindus, it has become clear that we must focus upon *the process of conversion*, that is, the process by which people come to repentant faith in Christ. The new birth is instantaneous, but the soul struggle to come to faith may take years. This was true even of Saul of Tarsus, who heard the gospel from the lips of those whom he persecuted and dragged into the courts. He heard Stephen's testimony and graphic confrontation. When the Lord Jesus appeared to him on the Damascus road, he said, "**It is hard for you to kick against the goads**" (Acts 26:14). Paul's conversion was not instantaneous, but his new birth was! However, the notion of irresistible grace leaves little room for such a protracted process. Thus the witness would not be inclined to understand the necessity for dogged persistence in witness. Some Calvinists do exemplify such persistence, but it is not because of their Calvinism but despite it.

Determinism complicates the simple gospel message.

If the deterministic doctrines of unconditional election and irresistible grace are true, then the simple gospel message of the apostles has been incredibly complicated and mystified. On the day of Pentecost when Peter confronted a nation which had crucified their Messiah, "**All of you must imperatively repent, . . . for the forgiveness of your [pl.] sins; and you [pl.] will receive the gift of the Holy Spirit** (Acts 2:38, Olson expanded trans.), there was no other unspoken implied contingency in Peter's promise, such as, "**if God has elected you**." A determinist's response would be that Peter was speaking to thousands and the promise was only valid for the elect among them. However, Paul's word to the Philippian jailor was primarily to an individual, "**Believe in the Lord Jesus, and you will be saved, . . .**" (Acts 16:31). If the deterministic doctrines are true, Paul had an unspoken, hidden agenda here, that is, "**Assuming that God has elected you.**" Even worse, the Lord Jesus had an unspoken reservation in His mind when He said to the Samaritan woman, "**Everyone who drinks of this water will thirst again, but whoever drinks of the water that I will give him shall never thirst; but the water that I will give him will become in him a well of water springing up to eternal life**" (Jn. 4:13b-14). We rightly object to the Arminians reading an unspoken conditional "if" into John 10:27-29. What right do we have to read an unspoken reservation into these blanket promises of the gospel?

Repentant faith is not some mysterious, mystical intangible, which God arbitrarily gives to some hell-bound sinners and withholds from others. It is the human response to God's ultimatum of the gospel, which men are commanded to do in simply receiving God's Son. How many millions of anxious sinners have been lost because nobody explained to them how simple and available the promises of the gospel really are.

In chapter 5 I have already shared Lightner's point that it is impossible to personalize the gospel to an individual sinner if one holds a deterministic theology. One must be vague and general about the terms of the gospel to avoid breaching one's sacrosanct theology.

Determinism is counterproductive of church growth.

Evangelist Robert Sumner has made an observation which I believe can be substantiated over and over again today and through the centuries: "Many, many more souls are being 'elected' into the family of God where a strong program of New Testament evangelism is in operation than in the *non*-evangelistic– and sometimes even *anti*-evangelistic– atmosphere of the 'tulip' churches."[39] If we look at the contemporary scene we see the rapid growth of Pentecostalism and some other Arminian churches, far outstripping Calvinistic churches. When one checks the television schedule it is obvious that Pentecostals have been way ahead in the use of modern media. In Latin America they have learned to harness the power of their 'street seminaries.' Observing the listings of evangelical Bible colleges over recent decades seems to show disproportionate Arminian growth. In short they have a more aggressive program of evangelism and missions and are seeing the fruit of it. Does this mean that their theology is right? Not necessarily, since many cults such as the Mormons have been using biblical methods of evangelism to great advantage. However, if unconditional election were true, should not God be electing at least as many, if not more people in Calvinistic churches than in Arminian? Some may say, "Gordon, you are a pragmatist!" Not at all! I am simply suggesting that we must test our theologies by its fruit, or lack thereof.

Henry Cook, in lectures delivered at Spurgeon's College, made an intriguing comparison:

> He [Whitefield] never spared himself either in England or in America. He swept though the countryside like a prairie fire. Yes, but it was like a prairie fire that soon burnt itself out. Multitudes heard him and were moved by him to decision. But practically nothing remained when he had gone. He seemed almost to spend his strength for naught and in vain. Wesley, on the other hand, was no great orator, and he never caused the sensation that Whitefield did. He was possessed of a deep religious experience and he preached with great earnestness, but he had none of the magnetic drive of Whitefield. Yet is was Wesley and not Whitefield that did the permanent work and left the permanent memorial.[40]

These two great evangelists were close friends. Neither one's theology is proved by his fruit. But Wesley simply used a biblical methodology of planting churches, which acknowledged that it was the evangelist's responsibility to follow up his converts by gathering them into fellowship groups. Apparently Whitefield's Calvinistic theology caused him to leave the follow-up to God's sovereignty.

Determinism raises serious missiological problems.

In this connection I remind the reader of two serious problems I raised in chapter 10: Why are some kind of peoples harder to reach than others if irresistible grace is true? Is is it fair of God to save more Americans than Mongolians, Muslims, caste Hindus, etc., if unconditional election is true?

CONCLUSIONS

In short I am arguing that there is not just inconsistency or paradoxical tension between deterministic theology and global evangelism, but a *serious disconnect and contradiction*, both logically, pragmatically, and historically. This does not disprove Calvinism or extreme Calvinism. But it should cause determinists to go back and check their theology to see if perchance they might have gotten it wrong.

I cannot close this chapter without raising the question as to how many millions are eternally condemned because of the failure of Protestant churches to pursue global persuasion evangelism from the Reformation until now? How many in India from 1517 until 1705 are condemned because Protestants' deterministic theology restrained missions and persuasion evangelism; how many in Africa; how many in Latin America? Indeed, how many European and American Protestants who desired to be saved were not because the simple offer of the gospel was not thought theologically appropriate? Some will respond that this was the sovereign will and decree of God. No, the responsibility is upon us Christians who have complicated the message beyond belief! **"The Lord is not slow about His promise, as some count slowness, but is patient toward you [Christians], not wishing for any to perish but for all to come to repentance"** (2 Pet. 3:9).

Note: This chapter is based on a paper given to the Eastern Regional of the Evangelical Missiological Society, Valley Forge, PA, May, 1992.

---

1. David J. Hesselgrave, *Communicating Christ Cross-Culturally* (GR: Zondervan, 1978), p. 55; He references J. I. Packer, *Evangelism and the Sovereignty of God* (Chicago: IVP, 1961), pp. 48-49, 413-23, and A. Duane Litfin, "The Perils of Persuasive Preaching, " *Christianity Today*, 21 (4 Feb., 1977):484-7.
2. Herbert J. Kane, *A Concise History of the Christian World Mission,* p. 76.
3. Gustav Warneck, *Outline of a History of Protestant Missions*, trans. George Robson, p. 38.
4. Ibid.
5. Thomas Coates, "Were the Reformers Mission-Minded?" *Concordia Theological Monthly,* 40:9, 600-11; Charles Chaney, "The Missionary Dynamic in the Theology of John Calvin," *The Reformed Review*, 17:64, 24-38; Samuel M. Zwemer, p. 206-16; Harry R. Boer, *Pentecost and Missions* (1961), p. 18. Boer faults all the Reformers but Bucer in this regard.
6. Coates, "Reformers," p. 604.
7. Martin Luther, *Sammtliche Schriften,* 2d ed., ed. Joh. Georg Walch (St. Louis: Concordia Publishing House, 1880-1910), vol. 14, p. 305.
8. Harry R. Boer, *Pentecost and Missions* (GR: Eerdmans, 1961), p. 18.
9. Coates, "Reformers," p. 601.
10. Martin Luther, quoted by Johannes Warns, *Baptism: Studies in the Original Christian Baptism,* trans. G. H. Lang (Paternoster, 1957), p. 248, 252.

11. There is a striking parallel between the 7 churches and 7 major epochs of church history. There may be a secondary application here.

12. Kane, *Concise History*, pp. 83-84.

13. Walter Bruce Davis, *William Carey: Father of Modern Missions* (Chicago: Moody, 1963), p. 105.

14. A. C. Underwood, *A History of the English Baptists*, pp. 134-35, cited by Fisk, *Calvinistic Paths*, pp. 143-44.

15. Cited by Richard Fletcher, *Barbarian Conversion: from Paganism to Christianity* (NY: Henry Holt, 1997), p. 1.

16. Fisk, *Calvinistic Paths*, pp. 141-154; Andrew Gunton Fuller, *The Complete Wordks of Andrew Fuller*, 2 vols.(Boston: Lincoln, Edmands, 1833); Fisk references A. C. Underwood (British Baptist historian); H. C. Vedder; Peter Toon; John T. Christian; NIDCC; *Eerdmans Handbook of the History of Christianity; The Oxford Dictionary of the Christian Church;* Schaff-Herzog Encyclopedia; Brooks Hays and J. E. Steely, etc.

17. Fuller, pp. 20ff.

18. Ibid, pp. 25ff.

19. Ibid, pp. 42-65.

20. Excerpts in Hawthorne and Winter, eds., *Perspectives*, rev. ed.(Pasadena, CA: USCWM, 1992) pp. B-94ff.

21. Kane, *Concise History*, p. 85.

22. Terry G. Carter, The Calvinism of William Carey and its Effect on his Mission Work," a paper delivered at ETS 2001 at Colorado Springs, Nov. 2001. Carter was looking for evidences of Carey's Calvinism and was quite disappointed not to find any.

23. Edward D. Griffin, *An Humble Attempt to Reconcile the Differences of Christians Respecting the Extent of the Atonement* (I have not located the original 1815 edition, but it is included with the essays in Edwards A. Park, ed., *The Atonement, Discourses and Treatises by Jonathan Edwards, John Smalley, Jonathan Maxcy, Nathanael Emmons, Edward D. Griffin, Caleb Burge, and William R. Weeks* (Boston: Congregational board of Publications, 1859), pp. 137-427, in which is also found Prof. Park's Introductory Essay to which I alluded; Joseph A. Conforti, *Samuel Hopkins and the New Divinity Movement*, p. 163.

24. O. W. Heick and J. L. Neve, *A History of Christian Thought*, 2 vols. (Phila.: Muhlenberg, 1946), II: 280. A good but somewhat biased summary pp. 276-80.

25. Walter A. Elwell, ed., *Evangelical Dictionary of Theology*, pp. 336-7, 415-6, 483-4, 761-2, 767-8, 786, 1070.

26. Conforti, pp. 3-5, 159-93, 227-232; Park, Ibid; Woodbridge, Noll, and Hatch, *The Gospel in America*, pp. 30-32.

27. Conforti, pp. 175-190.

28. Woodbridge, et al., pp. 107-8, 144.

29. Ibid, pp. 142-158.

30. John H. Hewitt, *Williams College and Foreign Missions* (Boston: Pilgrim Press, 1914) ad seriatim; Mark Hopkins, *A Discourse occasioned by the death of Rev. Edward Dorr Griffin* (Troy, NY: Tuttle, Belcher, Burton, 1837); Ansel Nash, *Memoir of Edward Dorr Griffin* (New York, Benedict, 1842); *The Haystack Prayer Meeting: An Account of its Origin and Spirit* (Haystack Centennial Celebration, 1906); Calvin Durfee, *Sketch of the Life of Ebenezer Fitch* (Boston: Mass. Sabb. School Society, 1865).

31. Brooks Hays and J. E. Steely, *The Baptist Way of Life*, p. 23, quoted by Fisk, p. 171.

32. Dan O. Shelton, *Heroes of the Cross in America*, p. 109, as quoted by Fisk, p. 172.

33. William Warren Sweet, *The Story of Religion in America* (NY: Harper, 1930), p. 257.

34. R. Pierce Beaver, *Pioneers in Mission* (GR: Eerdmans, 1966), p. 49.

35. Americans apparently appreciated Andrew Fuller more than the British did, since the first two editions of his complete works were published in America (1820-25 and 1833), the British edition coming belatedly in 1848.

36. Donald A. McGavran, *The Bridges of God* (NY: Friendship Press, 1955), p. 107; cf. *Understanding Church Growth* rev. (GR: Eerdmans, 1970).

37. Charles H. Spurgeon, cited by Iain Murray, *Spurgeon v. Hyper-Calvinism: The Battle for Gospel Preaching* (Carlisle, PA: Banner of Truth, 1995), pp. 112, 120, 127.

38. James Daane, *The Freedom of God.*

39. Robert L. Sumner, *An Examination of TULIP* (Murphreesboro, TN: Biblical Evangelism Press, 1972), p. 22.

40. Henry Cook, *The Theology of Evangelism* (London:Carey Kingsgate, 1951), p. 117, cited by Fisk, *Paths*, p. 170.

History, I think, is probably a bit like a pebbly beach, a complicated mass, secretively three-dimensional. It is very hard to chart what lies up against what, and why and how deep. What does tend to get charted is what looks manageable, most recognisable (and usually linear) like the wriggly flow of flotsam and jetsam, and stubborn tar deposits.

-Richard Wentworth

18

THE CONFIRMATION OF CHRISTIAN HISTORY: IS THIS A NEW DOCTRINE?

A score of years ago as I was increasingly becoming disillusioned with the biblical basis for deterministic theology, I was intrigued to find a lot of historical stimulus for my pilgrimage in Brian G. Armstrong's *Calvinism and the Amyraut Heresy*.[1] He showed the historical roots of a most significant reaction to extreme Calvinism, in the seventeenth-century Amyraldian movement of the Reformed churches of France. As I have broadened my historical study I have found that there is a substantial trail of historical movements which have been totally supportive of a "middle way," as Bishop Ussher sought in the sixteenth century. I was encouraged to find many historical antecedents for a mediate theology of salvation between determinism and semi-Pelagianism.

I must make it clear that ultimately this chapter says little about the truth or falsity of the position advocated here, since there is only one standard of truth—the Bible as the inerrant word of God. Christian history can only confirm and support the results of biblical exegesis; it should not be preliminary to, or even considered a parallel study to the biblical investigation. It must be considered only as a test or confirmation of the results of our theological endeavor. That is, if our results do not find any antecedents in the history of Christian thought, then we must go back and re-examine our biblical data to see where we might have gone wrong. But far too much theological study starts with the historical, which by the nature of the case is far more subjective than the biblical data.

There are a number of reasons that Christian historical study must be so limited. The first is the imperfection of the historical record. We know that a very significant proportion of the documents upon which we should be basing our study have long since perished. Whether it be the destructive incursions of the barbarians, persecutions by anti-Christian forces, the persecutions of a minority Christian group by the political majority church (whether Roman Catholic or Protestant), armed Muslim incursions, or just the ravages of time and bacterial action, much has been lost. And the loss has not been impartial. For example, most of what we know about Pelagius we know from his enemy, Augustine. So it is probable that the available data is skewed from the start. We know that there were significant persecuted evangelical groups during the medieval period, but how many leaders had opportunity to write theology, and how many of their works have survived?

Another limitation is the theological bias of the historiographer. The great Philip Schaff, in the preface to the first edition of his monumental history, naively states, "Having no sectarian ends to serve, I have confined myself to the duty of a witness—to tell the truth, the whole truth, and nothing but the truth;"[2] But as objective as Schaff tries to be, at times he goes far beyond the duty of a historiographer and frequently gives a theological refutation of the views of a particular historical figure. This is hardly objective historiography! The fact is that we all have our biases and our theological presuppositions. I make no bones about the fact that I come to this historical study with a bias. Because of my biblical studies I have concluded that an intermediate theology of salvation is true to God's word. Now I come to Christian history to see whether others before us have come to the same or similar viewpoints. The present study confirms that there are substantial antecedents for this middle way; indeed, it raises serious problems for the deterministic soteriologies which date back to Augustine.

AUGUSTINE, THE FIRST PREDESTINARIAN

The great hyatus

Early in my research in the church fathers I came across a startling statement by Reformed theologian Paul K. Jewett: "As has often been observed, the first true predestinarian was Augustine."[3] This may not have given pause to Professor Jewett, but the question immediately arose in my mind of almost four centuries of church history without any predestinarian teaching or emphasis, as other historians confirm. How could this be if it is a basic biblical doctrine, as Jewett states? If it is so basic, how could the disciples of the Apostles and their succeeding disciples for almost four hundred years have barely discussed the subject? But perusal of the pre-Augustinian fathers confirms this widely acknowledged fact. The fathers said much about free will, indeed, they coined the term.[4] But they said little or nothing about election or predestination.

We can understand this of those fathers who made limited use of

Paul's epistles. But even after his letters were widely accepted into the canon, the subject was ignored. Forster and Marston give extensive quotations from the fathers before the council of Ephesus (431) who held to free will: Justin Martyr (100-165), Irenaeus (130-200), Athenagorus (II), Theophilus of Antioch (II), Tatian of Syria (late II), Bardasian of Syria (154-222), Clement of Alex. (150-215), Tertullian (155-225), Novatian of Rome (200-258), Origen (185-254), Methodius of Olympus (260-311), Archelaus (d. 277), Arnobius of Sicca (253-327), Cyril of Jerusalem (312-386), Gregory of Nyssa (335-395), John Chrysostom (347-407), Jerome (347-420), Augustine in his early writings, and Cyril of Alexandria (376-444). Norman Douty references many of the above and adds names of others whom he documents as holding to general redemption: Eusebius (260-340), Athanasius (293-373), Gregory Nazianzen (324-389), Basil (330-379), and Ambrose (340-407).[5]

Those historians who address the problem tend to attribute it to the struggle against Gnosticism and Manicheanism, which were both fatalistic. This would be especially true in the eastern churches, which never did get into the doctrine of predestination, as did the western churches. This might go a small way toward explaining this vast omission, but in the main it still leaves this very serious problem for determinists unresolved. Those closest to the apostles were oblivious of a supposedly basic and important doctrine. But then, none of the apostles except Paul ever refers to foreordination, and Peter only refers to election three times. I have sought to show in previous chapters that the passages in John's Gospel usually connected with this doctrine are taken out of their broader context. There is no reference to foreordination in his epistles or the Revelation, nor in the synoptic Gospels, Acts, James, Jude, or Hebrews. Apparently these writers also did not feel that it was that basic or important either. Therefore, we should not be astonished if the early fathers omit reference as well.

Pejorative pigeonholing

As we survey the church fathers we find a significant problem in classifying their anthropology and soteriology. Usually three categories are considered: Pelagian, Semi-Pelagian, and Augustinian. As I studied the literature, I concluded that this was a gross oversimplification. Most Evangelicals agree that Pelagius was a heretic; both his anthropology and soteriology were seriously defective. But to attach his name to mediating fathers is clearly to use a pejorative and prejudicial term (Semi-Pelagian) of those who were not heretics. Would you like to be called a semi-heretic, just because you don't go all the way with Augustine? This along with pejorative and careless use of the term 'synergist' is very common in the literature. I concluded that many should be more accurately designated as semi-Augustinians. And then I noted that both Schaff and Neve do use that terminology and make that distinction to some extent (which Sproul and others do not do).[6]

But the more I dug into the diversity of viewpoints, I concluded that we should also distinguish two types of semi-Augustinians. While all semi-Augustinians held to Augustine's basic anthropology and emphasis upon God's grace in salvation, they did not want to follow him in his view of unconditional election and irresistible grace. Many of them emphasized God's initiative in salvation by some reference to prevenient grace (not necessarily universal). But others while stressing grace were not so sure that man did not have to take the first step by responding to the message of grace. So I would distinguish the prevenient grace semi-Augustinians from the human initiative semi-Augustinians. But all tended to see regeneration itself as fully a work of grace.

Semi-Pelagians, on the other hand, do not have a clear doctrine of regeneration and are synergistic. Pelagius (350-409), of course, was not even synergistic, at least as he was represented by his enemies. Ultimately, we can not be sure what he taught, since primary sources are minimal. Some historians like Neve, Walker, Williston, and Seeberg say that he had a much deeper concept of human guilt and of God's grace than usually represented. Schaff mentions that he understood justification in the sense of 'declaring righteous,' not like Augustine in the catholic sense of 'making righteous.'[7] This is a curious reversal.

Such distinctions are difficult to make before Augustine's time since few of those fathers wrestled with these issues. To be fair, it may be that Justin Martyr may be one of the few major fathers we could accuse (anachronistically) of being semi-Pelagian. Perhaps others of the more ascetic, legalistic fathers would fit into this category. But probably most of the early fathers fit better into a semi-Augustinian category, some more monergistic, some more synergistic. The anonymous Epistle to Diognetus (ca. 150), Tertullian (150-220), Hilary (300-366), and Ambrose (350-397) emphasized the gracious nature of salvation. Irenaeus (120-202), Origen (185-254), John Chrysostom (347-407), and Jerome (347-415) probably show more synergism, but should not be connected pejoratively with Pelagian heresy. This would probably be true of many of the better eastern church fathers. In any case it would seem clear that all believed in general redemption and to varying degrees in 'free will.'[8]

Pelagianism was rejected at the Synod of Carthage in 412 and again in 418, and that rejection was confirmed at the Third Ecumenical Council at Ephesus (431). Neve affirms, "But the rejection of Pelagianism did not mean the acceptance of everything in the Augustinian system. It was Augustine's doctrine of predestination which gave offense, to those even who otherwise favored him in his controversy with Pelagius."[9]

The triumph of semi-Augustinianism

There is no question that Augustine not only started a major battle with Pelagianism, which he won, but for a century afterward a major controversy continued among those who accepted his essential anthropology (original sin) and his emphasis upon grace in salvation. But other than his disciple and defender, Prosper of Aquitaine (d. 463), virtually no one accepted his views on predestination and irresistible grace, and even Prosper held to general redemption.[10] Confirming the absolute novelty of his views, his contemporaries like Jerome (347-415) and Ambrose (350-397) argued that very objection—these views were absolutely new and not held by any in the church before Augustine.

Augustine's view on election and irresistible grace spawned a strong reaction from many like John Cassian (d. 435), Vincent of Lerins (wrote "Commonitorium" ca. 434), Arnobius the younger (wrote about 460), Maxentius, Gennadius of Massila (d. ca. 495), Faustus of Rhegium (d. 495), Caesarius, Archbishop of Arles (502-542), and Avitius, Archbishop of Vienna (490-523). These should all probably be classed as semi-Augustinian, not semi-Pelagian. A number of anonymous works from the fifth century are clearly semi-Augustinian: "Hypomnesticon," "Predestinatus" (460), and "De Vocatione Omnium Gentium" (ca. 461), the last of which may be by Bishop Leo I of Rome.[11] Synods at Arles (472) and Lyon (475) sought to resolve the question and ultimately it was brought to the Synod of Orange (529), where the semi-Augustinians won the day against Pelagianism, but with no mention of predestination or irresistible grace. Bishop Boniface II of Rome affirmed the decision of the council, as did Gregory the Great (d. 604) subsequently. Vincent of Larins set forth his famous criteria of catholic doctrine that, only that which has been "believed always, everywhere, and by all" is orthodox. This was seen as excluding Augustine's theory of predestination as being novel and new.

While the Synod of Orange rejected semi-Pelagianism and affirmed much of Augustine's doctrine of grace, it departed from his views in the following particulars, as summarized by Neve:

1. The only statement about predestination was a rejection of predestination to perdition.
2. There was no affirmation of irresistible grace.
3. God foreknows all things, good and evil, but His prescience as such is not causative.
4. Prevenient grace is affirmed.
5. The grace of God and the merits of Christ are for all; God earnestly desires and wills the salvation of all men (1 Tim. 2:4).
6. Through the grace of God all may, by the cooperation of God, perform what is necessary for their soul's salvation.[12]

Thus Jewett is clearly wrong when he claims that a "milder

predestinarianism became the official teaching of the Latin church" after the Synod of Orange.[13] Schaff states:

> At the synod of Orange (Arausio) in the year 529, at which Caesarius of Arles was leader, the Semi-Pelagian system, *yet without mention of its adherents,* was condemned in twenty-five chapters or canons, and the Augustinian doctrine of sin and grace was approved, without the doctrine of absolute or particularistic predestination. (italics his)[14]

This also makes it clear that there is a valid semi-Augustinian position distinct from semi-Pelagianism. Additionally, it seems viable to distinguish those semi-Augustinians who hold to prevenient grace from those who see man taking the first step. I will not try to press the classification since some of them are quite ambiguous on this point.

Augustine's doctrinal limitations and problems

Since Augustine of Hippo was such a towering figure in the history of Christian thought by permeating both Roman Catholic and reformation theology, it is important to evaluate his impact for good or bad. It was a mixed bag. He did move Christian theology back toward Paul's doctrine of grace in a significant way. We praise God for that. But we must also recognize that there were some serious negative elements in his background, linguistic and exegetical skills, his perspective, and hence in his theology, which developed into absolute evils in the churches, both Catholic and Protestant.

His soteriology. It should be clarified at this point that Augustine's soteriology was little developed. It certainly did not include the teaching of justification by faith, let alone the *sola fide* of the Reformers. The reason was his sacramental view of salvation through baptism, the eucharist, and membership in the majority, politically approved Roman church. Beyond that there was no need for soteriology. Indeed it was his strong emphasis upon baptismal regeneration and an external organizational unity of the church allied with the state which set the pattern for the dead state-churchism of much of European Christendom over the centuries. I believe that this is *the* major heresy in Christendom today, through which hundreds of millions are "damned through the church." One of the most offensive views to his contemporaries was that unbaptized infants are damned.

Augustine had an incredible impact upon the medieval Latin-Catholic church, which clearly lapsed into scholasticism. Schaff states: "He ruled the entire theology of the middle age, and became the father of scholasticism in virtue of his dialectic mind, and the father of mysticism in virtue of his devout heart, without being responsible for the excesses of either system."[15] We all might not agree!

Coercive persecution of non-conformists. It was out of his controversy with the Donatists that Augustine not only moved to putting loyalty to the majority church above loyalty to the word of God, but actually began to advocate coercion in order to force the Donatist 'sectarians' back into the Roman church. He grossly misinterpreted the parable of the great wedding feast in Luke 14:15-24, with tragic consequences over the centuries. He misinterpreted 'compel' (*anagkazein*) as implying physical force and used it as a basis for persecuting the Donatists, who were probably closer to the truth than he was. Subsequently, Augustine's misinterpretation became the basis for the infamous inquisition and for the Reformers' persecution of the Anabaptists. That centuries of persecution of true and godly believers can be traced back to Augustine's careless exegesis is outrageous. It was not that Augustine was a creature of his times, because leading catholics like Athanasius, Chrysostom, Martin of Tours, Lactantius, Hilary of Poitiers and Ambrose were horrified and protested this kind of persecution. Tertullian said, "God has not hangmen for priests. Christ teaches us to bear wrong, not to revenge it."[16] Although the political and religious situation was much confused, considerable bloodshed resulted, the horrendous consequence of Augustine's misinterpretation of one verse of Scripture. See appendix L for more discussion.

Connected with this is his view of the organizational nature of the universal (Catholic) church, in contrast with the biblical view of its mystical, organic nature. He saw apostolic succession and tradition as more important than conformity to Scripture. He admitted that the Donatists were orthodox in doctrine, and the fact is that they were more concerned about a pure church than Augustine. Yet he persecuted them! Schaff concludes that in Augustine "the state church found not only the first Christian leader of importance to advocate the use of persecution against non-conformists, but they found the only Christian theologian of significance whose theological system could justify such persecution."[17] The reference here is to the relation of irresistible grace to coercion to faith.

Manichean influence. There seem to be two doctrinal areas in Augustine which can be traced back to his nine years in Manicheanism before his conversion. Clearly his ascetic view of sex and the Christian life came from this. To be fair we must recognize that the Manichean dualism of body and spirit not only influenced him but other church fathers as well. Manicheanism had become a major rival force in the West as well as in the East where it originated. A. H. Newman states, "Augustine . . . was for many years connected with the Manicheans and his modes of thought were greatly affected by this experience."[18] He traces asceticism, the exaltation of virginity, viewing all sex as sinful, pompous ceremonials in the church, sacerdotalism, and indulgences as coming into the churches through the influence of Manicheanism.

I would also suggest that there are Manichean roots to Augustine's deterministic theology as well. The usual explanation by church historians for the emphasis upon free will and the absence of deterministic theology before Augustine, is that the fathers were reacting against the determinism and fatalism of Gnosticism and Manicheanism. Certainly this is possible. However, it seems much more likely to me that the pervasive influence of Manichean thought, although resisted by the other church fathers, finally gained entrance into the church through Augustine. He was the Trojan horse for Manichean determinism. Indeed, this connection was made by Faustus after Augustine's death. In denouncing the error of predestination he "identified the current predestinarian doctrine with pagan and Manichean fatalism."[19] A millennium later the opponents of Flacius, a defender of the deterministic "Old Lutheranism" view, accused him of Manicheanism.[20] In fact the Catholic church continued to reject determinism for another eleven centuries after the Synod of Orange, but an Augustinian monk named Martin Luther capitulated to it under the guise of grace and set the Protestant Reformation on this erroneous path.

One other serious consequence of Augustine's determinism was his denial of assurance. He taught that the elect can only be known by perseverance to the end of life. And thus he robbed believers of the most precious salvation reality short of eternal life itself. This is not a light or historically limited issue. It continues to be a major problem among Christians today (cf. ch. 14).

The root of Roman Catholic accretions. It has been widely acknowledged that many of the errors of Roman Catholicism have their roots in Augustine. Sir Robert Anderson wrote, "Nearly all the errors prevalent in Romanism can be traced back to Augustine." Warfield conceded that Augustine was "in a true sense the founder of Roman Catholicism." Zanchius referred to him as one of the four legs supporting the papal chair.[21] We have already observed some of the specifics, such as infant baptism, baptismal regeneration, state-churchism, coercion to faith, and the damnation of unbaptized infants. Through these errors he laid the foundation for purgatory and the concept of limbo, and many others.

MEDIEVAL DETERMINISM

The Greek church ignored Augustine and never showed any inclination toward absolute predestination. John of Damascus held to absolute foreknowledge but rejected absolute election since God cannot foreordain sin and does not force virtue upon the reluctant will. Schaff's summary of the western church is quite pointed:

> The Latin church retained a traditional reverence for Augustine, as her greatest divine, but never committed herself to his scheme of predestination. [He documents Neander and Gieseler.] It always

> found individual advocates, as Fulgentius of Ruspe, and Isidore of Seville, who taught a two-fold predestination, one of the elect unto life eternal, and one of the reprobate unto death eternal. Bede and Alcuin were Augustinians of a milder type. But the prevailing sentiment cautiously steered midway between Augustinianism and Semi-Pelagianism, giving chief weight to the preceding and enabling grace of God, yet claiming some merit for man's consenting and co-operating will. This compromise may be called Semi-Augustinianism, as distinct from Semi-Pelagianism. It was adopted by the Synod of Orange (Arausio) in 529, . . . It was transmitted to the middle ages through Pope Gregory the Great, who, next to Augustin, exerted most influence on the theology of our period; and this moderated and weakened Augustinianism triumphed in the Gottschalk controversy.[22]

Gottschalk was a ninth century monk who unsuccessfully sought to revive Augustinian theology. The national synod of France (860) seems to have ended the controversy in the medieval period, except for the passing work of John Scotus Erigena. At the behest of Hincmar he wrote on predestination in 850. He held a single predestination, which was identical with foreknowledge.[23] It seems that the subject was not significantly raised again until after the Reformation. But it is clear that the Roman Catholic church, on the popular lever, drifted increasingly into semi-Pelagianism over the centuries before the Reformation.

THE REFORMERS AND THEIR SUCCESSORS

The German and Swiss Reformations

Undoubtedly the Protestant Reformation took place in a time of great ferment: intellectually, religiously, politically, and theologically. Mankind frequently tends to overreact in such times, and many examples of overreaction at that time could be cited. The evaluation as to what is reaction and what is overreaction depends upon the observer's point of view. For example, while I would sympathize with the Anabaptists' desire for a more radical reformation, most people undoubtably would agree that the Munster rebellion was an overreaction. In many areas we might criticize Luther for not going far enough. It is possible that in the area of predestination Luther overreacted to the semi-Pelagianism of the Catholic church, and clearly in the succeeding centuries, there were more than a dozen significant movements which sought to bring things back into better balance.

One also gets the impression that he never totally broke free from either his Augustinian background or the scholastic way of thinking. His rationalizations about the faith of infants, the ubiquity of the body of Christ, consubstantiation, etc., reflect a scholastic mode of thinking. See appendix

L for further discussion.

Luther was, after all, an Augustinian monk and after his conversion he found Augustine's emphasis upon grace most conducive to his newly recovered understanding of justification by faith alone. In that regard he undoubtedly remained an Augustinian throughout. He considered his writing of *The Bondage of the Will* as one of the major achievements of his ministry.[A] Additionally, he did not totally divest himself of Augustine's baptismal regenerationism either. Although Augustine knew nothing of justification by faith alone, his emphasis on grace seemed like a good fit to Luther. Although there is discussion as to how much Zwingli owed to Luther, probably he was influenced toward a more deterministic soteriology by Luther. There is no question but that Calvin was greatly influenced by Luther's determinism.

The Anabaptist modifications. Within a few years some of Luther's and Zwingli's colleagues had second thoughts. By about 1521 Zwingli had drawn to himself a number of gifted young intellectuals who were converted and joined with him in the Zurich reformation. Within a few years some, like Conrad Grebel and Simon Stumpf, were pressing Zwingli for a more thoroughgoing reformation. Dr. Balthasar Hubmaier joined them in their attack against the mass and other Catholic accretions. By 1524 a group of seven radical reformers had broken with Zwingli and the next year crystallized their opposition to infant baptism by baptizing each other. Thus began the Swiss Anabaptist movement.[24] There were many distinct strands of the Anabaptist movement, but regarding them Newman states:

> They were almost without exception opposed to the Augustinian system of doctrine, especially in its Lutheran and Calvinistic forms, insisting upon the freedom of the will and the necessity of good works as the fruit of faith, and regarding faith as a great transforming process whereby we are brought not simply to participate in Christ's merits, but to enter into the completest union with him in a life of utter self-abnegation.[25]

Thus although determinism was not the basic cause of the split with the Reformers, the Anabaptist leaders, many of whom were well versed in the original languages and the church fathers, felt that the Scriptures militated against the Augustinian component of reformation theology. Moveover, their unusually consistent Christian life and testimony could not be impugned by the Protestants and Catholics, who slaughtered them by the thousands. As they moved on to early martyrdom they must have felt

A I was greatly distressed at the tone of Luther's attacks on Erasmus in this work. Scholars have not been honest in referring to Erasmus's work as a "diatribe," since the Latin word means a "scholarly disputation." Actually Luther's work is the diatribe. Dave Hunt has devoted two chapters to this debate between Luther and Erasmus and affirms my conclusion that they were both badly in error, with the truth being in the middle (*What Love Is This?*, pp. 165-188).

doubly convinced that Augustine's contribution to the Reformation was totally negative, especially in regard to his teaching of coercion to faith. Unfortunately, few of the leaders survived long enough to write any theological analysis of the issues, although men like Dr. Balthaser Hubmaier were fully competent to do so. Concerning him Estep affirms:

> His own moral and ethical sensitivity led him to champion the freedom of the will, for without it he saw no basis for Christian responsibility. Neither the sovereignty of God nor the grace of God nullified for Hubmaier the necessity of an uncoerced response to the gospel. It was the Word and the Spirit that God used to bring salvation to fallen humanity.[26]

Hans Denck was a Bavarian Anabaptist leader who "was exceedingly trained in the word of the Scriptures and educated in the three main languages." Like many other Anabaptists his views were misunderstood and misrepresented, but his latest biographer, Kiwiet, has shown that he was not a universalist, but held that Christ's death was an atonement sufficient for all humankind, but efficacious only to the believer.[27] Other examples could be given since the available literature in English on the Anabaptists is growing substantially.[28]

Bullinger's modification of Zwingli. Henry Bullinger (1504-1575) was Zwingli's successor in Zurich. It seems clear that he did not go as far as Zwingli and Calvin on predestination. He was quoted by English Bishop John Davenant as holding to general redemption. Schaff, however, suggests that he came closer to Calvin's view later in his ministry.[29] Schaff also alludes to Theodor Bibliander, Bullinger's colleague, as the father of biblical exegesis in Switzerland and a forerunner of Arminianism, who opposed Calvin's rigid view.

Melanchthon's modification. It is general knowledge that Luther's chief associate, Philip Melanchthon (1497-1560), quite early on began to moderate Luther's extreme views. Since Luther depended upon Philip to draft most of the important doctrinal standards of the Lutheran churches, these increasingly began to show evidence of Philip's modifications. The Augsburg Confession, drawn up by Melanchthon in 1530 does not state that faith is involuntary or that prevenient grace is necessary to faith. In 1532 he revised his earlier comments on Romans, which had reflected Luther's views, now to state, "And it is manifest that to resist belongs to the human will, because God is not the cause of sin." In his *Loci Communes* (1535) he ascribes conversion to three causes: the Word, the Holy Spirit, and the human will. He sought to avoid conflict with Luther in his lifetime, but by 1550 he was accused of 'synergism.'[30] About the time of Luther's death in 1546 there was already beginning to be two parties in Lutheranism: Jena was the center of the ultra-Lutherans, and Wittenberg of the Philippists.

When Philip died in 1561 a collection of his writings was published which represented Philippism as opposed to Lutheranism. The subsequent 'Synergistic Controversy' between Pfeffinger of Leipzig and Matthias Flacius was really about Philip's views, even though he was apparently not personally involved. As mentioned previously, Flacius's defense of strict Lutheran views was essentially Manichean, as his opponents made clear. Flacius's followers went even farther in Manichean thinking. Salinger of Rostock taught that "original sin is the very substance of the body and soul of man," and that Christ assumed "flesh of another species."[31] Although the Formula of Concord of 1580 represented the old Lutheran doctrines, the divergence has continued in Lutheranism until the present. Indeed, very little of determinism is heard among Lutherans today since the tendency among evangelical Lutherans is more Arminian than Augustinian.

Calvin's actual views. There is considerable controversy over Calvin's actual views on many issues, which is surprising, especially in the light of the massive amount of writing he left us in his *Institutes*, commentaries, and many other writings. The reader might have noticed that a number of times in previous chapters I have found Calvin at odds with contemporary Calvinists, or at least undecided, whereas they are dogmatic.

The major issue is limited atonement. I have found over sixty passages in Calvin supporting general redemption, but seeing that about half of them have an element of ambiguity, I have culled them down to thirty quite unambiguous ones. On the other hand, there is only one passage Calvinists adduce to prove the opposite. Kendall, in his doctoral dissertation's appendix, has quoted Curt Daniel's doctoral dissertation in which he clearly shows that Calvinists have misunderstood this passage. Mind you, Curt Daniel himself is a five-point Calvinist. There is a growing body of doctoral level research, mostly done abroad, which supports the view that Beza and his associates carried Calvin's doctrines to their logical extreme conclusion by introducing the doctrine of limited atonement There is also some evidence that Calvin softened his views in his later commentaries, as he was immersed in expounding the Scripture itself, rather than systematizing a theological system. I cannot document this.

Beza's scholasticizing. One hardly needs to discuss the deterministic views of John Calvin in the main and his successor Theodore Beza (1519-1605), since there is no question about their views on unconditional election. I believe there is no question that Calvin owed much to Luther and Zwingli in this regard. However, over the years many scholars have questioned to what extent Beza developed Calvinism into a more rigid predestinarian system. In my own research into the specific areas of soteriology, whenever I have checked Calvin on a particular point I have been surprised to find that his commentaries are less rigid than contemporary Calvinists, and that at times he sounds positively Amyraldian or Arminian. I have no doubt that Beza developed Calvinism into a more scholastic form than the Calvinism of Calvin's later years. This is especially clear from the thirty quotations of Calvin on general redemption I have included in appendix E and the many dissertations done abroad supporting that view. See also my discussion in appendix K on the impact of philosophy in Beza's thinking.

The spread and modification of the Reformation

Beginnings in Great Britain. Early in the British reformation Bishop Hugh Latimer (c. 1485-1555), Miles Coverdale, the Bible translator, (1488-1569), and Thomas Cranmer, the Archbishop of Canterbury (1489-1556), can all be identified as holding to general redemption. Since they were contemporaries of the early Calvin, they probably did not get into the other issues of determinism. The 1553 version of the Articles of the Anglican Church clearly holds to general redemption. Some writers have referred to the "free-willers" in the Anglican church during this time as Calvinism made increasing inroads. In the 1590s there was considerable controversy at Cambridge and Peter Baro (1534-1599) was forced out for resisting Calvinism. In 1596 Nicholas Hemingius asked, "Do the elect believe or are the believers elect?" Richard Bancroft was non-predestinarian bishop of London. However, William Perkins' 1598 book, *The Mode and Order of Predestination* was supralapsarian extreme Calvinism. Arminius wrote a refutation but never published it because of Perkins' death.[32]

Toward the end of the sixteenth century there was a movement in England and Scotland to moderate the rigidity of the Calvinism which had been coming from Geneva. Richard Hooker (1553-1600) was described by Bishop H. C. G. Moule as a "moderate Calvinist." Archbishop James Ussher (1581-1656) clearly held to general redemption, and is quoted as telling Richard Baxter (1615-1691) that he brought Bishop John Davenant (1572-1641) and Dr. John Preston (1578-1628) to his view. Ussher is quoted as saying that there must be a "middle way" in soteriology, but that it was not yet clear to him.[33] Both Ussher and Davenant were delegates to the Synod of Dort. Davenant is a major source regarding the moderate Calvinistic views of his contemporaries. Bishop Joseph Hall (1574-1656) also held to general redemption.[34]

Most significant is the ministry of John Cameron (1580-1625) of Glasgow for his part in propagating a moderate form of Calvinism among the Huguenot Reformed churches of France. His connection with the moderate Calvinism of England is unclear, but the probability is great that he had some contact with one or more of the above named theologians. But I will come back to him later in connection with the Amyraldian movement in France.[35]

Arminius and the Remonstrants. James Arminius (1560-1609) had all the right Calvinist credentials to become the theology professor at the Reformed University of Leyden. He had studied for three years under Theodore Beza, Calvin's successor in Geneva. Before becoming pastor of one of the principal Reformed churches in Amsterdam, he had traveled in Italy and heard the lectures of some of the great Catholic professors. Newman states:

> By this time he was recognized as among the ablest and most learned men of his time. His expository sermons were so lucid, eloquent, and well delivered as to attract large audiences. He was called upon from time to time to write against the opponents of Calvinism, which he did in a moderate and satisfactory way. . . . Before this time [1602] his intimate friends had become aware of the fact that he was no longer in full sympathy with the extreme predestinarianism of Beza, and he had written an exposition of Romans 9 in an anti-Calvinistic spirit. This, however, was not published till after his death.[36]

Unfortunately after Arminius joined the University faculty in 1603 and studiously avoided any anti-Calvinistic utterances, his colleague Gomarus instigated the authorities to require him to deliver a series of public lectures on predestination. "He defended the doctrine in a way that would have been acceptable to moderate Calvinists; but Gomar thought it necessary to supplement these lectures with a course of his own." This precipitated a hostile controversy on campus, which soon exploded into a national debate, involving the government of the Netherlands. Although the Supreme Court declined to hear the issue, in 1609 Arminius and Gomarus were required to engage in an extended discussion (debate?) on the issue. Arminius took sick and died two months later. The following year his many followers set forth the five points of the Remonstrance, which were responded to by the Calvinists in their five points (the TULIP).

This controversy ultimately precipitated the infamous Synod of Dort (1618-9), attended by delegates from Reformed churches in several other countries. Since the Arminians were excluded, the result was a foregone conclusion—the Arminians were excommunicated. John Barneveld, a leading statesman and advocate of freedom of conscience, was accused of treason and executed five days after the end of the Synod. Episcopius, the leader of the banished Arminians, published extensively against the Synod and the intolerance of the government and reiterated the charge of Calvinism being "Manichean fatalism." This resulted in toleration being granted in 1625, and the establishment of an Arminian seminary in Amsterdam subsequently.[37] A century later the Wesleys developed a more evangelical form of Arminianism, which retained much of the Augustinian view of sin. The Wesleyan movement has become so significant and its impact so well known that I hardly need expand on it here. However, I should alert my readers to a distinct position called "Reformed

Arminianism," which holds to the original views of Arminius himself, unmodified by the Remonstrants or the Wesleys.[38]

Cocceius and Covenant Theology. Johannes Cocceius (1603-1669) was not the originator of Covenant Theology, but was certainly a major factor in its early development. Newman comments:

> He studied Greek with a Greek and Hebrew with a Hebrew and became easily the most accomplished biblical scholar of his time. . . . He was pre-eminently a scriptural theologian. . . . The dominating thought in his theology, as in his interpretation of Scripture, was the divine covenant. This was not a wholly new thought, but he developed it with such richness of scriptural citation, with such logical acumen, and with such an insight into historical relations, that he may properly be regarded as the father of the federal theology. His great work, "Summary of the Doctrine Concerning the Covenant and Testament of God," was first published in 1648 and may be regarded as the first serious attempt at the working out of a biblical theology. . . . It is noticeable that the doctrine of predestination does not figure in this system and the entire doctrine of divine decrees is kept in the background. The aim of Cocceius was evidently to show that man was so endowed and conditioned that he need not have fallen, that he was responsible for his fall, and that after the fall God placed salvation within the reach of all by covenant and actually provided redemption in Christ for all who would believe.[39]

Lyle Bierma, in a recent study, has sought to show that a generation earlier Caspar Olevianus (1536-1587) was the first to use the covenant idea as a sustained theological *leitmotif*, and that he recognized both a unilateral (divine) and a bilateral (divine-human) dimension to the covenant of grace.[40] Whether this was a reaction against extreme determinism is not clear. Be that as it may, Charles Ryrie confirms Newman's opinion that it was Cocceius, having been influenced by Melanchthon, who saw in the covenant theme a "way to blunt the sharp and highly debated views on predestination current in his day." He goes on to assess his contribution:

> . . . Cocceius expounded the concept of two covenants: the covenants of works and of grace. In both, he said, man had a part to play and a responsibility to meet. He made these covenants the basis, background, and substance of all God's dealings with man for his redemption. Thus, Cocceius's contribution was a detailing and systematizing of the idea of the covenants, giving a more prominent part to man in contrast to the rigorous predestinarianism of his day and making the covenant idea the governing category of all Scripture.

Ryrie then suggests that Herman Witsius (1636-1708) undermined Cocceius's intention by developing the idea of a Covenant of Redemption in eternity past, which in effect reverted Covenant Theology back to a deterministic mode of thought.[41] Thus it would seem clear that Cocceius represents another of the early reactions against the extreme determinism of the Reformers.

Modification at the Saumur seminary. Salmurian or Amyraldian theology can be traced back to John Cameron (1580-1625), who had studied in Glasgow under Andrew Melville, the "Scots Melanchthon." Cameron so excelled in his study of Greek, Hebrew, History, Rhetoric, and Logic that upon graduation he was appointed as regent in Greek. Logic was taught there from Ramus, who espoused a more inductive methodology, rather than from Aristotle's more deductive approach. By 1600 after only one year he migrated to France, which was to be the locus of most of his ministry. He taught and pastored in many cities: twice at Bordeaux, Bergerac, and Sedan and studied in Paris, Geneva, and Heidelberg, before beginning his teaching at the theological Academy at Saumur in 1618. His teaching there was so effective that in just three years his views on general redemption were accepted with alacrity by his students and successors on the faculty, especially Moyse Amyraut. There may be some question as to how much of Amyraut's theology is directly derived from Cameron, but as to the essentials of general redemption there can be no doubt. In any case the Reformed churches of France were grateful to Cameron for "his great services in the controversies against Arminians and Roman Catholics"[42]

Moyse Amyraut (1596-1664) proved to be such an effective exponent of Cameron's theology after his untimely death, that his name became attached to it. After studying law at Poitiers, Amyraut probably came to Saumur as a student in 1618 when Cameron began to teach. We have little biographical information from his early years, but his five years as a student probably involved studies at Leyden as well. Shortly after being called as minister at Saumur in 1626, he must have begun teaching at the Academy, since within a year he was appointed as rector. By 1631 he and Louis Cappel began full-time responsibilities, sharing ministry both at the church and Academy. Amyraut served as principal from 1641 until his death. Life for the Protestant Huguenots in France at that time was life under the Edict of Nante, which gave them certain civil liberties. In 1631 Amyraut won an outstanding victory in the exercise of those liberties, and was also partly responsible for attempts to improve relationships with the Lutherans. Amyraut became well known for developing good personal relationships with Roman Catholics while pursuing a strong apologetic for the Protestant faith.

It was in this connection that in 1634 he innocently started a controversy which was to become a central feature of his life for many years. He published what he entitled, *A Brief Treatise on Predestination* which was occasioned by a dialog with a Roman Catholic gentleman while at dinner with the Bishop of Chartres. This gentleman was "filled with horror by the doctrine of predestination as taught in our churches," and regarded it as "contrary to the nature of God and His gospel to say that He created the greatest part of mankind with the express purpose of damning them."[43] His treatise stirred up a "civil war" among the Reformed churches, not just of France, but also Geneva, Bern, Leyden, Groningen, Franecker, and Sedan, as well. He responded to the opposition by publishing, *Six Sermons on the Nature, Extent, Necessity, Dispensation, and Efficacy of the Gospel*, to which he prefaced a 75 page treatise to show that his doctrine was really that of Calvin. The attacks from the scholastic Calvinists eventuated in charges of heresy being leveled at Amyraut and Paul Testard in the national synod of Alençon in 1637. The charges focused on the universality and sufficiency of grace. Armstrong states, "It is certain that Amyraut barely escaped being deposed and having his writings condemned. In fact the opposition was so formidable that it seems unbelievable that he was not condemned."[44] Although they were honorably acquitted from the synod, there were a few stipulations. They were not to refer to Christ dying *equally* for all, since that was subject to misunderstanding. They had explained the reference to "conditional decrees" as an anthropomorphism and agreed not to use such expressions in the future.[45] There were also some questions about their terminology in reference to natural theology, but again their modifications satisfied the synod.

The synod decision did not end the controversy, however. Further debate was triggered in 1641 by Amyraut's treatise entitled, *Doctrinae J. Calvini de Absoluto Reprobationis Decreto Defenso . . .*, in response to an anonymous English Arminian writer. In this treatise Amyraut really sets out his own position rather than that of the 'orthodox' scholastic Calvinists. There was a continuing volley of voluminous books published by both sides to the controversy until 1649, when a Protestant prince arranged for a private meeting of the parties and extracted from them a commitment to halt the polemic writings. It was not totally effective, however, because in 1655 two Parisian pastors wrote works in support of the Amyraldian view. After this Amyraut did not take an active part in the debate, but focused his attention on other topics. In any case, one of those Parisian pastors was elected moderator of the Synod of Loudun in 1659, so it is clear that the Amyraldian view was growing in acceptability within France.

A score of years after Amyraut's death, the revocation of the Edict of Nantes (1685) caused many (perhaps most) of the Protestants of France to flee, many to the low countries and England, some even to America. Apparently the Academy of Saumur did not survive to perpetuate the Amyraldian theology. Thus it lost its geographical base and its adherents were scattered. Yet its impact can be traced right up to the present, even though its identity as a distinct theological school of thought has been seriously blurred. Amyraut's extensive writings are unfortunately available only in Latin and Old French.[46]

In Switzerland there seemed to have been a strong reaction against the Amyraldian theology. Nevertheless, even in Geneva men like Mussard, Morus, and Chouet were influenced by Saumur. Louis Tronchin and Philippe Mestrezat ultimately came out openly in sympathy with this theology. The impact can be traced into the 18th century. Although the Netherlands was the main source of opposition to the Salmurian theology, the French Reformed refugees flooding into the country after 1685 brought their theology with them. Nicole lists Venema, van Oosterzee, and Doedes as among the more recent advocates of this view there. In Germany there already were similar views present in Bremen, so it is difficult to evaluate Amyraut's impact there. In England John Davenant (1570-1641) already held views similar to Amyraut's. Richard Baxter (1615-1691), the great Puritan evangelist, openly professed Amyraldian views and lists a number of other men who did also. In Scotland James Fraser of Brea, Thomas Mair, the New Light Reformed Presbytery, James Morison and his group, and Ralph Wardlaw can be identified as Amyraldian. In the United States it seems clear that Amyraldian views influenced New Divinity (Samuel Hopkins, Edward D. Griffin, L. Woods), New School Presbyterianism (J. Richards), and among the Baptists E. Dodge, Alva Hovey, Pepper, and more recently A. H. Strong can be so identified.[47]

The Pietistic movement. Philip Spener (1635-1705) and August Franke (1663-1727) were the two key men in the beginnings of Pietism in the Lutheran state churches of Germany and Scandinavia. Spener sought to cultivate the spiritual life by small-group Bible study and prayer meetings and was grieved by the arid and bitter theological disputation and low moral state of the Lutheran state church. Franke helped found the University of Halle in 1694 out of which came the first Protestant missionaries and the Danish-Halle Mission in 1705. Although the pietistic movement did not stress theology, it definitely did not hold to the determinism of Luther.

The Moravian movement. Some persecuted followers of John Hus banded together with some Waldensians and Moravians to form the *Unitas Fratrum* (United Brethren) in 1467. Badly persecuted by the Catholics, a remnant under the leadership of Christian David (1690-1751) fled to the estate of the pietist Count Nicholas von Zinzendorf (1700-1760) in Saxony in 1722. Out of this Christian community, a most remarkable missionary movement developed. Between 1732 and 1760 this small movement sent out 226 missionaries to ten foreign countries, far outstripping all other Protestants combined. The Moravians stressed God's love for a lost world and bypassed the determinism of the Reformers.

Thomas Boston and the Marrow men. The Marrow controversy of the Presbyterian Church of Scotland in the 1720s might be characterized as conflict between the 'legalists' and the 'evangelicals.' Edward Fisher's earlier book published in England in 1645, *The Marrow of Modern Divinity*, was a source of the view of the 'evangelicals,' that all men may apply to Christ for salvation, if they will, and that "a gospel warrant existed for offering Christ to the whole world." Although both sides of the controversy were covenantal Calvinists, Thomas Boston (1677-1732) and his associates rejected the third covenant of Covenant Theology, the "covenant of redemption" in eternity past. A century later it led to the general redemption view of John McLeod Campbell (b. 1800), for which he was dismissed from ministry in 1831. He saw the Calvinism of his church as legalistic in denying that "all sinners are summoned to come to God with assurance of his love for them." Contrary to his view, "he refers to the theological systems of Owen and Edwards, in which they assert that God's justice is his essential attribute and is universal in its extent, while his love is arbitrary, and limited to the elect."[48]

The New Divinity movement. In the previous chapter I have already focused on the neo-Edwardsian New Divinity movement of the Second Great Awakening in New England. Although they called themselves "consistent Calvinists," they really were not such. Although holding to an extreme view of sovereignty and depravity, they not only held to general redemption, but also to the governmental view of the cross, which is really more harmonious with Arminianism. They were all successors of Jonathan Edwards, Sr. Of his immediate protégés, Samuel Hopkins became the theologian and Joseph Bellamy, the pastoral mentor. The junior Edwards moved even farther from his father's Calvinism, with grandson Timothy Dwight and his protégé Nathaniel Taylor laying the foundation for the theology of evangelist Charles G. Finney. Dwight and Taylor represent a distinct strain called the New Haven theology, which stressed human free will, the "power to the contrary." It can be demonstrated that both the Second Great Awakening in New England and the American foreign missions movement came out of the New Divinity movement. Most of the historians have overlooked the fact that the unifying factor of the movement was their view of general redemption.[49]

The Restorationist movements. Barton W. Stone (1772-1844) and Alexander Campbell (1788-1866) were two American Presbyterian ministers who early found "that Presbyterianism was not adequate for their revivalistic experience or for their theological views." In 1804 in Kentucky Stone began "to organize groups that would answer to no name but 'Christians'." In a similar way in 1811 in the Ohio valley Campbell started a movement rejecting traditional church forms and emphasizing New

Testament doctrine and polity. "In 1832 the followers of Stone and Alexander Campbell came into a loose alliance known as the 'Christian' or Disciples' movement."[50] By the early 20th century the movements separated again, but both have emphasized that water baptism is necessary for salvation and have been decidedly Arminian.

Modern advocates

Samuel Fisk has done yeoman's work in amassing the quotations of hundreds of scholars, commentators, Bible teachers, church leaders, and theologians in the 19th and 20th centuries who have been generally supportive of a mediate view of salvation truth. He has not included those with Arminian associations in his list. I will list only the names of those who hold to eternal security and to conditional election. Many others could be listed who seek to balance God's sovereignty and human responsibility in other ways.

At the end of the 19th century Baptists E. H. Johnson and Henry G. Weston wrote *An Outline of Systematic Theology* (Phila.: American Baptist Publ., 1895). The great French commentator, Frederick L. Godet's writings are quite explicit. Bishop Christopher Wordsworth, *The New Testament in the Original Greek, with Notes and Introductions* (London: Rivingtons, 1877); William Evans, *the Great Doctrines of the Bible* (Chicago: Moody, 1912). Nathan E. Wood was professor at Andover-Newton Seminary, *The Person and Work of Jesus Christ: An Exposition of Christian Doctrine* (Phila.: American Baptist Publ, 1908). W. H. Griffith-Thomas collaborated in the founding of Dallas Seminary, but died before he could begin teaching theology there. H. A. (Harry) Ironside, the pastor of Moody Memorial Church, was a special Bible lecturer at Dallas Seminary, but he died just before I began studies there, and I never got to hear him. His many books and commentaries are very supportive of mediate soteriology. The great expositor, G. Campbell Morgan's many commentaries and book are clear, as are those of F. B. Meyer. Among Southern Baptists are Edgar Y. Mullins's doctrinal works, and those of Hershel H. Hobbs. Others are W. E. Vine, E. Schuyler English, J. Sidlow Baxter, and Lehman Strauss. I am sure the list could be greatly expanded.

CONCLUSIONS

I believe that there are a number of very significant conclusions which can be drawn from our historical investigation:

1. Determinism has a very significant problem with the virtual silence of the church fathers regarding predestination and irresistible grace and their emphasis on free will before the latter years of Augustine (after 417).
2. Augustine's determinism, as well as some of his other errors, can probably be traced back to the impact of his nine years in

Manicheanism and possibly to his time in neo-Platonism, not to any careful biblical exegesis. His views were viewed by many contemporaries as radically new.

3. The majority of the church fathers, both before (anachronistically) and after, may be thought of as semi-Augustinian, not semi-Pelagian.
4. The ongoing controversy arising from the Augustine/Pelagius conflict was essentially settled for the church for a thousand years by the Synod of Orange (529), which took a semi-Augustinian position. There was only sporadic advocacy of Augustine's determinism before the Reformation.
5. Augustine's teaching and example on coercion to faith relate to his doctrine of irresistible grace and have poisoned the testimony of Christendom until the present, resulting in the martyrdom and torture of untold thousands of true Christians, both by Romanism and Protestantism.
6. Augustine was the source of many of the major errors of Roman Catholicism and of state-church Protestantism.
7. Although the major Protestant Reformers represent a recrudescence of Augustinian determinism, within a few years their associates and successors sought to modify and blunt their rigid determinism. Almost to a man these who sought to modify this extreme determinism were better versed in the original languages than the Reformers they followed.
8. Theodore Beza took the lead in reverting Genevan Calvinism to a more scholastic mode, which seriously innovated with the doctrine of limited atonement, which first surfaced in a creed in the Canons of Dort in 1619.
9. There have been at least a dozen significant reactions to the determinism of the Reformers, the outcome of which has continued to be a major force in evangelical Christianity. Much of the evangelism, church growth, and missions thrust of recent centuries has been spawned by these movements.
10. There have been hundreds of commentators and biblical writers in the 19th and 20th centuries who held a mediating theology of salvation.

Note: This chapter is based upon a paper given at the Eastern Regional of the Evangelical Theological Society at Lancaster, PA, in March 1998.

---

1. Brian G. Armstrong, *Calvinism and the Amyraut Heresy: Protestant Scholasticism and Humanism in Seventeenth-Century France* (Madison: Univ. of Wisconsin Press, 1969).
2. Philip Schaff, *History of the Christian Church*, 8 vols. (GR: Eerdmans, 1985 [1910]), I, viii.
3. Paul K. Jewett, *Election and Predestination* (GR: Eerdmans, 1985), p. 5; Boettner, p. 365.
4. Forster and Marston, *God's Strategy in Human History*, p. 244; Geisler, *Chosen But Free*, Appendix 1.
5. Forster and Marston, pp. 243-277; Norman F. Douty, *The Death of Christ*, pp. 136-138.
6. R. C. Sproul, *Willing to Believe: The Controversy over Free Will* (GR: Baker Books, 1997), pp. 69-86.

7. Schaff, III, 812; see also J. L. Neve, *A History of Christian Thought*. 2 vols. (Phila.: Muhlenberg Press, 1946), I, 143, where he references Loofs, *DG*, p. 419, and also W. Walker, *Church History*, p. 186, as showing that Pelagius taught justification by faith alone.

8. Forster and Marston, pp. 243-257; Douty, pp. 136-9.

9. Neve, I, 148.

10. Douty, p. 138, extensive quotes of Prosper on general redemption.

11. J. L. Neve, p. 150; Schaff, III, 864-7.

12. Schaff, III, p. 869; Neve, I, 151.

13. Jewett, p. 7.

14. Schaff, III, 866; Neve, I, 1151. It is interesting to note that Schaff, as a Reformed writer, selects for quotation those canons which are more deterministic in tone; Neve, as a Lutheran, selects the less deterministic canons of the Synod. But we must note the balance the Synod sought to attain.

15. Schaff, III, p. 1018.

16. Forster and Marston, pp. 281-7.

17. Forster and Marston, p. 283.

18. Albert Henry Newman, *A Manual of Church History*, 2 vols. (Phila.: American Baptist Publ., 1899), I, 197.

19. Ibid, I, 370.

20. Ibid, II, 323.

21. Sir Robert Anderson, *The Gospel and its Ministry* (GR: Kregel, 1978), p. 95; B. B. Warfield, *Calvin and Augustine*, ed. Samuel Craig (Phila.: Presbyterian & Reformed, 1956), p. 313; Jerom Zanchius, *The Doctrine of Absolute Predestination* (GR: Baker Books, 1977), pp. 168-9, as quoted by Laurence M. Vance, *The Other Side of Calvinism* (Pensacola: Vance Publications, 1991), pp. 18-19.

22. Schaff, IV, 523-4.

23. Ibid, IV, 525-543.

24. William R. Estep, *The Anabaptist Story: An Introduction to Sixteenth-Century Anabaptism* (GR: Eerdmans, 1996), pp. 11-21.

25. Newman, II, 154-5.

26. Estep, p. 97.

27. Jan J. Kiwiet, "The Life of Hans Denck (ca. 1500-1527)." *The Mennonite Quarterly Review* 31 (Oct. 1957) 24 2, as quoted by Estep, p. 110-1. The commendatory quotation above is in the words of a contemporary, Johannes Kessler, who misunderstood his theology.

28. See also Meic Pearse, *The Great Restoration: The Religious Radicals of the 16th and 17th Centuries.*

29. John Davenant, *The Death of Christ*, ed. Allport (London, 1832), II, 319, as quoted by Douty, p. 140; Schaff, VIII, 210-1, 618.

30. Newman, II, 322.

31. Ibid, II, 322-4.

32. Carl O. Bangs, *Arminius* ; O. T. Hargrave, "Free-willers in the English Reformation," *Church History*, XXXVII (1968), 271-280.

33. I have lost the documentation on Ussher.

34. A major source of these quotations is in Douty, pp. 143-149: Moule, *Outlines of Christian Doctrine*, p. 43; Francis Goode, *The Better Covenant* (1848), pp. 334f.; Morris Fuller, *The Life, Letters, and Writings of John Davenant* (London, 1897), p. 521; Davenant, *op. cit., p. 386*; Joseph Hall, *Works*, X, 474.

35. Armstrong, pp. 42-70.

36. Newman, II, 340.

37. Ibid, II, 339-349.

38. Stephen M. Ashby, "Reformed Arminianism," in J. Matthew Pinson, ed., *Four Views on Eternal Security* (Zondervan, 2002), pp. 135-187.

39. Newman, II, 575-6.

40. Lyle D. Bierma, *German Calvinism in the Confessional Age* (GR, Baker Book, 1997), p. 183.

41. Charles C. Ryrie, *Dispensationalism*, rev. ed. (Chicago: Moody, 1995), pp. 185-187.

42. Roger Nicole, "Amyraldianism" in *Encyclopedia of Christianity* (1964), I: 187. Most of the historical summary in this section is derived from Nicole's article and from Armstrong, pp. 42-119. At times their appraisals differ, but I have tried to focus on the agreed essentials regarding the background.

43. Amyraut, *Preface to Six Sermons*, i-ii, as quoted by Armstrong, p. 81.

44. Ibid, p. 96.

45. Roger Nicole expressed his opinion to me in a telephone conversation (December, 1981) that Amyraut held to conditional election. This is contradicted by Brian Armstrong and Leonard Proctor, and in a conversation with Dr. Nicole in 2001 he agreed that they may be right. Although Amyraut believed in unconditional election, he did not emphasize it in his system.

46. Amyraut was a very prolific writer, having produced 90 titles plus additional theses. His writings are in Old French and Latin and unfortunately very few have been published in English. A large number of them are in the Princeton Seminary library. I have tried to encourage Roger Nicole to translate them but he feels that Amyraut's views were too heretical to justify the effort, even though he wrote his doctoral dissertation on Amyraut. His earliest work on apologetic and polemics was published in 1631 and published in English in London in 1660 as, *A Treatise Concerning Religions* . . . . He wrote on justification by faith in 1638; the merit of works in 1638; the Lord's Supper in 1640; a polemic piece opposing the fideism of Roman Catholics in 1641; and the intermediate state, 1646, (English, 1660). In addition to the works mentioned above relating to the general redemption issue, there were many others which I will not attempt to list. Most significant was his six-volume work on Christian ethics totalling 4600 pages (1652-60). "It was the first major attempt within Reformed Protestantism to produce an ethical system." We should also mention his paraphrases of Psalms and most of the New Testament, and at least 72 sermons were published as well with great circulation. It is also noteworthy that at the time of his death, Amyraut had projected a work entitled, *Theologie francaise*, for which there are contemporary comments which might indicate that it was to be a diachronic Biblical theology. Roger Nicole found a manuscript copy of notes with that title, but its poor quality in his opinion made him doubt its identity with the project. If it had been completed, it is conceivable that he might have become the father of the Biblical Theology discipline.

47. Nicole, pp. 192-3.

48. M. Charles Bell, *Calvin and Scottish Theology*, pp. 153-161, 181-192.

49. The key evidence is in Edwards A. Park, *The Atonement: Discourse and Treatises by* . . . (Boston, 1859). See also Conforti, *Samuel Hopkins and the New Divinity Movement.*

50. John D. Woodbridge, Mark A. Noll, and Nathan O. Hatch, *The Gospel in America* (Zondervan, 1979), pp. 192-3.

Christ sent His disciples into all the world, and He instructed them to preach the gospel to every creature. If, then, election means that all those whom God has arbitrarily chosen will certainly get to Heaven, and that all those whom He has not chosen will certainly not get there, no matter how faithfully and frequently the gospel may be preached to them, then why be greatly agitated about it? True, we have the command to take the gospel into all the world; but if only some are thus 'elected,' why be greatly disturbed about it? -Henry C. Thiessen

19

WHAT DIFFERENCE DOES IT MAKE?

Is this whole book a tempest in a teapot? Or making a mountain out of a molehill? Perhaps many naive Christians or those who are not theologically oriented might think so. Granted that I have gone to great lengths to work out the details of a system which is critical of both Arminianism and Calvinism. It has taken considerable detailed study to substantiate both my critique of those systems and the defense of a mediate theology of salvation. It is my conviction that both of these systems, as systems, are seriously flawed. Each has some scriptural features and some unscriptural ones. But as systems they fail in far too many points. But what difference does it make, after all?

I won't have to convince theologically oriented Christians that it makes a world of difference in most areas of theology. Since doctrine and theology are the proper foundation for a sound Christian life, it makes a world of difference in how we live out our walk and service of God as well. It also has a major impact upon our witness of the gospel to the unsaved and the discipling of believers. We should have a concern for truth, not only in theological study, but also in the way Scripture is interpreted and preached in the pulpits of our churches. If in all of this our theological systems have deflected us from apprehending and fulfilling that which is the core of God's plan, this is a serious problem. If we have majored on the minor and minored on the major from God's perspective, we are in real trouble at the judgment seat of Christ.

As I write these words the secular media are filled with distorted images of evangelical Christianity, perhaps more than ever before in

America's history. Deterministic theology has given Evangelicals bad press for at least four centuries. We have a serious apologetic problem, whether in academia, the media, within Christendom, with Jews, Muslims, Hindus, and adherents of world religions, or cult members. We are viewed as gay bashers, abortionist killers, haters of Muslims, a threat to Jews, and the list goes on. We don't need to add to that the notion that we believe God is an angry, arbitrary despot, who has already destined the mass of humanity to hell quite irrespective of anything they or anybody else can do about it. There is a serious danger of adding offense to the very real offense of the gospel of Christ.

The Impact on the Christian Life

Let us start where we all live, the Christian life. The track record of both determinism and Arminianism in reference to a balanced Christian life has not been encouraging. The most significant area is the matter of the assurance of salvation as a basis for a stable Christian life.

Assurance. The major concern which energized Michael Eaton to write his *No Condemnation: A New Theology of Assurance* was the paradox that both Arminians and Calvinists have real problems with assurance of ultimate salvation. Arminianism is on record as denying that any Christian can be sure of ultimate salvation. Extreme Calvinism differs only in asserting that once we are genuinely saved we can be sure of ultimate salvation, if we can be sure that we are now genuinely saved. Asahel Nettleton was only one of a legion of Puritans who agonized until their dying day whether or not they were indeed regenerate members of God's family. This was not because of any defect in God's plan of salvation but because of faulty theology. Eaton gives extensive exemplification of the problem from a first-hand perspective among those whom he calls "developed Calvinists."

I was greatly blessed to have been saved through a witness outside my Arminian church, so thus I was not prone to accept its theology or lack thereof very readily. Nor was I really exposed to extreme Calvinism until I was grounded well enough to reject it. As a consequence I have never in over half a century since my conversion had a problem with assurance. I was blessed to have full assurance within a few months and to have come to the conviction of eternal security within some months after that. But the record shows that for far too many Christians lack of assurance undermines a stable Christian life.

Rationalizing sin. Extreme Calvinism has long struggled with the problem of rationalizing sin, for which the technical term is antinomianism. The Particular Baptists of Andrew Fuller's day had a serious antinomian problem as Fuller discovered early in his Christian life (see chapter 17). Indeed, this was what began to disillusion him with the hyper-Calvinism in which he was raised. Tobias Crisp was identified by Stokes as one of those antinomians who believed that: "The elect are discharged from all their sins. . . . The elect upon the death of Christ cease to be sinners, and ever since sins committed by them are none of their sins. . . ."[1] I can remember my shock when a Calvinistic colleague of mine prayed in the college chapel in reference to a sinful incident, that it was part of the sovereign purpose of God anyway. He was to the best of my knowledge a godly man, but I don't believe he understood the impact of that kind of thinking on the students. It was a slip into antinomianism. On the other hand, my early Christian experience of my Arminian pastor calling sin "a mistake" in order to maintain his perfectionist theology is a similar rationalization. Drop the bar low so that you can jump over it.

Prayer. The efficacy of prayer is another serious problem Calvinists struggle with. This is one of many areas in which the criticism of Calvinism by Open Theism is valid. Unfortunately both are in error. God does respond to the prayers of His people because the future is not set in concrete by any immutable decrees of God. God does not change as to His character, but He does change in His ways of dealing with people. He does actually respond to the prayers of His people; the Bible is unambiguous about this. I have already argued that God's foreknowledge is not determinative of the future. I remember an English professor who fancied himself a theologian of quite Calvinistic convictions. His statement in a faculty meeting that prayer does not really change anything but ourselves, left us wondering if he had ever read the many Bible statements to the contrary. I have already referenced Brother Andrew's suggestion that this is an Islamic or perhaps deistic way of thinking, but certainly not biblical. Remember the sun standing still when Joshua (ch. 10) prayed; Elijah's prayer to stop the rain for 3½ years (1 Kings 17-18; Jas. 5:17); and Moses' intercession for Israel (Num. 14). A myriad of others could be cited.

Conditional love. The limitations on God's love in determinism make a tremendous difference in the Christian life, whether it be the conditionality of His love found in both Calvinism and Arminianism, or the restriction of His love implicit in limited atonement. Some of the more extreme determinists have literature entitled, "Does God love you?" or something of the sort. How can we have a good relationship with a God whose love in conditional, limited, and arbitrary?

Legalism. Speaking of the conditionality of God's love raises the problem of legalism and inordinate introspection which Michael Eaton reported observing among extreme Calvinists. He found a study of Galatians liberating in this regard. All serious Christians must fight the tendency to fall into legalism, but the evidence seems clear that both the extreme Calvinists and the Arminians are especially prone to it. One of the worst legalisms is writing off struggling Christians as counterfeits because they don't measure up to some legalistic standard. Earlier in the day as I write this I heard a tape of the late James Montgomery Boice expounding Luke 9:23, to say that if one doesn't deny oneself and take up the cross and follow Christ, one is not a Christian. How much must we deny ourselves, how much must we mortify the old man, how closely must we follow Christ to martyrdom to qualify as true Christians? Certainly none of us qualify 100 per cent. This type of back-loading of the gospel with "discipleship salvation" is legalism. It caused great soul agony for the Puritans.

This type of interpretation is rife among Arminians also. How many of the Arminian denominations developed not only a lifestyle legalism, but also a legalistic understanding of the terms of salvation? The Lord Jesus said, "**For my yoke is easy and my burden is light.**" He was the enemy of pharisaic legalism. It is not conducive to a balanced Christian life.

Self-righteous pride. Pride was the original sin of Lucifer, which made him a Satan. We understand that pride was a major factor in the mindset of the Pharisees of Christ's day. When we unduly focus upon ourselves as God's 'elect,' there is a serious danger of denigrating both the 'non-elect' and those who do not agree with our deterministic theology. I already referenced R. C. Sproul's calling Arminians and others who believe in the priority of faith "barely Christian." I have met others of like mindset. As I sought to point out in chapter 8, the biblical references to 'elect' and election are precious few, certainly not replete enough to make this a governing category of our theology or concept of the Christian life. Rightly understood it is a glorious truth. Wrongly understood it is a source of spiritual pride. Yet this is usually portrayed as a view which magnifies God's grace. Perhaps this is why more humble Calvinists have wrongly hesitated to call themselves God's elect. I don't know. Evangelist John R. Rice has put it bluntly: "The heresy of extreme Calvinism is particularly appealing to people. . . . It appeals to the scholarly intellect, the self-sufficient and proud mind. So brilliant, philosophical, scholarly preachers are apt to be misled on this matter more than the humble-hearted Bible believer."[2]

On the other hand, Arminian sinless perfectionism also can be a great wellspring of pride. "I haven't sinned in ten years!" we hear. "I have received the second blessing and am now living on a higher plane of Christian experience." "I have been baptized in the Holy Ghost and speak in tongues." All of these expressions sound very intimidating to other Christians and seem far from humble from where I stand. Harry Ironside had an enlightening experience as a struggling young Salvation Army officer sent to a rest home. He found that those inmates who professed the least of "entire sanctification" were the most godly, and those who claimed the most showed the least evidences of the fruit of the Spirit.[3]

Irresponsible personal lives. Geisler spelled it out: "Extreme Calvinism leads logically (if not practically) to personal irresponsibility: if our actions are good action, they are such only because God has programmed us to do good; if evil, then we cannot help it because we are sinners by nature and God has not given us the desire to do good."[4] It was a defining moment in Andrew Fuller's early Christian life when the hyper-Calvinistic drunk Christian he confronted disavowed any responsibility for his own behavior. Edward Bowlen put it bluntly, "To say that one believes in man's responsibility, but not in free-will, merely begs the question since, obviously, there could be no responsibility if there were not first a free moral agent whose volitional choices implied and accrued responsibility. Free-will and responsibility are inseparable."[5] Calvinist Iain Murray wrote of the British hyper-Calvinists, "*Divine sovereignty was maintained and taught, not only in exaggerated proportions, but to the practical exclusion of moral responsibility*" (italics his).[6] What Murray does not grasp is that the problem is just as acute for any Calvinists who believe in all-inclusive decree(s) of God. Resort to antinomy or paradox does not really resolve it. Fisk has a score of excellent quotations from the whole spectrum of evangelicalism concerning this motivation-destroying notion, but one from A. H. Strong will have to suffice. "Denial that the will is free has serious and pernicious consequences in theology. On the one hand, it weakens even if it does not destroy man's conviction with regard to responsibility, sin, guilt and retribution."[7]

Blaming God. Non-Christians quite regularly blame God for every calamity which comes into their lives. Of course, they are ignorant of the fact that weather-caused calamities are a consequence of the inauguration of seasonal weather patterns after the Noahic deluge (Gen. 2:5-5; 8:22), which in turn was part of God's judgment upon mankind for its violence. Isn't it a travesty then that deterministic Christians also attribute everything that happens directly to God, since they believe that God's decrees are all-inclusive? However, I am convinced that not only is that Augustinian assumption grossly in error, but the dominant testimony of Scripture is that although we believe in God's providence in the life of the Christian, most of what happens in the world is a consequence of Satan and his godless forces and a fallen human race which is a part of his world-system. Did not the Lord Jesus call him the "prince of this world" and Paul refer to him as "the God of this world?" Most Calvinists would rationalize this by saying that Satan is already bound and God is sovereign. I remind the reader of Geisler's anecdote I quoted in chapter 3 of the Calvinist who got peace in affirming that "God killed my son." God gets enough blame from non-Christians without misguided determinists joining their ranks in blaming God.

Even things which are attributed to God He does or has done mediately, not directly. We are called His creatures, but the fact is that God only directly created two human beings, Adam and Eve. The rest of us all came into being through the sexual activity of our parents and ancestors going back to them. Those of us who are traducianists also believe that our soul-stuff was mediately received from our parents and was not directly created by God. So when we think as to how God does His work in the world, we realize that most of it He accomplishes mediately through human instrumentality. When we pray, most frequently we see God answer through some other person. Sometimes He chooses to work transcendently or directly, but this is not the norm. I am convinced that most of the time when we pray for God to work in someone else's life, He answers our prayer by using another person. When we pray for the salvation of a person to whom we have witnessed and to whom we do not have access, He will bring someone else into their lives to reinforce our witness. I could give some striking examples. It isn't that God zaps that person with irresistible grace. Sometimes when we pray for money, God moves someone else to give it. When I was a seminary student praying for summer employment, the next day a fellow-student asked me to hold down his drafting job for him for the summer since he needed the job for the fall. I was not only able to preserve his job for him, but I earned enough to buy my ticket to Pakistan to begin my missionary ministry. God normally uses human instrumentality.

Fatalistic, passive, unmotivated Christians. We have a hard enough time motivating most Christians to actively seek and do the will of God without introducing contrary notions into their minds. Even for those who are motivated, sometimes the motivations are not biblical. Too often Arminians are motivated by fear of losing salvation, but then again too often Calvinists are working hard to prove that they are among the elect. But even worse is to believe that God has already settled everything in His decrees and nothing we can do can change that. They may call it a "soft determinism" as Feinberg does, but it still amounts to fatalism when you come down to it. Terms like compatibilism do not really resolve anything.

The true motivation should be our gratitude for what He has already done for us and is ready to do for "whosoever will" (2 Cor. 5:10). There are many other motivations for godly living beside the "love of Christ" but certainly fear of hell is not one of them. Paul epitomized it: "**For the grace of God has appeared, bringing salvation to all men, instructing us to deny ungodliness and worldly desires and to live sensibly, righteously and godly in the present age . . .**" (Titus 2:11-12). It is clear that Calvin, trained in law not theology, expounded the ten commandments as the essence of the Christian life, unaware of this truth and that of Romans 7:6: "**But now we have been released from the Law, having died to that by which we were bound, so that we serve in newness of the Spirit and not in oldness of the letter [the Law].**" After reading Dave Hunt's account of how Calvin ruled Geneva as a despot, dictating minute details of the people's lifestyle,[8] I suspect that he was much like those legalists whom Paul excoriated in his letter to the Galatians.

The Impact on God's Truth

In our day of relativism most people do not believe in absolute truth. Most Christians really don't care much about doctrine and are very subjective in their Christian lives and faith. "Whatever turns you on," "whatever floats your boat,"–these are the mottoes of the day, even among Christians. Whatever seems to meet our material, emotional, and/or physical needs is acceptable, even if it is absolute heresy. But truth does matter! The Lord Jesus claimed to be absolute truth (Jn. 14:6) and He claimed that God's word is absolute truth (Mt. 5:18; Jn. 10:35). The Greek word for truth (*alētheia*) has as a key idea 'reality,' or 'actuality.'[9] So if we are prey to doctrinal error, we are living in a realm of unreality, believing things which are not actual or true. In this book I have focused upon the theology of salvation, but actually all the categories of theology are affected. As one might gather from chapter 3, the biblical view of God is vastly impacted, and from chapter 4, our understanding of man and sin. But there is also some impact on our view of the Bible and the person and work of Christ. Thus it bleeds through our whole view of God, Christ, man, sin, salvation, and even of the church.

Views of God. The subtitle of Dave Hunt's exposé of Calvinism indicates that he feels that "Calvinism's Misrepresentation of God" is the most serious problem. Although it is difficult to prioritize, I would tend to agree with him since all the other loci of theology flow from Theology Proper. Carl Henry also makes the point in his classic text on Christian ethics, that the whole of biblical ethics flows from the person and work of God.[10] If God is the author of evil, how can we blame Satan or any human for sin and rebellion? This goes back to the notion of a single decree of God, which in turn goes back to the absurd philosophical notion of the simplicity of God. Let Christian philosophers show me one verse of Scripture which teaches the simplicity of God. Deuteronomy 6:4 teaches the unity of God, but is is very clear that *echod* means a composite unity, not even a singleness, as proved by its usage in Genesis 2:24 and elsewhere.

The notion of the impassibility of God also meets with insuperable difficulties when philosophy is set aside and the simple Scripture text is examined. One can hardly read ten chapters in the prophets without finding God's emotional involvement with His people graphically portrayed. This cannot be explained away as anthropomorphism or even anthropopathism. How many of the prophets spoke of God's undying love for Israel? How often does the New Testament speak of God's love for the church, and even for a lost world (extreme Calvinists notwithstanding). Is not love an emotion? We use the fact that the Holy Spirit is grieved by our sin (Eph. 5:30) as a proof of His personality. It seems to me that the only ones who might be able to argue the impassibility of God are non-Christian philosophers who have never read the Bible. What a distorted picture! But it is out of this distorted image of God that the notion of a God who does not love lost sinners arises; of a God who can reprobate the majority of humankind to hell without any possibility of their being saved.

The God of Calvinism is an arbitrary, coercive God. He is a God who impelled Augustine to persecute the Donatists to the death with the sword of the Roman government, a God who impelled Calvin to not allow Servetus to be beheaded but to agree to his burning at the stake; a God who impelled Calvin to have Jacques Gruet tortured twice daily until he confessed to insulting Calvin, whereupon he was beheaded.[11] Today we would call such a person a "control freak," and such an epithet seems appropriate for the God Calvin portrayed by his theology and example. Calvin with his brilliant legal mind was applying an exaggerated view of the Mosaic Law to the New Testament church. If it be argued that Calvin was a creature of his times (a poor excuse), this cannot be said for Augustine, since the church fathers before and contemporary with him objected to the coercive use of force. This was one of the evils of Roman Catholicism which Calvin should have revolted against in the light of clear New Testament teaching. In chapter 3 I sought to show that there is absolutely no biblical basis for such a distorted concept of the sovereignty of God or of the fancied divine decrees which supposedly set His plan for the universe into fatalistic concrete.

During my presentations on Islam over the years, people have asked me, "Why do Muslim 'fundamentalists' do what they do?" My response is to look at the character of Allah and the example of his prophet, Muhammad. I am reminded of a recent comment by a British missionary in Pakistan to a visiting American pastor, "To be a good Muslim one must be angry for Allah." Allah is an arbitrary, angry, coercive God, not a God of love as frequently misrepresented.[12] I cannot avoid making the parallel.

On the other hand, we find that Arminians have tended to downplay the justice of God by seeing God's love as His primary attribute. As a consequence, the forensic, legal dimension of the cross was abandoned by the Remonstrants in favor of Grotius' governmental theory. Far more serious is the extreme Arminian view of Open Theism which denies the absolute foreknowledge of God through an attempt to redefine it in harmony with process theology. I have touched on the serious error of this view in chapter 3 and in appendix C.

Views of humanity. In chapter 4 I sought to show how the extrapolation of human depravity into *total* depravity and thence into total inability is without biblical warrant. This had its devastating impact upon global missions for centuries since the 'heathen' were represented as so depraved that it was useless to try to evangelize them. Even among nominally Christian British and Americans the notion of total inability was made the basis for opposition to any confrontation of sinners with the gospel of Christ since they supposedly had to find some "warrant" within themselves that God's irresistible grace had identified them as "elect." Some of those sinners were so anxious to get saved, that they were jealous of those who found that warrant, ignorant of the fact that the warrant is in the promises of the word of God not in man. As a result of this distortion of depravity and the gospel millions never came to the place of trusting Christ's finished work for salvation and others like Fuller and Griffin waited passively for God's irresistible grace (cf. ch. 17).

The general impact of all of this upon the Christian community was a pessimism for centuries about the possibility of salvation, both on the part of the sinner and on the part of the preacher. What a thrill it was for me recently to discover that the thousands and thousands who were converted to Christ in the Second Great Awakening in New England after the Revolutionary War, were in the main in the churches of the New Divinity pastors who preached that Christ died for all without exception. The reason? Not only was it that these pastors preached that "Christ died for **you,**" but for the first time in Calvinistic New England the common people were finding out that depravity did not mean inability to exercise repentant faith. There is a real sense in which this extrapolation of depravity and virtual denial of the *imago dei* tends to dehumanize man and makes him out to be less than God's word shows him to be, especially if he is viewed as being one of that fictional category called the "non-elect."

Views of the Bible. If my appraisal of the situation is correct, Arminians in general have a problem with the inerrancy of Scripture. I suspect that contemporary Arminianism finds the Scripture to be self-contradictory. I referenced Howard Marshall's admission of the serious tension between the promises of eternal security and the implication of the warnings to Christians as he understood them. Marshall is certainly highly reputed among Arminian scholars. When the interpretation of diverse passages of the Bible comes out with contradictory conclusions, trust in inerrancy is certainly undermined. Many Arminian denominations do not even have a position on inerrancy.

On the other hand, determinists also have a problem they have not realized or confronted. If the outworking of God's sovereignty and decree(s) is all encompassing, then how can it be that certain aspects of Scripture show the involvement of sinful human hands. I am not referring, of course, to the inerrancy of the autographa. I am referring to the preservation of the text, which all Evangelicals acknowledge is not perfect. Although there has been incredible preservation compared to other ancient documents, nevertheless, the text is not 100% perfect. Believing that God works mediately in many of His works in the world, I have no problem with that. But if God has decreed "all that comes to pass" why did He not arrange for the perfect preservation of Scripture? Even worse is the problem of translation. Why did God sovereignly allow that corrupt Vulgate version to dominate Christendom for over a millennium? It was the basis of many Romish errors and of the gross confusion of mainstream Protestantism. Why did God allow the KJV with its many mistranslations to dominate the

English-speaking world for so many centuries? Those of us who don't buy into the all-inclusive decree(s) of God, have questions, but these are minuscule compared to the problems of the determinists.

Views of Christ. There have been many distorted pictures of the Father and Christ in past theology. When Roman Catholic theology portrayed both Father and Son in a stern and wrathful way with Mary as the loving intercessor, the Lutherans sought to correct that by portraying Christ as the loving intercessor with a God of wrath. Both Lutheran and Calvinistic theology has tended to portray Christ as propitiating and reconciling a wrathful God. Nineteenth-century pietists in Scandinavia began to question that picture with the question, "Where is it written?"[13] Of course, a host of passages affirm the love of God in taking the initiative in salvation (Jn. 3:16; Rom. 5:8, etc.). But extreme Calvinism denies God's love for a lost world and similarly restricts the love of Christ to the 'elect.' The Gospels, however, do not portray the Lord Jesus as showing any limitation of His love and compassion for lost sinners. Mark recorded Christ's love for the rich young ruler, who may never have come to faith for all we know (Mk. 10:21). Did all those whom the Lord healed and delivered from demon oppression in His love and compassion–did they all come to faith in Christ and become 'elect?' This is highly improbable.

Views of salvation. The history of theology is one of human over-reaction. In chapter one I gave examples of how doctrinal error in one direction was overcompensated for in the opposite direction. Among the church fathers there was a drift away from the gospel of God's grace into various forms of legalism. Pelagius' man-centered distortion of salvation was countered by Augustine's inconsistent overreaction with his deterministic concept of God's grace, mixed with elements of legalistic church-centered salvation, which was incongruent. Although a semi-Augustinian resolution was arrived at in the synod of Orange (529), the medieval Catholic church drifted increasingly to semi-Pelagianism.

Luther and Calvin reacted by reverting back to an inconsistent repackaging of Augustine's deterministic concept of grace, retaining much of his church-centered concept of salvation, but restoring justification by grace from the Pauline epistles. There is good evidence that Calvin, coming a score of years after Luther, by increased dependence upon Augustine and Greek philosophy began a process of rescholasticizing the Protestant movement. Beza then took the lead among Calvin's successors in completing that process by introducing the doctrine of limited atonement. I have identified at least a dozen movements which were attempts to correct this over-reaction and move away from determinism. Among them Arminius' correction itself got hijacked by the Remonstrants who went far beyond his start.[14] The Wesleyan movement brought it back to a more evangelical position, although developing more unbiblical strains. The more modest correction of Cameron/Amyraut had a major impact until dispersed by the revocation of the Edict of Nantes, although perpetuated by Richard Baxter, the Marrow Men of Scotland, and the New Divinity of New England. The latter two movements also moved beyond Amyraut's Calvinism to an unstable compromise with some Arminian concepts.

Over these centuries there were constant universalist reactions against the narrow determinism of the Reformers and their successors. Those with a liberalizing mindset took the biblical truth of Christ's death for all, and failing to distinguish the objective ransom from the subjective liberation, sought to universalize salvation. This was clearly a reaction to the gross narrowness of determinism. I have not had opportunity to trace this from Reformation times, but it was clearly a problem in Great Britain in Andrew Fuller's day, and in New England as a reaction to Puritanism. Fuller's most widely applauded works were against Socinian universalism, just as Edward Griffin's Park Street lectures in defense of evangelical theology against Bostonian universalism were highly appreciated on both sides of the Atlantic. Universalism is clearly a reaction against determinism. Geisler rightly claims that it logically lays the ground for universalism: "*If God can save anyone to whom He gives the desire to be saved, then why does He not give the desire to all people?*" (italics his). If God is a loving God, why does He not use His irresistible grace to save all?[15] Calvinists have no answer to universalism except to deny God's universal love. No wonder universalism has flourished in heavily Calvinistic areas.

Here also Fisk has given substantial supporting documentation. Howard Hageman wrote: "Not only can such a view of predestination easily lead to universalism, it can just as easily lead to the blurring of all moral distinctions." Neve points out that the universalist leader, Hosea Ballou, was "a determinist, for, according to him, if the will of God to save all shall be carried out, the will of man must be denied the power of resistance." Nels F. S. Ferré was a universalist because of his belief in the sovereignty of God: "A theology based on sovereign love will uncompromisingly stand for universal salvation. Anything less would be inconsistent with God's love." Perhaps even more telling is extreme Calvinist Arthur Custance's leaning toward the probability of universalism.[16]

If unconditional election and irresistible grace are true, there is no good news of the gospel for sinners. There is just a message of resignation to the inexorable will of God. That sounds to me to be more like the Islam I heard in Pakistan. Islam is a religion of submission to the inexorable will of a sovereign Allah. Let me repeat, *there is no good news for sinners.* It is bad news for most. It is not just that Christians may differ as to the content of the gospel; there is no good news to discuss. The hyper-Calvinists with which Fuller and Spurgeon struggled were absolutely consistent–there is no need to preach to the unconverted. *If election is unconditional, then it can neither be contingent upon human preaching or the response of the sinner.*

On the other hand, Arminian denial of eternal security does leave us with a temporary salvation, more akin to probation than the full acquittal of justification by faith alone. In chapters 14 and 15 a brief defense of eternal security is presented in contradistinction to perseverance of the saints. The lynchpin of my treatment is a non-traditional exegesis of the warning of Hebrews 6 and the strong scriptural evidence of the preservation of the saints, as Howard Marshall admits. I believe careful exegesis of all relevant passages eliminates the tension so widely admitted by both Calvinists and Arminians. Such an insecure view of salvation held by both Arminians and extreme Calvinists is not a solid base for building a stable Christian life of assurance and blessing.

The Impact upon Preaching

Reformed homiletician and editor, James Daane, wrote his most significant critique of decretal theology because of his conviction that it is unpreachable.[17] Obviously Arminians are not preaching it, but he has observed that the Reformed are not preaching their Calvinism either because it is unpreachable. This caused him to reexamine the biblical basis of what he terms 'decretal theology.' Although I have not been a part of the Reformed tradition, I have sat under the ministry of at least three five-point Calvinists for an extensive period, one of whom even wrote a book on election. I cannot recall any one of the three giving any exposition of Calvinistic doctrine from the pulpit. Perhaps there were passing allusions to their Calvinistic doctrine, but nothing substantive. All three believed in evangelism and missions, inconsistently, I believe. Those Calvinists who believe in missions and evangelism are faced with an insuperable dilemma. Preaching their Calvinism along with the necessity of exercising repentant faith will prove counterproductive. Certainly Calvinism is not the gospel and preaching them together will not only seem contradictory, but also will be offensive to unregenerate hearers, far more than the simple offense of the cross. Harold Camping of Family Radio is one exception in that he preaches his Calvinistic doctrines since he perceives them to be the gospel, but his preaching does come across as adding offense to the gospel. Daane's solution to the dilemma is to move away from philosophically-derived decretal theology to a more biblically based doctrine of election, centering upon God's election of the Lord Jesus as the Messiah. Indeed, this is the goal of my whole book.

The Impact upon Apologetics

When I was first called upon to teach Christian evidences, I was appalled to find the oft-quoted contrarian statement by Spurgeon that since the Bible is like a lion, you don't have to defend it, you just let it go. I knew the references to the word of God being like a hammer, a mirror, a sword, etc. but I have never been able to find any biblical reference to the Bible being like a lion. Today lions are an endangered species in many parts of the world. So I have my doubts about Spurgeon's simile and its negative impact upon naive Evangelicals for over a century. Most of us see Spurgeon as a hero of the faith in carrying to the next generation Andrew Fuller's emphasis on confronting sinners with the gospel. However, I wonder if his commitment to essential Calvinism did not distort his perspective on the value of apologetics. Perhaps the root of Spurgeon's reticence toward apologetics goes back to Calvin. Hunt demonstrates by extensive quotes from Calvin that he had "little use for evidence and proof." In emphasizing the internal testimony of the Spirit, Calvin denigrates the external evidences for the inspiration of Scripture. Hunt points out that Muslims, Mormons, and others give their own subjective testimonies for the truth of their holy books since they lack any external objective support.[18] It is true that in the last century many Calvinists have been at the forefront of the use of apologetics. I suspect that with the devastating inroads of liberalism in their denominations, men like Machen, Warfield, and Wilson were forced to use the apologetic tools at their disposal to defend the faith, and men like Sproul, James Kennedy, and others have picked up the mantle. However, it really is inconsistent with their anthropology and soteriology. If man is dead in total inability, apologetic argument is not going to have any impact. In chapter 17, I argued that the biblical paradigm is for persuasion evangelism and that apologetics is a vital part of this.

A starting point in apologetics is in the arguments for the existence of God from creation. Starting with the premise of total inability it is obvious that if the word of God cannot impact the 'non-elect,' certainly the naturalistic arguments would be even more useless. I take it that this is the major reason why Reformed thinkers like Cornelius Van Til and Karl Barth had so little use for these arguments and why Buswell, as a very low five-point Calvinist, held such empirical evidences in high regard, albeit inconsistently. I am sure that the testimony of Dr. Viggo Olsen, MD, concerning the part that such evidences played in his conversion, can be multiplied many times over.[19]

I would also suggest, as I have above, that determinism seems so absurd to most non-Christians that it raises serious obstacles to their consideration of the gospel. Historically knowledgeable people already have a negative impression of Calvin and the Puritans, but when they learn about unconditional election, the turnoff is complete. A germinal experience in the ministry of Moyse Amyraut in seventeenth-century France was a discussion with a Catholic nobleman over dinner at the Catholic bishop's residence. His witness was squelched because this nobleman was "filled with horror by the doctrine of predestination as taught in our churches," and regarded it as "contrary to the nature of God and His gospel to say that He created the greatest part of mankind with the express purpose of damning them."[20] James Daane suggests that the problem of preaching decretal theology is reprobation. "Simply stated, reprobation gets in the way of every attempt to take election seriously because in the traditional Reformed theology *reprobation is always there.*" He pointed out how the Synod of Dort struggled to separate election and reprobation, but this is impossible.[21] I hasten to add in passing that the Aristotelian concept of the impassability of God works wonders to explain how God could be so cruel and unjust and unfeeling and helps to desensitize us to the horrors of reprobation.

Calvinists face the same problem with making God the author of evil and this is why the Westminster Confession was changed in crossing the Atlantic to mention plural decrees, that is, including a decree to *permit* sin. But according to Calvinistic interpretation of Ephesians 1:11, if God "works all things according to the counsel of His will," this would have to include sin.

In chapter 10, I raised the problem of the Calvinistic God being the ultimate discriminator of persons since He supposedly gives the gift of repentant faith to so few in many nations and to so many Americans. Not that many non-Christians would necessarily be aware of this "intractable problem," but then Calvinists also seem unaware of the problematic way it portrays God. Non-Calvinists have no difficulty here since we see the major part that human factors have in people coming to faith.

Resorting to Philosophical Sophistries

I am concerned with the deleterious influence of human philosophic systems upon theology. I found contemporary evidence of philosophical sophistries in Calvinistic theology. The heavy dependence upon words like antinomy, paradox, and mystery are highly troubling. Expressions like "soft determinism" and compatiblism as explanations for the contradictions of the system seem more like a smoke-screen than a logical explanation. Daane charges that commitment to decretal theology only produces "word games."[22] I faulted the widespread failure to make a simple distinction between God's *certainty* of the whole future and God's *determining* of the whole future, as a fundamental error of logic and language.

On the other hand, I have suggested that Craig's middle-knowledge view, not only has substantial biblical support, but also helps explain how God in a non-deterministic way can orchestrate the events of redemption history to bring the world to the conclusion which He has foreordained from eternity past. Augustine's radical reversal of the tradition of four centuries of the apostles' and church fathers' teaching of free will and human responsibility involved philosophical sophistry derived from his Manichean and neo-Platonist background supplemented by serious isogesis of Scripture. The whole biblical narrative is predicated upon fallen man's free will and responsibility for his actions, the delegation of divine authority to Adam, Noah, and Israel through Moses, and begins a pattern of divine self-limitation, which reached its epitome in the cross of Christ. Drawing from my engineering background, I have sought to point up the extreme theological recklessness of the *many extrapolations* of language and thought common among determinists. These involve such persistent subtle semantic shifts that I have no hesitation in calling them logical sophistries. They do not clarify God's truth; they only obfuscate.

Usurping the True Meaning of Scripture

The main body of my book has been devoted to the interpretation of crucial Scripture passages, by carefully examining the contexts, both immediate and comprehensive; the usage of key words in the secular, Jewish, and biblical, and patristic literature; the grammar and syntax of each sentence; the analogy of Scripture, without resort to parallelomania; and to some extent checking how Calvin and other Protestant interpreters have interpreted these passages. It has not been unusual to find Calvin at odds with the Calvinists, but ultimately we must not look to Augustine, Luther, Calvin, Arminius, Wesley, or any church leader as an authority in interpretation.

In chapter 1, I have sought to alert the reader concerning many of the ways we go astray in interpreting the word of God. The most serious is theological interpretation, that is, coming to Scripture with a theological position and seeking with a deductive methodology to harmonize the given passage with that viewpoint. Obviously, that approach has got it backwards. It is imperative to start with an inductive, exegetical approach. This is why we must be so careful to eliminate our presuppositions and biases when we handle the word of the living God. To fail to do so is to allow a theological or philosophical system to usurp the true meaning of God's word. In the parable of the soils the Lord Jesus spoke about the fourth kind of people, **"who have heard the word in an honest and good heart, hold it fast, and bear fruit with perseverance"** (Lk. 8:15). This must be the goal of every Christian. It is not only foundational to bearing fruit for God, but also essential in honoring His inerrant word. We bring discredit to God, His church, His word, and His gospel when we indulge in deductive, theological interpretation, which is Scripture twisting.

Missing the Heart of God's Great Plan

God's great plan of the ages is the redemption and restoration of His lost human race. The promises made to Abraham centered in the blessing to "all the families of the earth" through Abraham, his lineage of 'choice' people, and through his 'choice' seed, the Messiah. When the Lord Jesus began His ministry by announcing the future kingdom of God as the goal of God's redemptive plan, the key issue with the Jewish nation was whether or not He was the elect One of God, God's choice servant. In that great Pentecost sermon, the apostle Peter announced that the resurrection was proof that He is God's choice servant and that repentant faith in Him was the imperative condition for inclusion in that coming kingdom. As Christ's church developed as a preparatory "mystery" form of the kingdom, it reluctantly and with God's prodding broke free from its Jewish base and began to move out among "all the families of the earth." Now God's great predetermined plan is His "taking from among the Gentiles" a 'choice' people for His name (Acts 15:14) to be the citizens of that future kingdom.

Essential to the outworking of His plan is the delegation of God's authority and power to humanity to be His instruments in its implementation. Therefore He began by creating Adam and Eve in His image and delegating dominion to them. This progressive delegation of aspects of His sovereignty reached its peak in the appointment of the Lord Jesus as His regent King and attestation of this by His resurrection from the dead. As the unique Son of God, He now delegates the authority to become sons of God to those who by faith receive Him (Jn. 1:12-13) so that they might be trustees (stewards) of the good news. Since His image is being restored in this new humanity, they are accountable moral agents in the implementation of this plan by persuasion evangelism and global outreach. The content of the good news they bear is of highest importance in producing genuine fruit for God, fruit which will persist and survive the fires of God's judgments.

To what extent our theology of salvation is harmonious with that plan, to that extent it is the "whole counsel of God" (Acts 20:27); but to what extent it obscures or hinders that plan it will be burned up in the fires of God's judgments. May every Christian be found searching the Scriptures with an "honest and good heart" to verify, understand, believe, obey, and proclaim accurately God's great eternal plan for the salvation of people of "**every nation and *all* tribes and peoples and tongues**" (Rev. 7:9).

Conclusions

I, therefore, appeal to my Calvinistic readers to consider the possibility that Arminius may have gotten something right, that some of his reaction against Calvinism was biblical. I appeal to my Arminian readers to consider the possibility that Calvinistic doctrine may not all be false. I appeal to my Lutheran readers (although I have not focused much on you) to consider that the internal tensions in evangelical Lutheranism are resolvable by going beyond Luther and Melanchthon to a fresh exegesis of Scripture.

Let us break free from the destructive and divisive polarization of theology by getting back to the full inspiration, sufficiency, and priority of the Scriptures in developing our theology. Let us make sure that we have got a balanced theology, not majoring in the minor or perhaps even missing the major themes completely, but focusing on the heart of God's plan of the ages–the redemption of lost humanity through the all-sufficient blood of Christ's cross by confronting the lost with the imperative of response to his bona fide offer of grace by repentant faith. Let us make sure that we are "telling it like it is," not binding on earth what God has not bound in heaven, and not loosing on earth what God has not loosed in heaven. Only this will give the full glory to the Living God.

---

1. G. T. Stokes, *The Acts of the Apostles* (The Expositor's Bible; London: Hodder & Stoughton, 1891), I: 134-6, cited by Fisk, p. 194.
2. John R. Rice, *Predestined for Hell? No!* (Murfreesboro, TN: Sword of the Lord, 1958), p. 6, cited by Fisk, p. 198.
3. H. A. Ironside, *Holiness: the False and the True* (Neptune, NJ: Loizeaux).
4. Geisler, *Chosen but Free*, p. 132.
5. Edward C. Bowlen, *Concise Critique of Contemporary Coercive Calvinism* (Westfield, MA: Faith Bible Baptist Church, 1976), p. 2, cited by Fisk, p. 206.
6. Iain H. Murray, *Spurgeon v. Hyper-Calvinism: The Battle for Gospel Preaching* (Edinburgh: Banner of Truth, 1995), p. 127.
7. A. H. Strong, *Systematic Theology*, p. 511; among many cited by Fisk, pp. 206-10.
8. Dave Hunt, *What Love Is This? Calvinism's Misrepresentation of God* (Sisters, OR: Loyal, 2002), pp. 59-74.
9. Abbott-Smith, *Lexicon*, p. 20.
10. Carl F. H. Henry, *Christian Personal Ethics* (Eerdmans, 1957), pp. 145-71 (not just limited to these pages).
11. Schaff, VIII: p. 503.
12. C. Gordon Olson, "Evangelical Misrepresentations of Allah," a paper presented at Lanham, MD, at the Eastern Regional of the ETS, March 23, 2002.
13. P. P. Waldenstrom was a leader of the "readers" who questioned Lutheran theology and founded movements like the Mission Covenant and the Evangelical Free churches. Even though I left the Mission Covenant because of its growing liberalism, I appreciate many features of its heritage.
14. Stephen M. Ashby, "A Reformed Arminian View," in J. Matthew Pinson, ed., *Four Views on Eternal Security* (Zondervan, 2002), pp. 138, 150. See also the various writings of Carl Bangs. Ashby does not used the term 'hijacked,' but the significant differences between Arminius and later Arminians would justify this language. We could also say with equal fairness that Theodore Beza and his associates hijacked the Calvinistic movement.
15. Geisler, pp. 134-5.
16. Howard G. Hageman, *Predestination* (Phila.: Fortress, 1963), pp. 70-71; J. L. Neve, *HCT*, II:282; Nels F. S. Ferré, *The Christian Understanding of God* (NY: Harper, 1951), pp. 217ff., see also Arthur C. Custance, *The Sovereignty of Grace* (GR: Baker, 1979) the latter part of the book, cited by Fisk, p. 218-9.
17. James Daane, *The Freedom of God: A Study of Election and the Pulpit* (GR: Eerdmans, 1973).
18. Hunt, pp. 394-6, cites Calvin's *Institutes*, III: pp. 71-73.
19. Viggo Olsen, *Daktar/Diplomat in Bangladesh* (1975).
20. Moyse Amyraut, Preface to *Six Sermons*, pp. i-ii, cited by Armstrong, *Amyraut Heresy*, p. 81.
21. Daane, pp. 35ff.
22. Ibid, p. 73.

All the way my Savior leads me;
What have I to ask beside?
Can I doubt His tender mercy,
Who through life has been my guide?
Heav'nly peace, divinest comfort,
Here by faith in Him to dwell!
For I know whate'er befall me,
Jesus doeth all things well.

All the way my Savior leads me;
Cheers each winding path I tread;
Gives me grace for every trial,
Feeds me with the living bread;
Though my weary steps may falter,
And my soul athirst may be,
Gushing from the rock before me,
Lo! A spring of joy I see.

-Fanny J. Crosby

APPENDIX A

MY THEOLOGICAL PILGRIMAGE

Since I was saved half a century ago as a junior in engineering college, I have been on a theological pilgrimage. Shortly after my conversion, I became aware of the importance of at least one theological issue. I knew I was saved and that up to that point I had been lost. But now how certain and secure was my salvation? Was it valid for eternity or was it some kind of probation?

From childhood I had grown up in an Arminian church. The pastor whose ministry covered those years, while professedly evangelical, did not preach evangelistically in a forthright manner. As a result, although I always knew that Christ died for the sins of the world, I didn't understand the necessity of the new birth or a personal relationship with Christ. I had been christened, confirmed, and joined the church as a high-school senior ignorant of salvation truth.

When I was elected to be president of the youth group, I was embarrassed to realize that I had never read one book of the Bible and was really biblically illiterate, despite years of faithful attendance in Sunday School. So I started reading the Gospels and Acts, but when I got to Romans I didn't have a clue. After several attempts, I gave up. I was spiritually dead and didn't know it. It wasn't until two years later that the Lord used my closest buddy and classmate, Herb Hage, to bring me to salvation through hearing him ask his cousin whether he had been really born again. I don't think that I had ever heard about being born again before. My pastor didn't preach that. That summer I started again to read the New Testament to find out what it said about the new birth and salvation. I got some gospel tracts from my sister and looked up the references in my Bible, and when I returned to engineering college in the fall, I had the assurance of salvation. Herb and I joined a newly formed InterVarsity group on campus. My sister Harriet and I started taking courses in the Newark (NJ) evening Bible School.

The first doctrinal issue. Very soon the question of eternal security became the central focus of our discussion and study. Herb's church believed it, but he wasn't sure why. He had a Strong's concordance, and we began to study every verse in the Bible that seemed to relate to the subject. We realized that a major issue was the meaning of certain key words in those passages. So we used the concordance to see how those words were used in other contexts, in an attempt to see the range of meanings to discover the probable meaning in the passage in question. Herb's pastor, Bill Fisk, lent us a copy of J. F. Strombeck's *Shall Never Perish*, which helped us greatly to clarify the issues. After many months of study, both Herb and I became thoroughly convinced that our salvation was eternal, and that the Arminian denial of eternal security was not supported in Scripture. That conviction of mine has only grown stronger over years of theological study and teaching. I am grateful to the Lord that over the ensuing years, no matter what the spiritual struggle, I have never seriously doubted my own salvation or the scriptural truth of eternal security.

Calling to ministry. In that junior year in engineering I struggled with God's will for my life. Science and technology has always been my passion. In fifth grade after doing a chemical experiment in 'show and tell', I had astonished my teacher by balancing the chemical equation for it on the blackboard. With that kind of interest in science it wasn't hard for me to get the Bausch and Lomb honorary science award when I graduated from a large suburban high school. In engineering college I was an honors student and invited to join the honorary engineering society, Tau Beta Pi. But I had never asked the Lord whether or not I should become an engineer.

There were two remarkable providential events related to my summer jobs which set the scene at Campus in the Woods in Ontario for leading into ministry. An engineer friend wanted to get me a summer job with him in Schering Corporation and set up the appointment with the personnel director. It should have been a slam dunk. But I never heard from him after the interview. Years later I found out that I had offended him in the interview with an incredibly coincidental, inadvertent, and innocent comment. Instead, the college got me a far better job with a small company in Jersey City as assistant to the Chief Chemist, a very nice Jewish man. Then the second summer, when I asked my Jewish bosses if I could take August off to go to a training camp in Ontario, the President said, "My neighbor is going to that training camp." I was astonished at the coincidence. It was true that his neighbor, Jim, was going to Campus in the Woods, and this inclined my bosses to give me the month off. It was there through counsel with Ros Rinker and Charlie Hummel that I understood God's leading into ministry. And there I studied *Therefore Go* and became convinced of the centrality of missions.

Despite the lack of any apparent abilities related to Christian ministry (not being particularly articulate), I felt a growing conviction of the Spirit that I should go on to seminary after graduation. I took a battery of tests which NJIT then offered to graduating seniors and got the results from the guidance counselor: "Gordon, these tests show you are ideally suited to become a successful engineer. You scored in the top 10% of college graduates in vocabulary and in the top 1% in technical vocabulary. What are your plans?" When I told him that I was going to theological seminary, he was shocked. But when God calls He provides the ability, and I have never regretted the decision to go into ministry.

Theological education. At Dallas Seminary I was taught and accepted the 'moderate' Calvinism of Lewis Sperry Chafer, which I now know was essentially Amyraldian soteriology. I was privileged to take the last Spiritual Life course he taught and got much of my theology from his successor, John F. Walvoord. However, the soteriology was taught by a teaching fellow named Howard G. Hendricks. Even more important was being in the first class at Dallas in which he taught inductive Bible study methodology, as he had learned it from Merrill Tenney and Robert Traina. I also took some of the first Biblical Theology courses taught by Charles C. Ryrie.[1] Merrill Unger gave me a good foundation in Hebrew, and S. Lewis Johnson's "Introduction to Greek Exegesis" course was especially helpful. Many Bible books were taught in special lectures by Roy L. Aldrich, Jack Mitchell, and J. Vernon McGee. I majored in theology, and becoming concerned about the erosion in evangelical circles of the doctrine of verbal plenary inspiration, I wrote my master's thesis on the verbal aspect of inspiration, "A Definitive Study of Verbal Inspiration." Forty-five years of further study have confirmed the truth of the inerrancy of the Scriptures.

Missionary ministry. I had long had an interest in Muslim ministry, so when a Pakistani student at seminary became my close friend, God was able to use him as my 'man of Macedonia.' He shared the need of an evangelical student ministry in Pakistan and that burden grew. In 1956 I arrived in Pakistan as an independent missionary and working with my friend's contacts started the Pakistan Fellowship of Evangelical Students with a camp in the Himalaya foothills. He had told me there were 400 Christian college students, but I soon found out that very few of them had a personal relationship with Christ. Three years later, after marriage to Miriam Moffatt, a missionary nurse, we began to worship with a group of indigenous Brethren assemblies related to Bakht Singh, the Indian evangelist. Before long I was torn between demands of the student ministry and the assemblies, in addition to work with the Evangelical Fellowship of W. Pakistan and the Pakistan Bible Correspondence School. On furlough we joined the staff of International Fellowship of Evangelical Students. After eight years of ministry in English and Urdu, health complications forced our return home.[2]

Teaching theology. During the years of missionary service and brief pastoral ministry, no serious soteriological issues had been raised. In 1967 when I began to teach at Northeastern Bible College, I was assigned Bible Doctrine and Biblical Theology courses, among others. Our Executive Vice-President, Wesley A. Olsen had developed the Biblical Theology course based on Erich Sauer's and Geerhardus Vos's diachronic methodology, which has proved to be an excellent approach. Whatever other courses I taught, these two were my constant joy and challenge every year for 23 years.

Northeastern was somewhat unique with its emphasis upon inductive methodology in its Bible department due to the impact of William C. Lincoln and James G. Kallam, both students of Traina. We were all encouraged to stress an inductive methodology in our teaching.

In my second year I was asked to fill in by teaching an upper level Systematic Theology course as well. I used J. Oliver Buswell, Jr.'s one-volume textbook because it stressed an inductive and exegetical methodology. In the early 1970s I became increasingly dissatisfied with the deductive treatments in some of the Calvinistic theological works I was utilizing and began the exegetical research which is the substance of this present work. At that time a new theology teacher came on campus who held rigidly to extreme Calvinism, and dialog with him helped me to understand the unbiblical features of the system. Dr. Chafer had always started his theological discussion with a study of the determinative Scriptures, and I realized that this had to be my methodology.

A crystalizing soteriology. By 1981 I felt I was ready to present some results in a paper presented at the annual meeting of the Evangelical Theological Society in Toronto entitled, "Beyond Calvinism and Arminianism." Although it was to be in a parallel session in a small classroom, the subject attracted so many attenders that we had to move down to the chapel for the presentation. Although I was an unknown, perhaps half of about 300 attendees heard my paper; so great was the interest. Since then I have given papers on many aspects of the subject in national and regional ETS meetings. These papers are the substance of this book.

A number of other events helped to mold my thinking. Being that Northeastern was a small college, my teaching was quite diverse, and I was not afforded the luxury of specialization. In the beginning I even taught mathematics and logic. Over the years theology made up about half of my teaching load with missions and Bible making up the balance about equally. Teaching Christian Ethics and Christian Evidences from time to time rounded out the challenge. Beginning in the 70s I was assigned Life of Christ and the Book of Acts annually. As I wrestled with many contexts in the Gospels and Acts, I realized that they were totally in conflict with a deterministic soteriology. More than anything else this moved me toward a mediate position.

I hope you grasp the irony in my saying that it is wonderful how the Bible informs theology! It is also wonderful how missiological concerns can inform our theology and vice versa. Indeed this sort of cross-pollenization is extremely healthy. I am convinced that many scholars suffer from narrow specialization and lose the forest for the trees. Thus I do not apologize for not being a theological specialist.

For a decade it was my privilege to serve as a Bible answerman on a telephone call-in program on WFME, the Family Radio station in the metro New York area. Since it followed Harold Camping's Monday through Thursday Open Forum program, listeners would regularly put me on the spot by asking me to respond to Camping's extreme Calvinistic comments the previous nights. Wrestling with those questions forced me to reevaluate my position, because I found his harsh answers totally unacceptable (for which I was ultimately dropped from the program).

The reader might wonder just what denominational traditional bias I bring to this subject. I was ordained by an independent Bible church. I had taught an adult Sunday School class in a Methodist church for some months. In Pakistan I attended a United Presbyterian (pre-merger) church for 3 years while in language study and then began ministering with indigenous Brethren assemblies for five years. During furlough I joined the General Conference Baptist church through which I had been saved years earlier, and have since pastored two Conservative Baptist churches and had interim ministries in two independent Baptist churches. We were members of a Regular Baptist Church for many years (where two pastors were five-point Calvinists), and now we are members of an Evangelical Free Church. I suspect that my lack of denominational loyalty has been a strength rather than a weakness.

It is not that I don't have convictions. Over the years of teaching, my students saw me as very dogmatic. Most areas of my theology have changed very little in half a century, but I have always been willing to re-examine some of the difficult areas, such as the subject of this book.

I can assure the reader that I have not gone to press hastily with this book. Indeed much of my attention for the last decade has been focused on missions conferences, and writing, publishing, and updating my missions textbook, *What in the World is God Doing?*, which has enjoyed wide circulation.

In 1991 I suffered a massive heart attack and recovered remarkably well, resulting in the conviction that God had spared my life so that I might get this book to press. Providentially, in 1997, my cardiologist ordered a PSA test, which prompted cancer surgery. In April 2000 all alone in the Poconos, I passed out and fell flat on my face. After regaining consciousness and driving fifty miles to the emergency room, a double bypass was mandated. My cardiologist's analysis was that the hard compression on my chest probably saved my life. In January 2002 after jogging on Daytona Beach, I passed out on a stair with a pulse of 30, requiring the implantation of a pacemaker/defibrillator. Do I ever believe in God's providence! I am also thankful for the "common grace" of modern medicine.

I believe that I have dealt with the major exegetical issues and set the results of my research before you with the prayer that you may be challenged to re-examine your soteriology, no matter how dogmatically previously held.

Just to avoid any confusion, let me affirm that I am C. Gordon Olson, not Gordon C. Olson. I believe the late Gordon C. Olson of the Chicago area was an Arminian, perhaps even a precursor of Open Theism. We are not related, and there is no connection.

---

1. Merrill C. Tenney, *Galatians: The Charter of Christian Liberty* (GR: Eerdmans, 1951). Tenney studies Galatians using nine different Bible study methods. Robert A. Traina, *Methodical Bible Study* (Privately published, 1952). My late colleague, William C. Lincoln, studied under Traina at the then Biblical Seminary in New York City and wrote a more popular book, *Personal Bible Study* (Minneapolis: Bethany Fellowship, 1975). A number of Ryrie's courses led to the publication of: Charles Caldwell Ryrie, *Biblical Theology of the New Testament* (1959).

2. It was thrilling for me in February of 1997 to return to Pakistan for the first time in 33 years to see the most encouraging progress these ministries have made. The Pakistan Fellowship of Evangelical Students is flourishing.

APPENDIX B

CRITIQUES OF DETERMINISTIC WORKS

John Piper's *The Justification of God*

Most Calvinists probably feel that John Piper's 1993 book, *The Justification of God: An Exegetical and Theological Study of Romans 9:1-23*, is the capstone of their case. Piper is obviously a brilliant scholar and a major defender of Calvinism. Having his doctorate from the University of Munich, he is thoroughly conversant with the English and German theological literature. His use of the Greek and Hebrew and extensive citation of that literature is very impressive. I am sure that it gives Calvinists great security in knowing that a man of this caliber is leading the charge. However, I suggest that his work is badly flawed in a number of very significant ways.

His narrow focus. Right off on his first page, he defensively refers to those who will criticize his narrow focus upon only Romans 9:1-23 as guilty of a "stereotype," which will discount it as "too limited in its scope and blinded by its dogmatic concerns to the larger redemptive-historical issues" (p. 15). This is not at all a stereotype, but a serious concern, not only with the larger redemptive-historical issues, but also with careful consideration of the immediate context of the passage. This he seriously violates, as I shall show. He further claims that he is not losing sight of the forest while focusing on one tree (p. 16). However, it is clear to me that he has totally ignored the two trees in the forest right next to the tree upon which he is focusing (9:9-13 and 9:24–10:21). In so doing, he has cut the tree down and dragged it out of the forest and into the laboratory for a dissection, but in so doing has introduced various fungi from the pseudepigrapha, German scholarship, and a scholastic methodology

Paul's concern for Jews' salvation. He makes a good point regarding 9:1-6, that Paul has a major concern for the salvation of his individual Jewish brethren and that this informs the meaning of 9:6-23 as being concerned about the salvation of individuals, not just the roles of nations place in history. Since Paul comes back to the issue of individual salvation in 9:24–10:21, this does not prove that 9:6-23 is focusing upon individual election. These are distinct, yet closely related issues. Piper sets up a false dichotomy, and he denigrates the crucial role which Israel played in salvation-history, by use of the word "merely" (p. 56) . Obviously, the salvation of individual Jews had already been and has continued to be vastly affected by the dispensational transition of God's primary focus from the nation Israel to the Church as the bearers of the promise of salvation. He also misses the major Jew/Gentile issue throughout Romans, which is most important in understanding the issues which Paul is addressing, as I highlighted in chapter 3, pp. 72-3.

Ignoring the subsequent context. He only has a few passing references to 9:24–10:21, as can be verified by checking the references in the Scripture index (which I carefully did). There is no discussion at all of this important context. Since Paul's emphasis there is upon the cruciality of faith, which is an important theme of the whole book of Romans (60 references), how can he almost totally ignore this section and yet claim to do justice to contextual considerations? Over the years I fielded questions on WFME, I got many questions about Romans 9, and as a moderate Calvinist (at that time), I suggested that the callers also balance off Romans 9 with Romans 10. Now I see that the issue is more than balance, it is a crucial contextual consideration. Although he has extensive discussion of Romans 11, he jumps right over 9:24–10:21 in his long excursis on "The Theological Unity of Romans 9 and 11" (pp. 25-31).

Ignoring the foundational context. Even worse, if that were possible, is the way he skips over the crucial introductory context of 9:9-13 with a brief theological discussion (pp. 51-3). Since Paul is establishing the foundation for this whole section, it is exceedingly important to exegete it in sequence. Yet Piper lost it in the crack between pages 70 and 71. Indeed, the way that Piper jumps from one passage to another causes the reader to lose the sequence of Paul's argument. Most importantly, Piper quotes Genesis 25:23 three times, but only once gives the whole verse about "two nations are in your womb," and even then does not discuss the real implications of these words (pp. 61-2). Similarly, he obfuscates Paul's reference later to Jeremiah 18, under the heading, "*The traditions behind Romans 9:20, 21,*" by not only quoting two possibly relevant Isaiah passages, but also extensive discussion of references from the pseudepigrapha. He has no discussion of the national implications of Jeremiah 18:1-8, which is crucial (pp. 194-9). Piper is more concerned with the impact of extra-biblical "traditions" than he is with God's word to the nation Israel through Jeremiah, in a situation parallel to Paul's.

Mistranslating a key verse. Piper mistranslates 9:6b by moving the negative from the first clause to the second in the sentence. This violates a fundamental law of logic and totally changes the meaning of the sentence. His corruption: "For all the ones from Israel, these are not Israel" (pp. 58, 65, 67). The existing translations are all correct. Moving the negative *ou* to the second clause makes the verse into the converse of Paul's statement. A law of logic tells us that the converse of a statement may or may not be true. It is not true that no Jews are the true Israelites, since the early church was mostly Jewish. I am not clear what Piper's agenda was in this, but it is indefensible!

A defective, deductive methodology. Piper's whole methodology in the book is faulty and scholastic. He starts out with extensive theological discussion before really getting into the exegesis of the text. This biases the whole exegesis and is a reversal of the proper inductive theological methodology. We must always start with the inductive, exegetical data before we can even begin to do theology. Alan Clifford, in his survey of four major British theologians, criticizes the methodology of John Owen as being scholastic: "Theological arguments are advanced and debated first (albeit with some reference to relevant texts) and the major exegetical discussion follows" (cf. app. L). This is a deductive procedure and only give the appearance of sound exegesis.

Reading in predestination. Piper has a section entitled, "God's means of maintaining His purpose: predestination" (pp. 51-3). The word *proorizein* does not occur in this whole passage (ch. 9–11), and as I have shown in chapter 7, should never have been translated 'predestination.' Piper gratuitously assumes that election and predestination are synonyms.

Ignoring the early fathers. He states that "Schelkle has gathered relevant material from the early church fathers. We will not rehearse that discussion here" (p. 56). Although I am skeptical about building theology on the church fathers, the testimony of the early fathers is still significant as a confirmation. Did Piper decline because the early fathers did not see absolute election in Romans 9? I suspect from the material I have already adduced in chapter 18 that the early fathers did not in the least support his interpretations. Since his source is in German, he should have shared at least a summary with those who do not have access to the German.

Much more should be and could be said about Piper's book, but space and time do not allow.

Ray Ortlund, Jr.'s essay

Ray Ortlund, Jr. surveyed some Old Testament case studies on the sovereignty of God, which he claims the Arminians have overlooked ("The Sovereigty of God: Case Studies in the Old Testament" in Schreiner and Ware, I, pp. 25-46). Even though I hold no brief for Arminianism, I believe that Ortlund has not made his case either. First he quotes without specific comment five passages as being "striking testimonies to God's supremacy over us" (Ex. 4:11; Isa. 45:7; 63:17; 64:7-8; Lam. 3:37-38; Dan. 4:34-35). Since my mediate soteriology in no way questions God's supremacy over us, some of the passages do not require comment. The Isaiah 63-64 context is speaking about the severity of God's judgments of Israel in language reminiscent of Paul in Romans 1, referring to God giving up the heathen to their sin. It is in this judgmental sense that God had made Israel wander from His ways and hardened their hearts. It is not that God has sovereignly reprobated individual Jews to hell. Beyond that no comment is needed since he has not made his point.

Ortlund then gives an extensive discussion of Psalm 139, with an Augustinian spin. Commenting on the verse 5 reference to God hemming him in: "David is confessing his vivid awareness of God's unrelenting attentions bombarding the fortress of his soul from all sides. As a result, God has David under his control, as the second line implies. All David can do is yield." Certainly we can agree that God is actively involved in the circumstances and many details of David's life, including Nathan's confrontation of his sin. But was this exhaustive in God determining that David would sin? This is what Ortlund implies! Then in commenting on verse 14 he takes the phrase "your works" as a reference to the unfolding of events in David's life as being solely divine works. The immediately preceding context, however, is a reference to God's forming him in his mother's womb, so Ortlund seems clearly to be guilty of isogesis here. Then in verse 16 he focuses on the statement that David's days were ordained or planned by God, they were written in God's book. This is the heart of his argument: "He means that his life, considered not only as a whole but also right down to his daily experience, was determined (what other word fits?) ahead of time" (p. 32). Again, would Ortlund include David's sins with their terrible consequences upon the children of Israel in this? I should hope not. It should also be noted that his discussion hinges upon the meaning of *yatzar* in v. 16. He doesn't examine this word (which he ought to have done), but BDB lists: "2b. Fig. for frame, pre-ordain, plan (in divine purpose)"(p. 427). Yes, God has a plan for every believer's days. The RSV uses "formed," which may be on target since we can understand how our days are formed of God's workings and ours. Would he say that every detail of David's life was a direct work of the Holy Spirit. Even as Augustinian a writer as R. C. Sproul acknowledges that there is a synergism in the Christian life. Would Ortlund extrapolate this to say that the days of unbelievers' lives are also pre-ordained?

Secondly, Ortlund focuses upon God's statement to Jeremiah in 1:4-5: **"Before I formed you in the womb I knew you, before you were born I set you apart."** His whole argument hinges upon a deterministic spin on the common verb *yada'* based upon a few supposedly supportive usages in Gen. 18:18-19, Ps. 1:6, Hos. 13:4-5, and Amos 3:2, which I have already discussed in great detail (cf. ch. 7, pp. 155-6, & app. E). There is no linguistic basis for assigning a pregnant meaning to *yada'* in these few contexts. As to God's knowledge of Jeremiah before He formed him in the womb, it can be understood in the light of the parallel, **"before you were born I set you apart."** Certainly Jeremiah, like the Apostle Paul later (Gal. 1:15), was a unique instrument of God, so we should not extrapolate determinism from the statement that the omniscient God had set him apart for His service before he was born. Even if we extrapolate this statement to all believers being foreknown and set apart as God's witnesses in His omniscient mind even before we were born, this still does not justify the idea of unconditional election to salvation or of "sovereign" reprobation of the "non-elect." So when Ortlund states that "God does not foreknow events **with bare prescience**, so that he must look on as events unfold in history out of his control" (p. 45, emphasis mine), he is making a caricature of his opposition. God is not a mere observer, but neither does He pull the strings of mere puppets. The truth is in a mediate position.

Thirdly, Ortlund seeks to develop his view of sovereignty from the book of Jonah. Certainly God's sovereign dealings with man comes out clearly in this book, but not the Augustinian concept of sovereignty. Time and again God has to confront Jonah to move him to even minimal obedience. But never does He work any "irresistible grace" on Jonah. And this is the pattern in God's dealings with man over the ages—He has to confront mankind (Cain, the pre-flood peoples, Israel, Christians today, etc.) to bring about repentant faith and obedience. The book of Jonah says nothing about exhaustive control of humans. Indeed, did God in eternity past decree Jonah's disobedience? Ortlund then quotes Job 12:13-16 about how "God retains ultimacy in all things." He seems to imply that God is ultimately behind man's deceiving and being deceived, whereas Job's point more simply is that the deceiver and his victim are both in the hands of God, just as the song goes, "He's got the whole world in His hand." To conclude, I don't think Ortland's discussion has any force against a mediate soteriology, whatever force it may have against Arminianism.

R. C. Sproul's *Willing to Believe*

R.C. Sproul's 1997 book, *Willing to Believe: The Controversy over Free Will* must be responded to, since he is a leading spokesman for Reformed theology. He has admittedly rendered service in surveying the contemporary scene and nine distinct historical viewpoints on the issue. However, there is a strong bias, which comes through in the introductory chapter and in the selection of viewpoints. He polarizes the viewpoints rather than clarifying the issues. There are a number of serious methodological concerns to be mentioned.

In the introductory chapter he inveighs against semi-Pelagianism and Arminianism in pejorative terms. Indeed, he quotes Packer and Johnston approvingly that the present-day evangelical Christian has semi-Pelagianism in his blood (p. 22). He also states that Arminians (and the rest of us) are barely Christians because putting faith before regeneration is "fundamentally un-Christian." Is Sproul aware that Calvin did not come down unambiguously on the order of faith and regeneration, as I have shown in chapter 10, p. 212? I and hundreds of millions of other evangelical Christians take personal offense at such pejorative language. How can Sproul deal with the historical material in a balanced and unbiased way with such a narrow attitude of heart and mind? I would hardly call him barely Christian and his views as fundamentally un-Christian, even though I think them seriously wrong!

Throughout his book Sproul polarizes the discussion by recognizing essentially only three views: the Augustinian, semi-Pelagian, and Pelagian. This skews the discussion considerably since there are clearly at least four and probably many more distinct positions which can be identified, as can be seen from my historical investigation in chapter 18. There I have pointed out that both Schaff and Neve clearly identify a semi-Augustinian position as distinct from the semi-Pelagian. Sproul is aware of the semi-Augustinian position since he alludes to it in passing on page 76, but he chooses to ignore it in his discussion throughout the book. This is also pejorative and prejudices the case, especially if the semi-Augustinian position ends up being the biblical one, as I claim. It needs to be directly addressed, not ignored, especially since it has strong historical antecedents.

Then his selection of representatives similarly biases the discussion, since no mediate representative theologians are discussed. Why does he not have a chapter on the semi-Augustinians? Why no chapter on Phillip Melanchthon, who modified Luther's Augustinianism substantially, and out of whose teachings a whole school of Lutheranism developed? Why no mention of Moyse Amyraut and the whole general-redemption movement in the seventeenth-century Huguenot churches in France, or of a subsequent representative, such as Richard Baxter?

The closest he comes is in his treatment of Lewis Sperry Chafer, who was Amyraldian. He rightly shows some of the inconsistencies of Chafer's attempt to hold a moderate Calvinism. His treatment of Chafer is almost wholly derived from John Gerstner's highly pejorative treatment of Dispensationalism, in which Gerstner is not directly addressing Chafer's soteriology. Nevertheless, Gerstner raised the old chestnut that dispensationalists teach two ways of salvation, when in fact dispensationalists have repeatedly denied that charge for scores of years. In fact, dispensationalists teach different rules of life for believers in different ages, as Chafer made very clear. How can Sproul and Gerstner fairly deal with a theology which they have not honestly sought to understand?

Most significantly, I believe, is Sproul's failure to really get into biblical or systematic theology, per se. There is no biblical exegesis of the determinative scriptures. He does not even have a concluding chapter summarizing his own conclusions on the matter. Presumably he feels that Augustine's and Calvin's treatments represent his own position. Although Augustine's anthropology is probably satisfying to Sproul, I wonder if he would agree with his soteriology of salvation through the church and its sacraments. He probably feels that Calvin's writings represent him fairly, but in fact Calvin held to general redemption, as proved by Kendall, Armstrong, and Geisler, and the quotations of Calvin I have included in appendix E. The methodology of pitting polarized views against each other without doing any biblical exegesis is a flawed and unprofitable approach to arriving at theological truth.

APPENDIX C

A CRITIQUE OF OPEN THEISM

Open theism is a relatively new perspective on the character of God which has only been touted in the last quarter of the twentieth century, although there were some antecedents. It has also been called the new theism and extreme Arminianism. Its major proponents are Clark Pinnock, Richard Rice, John Sanders, William Hasker, David Basinger, and Greg Boyd. It was deemed significant enough that at least ten sessions of the Evangelical Theological Society annual meeting in Nashville in November, 2000, were devoted to the issue, mostly in refutation.

Advocates of open theism seem to have some valid concerns with the "Classic Concept of God" as held by the church fathers and the Reformers. However, it is clear to me that in resolving those concerns they have gone off the deep end and have seriously departed from an orthodox, biblical view of God. However, their concerns do represent a critique of the deterministic view of God held by Augustinians. Therefore, it is most helpful to examine their views in contrast with Augustinian determinism. Although they may not be totally unified in their view, there are a number of significant aspects of their position that are important to examine.

What is Open Theism?

The most significant departure from classic theism is their concept of a limited foreknowledge of God. They claim that God can only foreknow that which He determines. Since God has not determined everything, He could not have a complete knowledge of the future, since it is unknowable. They find that some aspects of the future were determined by God, but that most of the future is open. They claim that they do not deny foreknowledge, but only redefine it, since God knows everything that can be known about the future. They also claim to be clarifying the nature of future events, but in reality, they hold to a limited omniscience, which is a contradiction of terms. The classic concept of God holds that God is infinite in all His attributes and, thus, must be infinite in His knowledge of future events, especially since we understand that God is eternal and created time as part of the time-space universe. He is outside of time and can not be limited by it in His knowledge. This is confirmed by the use of the time-space word *aiōn* in reference to the universe in passages such as Hebrews 1:2.[1]

Open theists also believe that as God interacts with His creatures, He genuinely changes His mind and is not immutable in the classic sense. In a real sense, God is temporal, and as He interacts with His creatures in time, His knowledge changes and grows. God's relationship with His creatures is dynamic, not static. They emphasize that God's changelessness relates to His faithfulness to His word and not to a static personal changelessness.

In common with Arminians, they hold that love is the primary attribute of God and, therefore, find that the many representations of God's emotional involvement with His people make the classic concept of the impassibility of God untenable. They stress that Christ is the ultimate paradigm of God's character and attributes. Since His life was characterized by service and suffering, and not in power over others, this is an important aspect of God's character. Like many others who reject the determinism of Augustine, they hold to libertarian free will, the power of contrary choice. But this is not at all unique to their view.

What are their major concerns?

The Old Testament narratives. Open theists claim that their major concerns arise out of a number of Old Testament narrative texts which seem to indicate that God actually repents or changes His mind. In harmonizing these passages with the declarative statements that God does not repent or change His mind, their approach is the opposite of the classic view. Over the centuries, Christians have understood these narrative texts as figures of speech, as anthropomorphisms, that is, representing God and His actions in human terms. We understand that this is a kind of accommodation of God's communication to human sequential thought processes. Open theists, however, feel that these passages should be taken more literally, and that the other passages which describe God's foreknowledge and immutability must be reinterpreted to harmonize with a more literal reading of these texts.[2] The problem with their hermeneutics (interpretive principles) is that what they call a more literal reading, is actually what I call a 'crass' reading of the text.

If an interpreter ignores a recognizable figure of speech in a passage, this is crass interpretation rather than literal interpretation. A classic example of this is the Roman Catholic interpretation of Christ's words at the Last Supper, "**This is my body**." They ignore the obvious figurative language of his words, a metaphor, and assume that the piece of bread in His hands was actually His physical body. This is patently absurd! It is also just as absurd to believe that the bread consecrated by the priest mystically and magically becomes the physical body of Jesus Christ.

Similarly, we understand that some aspects of these narrative passages are figures of speech. Abram's intercession in Genesis 18:23-32, Moses' intercession in Exodus 32:12-14, and King Hezekiah's prayer for extended life in 2 Kings 20:1-6, etc., are not to be taken crassly. But are anthropomorphic representations. Although God is represented in the form of the Angel of Yahweh eating with Abram, interacting with his intercession for Lot, and going down to Sodom to check out its wickedness before destroying it, this is clearly an anthropomorphic representation, since God actually appears as a man. Otherwise, we end up questioning not just God's foreknowledge, but also His present knowledge and His omnipresence as well. Wayne House suggests that if we ignore the obvious figurative and accommodative nature of the narrative, we end up saying God did not know how many righteous people were in Sodom until he actually went down to Sodom to check it out. Thus, once we begin to question the infinitude of God's omniscience, we end up questioning the infinitude of His other attributes as well.[3]

Open theists should have started by doing a basic word study of the Hebrew word *nacham*, which is frequently translated "to repent, be sorry for." Richard Shultz did such and concluded that in those 34 usages of *nacham* in which God is the subject, 26 are general statements in the affirmative and 8 are used with a negative to express God's compassion in withholding deserved judgment. Even when men are the subject of the verb (7 times), only one involves the idea of repentance, and none involve a change of mind based on newly acquired knowledge. He concludes that the central idea of the word is "to relent, have compassion upon."[4] The point is that God in His compassion frequently relents from meting out the judgment mankind deserves. It is not that God is indecisive and actually changes His mind as He gets more information. Such a word study done early might have averted this whole dangerous theological movement.

Open theists make much of God's apparent change of mind in the book of Jonah. However, I am convinced that an overlooked factor in the narrative was Jonah's failure to announce the conditional nature of God's impending judgment on Ninevah. Jonah did not want them spared and, therefore, did not 'tell it like it is.' He truncated the message for his own agenda. This becomes clear from Jonah 4:2.

The problem of evil. Another concern of the open theists has been finding a better solution to the problem of evil than that forthcoming from Augustinian deterministic theology. If God has determined all that comes to pass, then God becomes the author of evil. They made a start in the right direction by affirming human libertarian freedom, but then pressed it too far in denying the absolute foreknowledge of God. The premise of that denial is that God cannot foreknow that which He has not determined. As discussed in chapter 3, it is presumptuous for anybody to say what God could or could not know. With the open theists, I affirm that God has not decreed all the evils which have befallen human history. But we must separate God's knowing from His determining. Open theists' limitation of God's foreknowledge was not only unnecessary, but it ended up undermining the very character of God.

Reprobation. Open theists, like Arminians and others, struggle with the problem of reprobation inherent in Augustinian theology. They rightly deny absolute predestination to either heaven or hell. But in seeking to defend libertarian freedom, they conclude that God cannot know the future free decisions of mankind and therefore end up with a future which is partly open and partly determined. The body of my book (cf. ch. 7) seeks to give a biblical answer to both the absurdity of reprobation and absolute predestination as found in the conditional nature of election. This should have been an adequate solution without resorting to a denial of God's foreknowledge. The open theists' problem is that they start with the same false premise as the Augustinians: that God cannot know that which He has not determined. There is nothing biblically or philosophically which requires this premise.[5]

Answered prayer. Another major area of concern, which open theists share with many others, is how, given a deterministic concept of God, there can be any objective reality to answered prayer. It becomes a mere subjective exercise for the Christian, if God does not actually respond to the prayers of His people. If God has made an exhaustive decree in eternity past, then either we are not exercising any freedom in asking God, or He doesn't really respond to our requests in any meaningful sense. This is a concern, not just of open theists, but of all Christians who reject Augustinian determinism.

God's will for our lives. Open theists also are concerned about the concept of God's blueprint for the life of the Christian which seems to be informed by the concept of God's eternal decree. They feel that such a rigid idea of God's will should be replaced with a more open-ended one. Greg Boyd suggests that it is very difficult to deal with a number of counseling situations based upon the rigid scenario and gives an extremely difficult case study to support his point.[6] However, the open theists are not the first to question the rigid blueprint concept. Gary Friessen's book on *Decision Making in the Will of God* rejects it explicitly. This is a problem only for the determinist. The rest of us are not bound to the blueprint concept of the will of God for our individual lives. So rather than being an argument for open theism, it is really an argument against Augustinian determinism.

The major errors of Open Theism

Limited foreknowledge. Open theists have had to explain how God can have only partial foreknowledge of the future by limiting the categories of future events which God determines and therefore knows. Boyd lists five: His chosen people, individuals, Christ's ministry, the elect, and some end-time events. Unless Scripture specifically mentions something that God foreknows, He cannot know it. They explain God's orchestration of those future events which He has determined, in terms of His knowledge of the character of the people involved and the setting up the circumstances which bring them to the desired decision and action.[7] Thus in effect, they end up inconsistently holding that God uses a coercive scenario to accomplish His will in these events, while leaving all the rest totally open. For instance, God knew Peter's character perfectly, so that He could set up the circumstances under which he would deny Christ three times in fulfillment of Christ's prophecy. One wonders, however, according to their scenario, how Christ could know that Peter would deny Him exactly three times, not two, or four, or more, and all before the cock would crow.

One of the early responses to the attack on divine foreknowledge by open theists was that of William Lane Craig in *The Only Wise God*. It is also the best, in that he deals also with the errors of determinism in the same treatment. He bases his discussion upon an excellent survey of the biblical data for God's absolute omniscience of the past, present, and future in chapter one. This treatment confirms what Christians, with little dissent, have held since apostolic times and what Stephen Charnock set out so clearly in 1682 in his classic, *The Existence and Attributes of God.* It is beyond the scope of my book to summarize all of this material, but the whole thrust of thousands of biblical prophecies is to validate God's absolute foreknowledge. Some of the key passages can be listed for study: Genesis 15:13-14; 40:8; Deuteronomy 18:22; 31:16-17; 1 Kings 13:2-3, 20-24; Psalm 139:1-6; Isaiah 41:21-24; 44:6-8; 46:9-10; Daniel 2:36-43; 7 and 11. These are just a small part of the Old Testament prophecies, let alone the many more in the New.[8]

Craig also responds to D. A. Carson's attempt to show from biblical evidence that God foreknows everything because He determines everything. He concludes:

> His foreknowledge of the future cannot be based on foreordination alone, for he foreknows our thoughts and intentions and even our sinful acts. Since God is not responsible for these human activities, it follows that he does not bring them about. They are therefore truly free acts, or contingents, and God's foreknowledge of them is thus foreknowledge of future free actions.[9]

Finally, Craig touts the concept of middle knowledge, that God not only knows the whole future, but that He also knows future counterfactuals. He rightly suggests that this is one of the more fruitful theological ideas ever conceived. He shows that it has solid biblical support (see app K).

Carl (not John) Sanders gave a paper at ETS 2000, in which he showed how open theism's treatment of Bible prophecy is totally inadequate to explain its specificity of persons, places, and events.[10] Although writers like Rice and Boyd try to deal with the issue, they have a vague and generalized view of prophecy which does not at all take into account the incredible detail of Messianic and other prophecies, which have all been literally fulfilled.[11] In spiritualizing and generalizing such prophecies, they have also emasculated them of their apologetic value as well. Especially through

Isaiah God makes claims for the apologetic value of prophecy. Over the centuries, Christians have so interpreted Bible prophecy, in the main.

Carl Sanders also pointed out the importance of biblical typology in demonstrating the absolute foreknowledge of God. It is extremely difficult, if not impossible, to explain how God could arrange not only the types and symbols of the Old Testament, but also the antitypical future events, if He does not possess absolute foreknowledge. The same can be said for examples of what is called "canonical interpretation." This means that the sequence of the writing of Bible books is significant for interpreting them. This would involve heavy orchestration on God's part, impossible if He does not know the whole future.

A Selective Sequential Bibliography

Richard Rice, *The Openness of God* (Minneapolis: Bethany, 1980).

Bruce Reichenbach, *Evil and a Good God* (New York: Fordham Univ., 1982)

Royce Gruenler, *The Inexhaustible God: Biblical Faith and the Challenge of Process Theology* (GR: Baker, 1983).

Norman L. Geisler, "Process Theology and Inerrancy," in Lewis and Demarest, *Challenges to Inerrancy* (Chicago: Moody, 1984).

David Basinger and Randall Basinger, eds., *Predestination and Free Will: Four Views* (John Feinberg, Norman Geisler, Bruce Reichenbach, and Clark Pinnock)(Downers Grove, InterVarsity, 1986).

William Lane Craig, *the Only Wise God: The Compatibility of Divine Foreknowledge and Human Freedom* (1987).

Ronald Nash, *Process Theology* (GR: Baker, 1987).

Greg Boyd, *Trinity and Process* (NY: Peter Lang, 1992).

Clark Pinnock, Richard Rice, John Sanders, William Hasker, and David Basinger, *The Openness of God: A Biblical Challenge to the Traditional Understanding of God* (Downers Grove: InterVarsity, 1994).

David Basinger, *The Case for Freewill Theism* (Downers Grove, InterVarsity, 1996).

Norman L. Geisler, *Creating God in the Image of Man* (Minneapolis: Bethany, 1997).

Millard J. Erickson, *God the Father Almighty* (GR: Baker, 1998).

Norman L. Geisler, *Chosen but Free* (Minneapolis: Bethany, 1999).

Greg Boyd, *God of the Possible* (GR: Baker, 2000).

Bruce Ware, *God's Lesser Glory: The Diminished God of Open Theism* (Wheaton: Crossway, 2000).

Note: This appendix is based upon a paper presented at the Annual Meeting of the Evangelical Theological Society at Colorado Springs, November 2001.

---

1. G. Abbott-Smith, *Lexicon*, p. 15.

2. Greg Boyd, *God of the Possible*, pp. 53-87; Richard Rice, "Biblical Support for a New Perspective," in Pinnock, et. al., *The Openness of God*, pp. 22-38.

3. Wayne House, "The New Theism: An Exegetical Response to Greg Boyd." ETS 2000

4. Richard Shultz, "A Semantic and Hermeneutical Analysis of *NACHAM*;" ETS 2000; Craig, *The Only Wise God*, p. 46.

5. Craig, pp. 39-48.

6. Boyd, pp. 103ff.

7. Ibid, pp. 35-39.

8. Craig, pp. 25-37.

9. Ibid, p. 48.

10. Carl Sanders, "Open Theism and Hermeneutics: Some Implications"; ETS 2000.

11. Boyd, pp. 33-45; Richard Rice, "Biblical Support," in Pinnock, et. al., pp. 50-53.

APPENDIX D

HUMANITY'S TRIPARTITE NATURE

This brings us to the age-old controversy over dichotomy versus trichotomy in man's original creation. In answering this question, we must not be distracted by the nature of fallen man, which is quite another question. This issue is significant to our understanding of the nature of spiritual death and of regeneration. The fact that a majority of theologians have opted for dichotomy has obscured these two essential truths. Let us revisit this old discussion and seek to clarify the issues.

A response to arguments for dichotomy

In essence, the major argument for the dichotomy view is the interchangeable use of soul and spirit in much of Scripture. This is not debatable, but it is explainable in harmony with trichotomy. Since most of Scripture is describing the anthropology of fallen man, this is not really direct evidence for the original condition of Adam and Eve. J. B. Heard suggested that another reason why the Old Testament does not show a distinction between soul and spirit relates to the progress of revelation. Since God did not choose to reveal His triune nature explicitly before the coming of the Messiah, there is a parallelism in His not revealing the tripartite nature of man. "It would be out of harmony with the 'analogy of faith,' if the tripartite nature of man were fully described in those books of the Bible which only contain implied hints of the plurality of persons in the Godhead."[1]

Therefore, Charles Hodge's objection that the creation account does not mention a distinct spirit (*ruach*) of man is easily explainable. Indeed, the reference to God blowing into man's nostrils the breath of lives (pl.) may well have been intended to communicate both the imbuement of physical life and breath and also the impartation of the human spirit. This is seen in two exegetical features. First, the word for breath (*neshmah*) also means 'spirit' or 'mind' as it is used in Proverbs 20:27: **"The spirit of man is the lamp of the LORD, searching all the innermost parts of his being."**[2] This truth is later reinforced by Paul: **"For who among men knows the *thoughts* of a man except the spirit of the man which is in him? Even so the *thoughts* of God no one knows except the Spirit of God"** (1 Cor. 2:11). Secondly, the word for life (*hayah*) is in the plural here. But God was only breathing one physical life into Adam. The breathing of physical life could well be not only a physical reality, but also a symbol of the imbuing of man with a distinct human spirit. The Lord Jesus gave us a later analogy on the day of His resurrection when He breathed on the apostles and said to them, **"Receive the Holy Spirit"** (Jn. 20:22). Contrariwise, some might argue from Genesis 6:17 and 7:22, where *ruach hayyim* seems to be used of animal life, that the above interpretation of *neshmah hayyim* in Genesis 2:7 is not cogent. However, the context is not at all clear in these two passages that *ruach hayyim* refers to animal life.

Thirdly, Hodge argues that soul and spirit are used indiscriminately of men and of irrational animals, for which he gives Ecclesiastes 3:21 as a proof text: **"Who knows that the breath of man ascends upward and the breath of the beast descends downward to the earth?"** This is indeed a flimsy basis for his point, since it is clear that Solomon is speaking phenomenally of life **"under the sun."** In its context, this question came out of a cynical stage in Solomon's thought processes. In Hodge's day there was little insight into the importance of genre in hermeneutics, so we can excuse this lapse. Hodge's fourth argument that humans lack consciousness of a division of their own immaterial nature is hardly a proof. The human psyche is very complex, and our lack of personal awareness of this division proves nothing. What counts is what God's word says about the immaterial part of man's nature.

Although Thiessen was a modified trichotomist, he gave a good summary of additional arguments for dichotomy. A fifth argument is that 'soul' is ascribed to God in a number of passages. These, however, can easily be understood as anthropomorphisms, since the Bible has many other such figures of speech.

A sixth argument is that the highest place in religion is ascribed to the soul in Mark 12:30, Luke 1:46, Heb. 6:18-19, and James 1:21. Christ's command to love God with **"all your heart, and with all your soul, and with all your mind, and with all your strength"** (Mk. 12:30) does not imply that the soul is the highest faculty of man, as alleged. Quoting from the law, the Lord is stressing that we must love God with all of our faculties, from the highest to the lowest. Other writers have argued, however, that if we were to press the point here, the Mosaic Law would be delineating a four-fold division of the immaterial part of man. However, at this point in the progress of revelation, it would not have been appropriate for God to give an analysis of man's constituent parts. The statement is designed to best communicate to contemporary Jews that man must love God with the totality of his being, without giving a theological breakdown. Neither is the wording of Mary's Magnificat (Lk. 1:46) a problem for the trichotomist. We should exalt the Lord with both our soul and spirit, and her coordinate usage does not imply synonymity at all. It is also appropriate for the writer of Hebrews to speak of our hope as **"the anchor of the soul"** since the soul, which probably includes the emotions of man, is the part of our personhood that most needs an anchor. James 1:21 is one good example of the Scripture's frequent use of synecdoche, a figure of speech in which a part, the soul, represents the whole of man.

Lastly, Thiessen lists the argument that body and soul are frequently represented as constituting the whole of man (Mt. 10:28; 1 Cor. 5:3; 3 Jn. 2) and that to lose the soul is to lose all (Mt. 16:26; Mk. 8:36-7). This is clearly a case of metonymy, a part for the whole. But there is significant other evidence for a distinction between the two in regenerate believers. The passages are well known to both sides, but generally dismissed as irrelevant by dichotomists in the light of their major argument of interchangeability. But these passages must not be lightly dismissed without careful examination.

Positive evidence for trichotomy

The Apostle Paul's most explicit statement is in 1 Thessalonians 5:23: **"Now may the God of peace Himself sanctify you entirely, and may your spirit and soul and body be preserved complete, without blame at the coming of our Lord Jesus Christ."** Hodge dismisses its significance by saying that Paul "only uses a periphrasis for the whole man."[3] This is possible, but we must also be open to other evidence that in Paul's mind soul (*psuche*) and spirit (*pneuma*) are distinct. This comes from the two passages in First Corinthians. In 2:11-15 we see a contrast between the adjectives derived from these two nouns, *psuchikos* and *pneumatikos*:

> **For who among men knows the *thoughts* of a man except the spirit of the man which is in him? . . . But a natural (*psuchikos*) man does not accept the things of the Spirit of God, for they are foolishness to him; and he cannot understand them, because they are spiritually appraised. But he who is spiritual (*pneumatikos*) appraises all things, yet he himself is appraised by no one.**

The development of Paul's logic in the passage confirms the reality of the distinction in Paul's mind. In speaking of the process of revelation in vv. 10-13, he compares the role of the Holy Spirit in searching God's mind to the human spirit, which searches man's mind. This implies a correspondence between the two in the revelation process. Then in 2:14 he describes the unregenerate man as a soulish (*psuchikos*) man. Man is merely soulish, not only devoid of the Spirit of God, but deficient in the corresponding realm of the human spirit as well. In total contrast, he sets the spiritual (*pneumatikos*) man in 2:15. Even if one does not accept this interpretation of the passage, at the very least, it would have to be acknowledged that Paul is using these two adjectives in marked contrast. Although Lewis and Demarest have made the most thorough-going attempt to refute trichotomy, they not only miss the full implication of this passage but totally skip any reference to the similar passage in 1 Corinthians 15:35-49:

> **It is sown a natural (*psuchikos*) *body, it is raised a spiritual* (*pneumatikos*) body. If there is a natural body, there is also a spiritual *body*. So also it is written, "The first man, Adam, became a living soul." The last Adam *became* a life-giving spirit. However, the spiritual is not first, but the natural; then the spiritual** (1 Cor. 15:44-46).

Again, the flow of logic of the resurrection passage in chapter 15 is important to the fullest implication relating to the distinction between the two adjectives, but at the least we can say that *pneumakikos* and *psuchikos* are distinct in Paul's mind, certainly not synonymous. After contrasting the different kinds of physical flesh of various kinds of bodies in vv. 35-39, he goes on contrast the various distinct types of celestial bodies (earth, sun, moon, and stars). This brings him in vv. 44-46 to the characterization of our present bodies as *psuchikos soma* and of our resurrection bodies as *pneumatikos soma*. Although our understanding of the resurrection includes some connection between our present bodies and our resurrection bodies, just as a seed connects with the plant (vv. 42-44), Paul in the main markedly contrasts the two. Thus it seems clear that in Paul's Spirit-guided mind the distinction between the soulish nature of our present bodies is in strong contrast with the spiritual nature of our resurrection bodies. Therefore, soul and spirit are distinct categories in Paul's mind.

Most significantly, we could say that the impact of Hebrew 4:12 has been denigrated by dichotomists. "**For the word of God is living and active and sharper than any two-edged sword, and piercing as far as the division of soul and spirit, of both joints and marrow, and able to judge the thoughts and intentions of the heart.**" Thiessen quotes Alford: "The *logos* pierces to the dividing, not of the *psuche* from the *pneuma*, but of the *psuche* itself and of the *pneuma* itself;"[4] However, the usually dependable Alford has erred here in not observing the anarthrous use of both nouns in the Greek. Note how he inserts the articles in the English. Arndt and Gingrich take the force of *merismos* as "division, separation," rendering the clause, "to the separation of soul and spirit, i.e., so as to separate soul and spirit Hb. 4:12."[5]

Two other significant passages are usually omitted from discussion by dichotomists. J. B. Heard, in his unique work, *The Tripartite Nature of Man: Spirit, Soul, and Body,* links together James 3:15 and Jude 19: "**This wisdom is not that which comes down from above, but is earthly, natural, demonic**" (Jas. 3:15); "**These are the ones who cause divisions, worldly-minded, devoid of the Spirit**" (Jude 19). Heard comments:

> We will class these two passages together as throwing light on the contrast between the natural and the spiritual man of I Cor. ii.14. In the first case, St James says of the wisdom that is from beneath that it is earthly, *epigeios*, and the two next predicates are thrown in to strengthen this affirmation, as well as to advance a climax. This earthly wisdom,

> unlike that which comes down from above, has its seat in the psychical nature only. As there is nothing heavenly about it, so it does not spring from the *pneuma*, but only from the soul, the seat of the affections and impulses. If it has any source of inspiration, . . . it is from beneath, and not from above. Satan, not the Holy Spirit, is the inspirer of this kind of wisdom; it is devilish, not godlike. In St Jude, we read of the scoffers that they separate themselves, being psychical only, and having not the Spirit. . . . men who act on psychical principles only, because they lack the pneumatical faculty.[6]

It would seem that many theologians are fearful of affirming trichotomy because of Plato's trichotomist view and the supposed association with ancient heresies, such as Gnosticism, Semi-Pelagianism, Annihilationism, and Apollinarianism. First, we should note that Plato's trichotomy bore no relationship to biblical trichotomy, since the parts do not at all correspond. He divided the soul into two parts: a rational, immortal soul and an irrational, mortal soul.[7] The other superficial associations and distortions of a biblical trichotomy in no way militate against it. Frequently, heresies are noted for the way in which they resemble or mimic the truth. So we should not let a superficial resemblance between biblical trichotomy and various heresies deter us in the least.

Although a majority of theologians seem to have opted for dichotomy, it would seem that as the theological center shifted from the Greek world to the Latin locus in Augustine's day that trichotomy fell into disfavor. It was suggested by Heard that this was because the Latin language does not easily cope with the distinction of soul and spirit.[8] In any case it may have been restored by Luther, as claimed by F. J. Delitzsch. The advocacy of men like Delitzsch, C. J. Ellicott, Henry Alford (tentatively), H. P. Liddon, and R. H. Lightfoot must not be ignored.[9] Thus all the data adduced for dichotomy are fully explainable in terms of trichotomy, but the New Testament data for trichotomy cannot be adequately explained by dichotomists.

Note: This appendix is part of a paper presented at the Eastern Regional of the Evangelical Theological Society at Myerstown, PA, March, 1999.

---

1. J. B. Heard, *The Tripartite Nature of Man: Spirit, Soul, and Body* (1866), pp. 67-68.
2. Brown, Driver, & Briggs, p. 675.
3. Charles Hodge, *Systematic Theology*, II, pp. 49-50.
4. Henry Alford, *The Greek Testament*, en. loc., cited by Thiessen, p. 227.
5. William F. Arndt and J. Wilbur Gingrich, *A Greek-English Lexicon*, p. 506.
6. Heard, pp. 81-2.
7. Ibid, p. 137.
8. Ibid, p. vii.
9. H. D. McDonald, *The Christian View of Man*, p. 76.

APPENDIX E

QUOTATIONS OF JOHN CALVIN ON GENERAL REDEMPTION

Isaiah:

"*He bore the sin of many.* I approve of the ordinary reading, that He alone bore the punishment of many, because on Him was laid the guilt of the whole world. It is evident from other passages, and especially from the fifth chapter of the Epistle to the Romans, **that 'many' sometimes denotes 'all'.**" Commentary on Isaiah 53:12

Ezekiel:

"As everybody knows, **all men are called to repentance and the hope of salvation is promised to them when they do repent.** . . . However, this will of God which He has set forth in His word does not stand in the way of His having decreed from before the creation of the world what He would do with each individual." Commentary on Ezek. 18:23

". . . God longs for nothing more sincerely than that whoever was perishing and rushing to destruction should have returned to the way of salvation. . . . the way in which God wills all to be saved must be noted, namely, *when they shall turn themselves from their ways.* . . . We hold, therefore that God does not will the death of the sinner **inasmuch as He calls all men indifferently to repentance and promises that He is prepared to receive them,** on condition that they earnestly repent." (*Calvini Opera*, 40:445-6, Armstrong's translation on p. 189, cf. Latin in footnotes.)

Matthew:

"*And to give His life a ransom.* As we have said, Christ spoke of His death to draw the disciples away from their perverse idea of an earthly kingdom. Yet He aptly and well expresses the power and fruit of His death when He declares that His life was the price of our redemption. From this it follows that our reconciliation with God is free, for the only price paid for it is Christ's death. And so this one word overthrows all that the Papists babble about their disgusting satisfactions. Moreover, since Christ won us as His own by His death, the submission of which He speaks is so far from derogating from His infinite glory that in fact it makes it more glorious. **'Many' is used, not for a definite number, but for a large number, in that He sets Himself over against all others. And this is its meaning also in Rom. 5:15, where Paul is not talking of a part of mankind but of the whole human race.**"

Commentary on Matthew 20:28

"The fruits of Christ's death have only made their lasting impression upon us when we know that He was not rudely snatched away to the cross by men, but that the sacrifice was ordained by the eternal decree of God, **to expiate the sins of the world.** Whence do we obtain reconciliation if it is not that Christ placated the Father by His obedience? So let us ever think of the Providence of God which Judas himself and all the ungodly (though they do not want it so, and act against it) must obey. Ever hold on to this, that Christ suffered because, by this kind of expiation, God was pleased. Christ says that Judas is not absolved from blame on the grounds that he did nothing but what was divinely ordained. Though God in His righteous judgement fixed the price of redemption for us as the death of His own Son, nonetheless Judas in betraying Christ, being full of treachery and greed, drew on himself a right condemnation. **God's will for the redemption of the world** in no way prevents Judas being a wicked traitor."

Commentary on Matthew 26:24

Mark:

"*This is my blood.* I have already warned, when the blood is said to be poured out (as in Matthew) *for the remission of sins,* how in these words we are directed to the sacrifice of Christ's death, and to neglect this thought makes any due celebration of the Supper impossible. In no other way can faithful souls be satisfied, if they cannot believe that God is pleased in their regard. **The word *many* does not mean a part of the world only, but the whole human race: he contrasts *many* with *one,* as if to say that he would not be the Redeemer of one man, but would meet death to deliver many of their cursed guilt. It is incontestable that Christ came for the expiation of the sins of the whole world."**

Mark 14:24 in *The Eternal Predestination of God,* IX, 5

John:

"And when he says *the sin of the world* he extends this kindness indiscriminately to the whole human race, that the Jews might not think the Redeemer has been sent to them alone. From this we infer that the whole world is bound in the same condemnation; and that **since all men without exception** are guilty of unrighteousness before God, they have need of reconciliation. John, therefore, by speaking of the sin of the world in general, wanted to make us feel our own misery and exhort us to seek the remedy. Now it is for us to embrace the blessing offered to all, **that each may make up his mind that there is nothing to hinder him** from finding reconciliation in Christ if only, led by faith, he comes to Him."

Commentary on John 1:28

"*That whosoever believeth on him should not perish.* The outstanding thing about faith is that it delivers us from eternal destruction. For He especially wanted to say that although we seem to have been born for death sure deliverance is offered to us by the faith of Christ so that we must not fear the death which otherwise threatens us. And He has used a general term, **both to invite indiscriminately all to share in life** and to cut off every excuse from unbelievers. Such is also the significance of the term 'world' which He had used before. For although there is nothing in the world deserving of God's favour, He nevertheless shows He is favourable to the whole world **when He calls all without exception to the faith of Christ**, which is indeed an entry into life.

Moreover, let us remember that although life is promised generally to all who believe in Christ, faith is not common to all. Christ is open to all and displayed to all, but God opens the eyes only of the elect that they may seek Him by faith. The wonderful effect of faith is shown here too. By it we receive Christ as He is given to us by the Father—the one who has freed us from the condemnation of eternal death and made us heirs of eternal life by expiating our sins through the sacrifice of His death, so that nothing shall prevent God acknowledging us as His children. Therefore, since faith embraces Christ with the efficacy of His death and the fruit of His resurrection there is nothing surprising in our also obtaining by it the life of Christ."

"For God sent not. This is confirmation of the former statement. For God's sending His Son to us was not fruitless. Yet He did not come to destroy; therefore it follows that the proper function of Son of God is that whosoever believes may obtain salvation through Him. None need now wonder or worry how he can escape death since we believe it was God's purpose that Christ should rescue us from it. **The word *world* comes again so that no one at all may think he is excluded, if only he keeps to the road of faith.**"

Commentary on John 3:16-17

"Again, when they proclaim that **Jesus is the Saviour of the world** and the Christ, they have undoubtedly learned this from hearing Him. From this we infer that in two days Christ taught the sum of the Gospel more plainly there than He had so far done in Jerusalem. And He declared that **the salvation He had brought was common to the whole world,** so that they should understand more easily that it belonged to them also. He did not call them as lawful heirs, but taught them that He had come to admit strangers into the family of God and to bring peace to them that were far off." Commentary on John 4:42

"'I am come a light into the world.' The universal particle seems to have been put in deliberately, **partly that *all believers without exception*** *might enjoy this benefit* in common and partly to show that unbelievers perish in darkness because they flee from the light of their own accord" Commentary on John 12:46

"For He delayed pronouncing judgement on them, because He had come rather for the salvation of all. We must understand that He was not speaking here of unbelievers in general but of those who wittingly and voluntarily reject the preaching of the Gospel exhibited to them. Why then did Christ not wish to condemn them? Because He had temporarily laid aside the office of judge and **offers salvation to all indiscriminately and** stretches out His arms to embrace all, that all may be the more encouraged to repent. And yet He heightens by an important detail the crime of rejecting an invitation so kind and gracious; for it is as if He had said: 'See, I have come to call all; and forgetting the role of judge, my one aim is to attract and rescue from destruction those who already seem doubly ruined.' Hence no man is condemned for despising the Gospel save he who spurns the lovely news of salvation and deliberately decides to bring destruction on himself." Commentary on John 12:47

"Christ's proper work was to appease the wrath of God **by atoning for the sins of the world,** to redeem men from death and to procure righteousness and life. That of the Spirit is to make us partakers not only of Christ Himself, but of all His blessings."

Commentary on John 14:16

"For in the word *world* is here embraced the whole human race. And there is but one Saviour who rescues and saves us from this dreadful slavery. . . . For it was God who appointed His Son to be the Reconciler and determined that the sins of the world should be expiated by His death." Commentary on John 14:30

"For he who seeks to be loved by God without the Mediator gets imbrangled in a labyrinth in which he will find neither the right path nor the way out. We should therefore direct our gaze to Christ, in whom will be found the pledge of the divine love. . . . Thus in Him, as in a mirror, **we may behold God's fatherly love towards us all**, since He is not loved separately, or for His own private advantage, but that He may unite us along with Himself to the Father."

Commentary on John 15:9

"I think that under the word *world* are included both those who were to be truly converted to Christ and hypocrites and reprobates." Commentary on John 16:8

Romans:

"That he should be heir of the world. Since he is now dealing with eternal salvation, the apostle seems to have led his readers to the world somewhat inopportunely, but he includes in the word *world* generally the restoration which was hoped for from Christ. **While the restoration of the life of believers was in fact the principal object, it was, however, necessary that the fallen state of the whole world should be repaired.** In Heb.1:2 the apostle calls Christ the heir of all the blessing of God, because the adoption which we have procured by His grace has restored to us the possession of the inheritance from which we fell in Adam. But since under the type of the land of Canaan not only was the hope of a heavenly life displayed to Abraham, but also the full and perfect blessing of God, the apostle rightly teaches us that the dominion of the world was promised to him." Romans 4:13

"But not as the trespass, so also is the free gift. For if by the trespass of the one the many died, much more did the grace of God, and the gift by the grace of the one man, Jesus Christ, abound unto the many. We should note, however, that Paul does not here contrast the larger number with the many, for he is not speaking of the great number of mankind, but he argues that since the sin of Adam has destroyed many, the righteousness of Christ will be no less effective for the salvation of many." Commentary on Romans 5:15

"Paul makes grace common to all men, not because it in fact extends to all, but because it is offered to all. Although Christ suffered for the sins of the world, and is offered by the goodness of God without distinction to all men, yet not all receive Him."
Commentary on Romans 5:18

Galatians:

"I would they were even cut off. His indignation increases and he prays for destruction on the imposters by whom the Galatians had been deceived. The word 'cut off' seems to allude to the circumcision which they were pressing for. Chrysostom inclines to this view: 'They tear the Church for the sake of circumcision; I wish they were cut off entirely.' But such a curse does not seem to fit the mildness of an apostle, who ought to wish that all should be saved and therefore that not one should perish. **I reply that this is true when we have men in mind; for God commends to us the salvation of all men without exception, even as Christ suffered for the sins of the whole world"** Commentary on Gal. 5:12

Colossians:

"First, he says that we have redemption, and immediately explains it as *the remission of sins;* for these two things belong together by apposition. For, without doubt, when God remits our sins, He exempts us from condemnation to eternal death. This is our liberty, this our glorying against death, that our sins are not imputed to us. He says that this redemption was procured by *the blood of Christ,* **for by the sacrifice of His death all the sins of the world have been expiated.** let us, therefore, remember that this is the sole price of reconciliation, and that all the trifling of Papists about satisfaction is blasphemy."

Commentary on Colossians 1:14

Hebrews:

"When he *says for every man,* he does not just mean that He should he an example to others, in the way that Chrysostom adduces the metaphor of a physician who takes the first sip of a bitter draught, so that the sick man will not refuse to drink it. He means that Christ died for us, because He took on Himself our lot, and redeemed us from the curse of death. So there is added that this was done by the grace of God, because the ground of our redemption is that immense love of God towards us by which it happened that He did not even spare His own Son" (Rom. 8:32). Commentary on Hebrews 2:9

"The apostle indicates that *the fruits of it do not come to any but* to *those who are obedient.* In saying this he commends faith to us, for neither He nor His benefits become ours unless, and in so far as, we accept them and Him by faith. **At the same time he has inserted the universal term 'to all' to show that *no one is excluded from this salvation who proves to be attentive and obedient to the Gospel of Christ"***

Comments on Heb. 5:9

"To bear the sins means to free those who have sinned from their guilt by His satisfaction. **He says many meaning all, as in Rom. 5:15.** It is of course certain that *not all enjoy the fruits of Christ's: death, but this happens because their unbelief hinders them"*

Commentary on Heb. 9:28

II Peter:

"Here is His extraordinary love toward man, **that He wills all men to be saved, and is prepared to bring even the perishing to salvation.** However we must notice this order—God is prepared to bring all men to repentance so that none may perish. For the means of obtaining salvation is indicated by these words. Therefore any one of us who aspires to salvation must learn to apply himself to this way." (Commentary on 2 Pet. 3:9 from *CO,* 55:475-76, as translated and quoted by Armstrong, p. 191, Latin in footnote.)

Sermons on Isaiah 53:

"That, then, is how our Lord Jesus bore the sins and iniquities of many. **But in fact, this word 'many' is often as good as equivalent to 'all'. And indeed, our Lord Jesus was offered to all the world.** For it is not speaking of three or four when it says: 'God so loved the world, that He spared not His only Son.' But yet we must notice what the Evangelist adds in this passage: 'That whosoever believes in Him shall not perish but obtain eternal life. Our Lord Jesus suffered for all and there is neither great nor small who is not inexcusable today, for we can obtain salvation in Him. Unbelievers who turn away from Him and who deprive themselves of Him by their malice are today doubly culpable. For how will they excuse their ingratitude in not receiving the blessing in which they could share by faith?"

The Institutes and Miscellaneous Writings:

"We must now see in what ways we become possessed of the blessings which God has bestowed on his only begotten Son, not for private use, but to enrich the poor and needy. And the first thing to be attended to is, that so long as we are without Christ and separated from him, nothing which *he suffered and did for* the *salvation of the human race* is of the least benefit to us" *(Institutes,* 3.1.1 or vol. I, p. 461.)

"He had commanded Timothy that prayers should be regularly offered up in the church for kings and princes; but as it seemed somewhat absurd that prayer should be offered up for a class of men who were almost hopeless (all of them being not only aliens from the body of Christ, but doing their utmost to overthrow his kingdom), he adds, that it was acceptable to God, **who will have all men to be saved. By this he assuredly means nothing more than that the way of salvation was not shut against any order of men; that, on the contrary, *he had manifested his mercy in such a way, that he would have none debarred from it.*"**

(*Institutes*, 3.24.16)

"It is no small matter to have the souls perish who were bought by the blood of Christ"

(The Mystery of Godliness, 83)

From Brian Armstrong, *Calvinism and the Amyraut Heresy,* pp. 137-8, footnote #58:

"There are many passages in which he [Calvin] makes the universal reference of Christ's atoning work quite explicit. In his "De aeterna Dei predestinatione" this topic arises and Calvin responds that the teaching that Christ died for all is beyond controversy: "Controversia etiam caret, Christum expiandis totius mundi peccatis venisse. Sed confestim occurrit illa solutio: Ut quisquis credit in eum non pereat, sed habeat vitam aeternam (Joann. 3,15). Nec vero qualis sit Christi virtus, vel quid per se valeat, nunc quaeritur: sed quibus se fruendum exhibeat" *(CO,* 8:336). Again, in his sermon on Isaiah 53 he say. "Ainsi donc il nous faut bien noter ces mots du Prophete, quand il dit que la correction de nostre paix a este sur nostre Seigneur Jesus Christ: d'autant que par son moyen Dieu est appointé et appaisé: car il a porté sur soy tous les vices et toutes les iniquitez du monde" *(CO,* 35:627). In his commentary on John 3:16-17 he states that God "has ordained His Son to be the salvation of the world" *(CO,* 47:66). In his commentary on Romans 5:10 he states that Christ's death was "an expiatory sacrifice through which the world was reconciled to God." And in his important sermon on I Timothy II:3-5 he repeats this sentiment often: ". . . Jesus Christ est venu pour estre Sauveur commun de tous en general, . . ." *(CO,* 53:149). "Pourquoy donc est-ce que maintenant nous sommes domestiques de la foy, enfans de Dieu, et membres de nostre Seigneur Jesus Christ? C'est d'autant qu'il nous a recueillis a soy. Or: n'est-il point Sauveur de tout le monde aussi bien? Jesus Christ est-il venu pour estre Moyenneur seulement entre deux ou trois hommes? Nenni: mais il est Moyenneur entre Dieu et les hommes" (*CO,* 53:159-160). Moreover, he can even lament that "it is no light matter that souls should perish who were bought by the blood of Christ" (Sermon on II Timothy 2:19). When this evidence is compared with what is presented in our chapter 4 notes 73, 81-83 and esp. 87, it would seem that the position is untenable which holds that Calvin teaches Christ died for the elect only."

SOURCES

Brian G. Armstrong, *Calvinism and the Amyraut Heresy: Protestant Scholasticism and Humanism in Seventeenth-Century France* (Madison: U. of Wisconsin Press, 1969).

Norman L. Geisler, *Chosen But Free* (Minneapolis: Bethany House, 1999), Appendix 2.

R. T. Kendall, *Calvin and English Calvinism to 1649*, second edition (Carlisle, Cumbria, UK: Paternoster Press, 1997), Appendix #1. This appendix is not in the first edition published by Oxford Univ. Press in 1979.

Note: Emphasis in the quotations is mine.

APPENDIX F

WORD STUDIES ON FOREKNOWLEDGE

CALVINISTIC CLAIMS

There is a strong tendency in Calvinistic theology to make foreknowledge and election/predestination close to identical in meaning. Berkhof is typical:

> The word *yada'* may simply mean "to know" or "to take cognizance" of someone or something, but may also be used in the more pregnant sense of "taking knowledge of one with loving care," or "making one the object of loving care or elective love." In this sense it serves the idea of election, Gen. 18:19; Amos 3:2; Hos. 13:5. The meaning of the words *proginoskein and prognosis* in the New Testament is not determined by the usage in the classics, but by the special meaning of *yada'*. They do not denote simple intellectual foresight or prescience, the mere taking knowledge of something beforehand, but rather a selective knowledge which approaches the idea of foreordination, Acts 2:23 (comp. 4:28); Rom. 8:29; 11:2; I Peter 1:2. These passages simply lose their meaning, if the words be taken in the sense of simply taking knowledge of one in advance, for God foreknows all men in that sense. Even Arminians feel constrained to give the words a more determinative meaning, namely, to foreknow one with absolute assurance in a certain state or condition. This includes the absolute certainty of that future state, and for that very reason comes very close to the idea of predestination. And not only these words, but even the simple *ginoskein* has such a specific meaning in some cases, I Cor. 8:3; Gal. 4:9; II Tim. 2:19.[1]

The hidden agenda here is to establish the doctrine of unconditional election vis-á-vis conditional election. If these words have a selective meaning akin to predestination, then there would be no direct scriptural indications of conditional election. However, if these terms do not have a selective meaning, then there are two passages which do indicate that foreordination/election is conditional.

The question is whether the word *proginoskein* has any selective implication. Thus lexical study of the usage of this word is of highest importance. It is my proposition that a lexical study of the usage of *yada, ginoskein,* and *proginoskein* uncovers not the slightest scintilla of hard evidence that there is such a selective connotation. Indeed, the Apostles Paul and Peter would be guilty of redundancy and illogic if Calvinists are right that these meanings are close to each other. Let us look into the linguistic data. Let it be clarified that when I refer to a "lexical study", I am not just referring to consulting the lexicons, but as the dictionary defines it: "1. of the words of a language as distinguished from its grammatical structure."[2] *This involves a careful study of the usage of these words*. I would not claim that the lexicons uniformly support my conclusions. The thorough theologian must not always depend upon the judgment of the lexicographers since they are sometimes guilty of egregious errors (as I show in appendix G). They rarely discuss each context in detail and defend their conclusions as I intend to do.

THE MEANING OF FOREKNOWLEDGE

A Word Study of *yada'*

The problem with Berkhof's analysis is that although it is remotely possible that these words can be so interpreted in some of these contexts, there is no purely linguistic supportive data for these more remote, hypothesized meanings.

The lexicons. The primary meaning of the Hebrew word *yada'* is 'to know to perceive, to consider,' and it is so translated overwhelmingly in most of the 944 times it occurs in the Old Testament. It is used of knowledge as a personal relationship in upward of one hundred of these usages. The Tregelles-Gesenius lexicon does not list "to choose" as a possible meaning for *yada'*. It does, however, list: "(7) Often used of the will, *to turn the mind to something, to care for, to see about*. . . . -(a) of God as caring for men; Psalm 144:3; Neh. 1:7; followed by *min* Amos 3:2, 'you only have I known (especially cared for) of all the nations of the earth.' Gen. 18:19, 'him (Abraham) have I known (cared for, chosen) that he may command,' etc. Compare Psa. 1:6."[3] Note that the meaning "cared for" fully satisfies the context, and that the meaning "chosen" slipped in by the parenthesis is neither called for by the context or any other. Therefore, the Brown, Driver, and Briggs edition drops even that passing word.[4] The KJV never renders *yada'* as 'to choose'. The Septuagint does not translate it as 'to choose' in any of the passages which Berkhof cites (Gen. 18:19; Amos 3:2; Hos. 13:5). Nevertheless, Bultmann in *TDNT*, as a parting shot in his discussion of the Old Testament usage says,

> Finally, the element of will in *yada'* emerges with particular emphasis when it is used of God, whose knowing establishes the significance of what is known. In this connection *yada'* can mean 'to elect', i.e., to make an object of concern and acknowledgment." Then without any other proof, he refers to five contexts in the footnote, "Gn. 18:19; Ex. 33:12; Am. 3:2; Hos. 13:5; Jer. 1:5.[5]

Careful examination of these passages shows that none of them **require** the rendering 'to elect, to choose', nor does the LXX render *yada'* as anything other than 'to know' *(oida, epistamai, ginosko)* except in Hos.

13:5 where *poimaino* is used. One would think that if *yada'* had a hint of such an idea, the LXX translators would have picked it up just once. Presumably they knew Hebrew better than Bultmann. Paul Gilchrist (Covenant College) in his article in the *Theological Wordbook of the Old Testament* does not refer to any selective factor in his discussion of the meaning of *yada'*.[6] I presume that he, coming from the Reformed tradition, did not show any Arminian bias in that omission.

The usage. As we examine the above contexts, it becomes clear that the emphasis upon God's intimate knowledge and care for individuals or the nation adequately satisfies the context. 'Choice' is not at all in view, even though remotely possible in some contexts. In reference to Gen. 18:19, we should observe that it was God's ongoing relationship with Abraham which gave promise of his commanding his children to keep the way of the Lord. Here the KJV renders the overwhelmingly primary meaning of *yada'* and is preferred over the NAS and NIV assumption of a remote secondary connotation: "**For I know him, that he will command his children and his household after him, and they shall keep the way of the LORD, to do justice and judgment; that the LORD may bring upon Abraham that which he hath spoken of him.**" God's choice of Abraham would not assure this result, since Jacob was similarly chosen and failed to so command his children in an effective way. God knew Abraham's heart, that he would instruct Isaac. Obviously, our Calvinistic friends would not want to say that God chose him because He knew how Abraham would behave. Unless they are willing to grant that, their insistence upon 'choice' seems an extremely remote possibility. Translators (and theologians) should always choose the primary meaning of a word unless a secondary meaning makes better sense in the context. But it is highly doubtful that this is even a secondary meaning of the word. Bertram (in *TDNT*) states that here "the LXX has the thought of omniscience instead of that of election."[7]

In Ex. 33:12 when God said to Moses, **"I have known you by name, and you have also found favor in My sight,"** it is doubtful that the meaning is that God had chosen him by name. Whatever would that mean? It is far more likely that God's ongoing relationship with Moses, since He had commissioned him years before, was the basis of the favor He continued to show him despite the sin of Israel. Verse 11 specifically mentions that face-to-face relationship: "Thus the LORD used to speak to Moses face to face, just as a man speaks to his friend."

Hosea 13:5 is the least likely context in which to find the meaning of 'choice', since it was in the wilderness that God cared for Israel (as the LXX renders it). "**Yet I have been the LORD your God since the land of Egypt; and you were not to know any god except Me, for there is no savior besides Me. I cared (LXX *poimaino*) for you in the wilderness, in the land of drought.** (Hos. 13:4-5, NAS). God did not choose Israel in the wilderness by any stretch of the imagination, so neither the LXX translators or the context support such a meaning here.

Amos 3:2 presents problems also for this unproven pregnant meaning. **"Hear this word that the LORD hath spoken against you, O children of Israel, against the whole family which I brought up from the land of Egypt, saying, You only have I known of all the families of the earth: therefore I will punish you for all your iniquities. Can two walk together except they be agreed?** (Amos 3:1-3 AV). Is the reason that God will punish Israel for their iniquities because He chose them or because he had an ongoing relationship with them? In both the preceeding and following verses He refers to that relationship. Context must decide for the primary meaning of the word. Which is a more reasonable basis for God's judgment upon Israel--His relationship with them or His choice of them? God's ongoing relationship with Israel over the centuries intervening on their behalf time and again brought awesome responsibility as a basis of judgment. But the fact of their choice by God (which we do not deny) is a less compelling basis of judgment. Amos 3:7 also raises a problem for the Calvinist. If 'choice' is in view and election is based upon some secret counsel of God, why then does He state, **"Surely the Lord God does nothing unless He reveals His secret counsel to His servants the prophets**"?

Lastly, we must consider Jeremiah 1:5: **"Before I formed you in the womb I knew you, and before you were born I consecrated you; I have appointed you a prophet to the nations"** (NAS). The sentence consists of two coordinate clauses, the first with the verb *yada'* and the second with the verb *qadash*. The assumption of the Calvinistic reading is that since the verbs are in a parallelism, they are roughly synonymous. But that is an unproven assumption. Another possibility is that there is a sequence of thought here. God is assuring Jeremiah that He knew him before he was even formed in the womb, and that He also set him apart for prophethood before birth. Since Jeremiah, like Moses before him, questioned his own ability to be God's prophet (1:6-7), the fact that God thoroughly knew him was important for Jeremiah to understand. God fully knew his limitations, and despite this, consecrated and appointed him to the awesome responsibility of being a prophet to the nations. There is nothing in the context which requires, or even hints at a parallelism between *yada'* and *qadash*.

Thus, in none of these contexts is there a sound contextual basis for reading the idea of 'choice' into *yada'*. One would think that if it were true, there would be one clear, indisputable context out of the 944 usages of the root which would require 'to choose'. It should also be noted that if the authors had wanted to communicate the idea of 'choose,' there is a most suitable word, *bachar*, which is regularly used of the divine choice of Abraham, Israel, and many individuals. In addition, none of the cognate languages, such as Assyrian, Aramaic, Syriac, Ethiopic, or Phoenician, evidence any such connotation. The Assyrian has a usage, "God has regarded him", but this is of course quite different from 'choose'.[8] Indeed, many Calvinistic writers make this subtle shift from "taking knowledge of one with loving care" to "making one the subject of loving care or elective love."[9] Theologically, this is a very significant shift. Of course, God takes knowledge of believers with loving care, but to say it means to *make* someone the object of His loving care is to read something radically different into the word. But there is no linguistic basis for this shift. C. W. Hodge's article in *ISBE* shows that there is a philosophical and theological basis for such oft-repeated statements, but gives no direct linguistic evidence for it. Indeed Hodge, like Berkhof, makes foreknowledge equivalent to foreordination.[10]

A Word Study of *ginoskein*

The lexicons. As we move into the Greek terms, we find that Bertram claims an elective connotation for *ginoskein* in the Septuagint, referring to Num. 16:5; Ps. 1:6; 36:18; Hos. 5:3; 11:12; Amos 3:2; and Nah. 1:7.[11] Upon closer examination, however, in most of these contexts the LXX differs significantly from the Hebrew, and in none of them does the LXX context even remotely suggest 'choice'.

The Septuagint text of Num. 16:5 reads: "*Epeskeptai kai egno ho theos tous ontos autou kai tous hagious*". Behind *egno* in the Greek is *yada'* in the Hebrew, in the sense of 'show' and in no way supports Bertram's claim. The idea of choice is found later in the verse but is not a rendering of either *yada'* or *ginoskein*. The Septuagint text of Hos. 11:12 reads: "*Nun egno autous ho theos*". Again the Greek shows little resemblance to the Hebrew text, so the only question is what connotation was in the mind of the translators. The temporal "now" makes it clear that choice is not in view here. The two references in the Psalms, Hosea 5:3, Amos 3:2, and Nahum 1:7 present a similar picture. The knowledge of relationship fully satisfies the context without resort to any such elective meaning.

In New Testament usage, we find that neither Thayer or Abbott-Smith give 'to choose' as a meaning for *ginoskein*. The three contexts usually cited as requiring some elective connotation are 1 Cor. 8:3, Gal. 4:9, and 2 Tim 2:19. However, in 1 Cor. 8:3 Paul is contrasting the proud knowledge of the Corinthian pseudo-philosophers with the infinitely more important truth that God knows the true believer: "**If anyone supposes that he knows anything, he has not yet known as he ought to know; but if anyone loves God, he is known by Him**" (1 Cor. 8:2-3). The conditional 'if' clause speaks of our love for God, so the fact that we are known by Him could hardly be referring to some unconditionally elective choice. Rather, it probably speaks of His loving care for His own.

The context of Gal. 4:9 is also easily understood without reading 'choice' into it. "**However at that time, when you did not know God, you were slaves to those which by nature are no gods. But now that you**

have come to know God, or rather to be known by God, how is it that you turn back again to the weak and worthless elemental things, to which you desire to be enslaved all over again?" (Gal. 4:8-9 NAS). For those legalistic Galatians who might be supposing that they had come to know God by their own works and initiative, Paul makes it clear that the plan of salvation rests upon God's knowledge of us and our relationship with Him. He took the initiative in sending His Son (4:4) and His Spirit (4:6). But this is not equivalent to an implication of choice. Of course, we do not deny that there are other passages and words which do speak of God's choice, but the truth of those passages must not be read into this verse and into the word *ginosko* in any context.

The third context is 2 Tim. 2:19: "**Nevertheless, the firm foundation of God stands, having this seal, 'The Lord know those who are His,' and, 'Let everyone who names the name of the Lord abstain from wickedness**" (NAS). Again the primary meaning of the word makes perfect sense here, and there is no contextual basis for resorting to a supposed secondary sense. It speaks of that special relationship between God and the believer as the firm basis for departing from wickedness. We have seen this consistent connection right from Genesis 18:19. Those who would see a supposed pregnant meaning here might point out that the Aorist tense is used. The NAS translators render it as a present, probably seeing it as a gnomic aorist, which is defined as, "A generally accepted fact or truth may be regarded as so fixed in its certainty or axiomatic in its character, it is described by the aorist, just as though it were an actual occurrence."[12]

A Word Study of *PROGINOSKEIN*

Usage. When we examine the usage of *proginoskein* itself, we find that nowhere in the classical, the Koine, or the Septuagintal usage does it mean 'to choose beforehand'. It uniformly means 'to know beforehand' referring to prescience.[13] There is one touted usage in Judith 9:5-6:

> "O God, my God, hear me also, a widow. It is you who were the author of those events [judgments upon Israel] and of what preceded and followed them. The present, also, and the future you have planned. Whatever you devise comes into being; the things you decide on come forward and say, 'Here we are!' All your ways are in readiness, and your judgment is made with foreknowledge" (New American Bible).

Although it is clear that Judith is speaking of God's programming of events, that in no way justifies reading a determinative force into her use of *proginoskein*. Indeed she has her own plan to assassinate Holofernes by guile and charm. There is nothing in the context which at all requires a sense other than mere prescience. It is, of course, a possible connotation. But if this were the case it would be the only such usage in the whole LXX, or indeed in any of the other Hellenistic Jewish literature. The Jewish writer Philo (De Somniis I:2) uses it in terms of knowing beforehand through dreams. Twice in Wisdom in the Septuagint (6:13 & 8:8) it is used of prescience. Josephus uses it of knowing something earlier than the time of speaking (Bellum Judaicum 6,8; Antiq. Jud. II, V:36).[14]

The classical usage is uniform. Hippocrates, Euripides, Thucydides, Plato, Xenophon, Demosthenes, and Aristotle, all use it in the sense of knowing beforehand. Jacobs and Krienke conclude that:

> The composite *proginosko* formed from the prefix, *pro-*, before, and the vb. *ginosko*, perceive, be acquainted with, understand, know, is attested from Euripides onwards and means to know or perceive in advance, to see the future. . . The corresponding noun *prognosis* (attested as a medical technical term since Hippocrates) denote the foreknowledge which makes it possible to predict the future.[15]

Subsequent to the New Testament, the church fathers until the time of Augustine also consistently use *proginoskein* in the sense of prescience. Justin Martyr, Hermas, 2 Clement, Ambrose, Origen, and Jerome could be cited.[16] Augustine in his earlier days understood it the same way, but later, based upon a misinterpretation of John 15:16, he began to give it a more determinative sense.[17] Since I have already given a detailed study of the usage in the seven New Testament passages in chapter 7, I will refer you back to that discussion to get the complete picture. This appendix is only supplementary to that discussion.

---

1. Berkhof, p. 111-2.
2. Eugene Erlich, et al, *Oxford American Dictionary* (New York: Oxford University Press, 1980), p. 381.
3. William Gesenius, trans. Samuel P. Tregelles, *Hebrew-Chaldee Lexicon to the Old Testament*, p. 334.
4. Brown, Driver, and Briggs, p. 394.
5. R. Bultmann in *TDNT*, I, p. 698.
6. Paul R. Gilchrist in Harris, Archer, and Waltke, eds. *Theological Wordbook of the Old Testament*, I, pp. 366-8.
7. Bertram in *TDNT*, I, p. 700, ftnte.
8. Professor Melvin R. Dahl, telephone conversation, Nov. 15, 1992.
9. Berkhof, p. 480.
10. Caspar Wistar Hodge in James Orr, *International Standard Bible Encyclopedia*, II, pp. 1128-31.
11. Bertram in *TDNT*, I, p. 700.
12. H. E. Dana and Julius R. Mantey, *A Manual Grammar of the Greek New Testament*, p. 197.
13. Bultmann in *TDNT*, I, p. 715.
14. Ibid, I: 715-6.
15. Jacobs and Krienke, *International Dictionary of New Testament Theology*, p. 692.
16. Bultmann in *TDNT*, I: 715-6.
17. Augustine, *On the Predestination of the Saints*, ch. 7 (NPNF, 1st, 5:500-1.); *On the Gospel of St. John* LXXXVI:2 (NPNF, 2nd, 7:352.)

APPENDIX G

WORD STUDIES OF REPENTANCE AND CONVERSION

As we move into the subjective aspect of salvation truth, the definitions of 'repentance' and 'conversion' are most important in constructing an inductive *ordo salutis.* In teaching systematic theology over the last thirty years, I have had a growing conviction that some of the standard theological works are imprecise or even erroneous in their definitions of these terms. However, in doing more in-depth research on these terms, I was utterly shocked to find that one of the theological dictionaries, which scholars depend upon, has basic and elementary errors, omissions of significant data, and misstatements of facts so simple that a novice seminary student could check them by use of a concordance. At a more advanced level, there are certain assumptions made by these scholars that, upon closer examination, are highly questionable. *The result of this is a biased attempt to equate repentance and conversion, rather that recognizing them as distinct biblical truths.*

Data distortions. First, I will state the distortions of data I have uncovered and then we will seek to reconstruct the definitions of these terms based upon the correct data. Then we will examine a fallacious presupposition which has led to a false conclusion.

J. Goetzmann in the *The New International Dictionary of New Testament Theology* states:

> The NT does not follow LXX usage but employs *metanoeō* to express the force of *sub* [*shub*], turn round. This change in meaning was prepared for by other Gk. translations of the OT and in Hellenistic Jud. (for evidence cf. J. Behm, *TDNT* IV 989).[1]

The fact, however, is that *shub* is never so translated in either the Septuagint or the New Testament. It seems that the authors of the articles in *NIDNTT* consulted each other rather than their Hebrew and Greek primary sources, because F. Laubach makes a similar erroneous statement a few pages earlier in discussing the renderings of *shub*: "The LXX translates these passages by *epistrephō*, *apostrephō*, *anastrephō*, but not, as in the NT, by *metanoeō*. The theological meaning of *sub* can be clearly traced in the NT."[2]

Before we proceed, let me state the linguistic facts, thus correcting the above misstatements:

1. *Shub* clearly means “turn round, return (qal), bring back, restore (hiph.)"[3]

2. *Shub* is never rendered as *metanoeein* in either the Septuagint or the New Testament.

3. *Shub* is predominantly translated as some compound of *strephein* in the Septuagint (the vast majority of the 1040 occurences), and in the New Testament (4 times).[4]

4. *Nacham* clearly means, “1. be sorry, moved to pity, have compassion,. . . 2. be sorry, rue, suffer grief, repent, . . . 3. comfort oneself, be comforted. . ."[5] It is rendered 14 times in the Septuagint as *metanoeein* and never translated in the New Testament, in any way.

5. Conversely, *metanoeein* is never found in the New Testament as the translation of any Hebrew term.

6. The secular Greek usage of *metanoeein* is clear: "to change, one's mind,. . . to change one's resolve or purpose, . . . to come to a different opinion, to change one's view, . . . if the change of mind derives from recognition that the earlier view was foolish, improper or evil, there arises the sense 'to regret,' 'to feel remorse,' 'to rue'"[6]

A hidden agenda. Thus we see that Laubach's statement is baldly erroneous. Goetzmann, however, seems aware of the facts and, fudges by saying, “**employs** *metanoeō* to express" rather than "translates", which reveals that he has a hidden agenda. He is trying to make a case for the idea that although the secular Greek literature uses *metanoeein* in the sense of “to change one's mind," there was a semantic shift in the Hellenistic Jewish literature and later Greek translations of the Old Testament from the force of *nacham* to that of *shub*, that is ‘conversion'. He cites Behm as authority for that shift so we must examine his treatment to get to the root of his agenda. Such cavalier treatment of the data clearly indicates a bias or an uncritical deference to Behm's opinion. But the distortion of the data is most significant.

Although Behm and Wurthwein do not make any factual misstatements in their treatment in *TDNT*, they load their discussion with a mass of irrelevant data which skews the conclusions. The question is whether the New Testament usage of *metanoeein* has shifted radically to the later Jewish Hellenistic usage as 'conversion.' After Behm surveys the secular Greek usage, cited above, Wurthwein surveys the penitential fasts of the Old Testament and the prophets' outlook on the possiblities for the conversion of Israel. He does not refer to *nacham*, however, and assumes the synonymity of repentance and conversion. Then Behm, in examining the Septuagintal usage, states:

> But *nacham* and *shub*, though they have different basic meanings, both denote movement away from a position previously adopted (whether lit. or fig.), and are thus often used as par. (Jer. 4:28; Ex. 32:12); religiously, they can be almost synon., cf. Jer. 8:6 with 31:18ff. The result is that in the LXX *metanoeo* and *epistrepho* seem to be related in meaning, Jer. 8:6, *Ier.* 38:18f., Isa. 46:8 (deviating from the Heb.). *Metanoeō* thus approximates *epistrephō* = *shub*, the OT tt. for religious and ethical conversion.[7]

Kaiser's principle. Behm goes on to refer to the later Greek translations of the Old Testament as manifesting this shift, the Apocrypha, Pseudepigrapha, Philo, Josephus, and Rabbinic literature as well. However, I would raise a vigorous objection to the pages of data he adduces as almost totally irrelevant to the issue at hand, written after the New Testament. Walter Kaiser has made a significant point well, in outlining the proper steps to be taken in a word study. He suggests study of:

> those contexts that illustrate its usage *prior* to the selected text we are exegeting. The principle here is the same as what we were advocating in our discussion of the 'Analogy of [Antecedent] Scripture.' What was written after the text in question is of no use or helpful only for the sake of comparison."[8]

When we consider the chronic externalism of Pharisaic rabbinic thinking in the pre-Christian era, which Christ exposed in no uncertain terms in the Sermon on the Mount, it is unthinkable that He, His herald, and His apostles would have had an externalistic concept of repentance. The New Testament Christian understands very clearly that it all must start with an internal working of the Spirit in the heart, which only then works its way outward into the behavior of the individual. Wurthwein himself points up the OT prophets' repeated warnings against merely going through the external rituals of penitence without a genuine repentance of heart. Thus it is unthinkable that the Lord Jesus and his ambassadors should be influenced by this rabbinic shift of meaning from the internal (repentance) to the external (conversion).

Is association synonymity? Behm's support for the synonymity of repentance and conversion as quoted above depends heavily upon the close association of *shub* and *nacham* in five Old Testament passages and later of *metanoeein* and *epistrephein* in two New Testament contexts. The false assumption is that close association or even coordination of terms argues for synonymity. This is a patently false assumption. Upon further examination of the OT contexts it becomes clear that none support synonymity. Jereremiah 4:28 is a simple coordination of the two words. God says, "I will not repent, nor will I turn back." First the change of mind is mentioned, and then the logical outcome is a change of action. Exodus 32:12 is the same simple coordination. Jeremiah 8:5-6: "They refuse to return *(shub)*. . . . No man repented *(nacham)* of his wickedness, saying, 'What have I done?' Everyone turned *(shub)* to his course, like a horse charging into the battle." Again proximity of the two words does not indicate synonymity, only relationship. Jeremiah 31:18f.: "Turn me *(shub)*, and I shall be turned, for you are Yahweh, my God. For after I had turned away *(shub)*, I repented *(nacham)*." Again proximity does not indicate synonymity, and we should note that the most proximate use of *shub* does not have to do with conversion, but with turning away from God, as the Septuagint rightly understands it. Isaiah 46:8 does not even have *nacham*, but is adduced by Behm because the Septuagint has both *metanoeein* and *epistrephein*, departing greatly from the Hebrew. The Septuagint refers to turning *(epistrephein)* the heart as coordinate with *metanoeein*, which even less proves synonymity. This is as inane as saying that apples and oranges means that apples equals oranges. Thus Behm is guilty of a serious logical error here. His unstated, erroneous premise is that coordinate use of two words proves that they are synonymous.

Behm carries over this faulty logic into his discussion of the NT associations of *metanoeō* and *epistrephō*:

> Again the NT use betrays certain peculiarities like the Jewish Hellenistic (*metanoeō* synon. of --> *epistrephō* , Ac. 3:19; 26:20; constr. with prep. *apo or ek*, Ac. 8:22; Rev. 2:21f.; 9:20f.; 16:11; Hb. 6:1; const. with *eis*, Ac. 20:21), and rests on the underlying Aramaic, the speech of Jesus and primitive Palestinian Christianity. Hence the only apposite renderings are 'to convert' and 'conversion.' [9]

In his subsequent discussion he further compounds the confusion of the internal work of repentance with the external by speaking of baptism effecting conversion, apparently advocating a baptismal regenerationist viewpoint.[10] However, John the Baptizer insisted that the Pharisees should "bring forth fruit worthy of repentance" (Mt. 3:8), thus distinguishing the internal from the external.

Theological implications. Some may accuse me of making too fine a point. But to confuse repentance as an internal matter of the heart with conversion as an external change of lifestyle is to confuse effect with cause and to bring serious theological error as well. An internal change of mindset, heart, and attitude is necessarily prior to the outward change of lifestyle. Indeed, the Lord Jesus Himself laid great stress upon the Pharisees' propensity to externalism rather than a heart relationship with God. To illustrate, if one is driving down the interstate in the wrong direction, first there must be a change of mind or attitude, a recognition that one is going in the wrong direction. Only then can one look for an exit and make a u-turn, which corresponds to conversion. If repentance and faith are integrally connected, as implied in Acts 20:21 and as most evangelicals recognize, then to confuse repentance and conversion is also to confuse faith and conversion. This confusion is frequently reflected in the theologies. For instance, Berkhof in discussing conversion identifies *metanoia* as the most common word for conversion in the New Testament and as the "most fundamental of the terms employed."[11] There is a real question in my mind whether repentance should even be discussed under the heading of conversion, as is customary in many theologies. If repentance/faith is a condition for regeneration (as discussed in chapter 10), and conversion is the human side of regeneration, then repentance and conversion should be given separate consideration. I believe that this is also a matter which relates to the presuppositions of the lordship salvation debate.

Before concluding, another clarification should be made. Repentance must be distinguished from remorse. Although lexicographers discuss whether there is a clear distinction between *metanoeein* and *metamelomai*, Matthew's use of *metamelomai* to refer to Judas in Matthew 27:3 strongly suggests that remorse is clearly intended. Obviously Judas did not repent in any real sense.

To summarize the reasons for clearly distinguishing repentance and conversion:

1) *Metanoeein* is never found as a translation of *shub*, either in the Septuagint or in the New Testament.

2) The shift in connotation of *metanoeein* evidenced in later Hellenistic Jewish literature is irrelevant to its New Testament usage.

3) The close association of repentance and conversion in a number of Old Testament and New Testament contexts does not at all imply that they are synonymous. Rather the logical sequence of repentance before conversion is always maintained.

4) Very few modern translators have followed *TDNT* in rendering *metanoeein* as 'conversion' or any synonym.

1. J. Goetzmann in Colin Brown, ed., *The New International Dictionary of New Testament Theology* (Grand Rapids: Zondervan, 1975), I, 357.
2. F. Laubach in Colin Brown, ed., op. cit., I, 354.
3. Goetzmann, I, 354.
4. Georg Bertram in *TDNT*, VII, 716.
5. William Gesenius, trans. & ed., Francis Brown, S. R. Driver, and Charles A. Briggs, *The New Hebrew and English Lexicon* (Peabody, MA: Hendrickson, 1979), p. 636.
6. Johannes Behm in *TDNT*, IV, 978-9.
7. Ibid., IV, pp. 989-90.
8. Walter C. Kaiser, Jr., *Toward an Exegetical Theology* (GR: Baker, 1981), p. 145.
9. Behm, IV, p. 999.
10. Ibid., IV, p. 1003.
11. L. Berkhof, *Systematic Theology* (GR: Eerdmans, 1953), p. 480.

APPENDIX H

IS BAPTISM ESSENTIAL FOR SALVATION?

One of the earliest errors to enter the church was the to make the ordinances into sacraments. Water baptism and the Lord's Supper began to be viewed as efficacious in the early centuries. In subsequent centuries this ultimately was crystallized in the development of the Roman Catholic Church with its doctrine of baptismal regeneration. It was understood that, in some almost magical way, the instant an individual is baptized, he is regenerated and forgiven. One question which naturally arose from that viewpoint was how to deal with post-baptismal sin, since presumably that had to be dealt with separately. But the root of the problem was thinking that baptism was an essential condition for salvation, which in effect made it a substitute for faith. The Roman Catholic Church today is the major advocate of baptismal regeneration. Certainly on the popular level, the average Catholic priest affirms that Roman Catholic baptism assures ultimate salvation.

The reformers did not make a total break with a sacramental view of the ordinances. Luther continued to hold to Christ's mystical presence in the elements of the Lord's supper and retained infant baptism with some connotation of efficacy. Thus Lutherans and Reformed over the centuries have come to believe in baptism as having some effect upon the infant, whether in regeneration or in inclusion in the covenant. The Anglican Church (Episcopalian in USA) has always tended toward differing degrees of efficacy in the sacraments, depending upon which segment of the Church is considered (Anglo-Catholic, Liberal, or Evangelical).

In America the scene was complicated by the Restoration Movement of the Campbellites (Churches of Christ and Christian Churches). Here additional millions moved toward understanding baptism as effecting the forgiveness of sins. Some within the Restoration Movement churches are very aggressive in convincing people that one must be baptized by them for the forgiveness of sins. What is the biblical data in answer to this most important question?

The arguments for baptismal regeneration usually derive from the Gospel accounts of John's baptism being a "baptism of repentance for the forgiveness of sins," from Christ's words to Nicodemus in John 3, from the Mark 16:16 wording of the Great Commission, from Peter's Pentecost sermon (Acts 2:38), from Ananias' words to Paul in Acts 22:16, and Paul's doctrinal statement in Titus 3:5. These are the 'proof-texts,' but there are also certain presuppositions held by baptismal regenerationists which need to be examined in our discussion. Another significant factor in at least several of the passages, is a lack of accurate translation in the KJV, which obscures the truth of the passages. The KJV translators were to a man Anglicans and mostly held to baptismal regeneration. This affected their translation. Unfortunately subsequent translators have not done a great job of giving a more precise rendering of those verses which would clear up the issue. The issue is not whether baptism is commanded of believers, but whether it is a necessary condition to becoming a genuine Christian. Let us look at the inductive and deductive data which bear upon the issue.

THE INDUCTIVE BIBLICAL DEVELOPMENT

The Old Testament background

The antecedent of the Lord's supper was the Passover remembrance of Israel's exodus from Egypt. This is clear since it was at a Passover celebration that the Lord Jesus modified and simplified the Passover seder (order) and commanded Christians to remember His death by its observance. Over the centuries before Christ, when the Jews observed the Passover, there is no indication that they viewed it as efficacious or other than a simple memorial of a mighty intervention of God. Indeed, Moses explained that the meaning of Passover was "**in order that you may remember all the days of your life the day when you came out of the land of Egypt**" (Deut. 16:3).

In a similar way the antecedent of baptism was clearly circumcision. It was initiatory into the people of God, whether for a Jewish male or a Gentile convert. Moses also explained its symbolism to a new generation of Jews about to enter the promised land, "**Moreover the LORD your God will circumcise your heart and the heart of your descendants, to love the LORD your God with all your heart and with all your soul, in order that you may live**" (Deut. 30:6). "**Circumcise then your heart, and stiffen your neck no more**" (Deut. 10:16), he exhorted them. Israel was not to trust in external circumcision but in a work of the Spirit on the sinful human heart. So when we come to the New Testament linkage of circumcision and baptism, we are not surprised to find that there are frequent warnings about trusting in physical circumcision and outward religious observances (Matt. 5:8; 6:1; 23:27; Acts 15:1-29; Gal. 5:2-3; 6:12-15; Rom. 2:25-29; 4:9-16; Col. 2:11-13). The Colossians 2 passage shows the connection of circumcision and baptism in Paul's thinking, but a circumcision wrought without hands, of the Spirit of God on the human heart. This is crucial background in understanding water baptism in the Gospel accounts.

The Gospel accounts

The ministry of John the Baptizer. John the son of Zechariah was called the Baptizer[A] because he initiated the ritual of water baptism. Scholars debate whether so-called proselyte baptism of the Jews originated before or after John. This is a moot point since it was not really baptism at all, but a self-immersion. John was the first person who immersed *another* person, and thus he was called the Baptizer, that is "the one doing the immersing" (note that the *-izo* ending in Greek is causal).

Let us examine the account in Matthew chapter 3. As John the Baptizer came announcing the impending kingdom of God and the coming of the Messiah-King, his ministry of preparation emphasized the absolute necessity for Israel to repent or to be judged (Matt. 3:2). When many hypocritical Pharisees and Sadducees came to make a show by being baptized by John, he warned them sternly that unless their repentance was genuinely from the heart, they would be cut off from the kingdom (3:5-10). To reinforce his point he stressed that the coming Messiah would not just perform external water baptism, but an efficacious baptism of the Spirit and of fire (3:11-12). One could put on an outward show of repentance in water baptism, but one could not get away with externalism when the Messiah comes. Unfortunately many have misinterpreted John's words in verse 11 to imply the opposite by ignoring the context, "**As for me, I baptize you with water for *(eis)* repentance**". Understood in its context, there is no way that John could be implying that baptism causes repentance. The Greek preposition *eis* could imply this when taken alone, but in the context grammarians have recognized that *eis* can mean 'because of' in a number of contexts like Mt. 12:41.[1] Thus John said, "**I baptize you with water because of (your) repentance.**"

When we turn to Mark's Gospel we find a brief statement, "**John the Baptist appeared in the wilderness preaching a baptism of repentance for the forgiveness of sins**" (Mk. 1:4). Luke also in 3:3 uses the same phrase to describe John's ministry: "*baptisma metanoias eis aphesin hamartion.*" The question is whether the forgiveness is conditional upon the baptism or the repentance? Baptismal regenerationists assume that it is conditioned upon baptism as well as repentance. This is an unfounded assumption. We must examine the relation between *baptisma* and *metanoias* since *metanoias* is in the genitive/ablative case. It could be a genitive of reference, which would be translated, "a baptism with reference to repentance for the forgiveness of sins."[2] It also could be an ablative of source, which Dana and Mantey describe as a noun which "owes its existence in some way to that which is denoted in the ablative."[3] Thus it would be a "baptism derived from repentance for the forgiveness of sins." In neither alternative does it imply that forgiveness is contingent upon baptism. None of the other usages of the genitive/ablative fit the context. Thus it is the repentance which brings forgiveness of sins, and this accords with

A. This is the accurate translation of *ho baptistes,* which is a noun of agency according to morphology, and of *ho baptizon*, which as a participle implies the one doing the action.

John's warning to hypocrites, which we have already noted.[B]

We should also note John's own stated purpose for which he baptized: **"but in order that He might be manifested to Israel, I came baptizing in water"** (Jn. 1:31). Thus he had the great privilege of baptizing the Messiah Himself. It should be obvious to all Evangelicals that the Lord Jesus was not baptized for regeneration since He needed none. He was baptized to identify with the repenting and believing remnant of Israel. It was to be an external witness of His messiahship to John, as God had told him, **"'He upon whom you see the Spirit descending and remaining upon Him, this is the one who baptizes in the Holy Spirit.' And I have seen, and have borne witness that this is the Son of God"** (Jn. 1:33-34). This identification with the godly remnant of Israel is further elucidated by the secondary, metaphorical meaning of the word *baptizo,* that is, "to be overwhelmed by something, to be identified with someone." This is clear from Christ's own usage in Mark 10:38f, **"Are you able to drink the cup that I drink, or to be baptized with the baptism with which I am baptized?"** He is referring to His death. Paul speaks of Israel's identification with Moses as they escaped from Egypt (1 Cor. 10:2). Christ's own baptism was an identification, not an efficacious ritual. Likewise our baptism is an identification with Christ, not an efficacious ritual (1 Cor. 12:13, etc.).

The ministry of the Lord Jesus Christ. After John was imprisoned, the Lord Jesus began His public ministry by preaching, **"The time is fulfilled, and the kingdom of God is at hand; repent and believe in the gospel"** (Mk. 1:15). As we search through all four Gospel accounts of Christ's preaching, we find this same message with absolutely no reference to baptism at all. Repentance and faith (trust) are emphasized over and over again, but there is total silence about baptism in His preaching. This would be extremely strange if Christ and the Gospel writers believed that baptism was a necessary condition of forgiveness and the new birth. Indeed, the only hint we have that Christ practiced baptism at all are the three references in John 3:22,26; and 4:1-2. In fact the word *pisteuo* (believe) is used 96 times in John's Gospel without ever being linked to baptism.

As we trace through Christ's ministry, we find numerous incidents where the Lord declared an individual's sins forgiven before there was any possibility of baptism. In Mark 2:1-12 we find the paralytic who was let down through the roof. Mark says that Jesus, seeing their faith, said to the paralytic, **"My son, your sins are forgiven."** Clearly his sins were forgiven apart from baptism. In Mark 5 we find the account of the woman with the

---

B. Some may question why John preached repentance rather than faith. It is clear that when the message went to God's chosen people Israel, the word 'repent' was used by John, Christ, and the apostles. This carries through in the book of Acts until the message began to be preached to the Gentiles, when the word 'believe' began to be used. From this it is clear that repentance and faith are the two sides of the one coin (Acts 20:21).

flow of blood. Christ's immediate words were, "**Daughter, your faith has made you well; go in peace, and be healed of your affliction**" (Mk. 5:34). A few moments later He told the synagogue official, "**Do not be afraid any longer, only believe**" (5:36). When the Lord commissioned the twelve apostles and sent them out to the lost sheep of the house of Israel, Mark states, "**And they went out and preached that men should repent**" (Mk. 6:12). None of the Gospel writers mentions baptism at this important point in Christ's instructions to the apostles. The last such case is necessarily that of the thief on the cross. The Lord took the genuine expression of repentance/faith on his part as an adequate condition for promising him, "**Today you shall be with me in paradise**" (Lk. 23:42-3). Neither did Christ mention baptism, nor was it possible for him to have been baptized.

Christ's words to Nicodemus. When we come to the much discussed account of Christ's interview with Nicodemus, we must be very careful to examine the exegetical possibilities of His imperative to be "**born of water and the Spirit**" (Jn. 3:5). Baptismal regenerationists again hastily assume that this is a reference to water baptism. They do not seriously consider the other interpretations which are more supportable from the context and the analogy of other Scripture. There are three other commonly-held views.

Some have held that the 'water' is a reference to natural birth and 'Spirit' to the contrasting new birth of the Holy Spirit. Of course, this view builds upon the fact that our natural birth is a watery birth in the bursting of the amniotic sac. This finds some strong support from the immediate context. Nicodemus's reaction to Christ's first statement about being born again (3:3) showed the limitation of his thinking to mere physical birth (3:4). Thus to correct his thinking the Lord said in effect, "you must not only be born naturally, but you must also be born of the Holy Spirit." This is further reinforced by Christ's clarification in verse 6, "**That which is born of the flesh is flesh, and that which is born of the Spirit is spirit**." This is an obvious contrast of the first, physical birth with the second, spiritual birth. Certainly this understanding must be given serious consideration.

Two other interpretations see the word 'water' as symbolic. One builds upon the other references in the New Testament to the Holy Spirit's use of the word of God to produce regeneration, such as James 1:18 and 1 Peter 1:23-4. Ephesians 5:26 speaks of Christ cleansing the church by "the water of the word." The weakness of this view is that it has to go far afield to find support.

Another more cogent symbolic interpretation sees water as representing the Holy Spirit and the reference to Spirit as clarifying the meaning of the symbol. Thus the *kai* (and) is better translated 'even' and is epexegetical. It is also taken by some commentators to be an example of hendiadys. Blass and DeBrunner explain, "The coordination of two ideas, one of which is dependent on the other (hendiadys), serves in the NT to avoid a series of dependent genitives: A[cts] 23:6."[4] This view receives strong support from the broader context of the fourth Gospel since the Lord used water as a symbol of the Spirit in his witness to the Samaritan woman (Jn. 4:10-14), and again at the feast of Booths when He gave that most dramatic invitation, **"If any man is thirsty, let him come to Me and drink. He who believes in Me, as the Scripture said, 'From his innermost being shall flow rivers of living water.'"** John clearly tells us that the Lord was speaking of the Holy Spirit (7:37-39). Another grammatical indication which tends to support this view is the fact that both 'water' and 'spirit' in the Greek do not have the article. This would seem to indicate that these are not two distinct entities. As Charles Hodge emphasized over a century ago that "the sign and the thing signified are often united, often interchanged, the one being used for the other." Hodge bases this statement upon the strong Old Testament symbolic usage of water. For example, Isaiah 12:3, "Therefore you will joyously draw water from the springs of salvation." See also Isaiah 35:6; 44:3; 55:1; Ezekiel 36:25; Jeremiah 2:18; Zechariah 14:8.[5] It would be an absurdity to read baptism into all of these passages. So the Lord Jesus, speaking to a very knowledgeable teacher of the Old Testament, built upon a familiar symbol of prophetic truth in explaining salvation.

Mark 16:16. The last passage for discussion in the Gospels is Mark's form of the Great Commission. Read superficially it might seem to indicate that baptism is a necessary condition: "He who has believed and has been baptized shall be saved; but he who has disbelieved shall be condemned" (Mk. 16:16). The key is to avoid reading into the statement what Christ did not say. This is a common failure of interpretive logic. Christ did not say that those who are not baptized will be condemned. Those interpreters take the converse of His positive statement to be true, that is, that those who are not baptized will be condemned. But an axiomatic rule of logic, found in all the basic textbooks, is that the converse of a statement may or may not be true. The only way we can prove whether the converse of a true statement is true or false is by depending upon other data. In this case, the other data from other Scripture references tells us that the converse is false —that those who are not baptized are not necessarily condemned. It should be noted that some other interpreters do not see this as a reference to water baptism at all, but to Spirit baptism. It should also be noted that this verse is not found in the oldest and best Greek manuscripts, and probably was not a part of the original text of Mark. But whether this be true or not, the Lord did not make baptism an essential condition of salvation.

The book of Acts

The book of Acts is crucial for our understanding of the place of baptism in the plan of salvation because we see here the early preaching and practice of the gospel message. Let us examine the key passages.

Peter's Pentecost sermon. The invitation which Peter gave at the end of his Pentecost sermon is most significant. Thousands of Jews were under the conviction of the Spirit because of his preaching of the word of God (Acts 2:37). Peter's command was twofold: "Repent, and let each of you be baptized in the name of Jesus Christ for the forgiveness of your sins, and you shall receive the gift of the Holy Spirit" (2:38). The question arises as to what the relationship is between repentance and baptism. Are forgiveness and the gift of the Spirit contingent upon repentance alone or upon baptism as well? Part of the problem of interpretation lies in the careless rendering of the KJV, which is partially corrected by the NAS quoted above. The NAS translators recognized that the break in thought between the two imperatives ought to be reflected in the translation. *Metanoesate* (Repent) is a second person plural active imperative and could be paraphrased, 'All of you must imperatively repent!' *Baptistheto* (let each of you be baptized) is a third person singular passive imperative, which is radically different in thrust. The shift from second to third person, from plural to singular, and from active voice to passive, is most significant. The third person singular imperative is a much weaker hortatory form as the NAS has rendered it.[6] This same usage is illustrated in Rev. 22:11. Because of that break in the grammar, we should really view the phrase about baptism as parenthetical: 'Let each of you who repents be baptized.' It should also be noted that the promise of forgiveness and the gift of the Holy Spirit are both phrased in the plural, so that its connection is with repentance, not baptism. Thus the force of Peter's words in the Greek was: 'All of you (pl.) must imperatively repent (and let him [s.] be baptized) for the forgiveness of your (pl.) sins, and you (pl.) will receive the gift of the Holy Spirit.' Alternatively, A. T. Robertson has suggested that this is to be understood as the use of *eis* to express the basis of forgiveness. Of course, three thousand converts were baptized that day. But it is clear from the grammar of the passage that they were not saved through that baptism.[C]

The ministry of Peter and others. This is confirmed by the subsequent pattern of gospel preaching we find as we walk through the Acts narrative. In Peter's second sermon, faith, repentance, and conversion are stressed, but there is no mention of baptism (3:16, 19). In the apostles' second confrontation with the Sanhedrin, Peter emphasized repentance and forgiveness without mentioning baptism (5:31). When Philip first preached to the Samaritans, he baptized those who believed, but they did not receive the Holy Spirit until days later when Peter and John came down from Jerusalem, so that Peter could use the keys and open the door of faith to Samaritans officially. Even though this is an anomaly explained by the dispensational transition involved, it clearly shows that baptism was not at

C. Robertson and Davis, p. 256: "Hence a case like Acts 2:38 *eis aphesin ton hamartion* can mean either *on the basis of forgiveness of sins* (cf. Mk. 1:4f. 'Confessing their sins') or *with a view to forgiveness of sins.* There is nothing in *eis* to compel either result. One will interpret it according to his theology."

all efficacious, even when true faith was present (8:12-17). The conversion of Cornelius and his household is a clear paradigm of salvation truth for Gentiles (10:43-48). Yet Peter's sermon concludes, "**that through His name everyone who believes receives forgiveness of sins**" (10:43). Immediately, *before* being baptized, they received the Holy Spirit. Indeed, Peter took the manifest reception of the Spirit as proof that they were fit candidates for baptism, although they were Gentiles. When Peter defended his actions before the Jerusalem church, he made that same point again quoting the words of Christ from 1:5, which contrasts water baptism with Spirit baptism (11:15-17). And in describing the founding of the Antioch church, Luke mentions that those who believed turned to the Lord, but does not mention baptism (11:21).

The apostle Paul's ministry. As the narrative shifts to Paul and Barnabas, we note their preaching in the synagogue of Antioch of Pisidia. Paul speaks of forgiveness through faith with no mention of baptism (Acts 13:38-39). When Luke describes the subsequent response there, he mentions believing as connected to eternal life, without reference to baptism (13:48). Thus we see that Paul really did tell the Philippian jailer the whole truth when he said, "**Believe in the Lord Jesus, and you shall be saved and your household**" (16:31). They did get baptized in obedience to Christ's command, but Paul very significantly left baptism out of the gospel message. He told it like it is. In subsequent narrative Luke refers several times to converts believing, without reference to baptism (17:12, 34; 19:18). Most significant is Paul's charge to the Ephesian elders, where he describes his preaching as, "**repentance toward God and faith in the Lord Jesus Christ**" (20:21), again without reference to baptism.

The account of Paul's meeting the dozen disciples of John the Baptizer is most interesting (19:1-7). Paul specifically asked them whether or not they had received the Spirit. Their answer was negative. Why did Paul rebaptize them? Certainly he did not denigrate John's baptism. But it was not Christian baptism of the New Testament church, the body of Christ founded on the day of Pentecost. John was a part of the previous dispensation or age (Mt. 11:11). So he needed to rebaptize these Jewish Old Testament believers from the previous legal dispensation to incorporate them into the New Testament body of Christ. They were an anomaly of geographic dislocation. But if baptism is for the forgiveness of sins, then Paul erred greatly. If John's baptism were efficacious, Paul had no need to baptize them over again. Some interpreters might say that John's baptism was ineffective and therefore had to be repeated. Their inconsistency becomes manifest in that these are the same interpreters who would claim Mark 1:4 as a proof text for baptism being for forgiveness of sins. They can't have it both ways. Either John's baptism was efficacious or it was not. These disciples were genuine in their repentance/faith as seen in their immediate reception of the Spirit at the laying on of hands. No, far better to understand this anomalous incident as part of the dispensational transition from Israel to the Church as the people of God. Thus the Spirit confirmed that they had now been incorporated into the body of Christ.

Paul's recounting before the Sanhedrin of his conversion testimony has occasioned much discussion because of the translation of Ananias' words to the newly converted Paul, "'**And now why do you delay? Arise, and be baptized, and wash away your sins, calling on His name**'" (22:16). Baptismal regenerationists understand Paul to be yet unsaved and needing to wash away his sins by baptism. If this were true it would be a serious anomaly and contradict the rest of the New Testament evidence. First of all, it is clear that Saul was already converted on the Damascus road three days earlier. His first response to Christ shows that he was instantaneously born again: "'**What shall I do, Lord?**'" (22:10). He called Jesus his Lord and submits to His instruction! However, Ananias had every right to be suspicious of this chief persecutor of the church, and assumes that he is yet unconverted.

The main difficulty with Ananias' words is translational. The participial phrase at the end of the sentence has been badly mistranslated by the KJV translators and those translations which followed in that tradition. *Apolousai tas hamartias sou epikalesamenos to onoma autou* ("wash away your sins, calling on His name.") This is a dangling participle, which is poor English, but good Greek. The relationship and force of these adverbial participial phrases are spelled out in the grammars. It seems clear that this is an instrumental participle, which indicates "the means by which the action of the main verb is accomplished."[7] Thus to make good English out of it, it should be properly translated: "**Wash away your sins by calling on His name**." The addition of the one little word 'by' corrects the abominably poor grammar of the English and fairly represents the force of the Greek.[D] This is in perfect accord with the truth of Joel 2:32 quoted by Paul in Romans 10:12-14, "'**Whoever will call upon the name of the Lord will be saved.**'" It is clear that we wash away our sins by calling on His name, not by getting baptized!

Lastly, we should note Paul's summary of his commission as he recounts it to Herod Agrippa, "**... to open their eyes so that they may turn from darkness to light and from the dominion of Satan to God, in order that they may receive forgiveness of sins and an inheritance among those who have been sanctified by faith that is in Me**" (26:18). Again we note that the omission of baptism in this summary of salvation truth is most significant. Likewise with Paul's statement, "**. . . that they should repent and turn to God, performing deeds appropriate to repentance**" (26:20).

D. I am continually amazed that a translational tradition (rut) has developed over the centuries which has resulted in such horrible English and significantly misses the point of the Greek syntax.

The New Testament epistles

Non-Pauline epistles. Both James and Peter give us definitive statements about the place of the word of God in bringing about the new birth. **"In the exercise of His will He brought us forth by the word of truth, so that we might be, as it were, the first fruits among His creatures"** (Jas. 1:18). **"For you have been born again not of seed which is perishable but imperishable, that is through the living and abiding word of God"** (1 Pet. 1:23). Neither mentions baptism. Peter's reference to baptism in 1 Peter 3:20-21 requires closer examination: **"And corresponding to that, baptism now saves you—not the removal of dirt from the flesh, but an appeal to God for a good conscience—through the resurrection of Jesus Christ, . . ."** Here the Greek word *antitupon* is most significant. Transliterated it is 'antitype'. Thus Peter is clearly stating that he is speaking figuratively. The flood of Noah was the type; baptism is the antitype. Then Peter, having stated this, realizes that his readers might interpret it crassly. So he breaks his line of thought to explain that he is not speaking of water baptism cleansing the body, but of the work of God upon the conscience. This is to follow the example of Moses (as already noted). Crass interpretation fails to recognize figurative language where it is so obvious.

Pauline epistles. The Apostle Paul gives us much grist for our theological mill in his letters. In his first letter to the church in Corinth he reflects on his early ministry in Corinth. **"I thank God that I baptized none of you except Crispus and Gaius, that no man should say you were baptized in my name. Now I did baptize also the household of Stephanus; beyond that, I do not know whether I baptized any other. For Christ did not send me to baptize, but to preach the gospel, . . ."**(1 Cor. 1:14-17a). It is extremely hard to see how Paul could write these words if he really believed that we are born again through baptism or that baptism was an essential condition of being saved. If it were so essential, Paul would certainly have made it a point to keep a roll of those he had baptized. Now just a few years later he can't even remember whom he had baptized. How could he thank God for so few he had baptized? How could he set baptism and preaching the gospel in such strong contrast if baptism is an essential part of the gospel of salvation?

Paul's great letter to the Galatian churches is extremely relevant to the issue. Legalists had sneaked into the Galatian churches to try to counteract Paul's gospel of saving grace (2:4-5). They insisted that circumcision and obedience to the Mosaic Law were necessary for both salvation and Christian morality. After refuting their viewpoint conclusively in the first four chapters, Paul warned them about the spiritual danger of those who trust in externalism: **"Behold I, Paul, say to you that if you receive circumcision, Christ will be of no benefit to you. And I testify again to every man who receives circumcision, that he is under obligation to keep the whole Law. You have been severed from Christ, you who are seeking to be**

justified by law; you have fallen from grace" (5:2-4). It is not that circumcision in itself was wrong, for Paul had had Timothy circumcised so that he might join them in witness to the Jews (Acts 16:3). It is trusting in the external ritual of circumcision which is spiritually dangerous. In a very real way trusting in baptism for salvation is the very same sort of externalistic legalism that Paul so clearly warned about. One would have to say that trust in an efficacious ritual of baptism for salvation puts one in the very same spiritual danger that Paul warns about. That is to sever ones self from Christ, rather than trusting in a personal relationship with Him. As Paul concludes his letter, "**For neither is circumcision anything, nor uncircumcision, but a new creation**" (6:15). It is not far afield to substitute the word 'baptism' for the word 'circumcision' in this verse and yet retain its main point.

Shortly after writing Galatians, Paul wrote the more reasoned theological statement–the book of Romans. He makes exactly the same point in the end of the second chapter (Rom. 2:25-29): "**But he is a Jew who is one inwardly; and circumcision is that which is of the heart, by the Spirit, not by the letter, and his praise is not from men, but from God**" (2:29). In defending justification by faith alone, Paul makes a major point that circumcision is just a sign and seal of faith, not in the least efficacious (4:9-16). His argument is based upon the fact that Abraham was a believer for many years before he was circumcised. His conclusion establishes an essential principle, "**For this reason it is by faith, that it might be in accordance with grace, in order that the promise may be certain to all the descendants**" (4:16).

Those who might question the connection we have noted between circumcision and baptism need to take note of Paul's words to the Colossian church, written some years later from house arrest in Rome: - "**And in Him you were also circumcised with a circumcision made without hands, in the removal of the body of the flesh by the circumcision of Christ; having been buried with Him in baptism, in which you were also raised up with Him through faith in the working of God, who raised Him from the dead**" (Col. 2:11-12). Since the circumcision was wrought "without hands," it is clear that the baptism is also that Spirit baptism of the heart, not the ritual of water baptism. Only this can be efficacious.

Finally we must note Paul's words to Titus in his last years of ministry: "**He saved us, not on the basis of deeds which we have done in righteousness, but according to His mercy, by the washing of regeneration and renewing by the Holy Spirit, whom He poured out upon us richly through Jesus Christ our Savior**" (Tit. 3:5-6). Based upon all the previous investigation, it is unthinkable that Paul is referring to baptism here. Those, like Ellicott, who make that assumption, base it upon the opinion that *loutron paliggenesias* is a possessive genitive, making baptism the cause of regeneration. Charles Hodge pointed out that this is not the only option grammatically. More likely it is a genitive of apposition, indicating that the washing is the internal washing of regeneration by the Holy Spirit. Indeed, "renewing by the Holy Spirit" must be epexegetical. Otherwise it is redundant.[8] One is biblically naive to think that baptism is the only washing referred to in the word of God, or even the most important washing.

THE DOCTRINAL CRYSTALLIZATION

Let us summarize the conclusions drawn from our inductive study.

Repentant faith is the only condition of salvation

A century and a half ago Charles Hodge pointed out that the New Testament everywhere teaches faith as the one condition for forgiveness and salvation.[9] More recently Lewis Sperry Chafer stressed that about 150 times in the NT, faith is the only condition of salvation.[10] If baptism were an essential condition, it would seem clear that it should have been emphasized in these 150 contexts, many of which we have already examined. Otherwise God is guilty of misleading communication of this central issue. For instance, did the Apostle Paul tell the whole truth when he told the Philippian jailer, "**Believe on the Lord Jesus Christ and you shall be saved**"? Did Paul omit an essential condition? The overwhelming support from 150 parallel passages confirms that Paul set out the one necessary condition for salvation and omitted nothing.

The few problem passages have been mistranslated or misinterpreted.

We have already examined how some passages which on the surface seem to make baptism a condition of salvation have been mistranslated or inexactly translated because of the theological bias of the King James translators, such as Matthew 3:11, Mark 1:4, Luke 3:3, Acts 2:38 and 22:16. We have noted that there is a serious logical fallacy in reading efficacious baptism into Mark 16:16. There are a number of promising interpretative possibilities in Christ's words to Nicodemus in John 3:5 which are much more cogent that the assumption that 'water' is a reference to baptism. That same assumption that Paul is referring to baptism in Titus 3:5 is totally unwarranted. Thus we see total consistency in the teaching of Scripture on this point (and every other point).

Many were given assurance of salvation and/or had received the Spirit before baptism.

We noted a number of examples in the ministry of Christ and the apostles where an individual was unquestionably saved without any possibility of baptism. In some cases they were baptized subsequently. The paralytic who was let down through the roof, the woman with the flow of blood, the thief on the cross, and Cornelius and his household, are some case studies examined. These have been seriously ignored by many interpreters.

Some individuals who were baptized did not receive the Holy Spirit.

We have noted two cases where individuals who had repented/believed did not receive the Holy Spirit until subsequently. In the case of the Samaritan converts of Philip, they (except for Simeon) genuinely believed and were baptized in water, but they did not receive the Holy Spirit until many days later (Acts 8:12-17). The second involved the dozen disciples of John the Baptizer (Acts 19:1-7), who although being genuine baptized converts of John did not receive the Holy Spirit for two decades after baptism. These are serious anomalies for baptismal regenerationists, and are best understood as being part of the dispensational transition from Israel to the New Testament church.

Regeneration is always wrought directly by the Spirit through the word of God.

We have examined a number of definitive statements about the new birth: John 3:3-18; James 1:18; and 1 Peter 1:23. All of them refer to the word of God and/or the Holy Spirit of God as the active agents. None of them mention water baptism. Salvation is frequently referred to in both testaments as a washing, but this washing is never accomplished by baptism. When the Lord Jesus washed the feet of the apostles, he used the symbolism of salvation as a washing (Jn. 13:1-20): "He who has bathed needs only to wash his feet, but is completely clean, and you are clean, but not all of you" (13:10). Salvation is the bath; the believer needs to cleanse his walk by confession of sin (1 Jn. 1:9). We noted Ananias' use of this symbolism (Acts 22:16). Peter's vision of the unclean food in Acts 10 speaks of Gentile salvation as a cleansing (10:15; 11:9). In 1 Corinthians 6:11 Paul refers to the Corinthian Christians as having been washed. It occurs again in Ephesians 5:26 and Titus 3:5. John speaks of forgiveness as a cleansing (1 Jn. 1:7,9). Finally, martyrs are said to have "washed their robes and made them white" (Rev. 7:14). This is always accomplished by the Spirit through the word without any reference to baptism. The symbolism is obvious and should not be ignored.

Failure to contrast water baptism with Spirit-baptism leads to serious error.

Both John the Baptizer and the Lord Jesus set water baptism in bold contrast with Spirit-baptism as to efficacy. The apostle Paul gave us the doctrinal explanation of Spirit-baptism in many contexts, which are erroneously assumed to be reference to water baptism. In both 1 Corinthians 12:13 and Colossians 2:11-13 Paul makes it clear that he is speaking of

Spirit-baptism, not water baptism. We must interpret the other passages (Rom. 6:3-4) in the light of these clear doctrinal statements. Spirit-baptism is efficacious for salvation; water baptism is not.

The apostle Paul minimized the cruciality of baptism.

Paul's thanksgiving to God that he baptized so few in Corinth, his lack of memory of whom he baptized, and his statement of his commission to evangelize—all are incomprehensible if baptism is some way effective in accomplishing salvation, or even a part of it (1 Cor 1:14-17). Baptism must be seen as a command to believers, not a means to become believers.

Requirement of baptism for salvation is tantamount to the legalism of the Galatian Judaizers.

The Pharisees were legalists because they believed that salvation is contingent upon ritual circumcision and law keeping. The Judaizers whose teaching fomented the Jerusalem Council insisted that circumcision was essential for salvation (Acts 15:1). The Council concluded that these people "unsettled the souls" of believers (Acts 15:24). In a similar way, the legalism of requiring the external rite of baptism as a condition for salvation unsettles the souls of Christians today. In so doing they change radically the whole nature of the Christian message. They also make it dependent upon ritualism and law-works. The only difference is that the Judaizers were still hung up in the Old Testament and hadn't moved into the New. Today's legalists draw from the New Testament command to be baptized, but by giving it undue importance in salvation have re-established the same principle as the Judaizers. Only now it is a different rite. This makes salvation no longer of grace (the unmerited favor) of God, and puts them in the same camp as the Galatian legalizers, who Paul says were bewitching the people (Gal. 3:1). Paul calls it a slavery and expresses concern for the salvation of those so deceived (Gal. 4:9-11, 5:1-4).

---

1. F. Blass and E. DeBrunner, *A Greek Grammar of the New Testament and Other Literature*, trans. Robert W. Funk, p. 112; A. T. Robertson and W. Hersey Davis, *A New Short Grammar of the Greek Testament* p. 256.
2. H. E. Dana and Julius R. Mantey, *A Manual Grammar of the Greek New Testament*, p. 76
3. Ibid., p.82
4. Blass and DeBrunner, p. 228.
5. Charles Hodge, *Systematic Theology* (Grand Rapids: Eerdmans, 1968), III. p. 593.
6. William D. Chamberlain, *An Exegetical Grammar of the Greek New Testament* (NY: Macmillan, 1952), p. 86.
7. Dana and Mantey, p.228.
8. Hodge, III, pp. 595-9.
9. Ibid, pp. 600f.
10. Lewis Sperry Chafer, *Systematic Theology* (Dallas: Dallas Seminary Press, 1948), III, p. 376.

APPENDIX I

RELATION TO PREMILLENNIALISM AND DISPENSATIONALISM

As I have been writing and reviewing the main chapters for this book, I have had a growing impression that a mediate theology of salvation in some way connects with my premillennialism and dispensationalism. I first wondered about this over a score of years ago while reading in Armstrong's *Calvinism and the Amyraut Heresy*, about what seemed to me to be Amyraut's incipient dispensationalism, since he clearly contrasted the Mosaic Covenant with the Covenant of Grace. As I was reviewing chapter 3, page 62 of my book, I realized that Augustine's millennial view of the Church as the kingdom now, led him to extrapolate the truth of God's sovereignty in a way which ignores God's delegation of the exercise of His sovereignty. This harmonized with his view of the union of church and state, which led to the persecution of the Donatists. I have not had leisure to research this, but I will list a number of connections that I have come across for further study. These are only suggestive and tentative.

1. The early church fathers, before Augustine, saw distinct ages in the history of salvation, and they also defended the teaching of free will against the determinism of Manicheanism and neo-Platonism.[1]

2. Augustine moved away from the premillennialism of the earlier church fathers and became the father of both amillennialism and postmillennialism[2] through his spiritualizing hermeneutic. I suspect that this colored his view of divine sovereignty, leading to the idea of God's exhaustive control of all that transpires in the universe. Therefore, since the majority Roman church was virtually equated with the kingdom of God, any professing Christians outside of that church needed to be coerced back into the Catholic Church by the government's power. A coercive God, who saves people by irresistible grace, would approve of the use of coercion in the church.

3. Calvin followed Augustine's amillennialism and state-churchism and thus used the governmental powers of Geneva to impose his brand of Christianity upon all the citizens, even to the point of execution.

4. Calvin's lack of understanding of the full implications of the distinction

between Israel and the church was the basis for his exposition of decalogue as the essence of the Christian life. Michael Eaton, in his experience in Puritan and Reformed practice and thinking, saw this as a reversion to Galatian legalism. My understanding of dispensational teaching is that the New Testament Christian is not under the Mosaic Law, including the decalogue, *as a system* (Rom. 7:6; 2 Cor. 3:3-11), even though we must affirm absolutes of morality from the New Testament "law of Christ" (1 Cor. 9:19-23).[3]

5. Cocceius sought to develop a more historical concept of the covenants of God, in order to blunt the growing determinism of the extreme Calvinism of his day. Unfortunately, the subsequent development of an ahistorical covenant, the Covenant of Redemption, in past eternity, undid Cocceius's effort and solidified the determinism of extreme Calvinism. See my discussion in chapter 18.

6. Perhaps there is a connection between the dichotomizing methodology of Pierre Ramus, which informed Moyse Amyraut's moderate Calvinism, and the tendency of dispensationalists to make significant distinctions in scriptural interpretation, such as, between salvation and rewards, between law and grace, between salvation and fellowship with God, between salvation and discipleship, and between the many dispensations, etc. Armstrong understood that Amyraut contrasted the Mosaic Covenant from the New Covenant of Christ's blood, which is a foundational idea of dispensationalism. Reformed theology tends to blur and/or deny such distinctions.[4]

7. Thomas Boston and the Marrow men of Scotland, in their move away from the legalistic concept of salvation in the Church of Scotland, distinguished the Mosaic Covenant from the Covenant of Grace.[5]

8. Most extreme Calvinists also hold to Covenant Theology and are hostile to Dispensationalism.

9. Although R. C. Sproul's *Willing to Believe* was intended to survey nine different views of sin and grace, his attack on Lewis Sperry Chafer's views ended up being mostly an attack on his dispensationalism.

1. Charles C. Ryrie, *Dispensationalism Today,* pp. 185-7; Forster and Marston, *God's Strategy,* pp. 243-257.

2. Loraine Boettner argued that Augustine was the father of postmillennialism, because he saw the church of his day in the thousand year millennial kingdom then and preparing the way for Christ's return about AD 1000. I have Dr. Boettner's letter in my files. Of course, he was also the father of amillennialism since he believed that the kingdom is now and tended to identify the Roman state church with the kingdom of God, which Roman Catholicism has also tended to do. I hold that most of the New Testament references to the kingdom of God can be understood as reference to Christ's bona fide offer of Himself as King to Israel and to that postponed future millennial kingdom.

3. Calvin, *Institutes*, I, 314-99; Michael Eaton, *No Condemnation: A New Theology of Assurance*, pp. 15-25, 37-161.

4. Brian Armstrong, *Calvinism and the Amyraut Heresy*, pp. 142-157.

5. M. Charles Bell, *Calvin and Scottish Theology,* pp. 151-203.

Behind the shameful apathy and lethargy of the church, that allows one thousand millions of human beings to go to their graves in ignorance of the Gospel, there lies a practical doubt, if not denial, of their lost condition.

-A. T. Pierson

APPENDIX J

THE ONLY LIGHT IN THE DEADLY NIGHT: THE FATE OF THE UNEVANGELIZED

The central issue in understanding the biblical basis and motivation for Christian missions is the uniqueness of Christ and the gospel He gave to His apostles to proclaim throughout the world. If Christ is not uniquely the Savior of the world, then there is little point to Christian missions! If other religions have a true knowledge of God and salvation, then why bother to send missionaries to them? If there is salvation to be found apart from the sacrificial death of Christ, then missions is a tragic mistake—indeed, Christ's death itself was a tragic mistake! So the essential basis of world missions is the uniqueness of Christ and His gospel and the lostness of the unevangelized.

However, with the massive immigration of third-world peoples, our western culture is becoming increasingly pluralistic. In our society we must defer to the sensibilities of not only Roman Catholics, Jews, atheists, and agnostics, but now Muslims, Hindus and others as well. "In a pluralistic world it is becoming increasingly difficult to maintain the uniqueness of the Christian faith." Kane goes on to highlight the problem:

> When we move into the non-Christian world, where the missionary has to operate, we find that the exclusive claims of Christianity are vigorously challenged by the non-Christian religions now undergoing an unprecedented resurgence. It is safe to say that the most offensive aspect of twentieth-century Christianity is its exclusiveness. Such a claim does not make sense to the Hindu, the Buddhist, or the Confucianist.[1]

The problem is not just outside the church. Even among evangelical Christians we find a serious erosion of biblical teaching in this regard. A number of surveys taken over the last twenty years indicate that a shockingly large percentage of Christians do not believe that Christ is the only way of salvation, and that the heathen are lost and will go to hell. A survey of Christian collegians attending the Urbana '67 missionary conference indicated that less than forty percent of the students, who were mostly from secular colleges, believed that a person not hearing the gospel is lost. Although in Christian colleges the picture is much better, there still is cause for concern. Richard Bailey's 1971 study showed that twenty-seven percent in Christian liberal arts colleges and nine percent in Bible colleges did **not** believe that the heathen are lost.[2] My own surveys of freshman Bible college students confirm that the situation has not improved in the intervening years, but has probably gotten worse.

How can Christians hold such views? Actually the problem has a long history. A third-century Alexandrian church father named Origen advocated universalism, which is the view that all men will ultimately return to God and be 'saved.' Over the centuries, however, this view never gained any popularity since his doctrine was deviant in other areas, and this so obviously goes counter to the Bible, the authority of which was not seriously questioned. In the last century or two, with the widespread attacks upon the authority of the Bible, universalism has been revived. Because of the connection between unitarianism (with its denial of Christ's deity) and universalism, the merged Universalist-Unitarian denomination is the major overt representative of this viewpoint. But there are many universalists in the old-line liberal denominations. Even among those who claim a more orthodox theology (Neo-orthodoxy) like Karl Barth, there has been a revival of universalism, which Robertson McQuilkin calls the "New Universalism." But it also is not based upon full acceptance of the authority of the Bible, as might be expected.

But even among those who more consistently acknowledge the authority of Scripture, there are those who, while admitting that not all will be saved, hold that the sincere seeker after truth who has not heard the gospel will not be condemned by God. Robertson McQuilkin calls this the "Wider Hope Theory." Even more recently some have adopted a variant of this, the "New Wider Hope Theory," which states that

> Those who live by the light they have will be saved on the merits of Christ's death. We recognize that this is a more conservative version of the New Universalism. It doesn't say that all will be saved on the merits of Christ, but that some may be saved on the merits of Christ through general revelation, apart from the special revelation of Scripture.[3]

A number of supposedly evangelical scholars have expressed such sentiments from time to time, but without any substantial defense of their viewpoint. It would seem to be fuzzy thinking arising from an emotional reaction rather than biblical fact. More recently Clark Pinnock and John Sanders have written and spoken extensively for this view, calling it "inclusivism."[4] It is very harmful in that it distorts Scripture and seriously undermines the missionary program of the church. Indeed a century ago a missions-minded pastor put it well: "Behind the shameful apathy and lethargy of the church, that allows one thousand millions of human beings to go to their graves in ignorance of the Gospel, there lies a practical doubt, if not denial, of their lost condition."[5] Since this was written a century ago the number has escalated to over three billion, but the root cause of the church's apathy has not changed. So it is imperative that we examine the uniqueness of the Christian faith, the lostness of non-Christian peoples, and the inclusivistic denials of these foundations.

THE UNIQUENESS OF CHRIST AND HIS GOSPEL

When we compare the Bible's statements with other religions, we find that Christ's claims are unique. Christ's person and work are also unique in backing up His unparalleled claims. The nature of the salvation He procured for us has no equal in the religions of the world—nothing even comes close!

The unique claims of Jesus Christ and His apostles

The Lord Jesus claimed to be a unique person. He claimed to have come from eternal existence with God the Father in heaven. He claimed equality with God. He used titles of Himself which are appropriate only to God. He claimed to have the attributes, offices, and prerogatives of deity. He accepted worship as God. The apostles also referred to Him in the same unique ways. Most striking is the title used by the apostle John, which is translated in the Authorized Version as the "only begotten Son of God." The Greek word used here is *monogenes* which means "'in a class by himself,' 'the only one of his kind,' or in other words 'unique.'"[6] The NIV translates it as "His one and only Son."

In addition, Christ claimed to be the only Savior of the world. His most direct statement is in John 14:6, "Jesus said to him, 'I am the way, and the truth and the life; no one comes to the Father, but through Me.'" The apostle Peter confirmed this in his words to the Jewish leaders, "And there is salvation in no one else; for there is no other name under heaven that has been given among men, by which we must be saved" (Acts 4:12). Later the apostle Paul also added his testimony: "For there is one God, and one mediator also between God and men, the man Christ Jesus" (I Tim. 2:5). If people can be saved apart from Christ, then Christ and his apostles made false claims.[7]

Sometimes we overlook the obvious. The astounding fact is that no founder of any world religion even made claims that compare with the claims that Jesus Christ made. Thomas Schultz's statement stands out boldly:

> Not one **recognized** religious leader, not Moses, Paul, Buddha, Mohammed, Confucius, etc., have [*sic*] ever claimed to be God; that

is, with the exception of Jesus Christ. Christ is the only religious leader who has ever claimed to be deity and the only individual ever who has convinced a great portion of the world that He is God.[8]

Although this statement is mind-boggling, it could have been made even stronger. Some of the founders of world religions didn't even have much to say about God at all. It seems that Gautama the Buddha, Confucius, and Lao Tse were essentially agnostics in the sense that they did not claim to know God or concern themselves with Him. Some of the religions, like Hinduism and Shinto, do not have identifiable founders. The two who came closest to a biblical concept of God were Zoroaster (Zarathustra) and Muhammad. Although Zoroaster may have gotten some concepts of God correctly passed down from Noah's day, his teachings were not written down until after Christ and those writings were undoubtedly influenced by the Christian view. In any case Zoroastrianism is a dying religion today with few followers.[9] It is a well known fact that Muhammad borrowed heavily from Jews and Christians and modified the concept of God considerably. In any case, none of them claimed sinlessness, deity, or the ability to save mankind. Even if any had, none of them would have been able to make their claims stick! Only Jesus the Messiah's claims are substantiated by His person and work.

His life supports His claims.

When one makes a careful study of the religions of mankind, one finds that there is no parallel to the person and work of the Lord Jesus. There are over a hundred detailed prophecies of His first coming that were fulfilled in His ministry.[10] Even though Isaac and John the Baptist were miraculously born of aged parents to prepare humanity's minds for the virgin birth, He was the only one in human history born of a virgin. He alone lived a sinless life. He alone revealed a loving, personal and holy Father-God with whom He had fellowship eternally. He confirmed His claims to deity by His unique miracles of love and compassion. God had confirmed the ministry of the Old Testament prophets by wonderful miracles, but none of them compares with Christ's. He alone made predictive prophecies which are continuing to be fulfilled, including a dozen of His own death and resurrection. And then He alone died as a sinless sacrifice for sin, which was sealed by His bodily resurrection from the tomb. His resurrection was not just a restoration of physical life, but His post-resurrection appearances in a glorified body made it unique. He alone ascended into heaven bodily with the promise to return in the same way to establish His rule upon the earth. **Not one of these things can be said for Zoroaster, Gautama the Buddha, Lao Tse, Confucius, Guru Nanak, or Muhammad.**

His unique salvation

The uniqueness of the fall. Just as striking as the unparalleled person of Christ, so also is His plan of salvation. Careful study of other religions uncovers nothing like it in any of its major features. Indeed, we could say that none of the world religions have any plan of salvation at all from sin and the fall. This is understandable since none of them, including Judaism and Islam, have any concept of man as a fallen creature under the sway of sin. All religions view mankind as essentially good, imagining that salvation by God is not necessary. Hinduism's *moksha* (realization) has to do with release from the cycle of life. Gautama the Buddha's *nirvana* (oblivion) has to do with release from the sufferings of life. Zoroastrianism and Islam do have a concept of paradise after death, but it is attained by human merit, not by the work of God.

The uniqueness of grace. This brings us to the key difference between evangelical Christianity and all other religions—salvation by grace. All other religions are based upon human merit, not the grace of God. But grace means 'unmerited favor.' We cannot earn it! Only biblical Christianity teaches that God reaches down to save sinful man. All the other religions see man struggling upward to God. The Sikhs of India use the word for grace (*parshad*) a lot, but they, like adherents of other religions, are striving to please God by their own works. Even the cultic corruptions of Christianity depart from the truth in this essential point, whether it be Mormons, Jehovah's Witnesses, or whatever. Roman Catholics also overwork the word 'grace' but do not understand salvation by grace alone. The Catholic tries to merit God's grace by baptism, confirmation, confession, attendance at mass, good works, and last rites. But salvation is not by human merit: "For by grace you have been saved through faith; and that not of yourselves, it is the gift of God; not as a result of works, that no one should boast" (Eph. 2:8-9).

Forgiveness and assurance. All systems of meritorious salvation undermine two important things: the forgiveness of sin and the present assurance of eternal life. No one can know for sure about salvation as long as it is based upon human merit. Indeed, unless it is claimed by faith in Christ, any sense of forgiveness is a deception. Although various religions differ in details, they are alike in striving to merit God's favor. For example, a tradition of Islam states that when Muhammad was dying, his daughter Fatimah asked him to pray for her salvation. His reply was, "Daughter, my prayer will do you no good! Only your own works will save you!" Muslims deny the cross of Christ and His redemptive sacrifice as a basis for forgiveness. This is typical of all other religions. Erich Sauer has well summarized the confused diversity of man's religions:

> Heathenism as a whole rests not only on error and deceit, but at the same time also on a spiritistic foundation. . . Through all this the heathen, under demon influence, became the "creator of his gods."
> . . .
> The Grecian says : Man, know thyself.
> The Roman says : Man, rule thyself.
> The Chinese says : Man, improve thyself.

The Buddhist says	: Man, annihilate thyself.
The Brahman says	: Man, merge thyself in the universal sum of all.
The Moslem says	: Man, submit thyself.
But Christ says and in HIM	: "Without Me ye can do nothing,"
the Christian says	: "I can do all things through Christ Who makes me mighty" (Phil. 4:13).

"In his religion the heathen expresses his *godlessness.* Religion is **the** sin, namely, the sin against the first command, the replacing of God by the gods;" "the most powerful expression of the opposition of man against God and contradiction within himself."[11]

An historical salvation. Christian salvation is also without equal in being based upon real, historical events that God wrought among men. Most of the oriental religions are filled with myths and legends about their many man-like gods. Shinto has its creation-myth. Hinduism has legends about Krishna and many other deities. We are not sure **whether** Lao Tse even existed. We really can't know **when** Zoroaster lived. But Christianity is a historical faith, based upon what God did in human history in the incarnation, ministry, and passion of Christ and the work of the Holy Spirit through the church. The human authors of the Bible frequently tied their narratives in with secular history. Archaeology can confirm the essential historicity of many events in the Bible. Islam makes the strongest claims of historicity among the religions. That doesn't matter much, however, since Muhammad claimed to be neither God nor Savior. He didn't claim to work any miracles or to have risen from the dead. It is even more astonishing to know that Muslims believe that Muhammad is buried in a tomb in Medina, whereas they believe that the 'prophet Jesus' is in heaven. Paradoxical, isn't it?

ARE THE HEATHEN REALLY LOST?

In order to answer this question intelligently we must first define the term, 'heathen'? The dictionary definition is, "an unconverted member of a people that does not acknowledge the God of the Bible; a pagan."[12] Actually the definition could be broadened to include any unchurched person in any country since there are pagans everywhere.

What do we mean by 'lost'?

People can be lost in many senses—geographically, intellectually, emotionally, etc. But what really counts is what God means by the word 'lost.' The Lord Jesus said that the basic purpose of His coming was "to seek and to save that which was **lost**" (Luke 19:10). The biblical picture is that man is lost in reference to God. The consequences of Adam's fall were devastating: all mankind became separated from God. Not only did Adam and Eve die spiritually when they sinned (Gen. 2:17), but they caused the whole human race to be born spiritually dead and under God's wrath, without hope and without God in the world, and alienated from the life of God (Eph. 2:1-3, 12; 4:18).

Eternally lost. Man is not only lost in that he is presently without God, but apart from Christ's salvation that separation becomes eternal death (Rom. 3:23; 6:23). It is the Lord Jesus Himself who had the most to say about eternal punishment. Herbert Kane well summarizes:

> The Bible clearly teaches that there are two destinies open to man. One involves everlasting happiness in the presence of God and the holy angels (Lk 15:10; Rev 22:3-5; 1 Thess 4:17), the other involves everlasting misery in the company of the devil and his angels (Mt 25:41). The New Testament speaks of two gates—one strait and the other wide; two ways—one broad and the other narrow; two destinies—one life and the other destruction (Mt 7:13-14). In the day of judgment the sheep will be separated from the goats (Mt 25:31-46), and the wheat from the tares (Mt 13:36-43), the good from the evil (Jn 5:29). And in the resurrection there will be a separation between the just and the unjust (Acts 24:15)[13]

Universal spiritual and physical death. The Bible is very clear about the universality of man's lost condition—none are exempted. Paul writes that God's law shuts every person's mouth, that all the world is guilty before God, and that "death spread to all men, **because all sinned**" (Rom. 3:19-20; 5:12). The aorist tense of the last verb is best understood as a reference to the fact that we all sinned in Adam, since the aorist tense looks at the action as a point in past time. The whole human race shared in the sin of Adam and shares spiritual and physical death because of that disobedience, not just because we sin. We sin because we are sinners. People are not becoming lost—they are already lost! "Whoever believes in Him is not condemned, but whoever does not believe stands condemned already because he has not believed in the name of God's one and only Son" (John 3:18 NIV). This is true both of people who reject the gospel and of those who have never heard the gospel. Unless people are saved through Christ, they will stay lost for eternity.

All mankind's need of salvation

The Lord Jesus made it abundantly clear that all men need to be saved. This was true of God's chosen people, the Jews. In commenting on people who had died suddenly and tragically, Christ said, "Unless you repent, you will all likewise perish" (Luke 13:5). Christ even told a very religious Jewish leader, Nicodemus, that he needed to be born again in order to enter the kingdom of God (John 3:5). If that was true of Nicodemus, it is certainly true of pagan peoples. The book of Acts records the conversion of the first pagan Gentiles, the Roman centurion Cornelius and his household (Acts 10:1—11:18). Even though Cornelius had already given up his Roman idolatry and prayed to the true God of Israel, yet the angel told Cornelius that when the Apostle Peter came he would speak words by which they would be saved (11:14). Even though this devout and sincere heathen's prayer was answered, he was not yet saved until he heard the message of salvation from Peter. The inclusivists would have us believe that Cornelius was a "pagan saint," already saved through general revelation. They ignore Cornelius' contact with the word of God through Judaism and Peter's explicit statement that they were to be saved through Peter's message.

On his second missionary journey the Apostle Paul had opportunity to preach the gospel to some very civilized and intellectual Greek philosophers in Athens. Note that universalists rationalize that Greek philosophy was as good a preparation for the gospel as the Old Testament and the inclusivists claim the Greeks had the truth of God through the Greek writers to which Paul alludes. However, Paul told them bluntly that, "God is now declaring to men that all everywhere should repent, because He has fixed a day in which He will judge the world in righteousness through a Man whom He has appointed, having furnished proof to all men by raising Him from the dead" (Acts 17:30-31). Later Paul explained that repentance in a limited Christian context when he described his ministry as "solemnly testifying to both Jews and Greeks of repentance toward God and faith in our Lord Jesus Christ" (Acts 20:21). He did not mean repentance within the context of any pagan religion, but only as it is linked with faith in Christ.

What about those who have never heard?

We have gone into considerable detail to show the clarity of Bible revelation about the universal and eternal nature of man's lostness apart from Christ because these are exactly the points that the various kinds of universalism and inclusivism deny. We have sought to show that God's condemnation comes to all men until they are saved by faith in Christ. It is clear that the universalists and inclusivists have to contradict the Bible to hold to salvation outside of personal faith in Christ. Indeed, they do not hold to inerrancy of Scripture. However, many would raise the valid question, "What about those who have never heard the gospel of Christ and had opportunity to believe and be saved? It isn't really fair of God to condemn them to hell, is it?"

The heathen have a revelation of God. It is not as if the heathen did not have any knowledge of God. The Apostle Paul mentions two kinds of revelation of God that all men have by nature, which we refer to as 'general revelation'. In Romans 1:18-25 he traces the reason for God's wrath falling upon the heathen. He points out that the heathen were not always heathen. They, like all of us, descended from Noah, who knew God. But they suppressed the truth in unrighteousness (1:18), didn't honor Him as God or thank Him, but in pride in their own wisdom indulged in foolish speculations (1:21-22). So generation after generation, they got farther away from the true knowledge of God and ultimately fell into idolatry and immorality (1:23-25) (probably at the Tower of Babel). Indeed, a number of pagan tribes have a tradition about once knowing God and His book, but having lost that knowledge.[14]

Paul also emphasized the fact that all men have been given a revelation of God in nature when he wrote:

> **Because that which is known about God is evident within them; for God made it evident to them. For since the creation of the world His invisible attributes, His eternal power and divine nature, have been clearly seen, being understood through what has been made, so that they are without excuse** (Rom. 1:19-20).

There are a number of impressive arguments philosophers have used for thousands of years for the existence of God. The cosmological argument reasons from the fact that this universe clearly had a beginning and therefore a Creator (Aristotle's "Unmoved Mover"). The teleological argument reasons from design and order in creation to show that there must have been a 'Designer God'. God's hand in creation is obvious to the unprejudiced mind. The more we learn about nature through modern science, the more we see design and order. Most of the Moody Science film series is based upon the teleological argument. But we don't need modern science to see this. King David saw it three millenniums ago: "The heavens are telling of the glory of God; and their expanse is declaring the work of His hands. Day to day pours forth speech, and night to night reveals knowledge. . . . Their line has gone out through all the earth, and their utterance to the end of the world" (Ps. 19:1-4). The heathen "are without excuse," Paul concludes, because they repress the truth about God and don't worship Him.

A second type of revelation is the human conscience—the law of God written on the human heart. Paul argues that men do not have to possess the written law of God to come under condemnation:

> **For all who have sinned without the Law will also perish without the Law; and all who have sinned under the Law will be judged by the Law; . . . For when Gentiles who do not have the Law do instinctively the things of the Law, these, not having the Law, are a law to themselves, in that they show the work of the Law written in their hearts, their conscience bearing witness, and their thoughts alternately accusing or else defending them, on the day when, according to my gospel, God will judge the secrets of men through Christ Jesus** (Rom. 2:12-16).

Although the human conscience is a marred and weak testimony to God and His Law, nevertheless man is responsible for its light. By it all men are condemned as sinners, since no one even lives up to his own conscience. Although God's general revelation in nature and human conscience is adequate to condemn men, there is no hint in the Bible that it is adequate for salvation. General revelation tells man nothing about God's plan of salvation. It is **our** responsibility to tell them. Inclusivists claim that general revelation is adequate for salvation without any explicit Scriptural proof of this notion.

God's holiness and judgment. Those who rationalize away God's judgment on heathen who have not heard usually appeal to God's love. "Could a God of love condemn the heathen?" they ask. But they forget God's holiness and wrath. Yes, God in His love gave His unique Son that whoever believes on Him should not perish (John 3:16). But the Bible has a lot to say about God's wrath and judgment upon sinners. Indeed it was Christ Himself who gave the fullest revelation about God's wrath and judgment (see the Kane quotation above). Remember that God's judgment is not based upon relative merit—as in the Muslim's concept of God's scales. One sin is enough to condemn us to hell. No man, heathen or nominal Christian, can be holy and righteous enough to escape condemnation (cf. Hab. 1:13). The inclusivists totally ignore the mass of Scripture which emphasize God's signal judgments upon mankind, such as the Noahic deluge which destroyed the whole human race, the judgment upon the idolatrous worship of the tower of Babel, the ten judgmental plagues upon the idolatrous worship of Egypt, the order to exterminate the idolatrous and immoral Canaanites, and the many prophecies in the prophets of God's coming judgments upon the pagan nations surrounding Israel.

However, it should also be pointed out that there are degrees of judgment in hell. The moral heathen will not be judged as severely as those who sin against greater light (Matt. 11:20-24). The parallel truth is that for believers there are degrees of reward for faithfulness (over and above salvation, which is by grace). God is fair and just!

Reductio ad absurdum. One useful way to examine the logic of a proposition is called *reductio ad absurdum,* which means reducing it to the absurd. If you start with the premise that only those who consciously reject the gospel will go to hell, you will see how absurd the conclusion comes out. If that were true (and it isn't), then missionaries would be bringing condemnation to most heathen who have not heard. The fact is that the majority of heathen who hear do not believe and get saved. Most reject the gospel. If that majority was not lost before the missionary came, then the missionary would have brought condemnation to more people than he brought salvation to. I was a missionary to a Muslim country. When I preached and witnessed to Muslims, very few accepted Christ to my knowledge. Thus I would have brought condemnation to most all I witnessed to. How absurd the whole missionary enterprise then becomes! Indeed, if many heathen were really seeking for the truth (as some maintain), why don't missionaries experience them believing upon the first hearing of the gospel. The fact is that most heathen (like most western

'Christians') have to hear time and again before they believe and are saved. This shows the effects of sin and depravity. The Apostle Paul spelled it out quite clearly, "And even if our gospel is veiled, it is veiled to those who are perishing, in whose case the god of this world has blinded the minds of the unbelieving, that they might not see the light of the gospel of the glory of Christ, who is the image of God" (2 Cor. 4:3-4).

This brings us to another dimension of the problem—Satanic and demonic involvement. Earlier in this chapter we showed that man's religions are not a help toward God. We must also note that religion is something Satan uses to keep men from knowing God. Paul expands on this: "But I say that the things which the Gentiles sacrifice, they sacrifice to demons, and not to God" (1 Cor. 10:20). Even apostate forms of Christianity are the Devil's tool to keep men from the true knowledge of God. In the Sermon on the Mount Christ put it bluntly:

> **Beware of the false prophets, who come to you in sheep's clothing, but inwardly are ravenous wolves. . . . Not everyone who says to Me, "Lord, Lord," will enter the kingdom of heaven; but he who does the will of My Father who is in heaven. Many will say to Me on that day, "Lord, Lord, did we not prophesy in Your name, and in Your name cast out demons, and in Your name perform many miracles?" And then I will declare unto them, "I never knew you; *depart from me, you who practice lawlessness*"** (Matt. 7:15, 21-23).

Objections answered

Isn't sincerity enough? It is granted that there are many sincere followers of other religions, and from the human point of view it might seem that God would honor that sincerity. The fact is that the Bible gives no hint that God is at all impressed with so-called sincerity. Our God is a God of truth. Other religions do not lead to the One God—they are all false (for further details see ch. 13). Both Cain and Abel were sincere in their worship, but God rejected Cain's offering because it wasn't according to truth. Cornelius, the Roman Centurion, was sincere, but he wasn't saved.

Illustrations of this from the medical world are frequently given. A patient may be given the wrong medicine very sincerely, but may die nevertheless. This is very personal to me because my brother died of polio because of the wrong advice of a doctor. He may have been well trained. I presume that he was sincere in telling my sister-in-law to keep him in bed at home, but he was sincerely wrong! The engineers who built those bridges which collapse in the wind or flood were probably very sincere. But people who die in such tragedies get no solace from their sincerity. If sincerity isn't enough in medicine or engineering, what indications do we have that it is enough in the far more important sphere of man's eternal destiny?

Is it really fair of God to condemn those who've never heard? Our problem so often is that we look at things from man's point of view and fail to see God's perspective—and that's the only one that counts! Remember that God would be fair and just in condemning all men to Hell. We are all by nature children of wrath. It is only of God's grace and mercy that any of us are saved. We with our limited perspective and knowledge may deign to criticize the justice of the omniscient God. But our questions arise from our ignorance of all the facts. But on what basis is man judged? The word of God is very clear: "Now we know that God's judgment against those who do such things is based on truth" (Rom. 2:2 NIV). When God's judgment came upon Sodom and Gomorrah, Abraham's words of intercession for Lot expressed the truth: "Shall not the judge of all the earth deal justly?" (Gen. 18:25)

Doesn't God apply the merits of Christ's death to pious heathen apart from hearing and believing the gospel? Inclusivist writers have suggested the possibility that the heathen might be considered like the Old Testament saints, who were saved apart hearing the gospel. First of all, we should note that the Old Testament saints did believe the promises of the revelation God had given them concerning the coming Messiah. Thus the parallel breaks down, since the heathen do not have such a special revelation. We should also note that not only is there no indication in Scripture that such is the case, but also this would contradict the direct statements of the Bible. Some have misunderstood Paul's statement in Romans 3:25: "because in the forbearance of God He passed over the sins previously committed." However, it is clear that Paul is talking about the sins of Old Testament saints being forgiven in anticipation of the cross (this is clear from Heb. 9:15).

There are many specific Scripture statements which exclude those who don't personally believe in Christ. We have already referred to many of them such as John 3:5,16-18, etc. Christ was even more explicit in John 8:24 when He said, "for unless you believe that I am He, you shall die in your sins." Paul also left no room for doubt in referring to the second coming of Christ: "dealing out retribution to those who do not know God and to those who do not obey the gospel of our Lord Jesus" (2 Thess. 1:8). This is not an easy doctrine. Indeed, it is very difficult! But we must never allow our feelings to dictate what we determine to be truth. Let us just believe what God has said and act upon it.

A Critique of Contemporary Inclusivism

It has been in the last decade that inclusivists like Lesslie Newbiggin, Clark Pinnock, and John Sanders, while claiming to be Evangelicals, have become increasingly vocal about their denial of the lostness of the unevangelized. They are getting a following from many who have not examined their lack of evangelical credentials. My own research has shown, for example, that Newbiggin, while touted as an ecumenical Evangelical, was neither an Evangelical nor a friend of Evangelicalism.[A] There are a number of responses from evangelical writers, who give a more thorough refutation than possible here.[15]

It has been clear for a score of years that Clark Pinnock has moved away from verbal, plenary inspiration of Scripture, and Ramesh Richard has shown additionally that his Christology is very defective[16]. Pinnock, despite his claim to have a high Christology, says that Christ's uniqueness and finality belong to Jesus *only derivatively* and he rejects an incarnational Christology as the norm.[17] Thus the foundation for his doctrine of salvation is exceedingly weak, even heretical.

Richard shows how one of the axioms of Pinnock's inclusivism is his optimistic view of the universal love of God based upon global covenants, like that with Noah, the so-called "pagan saints" outside of Israel before Christ, and God's continuing dialog with the nations. His second "particularity" axiom means that salvation is only through the cross of Christ, even though explicit faith in Jesus Christ is not a necessary condition of salvation. Indeed, salvation is not to be so narrowly defined as merely individual, spiritual salvation from hell, but is to be understood holistically and more corporately. Sanders speaks about the "faith principle" in the unevangelized world, which does not necessarily require explicit faith in the Lord Jesus. They see this exemplified in premessianic believers, like Enoch, Noah, Job, Melchizedek, and ultimately Cornelius, among others. They believe that these "pagan saints" had faith in the general revelation found in nature. Sanders suggests that the restrictive view is not the only motive for missions, and that there are other legs upon which the table can stand: the great commission and the needs of those who have only "implicit faith" (not explicit) and therefore haven't experienced the fullness of salvation we can share with them. There are many other details, but I believe I have fairly summarized their views.

A critique. I have already dealt with many of the issues earlier in this chapter. Additionally, we should note that the inclusivists' weak view of Scripture allows them to be very selective in the passages they treat. Their overly optimistic read on the universal love of God manifest before Christ significantly omits the very obvious judgments of God already alluded to earlier in this appendix. They also fail to take into account the substantial

---

A In 1980 I wrote "An Evaluative Review of *The Open Secret* by Lesslie Newbiggin" (1978), in which I showed his nonevangelical view of inspiration, Christology (many Christologies in the NT), and his almost universalist soteriology. He takes offense at the idea that we can have assurance of ultimate salvation, and carries his concept of "surprise" in the teachings of Christ to lead to the possibility that God is working through athiests, humanists, and Marxists and that they will be "surprised" to be included, while those who presume to think they are in will be surprised to find themselves excluded (pp. 196-8).

special revelation given to the so-called "pagan saints" of earlier dispensations and the passing down of the knowledge of the true God to the descendants of Noah, such as Job and Melchizedek. They were not dependent upon natural revelation alone by any means. Their faith was in the true God, Yahweh, and in the messianic expectation of salvation yet to be provided. As a dispensationalist, I would be quick to grant that they did not all have a clear understanding of the person and work of the Messiah as predicted and promised. Indeed, the prophets themselves searched to understand this salvation (1 Pet. 1:10-11). Charles Ryrie's suggestion is helpful that the content of faith required for salvation necessarily grew with each successive revelation and dispensation. In any case the New Testament clearly testifies that in this present age faith has to be put in Jesus the Messiah **explicitly**. Sanders questions, "A single statement by our Lord Jesus could have settled the controversy before it began."[18] The fact is that He did, and it is in the best know verse in the Bible, John 3:16, as well as a legion of other passages which stipulate that our trust has to be "in Him" (His one and only Son) in order that we should not perish. They cannot separate the objective, historical reality of the person and work of Christ from our subjective appropriation of that salvation by repentant faith in that divine Messiah. To do so is to violate the whole tenor of the New Testament proclamation.

The inclusivists tend to deal with generalities. Let's get specific. What about sincere religious Muslims, undoubtedly millions out of the one billion nominal Muslims in the world today? Muslims believe that to call the 'prophet Jesus' God incarnate is the greatest of all sins, a blasphemy. Therefore, the doctrine of the Tri-Unity of God is also blasphemous. They believe that the 'prophet Jesus' was not crucified, and that to see His substitutionary sacrifice as the basis for forgiveness of sin is heresy. Now what kind of "implicit faith" can a sincere Muslim have which might save him? Or let us consider sincere Hindus, who worship 33 million idolatrous gods and as pantheists deny the personality of God. They worship cobras, monkeys, rats, elephants, and especially cows. Remember what God did in judgment upon the religion of Egypt, where it was frogs, ibises, crocodiles, cats, and especially bulls which were worshipped, which worship was judged in the ten plagues. Or consider the hundreds of millions of Buddhists. At the end of the Congress of World Religions, which convened in Chicago in 1993, as they drew up a joint ethical statement, they had to leave out the word 'God' lest they offend the Buddhists, who do not believe in a personal God. Just who are these "pagan saints" of the inclusivists?

Note: This appendix is taken from *What in the World Is God Doing? The Essentials of Global Missions*, 4th ed., 1998.

---

1. J. Herbert Kane, *Understanding Christian Missions,* p. 105.
2. Richard Bailey, "Missions--Christian Collegians' Concepts," *Eastern Challenge*, 7 (July 1971), p. 3; MARC, *Christian Collegians and Foreign Missions* (1968).
3. J. Robertson McQuilkin, "The Narrow Way," in *Perspectives*, p. 128.
4. Clark H. Pinnock, *A Wideness in God's Mercy: The Finality of Jesus Christ in a World of Religions* (1992); "Toward an Evangelical Theology of Religions," JETS, 33 (1990):359-368; John Sanders, *No Other Name: An Investigation into the Destiny of the Unevangelized* (1992); Sanders, ed., *What About Those Who Have Never Heard? Three Views on the Destiny of the Unevangelized* (1995).
5. A. T. Pierson, *Evangelize to a Finish*, p. 12. Cf. also *The Crisis of Missions*, p. 291.
6. James Oliver Buswell, Jr., *A Systematic Theology of the Christian Religion,* 2 vols. (1962), 1:111.
7. For a good summary of these claims see Henry C. Thiessen, *Lectures in Systematic Theology*, revised by Vernon D. Doerksen (1979), pp. 92-96.
8. Josh McDowell, *Evidence That Demands a Verdict* (1972), p. 92, citing Thomas Schultz, "The Doctrine of the Person of Christ with an Emphasis upon the Hypostatic Union" (Dissertation, Dallas Theological Seminary, 1962), p. 209.
9. John B. Noss, *Man's Religions*, 4th ed. (1969), p. 344. Paul C. Haagen in his chapter on Zoroastrianism in Howard F. Vos, *Religions in a Changing World* (1959), pp. 207-12, naively shows parallels between Christ and Zoroaster, without clarification. He was apparently unaware that Zoroaster had a human father and that the *Zend Avesta* was not written down until centuries after Christ, thus allowing Zoroastrians to invent such comparisons..
10. McDowell, *Evidence*, pp. 147-84.
11. Erich Sauer, *The Dawn of World Redemption,* trans. by G. H. Lang (1951), p. 85 (quotations from unattributed German sources).
12. *Webster's Collegiate Dictionary,* 5th ed., s.v. "heathen."
13. Kane, *Understanding,* p. 130
14. Don Richardson, *Eternity in their Hearts* (1981), pp. 28-120.
15. Ramesh P. Richard, *The Population of Heaven* (1994); Millard J. Erickson, *How Shall They Be Saved? The Destiny of Those Who Do Not Hear of Jesus* (1996); Ronald H. Nash, "Restrictivism," in John Sanders, ed., *op. cit.* (1995); also, Ajith Fernando, *Crucial Questions about Hell* (1991); Larry Dixon, *The Other Side of the Good News: Confronting the Contemporary Challenges to Jesus' Teaching on Hell* (1992); William V. Crockett and James G. Sigountos, eds., *Through No Fault of Their Own? The Fate of Those Who Have Never Heard* (1991); Edward Rommen and Harold Netland, eds., *Christianity and the Religions: A Biblical Theology of World Religions* (1995).
16. Richard, pp. 47-55.
17. Pinnock, *Wideness*, p. 53-62.
18. John Sanders, *No Other Name: An Investigation into the Destiny of the Unevangelized* (1992), p. 19.

APPENDIX K

THE IMPACT OF PHILOSOPHY

I am neither a philosopher nor the son of one. I am an ex-engineer, the son of a carpenter. So I make no pretensions of great knowledge in this area. Therefore, I am dependent upon secondary sources. Experts in philosophy will probably find that my treatment lacks specifics. My comments, therefore, can only be general suggestions as to problem areas for further investigation. I am, however, greatly concerned about the impact of false philosophies upon our evangelical theology and at the same time the lack of simple logic in our exegesis of Scripture.[1]

Although the apostle Paul was well versed in Greek thought, he saw the great danger of Greek philosophy corrupting the simple gospel message he was proclaiming, and he traced the arrogance of some of the Corinthian Christians to their affectation of such:

> **For the word of the cross is foolishness to those who are perishing, but to us who are being saved it is the power of God. For it is written, "I will destroy the wisdom of the wise, and the cleverness of the clever I will set aside." Where is the wise man? Where is the debater of this age? Has not God made foolish the wisdom of the world? For since in the wisdom of God the world through its wisdom did not *come to* know God, God was well-pleased through the foolishness of the message preached to save those who believe. . . . but God has chosen the foolish things of the world to shame the wise, . . . so that no man may boast before God. . . . For I determined to know nothing among you except Jesus Christ, and Him crucified. . . . my message and my preaching were not in persuasive words of wisdom, but in demonstration of the Spirit and of power, . . .** (1 Cor. 1:18–2:4).

Paul's reason for writing the above becomes clear in chapter 15, where it is evident that some false Greek philosophy, probably that of Socrates and Plato, had caused them to deny the bodily resurrection, which he emphasized is central to our faith since it connects with the resurrection of Christ.

Later in dealing with a similar arrogance and speaking about the use of carnal weapons in our warfare, he wrote: "***We are* destroying speculations and every lofty thing raised up against the knowledge of God, and *we are* taking every thought captive to the obedience of Christ, . . .**" (2 Cor. 10:5). Even later as an incipient Gnosticism, which was a syncretism of Christianity with Greek philosophy, was creeping into the Colossian church, he warned: "**See to it that no one takes you captive through philosophy and empty deception, according to the tradition of men, according to the elementary principles of the world, rather than according to Christ**" (Col. 2:8). The apostle John's letters also show evidence of Gnostic influences coming into the churches. These concerns of God's apostles are still extremely relevant to the problems of modern evangelicalism. I am, however, in full agreement with the point that Norman Geisler has made over the years, that we must know philosophy in order to refute erroneous philosophies. We would all have to acknowledge our debt to Aristotle for some of his basic laws of logic without accepting his whole philosophic system. Our problem is with these human systems.

Some years ago I was appalled to stumble across Wolfson's two volumes on Philo of Alexandria in our county library and see firsthand the incredible syncretization of the Hebrew Scriptures with Greek philosophy and mythology by this Hellenic Jew. Indeed, there are indications that centuries earlier the Septuagint translators had the same mindset when they translated the Hebrew *nephilim* (fallen ones) in Genesis 6:4 with the Greek *gigantēs* (giants). This gross mistranslation is clear evidence of trying to read the superhuman gods of Greek mythology into their Greek version. This Alexandrian spiritualization of Scripture also influenced the church fathers, Dionysus, Clement, and Origen. From there a spiritualized hermeneutic spread to Augustine and the whole of medieval theology. Wolfson showed how centuries later it even infected the Muslim scholars' interpretation of the Qur'an and thus came full circle back to medieval Judaism.[2] In the medieval period Muslim theologians went through an extended discussion about the place of Greek philosophy in Islamic theology. I'm not sure that Christian theologians showed equal concern. In any case Gnosticism continued to be a major threat to the churches for centuries (and still is today with the discovered Gnostic 'gospels')

PHILOSOPHY'S HISTORICAL HEGEMONY

Augustine's relapse to determinism

Before his conversion Aurelius Augustine was a Manichean and a neo-Platonist, both of which are deterministic. For many years after his conversion he advocated the free-will views held by the church fathers for the first four centuries, but then sometime after AD 417 he reverted back to the determinism of his preconversion days, but now under the new guise of emphasizing grace.[3] Since he remained a stolid churchman who emphasized the baptismal regeneration of infants, the efficacy of the sacraments, and the restriction of salvation to those in the organized Catholic church, it is hard to understand how grace figured into his newly deterministic theology. Although his understanding of election as unconditional and of grace as being irresistible makes it sound like a gracious salvation, he did not hold to justification by faith alone as God's declaration of imputed righteousness.

Sahakian shows the philosophical roots of his theology: are important to understand. Sahakian states:

> "The psychical and spiritual that had displaced the material and the physical in the philosophy of Plotinus and Origen reached its full systematic development in the philosophy of Augustine. . . . Despite such occasional lack of consistency between Augustine's theology and his philosophy, his views exerted a potent influence not only upon the course of medieval thought, but even upon important trends in modern, including contemporary, philosophy. . . . Notwithstanding Augustine's strong affinity for Platonic and Neo-Platonic philosophy, he severely attacked the Skeptics of the Platonic School, . . ."[4]

Scholasticism's debt to Greek philosophy

I suspect that very few scholars would try to deny that medieval scholasticism was characterized by a heavy dependence upon Greek philosophy and a deductive methodology. McCoy's summary is good: "Scholasticism may be distinguished most clearly by its reliance on philosophy and its characteristic method of deducing a system of thought from one or more fundamental principles. These principles are derived from accepted authority and the reasoning based thereon is buttressed by reference to additional authority."[5] Armstrong identified four tendencies:

> (1) Primarily it will have reference to that theological approach which asserts religious truth on the basis of deductive ratiocination from given assumptions or principles, thus producing a logically coherent and defensible system of belief. . . . (2) The term will refer to the employment of reason in religious matters, so that reason assumes at least equal standing with faith in theology, thus jettisoning some of the authority of revelation. (3) It will comprehend the sentiment that the scriptural record contains a unified, rationally comprehensible account and thus may be formed into a definitive statement which may be used as a measuring stick to determine one's orthodoxy. (4) It will comprehend a pronounced interest in metaphysical matters, in abstract, speculative thought, particularly with reference to the doctrine of God.[6]

Daane described the historical process by which the medieval scholastics, who had only translations of Aristotle and Porphyry, wrestled with the question as to how:

> God the great Universal related to all the particularities of our world? Later the scholastics came into possession of the whole of Aristotle's writing, obtaining them from the Jews of Spain, who had obtained them from the Arabs. With the recovery of these writings scholasticism–getting an assist from the neo-Platonic tradition of Augustine–burst into the theological ferment with which many of the great names of medieval theology are associated.
>
> God continued to be regarded in terms of rationality. For Anselm all Christian truth is demonstrable. Aquinas did not agree, but he did contend that theology and philosophy are not at odds. (By philosophy Aquinas of course meant Greek philosophy as refined and corrected by Christian revelation.) Since both philosophy and theology come from God, they cannot be in contradiction. Aquinas conceived of God as the first cause of all things and the most real and perfect of all beings. Such considerations led him to a view of God's providence as all-comprehensive, and to his view of double predestination. . . .
>
> Sixteenth- and seventeenth-century Protestant scholasticism, which developed the decretal theology of the single decree, had its roots in this medieval scholasticism.[7]

I believe that our investigation will confirm the soundness of Daane's analysis and that we will see that the Protestant Reformation did not end the powerful influence of the various schools of Greek philosophy.

Sources for the classic concept of God

Although Open Theism as a system is unscriptural and borders on the heretical, its proponents have done evangelical theology a service by criticizing what they call the "classic concept of God." John Sanders has given us a most provocative essay in which he traces the roots of the classic concept of God to the philosophies of Plato, Aristotle, and the Stoics and shows how Philo was the bridge from them to the church fathers and then to the medieval scholastics and on to the Reformers.[8] Perhaps it is my philosophical naivety, but I cannot understand how Trinitarian Christians can follow Greek philosophers in affirming the simplicity of God, let alone the impassability of God. Even Calvinist Bruce Ware has very appropriately modified the classic view of the immutability of God.[9] And half a century ago Buswell among the Calvinists led the way in calling for a modification and redefinition of the classic concept of God.[10] I note that many evangelical theologians have not even attempted to defend the simplicity of God, they just ignore it. On the other hand Open Theists are greatly influenced by modern process philosophy, as they readily admit.

Calvin's dependence upon philosophy, legal thought, and Augustine

John Calvin's education was in law and humanistic studies. Although he was on a clerical benefice (scholarship) from the Roman Catholic church until 1534, at least a year after his conversion, he had never really studied theology before he published the first edition of his *Institutes* in 1536.[11] At the behest of his father he had transferred to law in 1528, which suited him since he did not find the scholasticism of theology appealing. The expanding editions of his *Institutes* were all full of multiplied quotes of Augustine, evincing a lifelong dependence upon this father of determinism (36 quotations in the first edition; 342 in the last). No doubt Calvin had read Luther, which probably contributed to his conversion to Protestantism, but Luther, as an erstwhile Augustinian monk, was also highly indebted to Augustine and his philosophy. Luther, however, was hostile to the use of Aristotle in theology, and although Calvin made minimal use of Aristotle compared to the medieval Scholastics, he did make "extensive use of Aristotle and of Aristotelian distinctions." McGrath has suggested a dependence on John Major, and Oberman concludes his careful study of the early influences on Calvin with these words: "In unfolding his biblical theology and in building his institutions, Calvin used a whole range of authors from Augustine to Luther, from d'Étaples to Budé, from Erasmus to Bullinger; and he reflected currents ranging all the way from Platonism to late medieval Scotism."[12] His breadth of reading is commendable, but the last two sources are a concern.

Protestant Scholasticism

Theodore Beza's education was very similar to Calvin's, in law and humanistic studies. However, he was somewhat naive of theology when, because of his connections, he began to serve the Genevan reformation as a negotiator. His ignorance of theology got him embroiled in several controversies as he negotiated with both the Lutherans and the Zwinglians.[13] He didn't understand the differences between their positions on the Lord's supper and his blunders ended his usefulness in seeking to bring about Protestant unity during Calvin's lifetime, or even after. One might say that he learned theology the hard way. But his indebtedness to Aristotelian philosophy is evidenced by his letter to Peter Ramus, who had applied to teach at the Academy in Geneva but was critical of Aristotle's philosophy. Beza made some explanations as to why he could not hire him, but ended the letter with an astounding statement, "I am committed to Aristotle."[14] He did not say, "I am committed to the word of God" or anything similar. To my mind this is 'a smoking gun' in explaining why Beza is the major culprit in the further scholasticizing of Calvin's theology.

Although Armstrong faults Martyr, Zanchi, Beza, de Chandieu, and Danaeus for the Protestant regression to a scholastic methodology, he believes that Beza was the most influential and supports it with extensive documentation: "It was he who was responsible for the return to Aristotelian philosophy as the basis of the Genevan curriculum in logic and moral philosophy."[15]

Alan Clifford 's evaluation of the place of John Owen's methodology and theology among English evangelical successors is most intriguing.

> A number of scholarly studies indicate that beside Theodore Beza, Peter Martyr Vermigli (1500-62) and Girolamo Zanchi (1516-90) were responsible for reintroducing scholastic patterns of thought into Reformed theology. Biblical theology thus assumed a significantly modified character by the late sixteenth-century. *It was expounded deductively rather than inductively, and theory took precedence over the textual data, an approach totally alien to Luther and Calvin.* Through the influence of William Perkins and others, Bezan scholasticism helped English Protestant theologians outgrow their earlier antagonism to Aristotle. . . . [John Owen's] *Death of Death*–an early work–reveals the scholastic influences then in vogue. . . . [It] is typically scholastic in its structure. Instead of providing an exegesis of the relevant scriptural data first, followed by various inferences and conclusions, the order is in fact reversed. Theological arguments are advanced and debated first (albeit with some reference to relevant texts) and the major exegetical discussion follows. There is evidence to suggest that Owen's arguments in the earlier parts of the treatise prejudice his biblical exegesis in the later sections. (emphasis mine)[16]

Moderate Calvinistic reactions

It is an interesting observation of the history of Calvinism that two attempts to hold the line at Calvin's view of general redemption in reaction against Beza's extreme view both ultimately foundered on a problem of logical consistency. John Owen had pressed Beza's view to the extreme in exaggerating the tension between substitution and general redemption by trying logically to eliminate the biblical option. The Marrow Men of Scottish Calvinism moved to a view of general redemption, but in struggling with logical consistency of Christ's death as a substitution for all mankind without going to universalism, ended up with a denial of substitution and the ultimate unjust defrocking of John McLeod Campbell. Campbell's desire to maintain the biblical truth of God's love seemed to contradict substitution.[17] As I delineated in chapter 17, the neo-Edwardsian New Divinity theology of New England faced the same problem. I have already suggested that the resolution is not found primarily in logic, but in exegesis of the usage of the distinct Greek words for the cross. The recognition of the objective/subjective dichotomy in the use of these words is a very simple and logical solution (cf. ch. 5 & 6).

This solution to one logical problem does not, however, remove all the logical inconsistencies of moderate Calvinism. I held to the four-point Calvinism of Chafer and Dallas Seminary for over a score of years, which I am now convinced is essentially the view of Calvin, Bishop Davenant, Cameron, Amyraut, Baxter, and a host of others. However, when I began to see that the doctrines of irresistible grace and unconditional election require regeneration to precede faith, I saw for the first time the obvious deductively derived errors of the whole system. Even worse was the contradiction between the conditional nature of salvation as Chafer biblically developed it (upon faith alone) and the notion of unconditional election. There is an essential clash of logic here. Both Samuel Fisk and Laurence Vance have pointed up the inconsistency of the position, as the extreme Calvinists are quick to emphasize. Fisk's objection is mostly exegetical, but he also points up the logical contradiction.[18]

Norman Geisler has sought to resolve it by suggesting that election is unconditional from God's point of view as the giver of salvation, but conditional from man's perspective as the recipient. This connects with his idea that foreknowledge and predetermination are coextensive and essentially "one in God," based upon the simplicity of God.[19] To my mind this only superficially softens the contradiction. If God has determined to give salvation to a particular sinner without any condition attached to the gift, and then should announce that only those who put their trust in His Son can receive the gift, there is a real problem of honesty both of intent and communication. How can something be unconditional and conditional at the same time? I must hasten to emphasize that my major objection to moderate Calvinism is exegetical and not primarily logical, as spelled out in this whole book. Since it is a hybrid system, its internal contradictions are too serious. Calvin never worked out the internal contradictions, and I suspect no one else can do so either. Why should we try to hang on to Calvin? When he wrote the first edition of his *Institutes* in 1535 he was a new convert of barely two years and only a year out of Romanism, with minimal theological studies under his cap.[20] He did not change his position in succeeding editions. Why have we allowed this theological novice (at that time) to set the whole of Protestant theology for almost five centuries?

ATTEMPTS AT LOGICAL RESOLUTION

Antinomy, paradox, and mystery in determinism

As a new Christian half a century ago, I was given an illustrative resolution of the paradox of divine sovereignty and human responsibility, which is still being circulated today. Over the outside of the gate of salvation is written, "Whosoever will may come," but after we enter the gate and look back, on the inside it is written, "Chosen in Him before the foundation of the world." Such an illustration does not of course resolve or prove anything. Determinists frequently use words like antinomy or paradox to deal with the apparent contradiction between individual unconditional election with its comprehensive determinism and, on the other hand, human responsibility. Frequently they will resort to the word 'mystery' in quoting Deuteronomy 29:29: "**The secret things belong to the LORD our God, but the things revealed belong to us and to our sons forever, that we may observe all the words of this law.**" MacDonald has aptly observed: "Moreover, it is a distortion of the doctrine of election to claim that God's will pertaining to salvation *still remains a mystery* after he has 'made know to us the mystery of his will' (Eph. 1:9), and after 'God has revealed it [his secret wisdom, hidden since time began] to us by his Spirit' (1 Cor. 2:7-10)."[21] It is not just that Calvinism struggles with a mysterious antinomy between God's sovereignty and man's responsibility, but also that the contents and basis of God's elective decrees are so mysterious to the Calvinist.

We would all acknowledge that there are truths in the word of God that go beyond human comprehension, but there is a real question as to whether the tension between these two paradoxical lines of biblical revelation is not made intractable and incoherent by deterministic theology rather than being intrinsic in the biblical teachings. I would not claim that a mediate theology of salvation has resolved all tension, but I would claim that it has reduced the tension dramatically. Certainly mediate theology has eliminated any tension between God's universal love and Christ's full substitution for sinners in the cross. Since election is conditional, salvation also must be conditional. With a proper definition of sovereignty and a recognition of man's free will or limited autonomy, we need not resort to antinomy or mystery. The Spirit's work of convicting the sinner fully explains God's initiative in salvation and safeguards the gracious nature of salvation.

Soft determinism or compatiblism

Compatiblism is an essential concept in defending the coherence of Calvinism. The idea is that God accomplishes all His workings in the world either directly or compatiblistically through human agency. God has ordained the means as well as the end. In resolving the tension between determinism and human freedom, John Feinberg refers to his view as soft determinism (whatever that is?) or compatiblism, "for genuinely free human action is seen as *compatible* with nonconstraining sufficient conditions which incline the will decisively one way or another."[22] This is based upon their understanding of Ephesians 1:11 in the main. Indeed, Feinberg virtually builds his whole case upon this one text.

They give the inspiration of Scripture as an example of compatiblism. There was, it is true, a kind of synergism between the Holy Spirit and the human authors, which guaranteed inerrancy. But since compatiblism is a term used by deterministic philosophers to soften their determinism of all events, some problems arise. Did the Spirit determine every word choice of the authors or did He simply guard them from error? The first option sounds like dictation and eliminates the human element in Scripture. More serious is the extrapolation involved. This is clearly a special case involving godly men. Extrapolating it to all the wicked deeds of godless humans and demons is totally irresponsible.

The crucifixion of Christ is another example usually given, since Peter affirmed both human involvement and God's "determinative counsel and foreknowledge" (Acts 2:23). The use of the term compatiblism implies a determinism and thus God's direct causation of the crucifixion. In this case it is clearly godless men who are the agents. Did God coerce them to do what they did? Non-determinists would focus rather on Peter's reference to God's foreknowledge as an adequate explanation without coercion, which I have discussed exegetically in chapter 7. Going beyond simple foreknowledge to middle knowledge helps even more to understand how God could bring about the cross without coercion. God in His infinite omniscience can manipulate circumstances to bring about the desired end without any coercion of the participants.

The question which needs to be discussed, however, is whether these touted examples of compatibilism can be extrapolated to encompass all activity in human history. These are obviously special cases. A medical researcher would call this evidence merely anecdotal. There must be a more comprehensive study of data, and Calvinists have not adduced any other Scriptural proof of wall-to-wall compatiblism other than their spin on Ephesians 1:11. This I have already discussed exegetically in chapter 3.

A root error of logic and philosophy

It is vital for me to reinforce my discussion in chapter 3 of a fundamental philosophical error which I was taught and accepted for many years until I began using Buswell's text in 1968, which exposed a root error of logic. Boettner argued, as did my professor, that God cannot know that which He has not already determined. Buswell's significant response was:

> *But it is presumptuous for man to claim to know what kind of things God could or could not know. There is a mystery in knowledge which will probably never be resolved for us. . . . For men to declare that God could not know a free event in the future seems to me sheer dogmatism*" (emphasis mine).[23]

I suggest that this error is common to both extreme Calvinism and extreme Arminianism, the open theism view. Since God is *EL OLAM*, the eternal God, He is not limited by the time dimension of the created universe and can easily foresee the free events of the future. The problem with the Calvinists is that they deny that there are any free events in the future since they hold to exhaustive determinism. Even worse, the open theists deny God's foreknowledge.

But I must insist that failure to distinguish the difference between

***certainty* of the future and *determinism* of the future is a simple error of logic and language.** Our eternal God is so infinite in His attribute of omniscience that He surely can know future free events without having first determined them. Any claim that we can limit God's foreknowledge in any such philosophical ways is arrogant. Additionally, it makes an attribute of God (His omniscience) contingent upon something He does (He wills), which is a total reversal. Imad Shahadeh identified this as an error of Islamic theology, but we must root it out of Christian theology. Unfortunately, even the great Jonathan Edwards was among a host who apparently did not see this simple distinction.[24] William E. Gladstone (certainly a brilliant Christian leader) has put it so aptly: "But, surely as vision is a thing totally separate from causation, so is prevision: and *it is a confusion of ideas to mix certainty with necessity*" (emphasis mine).[25]

Perhaps an illustration will help. As I write these words the weather forecasters are certain that a cold front with heavy cells of thunderstorms will arrive this afternoon. How can they be so certain? It is a massive front confronting a hot, humid mass of air, and they can see it on the radar approaching from the west. They did not determine the weather (although at times they talk like they control it). There is a slight possibility that they could be wrong in this case. But our God has far better resources than radar to prognosticate–His omniscience. Indeed, biblical prophecy is very explicit and 100% accurate, both as far as free future events and also for those events which He has determined will happen. Some determinists try to make foreknowledge and foreordination synonymous, but this would be to accuse Paul of a lapse into tautology in Romans 8:29, because he uses two distinct words (cf. ch. 7). So both the determinists and the open theists are in error.[26] Four centuries ago, James Arminius was moved by simple logic to see this most important point as expressed in his disputation with Gomarus. Bangs explains: "One of the principle arguments was that the foreknowledge of God does not predetermine what is known."[27] I suggest that middle knowledge helps resolve the problem since it affirms on a biblical basis the fact that God has knowledge of counterfactuals, which He predicts but clearly does not determine.

Help from middle knowledge

William Lane Craig has been a major modern proponent of the concept of middle knowledge. Not only did he write his doctoral dissertation on it but also a more popular book, *The Only Wise God*.[28] Although this concept first surfaced from the writings of a sixteenth-century Jesuit, Luis de Molina, it has much to commend it in the Scriptures. It was most interesting to note that in the many discussions of Open Theism at the ETS 2000 annual meetings in Nashville, a number of presenters of diverse viewpoints were positive about middle knowledge.[29] Apparently Craig's advocacy is having an impact. Essentially this view holds that God has more than simple foreknowledge, but also a knowledge of future counterfactuals.

The best evidence comes from the account in 1 Samuel 23:6-13 about David's flight from Saul to the walled city of Keilah. David found out that Saul knew he was in Keilah, so he inquired of the Lord as to whether Saul would come down and besiege the city and whether the men of Keilah would surrender him into his hands. God gave him a positive answer to both questions so David and his 600 men fled. Therefore Saul did not bother to come down to Keilah. Here is a clear example of God's foreknowledge of counterfactuals. Another passage appealed to is Matthew 11:20-24, where the Lord Jesus stated that if the mighty miracles He had performed in Galilee had been performed in Sodom and in Tyre and Sidon, they would have repented long ago. This was not just an educated guess based upon His knowledge of the probabilities, but it must be taken as evidence that His omniscience extended to counterfactuals. The apostle Paul also evidenced middle knowledge by the Holy Spirit in his statement of 1 Corinthians 2:6-8 that if the rulers of this age had understood God's previously hidden wisdom of the gospel of Christ, "**they would not have crucified the Lord of glory**." Later in the chapter (2:10-16) Paul affirmed that verbal, plenary revelation which enabled him to speak so dogmatically about a counterfactual.

A chess game is a poor illustration of middle knowledge, but it may help. A chess player has to constantly try to understand all the option his opponent will be considering, even though only one of them will eventuate. The game is built upon prescience of counterfactuals. The chess player with no real prescience is working with probabilities. God, however, has real prescience of both events that eventuate and counterfactuals. This helps us understand how in a general way God can manipulate history to what extent He desires without coercion of the players involved. By virtue of middle knowledge God can work out His plan of redemption of humanity without being a puppeteer, pulling the strings.

If middle knowledge is true, it totally destroys Open Theism, which does not even acknowledge simple foreknowledge. Those Arminians who opt for simple foreknowledge need to get on board with Bill Craig. But if Calvinists continue to argue that God cannot know that which He has not determined, then they also have a serious problem with middle knowledge. Obviously, God has not determined these counterfactuals, since they have not and will not eventuate. According to their reasoning God can not know them. Obviously He does!

Geisler's defense of free will

Norman Geisler, as a very moderate Calvinist, has done an excellent job of defending free will logically and from the church fathers of the first four centuries. Please see chapter 18 for a list of the fathers and chapter 4 for my biblical discussion. Here is a summary of Geisler's arguments:

> Much, if not most, of the problem in discussing "free will" is that

> the term is defined differently by various persons in the dispute. As explained in chapter 2, logically there are only three basic views: self-determination (self-caused actions), determinism (actions caused by another), and indeterminism (acts with no cause whatever). Indeterminism is a violation of the law of causality that every event has a cause, and determinism is a violation of free will, since the moral agent is not causing his own actions.
>
> There are, of course, several varieties of self-determinism. Some contend that all moral acts must be free only from all external influence. Others insist they must be free from both external and internal influence, that is truly neutral. But they all have in common that, whatever influence there may be on the will, the agent could have done otherwise. That is, they could have chosen the opposite course of action.[30]

I will not try to summarize his answers to a number of objections to self-determinism which have been raised, but refer you to his appendix 4.

In his second chapter, alluded to above, Geisler raises the question occasioned by that catch phrase that the late comedian, Flip Wilson, constantly used: "The Devil made me do it." Judas might be able to get away with that excuse, but surely that holy angel Lucifer cannot use it and we can't blame God either for causing him to rebel and become the Devil. Some extreme determinists, including Luther, have attributed Satan's sin to God, but it is contradictory to think that God is causing beings to act in opposition to Himself. An intrinsic attribute of God is His goodness and holiness; He cannot sin, or even look with approval upon sin (Hab. 1:13). **"Let no one say when he is tempted, 'I am being tempted by God'; for God cannot be tempted by evil, and He Himself does not tempt anyone"** (Jas. 1:13). Certainly God created Adam good with free will or self-determination. But then how do the determinists solve the problem of where Lucifer and Adam got the desire for their first sin. Geisler notes that R. C. Sproul call this an "excruciating problem,"[31] but it is such only to determinists who deny self-determination and genuine free will. Geisler continues, "... if the followers of Jonathan Edwards insist on clinging to their flawed view of human freedom, then their God must take the rap for giving Lucifer and Adam the desire to sin."[32] In chapter 17 I have related how many of Edwards' proteges and even his own son moved to a neo-Edwardsian New Divinity view, which greatly moderated his Calvinism. They were right in abandoning limited atonement, but wrong in abandoning substitution in the cross. They should have also scrapped their determinism.

In answering the objection that since God is the ultimate cause of all things, nothing can be self-caused, Geisler makes a very important distinction between the impossibility of a self-caused *being* (except for God) and the possibility of a self-caused *action*. Lucifer's sin is proof of a self-caused action. Sometimes such simple distinctions can be exceedingly important in clarifying these issues. Since God created angels and humans as moral beings with free will and responsibility for their actions, self-caused actions must be a reality in this universe. Remember in chapter 4 how I developed the evidence from the earliest chapters of Genesis that God delegated responsibility to Adam, and subsequently to all mankind, by which He was limiting the exercise of His own sovereignty.

Indeed, Geisler develops the fact of responsibility and man's ability to respond despite the inherited sin nature. All Evangelicals agree "that God holds free creatures morally responsible for their free choices." He references Lucifer, the other angels, Adam and Eve, and all humans since the Fall.

> However, sound reason demands that there is no responsibility where there is no ability to respond. It is not rational to hold someone responsible when they could not have responded. And God is not irrational. His omniscience means God is the most rational Being in the universe. Therefore, reason also demands that all moral creatures are morally free; that is, they have the ability to respond one way or another. . . . logic seems to insist that such moral obligations imply that we have self-determining moral free choice. For *ought* implies *can*. That is, what we ought to do implies that we can do it. Otherwise, we have to assume that the Moral Lawgiver is prescribing the irrational, commanding that we do what is literally impossible for us to do.[33]

I must reiterate that I hold to free will primarily because of the *prima facie* indications of the whole biblical history of redemption, buttressed by exegesis of the doctrinal passages. Geisler's discussion of the logic of it is good corroboration.

Determinism as a massive extrapolation

An alert reader will note how many times I have used the word 'extrapolation' in this book. This is because I am convinced that Calvinism is itself a massive extrapolation of the biblical data. It is "off the chart." In every other area of thought extrapolation is exceedingly dangerous and it is even more dangerous in theology.

1. It extrapolates the sparse biblical data on God's decrees as the basis for a whole system.
2. By ignoring God's self-limitation of the exercise of His sovereignty, it extrapolates the impact of His sovereignty in the world.
3. It extrapolates human depravity to *total* depravity and thence to total *inability* to respond to God's claims and gospel.
4. By ignoring the provisional nature of the cross, it extrapolates its efficacy upon the elect, while restricting it from the "non-elect".
5. By making God's foreknowledge contingent upon His will, it

extrapolates the importance of God's will in the whole of theology, even above His attributes.

6. It extrapolates the biblical/linguistic data for foreknowledge to make it essentially equivalent to predestination.
7. It extrapolates the biblical/linguistic data for preappointment/foreordination to make it predestination.
8. It extrapolates God's effectual calling to be irresistible grace.
9. By assuming that election is individual and unconditional, it extrapolates its significance in the plan of salvation.
10. By ignoring the place of the conviction of the Spirit in conversion, it extrapolates the domain of the new birth to become the cause of faith.
11. It extrapolates the touted examples of compatibilism to all events in the universe.
12. It extrapolates the applicability of Ephesians 1:11 to every event in the universe.
13. It extrapolates the marginal biblical data on election to be the central motif of its theology.

CONCLUSIONS

There is an intellectual appeal of a difficult and labyrinthian system of theology which seems to be based upon the subtle nuancing of certain Scriptures not obvious to the simple reader and upon abstruse philosophical reasonings. This is a point which Dave Hunt makes repeatedly in his recent refutation of Calvinism, *What Love Is This? Calvinism's Misrepresentation of God*. This is why Calvinism has attracted some of the most brilliant minds over the centuries and currently tends to be at the forefront of evangelical scholarship. Many of these subtleties are not accessible to the simple reader of Scripture, nor is their gospel the simple gospel accessible to the babes. Those of us who don't have that intellectual brilliance can take comfort in the prayer of the Lord Jesus: **"I praise You, Father, Lord of heaven and earth, that You have hidden these things from the wise and intelligent and have revealed them to infants. Yes, Father, for this way was well-pleasing in Your sight"** (Mt. 11:25-26). It is not mere fideism to give priority to biblical exegesis and leave the abstruse reasonings to the philosophers. It is being responsive to the warnings of Christ and His apostles.

1. It was a major challenge to me, early in my teaching ministry, to attempt to teach college mathematics. But one of the great assets of the text I used was an extensive section on the relationship of set theory, Venn diagrams, and symbolic logic: Wendell G. Johnson and Luke N. Zaccaro, *Modern Introductory Mathematics* (McGraw-Hill, 1966). This has been most helpful to me in avoiding erroneous interpretations of Bible texts.

2. Harry A. Wolfson, *Philo*, 2 vols.

3. Norman Geisler, *Chosen, But Free*, pp. 161-174.

4. William S. Sahakian, *History of Philosophy* (Barnes and Noble Books, 1968), p. 88-9. I presume that as a secular writer he had no theological axe to grind.

5. Charles S. McCoy, "Johannes Cocceius: Federal Theologian," *Scottish Journal of Theology*, 16:365.

6. Brian G. Armstrong, *Calvinism and the Amyraut Heresy*, p. 32.

7. James Daane, *The Freedom of God*, pp. 153-4. Since Daane served as the editor of the *Reformed Journal*, his appraisal must be given great weight.

8. John Sanders, "Historical Considerations," in *The Openness of God*, pp. 59-100.

9. Bruce Ware, "An Evangelical Reformulation of the Doctrine of the Immutability of God," *Journal of the Evangelical Theological Society*, 29:4, pp. 431-449.

10. Buswell, *Systematic Theology*, , vol. I, pp. 46-64.

11. Robert M. Kingdon, "Theodore Beza" in McKee and Armstrong, eds., *Probing the Reformed Tradition* (Louisville: John Knox, 1989), p. 239; Timothy George, *The Theology of the Reformers*, p. 170, mentions that Calvin began study of scholastic theology at College de Montaigu, but acquired a distaste for the scholastic method and soon left it in 1528 to study law at his father's behest; Heiko A. Oberman, "*Initia Calvini*," in Neuser, *Calvinus Sacrae Scripturae Professor* (Eerdmans, 1994), p.119.

12. A. N. S. Lane, ed. in the introduction to John Calvin's *The Bondage and Liberation of the Will* (Baker, 1996), pp. xxiv-xxvi; Oberman, pp. 121-2, 153.

13. Kingdon, pp 241-243.

14. Theodore Beza in a letter to Pierre (Peter) Ramus, cited by Carl Bangs, *Arminius*; cf. Armstrong, *Amyraut*, p. 38.

15. Armstrong, p. 38.

16. Alan C. Clifford, *Atonement and Justification: English Evangelical Theology (1640-1790) an Evaluation* (Oxford: Clarendon Press, 1990) pp. 95-96. The studies he references are Armstrong, *Amyraut Heresy*, pp. 38ff, 127ff; A. E. McGrath, *the Intellectual Origins of the European Reformation* (Oxford, 1987), pp. 191-6; I. McPhee, "Conserver or transformer of Calvin's Theology? A study in the origins and development of Theodore Beza's thought, 1550-1570", (Cambridge: PhD thesis, 1979) pp. 354ff.

17. John Macleod, *Scottish Theology* (Edinburgh: Banner of Truth Trust, 1946), pp. 145-166; M. Charles Bell, *Calvin and Scottish Theology: A Doctrine of Assurance* (Edinburgh: Handsel Press, 1985), pp. 151-203.

18. Vance, pp. 147-8; Fisk, *Calvinistic Paths*, pp. 49-65.

19. Geisler, pp. 67-68; 52-53.

20. John T. McNeil, *The History and Character of Calvinism* (NY: Oxford, 1967), pp. 107-121.

21. William G. MacDonald, "The Biblical Doctrine of Election," in Pinnock, ed., *The Grace of God*, p. 225.

22. John Feinberg, "God Ordains All Things," in Basinger and Basinger, *Predestination and Free Will*, pp. 24-25.

23. Buswell, I:46.

24. Jonathan Edwards, *Original Sin*, p. 431, cited by James D. Strauss, "God's Promise and Universal History," in Pinnock, ed., *Grace Unlimited*, pp. 246-7.

25. W. E. Gladstone, in a footnote in his edition of Butler's *Analogy*, p. 131, cited by Fisk. *Sovereignty*, p. 83..

26. William Lane Craig, *The Only Wise God: the Compatibility of Divine Foreknowledge and Human Freedom* (Baker, 1987), pp. 31-34.

27. Carl Bangs, *Arminius: A Study in the Dutch Reformation*, p. 253. This was a disputation on July 10, 1603.

28. Craig, *The Only Wise God*; and *Divine Foreknowledge and Human Freedom: The Coherence of Theism* (Leiden: E. J. Brill, 1991).

29. My notes taken from tapes of various sessions indicate that Terrence Tiessen was positive, Dave Hunt seemed quite open to it, and Craig advocated it.

30. Norman L. Geisler, *Chosen But Free*, p. 175.

31. R. C. Sproul, *Chosen by God* (Wheaton: Tyndale, 1986), p. 31.

32. Geisler, pp. 19ff.

33. Ibid, pp. 29-30.

APPENDIX L

THE CHARACTER OF THEOLOGIANS

Over the years, I have been brainwashed to think that *ad hominum* argument in theology is invalid. This derives from the discipline of philosophy, in which the character of the philosopher is deemed to be irrelevant to the validity of his philosophical thinking. Abstract reasoning in philosophy may be totally divorced from the morality of the philosopher. Whether this is true or not, I cannot say. I have some suspicion that the morality of the philosopher does bleed through to his philosophy.

However, I have recently come to the realization that this is an invalid transfer to the discipline of theology. Forty years ago, I struggled with the extensive passages in 2 Corinthians in which Paul defended his own character to that church (1:8-14; 2:17–3:6; 4:7-15; 5:11-13; 6:3-13; 7:2-4; 10:1–12:13). Why was Paul so defensive? We tend to think that there is something wrong with a person who manifests significant defensiveness. As I struggled with this problem, it began to dawn on me that the credibility of the gospel message and Paul's teaching was dependent upon his character. If the false, "super-apostles," who were trying to undermine his spiritual authority with the people in Corinth–if they should succeed, then the truth of the word of God would also be undermined. The credibility of Paul's message is greatly dependent upon his own personal, moral credibility. If Paul was a phony, then his gospel would also be seen as phony! If he did not exemplify the message, then the message itself would be called into question. This is because the message he brought had a strong ethical dimension. His message was a message of a transformed life, and if his life did not manifest that transformation, his hearers had every right to question his message.

This probably explains why, in the last century or so, the liberals have been so prone to attack Paul's character and paint him as having an attack of epilepsy on the Damascus road, and having moved far away from the teachings of Jesus of Nazareth. This is why Gresham Machen felt he had to write *Jesus and Paul*, in defense of Paul and his gospel.

This is why the consistent character of pastors, evangelists, and missionaries is so important. Think of the damage done to the truth of the gospel of Christ by the sins of Jim Bakker and Jimmy Swaggart. Evangelists are characterized by the world as Elmer Gantrys. Why should theologians and Reformers be exempt from such scrutiny?

My point is that the character of the great theological figures, who have molded the theology of western Christendom, is of tremendous importance. In this connection, my historical research for this book has absolutely shocked me–even shaken me. The conduct of some of the great "worthies," such as Augustine and Calvin is absolutely shocking! Before Paul was converted, he was the principal persecutor of the church. Years after Augustine was converted, he became the major persecutor of the very vital Donatist churches of North Africa (cf. p. 402). I suspect that most of us, as Evangelicals, could identify far more with the persecuted Donatists, than with the politically approved, corrupt Roman church, of which Augustine was a leader. But Augustine had many other serious problems of doctrine, practice, and ethics, which can't be swept under the rug.

1. He was first to maintain infant baptism and to attack believer's baptism with the power of civil law (Armitage, *History of Baptists*, pp. 100, 217).
2. He taught that infants are damned without baptism (Berkhof, *History*, p. 256; Schaff, 8:556).
3. He developed the error of purgatory (Armitage, p. 149; Boettner, *Immortality*, p. 135).
4. He held that the first resurrection is the new birth, in contradiction of 2 Timothy 2:17-18 (Walvoord, *Millennial Kingdom*, p. 20.).
5. He held to baptismal regeneration (Schaff, 3:1020).
6. He held to worship of Mary (Schaff, 3:1020-1).
7. He held that Adam and Eve's sin was sex, that sexual intercourse is intrinsically sinful, that procreation is the only justification for sex, and advocated asceticism as the ideal for the Christian life (Forster and Marston, p. 272; Richardson and Bowden, p. 58).
8. He advocated the Apocrypha as canonical Scripture (Westcott, *The Bible in the Church*, p. 184-5).

The major problem of Augustine was with his handling and interpretation of Scripture. This is the root of most of his other errors. He expanded allegorical hermeneutics (Richardson and Bowden, p. 237; Terry, p. 44; Farrar, pp. 24, 235-8). B. F. Westcott wrote: "Augustine . . . was not endowed with critical sagacity or historical learning. He had very little knowledge of Greek, and fully shared the common prejudices which were entertained against a new translation of the Old Testament from the original."[1] Milton Terry says: "Not a few of his theological arguments are built upon an erroneous interpretation of the Scripture text. . . . His Evangelical Inquiries are full of fanciful interpretation."[2] F. W. Farrar is even more blunt:

> The exegesis of Augustine is marked by the most glaring defects. Almost as many specimens of prolix puerility and artibrary perversion can be adduced from his pages as from those of his least gifted predecessors. . . . Old Testament history is throughout treated as an allegory. Poetry and prophecy are similarly handled, till even Augustine's contemporaries were driven to complain. . . . Even the Gospels are not safe from this faithless invasion of predetermined dogmatism."[3]

Forster and Marston have an extensive discussion of the way in which Augustine's faulty hermeneutics affected his theology and led to his persecution of non-Catholic Christians.[4] Dave Hunt has carried this issue a step farther in tracing these errors through the medieval period down to John Calvin. He has two devastating chapters in which he surveys Augustine's influence upon Calvin in his "Irresistibly Imposed Christianity." It is, as I said before, shocking, and I would encourage every reader to acquire Hunt's recent book and read the details for onesself.[5]

I think that if most of today's Calvinists were forced to live under the dictatorial regime of John Calvin in Geneva, they would have second thoughts about their Calvinism. Most are aware of the Servetus execution, and are shocked that Calvin preferred to have him burned at the stake, rather than beheaded. But how would we think, as residents of Geneva, to know that Jacques Gruet was being tortured twice daily for thirty day to get him to confess to having put a placard on Calvin's pulpit, which accused Calvin of hypocrisy. After his forced confession, on July 16, 1547, he was beheaded.[6]

Contrast this with the character of the leaders of the dozen movements which I have listed in chapter 18, pages 406-416, who moved away from the determinism of Augustine and the Reformers. Although I have not emphasized their spiritual and scholarly qualifications, as seen in my sources, I probably have mentioned enough to give an impression. The early Anabaptists, such as Hubmaier and Denck, were outstanding in their moral and scholarly credentials. Philip Melanchthon was recognized as more qualified than Luther as a scholar, and with unimpeachable character. James Arminius, also, had outstanding qualifications and consistency of lifestyle. Johannes Coccieus's scholarship was likewise unimpeachable. The spiritual impact of Spener and Franke, the founders of the pietistic movement is incalculable. The same could be said for Christian David and Zinzendorf of the Moravian movement. My research was much more in-depth into the neo-Edwardsian, New Divinity movement of the Second Great Awakening and its impact upon the genesis of American foreign missions. I have been astonished at the incredible impact of one unheralded man, Edward D. Griffin. He and his mentors, associates, and disciples, were soul-winners, evangelists, and pioneer missionaries, as well as manifesting substantial scholarly qualifications. These men practiced what they preached. As I have pointed out many times in this book, when the Lord Jesus warned, "**So then, you will know them by their fruits**" (Mt. 7:20), He was referring to religious teachers, and this applies to this whole situation.

---

1. B. F. Westcott, *The Bible in the Church*, pp. 184-5, cited by Fisk, *Calvinistic Paths*, p. 96.
2. Milton S. Terry, *Biblical Hermeneutics*, rev. ed. (NY: Eaton & Mains, 1890), p. 44.
3. F. W. Farrar, *The History of Interpretation* (NY: Dutton, 1886), p. 235-8, cited by Fisk, *Calvinistic Paths*, p. 97.
4. Forster and Marston, *God's Strategy in Human History*, (Minneapolis: Bethany House, 1973), pp. 257-95.
5. Dave Hunt, *What Love Is This?* (Sisters, OR: Loyal Publishing, 2002), pp. 45-74.
6. Philip Schaff, *History of the Christian Church*, II, p. 502; George Park Fisher, *The Reformation*, p. 22.

Scripture Index

SUBJECT INDEX

SELECTED BIBLIOGRAPHY

Alexander, Archibald (1772-1851). *Thoughts on Religious Experience.* Carlisle, PA: Banner of Truth, 1967 repr.
Alexander, W. Lindsay. *A System of Biblical Theology.* 1888.
Alford, Henry. *The Greek Testament.* Chicago: Moody, 1958.
Allen, Ronald B. *The Majesty of Man: The Dignity of Being Human.* rev. ed. GR: Kregel, 2000.
Anderson, Sir Robert. *The Gospel and its Ministry.* GR: Kregel, 1978.
_________. *Redemption Truths.* GR: Kregel, 1980 (reprint).
Andrew, Brother. *And God Changed His Mind . . . Because His people dared to ask.* Tarrytown: Revell, 1990.
Arminius, James. *The Works of James Arminius,* trans. James & William Nichols, 3 vols. GR: Baker, 1986.
Armstrong, Brian G. *Calvinism and the Amyraut Heresy: Protestant Scholasticism and Humanism in Seventeenth-Century France.* Madison: Univ. of Wisconsin Press, 1969.
Bakker, Jim. *I Was Wrong.* Nashville: Thomas Nelson, 1996.
Bangs, Carl O. *Arminius : A Study in the Dutch Reformation,* 2nd ed. GR: Zondervan, 1985.
Barnes, Albert. *The Atonement.* Minneapolis: Bethany Fellowship, reprint of 1860.
Basinger, David and Basinger, Randall, eds. *Predestination and Free Will: Four Views of Divine Sovereignty and Human Freedom.* Downers Grove, IL: InterVarsity, 1986.
Baxter, Richard. *The Practical Works of Richard Baxter: Select Treatises.* GR: Baker, 1981.
Beaver, R. Pierce. *Pioneers in Mission.* GR: Eerdmans, 1966.
_________. *To Advance the Gospel.* GR: Eerdmans, 1967.
Beilby, James K. and Eddy, Paul R. eds. *Divine Foreknowledge: Four Views.* Downers Grove: InterVarsity, 2001.
Bell, M. Charles Bell. *Calvin and Scottish Theology :Theologyof Assurance.* Edinburgh: Handsel Press, 1985.
Berkhof, L. *Systematic Theology.* GR: Eerdmanns, 1953.
Berkouwer, G. C. *Faith and Justification.* GR: Eerdmans, 1954.
Best, W. E. *Justification before God (Not by Faith).* Houston: W. E. Best Book Missionary Trust, n. d.
Bierma, Lyle D. *German Calvinism in the Confessional Age.* GR, Baker Book, 1997.
Bloesch, Donald G. *Essentials of Evangelical Theology,* 3 vols. Peabody, MA: Prince Press, 1982.
Boer, Harry R. *Pentecost and Missions.* GR: Eerdmans, 1961.
Boettner, Loraine. *The Reformed Faith.* Phillipsburg: Presbyterian & Reformed, 1983.
_________. *The Reformed Doctrine of Predestination,* 5th ed. GR: Eerdmans, 1941.
Boice, James Montgomery. *Awakening to God.* Downers Grove, IL: InterVarsity Press, 1979.
Brown, Colin. ed. *The New International Dictionary of New Testament Theology,* 3 vols. GR: Zondervan,1967.
Bryson, George L. *The Five Points of Calvinism.* Costa Mesa, CA: The Word for Today, 1996.
Buswell, Jr., James Oliver. *A Systematic Theology of the Christian Religion.* Grand Rapids: Zondervan, 1962.
Cairns, Earle E. *Christianity Through the Centuries: A History of the Christian Church.* GR: Zondervan, 1996.
Calvin, John. *Institutes of the Christian Religion,* trans. By Henry Beveridge. GR: Eerdmans, 1964.
_________. *Commentaries,* trans. William Pringle, 22 vols. GR: Baker, 1979 reprint.
Caragounis, Chrys C. *Peter and the Rock.* Berlin: DeGruyter, 1990.
Carson, D. A. *Exegetical Fallacies.* Grand Rapids: Baker, 1984.
_________. *The Difficult Doctrine of the Love of God.* Wheaton: Crossway, 2000.
_________. *Divine Sovereignty and Human Responsibility: Biblical Perspectives in Tension.* GR: Baker, 1994.
Carson, D. A., Moo, Douglas, and Morris, Leon. *An Introduction to the New Testament.* GR: Zondervan, 1992.
Carson, D. A. and Woodbridge, John D. eds., *Hermeneutics, Authority and Canon.* GR:Academie, 1986
Chafer, Lewis Sperry. *Systematic Theology,* 8 vols. Dallas: Dallas Seminary Press, 1947.
Chantry, Walter. *Today's Gospel: Authentic or Synthetic?* London: Banner of Truth, 1970.
Clark, Gordon H. *The Atonement,* 2nd ed. Jefferson: The Trinity Foundation, 1987.
_________. *Predestination.* Phillipsburg, NJ: Presbyterian and Reformed, 1987.
Clifford, Alan C. *Atonement and Justification: English Evangelical Theology (1640-1790) an Evaluation.* Oxford: Clarendon, 1990.
Cocoris, G. Michael. *Lordship Salvation—Is It Biblical?* Dallas: Redencion Viva, 1983.
Conforti, Joseph A. *Samuel Hopkins and the New Divinity Movement.* GR: Eerdmans, 1981.
Craig, William Lane. *The Only Wise God: The Compatibility of Divine Foreknowledge and Human Freedom.* Baker, 1987.
_________. *Divine Foreknowledge and Human Freedom: The Coherence of Theism* (Leiden: E. J. Brill, 1991.

__________. *Time and Eternity: Exploring God's Relationship to Time.* Wheaton: Crossway, 2001.
Crampton, W. Gary. *What Calvin Says.* Jefferson, MD: Trinity Foundation, 1992.
Custance, Arthur C. The Sovereignty of Grace. GR: Baker, 1979.
Daane, James. *The Freedom of God: A Study of Election and Pulpit.* GR: Eerdmans, 1973.
Daille, Jean. *A Treatise on the Right Use of the Fathers* (1631), trans.T. Smith. Philadelphia: Presby Board,1842.
Davenant, John. *The Death of Christ*, ed. Allport. London, 1832.
Davis, Walter Bruce. *William Carey: Father of Modern Missions.* Chicago: Moody,1963.
Demarest, Bruce. *The Cross and Salvation: The Doctrine of Salvation.* Wheaton: Crossway, 1997.
Derickson, Gary and Radmacher, Earl. *The Disciplemaker: What Matters Most to Jesus.* Salem, Charis, 2001.
Dillow, Joseph C. *The Reign of the Servant Kings.* Miami Springs: Schoettle Pub., 1992
Douty, Norman F. *The Death of Christ.* Irving, TX: Williams & Watrous Publishing, 1978
Dowley, Tim. *Eerdmans Handbook to the History of Christianity.* GR: Eerdmans, 1977.
Dunning, H. Ray. *Reflecting the Divine Image: Christian Ethics in Wesleyan Perspective.* InterVarsity, 1998.
Duty, Guy. *If Ye Continue: A Study of the Conditional Aspects of Salvation.* Minneapolis: Bethany House, 1966.
Eaton, Michael. *No Condemnation: A New Theology of Assurance.* Downers Grove, IL: InterVarsity Press, 1995
Elwell, Walter A. ed. *Evangelical Dictionary of Theology.* GR: Baker, 1984.
Enns, Paul. *The Moody Handbook of Theology.* Chicago: Moody Press, 1972.
Erickson, Millard J. *Christian Theology*, 3 vols. GR: Baker, 1983
Esposito, John L., ed. *The Oxford History of Islam.* NY: Oxford Univ. Press, 1999
Estep, William R. *The Anabaptist Story: An Introduction to Sixteenth-Century Anabaptism.* GR: Eerdmans, 1996.
Feinberg, John S. *No One Like Him: The Doctrine of God.* Wheaton: Crossway, 2001.
Fisk, Samuel. *Divine Sovereignty and Human Freedom.* rev. ed. Eugene, OR, Wipf and Stock, 2002.
__________. *Calvinistic Paths Retraced,* Murphreesboro, TN: Biblical Evangelism Press, 1985.
Fletcher, Richard . *The Barbarian Conversion: from Paganism to Christianity.* NY: Henry Holt, 1997
Forster, Roger T. and Marston, V. Paul. *God's Strategy in Human History.* Minneapolis Bethany House, 1973.
Fuller, Andrew Gunton. ed. *The Complete Wordks of Andrew Fuller*, 2 vols. Boston: Lincoln, Edmands, 1833.
Geisler, Norman L. *Chosen But Free.* Minneapolis: Bethany House, 1999.
George, Timothy. *The Theology of the Reformers.* Nashville: Broadman, 1988.
Gerstner, John H. *A Primer on Dispensationalism.* Phillipsburg, NJ: Presbyterian & Reformed, 1982.
__________. *Wrongly Dividing the Word of Truth.* Brentwood, TN:Wolgemuth & Hyatt, 1991.
Gray, Janet Glenn. *The French Huguenots: Anatomy of Courage.* GR: Baker, 1981.
Grudem, Wayne. *Systematic Theology: An Introduction to Biblical Doctrine.* GR: Zondervan, 1994.
Hageman, Howard G. *Predestination.* Phila.: Fortress, 1963
Harrison, Everett F. *Baker's Dictionary of Theology.* GR: Baker, 1960.
Hawthorne and Winter. *Perspectives of the World Christian Movement*, rev. ed.Pasadena, CA: USCWM, 1992.
Heard, J. B. *The Tripartite Nature of Man: Spirit, Soul, and Body.* Edinburg: T. & T. Clark, 1866.
Heick, O. W. and Neve, J. L. *A History of Christian Thought*, 2 vols. Phila.: Muhlenberg, 1946.
Helm, Paul. *The Providence of God.* Downers Grove, IL: InterVarsity, 1993.
Henry, Carl F. H. *Christian Personal Ethics.* Eerdmans, 1957.
Hesselgrave, David J. *Communicating Christ Cross-Culturally.* GR: Zondervan, 1978.
Hewitt, John H. *Williams College and Foreign Missions.* Boston: Pilgrim Press, 1914.
Hodge, Archibald A. *The Atonement*, GR: Baker, 1974 reprint (1867).
Hodge, Charles. *Systematic Theology*, 3 vols. GR: Eerdmanns, 1968 reprint.
Hodges, Zane C. Hodges, *The Hungry Inherit.* Chicago: Moody, 1972.
__________. *Absolutely Free* GR: Zondervan, 1989.
__________. *Harmony With God.* Dallas: Redencion Viva, 2001.
__________. *The Gospel Under Siege: A Study on Faith and Works.* Dallas: Redencion Viva, 1981.
Hoekema, Anthony A. *Saved by Grace.* GR: Eerdmans, 1989.
Hoitenga, Dewey J., Jr. *John Calvin and the Will.* GR: Baker, 1997.
Hopkins, Mark. *A Discourse occasioned by the death of Rev. Edward Dorr Griffin.* Tuttle, Belcher, Burton, 1837.
Hull, J. Mervin. *Judson the Pioneer.* Phila.: American Baptist Publications, 1913.
Hunt, Dave. *What Love Is This? Calvinism's Misrepresentation of God.* Sisters, OR: Loyal, 2002.
Ironside,H. A. *Holiness: the False and the True.* Neptune, NJ: Loizeaux Bros.
Jenkins, Philip. *The Next Christendom: The Coming of Global Christianity.* Oxford: Oxford Univ. Press, 2002.
Jewett, Paul K. *Election and Predestination.* GR: Eerdmans, 1985.
Judson, Edward. *The Life of Adoniram Judson.* New York: Randolph, 1883.
Kaiser, Walter C., Jr. *Toward an Old Testament Theology.* GR: Zondervan, 1978.

__________. *Toward an Exegetical Theology*. GR: Baker, 1981.
Kane, Herbert J. *A Concise History of the Christian World Mission*. GR: Baker, 1978.
__________. *Understanding Christian Missions*. GR: Baker, 1974, 1982.
Kendall, R. T. *Calvin and English Calvinism to 1649*, 2nd ed. Carlisle, Cumbria, UK: Paternoster Press, 1997.
__________. *Once Saved, Always Saved*. Chicago: Moody, 1985
Klein, William W. *The New Chosen People*. GR: Zondervan, 1990.
Kuiper, R. B. *For Whom Did Christ Die? A Study of the Divine Design of the Atonement*. GR: Baker, 1959.
Ladd, George Eldon. *A Theology of the New Testament*. Eerdmans, 1974.
Lane, A. N. S., ed. Introduction to John Calvin's *The Bondage and Liberation of the Will* .Baker, 1996.
Latourette, Kenneth Scott, *A History of Christianity*. NY: Harper & Row, 1953.
Lewis, Gordon R. and Demarest, Bruce A. *Integrative Theology*. Grand Rapids: Zondervan, 1990.
Lightner, Robert P. *The Death Christ Died*. Des Plaines, IL: Regular Baptist Press, 1967.
__________. *Sin, the Savior, and Salvation: The Theology of Everlasting Life*. Nashville: Nelson, 1991.
Lovelace, Richard F. *The American Pietism of Cotton Mather*. Christian University Press, 1979.
Luther, Martin. *Sammtliche Schriften*, 2d ed., ed. Joh. Georg Walch. St. Louis: Concordia, 1880-1910.
__________. *The Bondage of the Will, trans.* J. I. Packer & O. R. Johnston. Old Tappan, NJ: Revell, 1957.
__________. *Martin Luther's Basic Theological Writings*, ed. Timothy F. Lull. Minneapolis: Fortress, 1989.
MacArthur, John F., Jr. *The Gospel According to Jesus*. GR: Zondervan, 1988.
__________. *Faith Works: The Gospel According to the Apostles*. Dallas: Word, 1993.
Macleod, John. *Scottish Theology*. Edinburgh: Banner of Truth Trust, 1946.
McClain, Alva J. The Greatness of the Kingdom. Chicago: Moody, 1 959.
McDonald, H. D. *The Christian View of Man* Wheaton: Crossway, 1981.
__________. *The Atonement of the Death of Christ: In Faith, Revelation, and History*. GR: Baker, 1985
McGrath, Alister E. *Institia Dei: A History of the Christian Doctrine of Justification: English Evangelical Theology (1640-1790) an Evaluation* Oxford, 1987.
McKee, Elsie Anne and Armstrong, Brian G., eds. *Probing the Reformed Tradition*. Louisville: John Knox, 1989
McNeil, John T. *The History and Character of Calvinism*. NY: Oxford, 1967
Marshall, I. Howard. *Kept by the Power of God*, 3rd ed. Carlisle, UK: Paternoster, 1995.
Mell, Patrick H. *A Southern Baptist Looks at Predestination*. Cape Coral: Christian Gospel Foundation, n.d.
Moody, Dale, *The Word of Truth*. GR: Eerdmans, 1981.
Morris, Leon. *The Apostolic Preaching of the Cross*, 3rd ed. GR: Eerdmans, 1965.
Murray, Iain. *The Puritan Hope: Revival and the Interpretation of Prophecy*. London: Banner of Truth, 1975.
__________. *Spurgeon v. Hyper-Calvinism: The Battle for Gospel Preaching*. Carlisle: Banner of Truth,1995.
Murray, John. *Redemption: Accomplished and Applied*. GR: Eerdmans, 1955.
Nash, Ansel. *Memoir of Edward Dorr Griffin*. New York, Benedict, 1842.
Nash, Ronald H. *Life's Ultimate Questions: An Introduction to Philosophy*. GR: Zondervan, 1999.
Neuser, Wilhelm H. ed. *Calvinus Sacrae Scripturae Professor*. Eerdmans, 1994.
Newman, Albert Henry. *A Manual of Church History*, 2 vols. Phila.: American Baptist, 1899.
Nettleton, David. *Chosen to Salvation*. Schaumburg, IL: Regular Baptist Press, 1983.
Noll, Mark A. *The Old Religionin a New World: The History of North American Christianity*. Eerdmans, 2002.
Nichols, James. *Calvinism and Arminianism*, 2 vols. London: Longmans, et al, 1824.
Olsen, Viggo B. *Daktar: Diplomat in Bangladesh*. Chicago: Moody Press, 1973.
Olson, C. Gordon. *What in the World Is God Doing? The Essentials of Global Missions* , 4th ed., 1998.
Olson, Roger E. *The Story of Christian Theology: Twenty Centuries of Tradition & Reform*. InterVarsity, 1999.
Orr, James, ed. *The International Standard Bible Encyclopedia*, 5 vols. GR: Eerdmans, 1955.
Owen, John. *The Death of Death in the Death of Christ*. Carlisle: Banner of Truth, 1959 reprint (1852).
Packer, J. I. *Evangelism and the Sovereignty of God*. Chicago: IVP, 1961
Packer, J. I. & Johnston, O. R. "Introduction ," in Luther's *Bondage of the Will*. Revell, 1957.
Paine, Gustavus S. *The Men Behind the King James Version*. GR: Baker, 1977.
Palmer, Edwin H. *The Five Points of Calvinism in the Light of Scripture*. GR: Guardian Press, 1972.
Park, Edwards A., ed. *The Atonement, Discourses and Treatises by Jonathan Edwards, John Smalley, Jonathan Maxcy, Nathanael Emmons, Edward D. Griffin, Caleb Burge, and William R. Weeks*. Boston: Congregational Board of Publications, 1859
Pearse, Meic. *The Great Restoration: The Religious Radicals of the 16th and 17th Centuries*. Paternoster, 1998.
Peters, George W. *A Biblical Theology of Missions*. Chicago: Moody Press, 1972
Pfeiffer, Charles F., Vos, Howard F., and Rea, John, eds. *Wycliffe Bible Encyclopedia*,2 vols. Moody, 1975.
Pink, Arthur W. *The Satisfaction of Christ*. GR: Zondervan, 1955.

__________. *The Sovereignty of God.* rev. ed. Carlisle, PA: Banner of Truth, 1961.
__________. *Eternal Security.* GR: Baker, 1974.
__________. *Gleanings from the Scriptures: Man's Total Depravity.* Chicago: Moody Press, 1969.
Pinnock, Clark H., ed. *The Grace of God, The Will of Man: A Case for Arminianism.* GR: Zondervan, 1989.
__________. ed. *Grace Unlimited.* Minneapolis: Bethany, 1975.
Pinson, J. Matthew, ed. *Four Views on Eternal Security.* GR: Zondervan, 2002.
Piper, John. *The Justification of God,* 2nd ed. GR: Baker, 1993.
Radmacher, Earl D. *What the Church Is All About: A Biblical and Historical Study.* Chicago: Moody Press, 1978.
__________. *Salvation.* Nashville: Word, 2000
Rice, John R. *Predestined for Hell? No!* Murfreesboro, TN: Sword of the Lord, 1958.
Richards, James. *Lectures on Mental Philosophy and Theology* (1846)
Ryle, J. C. *Expository Thoughts on the Gospels.* NY: Robert Carter, 1875.
Ryrie, Charles C. *Basic Theology.* Wheaton: Victor, 1986.
__________. *Dispensationalism Today,* rev. ed. Chicago: Moody, 1995.
__________. *So Great Salvation: What It Means to Believe In Jesus Christ.* Wheaton: Victor, 1989.
Sahakian, William S. *History of Philosophy.* Barnes and Noble Books, 1968
Sauer, Erich *The Dawn of World Redemption: A Survey of Historical Revelation in the Old Testament.* London: Paternoster, 1951.
__________. The Triumph of the Crucified. GR: Eerdmans, 1951.
Seaton, W. J. *The Five Points of Calvinism.* Edinburgh: Banner of Trusth, 1970.
Schaff, Philip. *History of the Christian Church,* 8 vols. GR: Eerdmans, 1985 [1910].
Schaff-Herzog Encyclopedia
Schreiner, Thomas R. & Ware, Bruce, eds. *The Grace of God/ The Bondage of the Will,* 2vols. GR: Baker, 1995.
Shank, Robert. *Life in the Son.* Springfield, MO: Westcott, 1960.
__________. *Elect in the Son.* Springfield, MO: Westcott, 1970.
Shedd, W. G. T. *Dogmatic Theology.* Nashville: Thomas Nelson, 1980 reprint.
Shelley, Bruce L. *Evangelicalism in America. Eerdmans, 1967.*
Shelton, Dan O. *Heroes of the Cross in America.* NY: Young People's Missionary Movement, 1904.
Spencer, Duane Edward. *TULIP: The Five Points of Calvinism in the Light of Scripture.* GR: Baker, 1979.
Sproul, R. C. *Willing to Believe: The Controversy over Free Will.* Grand Rapids: Baker, 1997.
__________. *Grace Unknown: the Heart of Reformed Theology.* GR: Baker, 1997.
__________. *Faith Alone: The Evangelical Doctrine of Justification.* GR: Baker, 1995.
__________. *Chosen by God.* Wheaton: Tyndale, 1986.
__________. *Getting the Gospel Right.* GR: Baker Books, 1999.
Stanley, Charles. *Eternal Security: Can You Be Sure?* Nashville: Nelson, 1990.
Steele, David N. & Thomas, Curtis C. *The Five Points of Calvinism.* Presby. & Reformed,1963.
Stein, Robert H. *Difficult Passages in the New Testament.* Grand Rapids: Baker, 1990.
Storms, C. Samuel *Chosen for Life.* GR: Baker, 1987.
Strobel, Lee. *The Case for Faith.* GR: Zondervan, 2000.
Strombeck, John F. *Shall Never Perish.* Moline, IL: Strombeck Agency, 1936.
Strong, Augustus Hopkins. *Systematic Theology,* 2nd ed. Philadelphia: Judson Press, 1906
Sumner, Robert L. *An Examination of TULIP.* Murphreesboro, TN: Biblical Evangelism Press, 1972
Sweet, William Warren, *The Story of Religion in America.* NY: Harper, 1930.
Tenney, Merrill C. ed. *The Zondervan Pictorial Encyclopedia of the Bible. 5 vols.* GR: Zondervan, 1975.
Thiessen, Henry C. *Lectures in Systematic Theology.* GR: Eerdmans, 1949.
Tiessen, Terrance. *Providence and Prayer: How Does God Work in the World?* Downers: InterVarsity, 2000.
Tidball, Derek. *The Message of the Cross.* Downers Grove: InterVarsity, 2001.
Tuttle, Robert G., Jr. *John Wesley: His Life and Theology.* GR: Zondervan, 1978.
Underwood, A. C. *A History of the English Baptists.* London: Baptist Union, 1970.
Vance, Laurence M. *The Other Side of Calvinism.* Pensacola: Vance Publications, 1991.
Vos, Geerhardus. *Biblical Theology: Old and New Testaments.* GR: Eerdmans,
Vos, Howard F. *Religions in A Changing World.* Chicago: Moody, 1959.
Walvoord, John F. *Jesus Christ, Our Lord.* Chicago: Moody, 1969.
__________. *The Holy Spirit.* Wheaton: Van Kampen Press, 1954.
Warfield, B. B. *The Plan of Salvation.* Eerdmans, 1935.
__________. *Calvin and Augustine,* ed. Samuel Craig. Phila.: Presbyterian & Reformed, 1956.
Warneck, Gustav. *Outline of a History of Protestant Missions.* trans. by George Robson. NY: Revell, 1901.

Warns, Johannes. *Baptism: Studies in the Original Christian Baptism,* trans. G. H. Lang. Paternoster,1957.
Wayland, Francis. *Memoir of Judson.* Boston: Philips and Sampson, 1853.
White, James R. *The Potter's Freedom.* Amityville, NY: Calvary Press, 2000.
Wiley, H. Orton. *Christian Theology.* Kansas City, MO: Beacon Hill, 1952.
Wilkin, Robert N. *Confident in Christ: Living by Faith Really Works.* Irving, TX: Grace Evangelical Soc., 1999.
Wills, Garry. *Saint Augustine.* NY: Viking Penguin, 1999.
Wolfson, Harry Austryn. *Philo: Foundations of R eligious Philosophy in Judaism, Christianity, and Islam,* 2 vols. Harvard Press, 1947.
Woodbridge, John D. ed. *Great Leaders of the Christian Church.* Chicago: Moody, 1988.
Woodbridge,John D., Noll, Mark. A., and Hatch, Nathan O. *The Gospel in America.* Zondervan, 1979.
Woodbridge, John D. and McComiskey, Thomas E., eds. *Doing Theology in Today's World.* Zondervan, 1991.
Wright, R. K. McGregor. *No Place for Sovereignty: What's Wrong with Freewill Theism.* InterVarsity, 1996.
Zanchius, Jerom. *The Doctrine of Absolute Predestination.* GR: Baker Books, 1977.

COMMENTARIES:
Alford, Henry. *The Greek Testament.* orig. 4 vols. Chicago: Moody, 1958 [1849].
Gundry, Robert H. *Matthew: A Commentary on his Literary and Theological Art.* GR: Eerdmans, 1982
Henrichsen, Walter A. *After the Sacrifice.* Zondervan, 1979
Howley, G. D. C. ed. *A New Testament Commentary.* GR:Zondervan, 1969.
Nichol, W. Robertson. ed., *The Expositor's Greek Testament.* GR: Eerdmans, 1961.
Strauss, Lehman. *The Book of the Revelation.* Neptune, NJ: Loizeaux Bos., 1964.
Walvoord, John F. and Zuck, Roy B., eds. *The Bible Knowledge Commentary.* Wheaton: Victor, 1983.

LINGUISTIC TOOLS:
Abbott-Smith, G. *A Manual Greek Lexicon of the New Testament,* 3d ed. Edinburgh: T. & T. Clark, 1937.
Arndt, William F. and Gingrich, F. Wilbur. *A Greek-English Lexicon of the New Testament and Other Early Christian Literature.* Zondervan, 1957.
Blass, F. and DeBrunner, E. *A Greek Grammar of the New Testament and Other Literature,* trans., Robert W. Funk. Chicago: Univ. of Chicago Press, 1961
Brown, Francis. *The New Brown-Driver-Briggs-Gesenius Hebrew and English Lexicon* Hendrickson reprint, 1979.
Burton, Ernest DeWitt. *Syntax of the Moods and Tenses in New Testament Greek.* Edinburgh: T.& T. Clark,1898.
Chamberlain, William Douglas. *An Exegetical Grammar of the Greek New Testament.* NY: Macmillan, 1952.
Cremer, Hermann. *Biblico-Theological Lexicon of the New Testament Greek.* J. & J. Clark. 1883.
Dana, H. E. and Mantey, Julius R. *A. Manual Grammar of the Greek New Testament.* NY:Macmillan, 1927.
Davidson, A. B. *Hebrew Syntax,* 3rd ed. Edinburgh: T. & T. Clark, 1901.
Demosthenes, 31,4, *Against Onetor.*
Harris, R. Laird, Archer, Gleason L., Jr. & Waltke, Bruce K., eds.. *Theological Wordbook of the Old Testament.* Chicago: Moody, 1980
Jastrow,Marcus. *Dictionary of the Targumim, Talmud Babli, Yerushalmi and Midrashic Literature.* N.Y.: Judaica Press, 1982.
Kidd, D. A. *Collins Gem Latin Dictionary,* 2nd ed. Harper-Collins.
Kittel, Gerhard, ed. *Theological Dictionary of the New Testament.* Grand Rapids: Eerdmans, 1964.
Lampe, G. W. H. *A Patristic Greek Lexicon.* Oxford, 1961.
Liddell, Henry George, Scott, Robert, and Jones. *A Greek-English Lexicon,* 9th ed. NY: Oxford Univ., 1996.
Moulton, James Hope, and Milligan, George. *The Vocabulary of the Greek Testament* . London: Hodder & Stoughton, 1914-1929.
Parkhurst, John. *A Greek and English Lexicon of the New Testament,* ed. by Hugh James Rose. London: 1829.
Robertson, A. T. and Davis, W. Hersey. *A New Short Grammar of the Greek Testament* 10th ed. Harper, 1958
Robertson, A. T. *Word Pictures in the New Testament* , 6 vols. Nashville: Broadman, 1930.
___________. *A Grammar of the Greek New Testament in the Light of Historical Research.*
Rogers, Cleon L. Jr. and Cleon L. III. *Linguistic and Exegetical Key to the New Testament.* Zondervan, 1998.
Ross, Allen P. *Introducing Biblical Hebrew.* GR: Baker, 2001.
Thayer, John Henry. *A Greek-English Lexicon of the New Testament.* NY: American Book, 1886.
Tregelles, Samuel P. *Gesenius' Hebrew and Chaldee Lexicon of the Old Testament Scriptures.*
Turner, Nigel in Moulton, James Hope. *Syntax,* vol. III
Wallace, Daniel. *Greek Grammar Beyond the Basics: Exegetical Syntax of the New Testament.* Zondervan,1996.
Watts, J. Wash. *A Survey of Syntax in the Hebrew Old Testament.* Nashville: Broadman, 1951.

Young, Robert. *Analytical Concordance to the Bible*. GR: Eerdmans, 1936.

ARTICLES:

Aldrich, Roy L. "The Gift of God," *Bibliotheca Sacra.* 122:487.
Berg, J. Vanden. "Calvin and Missions," in Hoogstra, ed. *John Calvin: Contemporary Prophet.* GR: Baker, 1959.
Berkouwer, G. C. "Election and Doctrinal Reaction," *Christianity Today.* 5:586.
Chaney, Charles. "The Missionary Dynamic in the Theology of John Calvin," *Reformed Review*, 17:64, 24-38
Coates, Thomas. "Were the Reformers Mission-Minded?" *Concordia Theological Monthly,* 40:9, 600-611.
Constable,Thomas L. "The Gospel Message" in Campbell, Donald K. ed, *Walvoord: A Tribute.* Moody, 1982.
Gerstner, John H. & Jonathan N. "Edwardsean Preparation for Salvation," *Westminster Theol. Jour.*, 42:5-50.
Godfrey, W. Robert. "Reformed Thought on the Extent of the Atonement to 1618," *Westminster Theological Journal* , 37 (Winter 1975) 133-171..
Gundry, Robert H. "The Language Milieu of First-Century Palestine." *Jour. Biblical Literature* 83 (1964): 404-408.
Hall, Basil. "Calvin Against the Calvinists," *John Calvin: Courtenay Studies in Reformation Theology.* 1966.
Hargrave, O. T. "Free-willers in the English Reformation," *Church History*, XXXVII (1968), 271-280.
Hoehner, Harold. "Chronological Aspects of the Life of Christ: Part V," *Bibliotheca Sacra* 524 (Oct. '74) pp. 340-8.
James, Edgar C. "Foreknowledge and Foreordination," *Bibliotheca Sacra* (July 1965).
Klooster, Fred H. "Missions–The Heidelberg Catechism and Calvin," Calvin Theological Jour., 7:181-208 (1972).
McCoy, Charles S. "Johannes Cocceius: Federal Theologian," *Scottish Journal of Theology*, 16:365.
Nicole, Roger. "Amyraldianism" in *Encyclopedia of Christianity.* (1964).
Olson, Roger. "Don't Hate Me Because I'm an Arminian," *Christianity Today.* 43 (Sept. 6, 1999) pp. 87-90, 92-4.
Sapaugh, Gregory. "Is Faith a Gift? A study of Ephesians 2:8, " *Journal of the Grace Evangelical Society*, 7, no. 12 (Spring 1994), pp. 39-40.
Steffens, Nicholas M. "The Principle of Reformed Protestantism and Foreign Missions." *Presby. & Reformed Review,* 5:241-53 (April, 1894).
Ware, Bruce. "An Evangelical Reformulation of the Doctrine of the Immutability of God," *Journal of the Evangelical Theological Society*, 29:4, pp. 431-449.
Zwemer, Samuel M. "Calvinism and the Missionary Enterprise," *Theology Today* 7:206-216 (July 1950).

THEOLOGICAL PAPERS:

Carter, Terry G. "The Calvinism of William Carey and its Effect on his Mission Work," a paper delivered at ETS 2001 at Colorado Springs, Nov. 2001.
Edgar, Thomas R. "The Meaning of *PROORIZO*," a paper given at ETS Eastern Sect., March 30, 2001 at PBU.
Olson, C. Gordon. "Evangelical Misrepresentations of Allah," a paper presented at Lanham, MD, at the Eastern Regional of the ETS, March 23, 2002.
Imad Shahadeh. "Panel Discussion" at ETS 2000, Nashville, TN, November 2000.

BIBLE TRANSLATIONS:

The Amplified Bible. GR: Zondervan, 1965.
Bruce, F. F. *The Letters of Paul: An Expanded Paraphrase.* Eerdmans: 1965.
Lamsa, George M. *The Holy Bible from Ancient Eastern Text: Translations tfrom the Aramaic of the Peshitta.* San Francisco: Harper and Row, 1985.
The English Standard Version. Wheaton: Crossway, 2001.
Knox, R. A., Msgr. *The New Testament: A New Translation.* NY: Sheed & Ward, 1953.
The New American Bible. NY: Catholic Book Publishing, 1970.
The New English Bible: New Testament. Oxford: Oxford Univ. Press, 1961.
The New Living Translation. Wheaton: Tyndale House, 1996.
Phillips, J. B. *The New Testament in Modern English.* NY: Macmillan, 1962.
The Revised Standard Version. NY: Nelson, 1957.
Rotherham, Joseph Bryant, *The Emphasized Bible.* Cincinnati: Standard Publishing, 1897.
The Septuagint Version of the Old Testament, with trans. By Brenton. London: Bagster, n.d.
Verkuyl, Gerritt, ed., *The Modern Language Bible: The New Berkeley Version* (rev. 1969).
Way, Arthur. *The Letters of St. Paul*, London: Macmillan, 1926.
Weymouth, Richard Francis, *The New Testament in Modern Speech.* Boston: Pilgrim, 1943.
Williams, Charles B. *The New Testament.* Chicago, Moody Press, 1958.

An additional bibliography of Open Theism is on page 452.